LIFE IN THE WRITINGS OF STORM JAMESON

Cultural Expressions of World War II
Interwar Preludes, Responses, Memory

Phyllis Lassner, Series Editor

LIFE IN THE WRITINGS OF STORM JAMESON

A BIOGRAPHY

ELIZABETH MASLEN

NORTHWESTERN UNIVERSITY PRESS | EVANSTON, ILLINOIS

Northwestern University Press
www.nupress.northwestern.edu

Printed in the United States of America

10 9 8 7 6 5 4 3 2 1

Library of Congress Cataloging-in-Publication Data

Maslen, Elizabeth.
    Life in the writings of Storm Jameson / Elizabeth Maslen.
      pages cm. — (Cultural expressions of World War II : interwar preludes,
    responses, memory)
    Includes bibliographical references and index.
    ISBN 978-0-8101-2979-5 (cloth : alk. paper) — ISBN 978-0-8101-6767-4 (ebook)
    1. Jameson, Storm, 1891–1986. 2. Women authors, English—20th century—
Biography. 3. Authors, English—20th century—Biography. 4. London Centre of
the International P.E.N.—Biography. 5. English Centre of International PEN—
Biography. 6. Pacifists—Great Britain—Biography. 7. Socialists—Great Britain—
Biography. 8. Feminists—Great Britain—Biography. I. Title.
    PR6019.A67Z78 2014
    828'.91209—dc23
    [B]
    2014011598

For my children and grandchildren,
with gratitude

CONTENTS

ACKNOWLEDGMENTS

I should like to thank the Institute of English Studies, University of London, and particularly its director, Professor Warwick Gould, for funding of travel to archives and libraries; and I am more than grateful for the Research Fellowship granted to me in 2005 by the Harry Ransom Center of the University of Texas at Austin, and for the help given to me there by Patricia Fox. All the archivists and librarians at the many archives and libraries I have visited have been unfailingly kind and helpful, providing advice and encouragement far beyond the line of duty. And I am particularly grateful to Christopher Storm-Clark for his generous help.

The individuals who have helped me are legion. I would particularly like to thank the staff at Senate House Library, University of London, at the London Library, and at the Whitby Literary and Philosophical Library. Special thanks go to Janet Allan, Rosalind Barker of Whitby, Mike Bott, John Chalker, Peter Conradi, Anthony Davey, Alison Gage, Feona Hamilton, Mr. Harrison of Whitby, Jenny Hartley, Stephen Knight, Catherine Maxwell, Michael Rhodes, Chris Richards, Jean Rose, Ashlie Sponenberg, Parry Thornton of Whitby, and of course my family, especially Jess for her professional help with photographs. I have been very reliant on James Griffiths for his technical support, which has been most generous. And without Phyllis Lassner's unfailing support and encouragement this project would never have reached completion. I have been enormously blessed in the many friendships the work on this book has brought me.

The unpublished correspondence of Storm Jameson and the unpublished typescripts of *Journey from the North* (copyright Storm Jameson), reprinted by permission of Peters Fraser & Dunlop (www.petersfraserdunlop.com) on behalf of the Estate of Storm Jameson.

Extracts from two unpublished letters by Arthur Koestler to Storm Jameson, reprinted by permission of Peters Fraser & Dunlop (www.petersfraserdunlop.com) on behalf of the Estate of Arthur Koestler. Permission also granted by Joseph Marshall, Rare Books Librarian, Centre for Research Collections, Edinburgh University Library.

Extracts from one letter by Rebecca West to Storm Jameson, reprinted by permission of Peters Fraser & Dunlop (www.petersfraserdunlop.com) on behalf of the Estate of Rebecca West.

Extracts from Storm Jameson material held in Leeds University Library, Brotherton Collection, MS 20c Dobrée; MS 20c Moult; MS 20c Shorter.

Extracts by A. D. Peters from A. D. Peters archived material in the Harry Ransom Center, University of Texas, Austin, reprinted by permission of Peters Fraser & Dunlop (www.petersfraserdunlop.com) on behalf of the Estate of A. D. Peters.

Letters and documents held in the private collection of Christopher Storm-Clark, reprinted by permission of Christopher Storm-Clark.

Extract from letter by Storm Jameson to Frank Swinnerton, August 14, 1937. Frank Swinnerton Collection. Permission to reprint granted by Special Collections, University of Arkansas Libraries, Fayetteville.

Extracts from material held at the BBC Written Archive Centre, Caversham Park, reprinted by permission of Monica Thapar on behalf of the Centre.

Extracts from letters by Storm Jameson to E. J. Thompson held in the Bodleian Libraries, University of Oxford, MS. Eng. lett. c. 5292 (Thompson), fols. 14–15, 17–20, 28, 41–42, 49, 56, 58, 64, reprinted by permission given by Colin Harris on behalf of the Keeper of Collections, Dr. Chris Fletcher.

Extracts from letters by Storm Jameson to Walter de la Mare held in the Bodleian Libraries, University of Oxford, July 5, 1925, September 7, 1925, September 21, 1925, de la Mare [box] B72 [uncat], reprinted by permission given by Colin Harris on behalf of the Keeper of Collections, Dr. Chris Fletcher.

Extracts from letter by Storm Jameson to Henry Nevinson held in the Bodleian Libraries, University of Oxford, MS. Eng. lett. d. 278 (Nevinson), fol. 143, reprinted by permission given by Colin Harris on behalf of the Keeper of Collections, Dr. Chris Fletcher.

Extracts from a letter by Storm Jameson to H. E. Bates, reprinted by permission of Navpreet Kundal of Pollinger Ltd., for the Estate of H. E. Bates.

Extracts from letters by Storm Jameson to Jacquetta Hawkes, reprinted by permission of Alison Cullingford, Special Collections Librarian, J. B. Priestley Library, University of Bradford.

Extracts from a letter by Storm Jameson to Sir William Emrys Williams, reprinted by permission of Penguin Books Ltd.

Extracts from letters by Storm Jameson to members of the Macmillan Publishing Press, Macmillan Letter Books (Third Tranche), reprinted by permission of the British Library Board. Permission also granted by Palgrave Macmillan.

Extracts from letters by Storm Jameson to Eleanor Farjeon in the Farjeon archive, ADD 83146, unbound, reprinted by permission of the British Library Board.

Extracts from talks given by Storm Jameson, reprinted by permission of the British Library Board.

Extracts from letters by Storm Jameson to Nancy Cunard, reprinted by permission of Robert Bell for the Estate of Nancy Cunard.

Extracts from letters and manuscripts by Storm Jameson, reprinted by permission of the Harry Ransom Center, University of Texas, Austin.

Extracts from (1) a letter dated January 27, 1961, by Storm Jameson to Secker from the Secker Mss; (2) a letter dated August 8, 1941, by Storm Jameson to Irvine from the Irvine Mss; and (3) sixteen letters by Storm Jameson to Ruth Crawford Mitchell dated between 1949 and 1969 from the Crawford Mitchell Mss, reprinted by courtesy of the Lilly Library, Indiana University, Bloomington.

Extracts from letters by Storm Jameson to Rosamond Lehmann in the Rosamond Lehmann archive (misc 42A/35), reprinted by permission of Patricia McGuire, archivist of King's College Library, Cambridge.

Extracts from papers held in the Liddell Hart Centre for Military Archives, reprinted by permission of The Trustees of the Liddell Hart Centre for Military Archives.

Extracts from letters by Storm Jameson to Vera Brittain and other mate-
rial from the Vera Brittain archive, reprinted by permission of the
McMaster University Library, Hamilton, Ontario. Extracts from Vera
Brittain's letters to Storm Jameson are included by permission of Mark
Bostridge and T. J. Brittain-Catlin, Literary Executors for the Estate of
Vera Brittain, 1970.

Extracts from letters from John Galsworthy to Storm Jameson, reprinted
by permission of Christopher Sinclair-Stevenson on behalf of the Estate of John Galsworthy.

Extract from a letter by Storm Jameson to Mr. Shorter, March 27, 1922,
in the "English Literary Authors" Collection (Clement King Shorter),
reprinted by permission of the Special Collections Library, University
of Michigan, Ann Arbor.

Extracts from letters by Robert Neumann to the English PEN Centre, reprinted by permission of the Liepmann AG, Literary Agency, Zurich.

Extracts from letters by Storm Jameson to Miss Atkinson of Jonathan Cape,
July 17, 1933; to Raymond of Chatto & Windus, December 12, 1931;
and to Norah Smallwood of Chatto & Windus, June 21, 1960, held in
the Random House Archives and the Library of the University of Reading, and reprinted by permission of the Random House Group Ltd.

Extracts from letters by Storm Jameson to Hilary Newitt Brown and Harrison Brown, reprinted by permission of the Simon Fraser University
Special Collections, Burnaby, British Columbia.

Extracts from letters by Storm Jameson to Michael and Bet Sadleir
housed in §11033 Michael Sadleir Papers at the Rare Book Literary
and Historical Papers, Wilson Library, University of North Carolina,
Chapel Hill, reprinted by permission of the Wilson Library, University
of North Carolina, Chapel Hill.

Extracts from letters by Storm Jameson, reprinted by permission of the
Allison-Shelley Collection, Special Collections Library, Pennsylvania
State University Libraries.

Extracts from Margaret Storm Jameson correspondence, Coll. No.
1987.002, reprinted by permission of the Department of Special Collections and University Archives, McFarlin Library, University of
Tulsa, Oklahoma.

Extract from letter by Storm Jameson to George Orwell, reprinted by permission of the Orwell Archive, UCL Library Services, Special Collections, University College London.

Extracts from letters by Storm Jameson to Livia Gollancz, reprinted by permission of the Modern Records Centre, University of Warwick Library.

Extract from letter by H. G. Wells to Storm Jameson, June 26, 1937, reprinted by permission of the Literary Executors of the Estate of H. G. Wells, A. P. Watt Ltd.

Extracts from letters by Storm Jameson to Czesław Miłosz held in the Czesław Miłosz Papers, General Collection, Beinecke Rare Book and Manuscript Library, Yale University, reprinted by permission of Christopher Storm-Clark.

Extract from letter by Margaret Lane, Countess Huntingdon, reprinted by permission of Selina Hastings.

For reference to material held in their collections I am grateful to the National Collections of Newspapers and Periodicals in the British Library at Colindale; the Guy Chapman archive (JMON2) in the Special Collections, Churchill College; the Winifred Holtby Archive, Hull Central Library; the Jameson Henley Papers, Liverpool Record Office, Central Library; the Women's Library, London Metropolitan University; the R. H. Tawney archive, CND archive, and Fabian Society archive, Special Collections, London School of Economics Library; the National Portrait Gallery; the Storm Jameson Author file, the Heinemann archive, Random House Archive; special papers at the Royal British Legion HQ; the SCR Archive (Society for Cultural Relations between the Peoples of the British Commonwealth and the Union of Soviet Socialist Republics), 320 Brixton Road, London SW9 6AB; the Society of Authors Archive, ADDMSS; the Labour Party Archive, People's History Museum, University of Central Lancashire; the University of Leeds, Personalia, STU/001 [committees document], the Women's Representative Council 1902–14; the Archive Services Center, University of Pittsburgh; the Bodley Head/John Lane files, Chatto and Windus files, Allen and Unwin files, Hogarth Press files, Jonathan Cape files, Routledge files, and the Herbert Herlitschka archive, Special Collections, University of Reading; the Elton/Ehrenberg papers and the Monk House papers, Special Collections, University of Sussex.

Despite every effort to trace and contact copyright holders before publication this has not been possible in every case. If contacted, the publisher will be pleased to rectify any errors or omissions at the earliest opportunity.

ABBREVIATIONS

AAK	Alfred A. Knopf
ADP	A. D. Peters
AK	Arthur Koestler
AM	Alan Maclean
ARO	A. R. Orage
BD	Bonamy Dobrée
BK	Blanche Knopf
CM	Czesław Miłosz
CSC	Christopher Storm-Clark
DC	David Carver
EJT	E. J. Thompson
GC	Guy Chapman
HM	Harold Macmillan
HO	Hermon Ould
HRC	Harry Ransom Center, University of Texas, Austin
IR	Irene Rathbone
JH	Jacquetta Hawkes
JM	John Montgomery
KLH	Kathleen Liddell Hart
LD	Rache Lovat Dickson
LG	Livia Gollancz
LH	Basil Liddell Hart
MS	Michael Sadleir
MW	Marjorie Watts
NC	Nancy Cunard
RC	Ruth Crawford Mitchell
RHT	R. H. Tawney
RL	Rosamond Lehmann
SJ	Storm Jameson

√B	Vera Brittain
VD	Valentine Dobrée

Works

AKOS	*A Kind of Survivor*
AOL	*The Soul of Man in the Age of Leisure*
BL	*Black Laurel*
BTC	*Before the Crossing*
CJ	*Civil Journey*
CM	*Cloudless May*
CP	*Company Parade*
CTD	*Challenge to Death*
CTT	*A Cup of Tea for Mr. Thorgill*
DAF	*The Diary of Anne Frank*
DM	*Delicate Monster*
ELSH	*The Early Life of Stephen Hind*
ETL	*Europe to Let*
ETW	*The End of This War*
FNWD	*Farewell, Night, Welcome, Day*
FTY	*Farewell to Youth*
GNMR	*The Georgian Novel and Mr. Robinson*
HCAC	*Here Comes a Candle*
HH	*The Happy Highways*
ITSY	*In the Second Year*
JMHR	*The Journal of Mary Hervey Russell*
JN	*Journey from the North*
LC	*London Calling*
LIW	*Love in Winter*
LM	*Loving Memory*
LRP	*Left Review Pamphlet*
LS	*The Lovely Ship*
LSAL	*Lady Susan and Life*
MDIE	*Modern Drama in Europe*
NC	*The New Commonwealth*
NCL	*The Novel in Contemporary Life*
NEW	*New English Weekly*
NTB	*None Turn Back*

NTLTP	*No Time Like the Present*
NVFTS	*No Victory for the Soldier*
PB	*The Pot Boils*
PW	*Parthian Words*
RTS	*The Road to Success*
SS	*Speaking of Stendhal*
TC	*The Clash*
THR	*The Hidden River*
TI	*The Intruder*
TK	*Three Kingdoms*
"TLN"	"The Last Night"
TLS	*The Times Literary Supplement*
TMIM	*The Moon Is Making*
TMS	typed manuscript
TOT	*Triumph of Time*
TPW	*The Pitiful Wife*
TSH	*The Single Heart*
TVH	*The Voyage Home*
TWE	*Tale without End*
TWS	*The Writer's Situation*
TWSHS	*Then We Shall Hear Singing*
TWSI	*There Will Be a Short Interval*
TWY	*That Was Yesterday*
WC	*The White Crow*
"WCS"	"The Writer in Contemporary Society"
WE	*The World Ends*
WIS	*What Is Happiness?*
"YP"	"The Young Prisoner"

LIFE IN THE WRITINGS OF STORM JAMESON

Prologue and Apologia

> Even an inhabitant of the neighbouring county of Lancaster
> is struck by the peculiar force of character which the
> Yorkshiremen display.
>
> — ELIZABETH GASKELL ON CHARLOTTE BRONTË

> The art of biography is more difficult than is generally
> supposed. Brother Juniper found that there was least to be
> learned from those who had been most closely associated with
> the subject of his inquiry.
>
> — THORNTON WILDER, *The Bridge of San Luis Rey*

This book explores the life and writings of an extraordinary woman. Margaret Storm Jameson was a leading figure in the literary, cultural, and political life of the interwar period and World War II, and continued to write distinguished novels for many years after that. She was a novelist and theorist of the novel admired by many of her peers, a political activist throughout the 1930s and a champion of many refugees before, during, and after World War II; and yet, in her old age and after her death, she sank into the kind of invisibility she half craved, half resented. Again and again throughout her life she noted with satisfaction that she had destroyed records of her life and letters from friends, and she said repeatedly that she wished to be forgotten. So why resurrect her?

We have over recent years established certain women as representative of the twentieth century, culturally, socially, or politically, so providing a plot for one version of the twentieth century. But that should not obscure or silence voices of others who present a different but equally valid account. And the more we explore the writings of Storm Jameson, the more interesting her voice is and the more it communicates with surprising ease to the twenty-first century. We learn of her anxieties as a married woman, about her husband, her child, and the problem of balancing the needs of these with a career. Hers is a voice representing a different quarter from those of the Woolfs, the upper classes, or the products of Oxford and Cambridge: she is one of the first women to graduate from a provincial university and establish a career in the literary world of London. Hers is a voice questioning, from the moment it is first heard, the widely honored shibboleths of her age; she is an eloquent precursor of the Angry Young Woman that Doris Lessing would be in the 1950s. And she has her finger on the pulse of her generation and its relation to the world in which it grew up, matured, and grew old. Her crucial engagement with and understanding of Europe sprang out of her own experiences abroad and with the many refugees she knew and helped in England and beyond, giving her unusually powerful insights into crises affecting a wide swath of the Continent. This is a woman who was fully engaged with the conflicts and tensions of her time, and who addressed them in her writings with insight, compassion, and a finely honed prose, always seeing a writer's responsibility as an interpreter of his or her own time, and constantly putting forward ideas on how best the novel should function as a vehicle for ideas.

A number of women writers of her time could be called iconoclasts, dissecting the received wisdoms of their own and the preceding age from a woman's point of view. They are involved, engaged, their work political as well as about relationships; they see very clearly the ways in which the private and public worlds interact. They are involved in public debate. There, for instance, is Mary Agnes Hamilton, and there is Ellen Wilkinson, both Members of Parliament, both writers. There are Vera Brittain, Winifred Holtby, Rebecca West, Phyllis Bottome, and Ethel Mannin, writing well and regularly about social and political issues, and active in various organizations. And Storm Jameson should be right at the top of the list, as an eloquent commentator and observer of the dilemmas of her age, those of a woman brought up as a Victorian, living through World War I, the rapidly changing, turbulent interwar years, to World War II and beyond. Her novels are always broad in scope, never tied to the purely provincial, and she is unafraid, like Honoré de Balzac, of analyzing unpleasant characters. She reveals her contemporary world, warts and all. Her sense of the universal embedded in the particular is reminiscent of Stendhal, and the invisibility her work suffered for a number of years recalls his fate in the nineteenth century. For in many ways she was ahead of her time, closer to a European tradition of a fiction of ideas and vision, and closer too to those postcolonial writers who, like Lessing, assessed and reassessed attitudes of mind that the metropolis had taken for granted.

She was a complex character. In her late autobiography, *Journey from the North*, she does not accept her own public persona, instead letting us into her dark side. Yet letters that friends kept over the long years of her life tell of a woman who knew passion and lasting love, enjoyed gossip, was witty and mischievous, with each letter crafted like a conversation suited to each correspondent. She could be open one minute, reticent the next; she was warmly generous to those she loved but could also be demanding. She did not suffer fools gladly if they antagonized her, but could be endlessly compassionate to those in need.

Her fiction was frequently maligned by contemporary critics (particularly after World War II) who did not appreciate her insights into crises of their age and her astuteness about European concerns. Yet a close reading of her work shows someone with an ear for the voices of her time and the capacity to capture them. She was equally committed to issues at home and abroad. She probes ways in which the zeitgeist affects the individual, while she can sketch the natural scene or the city street with a poet's eye. And she reinterprets realism as a vehicle for her concerns, always as a vehicle, a servant for her ideas and vision, always molded to fit the content. Her vision, her craft, and her personal life, so firmly committed to the problems of a rapidly changing world, make an extremely important contribution to our understanding of the twentieth century.

In this book, the aim has been to allow her personality to emerge from her letters and from comments by her friends. I have tried to avoid speculation, as there is real danger of fiction taking over from fact once imagination gets to work, and of putting one's own priorities to the fore, instead of those germane to the subject and the context in which the subject operated. Instead, I have occasionally raised questions and left them hanging; the reader has as much right to shape possible answers as I have. Where I have not been able to find or gain access to documentation on a particular issue, I have tried to resist filling the gap. It is of course tempting to speculate, for example, on Jameson's compulsion to destroy so many papers throughout her life, on why she felt responsible for so many people, or on her attitude to old age. I have tried to resist such temptations, as too much speculation, too many judgments, can undercut the emergence of a fascinating personality — and obscure the fact that part of that fascination will always be those facets that resist our determination to offer a definitive explanation. One reason why biography is so intriguing is that no two books on any one person come to the same conclusions; just as in life, close friends may have different views about someone they both know, or think they know, intimately. As it is, I have found much to puzzle and intrigue in Jameson's rich and varied writings, and hope the reader will come to share my admiration of this remarkable woman.

PART I

1891–1930

CHAPTER 1

Childhood and Adolescence

Margaret Storm Jameson was born in the small town of Whitby on the northeast coast of Yorkshire, on January 8, 1891. In one sense, this is simply a statement of fact about place and time, but it is by no means only that. For Whitby would hold a key place in both Margaret's life and her work as a writer: indeed Whitby, or the Whitby of her childhood that her memory shaped and cradled, was to become her mind's sanctuary in a wandering life. In both her fiction and nonfiction, she paints it with words. It is there at the end of her first novel, written during the early years of World War I:

> Darkness, peering over the rim of the sea, topped the ribbed waves and rested on the shoulders of the cliffs. In the murmuring shadows of the little town lights gleamed like fallen petals. Beyond the old dockyard scattered lights clung to the hillsides: far up the valley a single light marked the turn of the road that twisted to the moors, and on the quiet waters of the upper harbour the boats were slender shadows in the chequered dusk.[1]

On August 13, 1931, she recalled:

> At dusk the fields of under-sea show grey under the blue. In sunshine the surface of the water is green and silver like the back of a fish. Sometimes the old Church is unsubstantial, like beauty in a dream. On another day, in another light, it grips the edge of

the cliff, squat and sullen. The air is thin, and on a clear, wind-less day you see a long way: it seems further than you can see in other places.[2]

And Whitby is still there at the close of her last novel, as the protagonist drifts into unconsciousness:

> His sight darkened. In yet another dimension the North Sea flowed towards and past him, grey, cold, restless, lipping a known shore. He stirred. . . . I should have gone home. . . .[3]

However, the Whitby of Margaret's childhood was a place of powerful paradoxes. The legacy of the town's shipbuilding past was still strong when she was born, and it was proudly remembered, for instance, that Captain Cook had used converted coal-carrying ships, built in Whitby, for his voyage to Australia in 1769–70. By the time of Margaret's birth, shipbuilding was drawing to a close, and modern facilities were being developed farther north on Tyneside. Despite this, Whitby's ships still voyaged widely, its sailing community familiar with ports ranging from Europe to South America. By contrast, on the landward side, the town was virtually separated from the rest of Yorkshire by the steep slopes of the moors; even the advent of the railway did not altogether change this separation, as bad weather could, and still can, close the line. So the young Margaret was the product of a community that both looked abroad and had a sense of apartness from the rest of the country. There is still a local saying which might be her motto, "There's a right way, a wrong way, and a Whitby way," and this proud sense of identity had always been jealously guarded. When Alfred Tennyson was tempted to take a house there, the chair of the street commissioners "had no time to bother with 'run-a-countrys' as all strangers were styled, and received the great man coldly."[4] No *Idylls of the King* were written in Whitby.

Yet despite this sense of apartness, Whitby had moments in its history which had huge implications for England as a whole, and which were important aspects of Margaret's inheritance. On the headland high above the town, behind the parish church, is the site of a seventh-century monastery founded by a learned and influential woman, Hild of Whitby. Here Hild hosted the great Synod of Whitby that would finally resolve a key difference between the Celtic Church and the Church of Rome as to the dating of Easter and would greatly strengthen England's links with Europe, culturally and politically, for centuries to come. Hild was a strong woman, and in the small town below the abbey, over the centuries, strong women were the norm: when their menfolk were at sea, many women ran the coal ships and kept the businesses going. Margaret herself would proclaim in 1978: "As the daughter of a matriarch, a Yorkshire matriarch at that, I was never, from my earliest grasp of reality, in any doubt that talent for talent, wit for wit, women are the equals of men."[5]

Throughout her life, Margaret would deplore any modernizations of the Whitby of her childhood that she had come to idealize. Yet she did not idealize Whitby's inhabitants. In her novel *That Was Yesterday* (1932), considering Danesacre, the name Margaret frequently used for Whitby in her fiction, the protagonist reflects that this isolated town

> bred a kind of savagely individual race like none other in England, no man like his neighbour, except in so far as they were all hard, stubborn men. A great many of them were violently eccentric judged by any standards, even their own.[6]

Certainly what can be gleaned about Margaret's own family tree suggests something of the hard life that bred this toughness. Her paternal grandfather, William Jameson (c. 1828/29–65), a Master Mariner, was drowned on a crossing to Holland on July 29, 1865, aged thirty-six, leaving a widow and three surviving children.[7] His wife, Hannah, came of a long line of Storm ancestors, an old established Whitby family, although its roots were no doubt Norwegian: in the Whitby Public Library a note claims that the first record of the name Sampson Storm occurred in 1739. Hannah's father, another Sampson Storm (1803–65), kept the Golden Fleece Inn in Church Street when he retired from the sea, but retained an interest in several ships. For ship-owning was common in the Whitby of the day, although not usually on a grand scale: regularly men would own a share in a ship or ships when Whitby was a flourishing trading port.[8] William Jameson and Hannah had four children, according to the census of 1871, of whom William Storm, born October 2, 1854, would later be Margaret's father. So Margaret's father was ten when his father was drowned, and was sent to sea himself about three years later, before his mother married again, a marriage which would mirror both the good and the bad of the closeness of the Whitby community, as will become clear.

On Margaret's mother's side, the Gallilees seem, like the Storms, to have roots outside Whitby: certainly there were Gallilees on Tyneside at the end of the seventeenth century, according to a civilian census of the time, but when the first Gallilee came to Whitby is uncertain. George's father was simply recorded as "Seaman" when George himself married for the second time.[9] George was born in 1829, and the census of 1871 describes him as living at 13 Silver Street, as a sailmaker employing one man and twelve boys. He was also by then a widower. His wife, Sarah (née Clarkson), Margaret's grandmother, had died in 1870 aged forty-two. She had produced six children.[10] At least, six children are registered in the census, although both Margaret's mother and Margaret herself maintained there were seven, maybe remembering a child who died before the census.[11] The six recorded are Mary, Sarah, George, William, Hannah M. (Margaret's mother), and Jane (Jenny). And here the complications start for Margaret's family: when George married again on November 13, 1872, his wife was none other than the widow Hannah Jameson (Whitby parish church register). So Margaret's grandmother on her father's side was her step-grandmother on her mother's side.

In the Whitby Archives and Heritage Centre, George Gallilee is described as both sailmaker and shipowner or overseer, while a local historian states that he was a "sailmaker, who afterwards became a steamship manager in partnership with the late Mr. Harrison Baxter."[12] In her late autobiography, Margaret asserts she hardly knew her grandfather, as he was ill for many years; he did not die until 1914, when she was twenty-three, so it may have been that the illness incapacitated him mentally. In the same work she says he "had the reputation of a hard stubborn man, arbitrary, incorruptibly honest, with a violent temper kept, for the most part, under control. . . . He was bookish and extremely fastidious."[13] In 1933, she recalled her mother's memories of a strict, harsh upbringing with no toys, the children not living with George and his second wife, but in a separate house, because stepmother Hannah drank. In this work, Margaret says that his thrashings were merciless "and the noise terrified my mother" — a poignant comment, given that Hannah would beat her own children just as mercilessly in later years, cruelty breeding cruelty.[14]

Hannah married her stepbrother, William, on December 31, 1883, in the parish church (Whitby parish church register). Was this more a longing for escape than a love match? William's seagoing life had left him little time for the refinements that his young, fiery-tempered wife cherished, and his formal education had been minimal. Margaret gives no clue as to why they married, and those novels based on her family, while they tempt speculation, are nonetheless dangerous as sources for fact. In her autobiographical writings, much more is said about how ill matched the couple were, and how, despite the first years when Hannah went on voyages with William (she shared many long voyages, to South America, Vera Cruz, New Orleans, Odessa, the gulf of Archangel, and Norway), she fretted in her later domestic role as housebound wife and mother (*NTLTP*, 29). She could not give vent to her independent mind by running a business as other Whitby women had done down the ages, for William owned nothing on land; he was master of a ship but that ship had other owners. Margaret comments in 1933 that her mother "could have managed a business or made a success of any career in which courage, intelligence, and an abnormal energy are the conditions of success" (*NTLTP*, 33). Unfortunately, she had neither the education nor the opportunity and, until her father's death in 1914, little money of her own. So, as her children grew up, Hannah was caged by the notions of middle-class respectability that had now penetrated the Whitby community; she was without a role outside the home, with little money, and so staked all her hopes for life on her children.

What facts remain concerning the Storms, Jamesons, and Gallilees suggest lives ruled by both wide-ranging shipping and a communal and domestic claustrophobia that often bred violence, an atmosphere which Margaret would re-create in her novel based on old Whitby, *The Moon Is Making* (1937). Certainly the graves in Larpool Cemetery tell a tale of family ties that were as complicated as they were close. In 1914, George joined Sarah in the Gallilee grave, while Hannah was returned to her first husband when she died in 1909, a traditional way of solving the problem of first and second marriages.[15] Later, however, with no such rationale, Margaret's own mother, Hannah, would be buried with her Gallilee parents while William would be returned to the Jamesons when he died in 1942, this separation reflecting their dysfunctional marriage.[16] It is tempting to speculate that Bram Stoker sensed something of the deep currents of unease underlying the outward shows of respectability in Whitby when he had his Dracula land there in the novel published six years after Margaret was born.

Margaret arrived in this far from placid community at 26 Gray Street on January 8, 1891.[17] She was registered in the March quarter of that year and baptized in St. Michael's Church as Margaret Ethel, although by the 1901 census she is listed simply as Margaret Jameson. Later she adopted the name "Storm," at least partly for professional purposes, although in a BBC interview of 1970 she claimed that, her father being William Storm Jameson, she was given the name Storm as the eldest child — an amusing example of the narratives that "memory" can weave.[18] There is no such confusion about the pronunciation of her surname: "I am Jimmison only in Scotland. I was born Jameson with a long 'a' and two syllables."[19] She was, for her first fifteen years, the eldest of three, her sister Winifred being born when Margaret (nicknamed "Daisy" throughout childhood and adolescence) was four, her brother Harold a year later. These three children bore the brunt of their mother's thrashings, which appear to have been as much an outlet for her own frustration and boredom as punishment for any perceived fault. Margaret, for one, would be scarred for life.

Margaret rarely drew on her childhood in her fiction. What emerges from her autobiographical writings is a bright child who read voraciously, made few friends, and had little in common with her two siblings; the bond with Dorothy (Do), the young sister born in December 1906 when Margaret was almost sixteen, would be the strongest, if the most tempestuous. In her memoirs, Margaret would recall (though not in great detail) the voyages she made with her mother on her father's ship when very small; and she remembered her anguish on the first occasion, the first of many, that her mother went on a voyage without her, after Harold's birth. By her late twenties Margaret would claim to have very few memories of her early years, although she did "remember running madly down a street with a small flag when Mafeking was relieved. And standing on the quay at Antwerp, being told that the Queen was dead and being suitably depressed."[20] But what haunted her life and work, alongside warm memories of the town itself, was the cruelty first experienced in those mindless beatings, the desperate need to win her mother's approval, the constant sense of falling short.

The second house the family lived in, 5 Park Terrace, was Margaret's favorite, a redbrick, three-story house on the steep southern slope running up from the inner harbor. At five, she was sent next door to the kindergarten kept by the Corney family, where she was taught to write, count, and learn by heart. From the Corneys, she graduated to a school run by three sisters, the Miss Inghams, in the elegant, eighteenth-century Esk House. This small school offered her art, music, geography, history, selected books of the Bible, large amounts of poetry to be learned by heart, French, Latin, and arithmetic, although apparently this last was not a strong point. Overall, Margaret would later maintain, she gained "a rich and fascinating variety of information about the world, and . . . behind the serried ranks of facts, my imagination sat quietly with folded hands waiting for its moment."[21]

In the spring of 1903, the family moved to a newly built house in Ladysmith Avenue on West Cliff, close to the cliff top. It was named Saxonville after Margaret's father's ship, *The Saxon Prince*. There, in November 1906, the youngest child, Dorothy, was born, their mother's "last and overwhelming passion. They were laughably alike" (*JN*, 1:42). Margaret herself, now in her early teens, was proving to be intelligent, reading fast and avidly — and longing to get away. For the lack of close friends continued, her mother's possessiveness no doubt contributing to her isolation. Perhaps, too, the advent of her mother's adored last child, the child who was not subjected to those merciless thrashings, increased the wish to leave. Margaret did well in the public examinations she took at Esk House, but the little school could not prepare her for the matriculation she would need if she were to go to university, something her ambitious mother saw as perfectly achievable. Hannah saw Margaret as quite capable of winning one of only three university scholarships available for the whole of the North Riding of Yorkshire. This kind of ambition was extraordinary at such a date, in such a small enclosed town, and for a girl at that. Hannah, however, was undeterred, writing off to the Municipal School in Scarborough when Margaret was sixteen, and gaining an interview with the headmaster, A. S. Tetley, for herself and her daughter. There Hannah insisted that Margaret should spend a year at the school preparing for her matric the following June so as to qualify for a scholarship. The matric of those days was very demanding, requiring high marks in English language or literature, English history, math, three languages, a choice of sciences or mechanics, geography, and natural history. For a young girl from a small private school to achieve this in one year would be a tall order, but Hannah never appeared to doubt that what she had decided would happen; and the headmaster, whatever he thought of Margaret's prospects, agreed to Hannah's terms.

Accordingly, from September 1908, Margaret traveled daily by train to the school in Scarborough for two terms. Then, for the crucial examination term, she lived in lodgings in the town, an independence that hugely appealed to her. Much later she recalled those few final weeks as a time when "the habits of a vagabond and a solitary rooted themselves in me firmly" (JN, 1:48). Certainly her time at the Municipal School offered her things she had never experienced before: a genuinely challenging education and, above all, friends. The two Harland brothers, Sydney (later an eminent geneticist) and Oswald (who would become a novelist), came from a very poor background, with none of the middle-class values Hannah embraced. Yet, as Sydney tells in his autobiography, it was the boys' mother, like Margaret's, who fought for their education, so that they gained scholarships to the school in Scarborough.[22] This school was at the forefront of the drive to give a secondary education to children who would normally have left school at fourteen; it had been founded in 1899, less than a decade before Margaret arrived. The founder, A. H. D. Acland, particularly favored the sciences, so there were first-rate laboratories and workshops, but the education was broad, the current headmaster, Tetley, having the great gift of rousing enthusiasm for whatever he taught: even in old age, Margaret remembered his teaching of Milton's "Lycidas" (JN, 1:49). Did this play its part in her decision to read English at university?

In his autobiography, Sydney tells how Margaret's arrival at the school broke through his antisocial reserve:

> She looked . . . gauche, shy and uncomfortable, but there was something about her—I can't describe it; I can only say she shone. She sat down, put her books on the desk and began to work rapidly and with great concentration. . . . Oswald and I took her in hand to educate her privately—that is, to put revolutionary ideas into her head. . . . Oswald and I were red-hot socialists. She listened, but said very little. . . . We became close friends, and I confided in her about the girls I was interested in. She advised me about them in a friendship entirely without passion. . . .

> Margaret Daisy, as we called her, was a remarkable combination
> of innocence and common sense. (Harland, 24–25)

Just as Margaret's personality, her ability to listen, and the evident diplomacy in her comments on Sydney's girls made a deep impression on him and on his brother, the friendship with these two boys must have been a breath of fresh air for Margaret after the claustrophobia of home. The Harlands were brilliant, anarchic, absorbing everything they read in the school and local libraries and questioning what they found there. And Margaret drank it all in, attracted by their rebellion against ideas and values that displeased them, and their strong political convictions. Later, she recalled how one of the masters told her "your temperament gives a great deal of anxiety. And the Harlands are not good friends for you."[23] No doubt, in the early twentieth century, this girl's friendship with the eccentric, rebellious brothers raised eyebrows, but it would lay the foundations for many of Margaret's own decisions and directions in her early writing life (JN, 1:49). Nor did the friendship damage her studies: in June she achieved the matric, and in September she heard that she had indeed won one of those three scholarships that would open the way to university admission. However, the scholarships were modest, at sixty pounds apiece, and could not cover living expenses. Oxford or Cambridge was beyond her mother's means and William appears to have played no part in his children's education. So in the autumn of 1909, Margaret stayed in Yorkshire, at the University of Leeds, the only girl from the school to go on to higher education.[24]

CHAPTER 2

Student Life in Leeds and London

The year 1909 held many changes for Margaret: the family moved to a new home, Ryedale, on Chubb Hill, and in September of the same year she had her first experience of death in the immediate family. As it happened, Hannah Gallilee (formerly Hannah Jameson), her grandmother and step-grandmother, was not much mourned, although memories of her tough, manipulative personality would add flavor to her granddaughter's novels set in Danesacre. The departure for Leeds that autumn was a far more momentous event in Margaret's life, introducing her to a very different environment from the coastal towns she knew. Later, she described the Leeds of those days, with its "disenchanting grime, the ring of steel furnaces and mills belching smoke by day and flames by night, the ceaseless beat of industry in our ears" (JN, 1:51). She recalled too that "scholarship for its own sake was not usual among us," as life in the midst of factories, with very little money in students' pockets, meant that the economic facts of life loomed large: "You cannot set a university in the centre of an industrial region and think it will become cloistral" (JN, 1:52).

For her, this would be the most telling difference between the world of Oxford and Cambridge that she would learn about later, and the Leeds she experienced herself. "For most of us, a degree was the only gateway to a tolerable life," as it was not, she implied, for those who lived among dreaming spires (JN, 1:52). The Yorkshire College, together with the Leeds School of Medicine, had only been elevated to university status in 1904, so, as at school in Scarborough, Margaret was benefiting from new advances in education that gave opportunities to a wider range of potential students. Indeed, her undergraduate career would span a time of dramatic developments in Leeds as a city and in the university itself. The first vice-chancellor, Sir Nathan Bodington, died in May 1911, toward the end of Margaret's second year, and he was succeeded by Professor Michael Sadler, a dynamic educator, who shared with his son Michael a passionate commitment to contemporary art. His arrival in Leeds, at the beginning of Margaret's final year, would have considerable impact on the cultural life of the city, even as the university campus was expanding, the student numbers growing, and the potential of the new university coming to fruition.

Hannah did not accompany her daughter to Leeds, saying her farewells in Scarborough; so Margaret was on her own when she was assigned lodgings. The number of women students was still small as she arrived, and there was no hall of residence for women students in 1909; the first would be opened the following year. If a memoir of 1979 is to be believed, she spent her first week, before lodgings were assigned, "in some sort of religious community where I attended Compline for the first and only time in my life, wearing a borrowed veil over my hair."[1] Subsequently, the university records register three lodgings for her between 1909 and 1911.[2] Her experience as a woman student appears to have been rather different from the protective environment existing in most other universities of the day.[3] In the 1979 memoir she would claim that there was none of the pastoral care available to women students at Oxford or Cambridge. "Apart from my work," she asserted:

> I was, as far as I ever knew, completely unsupervised. I lived as I pleased, idled on the tennis courts on warm June days, spent whole days reading in the library outside my curriculum, neglecting prescribed books for what I took to be more advanced and therefore more exciting others. . . . Outside university activities I had few other diversions: if I went once during term to a restaurant in town or to a theatre, it was all. ("ULeeds 1909–12")

Independence, even the freedom to make mistakes, as will become clear, was a key feature of her experience as she remembered it, far beyond the reach of her contemporaries at Oxford or Cambridge, much as she would come to envy the greater entrée to cultural and political circles that the old universities ensured. Poverty shaped what she could and could not do: her mother contributed a pound per week in her first year, rising to thirty shillings by her second year, eighteen shillings of which went to her rent and a breakfast and meager supper. Living expenses and the cost of the books she could not resist buying left little over for luxuries.

Margaret's first term began on Monday, October 4, 1909. She registered the next day, signing herself as Margaret Ethel Jameson, student 7135. She paid a one-guinea entrance fee, giving as her proposed future career the standard one for a woman student of the time, "teacher," and registering for an honors degree in English studies. As a first-year student, she had to take four subjects, opting for Latin, French, European history, and English language and literature. English was still a relatively new academic subject at university level and as yet, the English Language and Literature Department in Leeds had only two members of staff: Professor Charles E. Vaughan and Assistant Professor Frederic Moorman. In her late reminiscences, Margaret said of these two men:

> I was . . . very fortunate, although he coldly disapproved of me, in having two years or a little longer under that severe and distinguished scholar, Professor C. E. Vaughan. . . . I never cut a lecture of his: after my first year I began occasionally to cut others, but not his. It was very apparent that he disliked having to teach young women reading for Honours. . . . It would never have entered my head to seek his advice on a problem, even scholastic, let along [sic] personal. If, rarely, I had a problem of sorts, . . . I took it to Professor Moorman, sure of being gently helped out of trouble. ("ULeeds 1909–12")

In her second year, 1910–11, Margaret concentrated on English literature, with subsidiary courses in English language, philosophy, and French. Now she became increasingly active in a number of student societies. She was a committee member of the Women's Representative Council, which promoted "the interests of the women students, and [undertook] the control of the common room."[4] She was elected joint secretary of the Society for Social Study, "formed for the purpose of obtaining a good understanding of social questions and schemes of social reform by means of lectures, discussions and other methods" ("ULeeds 1909–12").

In the first term of her second year (1910) she had also become a member of the *Gryphon* Committee, responsible for the students' journal. The majority of the articles printed in this lively little magazine were either anonymous or pseudonymous, so we can only guess at Margaret's contributions. However, the journal also recorded any talks that were given and, despite her dread of public speaking in later years, Margaret was an active member of the Union Debating Society from the moment of her arrival. In the first term of her first year, she had spoken on the motion "That a system of separate Universities for women is desirable"; later that academic year she voiced her opposition to the motion that "Socialism tends to destroy the moral fibre of a nation," and on another occasion argued that "Trade Union movements amongst women are most desirable at the present time."[5] Clearly, her "education" by the Harland brothers in matters political and social continued to bear fruit, supplemented by the strong socialist ethos prevalent among both staff and students in Leeds.[6] In December, the *Gryphon* recorded that Margaret had used the debate on trade union movements to appeal for "'Votes for Women.'" And in the same issue, the Debating Society report announced that the motion "Women's Suffrage on the lines of the Conciliation Bill should be granted" was passed by sixty-five votes to thirty-six, and that Miss Jameson, who proposed the motion, had made "an eloquent appeal."[7] The Conciliation Bill, bidding to enfranchise about one million women voters with sufficient financial means, was a Private Members' Bill that had been brought every year since 1900; in 1910 the bill was actually passed in June, only to be dropped when another election was called in November. There was a furious suffragette reaction, notably on Black Friday, November 18, when there was a six-hour struggle in London between the police and the Women's Social and Political Union (WSPU).[8] So Margaret's "eloquent appeal" aligned her with committed feminists; she would soon, however, voice greater concern for the plight of the poor, and would come to regard gender issues as less urgent than the eradication of poverty.

By her second year, she had made many friends and fell seriously in love with a classics student in the year above, whom her closest friend, "a dark handsome girl, whose nature had already the firmness and balance mine lacked," did not like (*NTLTP*, 58). This young man, Charles Dougan Clarke, is strangely elusive. His birth certificate states that he was born in Northern Ireland, on June 15, 1889, and that the birth was "entered at the monthly meeting of the Society of Friends in Lurgan, 14 August 1889," suggesting that the family were Quakers.[9] His parents, Charles G. Clarke and Lydia Ellen Clarke, were both American citizens, the father's "Certificate of Registration of an American Citizen" stating that he left the United States with his wife on April 20, 1904, and arrived in London on February 10, 1905, to practice medicine. Nothing is said of a child; it can only be inferred that there had been a previous residence in Northern Ireland, a return to the States, and a subsequent arrival in London when the boy was fourteen. Charles only appears in his own right when registering as a student at Leeds on April 29, 1907. What Margaret says of him in later memoirs is inevitably colored by the end of their relationship, but he was clearly very bright, left wing like herself, and readily participated in debate. Perhaps, when they met, Margaret saw in him some of the traits that had attracted her to the Harland brothers. In her late memoirs, she says she was flattered when he noticed her on a Debating Society visit to another university. She tells how they took long walks together and how, "one February evening, the affair came to a head." Despite his saying, all too prophetically, that he would make her unhappy, despite frequent quarrels, she recalls, "I was sensually and imaginatively obsessed, and as imprudent as possible" (*JN*, 1:56–57). Charles Clarke, known as Karl, graduated in 1911 with second-class honors and for a time moved out of Margaret's life; she would toy with another relationship in her third year, with a theological student from Mirfield, but there was nothing here to match the intellectual and sexual attraction that had drawn her to Charles.

In her third year (1911–12), as well as being vice president of the Society for Social Study, Margaret was elected honorary secretary of the humbler Women's Representative Council: during this year she wrote letters to the new vice-chancellor, Michael Sadler, about provision for bicycle accommodation and the installing of a telephone, receiving encouraging responses to both approaches.[10] She undertook still more responsibilities in this final year. She was one of three women representatives on the Students' Union Committee, she was still on the *Gryphon* Committee, and was also on the Entertainments and Dance Committees. She gave a number of talks during the year as well: in November, she spoke on "William Morris" at the Literary and Historical Society; the Women's Discussion Group reported in February that "later in the session Miss Jameson will give a paper on 'Infant Mortality,'" while in March, announcing forthcoming lectures, the *Gryphon* referred to jokes arising from "the announcement that Miss M. E. Jameson is to speak to the Social Study Society on 'How to keep a family on £1 per week.'"[11] Margaret may well have been better informed than was realized by her peers. For the meticulous research she would undertake in future years when preparing to write an article or novel may already have manifested itself; there were books available on the topics she spoke on and she may have read such works as Bessie Leigh Hutchins's *The Working Life of Women* (1911), Olive Schreiner's *Women and Labour* (1911), and Mrs. Pember Reeves's *Family Life on a Pound a Week* (1912).

Despite all these activities Margaret's studies did not suffer. In addition to her final examinations, she wrote a long essay on William Blake, whose revolutionary aspirations for a better society must have appealed to her, although she would be scathing about her essay later (*JN*, 1:55). At the time, she proved her academic potential, becoming the first woman at Leeds University to be awarded a first-class honors degree in English. But at this point her budding desire for an academic career was thwarted. We get a hint of her reputation among her peers in the *Gryphon*'s mischievous end-of-session piece, "Popular Plays and Books of Prominent Persons," where "Miss Jam-son" as "The Bohemian Girl" figures alongside the new vice-chancellor, Michael Sadler, as "The Man of Destiny."[12] Amusing as this was, a young woman's bohemian reputation at this date would not suggest a promising academic career to the male academics she needed to impress. So maybe as a result of Vaughan's dislike of women, maybe as a result of the image she was projecting, the academic post Margaret might have been offered at Leeds was given to a male contemporary, while she was awarded the John Rutson research scholarship. This scholarship enabled her to study for a Leeds M.A. that would not be supervised in the fledgling university but at University College London. So in the autumn of 1912 she left for the south, later recalling that she "was in debt to a bookseller at the Boar Lane end of Briggate [in Leeds]. The temptation to buy more books than I could afford was too strong. It took me four years to pay off a debt of less than fifteen pounds" ("ULeeds 1909–12"). The slow repayment gives some sense of Margaret's lack of funds as a student; but the debt also offers an early glimpse of her disastrous habit of living far beyond her means, a habit that would plague her throughout her life.

The John Rutson scholarship meant that Margaret was expected to write her M.A. thesis on pantheism in French and German literature, supervised by the eminent scholar Professor W. P. Ker. However, she was already, as her friendship with the Harlands and her speeches at Leeds suggest, much more attuned to her contemporary world. By the middle of her first term in London, she could no longer pretend to like the assigned topic, and told Ker that she wanted to write on modern European drama. Ker did not dissuade her, sending her off to the British Museum to work on a synopsis, which she submitted to him by the end of the term (JN, 1:68). But even more important, from Margaret's point of view, the move to London meant that she was reunited with her beloved Harland brothers, living with them in their lodgings, where she would meet Archie White, also from Yorkshire, who would become another lifelong friend. Before the end of 1912, she was attending lectures at the Harlands' college, King's on the Strand, at a time when there were fewer than a dozen women students there (JN, 1:64). At King's, the boys belonged to a small all-male society, the Eikonoklasts, that met once a week in the men's common room to talk about political and social issues and to drink beer, and within a month of Margaret's arrival, the Harlands insisted she should be admitted. The Eikonoklasts must have been very much to her taste: they were "sceptics, unavowed anarchists, self-dedicated to the unmasking of hypocrites, politicians, clericals, reactionaries, bigots and dogmatists of all ages and conditions" (JN, 1:65). They admired A. R. Orage, H. G. Wells, Sigmund Freud, and the witty satirist Anatole France, all writers who challenged their young admirers to address social, political, and psychological issues and to dream of a better world to which they might contribute in the future.

Back in Scarborough, Sydney and Oswald had introduced Margaret to the left-wing journal the New Age, bought in 1907 by A. R. Orage, a fellow Yorkshireman. Orage's intellectual range appealed to both the boys and Margaret: economics, literature, philosophy, and metaphysics were all addressed in his journal, as Orage believed everything cultural contributed to the understanding and solution of social problems, and Margaret was clearly stimulated by his insistence on the paramount importance of economics, given the working-class poverty in the Britain of her day. She no doubt disapproved of his ideas on the role of women, given his confident assertion that "double men's wages tomorrow, and the women's movement would die in euthanasia the day after," for she herself was one of the new generation of women aspiring to a good deal more than a financial security provided by the male of the species.[13] But in her third-year debates in Leeds, she had, like Orage, prioritized poverty issues above the struggle for the vote, as was shown by the topics she chose to speak on. She would continue to argue for many years that simply having the vote would not cure the desperate hardship endured by both men and women of the working class whose income could barely sustain them.

Orage's journal also championed the arts. He encouraged coverage of recent developments: imagist poetry, the implications for art of the postimpressionists, and, significantly for Margaret, reviews of Continental drama. His defense of realism in fiction as having dynamic potential rather than being backward looking would also be reflected in Margaret's future choices as a novelist. She clearly responded to his insistence on the skill "necessary to convey, and not merely to express, ideas that are likely for any reason to be resisted by our readers. To accomplish this is the noblest use of the art of writing. Every other use of the art is utilitarian or dilettante."[14] Orage had no time for art for art's sake; for him as for Margaret, the novel had a duty to engage with and reflect on the issues of its day.

Alongside Orage, another independent-minded socialist, H. G. Wells, had inspired Margaret and the Harlands since their school days; but the work that thrilled them as university students was his 1911 novel, *The New Machiavelli*. Margaret, looking back at these student days in London, remembered the excitement they felt in those "queer, lively years":

> The arts, we thought, were stirring in their sleep. Even the novel — you can't conceive the effect on us of *The New Machiavelli*. It scarcely seems possible now that we took that so hard. But think that to us the rigid Victorian code was still real. It was something we had consciously to reject.[15]

Wells's novel explored the tensions in both public and private life between Victorian patriarchal values and the urge to break free that Margaret and her friends were experiencing. They, too, scorned "your damned shirking, temperate, sham-efficient, self-satisfied, respectable, make-believe, Fabian-spirited Young Liberal" (Wells, 301), while remaining passionate about an end to poverty. Wells's ebullient, wholesale contempt for what he thought was wrong with those he presented as more addicted to debate than to action could not but appeal to the young Eikonoklasts. Yet importantly, when Wells's protagonist and his lover go off together, they are not the Lawrentian lovers of *Sons and Lovers*, published two years later. Wells's lovers are haunted by their betrayal of society's values, just as Margaret maintained she and her friends were:

> We talked of our freedom from this, that, and the other, but in our minds the Victorian habit persisted, like an old coat hung behind the door, that we shall one day take down and put on. ("Student Days," 164)

Rebellion against imperialist and capitalist ideas, and particularly against the puritanical sexual mores of the Victorians, was profoundly attractive to Margaret and her student friends but, as she herself would soon find, far from easy to sustain when confronted by the disapproval of family and the still potent Victorianisms endemic in the society of their day.

For the time being, however, all was fresh and exciting. Under the boys' guidance, Margaret explored the streets of London and visited art galleries: Sydney and she had their first joyous encounter with post-impressionism, Oswald disapproving as it was not, he maintained, an art accessible to the people. They went to concerts, although Margaret did not share Archie's love of Wagner, and they treated themselves to the music hall to see Marie Lloyd, who delighted Margaret:

> The very way she glanced at you, with that mingling of hard cynical mirth, boldness, and an indescribable air of having been *used*, was like being slapped in the face by life. ("Student Days," 165)

The charismatic Lloyd, vulgar and ebullient, had much in common with the richly earthy Whitby characters whose peasant strengths would always, for Margaret, hold the key to the human capacity to survive, however hard the challenge it faced. Overall, the sheer variety that London offered, in entertainment, in street encounters, in the harsh contrasts between rich and poor, thrilled and provoked her. All was not simply observation, however. She answered an appeal for tutors in a newly established Working Women's College at Earl's Court, the brainchild of Mary Bridges Adams. This woman had been one of the signatories of the 1885 manifesto of the Socialist League and fiercely believed that the working class should be independent. It was this aspiration that prompted her to set up a college where a few poor women from the mills and factories could have two or three months of an education.[16] The project appealed to Margaret and accordingly here she worked, on and off, for a year (JN, 1:65).

CHAPTER 3

Marriage and War

Already in Margaret's first term in London, there were signs of her idyll's
end. Charles (Karl) Clarke, the love of her second year in Leeds, re-
appeared; the Harlands and Archie White did not like him, but Margaret
was still in love, and their affair continued. Then disaster struck. Up in
Whitby, Hannah found compromising letters that Margaret had kept,
and rushed up to London to demand that Karl and her daughter marry.
The Victorian code of sexual morality that the Eikonoklasts had rebelled
against proved too strong for Margaret and her lover: on January 15, 1913,
Margaret and Karl were married. Her time of total freedom had been all
too short, and she was also without a grant, as the university authorities in
Leeds (although not her own professors) had not approved of her change
of topic (*NTLTP*, 85). But for a time at least, her marriage did not cause
drastic changes. She continued to live with her friends, moving with
them from Herne Hill to Shepherd's Bush. She read hundreds of plays
for her thesis, and on March 20, Orage, always well disposed to young
critics, published her blistering attack on George Bernard Shaw, written
with all the high-flown rhetoric typical of an inexperienced but highly
intelligent student.[1] This article was extracted from her thesis, which
she would later dismiss as simply "a joyous exercise in iconoclasm" (*JN*,
1:67). Her critical confidence was high, demonstrating that the younger
generation of her day could be quite as savage as the Angry Young Men of
the 1950s in mocking the shibboleths of an earlier generation.

Then the realities of her marriage caught up with Margaret. By the
end of the summer, she was living with Karl in a squalid room in Shep-

herd's Bush, not far from her friends physically but worlds removed psychologically. She would later say that Karl

> corrupted me in the sense that he worked unscrupulously on my senses and emotions . . . every day I was mortgaging my energies, my unlucid ambitions, my chances, poor as they were, of steadying myself, my whole future — mortgaging them to an egoism less tough than my own, but far more insidious. (JN/TMS, 1:57)

It would seem, from what she recalls here, that Karl felt the need to subdue his highly intelligent wife, making sure that she served his own needs, and in the process eroding her confidence in her own abilities. He must also have revived memories of her mother's abuse, which would always resurface whenever Margaret's confidence took a beating. Their situation was not easy for either of them, of course; they had been scolded into an improvident marriage, and were desperately poor. They quarreled constantly (there is no record of Karl having a job) and Margaret, struggling to finish her thesis and trying to make ends meet, attempted suicide. Karl was unsympathetic, the doctor who treated her contemptuous (JN, 1:74). Unsurprisingly, by the end of 1913, she was back in Whitby, while Karl returned to his parents in London, who strongly disapproved of his wife. It was poverty that parted them for the time being, but already the marriage was under strain. Karl needed to feel superior, and Margaret's Whitby toughness did not suit her to the role of subservient wife. Her depression was inevitable as she lost hope of developing the intellectual skills she had delighted in. Back in Whitby she did recover sufficiently to finish her thesis, and in June 1914 was awarded a Leeds M.A.; but her future looked bleak, with a husband who was undermining her confidence and losing her trust, for like her father, he was given to lying.

Margaret was not entirely defeated: in April 1914, Orage published another article adapted from her thesis, and between January and April she had four pieces published by Dora Marsden in the *Egoist*. Marsden, brilliant and volatile, had recently joined forces with Harriet Shaw Weaver, whose money and more stable talent underpinned the *New Freewoman*. This publication took over from Marsden's struggling journal the *Freewoman* in the late summer of 1913, the title changing to the *Egoist* in January 1914. The new journal rapidly developed different priorities from the *New Age,* although the two publications initially shared some contributors: Ezra Pound's ideas were at first close to Orage's, although he would become increasingly elitist in his writings for the *Egoist* as the journal became more deeply committed to avant-garde works. The *Egoist* serialized James Joyce's *Portrait of the Artist* from February 1914, and published poems by D. H. Lawrence in April of that year; by June, Pound and Wyndham Lewis were regular contributors. The *Egoist,* modernist in its priorities, had none of the social commitment of the *New Age.*

In 1913, when she was still in London, Margaret had met Marsden, and had also caught the eye of Weaver. A young man recalled visiting Weaver's apartment and seeing Margaret there, "the spirit of youth wrapped in a decorative long dark blue cloak."[2] So here she was in bohemian guise, writing alongside the avant-garde of the literary scene, a young writer brought up on Orage's commitment to an aesthetic inextricably linked to social issues. Her first article, published on January 15, 1914, attacked Henrik Ibsen's imitators for failing to see that "reality is of the spirit, born of a need to give form and meaning to the disorder confronting the inartistic view of life."[3] Sweeping though this early comment is, it is clear that Margaret already knew that journalistic skill in recording contemporary life was not enough to qualify as art. Sensitivity to form and pattern, an aesthetic vision, must be present. This did not mean that Margaret was prepared to water down social commitment, as her next article showed. On April 15, she used the review of a play to attack a suffragist anathema, the parasitic woman: the play's protagonist, she said, was simply "taking advantage of the modern admiration for the female presuming upon its femininity"[4] This pugnacious style of criticism must have appealed to Weaver, as she wrote offering Margaret a job on the journal, which the young woman eagerly accepted. As Weaver's biographers note:

> Harriet's offer was no doubt partly inspired by a wish to help Miss Jameson, but it also shows that she could choose . . . people who were worth helping. There was now no one on the paper with a journalist's flair for topical treatment of topical subjects, and Storm Jameson could have filled this gap. (*Miss Weaver,* 90)

Margaret's delighted acceptance, however, soon had to be rescinded; tough though she could be in some things, she could always be manipulated by her mother. This time Hannah put on a fine display of emotional blackmail: she was lonely, she said, not well, needed her daughter at home until Karl could get a job. And Margaret gave in, reluctantly refusing Weaver's offer, well aware that this was a decision that would leave her in the role of a wife struggling to make ends meet.[5]

At last, Karl achieved a teaching post, which took him first to Kettering and then, in the autumn of 1914, to Liverpool, where, by December, Margaret found herself a housewife in a garden suburb. Here her detestation for domesticity took root and would never leave her. Such was the intensity of her sense of entrapment, generated by their poverty and constant quarrels, that it appears to have loomed larger in her mind than the advent of World War I. Later she would recall the domestic battles and, importantly, link them to the experience of "the child *accustomed* to thrashings, and to be consoled afterwards. I had acquired a habit" (*JN/ TMS*, 1:90). For Karl, like Hannah, knew how to play on her emotions: "He had only to weep for himself and his unkindness and all my mortification and resentment melted in a flame of tenderness and pity" (*JN/ TMS*, 1:90). So she was too preoccupied with the struggle to maintain her own sense of self to feel the full impact of the war, at least initially. Her husband was not involved as yet, and while she wrote to Archie, away at the front and having found his métier there, the full awfulness did not touch her until, as for many others, it impinged on her family and friends.

To block out the rows, her loathing of domesticity, and the ever-present worries about money, she was reading avidly: Allen Upward's *The Divine Mystery*, a work examining Christian mythology through an anthropological lens, and Anatole France's novel of 1914, *La révolte des anges*, were two of the works that impressed her. But while the wit in France's novel delighted her, his work was haunted, like Wells's *New Machiavelli*, by the fear that any rebellion is in danger of reverting to the very situation it has fought to escape. Margaret picked up on this fear, which chimed in with her own experience, and she challenged it in another piece for the *Egoist*. In this article she dismissed an imagist poet as nothing more than "Tennyson turning in his grave," while writers like Pound and Richard

Aldington, she said, were out of touch with the real-life issues of their time.[6] Art, for her as for Orage, must be firmly grounded in the realities of its age, and this was something she had started to put into practice, as she had begun work on a novel in those early, fraught months of 1914. The aspirations of her student contemporaries for a better society would provide the core of her book. Furthermore, the turn to fiction gave her the chance to set ideas of her time in debate, as well as to re-create the student atmosphere of her time, while the student frame of mind, its rebellious liveliness, must have provided some solace for her present predicament, as her hopes for the future diminished under the stresses of marriage and domesticity.

This first venture into fiction, however, was soon to be put on hold as, by the autumn of 1914, Margaret was pregnant. She went back to Whitby for the birth, to the house in Ruswarp where her mother now lived, and on June 20, 1915, her son, Charles William (Bill) Storm, was born. When he was six weeks old she took him back to Liverpool and, for a time, he was the focal point for all her energies. Years later, she would recall how little she thought of the young men dying at the front, absorbed as she was by her child (JN, 1:93). But one was enough: when she became pregnant again, she took dismayingly primitive steps to abort, and by the end of the year returned to Whitby with her six-month-old baby and the manuscript of the novel. The child and the novel now shared her time: when Bill caught whooping cough from Margaret's young sister Dorothy, his mother would write at night in his sickroom. After Christmas they went back to Liverpool, and Margaret completed the novel in the spring of 1916 (JN, 1:99).

This first novel, *The Pot Boils*, is, unsurprisingly, an apprentice piece, but for all its unevenness, it is a more accomplished work than Margaret would later allow. Its structure is shaped by the movement from the optimistic idealism of student life in 1912 to the sobering effects of entry into the world of work, offering a vivid account of an idealism continually threatened by poverty. It draws on Margaret's delight in the drama of ideas, being shaped episodically, like scenes in a play. The debates of the student characters, first in a northern university and then in London, are interspersed with scenes dissecting the activities of a woman reformer whose attitude to the poor is one of benevolent patronage. Other scenes offer biting observations on a woman aesthete whose salon and flirtations are conducted at her husband's expense; Margaret's detestation of the parasitic woman would remain constant. In places, Margaret describes the world of nature as sensitively as Lawrence, just as she shared many of his political priorities, and the sensual thread of the love between Athenais and Thurlow is well drawn. The students in the novel have the vitality evidenced in so many widely different movements of the period: the futurists, the postimpressionists, and the vorticists, for example. Indeed, the novel's hectic, uneven progress heralds Margaret's arrival as the document maker of her age. Thurlow comments: "We of the northern universities are nearer life and the rebel spirit than you will allow. At least we are nearer than Oxford or Cambridge. The grime and strife of the world comes up to our very doors" (*PB*, 44). And while he and his fellow students are indebted to the thinkers of their time, they dissect, analyze, and criticize the thinkers' ideas: militant suffragettes, for instance, are attacked by Athenais herself for taking up too much space in the journal she works for with arguments for the vote, "as if they had the right, while there is one ill-paid, ill-fed working woman in England" (*PB*, 244). This attack shows Athenais on the side of the suffragists rather than the militant suffragettes. For while the suffragettes predominantly fought for the vote, the suffragist movement as a whole prided itself on a number of initiatives to help the poor.[7]

It is noteworthy that Margaret has Athenais take a degree in economics after her English degree, for economics would always be an area she herself was drawn to, and in this novel we find many comments showing how middle-class ideas about the alleviation of poverty, however well intentioned, must sound to the poor. Crucially, the representative of the working class, Poskett, the one character in the novel Margaret would later recall with approval, exposes the misreadings of the poor that reformers fall prey to. And he would retain his importance for Margaret, having successors as yardsticks in later novels, such as Thorgill in *A Cup of Tea for Mr. Thorgill*. Meanwhile in this first novel, the new order Margaret's students dream of will not necessarily follow the precise model of any of the thinkers whose ideas they debate. As Athenais says:

> I see all these people, Fabians, Democrats, New Tories, Suffragettes, New Aristocrats, every kind of reformer, all going somewhere, all trying for . . . something they call the good of man.

But each goes a different way, each looks for a different good. . . .
I wanted to understand, to test all these people and their ways,
and so perhaps to find a key to their confusion of tongues. (*PB*,
123–24)

In the end the sheer vitality of the book overrides its weaknesses. Its iconoclasm chimes in with that of Wyndham Lewis's journal *Blast*, founded
as Margaret began to write her novel in 1914, while its hopes and plans
for a better world would be wistfully remembered by its author as World
War I culled so many of her young friends.

By the time Margaret had finished the book in 1916, the war had
come closer to home. That spring, her father's ship, *The Saxon Prince*,
had been sunk off the Irish coast, and he and his crew would be consigned to a civilian concentration camp. Margaret's brother, Harold, was
in the Flying Corps, promoted to pilot by the summer, having already
won a Distinguished Conduct Medal for his missions as a wireless opera-
tor; her sister Winifred was working for the censorship office. Harold now
warned Margaret that Karl's exemption from military service because
he was a school master was unlikely to continue, given the losses on the
Somme; he offered his help to get Karl a job as an equipment officer.
Harold himself was awarded a Military Cross in December (*JN*, 1:101).
But in January 1917, when Hannah and young Dorothy were staying
with Margaret in Liverpool, a telegram was forwarded from Whitby:
Harold had been killed. Margaret's grief was as much for her mother as
for the young brother: later she recalled Hannah's "cry from an empty
womb" (*JN*, 1:101, 103).

Nevertheless, while Margaret the daughter grieved for her mother's
loss, Margaret the writer moved on. She had sent her novel to the Duckworth publishing house; their reader's report commented: "If this is a first
book, it shows considerable promise. . . . The man can write and is worth
watching."[8] Despite this, Duckworth rejected the book, and Margaret
considered whom next to approach. There was, however, a more pressing
decision to make. In the spring of 1917, as conscription cast the wider
net that Harold had predicted, she encouraged Karl to try for a job as an
equipment officer; a friend of Harold's supported him, and he was duly
posted to Reading. Karl left in March, while Margaret stayed behind to
pack and put furniture in store. She sent her novel off again, this time

getting an interview with a patriarch of publishing, Fisher Unwin, who suggested a contract for her next six novels, and then, disastrously, gave her a copy of Ethel M. Dell's Indian romance, *The Way of an Eagle*, as an example of how a novel that would attract a wide readership should be written. No doubt, he meant it as an example of the kind of popular novel a woman should write. Whatever his intention, Margaret had no interest in simply becoming popular by writing entertaining tales of love and adventure; she aimed to address ideas of her time, to be taken seriously by men and women alike. On the way back to Reading, she threw Unwin's gift out of the train window, and did not take up his offer (*JN*, 1:111).

For the next few months Margaret and the child followed Karl from one posting to another, ending up in Church Farm, situated a good three miles from the airfield at Chattis Hill in Hertfordshire, where Karl's squadron was based. It was a place she came to love both for its simple country life and for the fact that she faced none of the torments of domesticity there. The move also took place just as her novel had found a sympathetic reader who would ensure that she finally achieved publication. She had sent it to yet another publisher, Constable; she had sent it under Karl's name, thinking that an officer in the Royal Flying Corps might carry more weight with an editor, but when he was called for an interview, Karl blew her cover (*JN*, 1:116). So Margaret herself was invited to dine by a reader for the firm, Michael Sadleir, at that time working for the War Office, later to become a junior partner in the firm. And here began a fruitful friendship with both him and his wife, Bet. Margaret would remember Sadleir as very good-looking, "kind and sweet-tempered and loyal," seeing him as, like her, a "flawed rebel" against a strict background, and both "romantic and shrewd" (*JN*, 1:159). He would be a very different kind of friend from the Harlands. There was a link with Margaret's past in that he was the son of Michael Sadler, vice-chancellor of Leeds University in her final year, the son eventually spelling his name differently, to avoid confusion. There is no precise record that Margaret came across the younger Michael in Leeds, and his firm was not the first she approached with her novel, but her first letter to him suggests that she may have met him there, since she says: "I did not know [my book] would fall into your hands when I sent it to Constable and Co. The good fortune is mine" (SJ to MS, 11.13.17). What is certain is that Sadleir would share with Margaret his own cultural loves. He was a keen collector of nineteenth-century books and very knowledgeable about furniture. He and his father were also passionate about the postimpressionists, the son writing articles and reviews on modern art for *Art News* and *Rhythm*, the latter, of which he became coeditor, founded in 1911 to give a platform for the Anglo-American Fauves.[9]

Margaret's letters to Sadleir are the first to show her ability to evolve a personalized voice for each correspondent. In letters, her capacity to establish the right tone for each individual was honed to perfection, a skill that would enrich the voices of characters in her novels. The letters to Sadleir start as those of a bright young writer who is naive but willing to learn, they evolve into the outpourings of a young sister. That initial naïveté must have amused him; a few days after dining with him in November 1917, for instance, she felt sufficiently at ease to ask if Constable's would buy her book outright for one hundred pounds, since Karl was going abroad sooner than expected (he didn't), and "I'd like to have one 'pukka' fortnight in town before he goes" (SJ to MS, 11.29.17). Here is another early sign of Margaret's disastrous insouciance about money — and a disarming innocence in making such a suggestion for a first novel. Against the odds, Sadleir agreed to negotiate for the sum she asked, without taking up her offer to sell the book outright: he must have found her as refreshing as Sydney Harland did a decade earlier.

The years 1917 and 1918 were years of change on many fronts. While still in Liverpool, Margaret had written an article for the *Egoist*, "The Scene-Models of Norman MacDermott," focusing on the great stage designer's "simplicity, that is, the insistence on essentials, the creations of a clear, significant image" which "is the first condition of art."[10] Clearly, as critic, Margaret already valued simplicity and the use of clean lines in visual images, skills she would develop over the years in her descriptions of landscape and cityscape. Her bond with the *Egoist*, however, was not to last; when T. S. Eliot was appointed as assistant editor from June 1917, the volatile Dora Marsden did not offer her young critic any more space on the journal. This was not as painful as it might have been, as Margaret had already embarked on another novel, in which she aimed to respond to Sadleir's suggestions for *The Pot Boils*. This novel would soon be laid aside as yet again a personal crisis intervened, a crisis of considerable proportions that could have nipped her career as a novelist in the bud. For her marriage was already failing, leaving her emotionally vulnerable, while Karl was happy to spend long hours at his base. In June 1918, a squadron of the American Air Force arrived in Chattis Hill, and Karl made friends with their commanding officer, a Texan, Jesse (Jess) Fry. Almost as soon as they met, Margaret fell passionately in love with him, and he with her. She had few illusions about him: he was uneducated, there was a sense of violence behind his politeness, he had no moral sense and was all for physical excitement and money. Some years later, true to her reading of him, he would sell arms to both sides in the Sino-Japanese War (*JN*, 1:121). But at the time she was caught between her desire for him, her longing to escape an unsatisfactory marriage, her sense that she should not abandon Karl — and her anxiety not to lose her son.

For a time, decisions were put on hold: in September the American squadron left for France, and in October Karl was posted first to Canterbury and then to Oxford. Margaret, waiting for Karl to find lodgings for her, returned to Whitby with Bill to another dysfunctional household. Her father had just been repatriated, but Hannah rejected him, unable to forgive him for what she saw as his uncaring attitude to their dead son: from now on, when he was home, they lived separate lives under the same roof. Now Hannah's hopes were all bound up in Dorothy, the child who mirrored her own passionate, volatile nature. Meanwhile Margaret was marooned here, at Hannah's beck and call, coping with Do's jealousy of Bill; for Karl, quartered comfortably in Oriel College, wrote to say he could not find any rooms for his wife and child. He sent no money that October, nor did he show any sign of wanting to be demobbed. So the end of World War I found Margaret stranded in the uneasy family home in Whitby, with little money and a growing anxiety about the future.

Despite the emotional turmoil of the second half of the year, Margaret managed to finish her second novel, *The Happy Highways*, although she thought it less good than *The Pot Boils*, dissatisfied with her efforts to render it less episodic: "This connected narrative business is a bore, and I can't do it anyway. It's the old difference between the epic and the dramatic, of course — reduced to the low plane of novel writing."[11] Concerns that would become familiar throughout her career were already bothering her: she would always maintain that the novel was a lesser form of art than poetry or drama, the two literary media in which classical Greece and Rome excelled. The epic could be seen as connected narrative, drama as a series of scenes; Margaret's first novel had mirrored the scenic structuring of the drama she loved, but now, as she experimented with the "connected narrative," it was striking that she chose to see her model as a poetic form rather than as a simple continuation of nineteenth-century fictions. Be that as it may, she was right about this second novel: Sadleir, while encouraging, found the manuscript unwieldy, and Margaret set about cutting it down. Her letters to Sadleir, initially reporting her progress, soon became more relaxed in tone, and by the time he was posted to Paris for the peace talks she was writing friendly informal accounts of incidents that might amuse him. In one letter, she told him about a visit to the Tomorrow Club, founded in 1917 by Amy Dawson Scott (known as Sappho), to encourage young writers. Margaret was not impressed. She had already lampooned a literary salon in *The Pot Boils* and would often satirize them in future novels. She told Sadleir that "May Sinclair, who seemed rather a dear, read a paper on one Dorothy Robinson" (SJ to MS, 12.3.18). This was a misnomer, as clearly Margaret had not yet heard of Dorothy Richardson, whose first "chapter" of *Pilgrimage* had appeared in 1915, and for whose style May would coin the phrase "stream of consciousness." Nonetheless, May's talk had been the high point of the evening, for Margaret was dismissive of the aftermath: "The rest of the company indulged heavily in soul communion, a game in which I have small skill and less practice. I was rather out of things" (SJ to MS, 12.3.18). She would find Sappho's next venture more congenial: the PEN Club would be founded in 1921 and would shape Margaret's life in years to come.

Revisions all done, Margaret submitted *The Happy Highways* to Constable's, who accepted it but put it on hold until after the publication of *The Pot Boils*. This second novel is an altogether darker book than its predecessor. The first-person narrator, Joy, is a young man blinded in the trenches, looking back at his prewar world and what came after. As Sadleir saw from the outset, however, Margaret was trying to cover too much ground. Stylistic ideas that would mature in later work jostle a number of themes: intellectual meditation on concerns already fading into the past sit alongside searching and sensitive analyses of love and friendship, and toward the end of the work, passionate debates about what constitutes a just war or justifies holding out for peace. For war, the novel shows, brings out very diverse attitudes to patriotism, nationalism, and pacifism. The reality administers shocks: Kersent, the ardent pacifist who believes in the sanctity of life and is committed to the fight against poverty, is sent to prison for his beliefs and dies there. Importantly, he is the one pacifist the novel treats with respect for his integrity as opposed to those who simply claim the high moral ground; Margaret would always savage those who struck attitudes as against those who were true to their beliefs. In this novel the powerful meditation on the justifications for war as against pacifism shows her already aware of a debate that would increasingly claim her attention throughout the interwar years.

This was a novel written in the second half of the war, while Margaret's own private life was in chaos. She was searching not only for a direction but also for a voice, and in the text the protagonist meditates on aesthetic preoccupations that may well echo those of the author. For at one point he contemplates, with his natural skepticism, matters that were influencing modernist thinking:

> In a metaphorical burst of unwonted audacity, psychologists and philosophers have likened the mind to a stream. . . . The more geologically inclined talk of the strata of the mind. These similes and phrases seem too simple and tidy. . . . I do not believe that the creatures of the mind . . . inhabit an orderly mansion with the least reputable confined in the lowest dungeon, to emerge only at catastrophic moments. (*HH*, 108)

In her early novels, Margaret wrestles with the ideas of Freud and Alfred Adler, the aesthetics of Dorothy Richardson and a little later of Virginia Woolf. She is aware of modernist developments in such works as Joyce's *Portrait of the Artist,* serialized in the *Egoist* when she was a contributor, and however much she disapproved of the Tomorrow Club, she must have listened to aesthetic arguments there, as when she heard May Sinclair speak. But she was never one to accept blindly the pronouncements of others, and the issues debated in her early work, both social and aesthetic, are linked by clear, strong threads to the best of her mature work.

CHAPTER 4

Entry into the World of Work

By the end of 1918, Karl's unwillingness to return to civilian life was making Margaret's life increasingly difficult. She heard about jobs at an advertising firm in London, suggested that Karl should apply, and, when he "tetchily" refused, applied herself and was accepted (*JN*, 1:132). Accordingly, she announced to Michael Sadleir that she would be in London on December 30. There was no mention in her letter of the decision that would haunt her over the years, the leaving of little Bill with a woman who ran a small school in Whitby; for Hannah did not have the strength or inclination to look after the child at home. Instead, Margaret made light of what might be Karl's reaction:

> I see myself meeting Karl in Bond Street. He will be really delighted to see me and say — "Why, my dear old thing, why didn't you say you were coming up? What are you doing?" And I shall reply after the best French models — "Nothing — oh, how close it is — let us sit down." (SJ to MS, 12.16.18)

In early January, on paper headed Carlton Auxiliary, Carlton Studios, she told Sadleir (now calling him "Michael") that "by a series of accidents," she had found herself homeless when she arrived in London, sleeping that first night in the church of St. Martin in the Fields with members of the Women's Auxiliary Army Corps, and ending up in a squalid temperance hotel, where she remained until she could find something better (SJ to MS, n.d.). She was already depressed by what the job asked of her: "To fly from domesticity and then be asked to spend days thinking of Pear's Soap" was disillusioning (SJ to MS, n.d.). Eventually, she found lodgings in Kensington: "one vast room at a quite preposterous rent in a queer house full of Poles and things" (SJ to MS, 1.24.19). Maybe spurred on by her example, Karl was now starting to apply for jobs (he was unsuccessful), and she offered a rare insight into his abilities:

> Curiously enough, he has rather a genius for organisation in queer contrast to the haphazard way in which he runs his personal affairs. He can make order in chaos in the shortest possible time and is full of weird American efficiency ideas. He really can organise and I hope he gets his chance. (SJ to MS, 1.24.19)

But he remained in Oxford, and there was no antidote to her loneliness and increasing dislike for her job: "not a bit of use talking to Karl — he'd forget to answer" (SJ to MS, 1.24.19).

Her letters to Michael became longer. On one occasion she offered him a lively account of an incident in her lodging house. One of the lodgers, an Australian officer, arrived drunk in the early hours and shot one of the Poles, waking Margaret. Grabbing a coat she "dashed for the fire zone," found Czech lodgers milling around in fright, the Australian still with his gun, and the landlady begging everyone to keep quiet as she did not want any police or journalists (SJ to MS, 1.30.19). Margaret assured Michael she wandered over to the gunman talking "in a transatlantic middle-west accent Jess Fry couldn't have bettered," got the gun, calmed everyone down — and then, realizing what a fright she looked, "my hair an inglorious tangle, my nightgown too thin and my Burberry too short," she fled (SJ to MS, 1.30.19). It turned out the bullet had only grazed the Pole's temple, and she persuaded the Czechs not to go to the law. The telling of this tale, whether strictly true or not, revealed another of Margaret's gifts: a ready capacity for comedy.

When *The Pot Boils* was published, reviews were mostly encouraging.[1] Margaret's reaction to them was fairly buoyant, and in her letters to Michael, still in France, other concerns were given priority. Her arrival in London coincided with a wave of strikes, disputes having escalated since the end of the war, and she gave Michael an entertaining account of her struggle to get to work on time. She told him about a meeting in the Albert Hall, where she heard the Bolshevist John Maclean, and "the pure childish voice of Sylvia Pankhurst," a meeting where she confessed that

> for at least two hours I believed in the immediate possibility of Revolution. And when I reflect that a number of people are believing in it all the time with a fervency more untroubled than mine, I remember that other faith which was a grain of mustard seed and in a few years destroyed Rome and un-made a world, and I think that you are making peace on the very edge of a volcano. (SJ to MS, 2.6.19)

Margaret was no fool. She was already aware of the unease below the surface in Europe since Michael was privy to the Peace Conference at Versailles, where the Western leaders grappled with this unease.[2] No doubt aware of the tensions he was witnessing, Margaret tried to keep the prevailing tone in her letters entertaining, as here:

> I am now advertising the Auto Strop which yearns to be "human." That means a beautiful young man with a girl's eyes fixed adoringly on his chin — "A skin you love to touch" — or "Moments when a man's chin matters." I progress, oh yes I progress — Rake's Progress. (SJ to MS, 2.6.19)

She may have been good at her job, but her dislike of advertising was growing. Moreover, the Spanish flu epidemic had claimed half the staff of the Carlton "and we are working every evening and all Saturday to cope with accumulated work" (SJ to MS, 2.22.19).

What Margaret really wanted was a place "where I can write at night. And I want Billy" (SJ to MS, 3.16.19). In April, however, just as this hope became reality, she and her son installed at a house in Ruislip, she was headhunted. Frederick Thoresby, a retired businessman, had bought the long-standing weekly the *Christian Commonwealth and Brotherhood World*, his intention being to turn this journal into a vehicle for his own views, renaming it the *New Commonwealth*. He had approved of what he found in *The Pot Boils*, and invited Margaret to meet him. He was, she said:

middle-aged and judicial-minded. He wants to found one of those funny weeklies that "appeal to the sane elements" (who are the sane elements?) and invited me to sit on the editorial board. He is an Independent Liberal gone wrong. (SJ to MS, 4.12.19)

But she hesitated, as her private life was as tangled as ever, the Texan having returned. Karl, she told Michael,

gave me ten pounds and the next day borrowed six of it back again. The Colonial [Jess] took me out to dine and spoiled a perfectly good dinner by telling me he loved me. (SJ to MS, 4.16.19)

Not very surprisingly, she had a new idea for a novel (called at this stage "Jess and Caroline," ultimately *The Clash*) but no time to write. At least confusions provided copy, as she would ruefully admit.

Margaret's relationship with her Texan was clearly causing the Sadleirs anxiety. In early May she wrote defensively to Michael:

Of course I didn't encourage the Colonial. The man is impossible. . . . Give me credit for a caviare [*sic*] taste. . . . Jess has now gone back to U.S. for good. What an odd episode! This is the grin of the tragic mask, I think. (SJ to MS, 5.9.19)

While she strove to keep her tone light, she was far from happy. As she found herself unable to write, Michael encouraged her to cull articles from her drama thesis and to offer them to the *New Europe*, the editor of the journal being a friend of his. She was not enthusiastic, but the articles were duly extracted and accepted. She also managed, no doubt on the basis of discussions with Jesse and with Michael, and her own voracious reading, to write some articles on America, a matter of keen topical interest because of President Wilson's major role at the Versailles peace talks. At the same time, she toyed with the idea of publishing her thesis as a book. Unhappy in advertising and contemplating Thoresby's offer, she had settled Bill back in Whitby and was living in London with friends at their home in St. John's Wood. John Gleeson, a doctor, had been one of her group at King's, and his wife, Elizabeth, had now become one of

Margaret's closest friends: "I walked straight into an intimacy which fitted me like a comfortable old glove," she would recall (*JN*, 1:150).

Pleasant though this friendship was, Margaret was increasingly worried about being overworked and underpaid, and about whether to accept Thoresby's offer. He had

> offered me £5 a week to rewrite his new paper for him. I mean that he would write the 10 columns for which the editorial staff would be responsible and I would rewrite them in the best Storm Jameson style. Most degrading business but it might be worth it for a while until I amassed a little money. (SJ to MS, 5.21.19)

In the same letter, she also worried about the fate of her second novel, "buried in a Constable safe." The reason for the publisher's prevarication may not have been solely financial: there was the question of the novel's debate about pacifism. True, in 1916 two novels about pacifism had been published without a hitch: Rose Macaulay's *Non-combatants and Others* explored ideas about a just peace, and Mary Agnes Hamilton's *Dead Yesterday* had a similar theme. But by 1918, the climate had changed: Rebecca West's tragic portrayal of shell shock in *The Return of the Soldier* had no adverse reaction, for her damaged soldier would return to the trenches, but hardening attitudes to pacifism brought the publishers of *Despised and Rejected* by Rose Allatini (under the name A. T. Fitzroy) to trial and the firm was heavily fined.[3] Although this novel was also censured because it had lesbian and gay protagonists, the Constable editor, Mr. Kyllman, may well have been made nervous by the judgment. Whatever the editor's reason, Margaret now withdrew her book, approaching other publishers.

Some time before, she had told Michael about some "more or less Freudian" tales she had written; she had sent them to an agent, but he had found them too morbid (SJ to MS, 9.2.18). Michael, now home from France, liked one of them, including it in the first of a new series of tales he was editing anonymously for Blackwell's: *The New Decameron*, based loosely on Boccaccio's original concept. Margaret's contribution is a tale within a tale. The woman doctor's tale explores intolerance breeding intolerance; her sick father's tale, which she recounts, is gothic in style, exploring a disastrous mother-son relationship.[4] The father's tale evokes the Victorian era not just in theme but also in its nineteenth-century style, but the doctor daughter, her tale written in a contemporary mode, is said to have been seduced by "the modernist novelist's custom of stretching friends and enemies on the bed of pithecoid psychology" ("Woman Doctor's Tale," 79). Interestingly it is the old man's defense of old-fashioned values that, despite his old-fashioned style, converts his daughter to tolerance. Margaret, when contemplating ethical clashes, would again use style to evoke period in such novels as *The Lovely Ship* and *The Pitiful Wife*.

By the end of August, Margaret had revised her thesis and left the Carlton with some regret; she had liked her boss and some of her colleagues. She started work with Thoresby on September 2 (SJ to MS, 8.13.19). She soon found her subordinate position trying, complaining that a column she had written on America for the first issue had been drastically watered down, and that the serial she had started had not met with the editor's approval (SJ to MS, 9.24.19). But an eloquent attack on the divorce laws was approved, and she must have been responsible for writing or reworking many other unsigned pieces. The printing of the journal was also one of her responsibilities: in a late letter to Alfred Knopf she gave a vivid account of working alongside the printers until the early hours of the morning, and walking back through the silent streets of London without fear.[5] But at the time she told Michael tempestuously: "I *hate* journalism. Advertising was far better. I'm quitting in May or April. I want to write a million things, and I've no damned time" (SJ to MS, 10.3.19). Yet all was not lost: in the second issue, her keen interest in economics was given free rein in a signed article on profiteering. This must have pleased her; moreover, it offers proof that this interest in economics was well established before R. H. Tawney published *The Acquisitive Society*, the work that would harmonize with many of her ideas. Margaret worked hard for the journal, and helped other emerging writers where she could. In November, she advised Tom Moult, who had applied for the post of literary critic, about his forthcoming interview with Thoresby. He must at all costs avoid any reference to contemporary or near-contemporary avant-garde movements: "[Thoresby] dislikes Futurists and Imagists: no-one has ever told him about Vorticists, but if you say it to him he won't like it."[6] Moult must have paid heed, for he got the post.

Margaret had now placed three articles on America with the *New*

Europe, as well as the articles on drama (SJ to MS, 10.18.19). The editor, R. W. Seton-Watson, was a valuable contact for her, as he was something of a polymath; moreover he was keen to promote the interests of the newly established republic of Czechoslovakia. He was a friend of its first president, Tomáš Masaryk, and was passionate about Eastern European affairs. So Margaret was benefiting both from Michael's experience at the peace talks and from Seton-Watson's interests, and her eyes would turn increasingly to issues outside England as well as to the local causes already close to her heart. Meanwhile, her stories and articles were finding outlets. At Michael's request, she had submitted another short story, darkly erotic, for the second volume of *The New Decameron* (SJ to MS, 10.30.19).[7] And in the journal *Theatre-Craft*, she appeared alongside Ezra Pound and Harold Monro, with "Nietzsche in Modern Drama," the first chapter of her forthcoming book on drama.[8]

On November 28, the *New Commonwealth* gave its front page to a passionate article on the starving children in Vienna; the article was unsigned but later Margaret would claim that this matter so affected her that she mentioned it in every issue (*JN*, 1:157).[9] She was writing more attributed articles now, also using her grandfather's name, George Gallilee, as a pseudonym; and, while *The Happy Highways* was still going the rounds of the publishers, it was serialized in the journal.[10] In January 1920, Thoresby reintroduced the *New Commonwealth* as a new series, with a more attractive layout and more signed articles. One issue carried a front-page article on venereal disease, anonymous, but one that Margaret would later claim as her own.[11] The serialization of *The Happy Highways* continued, alongside one of her melodramatic tales, "A Cloke for Two" (*NC*, Jan. 9, 1920). But despite some eminent contributors, the journal, like the *New Europe* and many other publications, was struggling in the worsening economic climate. By March it was coming out monthly, although Margaret herself was now named as covering theater matters, and given a full page; and in the April issue she and Thomas Moult shared a "Special Literary Supplement." Here, Margaret wrote on the modern novel, offering qualified admiration for Wyndham Lewis's *Tarr*, and encapsulating Joyce's *Portrait of the Artist* in a grandiose metaphor: "Watered wine in the goblet of a Cellini" (*NC*, April 1920). Presumably she admired the style but was less impressed by the content. She was unimpressed by Virginia Woolf's second novel, *Night and Day*, finding the characters "entirely devoid of humour and of its cultured brother, wit. . . . They are not born — birth is vulgar — they are made" (NC, April 1920). But she was not so hard on Dorothy Richardson, saying of her, Joyce, and Wyndham Lewis that, even if not to one's taste, "it is impossible to deny to these writers a conscious attempt to develop word-craft in the novel, as distinct from the craft of character-drawing and plot" (NC, April 1920). However, she found them inferior to Joseph Conrad and D. H. Lawrence, who were for her the "supreme stylists." For her, Joyce, Lewis, and Richardson fell short, "due less to any lack of skill in words than to their spiritual and mental impoverishment" (NC, April 1920). The whole of this article makes Margaret's priorities clear; she was wary of any work where a writer struck her as more concerned with expression than with subject matter. The subtleties and complexities of human behavior and their social repercussions must in her view be paramount.

But Margaret's job was in the way of her novel writing. At least her decision to remove *The Happy Highways* from Constable's safe had finally paid off. Charles (Charley) Evans of Heinemann's sent it to John Galsworthy to read, and received a very favorable response:

> This authoress has done what none of the torrential novelists of the last ten years has achieved — given us a convincing . . . summary of the effervescence, discontent, revolt, and unrest of youth: the heartache and the beating of wings. . . . To an old-fashioned brute like me, of course, the lack of form and line and the plethora of talk and philosophy pass a little stubbornly down the throat and stick a little in the gizzard; but the stuff is undeniable, and does not give me the hollow windy feeling I get from a German novel — say; nor do I feel suffocated by the crude ego that stalks through most of their novels.[12]

Accordingly, Evans accepted the book, and on January 9, 1920, Margaret signed the contract.[13] This was just as well, as it would seem she had yet again succumbed to what was fast becoming a habit: living beyond her means and borrowing lavishly. For, in return for money loaned to her by her editor, on January 28 she agreed to an indenture between herself and Thoresby, giving him all the profits on *The Happy Highways* up to the value of £441 — a huge sum for the period.[14]

Her private life was also changing. Demobilization was virtually complete by February 1920, and Karl was returning to civilian life.[15] For a time, he seems to have lived on his gratuity; when he did apply for teaching posts, he was told he had stayed in the air force too long and was rejected. So Margaret provided a solution: she persuaded Thoresby to take Karl on as subeditor in her place (*JN*, 1:166). Later, she would be vague about the exact date she handed her job to Karl, but it seems likely that the April edition with its literary supplement was her last in the post: it may well be significant that Thoresby only forwarded news of the indenture to Heinemann on April 10, no doubt to make sure of recovering his loan.[16] Certainly by May, as letters to the Sadleirs show, Margaret was not living in London but had returned to Whitby, where she would be based until July. No doubt she had retired north to write, although she told Michael tersely, "Karl talks of my 'writing plans' when he means hopes. I do not know when I shall start writing again, but I shall die of suppressed talent if I don't start soon" (SJ to MS, 5.21.20). She had completed the revision of her thesis and had placed it with Collins, while *The Happy Highways* came out in early June, to mixed reviews; Michael's justifiable view that Margaret had attempted too much in this novel was on the whole shared by the critics.[17] Meanwhile, Karl, as subeditor, would be overseeing production of the *New Commonwealth* as Margaret had done, but she continued to supply large quantities of copy. In the summer, she came south, as the Sadleirs had generously lent their London house to herself and Karl; and despite working on her thesis and on Thoresby's journal, she had managed to finish her third novel, *The Clash*. She had already offered it to Heinemann, but this did not prevent her from sending it to Michael for his reaction as a friend she trusted, saying rather desperately:

> It is bad because it's really two books. The book I'd have written if I'd been able to write it in 1916 when I wanted to, and the book I had to write now, while [*sic*] all the differences and all the experiences of 1916–20. (SJ to MS, 8.13.20)

She was nearly incoherent in this letter, overburdened as she was with work, writing "rot for that cursed *New Commonwealth* — 10000 words of it, my dear Michael!" and typing 6000 words a day (SJ to MS, 8.13.20).

Fortunately, the monthly toil for the *New Commonwealth* was coming to an end. Thoresby's editorial in October 1920 announced that this was the last number under his editorship as the paper had "completed the object with which I started the paper in October 1919." As his original objective had been to set up a National Union of Citizens for those outside the confines of the existing Trades Unions, it is not clear what he felt he had achieved; but he now urged his small band of subscribers to read the *Daily Herald*, the newspaper supporting the Labour movement. Puzzlingly, the journal lingered on until early 1922, bringing out one article a month, at two pence. But Margaret was free of it and, relieved of her heavy journalistic commitment, was back in Whitby again. She complained to Michael that William Heinemann had not made up his mind about *The Clash*, and had not let the more amenable Charley Evans see it. But in fact she sounded more concerned about entering the antiques market, asking Michael's advice on the selling of an old chest of drawers she had rashly bought from a Whitby family (SJ to MS, 10.5.20). By the end of the month she sounded more anxious about the publication of her novel, and with good reason; she had overstretched her finances yet again by the purchase of the chest of drawers, confessing "my lacquer extravagance rather worries me. I've bought a new frock and I miss the N.C. cheque." But her spirits were not unduly affected, for she went on to tell Michael, "I had a three volume cable from Jess. I don't think I shall marry him; he is so extravagant" (SJ to MS, 10.31.20). Clearly this was good for morale.

That same month, *Modern Drama in Europe* was published. A revised version of her M.A. thesis, it was fiercely critical of what Margaret saw as drama's "slow descent to disintegration and unproductive repetition" after the excellence of Ibsen and Strindberg.[18] She set Nietzsche alongside these masters of their craft as having the "same intolerance of mediocrity: the same questioning of accepted creeds and faiths" (*MDIE*, xv), and her own credo, already proclaimed in a number of articles, chimed in with her reading of theirs:

> This is not a demand that art should instruct. . . . But it is a demand that art should present life as worth living, should glorify it for us, give us inspiration, strength and faith in the power of the human spirit. For this reason the cry of art for art's sake is an unmeaning phrase. (*MDIE*, xxiv)

This book had the brilliance of a fine thesis, concentrating on identifying how "realism" could or should be defined and evolve in the modern era, assessing those who resisted realism, and analyzing each dramatist's strengths and weaknesses by her own passionately articulated criteria. Its range was formidable, embracing dramatists from Scandinavia, Germany, Spain, Italy, France, Russia, and England, with no critic at that date to guide Margaret on such a wide-ranging quest. Rather to her surprise, since she saw it merely as the reiteration of ideas she had in her youth, the book was taken seriously, even if most reviewers disapproved of her iconoclastic approach.[19]

The following year brought mixed fortunes. Michael had introduced her to Naomi Royde-Smith's Thursday evening literary salon, and although Margaret would never be at home in such gatherings, and would frequently satirize them in her novels, they did provide some introductions she would value. Naomi was at this time editor of the *Saturday Westminster Gazette* and, while not attracting the kind of talent orbiting Bloomsbury, was respected as a patron. Rose Macaulay, who shared a flat with her, was kind to Margaret at that first meeting and would become a friend, as would elderly, unworldly Walter de la Mare. On the negative side, the prevailing tone gave no hint that the world of 1913 was "shrivelled and in ruins, like the forms of Georgian poetry," forms of poetry that appeared frequently in the *Westminster Gazette*, forms that Margaret saw as no longer appropriate for the postwar world (*JN*, 1:160). The great figures of this salon were not iconoclasts: there was Arnold Bennett, not Lawrence, Eliot, or Pound. Margaret gained little aesthetically or intellectually: the ethos of this salon was not hers.

More to her taste than the literary salon had been the annual conference of the Labour Party in January 1918, where it had been decided to open party membership to individuals, with particular emphasis on women, who were not members of Trade Unions, and also to encourage the formation of more local Labour branches.[20] Margaret, eager to be fully involved, was one of the earliest to gain individual membership.[21] By 1920, when she was up in Whitby, the Scarborough and Whitby Local Labour Party (in the North Riding grouping) was recorded as paying its dues to the Labour Party, and Margaret would maintain close links with this branch for a number of years. Moreover, 1921 saw the publication of a book by the socialist thinker whose ideas were in tune with her own,

R. H. Tawney's *The Acquisitive Society*. In the spirit of John Maynard Keynes, this work urged the importance of capitalism addressing the needs of the workforce, insisting that "labour consists of persons, capital of things. The only use of things is to be applied to the service of persons" (Tawney, 114). Tawney, like A. R. Orage, like Keynes, was wrestling with the problem of poverty in a capitalist economy. Some of their suggestions, like Orage's and, at this stage, Tawney's Guild Socialism, proved blind alleys, while others were more fruitful; and Margaret had already entered this debate, now all the more urgent, given the effects of war on the societies emerging from it.

As a serious journalist, Margaret was fast learning the professional writer's skill in using material more than once for different readerships. In February, the *English Review* printed, with minor changes, the "England and America" article originally published in the now-defunct *New Europe*, the second article spanning the March and April issues.[22] In May, a further article, "England and America: European Reconstruction," appeared: it insisted upon the importance of food production alongside industrial growth, since starvation in Europe remained one of Margaret's prime concerns, and it also argued the need for discipline in the rethinking of social policy on both sides of the Atlantic. But, while stressing the importance of workers as against Big Business, Margaret showed some exasperation with what she saw as a wrong emphasis in Labour policy: the large numbers of strikes since the war.

> So far, the only part of Labour's power over the wheels of production which Labour has shown itself capable of using is the power to stop the wheels altogether. Is it conceivable that it will never learn that wheels were made not to be stopped but to be used?[23]

She would always be wary of strike action, although far from unsympathetic to the desperation of the ill-paid workers who took part in them. It was their leaders she found wanting, not the workers themselves, as she would show in her two trilogies, *The Triumph of Time* and *The Mirror in Darkness*.

Margaret was now attracting notice: in June, the *Bookman* printed a photograph of her looking rather sultry, in a fashionable hat.[24] And importantly, she now met someone who, very soon, would become a major presence in her life, Blanche Knopf, wife of Alfred A. Knopf, whose young publishing firm was rapidly establishing itself in New York. The two women got on well, and Margaret was soon in correspondence with Blanche, recommending fellow writers to her as the Knopfs sought to expand their overseas list. Michael, whose work Margaret often analyzed perceptively in her letters, also showed increasing respect for her critical judgment, even while recognizing that her priorities were not always his. Margaret would later recall how he sent her a typescript, saying, "This is no use to Knopf, but the young woman can write, and you will like it — I daresay better than I do."[25] The young woman was Annie Winifred Ellerman, known as Bryher; Margaret met her and her partner, H.D. (Hilda Doolittle), when they returned from the States after Bryher's tactical marriage to Robert McAlmon. Margaret found her "charming to look at" although "worse than eccentric," and for a time they were friends: "[Bryher] was quickly generous, and clever, shrewd, self-willed, a little ruthless — the ruthlessness of a child rather than an adult" (*JN/TMS*, 1:247). Margaret knew her and H.D. well enough to be entrusted with their address in Zermatt — "I rather think her address is supposed to be a secret" — and to liaise with Michael over a typescript of Bryher's (SJ to MS, 6.16.21).

Margaret was still spending time in Whitby, where she could be with her son and concentrate on her writing, and she also spent time with her old friends, John and Elizabeth Gleeson, now living in Portsmouth. She seems to have been in London with Karl fairly regularly, but his work on the etiolated *New Commonwealth* could not have been very lucrative, their digs were cramped and noisy, and their relationship increasingly semidetached. However, still in thrall to her mother's Victorian values, still worried that she might well lose her son if she broke free, she was trying to preserve the marriage: in a March letter to Michael, she angled for a loan of his house in the summer if he and Bet were going away, so that she and Karl could enjoy more relaxing surroundings. In passing, she told Michael she was learning to drive, but "today I rammed a tram. Everyone was annoyed with me" (SJ to MS, 3.15.21), for a now-established ingredient in their correspondence was that she should appear scatty, he wise and judicious.

Margaret was far from scatty as a writer as she became more involved in the literary scene. When in London, she often went to Naomi's salon, sometimes finding congenial company like the writer and editor Frank Swinnerton, and in May she was elected to the Society of Authors. She was also increasingly active politically, although not yet as skilled as she would be: when in July she asked Galsworthy if he would be one of twelve writers to sign a letter for the papers about the Irish situation, his reply gently pointed out the need for focus:

> The really serious thing about Ireland is, or has been, Governmental adoption and justification of reprisals, involving the innocent. That is a question of world-ethics, against which the voice of Letters should be raised.[26]

Galsworthy was pointing to the violence the British government condoned in the months before the signing of the peace treaty that would pave the way for the establishment of the Irish Free State at the end of 1921. In particular, one of the paramilitary units, the Black and Tans, set up by the Royal Irish Constabulary specifically to deal with the rebellion, became a byword for indiscriminate brutality. Galsworthy's wise words were certainly heeded; in the next few years Margaret would hone her skills fast, as her political involvement grew. Meanwhile, although she was publishing some articles and reviews, the need to earn more money was becoming acute. Accordingly, she accepted an offer of fifty pounds to undertake a month's research for Margaret Sanger. Sanger, an American advocate of birth control, had written a book full of statistics on population, income, venereal disease, and related topics as found in the United States (*JN*, 1:171). Unfortunately, publishing on birth control in the States could still lead to prosecution, while England, on this subject, was more tolerant: Christabel Pankhurst's powerful tract on venereal disease, for instance, had been published in London, unscathed, in 1913.[27] So Sanger brought her book across the Atlantic. As a result, her statistics had to be made relevant for an English readership, so she employed Margaret to effect this; the job was meant to be finished in one month, but took longer, and the fee was doubled.

August that year, as Margaret toiled over her figures in London, was extremely hot. Karl went away to Dorset for a fortnight and, when he returned, she discovered that the affair he had begun with a young woman he had met in Canterbury was still going on. He had even brought her to the *New Commonwealth* as his secretary. Margaret began divorce proceedings, a brave move, since her article in the *New Commonwealth* had shown that she was fully aware of the humiliation women could suffer under the current legal system (*JN*, 1:173–77). She was aware of the stigma of divorce, too, asking Michael not to tell his wife what she was attempting (SJ to MS, 8.22.21). But she was soon confronted by a more formidable obstacle: when John Gleeson ran her up to Whitby to tell her mother about the intended action, Hannah, manipulative as ever, reacted badly. She

> persisted in a heart attack until I promised to postpone my divorce until she was dead ("Soon, so soon", don't you know!) The sad thing is that although she brings on the attacks deliberately they are real enough and dangerous. (SJ to MS, 9.17.21)

Predictably, Margaret bowed to Hannah's pressure and abandoned divorce proceedings, keeping her semidetached life, sometimes with Karl, sometimes on her own, with Bill sometimes with her and sometimes left in Whitby. But the emotional toll made her ill, and she was behind on a number of promised pieces. At the end of September, she took up Michael's offer to look at *The Clash*, and also sent it, with a deprecating note, to Blanche Knopf (SJ to MS, 9.27.21, 11.3.21).[28]

By this time *The Clash* had undergone a year of considerable revisions; and it was now mischievously dedicated "To My Husband." Margaret had felt from the outset that it was in essence two novels, and certainly it is a novel of contrasts.[29] The first part sets out the background of Elizabeth, the protagonist, sole child of an unhappy marriage, in a northern port with its own brand of barbarism, and charts her escape to a more sophisticated life. The next section is very different in tone and substance: "Grant me a facility in turning my own emotions to account!" she commented wryly to Michael (SJ to MS, 10.11.21). It covers the passionate love affair of Elizabeth and the Texan captain Jess Cornish, drawing heavily on Margaret's own experience. Margaret analyzes unsparingly the difference between loving and being "on fire" (*TC*, 198) and the problem of continuing loyalty to a husband who is more son or brother.

Toward the close of the novel, there is a bitter appraisal of the state of Europe, centering on the Paris Peace Conference. Margaret's view no doubt owed something to Michael, and also to Keynes's gloomy *Economic Consequences of the Peace*:[30]

> Liberty, with a bloody pate, stalked famished on the icebound
> Neva. Grand Dukes and generals ran about the two hemispheres
> crying Murder, revenge, and moved by the thought of so much
> suffering, the victors of the war blockaded Russia. . . . Lord We-
> verbridge groaned in travail and the new world was born, by the
> fecund will of one terrible old Frenchman and passionate lover
> of his country. . . . Loves meaner than his, and greeds poorer,
> served him. (*TC*, 251)

In one paragraph, Margaret encapsulated the suffering of the Continent
after World War I. Instead of addressing the wide-ranging poverty and
starvation in Europe, the West sent troops to Russia to aid the former
imperial forces against the new Communist regime, while the French
were keen for reprisals against Germany and its allies. Margaret was one
of those who saw the heartlessness of these priorities; reprisals, as in Ireland, would prove nihilistic, leaving the future in jeopardy. In *The Clash*,
Elizabeth hears of the slaughter of thousands of Jews after the armistice,
of growing anti-Semitism, of the simmering Irish question, sees the treatment of returning soldiers — and finds Jess's easy moralizing exasperating.
The novel ends with Jess himself receiving a lesson: he meets an old
English farmer who has lost four sons but is getting on with the harvest.
Jess "felt the presence of a strength beside which his own strength stood
abashed" (*TC*, 296). The man rooted in the land already stood for continuing life in this novel, something that would become a leitmotif in
Margaret's future works. By the end of November, she reported delightedly to Michael that Heinemann was publishing *The Clash*, "without
cutting a word" (SJ to MS, 11.24.21).[31] Little, Brown, her publishers in
the States, also accepted the book, but insisted that, in the American
edition, there should be a foreword asserting that she meant the book to
increase understanding between the nations, accepting differences in a
positive spirit.[32]

Financial pressures were growing again. In early 1922, the *New Commonwealth*, in its one-article format, finally died, so Karl was again unemployed; nevertheless, Thoresby, despite having lost a lot of money in

the venture, treated him generously. For some months, Karl appears to have lived off Thoresby's money, his wife, and his friends. At some point during these months, Margaret wrote another story for *The New Decameron*, "The Tale of the Solitary English Girl: The Pitiful Wife," a story both drawing on material used in *The Clash* and anticipating her next novel, *The Pitiful Wife*.[33] Produced out of Margaret's own emotional turmoil, it made no concession to delicacy of feeling: the presentation of a woman's passion was frank and quite brutal. It is revealing to compare this with Lawrence's tale, "Wintry Peacock," in the same volume, where the men make light of the suffering of the women they have taken. In her tale, Margaret captures the dark call of the blood from a woman's point of view; this is an intensely physical tale, with nothing about the mind. The reviewers in the major journals heaped praise on the volume, and in February she gratefully acknowledged the fee of £15.15 for the story (SJ to MS, 2.9.22). But she was better paid when she had access to the serious journals, and she needed more outlets. At Michael's prompting, she wrote to Clement King Shorter, a vastly experienced editor and founder of the *Tatler* and the *Sphere*. He was patron to a number of avant-garde writers such as Richard Aldington and H.D., and Margaret wrote asking for advice on what would be acceptable to editors of "good journals," as

> novels, it seems to me, are a luxury for the young author. . . .
> I should be a moderately well equipped critic and am a philosopher of sorts. If one is not an Oxford man are these qualities any use in the literary market?[34]

Her query shows a rueful realization that a provincial university did not secure the entry into the literary world that Oxford and Cambridge ensured in the 1920s.

There were other avenues, with no financial rewards, which appealed to Margaret's social conscience. She joined the English PEN Centre in 1922. The year before, Amy Dawson Scott (Sappho), moving on from the Tomorrow Club which had so failed to impress Margaret, had founded a Dining Club for the PPEN (Poets, Playwrights, Editors, and Novelists), soon to be known as the PEN. She dreamed of it becoming an international society, and this was quickly realized: by 1922, an International

Executive Committee had to be set up "to organise and maintain contact with the centres" that were springing up overseas.[35] John Galsworthy was the first president of the English Centre, presiding over other writers living in England who had international contacts.[36] Rebecca West was one of these founding members, as was Hermon Ould, who would become Margaret's close colleague and friend in future years. Ould, shy and profoundly idealistic by temperament, had begun to make his mark as a dramatist by the beginning of World War I; as a conscientious objector, he had worked for the Society of Friends' War Victims Relief Committee. When attitudes to pacifists hardened in 1917, he was arrested, ending up in the Dartmoor high-security prison, and in his memoirs he lightly touched on the brutal treatment handed out to people like himself. Ould would also recall how, in 1921, "it was not easy . . . to find people ready to accept the proposition that Germans, too, were human."[37] But some were more human than others: that same year, working with the Friends in Germany, he saw omens of the future, as in a sign outside a Munich cinema: "Juden sind nicht Erwünscht" (Jews are not wanted) (Ould, 53). Such experiences encouraged him to embrace the aspirations of Dawson Scott from the start, and he sacrificed his career as a playwright to the defense of free speech that was at the core of the PEN ideology. Margaret had been one of the contributors to his and Horace Shipp's journal *Theatre-Craft*, so her name would be known to him when she joined the PEN. Neither could know at this stage how much closer their work for the center would bring them, or how important that work would be.

For the time being, Margaret kept her professional base in Whitby: she was "reading" now for publishers, the flow of manuscripts taking a disproportionate amount of her writing time, although she was trying her hand at a play (SJ to MS, 7.8.22). Her love of drama was and would remain deep rooted; often she would try out future ideas as plays before turning them into novels. She still found time to be with Karl in Cornwall, or near the Gleesons in Portsmouth, still trying to keep her marriage alive. In April she ruefully declined the Sadleirs' offer of their cottage for May and June, as she wanted to look for a house for herself, her son, and her "unemployed, dilettante husband" (SJ to MS, 4.28.22).

The Clash was published on April 27, but reviewers were on the whole dismissive.[38] However, at least two fellow writers of Margaret's generation begged to differ: Winifred Holtby, in a 1922 letter, wrote:

Have you read *The Clash*, by Storm Jameson? A curious book, in some places showing real genius. Her descriptions are exquisite, wonderful. Her people are queer, sinister puppets, with the strange life of puppets. They move in a sharp, uncanny light like the light under the sea. They talk with disturbingly clever talk, such as one never really hears, and it's all shockingly, disquietingly alive.[39]

Vera Brittain would agree, remarking later in a letter to Margaret that reading Holtby's letter in her posthumous book

reminded me of the excitement [*The Clash*] produced in us when we read it just after leaving college. It was a wild book and its construction was nil, but it had a touch of real genius — a crazy, intense, "Wuthering Heights" atmosphere, which made other novels pale beside it.[40]

Whatever literary faults *The Clash* might have, its sheer vitality clearly spoke to these young, postwar women as they began to experiment with fiction themselves.

Storm clouds were gathering again for Margaret; the Texan had returned by the beginning of June, and she soon had to defend herself against rumors of a scandal that had reached the Sadleirs. She assured them that the Texan would not contemplate running away with her, but clearly he had come right back into her life (SJ to MS, 6.1.22). Her letters suggest that Karl was caught between resentment, self-pity, and his own admiration of Jess; she was in two minds about staying with Karl or escaping with Jess herself (SJ to MS, 6.20.22). At the beginning of July she tried to leave Karl, but caved in to his pleas that he was lonely. She told Michael he was to spend the summer with the Gleesons, and planned to read for a B.Litt. at Oxford "if I do really intend to abandon him. I wish he would" (SJ to MS, 7.12.22). So far, Margaret had kept her letters light in tone, but a fortnight later she poured out to Bet how hard she had tried during the nine years of her marriage, adding, in an effort to be fair: "I don't mean that Karl hasn't been kind and helpful and given me money . . . but the thinking and planning and worrying has [*sic*] been all mine." It had been hard for Jess too, "that he should come back and have me fling myself into his arms because I'm tired" (SJ to Bet Sadleir, 7.21.22). Karl, she said, was definitely going to Oxford; when she suggested she and Bill could live nearby, he seemed to agree but then said, "My opinion is that you'd be foolish not to marry Jess." She insisted it was not that Karl didn't care, but "he knows I'm about all in and it frightens him." This painfully honest letter ended in a tumble of words deploring her own unfairness to Jess and to Karl, yet pleading her own torment; she was hysterically unhappy, still haunted by the Victorian code that Hannah had so disastrously invoked when she insisted that Margaret should marry Karl.

By the autumn, Jess appeared to have gone for good, and for the time being Margaret would remain married to Karl. She had managed to start work on her next novel, renting a cottage for herself and Bill in the small village of Ballinger (SJ to MS, 10.6.22). But the emotional turmoil of the summer had taken its toll. Karl had set off for Oxford: "He looked about 17—all fluffy and new-born—when Elizabeth and I saw him off at Paddington," but soon Margaret had to return to Whitby with "a badly strained heart" (SJ to MS, undated). She had to stay there, living quietly, for the rest of the year, and continued to work on the novel, *The Pitiful Wife*, taking time out to revel in the action-packed works of John Buchan. Writing to Bet in December, she mocked her own novel as

> the day's output of slosh. . . . Downright slosh about love and beauty and hawthorn and birds and bubbling brooks—with a horrid old man as background to the innocents in the foreground. (SJ to Bet Sadleir, 12.10.22)

She had rented rooms in a house on the edge of Ruswarp, the village where her mother lived and where Bill had boarded off and on for so long. She lived there with him, Karl joining them for Christmas, and tried, not very successfully, to follow the regime of rest prescribed for her heart condition. She was still unwell in January, but the writing continued unabated. A few months earlier she had written a couple of comic tales about "Lady Susan," and the *Sketch* "think they have discovered a new humourist and said they'd take a dozen sketches" (SJ to MS, 1.9.23). She struggled to meet their order as she needed the money, yet still, by mid-February, was close to finishing the first draft of her novel, telling Michael:

> I have a feeling that this is the last book I shall write in such a feverish manner. . . . If I write any more they'll be quieter and not go delving into wild or tragic emotions. . . . I'm not serene, but fevered, which is bad art. (SJ to MS, 2.15.23)

This was an important insight, and one she had achieved for herself, whatever she might say later about her second husband, Guy Chapman, being the one who opened her eyes to the "slosh" of this novel. Her comments to Michael show that she had already seen for herself the value of standing back, of detachment, although she would not articulate this insight in critical articles for some time.

The year 1923 saw an important shift in Margaret's fortunes. The New York publishing house founded by Alfred A. Knopf in 1915 had expanded rapidly. By 1920, its British list was already impressive, including E. M. Delafield, Gilbert Frankau, Robert Graves, Wyndham Lewis, Ezra Pound, and Dorothy Richardson, and growth would be explosive over the next decade. In 1921, Alfred and Blanche traveled to Europe in search of fresh talent, and soon established themselves as the premier American publishers of European, Asian, and Latin American authors. Since their first meeting, Margaret and Blanche had corresponded, Blanche relying increasingly on Margaret's critical judgment of writers in England, and by March 1923, Margaret had been appointed representative of the Knopf publishing house in London. While still basing herself in Whitby, she set to work, corresponding with and visiting authors, literary agents, and publishers, traveling to London and back. By June she was in full flow, writing to Blanche with details of a translator she wanted, recommending a book on Einstein by the scientist J. W. N. Sullivan, saying she had a promise from Bertrand Russell for a future book, liaising with the publishers Victor Gollancz and Stanley Unwin, and chasing plays and memoirs (SJ to BK, 6.13.23). She felt confident enough to offer *The Pitiful Wife* to Knopf, which was accepted. She even risked asking for an advance of £150 (Constable had offered £100), and, unusually, Knopf agreed (SJ to BK, 6.29.23).[41]

That same month Margaret visited Karl in Oxford, although he was more absorbed by student life than by his studies, not showing much interest in his wife. She corrected the "beautifully printed" proofs of *The Pitiful Wife*, only lightheartedly objecting to the compositor's inclusion of "vast quantities of commas — quite unjustifiably supposing I do not know how to punctuate. . . . I am in fact one of nature's punctuators." But she was concerned that Michael had commented that if he had been Karl, he would have shot himself after reading the novel:

> That worried me. . . . I had thought — one is so ready to think the best of oneself — that it must be much better for Karl to have me get it said in a book rather than go on saying it aloud. (SJ to MS, 6.18.23)

Was she really so naive, or was she simply anxious to mask any malice when writing to a friend? Her dedication of *The Clash* to Karl, together with the barely disguised use of autobiographical material in *The Pitiful Wife*, surely sprang from a writerly delight in revenge for the long attrition of her marriage.

Compared with her mature work, *The Pitiful Wife* was still very much an apprentice piece, but it was an experiment of a different kind from her previous novels.[42] It is the tale of Jael, named after the biblical heroine remarkable for a savage murder, and her love for a young sculptor. It has strong autobiographical elements as have all Margaret's early works, but the experiments with style call to mind the evolution of the novel from the second half of the nineteenth century. The moorland world of the first book evokes a Brontëesque landscape rooted in the past, both by its nineteenth-century rhetoric, its brushstrokes that call up a gothic darkness and hugeness, and by the character of John Trude, malicious and physical. At fourteen his child Jael meets the androgynous, elvish boy Richmond; the action moves through the Pre-Raphaelite period, as the children read Sir Thomas Malory, to the era of early W. B. Yeats, and of the years before World War I. Richmond's art is alive because "nothing that lives is still" (*TPW*, 74), an echo of Margaret's view of Gordon Craig's designs for theater, while Jael responds like a fairy bride. By the end of the second book they marry, and have a son. But then war intervenes, and the style of the work evolves to match it; on leave, Richmond won't go near his studio as it is "like a song in a charnel house" (*TPW*, 128). When he finally comes home, Jael seems apart, more concerned for their child than for him, while Richmond's artistic focus is no longer on his wife but on the aging gargoyle, her father, representing for him mortality, "and all things, even beauty, sprang from his vileness" (*TPW*, 176). The final books reveal Richmond's other love, the woman he met while still in the forces, one of the things, but not the only one, that have come between himself and Jael. Jael's outpourings of jealousy and reproach are brutally modern, the language colloquial, far removed from the romanticism of the early books, but in the end she accepts him back. While the experimentation in this novel is clear after a few readings, the storyline does not sit comfortably with the shifts of style and tone, although structuring, patterning are there; those reviews that did not pick up on such aspects were mixed.[43] However, whatever the critics' verdicts, the sales of the book were excellent; in October, the *Adelphi* for one had the novel on its "Books to Buy" list, and Margaret had indisputably arrived as a writer to watch, although she was no doubt aware that the elements of "slosh" in the work had taken her close to the popular Ethel M. Dell, whom old Fisher Unwin had advised her to adopt as a model.

Margaret's attention was otherwise engaged for a time, as Whitby was experiencing a diphtheria epidemic; Bill had contracted what turned out to be a mercifully mild dose in July and she opted to nurse him at the isolated Ruswarp house as hospitals, in the years before antibiotics, were as likely to kill as to cure virulent diseases. His convalescence was slow, meaning she could not join Karl in Launceston where he had now established himself, abandoning Oxford and the chance of a further degree after one year. On November 11, Margaret joined her mother for the Armistice Day service at Whitby's cliff-top church, going up to the gallery, past the memorial tablet she had set up for her young brother, and looking down on her grandfather's box pew, reflecting on how "this church is a part of my life" (*JN*, 1:190). Back at her mother's house, she fainted: the diphtheria epidemic had claimed another victim, and she stayed there, nursed by her sister Winifred. Much later she would claim that she continued to write to publishers and writers throughout her illness, adding a postscript warning them of her infection. As a result, John Buchan, whose work had absorbed her during her last illness, sent her a copy of his latest book, while John Middleton Murry, whose wife, Katherine Mansfield, had died in January, offered money if she needed it, as her review of a story of Mansfield's had so delighted the writer when she was herself ill (*JN*, 1:190–92).

During 1923, Margaret had been writing the comic stories about Lady Susan promised to the *Sketch*. It was a journal that printed pictures of society weddings, catered to sport, and offered mildly saucy views of the theater. But it was not all frippery: in 1922 it printed Katherine Mansfield's "Taking the Veil," and in early 1923, Wyndham Lewis's "Portraits of Society People" and E. M. Delafield's "The Bond of Union," while the young Agatha Christie would become a regular contributor from March 1923. From May to July, Margaret provided weekly episodes of Lady Susan's follies, and toward the end of the year, Chapman and Dodd brought out a collected edition, *Lady Susan and Life: An Indiscretion*, comprising the twelve pieces written for the journal.[44] The tales are witty and mischievous, about a fluffy, cunning woman, totally unintellectual, complacently confident in her own beauty. They mock, among other things, the earnestness of the young, the pretentiousness (as in some of her novels) of some socialists, and D. H. Lawrence (from a silly woman's perspective). The lady's one lapse from propriety is typical of the tone: kissed by a Russian Bolshevist, she found him "so beautiful and simply covered in red hair," and his calling her his little spotless white cow, prompts the thought "so pastoral. Quite like Rousseau" (*LSAL*, 37). Lady Susan's voice comes through clearly, alongside her long-suffering tycoon husband. The lighthearted whole springs from Margaret's sense of comedy and pure fun, and those reviewers who noticed the book on the whole responded well.[45]

In December, Margaret had an offer that would finally lead to the end of her marriage. She met Alfred Knopf's father, Samuel, treasurer of the publishing firm, on a visit to London; after taking her to dine at the Carlton and giving her a Christmas present, jade and pearl earrings, from Blanche and Alfred, he told her he meant her to have an office in London (SJ to MS, 12.25.23). Accordingly, she consulted Michael about schools for Bill, and in January 1924 moved to Weybridge, forty minutes from London by train, and threw herself into the London scene. Much had happened in the last two years. Proust had died in 1922, the year Joyce's *Ulysses*, Eliot's *The Waste Land*, and Woolf's *Jacob's Room* were published. In the literary circles that took their cue from Bloomsbury, high modernism had arrived, even as in society at large, there was economic stagnation and growing unemployment. In December 1923 there was a snap general election, and Ramsay MacDonald, leader of the Labour Party, was asked to form a minority government, but did not have the weight in Parliament to effect major changes. On the European front, he had fought to persuade the French not to occupy the Ruhr in 1923, as Britain, with its worsening unemployment, needed Germany to be restored as a trading partner; but French policy would in part prevent a German renaissance.[46]

Many writers felt impelled to engage with the increasingly dire social situation at home and worrying developments in Europe, and among them were a good number of formidable women. Rebecca West was establishing herself as both novelist and journalist; Vera Brittain and Winifred Holtby, recent graduates from Oxford, would soon follow suit. These women, like Margaret, were iconoclasts, rebelling against the conventions. There were also prominent women like Mary Agnes Hamilton and Ellen Wilkinson, both MPs, both writers, conspicuously debating major issues of their time. There was Ethel Mannin, from a working-class background, soon to be writing regularly about social and political matters; and Woolf herself, while she shared her circle's "passionate commitment to aesthetic form," would produce over the next decade a fiction that "wrestled backwards and forwards between an ideal of formal beauty and social commitment, between abstraction and instruction, between imagination and history."[47] Amabel Williams-Ellis, one of the Strachey clan and soon to become a close friend of Margaret's, had addressed this problem in 1922, asserting:

> Ugly facts of the material world, or of the poet's or his characters' natures, must not have a blind eye turned to them. If we never look at them, how can we know if they are good or bad? We should have only a tradition instead of evidence.[48]

World War I had revealed all too clearly that the days of cozy romance were numbered, and the traumas it had left in its wake, both social and personal, must be confronted and assessed, as Amabel and others of her kind were urging.

Margaret was moving into an intellectual atmosphere that would suit her temperament, where rival priorities were being tested and explored in the arts as in social and political arenas. Her northern independence of mind would make its contribution, just as contemporary artists from the dales and industrial towns of Yorkshire, Herbert Read, Henry Moore, and Barbara Hepworth, would challenge the metropolitan aesthetics of the Bloomsbury Group.[49]

CHAPTER 5

Margaret and Guy

Improbably, it was *Lady Susan and Life* that would have the greatest impact on Margaret's life as she moved to London. She had not placed this
book with a major publisher, but with a small firm, Chapman and Dodd.
The London manager had written to her in Whitby, asking her to write another book for them, but had not liked her proposal. So soon after settling
herself and her son in Weybridge, Margaret visited the London office and
met the manager, Guy Chapman. For both, it was a momentous meeting:
almost immediately they began a relationship that, against all probability,
would last. Chapman was, in many ways, very different from Karl or Jess.
Born in 1889, educated at Westminster School and Christ Church, Oxford, he had wanted to be a historian, but his father insisted on the law.
However, when the father died suddenly in 1913, Guy turned to publishing, and then, some time after the outbreak of war, joined the Royal Fusi-
liers. In November 1914, against the wishes of both families, he married
Doris May Bennett before being posted to France. His experience there
would change him forever. The ordeal of the trenches drew him and his
men into a relationship of the deepest kind, as he would say later:

> All I am clear about is that it is sharper than any other sort of
> love, in an indefinably different way as strong and deep as my
> love for Margaret, my wife. Incidentally the only woman I have
> ever known who could, if not imagine such love, understand it.[1]

His marriage did not survive the war. Guy had been gassed, and as was
true for many, he was not the man his wife had married. She refused to

join him in Germany in 1919, where he was serving with the Army of Occupation under Bernard Law Montgomery; when he was demobbed in 1920, Doris told him she was in love with another man, but needed to continue to live with him until the danger of scandal was over. His loneliness and disillusionment were complete, and when Margaret met him some time later, she had much to contend with. She learned to accept that she must share him with a memory, not of his first wife but of his battalion (GC, AKOS, 120). In a passage cut from her late memoir, Margaret quoted a piece she wrote in 1924, soon after their relationship began, and it is poignant in its clear-eyed view of the sacrifices as well as the gains this relationship would bring. She meditated on love, "the three kinds of love, sensual, intellectual, imaginative," and recalled her sensual love for Jess, and the ease of being strongly drawn to a man "neither her intellect nor her heart approve for an instant" (JN/TMS, 1:49). Guy presented her with something very different:

> Do I know anything about intellectual love? Is it possible that Guy is capable of nothing more? Yes, it is possible. Love of this second kind is easy for men and women in whom quick minds are joined to a low vitality. Such people are charming companions, sensitive, witty, sympathetic. To be happy they need nothing but the good fortune to fall in love with one of their own kind. I could perhaps sergeant-major myself into becoming one of this kind. (JN/TMS, 1:49).

But Margaret found herself now committed to a rare kind, what she termed "imaginative" love, and which she found in Stendhal's *La chartreuse de Parme*, involving total commitment:

> To the last farthing, to uphold, to approve, to impoverish oneself, may be for nothing. One can be sure of nothing in this life — the only thing one *can* be sure of! Here, for the first time in my life, I have no doubts. (JN/TMS, 1:256)

Margaret may have had no doubts, but the price was heavy. Moreover, this definition of commitment to Guy throws some light on the kind of commitment she would have to those other people and causes that she undertook with such dedication as life went on.

Neither of them had money, so Margaret worked on various projects that prevented her from writing another novel. The Knopfs had put her in touch with Ernest Boyd, who had been on the editorial staff of the *Irish Times* and was now based in New York; one of his current projects was the translation of Guy de Maupassant's short stories. For the next few years Margaret would collaborate with him on this enterprise, a number of volumes being brought out both in the States and in England. She also wrote an introduction for Eric Sutton's translation of Jacques Cazotte's tales, along with the occasional review. But her main task was her work for the Knopfs. In April, Alfred wrote a round letter to his London counterparts, urging them to act through her, as a number were trying to deal directly with New York. Knopf praised her critical faculties and spelled out her right to make judgments on the firm's behalf.[2] In May, Blanche asked her to extend her brief by taking on difficult writers already on their books, naming the American writer Mary Borden Spears, married to an Englishman, and the Bloomsbury writer and publisher David Garnett (BK to SJ, 5.22.24). Clearly Margaret's skill at dealing with people had impressed the Knopfs. Her letters to the Knopfs were always businesslike; she handled her authority astutely, referring decisions to the Knopfs when she did not want to give offense to touchy London publishers, and she made her own decisions where appropriate. But she was not writing a novel.

The main distraction, of course, was her growing closeness to Guy, with all the problems that brought: they were both married, though each lived alone. More important, Margaret had to come to terms with the realization that, as a result of his war experiences, Guy was already "occupied territory," emotionally drained, and that "fatigue made him cruel." Fairly soon she learned to accept the alienated voice of his "exhaustion and fear of failure," and to welcome its fellow, the one that convinced her she was loved and needed (*JN*, 1:209–10). The problem of Karl had to be confronted too; sometime in the spring he came to London and made trouble, despite the fact that he had never abandoned his own affair. Yet there was the odd respite: in April, Guy shared his lifelong love of Scotland with her, taking her for a holiday in the Cairngorms (GC, *AKOS*, 113). But this was all too short a break: by July, he was busy setting up his own publishing house, an ill-fated venture, as in many ways his view of publishing harked back to the prewar days. Over the years it would become clear that he was no better at managing money than Margaret.

She now planned to move right into London, while Bill boarded in Weybridge. She could never resolve the clash between career and motherhood, and while she poured out money for her son, his schooling involved constant shifts and changes, sometimes living with her, more often not. Over the summer Karl, knowing how to play on her fears, threatened to take Bill from her, but eventually agreed to a divorce that would cite herself and Guy as the guilty parties. Once this was decided, Margaret made the move to London, renting the first floor of a house where the young Noel Streatfeild, an actress and a romp at this stage, had rooms.[3] In November, Guy and Margaret suffered the preliminary indignities legally required for a divorce in the 1920s: standing together by a window while four witnesses walked past. Guy was no support, fleeing as soon as it was over, and Margaret felt she should console Karl with tea and a dance; she had not yet broken completely free of him in her mind, while she was also acutely aware that she was choosing "a difficult self-centred lover" (JN, 1:223). In this, Guy had disturbing echoes of Karl, but Margaret's commitment would now be complete, whatever difficulties and exasperations she faced in the future. Taking Bill back to Whitby for Christmas, she told her mother about Guy. To her surprise and relief, the news did not provoke another heart attack, Hannah even accepting that Margaret and Guy might live together before they could marry. Accordingly, straight after Christmas, she gave in to Guy's pleas to come back before the end of the year, left Bill with his grandmother, and moved from the noisy London house full of women to quieter lodgings, making it easier for herself and Guy to be together.[4]

The following year was difficult, as each of them waited for their divorces to be finalized. Margaret continued to act as the Knopf London agent, bargaining intelligently, and sorting out any differences of opinion between Knopf and English publishers.[5] She continued to translate the Maupassant stories, and wrote another story for the fourth volume of The New Decameron series.[6] But she was still not writing a novel. In later life, she would insist that Guy's comment on the one she had first shown him ("I'm so sorry — I couldn't read your novel, you write so emotionally, writing should be clear and direct") had shaped her subsequent writing.[7] However, since the novel she most likely showed him was the recently published The Pitiful Wife, those letters to Bet and Michael, written before she ever met Guy, had already deplored "slosh" and said writing at fever pitch was bad art (SJ to MS, 2.15.23). And as her approving comment on Bryher's lucid style also showed, Margaret was critically mature long before meeting Guy. The "sloshy" style of her fourth novel had been something she needed to get out of her system, and would not occur again. It was in later life, when Guy was already ill and inclined to feel he had accomplished nothing, that she would give him credit for all her writerly virtues.

At Easter, she took Bill out of his Weybridge school and, worrying about his health, braced herself for the likely battle to persuade her mother to keep him in Whitby. Hannah, rather surprisingly, agreed: maybe she was missing Dorothy, who was now at university, for she even gave him Harold's old room (JN, 1:228–30). This must have been an enormous relief for Margaret, as she had enough of a problem, learning to cope with Guy. Moreover, divorce, as she had realized at her first attempt, was or could be a social stigma: there was always the danger of being ostracized. In July, she wrote anxiously to her beloved de la Mare, apologizing for not having visited him "because I have been getting divorced, and I didn't — and don't — know if you mind."[8] Typically, he was not judgmental, and by September she was writing happily to ask if they could visit him — "I have bought a little car and I don't hit many things with it now"; Susan (the car) would bring them, despite the fact that "Guy ran her into a large wall not long ago" (SJ to de la Mare, 9.7.25, 9.21.25).

By now, Guy's publishing venture was encountering severe financial problems, despite his having taken on a wealthy pupil, Dennis Cohen. Other than this pupil, Guy's only staff was his secretary, Mrs. Boyce, "a good-natured florid Cockney" whom he trusted implicitly (JN, 1:231). He and Margaret were now living together, moving from one rented flat to another. Guy could be remote, Margaret hated domesticity; and yet she had no doubts that this difficult man was right for her. By the end of the year they had two choices: Guy could keep his firm going if his wealthy pupil came into partnership, or he and Margaret could accept an offer from the Knopfs, who wanted to start their own house in London with Guy as manager. Rightly or wrongly, they accepted this offer, and were summoned to New York to finalize arrangements. Margaret was at first adamant that she must spend Christmas with Bill, so Guy set off alone; but she had barely arrived in Whitby when she was cabled by the

Knopfs to take a fast boat, the *Homeric*, on December 23. She felt she had no option as the job must come first and she was anxious not to offend, for she was also learning that, despite their generosity, the Knopfs could be imperious and demanding. She and Guy were in New York for nine days, during which time it was decided that Margaret should work for half a week, earning half the salary offered to Guy. In fact, as she would soon find, she would be working for five days most weeks, and Guy's somewhat old-fashioned views on what the firm could achieve, echoing his priorities for his own publishing company, would prove incompatible with the Knopfs' ideas on profit and the sale of American books in Britain (*JN*, 1:234). However, the partnership began positively. An agreement was signed on January 4, 1926, showing that Guy and Margaret agreed to establish a branch of the firm on or before April 1, 1926 at 38 Bedford Place (AAK to SJ, 3.6.67); and on January 9, they left New York on the Cunard liner *Berengaria* (SJ to BK, 1.13.26). A frantically busy time lay ahead, but Margaret somehow managed to complete a fifth novel, *Three Kingdoms*. What was more, squeezed in between the preparations for the new branch and other commitments, she and Guy were married on February 1 at the Registry Office in Chelsea, although in a letter to Blanche on February 5, Margaret maintained they were married the day before at the Royal Chapel of the Savoy — a tongue-in-cheek bow, perhaps, to American delight in London high life (SJ to BK, 2.5.26).[9]

Three Kingdoms was published in March, dedicated to Blanche Knopf, "my friend."[10] It was a novel that sprang out of Margaret's very modern problem: how to manage marriage, a child, and a career. The female protagonist has the name Laurence Storm, amalgamating Margaret and her admired D. H. Lawrence. Laurence marries the upper-class Dysart while still a student, has a child in 1915, and when he is a few months old, gets a job in a London advertising company. The novel follows Laurence through a platonic affair and other passing attractions, as she and Dysart drift apart. The dialogue is witty and crisp, while Margaret shows her skill at conveying the undertones of what is said. At one point Laurence has the unspoken thought that "men were irresponsible really, the hunters and fighters and players. . . . It was women who had to answer to life, women who were bound as by a secret navel cord to the dark secret root of life" (*TK*, 112–13). Here again, as in Margaret's short story for the third volume of *The New Decameron*, is a clear female response to a central

D. H. Lawrence theme. On the job front, advertising, its strategies and scheming, is dissected, while the effect of career on Laurence's private life is disturbingly bleak: "She had asked for freedom, and this was freedom and lonely enough" (*TK*, 339). In the end, Laurence reaches a compromise, and Dy has his share in this: "I don't care for domestic women," he says (*TK*, 406). This was one of the first novels to depict a woman really at work, at her desk, and as such was breaking new ground: the reviews were on the whole approving.[11] Margaret was taken increasingly seriously now, as a writer, and as someone with influence in the literary world. Significantly, in the *Finnegans Wake* Notebook for 1926, James Joyce listed names of worthwhile contacts: alongside Konrad Bergovici, André Suares, Mina Loy, and others, Storm Jameson was mentioned, more than once.[12]

The preparations for the new branch of Knopf went according to plan: the Chapmans were installed in Bedford Place by the April deadline, the initial business arrangement being that books would go to Guy, bills to Margaret.[13] However, it was not a conducive time for the setting up of a new business: Britain was in the grip of relentless industrial decline, and a general strike was called in May. Guy and Margaret were, as so often, struggling financially, and Margaret, anxious to nurture her growing reputation, intended to begin a new novel soon (SJ to BK, 5.31.26). But she was pushing herself too hard. By mid-June, she was ill, worrying that she must keep going as Guy could not cope with the business alone (SJ to BK, 6.14.26). By July 1 she was forced to retire, exhausted, to the Spreadeagle, an inn in Thame, near Oxford, its Falstaffian proprietor, John Fothergill, enjoying a growing reputation among writers; the Knopfs came to see her there on their visit to England, by which time Margaret had written half a novel, which Guy liked, and was feeling better (SJ to BK, 7.1.26, 7.19.26). Rest for her was always relative, and the pattern of driving herself beyond her strength and then collapsing was already establishing itself.

She spent the summer in Whitby, finishing the book, but there was trouble brewing in London. Guy was feeling the strain of confronting the Knopfs' different vision for the publishing house, and in September, seemingly acting as go-between for her husband, Margaret went so far as to suggest that the Knopfs might want to put in two people from New York (SJ to BK, 9.8.26). That particular storm seems to have blown over, but business relations would never be comfortable, and Margaret would become increasingly anxious about Guy's limited strength under stress; the gassing he had suffered in World War I had severely damaged his constitution. She and Guy did make at least one contact they would value highly as writer and friend, E. J. (Edward) Thompson, whose novel *An Indian Day* came on to their list in September.[14] Margaret's friendship with Amabel Williams-Ellis was also growing, Amabel's left-wing views chiming in with her own, and through her, the Chapmans visited the Hotel Portmeirion, Penrhyndeudraeth, in the village that Amabel's flamboyant architect husband, Clough Ellis, was currently building in North Wales. This place would soon become a regular retreat for the Chapmans, where they both felt at home. For Margaret's love of her hometown was one, she had quickly found, that was not shared: Guy could never settle comfortably in Whitby with its fiercely northern character. Back in London, the PEN began to have some impact on Margaret's life: she and Amabel attended the English Centre's dinner in December, whereupon Hermon Ould, who had recently taken over as secretary for both the English and International PEN, set about involving Margaret further.[15]

As she had now drawn back from being a frontline employee of the Knopfs, Margaret turned again to the journals to supplement her income, and soon found outlets for short stories. But she wanted a steadier income and so, like many of her contemporaries, she was tempted by the lucrative contracts offered by the London evening papers for both individual pieces and series of articles. When she started to write for the *Evening Standard* in December, she was not in poor company; during the 1920s, contributors included Ronald Knox, Alec Waugh, Rose Macaulay, Robert Boothby, MP, G. B. Sterne, John Drinkwater — and even Wyndham Lewis contributed the odd article. Women writers, however, did not always have an easy time with the literary editor of a newspaper: they were expected to stick to topics appropriate to a distinctly conservative view of their roles. Despite their strictures, Margaret was not to be cowed. She began a series of regular full-page articles in November with a witty piece titled "The Price of a Career: How Women Pay for Success."[16] She was very much the feminist in this piece, disparaging commitments to domesticity and subservience to a man's career, even while, in life, she would always distance herself from the overtly feminist societies, preferring to concentrate on injustices like poverty, affecting both men and women. And she would always put Guy's needs above her own, although the views she often expressed in her articles may give some clue to a resentment she resolved to keep firmly in check.

Margaret had submitted the typescript of her new novel to Constable's, but when Michael Sadleir prevaricated, she turned to Charles Evans of Heinemann again and, far from resenting her earlier defection, he accepted the book unseen, even giving her a generous advance.[17] *The Lovely Ship* was a tribute to the Whitby of the past, drawing in part on family history: Hannah's cousin, Sampson Storm Harrison, for instance, had left for Hartlepool to work on steam ships after being a sailmaker in Whitby, and became a foreman in a shipbuilding yard.[18] Yet the central character of this novel, Mary Hervey, while drawing on the strong businesswomen of Whitby's past, was an impressive invention of Margaret's own, not based on either of her own grandmothers. Indeed, this woman could well be a response to Elizabeth Barrett Browning's lament for a missing role model: "I look everywhere for grandmothers and see none."[19] In the course of the three novels that would develop her life, Mary competes in the masculine business world of the nineteenth and early twentieth century, while the novels also explore how her choices affect her as wife and mother.

Part 1 of *The Lovely Ship*, like the first part of *The Pitiful Wife*, establishes Mary's roots, harking back in tone and theme to a Victorian world, to a time when the traditions of the eighteenth century were on the verge of vast changes, as the world of industry moved into an age of increasing mechanization. This part acts as a prologue: the narrative really takes off when Mary settles in Danesacre, where her uncle owns a shipyard. Strikingly, Margaret sets this part of the novel in a context Mary is blind to: Charles Darwin, the death of Prince Albert, the laying of the Atlantic cable, huge social changes as rural life is overtaken by towns and cities. In the process, Margaret highlights one of her constant concerns, that women fighting for liberation can be so set on their own mission as to turn a blind eye to the sufferings of the poor and exploited. For Mary "never saw anything in the workers' uprising but a shameful manifestation of human wickedness" (*LS*, 97). She ignores the starving unemployed; as a woman she is absorbed in her own different battle for a recognition that, ironically, alienates her from the poverty of the working men. Yet she does not stand for women's rights in general, only for her own survival; her mother comes to represent for her "all the wilful extravagant helpless women created by a masculine world and broken by it" (*LS*, 107).

Overall, this book and its two sequels show that Margaret never espoused the idea that the world would necessarily be a better place with women in charge, preferring to analyze the dilemmas they faced as they made the choices that shaped them. Her Mary takes on many of the traits of the businessmen of her time, remaining vulnerable only when her emotional life reminds her of her femininity, yet driven to sacrifice domestic happiness to her overriding vision and ambition. The reviews were on the whole positive, but most missed the significance of the woman as shipbuilder, excelling in a business that was overwhelmingly a man's world. Instead, they lamented that there should have been more about Mary in love, as if here alone was she truly female and, by implication, here was the sphere most suitable for a novel by a woman.[20]

Whatever the reviewers' response, Margaret's own world was one where she was locked in a struggle with her many commitments. Well paid though the *Evening Standard* pieces were, the requirement to write regularly was irksome, given the limited range of subject matter she was allowed, although she sometimes drew on the contemporary issues that underlay her two most recent novels. In January, she wrote wittily on "Man the Hero — in Books. As Our Women Novelists See Him," but her February piece had a darker theme, insisting, as Laurence did in *Three Kingdoms*, that men, not women, were the incurable romantics:

> That, and not patriotism or any poorer motive, enticed thousands of proper men from their comfortable homes to stand in Flanders mud to be shot at. That is what keeps war going, not policy or necessity.[21]

Here was the strongest statement yet of Margaret's growing antiwar views. But increasingly she had a sense that she was demeaning her talent by this kind of journalism, despite the fact that so many of her contemporaries were following the same course.

Although Margaret was supposedly taking a back seat in the Knopf publishing business, she was still offering considerable assistance, not helped by the couple's constant moving between rented homes and hotels. The friendships formed continued to provide some compensations. E. J. Thompson was becoming one of Margaret's confidants, and Valentine Dobrée would soon become another. Valentine was married to the scholar Bonamy Dobrée, a friend of Guy's from their time in the army. She herself was an established artist, exhibiting with the London Group in 1920, before moving to the Pyrenees with Bonamy for a few years, when she exhibited at the Salon des Indépendants. She was close to the Bloomsbury Group, and experimenting with surrealism when Margaret first came into contact with her, persuading the Knopfs to take her novel, *Your Cuckoo Sings by Kind*, even though they knew it would not sell well. Valentine was brilliant, intense, passionately left wing, and wrote with a painter's eye. The two women soon became firm friends.

Margaret had been suffering pain stoically for some time, but now was forced to have an operation, a hysterectomy, perhaps as a result of her primitive efforts to abort a second child back in the war. Recovery was slow. During her convalescence, she began to correspond with another writer whose friendship would figure largely for several years. Vera Brittain, highly strung, hypersensitive, had, like many others, encouraged her brother to enlist in 1914, something she could not admit in her *Testament of Youth*. However, when the full horror of war struck her, she left Oxford University to join a Voluntary Aid Detachment (VAD) and nurse the wounded.[22] She returned to Oxford in 1919, where she met Winifred Holtby. Both were committed feminists, members of the Six Point Group, a women's action group founded by Lady Rhondda, and each had her first novel rejected in 1922. Vera was increasingly committed to peace, becoming a League of Nations Union speaker, and leaving the Liberal Party for Labour, primarily to pursue her feminist and pacifist concerns. Winifred shared most of her friend's commitments, supporting Vera from their student days through the early years of her marriage to George Catlin.

Margaret had admired Vera's first novel, *The Dark Tide*, and had tried, without success, to interest the Knopfs in it. Convalescing after her operation in late September 1927, she saw Vera's name in the *Daily Mail*, and decided to write to her. She had followed Vera's increasing reputation as a journalist, and knew of her membership in the Six Point Group. But strangely, she gave false information about herself in this letter that would have repercussions later. She said, "Probably, since I was married before

I was 19 and had a son before I was 20, I am older in effect if not in truth than you" (SJ to VB, 9.30.27). Why did she offer such a fiction? She may have met Karl when she was nineteen, in her second year at university, but they did not marry until she was twenty-two in 1913, and she had Bill two years later, which exempted her from war work. Had she for a moment adopted Laurence's persona in *Three Kingdoms*, who did marry at nineteen, had a son a year later, and left him abruptly to take a job at the end of 1916? Certainly Vera would, some years later, interpret this letter as showing Margaret was self-seeking, for Margaret's misrepresentation made it appear that she had opted for paid employment in the middle of the war, rather than volunteering for war work like Vera herself.[23]

Whatever her later view of things, when she received this letter in 1927, Vera responded warmly, and Margaret wrote back with more details of her career, suiting her comments to what she knew of her correspondent: "I didn't want to write — I've never been able to regard writing as a serious job — I wanted a career in the world." In this letter she was responding in kind to Vera's own priorities, engaging with feminist arguments of the time:

> I resent furiously that when I and my husband both want a career, he is set free for his and I am only freed for mine after I have arranged the domestic side of our joint lives. I am bored by looking after children, and yet I wish I'd stuck that out. You see, it's neither as easy as my smug articles in the Evening Standard pretend, nor so simple as the Time and Tiders imagine. I wrote a novel about it called "Three Kingdoms," but so far as I know no one observed that the story of Laurence Storm broke off just when it was entering on its most troublesome period. (SJ to VB, 10.8.27)

Margaret was learning, in her difficult second marriage, that she had to make many compromises; but she would never find this easy, paying in old age for her rebellious thoughts with a guilt she could not shake off.

Working for the Knopfs was becoming increasingly enervating; Margaret confided to Thompson that Guy "is worn to a bare nerve by Samuel Knopf. I wish I could get him away" (SJ to EJT, 11.1.27). However, Blanche and Alfred, though demanding, were not heartless. Alfred offered a flat above the office to make life easier, although the Chapmans decided against it, no doubt feeling this would tie them irrevocably to a situation that was fast becoming unendurable. Samuel Knopf, Alfred's father, was first and foremost a businessman, and pushed Guy to take on books that would sell; conversely, Guy still held to a publishing tradition that took risks with works of literary excellence. Margaret would mediate between them, but there seemed to be no middle way. Yet despite all, Margaret was working on her next novel, *Farewell to Youth*: by mid-November, she had reached the halfway stage (SJ to BK, 11.10.27). She must have been heartened when, the following month, *The Lovely Ship* was one of three short-listed by the *Femina* Committee for its annual award for a book on English life.[24] Nonetheless, while she finished her new novel by the end of January, the constant need for money was still driving her to well-paid journalism.

She had now accepted a contract with the *Evening News*, which would be continued throughout 1928, sapping her creative energies and her self-esteem. It is tempting to think that she used these articles to debate issues close to her own heart, since she was having to learn on the hoof how to have a career while supporting a husband and child; but how far they were meditations on a pilgrim's progress it is impossible to be certain. By February, she was already starting to count the cost of this money-making commitment, telling Blanche she could not start another novel before June (SJ to BK, 2.6.28). She might write lightly, but she was increasingly worried by the Knopfs' demands, and their effect on Guy's health: she confided in Valentine that he meant to resign.[25] This explains the amount of journalism she had shouldered: for on February 20, the *Evening News* announced the new series of exclusive weekly articles by Storm Jameson, a demanding commitment (Feb. 20, 1928, 8). Every seven days, Margaret had to produce an article on women's issues, although, as the pressure mounted, their exclusivity was inevitably compromised by skillful reworkings of material she was using elsewhere. They featured divorce and separation, problems of combining marriage, children, and career, and other topics deemed to appeal to women. She was hamstrung by the paper's policy when it came to choosing what to write about, and let Valentine know how she felt about her predicament, citing "an article entitled (though not by me) 'Can a wife say: "You *shall* be mine?" . . . And another (unpublished) called: 'The Damnation of

Storm Jameson'. Why in the name of God have I no self respect?" (SJ to VD, 3.3.28). Clearly lowbrow editors and their fatuous titles for her articles were getting on her nerves, and she was fed up and depressed by indulging in newspaper journalism.

By March, Guy had submitted his resignation to the Knopfs, although he would remain in office for a further six months. Margaret had sent off the typescript of her novel and had written a lecture titled "The Georgian Novel and Mr. Robinson," which she would eventually deliver in November. The weekly articles dragged on. Occasionally she injected a challenging element: she had recently supported a friend in the Divorce Court, where, despite the rituals to which she and Guy had been subjected, she told Valentine she was

> stunned by contact with a vocabulary and a moral standard that I simply did not know existed. I shall never be able to use certain adjectives again without feeling that I am being obscene. (SJ to VD, 3.3.28)

The resulting article caused an anxious editor to write that Storm Jameson "in this article expresses her strong individual view" since, fresh from her recent experience in the Divorce Court and recalling her own ordeal, she attacked current practice and the current religious view that condemned divorce (March 19, 1928, 8). The next week she was equally challenging, arguing that the next war would not be won by the nation with the strongest soldiers, but the one with "the cleverest scientists and inventors of killing gases" (March 26, 1928, 8). As she wrote, the League of Nations Union was setting up the Disarmament Campaign Committee, and the universal franchise won later that year would bring with it, for writers like Margaret and Vera, an increasing urge to debate responsibilities as well as rights. At the end of April, Margaret wrote again about the threat of war. Women should fight during peace against the prospect of war, she insisted. However, while she savaged women who had handed out white feathers during the last war, and those who prided themselves on "giving their sons to conflict," she admitted to having no sympathy for the pacifist in wartime; he might be necessary as a reminder of the "monstrous fatuity of war. But I do not like him" (April 16, 1928, 8). This sense that the pacifist's aim should be preventative, but that under war conditions his role was more problematic would increasingly trouble her in the years to come.

In May, the *Evening News* published a further series of articles by women, Margaret contributing the third, "Dreams — and Disillusion," which suggested much about her state of mind. She presented herself as having been a girl "swallowed up" by the war: "So much learned in so brief a time, so much tried for, so little done, so much bitterness, so many unexpected and unearned joys, so many failures" (May 21, 1928, 8). The self-flagellation that would become increasingly common over the years whenever Margaret's energy flagged was already well established, and her tone was bleak. Her loneliness, even in a marriage that she insisted suited her, was poignantly apparent, and she was desperately anxious to get Guy away before the end of his contract with the Knopfs. However, despite being a difficult employer, the firm was helping another member of her family: Samuel Knopf had agreed to pay Margaret's sister Dorothy five pounds a week, as she was taking on the reading of French and German manuscripts as well as secretarial work under Margaret's replacement.[26]

Farewell to Youth came out at the end of May, and showed how much Margaret had matured as a novelist in the past two years.[27] Its protagonist, Nat, drew on Guy's experience of war, his first marriage, and what he brought to his second. But the personal elements were set within a broad social and political context, with a wide range of characters from different backgrounds, looking forward to Margaret's later, increasingly complex works. The novel centers on the legacies of war, in England and in a blood-soaked Europe, as Nat's father, an idealist, is hounded for having German and Jewish friends, both publicly and by his materialistic, ambitious brother. Business is the new religion, and Nat is sickened both by this and by the terms of a peace that cause children in Austria and Central Europe to starve. Gradually, as his early marriage crumbles, Nat is drawn to his cousin Ann, but she has to cope with what war has been for him; he is one of the "lost generation . . . lost and restless in a world that changed when we had our backs to it" (*FTY*, 192). So now Ann has to accept second place to the war, just as Nat's mother had to accept second place to the ancestral home, each woman's love partly blighted by a legacy that binds their men to the past. This novel, while still drawing heavily on autobiographical material, shows not only Margaret's growing certainty that public and private lives are inextricably linked, but also her growing concern for developments in Europe. The latent intolerance and racism in the England of the 1920s surfaces in the way Nat's father is treated, while Nat's own priorities in the wake of World War I have changed, reaching beyond his own society to the sufferings of Europe. These would be themes that Margaret would develop in her novels of the 1930s, where she would find her ideas running parallel with a number of American and European writers, as will become clear. She was truly coming of age. Ironically, a number of reviewers centered their criticism on Nat's character, finding it unconvincing, especially in his generous attitude to his first wife, a part of the tale that was quite literally based on Guy's own first marriage and its aftermath.[28]

Meanwhile, Margaret's articles in the *Evening News* were attracting lively responses. By the end of May, there had been a mass of correspondence about her comments on the "next war," including many letters from women who wanted to join a peace league. So Margaret returned to the subject, urging her women readers to become more knowledgeable about European affairs, and about America's position. She told them to write to their MPs and talk to their friends, and she insisted that this was the most important initiative since the war, more important than the League of Nations, which the United States had refused to join, "because without America the League, for all its splendid, its invaluable work, is utterly helpless against the danger of war" (*Evening News*, May 29, 1928). In this article she went on to claim that any party with an active peace policy "would sweep the country," while a party backing the Kellogg-Briand Pact of Paris, outlawing war as an instrument of policy, "will deserve the gratitude of every woman with a vote." She said, moreover, she would like to see the formation of a Women's Anti-War Union with branches in every city, town, and village in England: "What every woman wants is not a world made soft for her sons but a world made decent." This was fighting talk, while Margaret was now openly distancing herself from a number of feminist causes:

> I have less sympathy and admiration than I ought to have for the various estimable women who are working for social and political reforms because I feel that there is a more urgent job ready to their hands. (*Evening News*, May 29, 1928)

She ended this important article by positioning herself as a mother and as a member of the Lost Generation of World War I: "We have more ghosts than friends. . . . It is because of my ghosts, because of my son, that I loathe and fear war." This reminder of the huge numbers of young men lost in the last war would fuel the pacifist movement of the interwar years. Moreover, this article shows that this was Margaret at her most eloquent, her deliberate use of heightened rhetoric proclaiming the priorities that would dominate her actions and thinking for much of the next decade. She was becoming a voice to be reckoned with, despite those reviewers who would have preferred her to stick to love stories. In June, delighted with her success in drawing her readers to the paper's columns, the *Evening News* renewed her contract for a further series of articles. Indeed, by June 20, the paper was announcing her article on the front page, saying her new series would be "on topics vitally interesting to the modern man and woman," delivered with "the frankness which is always characteristic of her brilliant writing" (*Evening News*, June 20, 1928). The response to her arguments had clearly overridden earlier editorial preconceptions about what was suitable for women readers; she was now being treated as a writer who would appeal to both sexes, given her skill in addressing issues of key importance to both.

Margaret soldiered on, often recasting topics she had previously addressed in her *Evening Standard* articles, with rather more bite and willingness to be controversial. In July, she maintained that the early feminists actually created the image of the downtrodden woman, an image taken up by the suffragists, who thus drew "a picture of Victorian womanhood which few Victorian women would have recognized" (*Evening News*, July 24, 1928). For, she went on: "*My* grandmother was a very ordinary Victorian — and a dignified autocrat who ruled her husband and her family with a rod of iron" (*Evening News*, July 24, 1928). This was certainly true of the old businesswomen of Whitby — but was it really true of her mother's mother, as true as it was of Mary Hansyke, Margaret's creation in *The Lovely Ship*? It was certainly not true of George Gallilee's alcoholic second wife, the only grandmother Margaret had known. However that might be, Margaret's article goes on to paint a wry picture of the liberated woman: she may have economic independence, but as a result, men hand over many responsibilities, the masterful man beloved by romantic novelists and which she said she despised disappears, and women are left strangely dissatisfied. Here too she wrote from experience; in both of her marriages, she paid a considerable price for economic independence, an independence on which both her husbands came to rely.

Alongside the demands of her weekly articles, there were other claims on Margaret's time. Dora Marsden's increasing volatility and demands for attention were putting relations with Harriet Shaw Weaver under strain. Harriet had closed the *Egoist* in 1924, and now concentrated on supporting Joyce. Left adrift, Dora asked for Margaret's help with the book she was obsessively, frantically writing. Margaret, remembering how in the early days of the *Egoist* Dora had supported her, went into action, trying to find her a publisher, although she soon had to ask Dora not to keep writing to her or rushing up to London to help her sell the book. After several publishers had rejected the work, Margaret had to defend herself against Dora's reproaches, yet treated her sense of betrayal gently, when Harriet and Dora finally quarreled violently (*Miss Weaver*, 281). Years later, Margaret would continue to defend Dora, ignoring, unlike Rebecca West, her mental problems and concentrating on her own "profound respect" for the former editor and her "humility before Dora Marsden's intellect."[29] These were generous comments about someone who, years after dispensing with her services, had given her several months of troublesome work.

Margaret finally got Guy away to the Yorkshire dales in June, and to the Dobrées in July, two welcome breaks as he was winding up his work with Knopf. In July, her one-act play, *Full Circle*, was "selected for publication" by the Reading Committee of the British Drama League.[30] Well constructed, with good dialogue, it was based on her own affair with the Texan and the discovery of her husband's betrayal. The weekly articles for the *Evening News* went on, and Margaret also supplied a few short stories to the *Sunday Dispatch*, a paper having Aldous Huxley, G. B. Shaw, and D. H. Lawrence among its contributors. The paper announced the first in August, proclaiming that "as a writer of psychological and social studies and as a novelist, Storm Jameson is in the very front rank."[31] Despite this accolade, the stories were to be consigned to the women's page. Accordingly, the short stories Margaret produced for the paper were so professionally attuned to the style of this page that it is hard not to see them as accomplished parodies of popular romantic tales; they had none of the punch that her best articles demonstrated, but catch the romantic tone neatly. Given their tendency to end with the heroine sighing in the arms of the hero, they must have been written tongue in cheek.[32]

On September 30, Guy finally left Knopf, and a week later he and Margaret went by car to Edinburgh to work together on the author who would remain a passion of his for the rest of his life, the politician, novelist, and patron of the arts William Beckford (1760–1844). Meanwhile Margaret had accepted yet another contract with the *Evening News*, but the tone of her contributions reflected her growing fatigue with the weekly demands on her time. Wit was scarce, and the achievement of universal franchise went unacknowledged, as she repeated comments on divorce and marital relations she had made before. She was getting to the end of her tether over her enslavement to what she considered hack writing.

In November there was a happening that divided the literary world. Jonathan Cape was prosecuted for publishing Radclyffe Hall's tale of lesbian love, *The Well of Loneliness*. When it came out in June, the book had sold steadily, but on August 19, the editor of the *Sunday Express* attacked it, and on August 23, the Home Secretary wrote to Cape saying he had read it and found it obscene despite the fact that it was more about loneliness than sex and demanding that Cape withdraw it, which he did. The trial began on November 9. Forty witnesses were summoned by the defense counsel, Norman Birkett, but not all were willing to appear, Galsworthy being one of "a larger number of well-known writers who declined to jeopardize their reputations by supporting an unpopular cause" (Berry and Bostridge, 228). However, others stepped forward: E. M. Forster, for instance, Desmond MacCarthy, Vera Brittain, Vita Sackville-West, Virginia Woolf, and Margaret. Given the mores of the period, the decision to appear was not taken lightly: when Virginia agreed to stand as a witness, for instance, both Leonard Woolf and Vanessa Bell urged that she should not testify as it would cast a shadow over Bloomsbury.[33] In old age, Margaret would recall how she herself visited Virginia Woolf to ask if they would have to testify that the novel was a supreme work of literature since Hall had insisted her work should be rated as a work of art. Woolf had assured her that would be unnecessary, as its literary quality was not the issue. Accordingly, the witnesses turned up at court, where Margaret recalled she had a conversation with Hall, who, she maintained: "alarmed me by saying in a powerful voice: I stand for perversion, mental and moral. All the same I felt a genuine respect for her forthrightness and plainness."[34] However, the magistrate refused to hear any of the expert witnesses and adjourned the case so as to read the book himself. On November 16 he ruled, in explicitly homophobic terms, that the book was an obscene libel and should be destroyed; a subsequent appeal in December was dismissed. The day after the ruling, Margaret wrote to Valentine, reporting that she had read Woolf's *Orlando*, which had almost converted her "to your reverence for her work. But something is missing" (SJ to VD, 11.17.28). Reading this work, she must also have felt the irony of Woolf's mischievous play with sex attracting no such hostility as Hall's ponderous novel.

Guy, now unemployed, was happily working on his "dear War" (SJ to VD, 11.17.28). His memoir would eventually appear as *A Passionate Prodigality*, while Margaret, the sole breadwinner, continued to write those short stories which, along with her *Evening News* contracts, were necessary money spinners. Then, on November 23, she gave the paper she had written in the spring, "The Georgian Novel and Mr. Robinson," to the Literary Circle of the National Liberal Club, and a fortnight later signed a contract for it with Heinemann.[35] She worried that financial pressures had made her rush into print, as it was her first major contribution to the ongoing debate of the 1920s about the role of the novel and the intellectual in the contemporary world. For in 1923 and 1924, Virginia Woolf had refined her position in the various versions of "Mr. Bennett and Mrs. Brown" (Briggs, 123–25). Then came E. M. Forster, who, in *Aspects of the Novel*, saw "story" as fundamental, while suggesting that "the more the arts develop, the more they depend on each other for definition."[36] Virginia Woolf, reviewing his book, concluded that he really wanted writers to keep close to "life": "It is the humane as opposed to the aesthetic view."[37] She challenged what she saw as his very English unwillingness to discuss the medium of words in which the writer works, pointing to Europe as the place where the medium was treated seriously. In January 1928, the critic Desmond Shaw argued that the novelist of the future would be "the artist-philosopher," while structure and technique were only of major importance to the "tradesman-novelist."[38] Rebecca West, in *The Strange Necessity*, expressed her admiration both for those who explored the inner life and those who analyzed the world around them.[39] Meanwhile, the responsibility of the artist and intellectual was the theme of Julien Benda's *La trahison des clercs* (*The Treason of the Intellectuals*), a work by the French philosopher that would have a profound effect on many writers of the time, both abroad and at home. The core of his message was that intellectuals whose prime purpose was to defend disinterested values like justice and reason — the "clercs" of his title — had betrayed this purpose, aligning themselves, in this age of "the intellectual organization of political hatreds," with pragmatic interests (Benda, 27). For Benda, writers, whether producing fact or fiction, should be responsible advocates for their age.

The Georgian Novel and Mr. Robinson was published in February 1929. In it, Margaret confronted those critics who saw the novel at an impasse, naming a range of contemporary writers who were extending the novel's territory, including Lawrence, Woolf, T. F. Powys, and Aldous Huxley. She argued that while story and particularly character were essential, they must persuade the reader with "some idea, some philosophy of life, some *faith*, perhaps, . . . which is the pattern" (GNMR, 10). She admired Woolf's "new methods of lighting" in *Mrs. Dalloway* (GNMR, 24), and the ease and fluidity Huxley and Woolf had in treating character: "a novel should be, above all, about people" (GNMR, 45), as in a few contemporary works including Woolf's *Orlando*. For Margaret, pattern was not something imposed from outside as in late James, but something organic: "the expression of the novelist's attitude to life, his fellow-men, and to God" (GNMR, 53). For her, "God" stood for humankind's quest for meaning, purpose. In the end, she concluded, "unrest, discomfort, danger, none of these qualities of an age have ever choked the breath out of its art. But scepticism, the failure of hope, is a deadlier and more withering spirit than any of these" (GNMR, 70). The great novelist, and here she was taking issue with West, did not need intimate knowledge of the scientific achievements of his age, but he "should be awake to the spirit that is producing these achievements, able to breathe the air of the world which is being created by them" (GNMR, 71).

Given the liveliness of the current debate, the reviews were unsurprisingly mixed, while critical response to the debate as a whole could at times turn wonderfully vitriolic.[40] H. C. Harwood, the curmudgeonly critic par excellence, dismissed Lawrence and Huxley as not having the technique of the novelist, while Virginia Woolf's egotism was less that of "the prophet than the introvert," and Forster, while not bad, would not last.[41] He then lambasted two promising writers, Clemence Dane and Margaret, for prostituting their promise by writing for the evening papers: "The crude vulgarity of adjacent columns has been too strong for them. One cannot, it is said, touch pitch without being defiled" and so they have become "coarse hucksters of the second-rate" (Harwood, 331). He seemed not to have noticed that most of the major writers of the day were also writing for these papers; but then, for him, major writers were exceptionally thin on the ground.

CHAPTER 6

Work Takes Over

It had indeed been uncharacteristic for Margaret to rush *The Georgian Novel and Mr. Robinson* into print, since she was by temperament a meticulous reviser, but a letter to Valentine explains why. Their "excellent invaluable Mrs. Boyce," who had been Guy's cashier, "entrusted with the business of closing up the Guy Chapman firm," and who had followed him to Knopf, had robbed Knopf of three hundred pounds, and also robbed Guy. He was now penniless and in debt, for Mrs. Boyce had destroyed letters to him without his seeing them, and had destroyed letters to Margaret too: "I shall have to do more journalism (Just when I was staggering to the end of my Evening News contract!)" (SJ to VD, 12.8.28). She and Guy were both devastated, too disheartened to prosecute the woman, who was allowed to disappear.

By the beginning of January, desperate for money, Margaret had finished her last article for the current *Evening News* contract, had three to write for the new women's journal *Britannia and Eve*, and was struggling with a story for a British Legion book. It would take the Chapmans five years to recover from their financial losses, and the mental price was very high, as she told E. J. Thompson: "Don't ever let anyone persuade you into Fleet Street. I've been trying my first piece of real writing for a year and agonising over it like any Bloomsbury devoué. Fleet Street chokes your brain" (SJ to EJT, 1.8.29). Moreover, she and Guy were still moving restlessly from place to place, dreaming of a permanent home but never settling on a plan that suited them both.[1] Bill's education was also an anxiety: at one point, they determined to live in Tonbridge for five years, sending Bill to the excellent school there (SJ to FS, 3.6.29, 3.18.29). But while Bill did start at the school, Margaret still shuttled between Whitby and a Tonbridge hotel for some months. Indeed, since Guy's resignation from Knopf, Margaret had been hard to track down: in March, she told a gently reproachful Hermon Ould that his PEN files were five addresses behind, and it was only safe to write to Ryedale. Three months later, she was in trouble with PEN again, this time over forgetting her subscription. She tried to make light of her chaotic lifestyle, offering, in lieu, their "large beetle-y house" in Tonbridge, a house they would never live in.[2] They did eventually come to rest in a hotel, without a car, to be near Bill for a time. By the autumn of 1929, all thoughts of settling in Tonbridge would be forgotten, as Margaret would return to her roots, buying a house, Mooredge, "high on the side of a hill above the Esk valley," near Whitby (JN, 1:248).

She had been struggling to write another novel since the beginning of 1928, but had been frustrated by those necessary forays into journalism. A more prestigious article, written for the *Nation and Athenaeum*, gave her pleasure and boosted her self-respect if not her bank balance:

> A real "middle" — the first I ever wrote. I have quoted Schiller and made my head ache and I suppose I shall get five guineas for it. As many words in the Evening News on "Should Women Love (or Live)" would bring in fifty. (SJ to EJT, 7.17.29)

This was why, she told Thompson, she was more usually tied to what Bill as a small boy had called "inking for money." Her output included, for instance, a short story for the *Sunday Graphic* and those articles for *Britannia and Eve*, and she was even desperate enough to agree to judge, alongside Ethel Mannin, snapshots for a Pears' Soap "Golden Glory" competition, "to discover the most charming woman in the British Isles" (SJ to EJT, 7.17.29).[3] At least the article for the *Nation and Athenaeum* had been satisfying to write, a thoughtful continuation of her thinking in *The Georgian Novel and Mr. Robinson*, this time responding more fully to West as well as to Forster and Woolf. She opened with a paradox: "Never has the novel reached so high a level of technical perfection, never has it displayed more subtlety and acuteness of perception, more grace of manner," but never had it been so little regarded except by novelists and reviewers.[4] Biographies were preferred, especially the war memoirs now emerging. She engaged, like West, with Pavlov's theory of "conditioned reflexes," but felt this was simply an example of "that hostility to 'the imagined thing,'" that kept writers who had fought in World War I tied to the past (*CJ*, 31). She speculated that the war had perhaps turned people from fiction to fact "like children who have been undeceived about certain legends in which we firmly believed"(*CJ*, 31). She asked how, if we prefer actuality to let's pretend, can we dismiss works like the *Agamemnon*, "in which the characters are symbols of an otherwise unimpartable reality" (*CJ*, 32); and she speculated as to whether fiction was not in fact the vehicle of this higher reality "which sleeps in all our minds," and can only be evoked in the form of symbols (*CJ*, 33). This article showed a Margaret fully engaged with current debate, however bogged down she was in lightweight journalism.

In *The Glory That Was Grub Street*, the critic St. John Adcock was undeterred by Margaret's commitment to the evening papers, setting her alongside the likes of Huxley, West, A. E. Housman, and Mary Webb. He saw her as bordering on the propagandist, but acknowledged that her novels had "a breadth of human charity and a prevailing sense of reality," deserving to occupy "so sure and high a place among living novelists" as she now did (Adcock, 170). This was no mean feat at the end of the twenties. The novel, as Margaret herself saw, had to compete with a number of impressive books on the late war. As well as works by Edmund Charles Blunden and Siegfried Sassoon, Richard Aldington's *Death of a Hero* and Robert Graves's *Goodbye to All That* came out; the German writer Erich Maria Remarque's *All Quiet on the Western Front* had reached English language readers, while his fellow German Ludwig Renn, one of Margaret's favorite novelists, had produced *War*, translated by Willa and Edwin Muir. But despite those who saw the novel at an impasse, experimenters were prolific, both in style and content: Olive Moore's mischievous *Celestial Seraglio*, Patrick Hamilton's *The Midnight Bell*, a study in claustrophobia set in a poor London pub, and Valentine Dobrée's elegantly witty fable *The Emperor's Tigers* all came out in 1929.

The Heinemann contract for Margaret's next novel, *The Voyage Home*, was signed on November 19, with an impressive advance of £750.[5] This novel continued the saga of Mary Hansyke, who was now selling the shipyard in Danesacre and, following the actual history of shipbuilding, moving north to the river Tees. With an echo of her own time since Wall Street had crashed in October 1929, Margaret depicted the desperate deprivations of workers in the late nineteenth century, interwoven with glowing natural descriptions. Characterization was increasingly deft, as people emerged through their views of themselves or each other, rarely through the narrator. Central to the work is how Mary fares in the man's world of shipbuilding, balancing business, marriage, and children. The theme of so many of Margaret's newspaper articles was here explored in depth, while remaining true to historical context. Mary's dilemma is captured concisely: "She who had seen, and made, so many changes, now could not face change" (*TVH*, 134). Old-fashioned security was longed for, even by an innovator who could be ruthless to workers, family, and lovers. While the *TLS* reviewer was polite but dismissive, others saw much more. Margaret Wallace in the *New York Times Book Review* pointed to "a depth and insight in her writing which evoke — in Henry James's hackneyed but valuable distinction — the emotion of recognition"; while L. P. Hartley in the *Saturday Review* spoke approvingly of the way Margaret "studies the external world in the mirror of her own consciousness." He went on to say she evoked the shipyard "not by an exhaustive description of its physical appearance but by its myriad intrusions into the lives and thoughts of those who subsisted on it."[6]

Guy also had a novel out in January, after a long search for a publisher. *A Painted Cloth* drew on his own experiences of the war, the changing world of publishing, of changing values as war intervened, and of love and marriage. It was a straightforward tale, verging at times, as in the long description of a libel case, on the pedantic, but it did light up in its descriptions of war. Here Guy could enter the mentality of those who learned to live for the day, not thinking of the future, while coming to accept the horrors around them as the norm. Overall, however, it was flat, its realism harking back to nineteenth-century models, not the new realism being molded by his wife.

Despite the need to make money, Margaret had now stopped writing articles for the popular press, while still placing short stories in a range of journals; but she had hit a frighteningly "dry" period:

> Lately, I have lost what small stock of self-confidence I ever had. . . . I think I shall try to get a job, but I can't face journalism

again. . . . What a fool I was to run after the meretricious and fading rewards of novel writing. (SJ to VD, 3.14.30)

Her state of mind was not helped by her anxiety about Bill, who had
returned from his excellent school in Tonbridge looking pale. Panicking,
Margaret sent him off to the English School in Switzerland, a move that
drained her finances, while the school proved to be academically mediocre, and encouraged a dilettante streak in Bill that she would later regret
(*JN*, 1:286). Guy must also have been a worry: he still had no full-time
job although he was involved in some editing for the publishing firm
Eyre and Spottiswoode, and his novel was not a success. He had finished
his excellent memoir of the war but could not find a publisher, and his
research on Beckford had met obstacles that were, for the moment, im-
passable.

All these worries resulted in Margaret being persuaded to write a book
about the origin of modern-day economics in the sixteenth and seventeenth centuries.[7] This meant that she could call on Guy's help and revive his interest in his old love, history. Her own interest in economics
was established early in her career, as her links with A. R. Orage and
her articles for the *New Europe* had shown, and now was a time when
the economy was being debated with ever-growing anxiety, as unemployment was steadily increasing. Margaret chose in this book to draw on the
ideas of R. H. Tawney, now professor of economic history at the London
School of Economics and established as a key intellectual on the left.
His most recent book, *Religion and the Rise of Capitalism*, published
in 1926, appealed to both Margaret and Guy, tracing as it did the rise of
individualism and the metamorphosis of Puritanism. Margaret's book,
The Decline of Merry England, dedicated to Guy, did not pretend to be
an original work, as her preface made clear. She frankly acknowledged
her huge debt to Tawney's book, her own aim being to offer an accessible way into an area of contemporary thought for the general reader.
Accordingly, she wrote in a lively style, with snippets of dialogue, vivid
images, and wide-ranging quotations from texts of earlier centuries. The
ideas on how responsibilities to society had been lost sight of in the rise
of the individual and the struggle for rights chimed in with Tawney's, as
she readily admitted. But the vitality of the style was her own. Moreover,
importantly, Guy's research in chasing down quotations and discussing

implications had reignited his enthusiasm for history, paving the way for his application to study at the London School of Economics the following year. The book was on the whole well reviewed; it was seen as part of a much-needed reassessment of past eras that was gathering pace since the war.[8]

Margaret had also managed to finish the final volume of the Mary Hansyke saga, *A Richer Dust*, signing the contract with Heinemann in October.[9] Gradually, after those first dry months of 1930, Margaret was recovering her confidence; on October 8 she delivered a lecture on "The Future of the Novel" to the Thirtieth Inaugural Meeting of Librarians, held at the London School of Economics.[10] The thoughts she offered showed her growing commitment to the novel of ideas. She praised Huxley and Lawrence as masters of this kind of fiction but although she spoke admiringly of *Ulysses*, she was not sure it was a novel; and while she also admired *Mrs. Dalloway*, she had reservations: despite Woolf's gifts of humor, insight, and perception, Woolf's work seemed to her, she said, to lack vitality, prioritizing the way it was written rather than what was written about.

PART II

1930-1938

CHAPTER **7**

Dawn of a Critical Decade

As 1930 drew to a close, what with Guy out of work and Bill being at a very expensive school, Margaret was yet again struggling to pay the family's bills. She had to forgo her membership in the Society of Authors, to which she had been elected in 1921, ceasing to pay into their pension fund; but she kept her PEN membership.[1] Her involvement with the PEN's English Centre and so with writers from Europe was increasing, slowly but surely: in December, for instance, she agreed to sit on the selection committee for an international literary prize. The PEN had grown hugely since the early twenties: no less than forty-four centers would each select a work to be submitted by June 1931.[2]

Margaret's next novel, *A Richer Dust*, came out early in the new year.[3] Charting Mary Hansyke's later years, it was the longest of the trilogy, developing a range of characters from the earlier works and introducing Mary Hervey Russell, old Mary's grandchild and her spiritual heir. Central to the work is Mary's grandson, Nicholas, who is born to resist his Victorian grandmother's determination to mold him in her own business image. War makes relationships shift and change: Nicholas mirrors Guy's emotional exhaustion, still in thrall to the world that war revealed to him. The melancholic spirit of Eliot's *Prufrock* and *Waste Land* pervades the postwar in this novel, by quotation and echo, while the sense of rootedness as balm remains very strong, a theme that would be a leitmotif throughout Margaret's work, making her peculiarly sensitive to the loss involved in exile. There is, as always, quiet delight in what is unchanged in landscape and seascape, untouched by the troubles that haunt human society. Margaret sketches Mary's delight in the old town and its surroundings, when she returns to Danesacre:

> She saw the crouched grey church, the green cliff-top lozenged with gravestones, the involute tracery of roofs, and all the unmeant loveliness of the old half-forgotten port, lustred on it through the centuries. (*TOT*, 1156)

Yet despite this return to her childhood home, Mary is increasingly alone, finding solace for her estrangement from so many in her family by endowing hospitals and training centers with huge sums drawn from the wealth she accumulated before and during the war. These positive moves are set against Nick's mockery of the unrealistic reparations the Allies were demanding from Germany, their erstwhile enemy. Like Lawrence, like Woolf, Margaret leaves her novel thematically open-ended, even as Mary dies, and her granddaughter walks away to confront the postwar world.

In all, the three works of *The Triumph of Time* demonstrate Margaret's growing skill in choreographing a range of characters from different strata of society, a skill that would develop further in her next trilogy, *The Mirror in Darkness*. Moreover, the character of Mary Hansyke herself is the first female protagonist not primarily based on Margaret herself. She is a character from an earlier generation, imaginatively conceived, responding to the changing world of the second half of the nineteenth and early twentieth century, and revealing the triumphs and perils of that time for a woman fighting her way into a male-dominated business world. She is very much alive, and most reviewers, especially those who had kept pace with the trilogy, were impressed.[4] Despite their praise, however, the book did not sell and Margaret was impelled to press on with another novel, which, she told Valentine, was "so gloomy that it positively drips" (SJ to VD, 2.21.31). This, it would seem, matched Guy's mood at the time, as he was desperate to move back from Mooredge to London; as a southerner, he could never feel at ease in Margaret's hometown, where the sense of belonging was so jealously guarded (SJ to VD, 3.3.31). He and Margaret did manage a holiday in France in April, taking Bill with them, but then it was back to work, the first draft of the novel being finished "by forced marches" in mid-June (SJ to VD, 6.19.31). Margaret was dismissive about it, as she so often was, although she was experimenting with a "modified, un-Joycean 'stream of consciousness' method," as the final version would reveal (SJ to VD, 6.19.31).

Despite the need to keep writing and the long hours at her desk which that involved, Margaret was not living in an ivory tower. In a passage cut from her late memoirs, she tells how, while living in Mooredge, she was elected chairman of the local Labour Party. This party was very much to her taste: it stood for social justice, for fair wages and the end of poverty, and, up to a point, for women's rights. Margaret recalls how her local branch fought the election in May 1931, "without help from headquarters" and with a raw candidate "willing to fight without hope":

> We campaigned with enormous energy and gaiety, . . . and for the first time in that constituency, bottom of the poll though he was, the Labour man did not lose his deposit. (JN/TMS, 1:203)

An article she wrote for *Everyman* at this time was in praise of Whitby, where still "the town remains a triumph (but a near thing) of nature over man."[5] She recalled the Whitby of her grandfather's day, its fierce independence savagely defended, its hostility to strangers, and its loveliness; the next day the article was reviewed with evident approval in the *Whitby Gazette*.[6] Margaret, in her moorland cottage, was at home.

As the economic climate, both in Britain and Europe, was worsening, leading to the growth of extremism both on the right and on the left, Margaret's life in Mooredge gave her at least a temporary illusion of stability. In September, she signed one of her last contracts with Heinemann, for "A Picture in the Margin," the novel that would be published as *That Was Yesterday*. The royalties would remain at 20 percent at home, 10 percent abroad, but as the sales of *A Richer Dust* had been lower than expected, her advance was reduced to five hundred pounds.[7] Given her continual need for money, this must have been a blow.

And this personal blow coincided with a blow to all supporters of the Labour Party. Ramsay MacDonald's Labour government fell after three months, and when the king refused to accept MacDonald's resignation, he took a momentous step, forming a national government with Liberals and Conservatives to deal with the economic crisis. Inevitably, he was accused of betraying his party and was expelled a month later; as a result of his move, Labour would remain strong in the country but not in

Parliament until after the next war. When Margaret went as a delegate to the Labour Party Conference in Scarborough that October, she echoed the clear grief in the chairman's speech about "Mr. MacDonald's new friends."[8] However, there was one compensatory factor for her. She was asked to look after a young German Social Democrat, Lilo Linke, who had come to the conference to see what her "English comrades" stood for.[9] Margaret found her friendliness and positive energy appealing and invited her back to Whitby, so beginning a friendship that would increase Margaret's understanding of the complex situation in Germany that was allowing Hitler to gain power.

By the end of October, buckling under her relentlessly heavy work schedule, Margaret was again unwell. She managed a review of Woolf's *The Waves*, her analysis of the novel expressing her admiration by mirroring its poetic tone. Yet she criticized the now-established label "stream of consciousness" as inadequate:

> It describes only the surface of the book, which is a succession of flashes, some long, some brief, as if the bird skimming the stream were now impatient, darting down and away again, and now content to fly for long minutes directly above the water, noting every stone on the bed and every blade bent by the current. Images recur, as a turn of the stream recalls an earlier one.[10]

She saw Woolf as preoccupied, not with appearances, despite exquisite descriptions of natural beauty, but with what lay beneath. Margaret wrote that Woolf's prose had become "more incisive and sinewy"; she did not simply attempt to paint in words, but offered "the image suggested to her mind by the picture-words and written down in their place." However, to achieve this, Margaret concluded, Woolf had made large sacrifices:

> She is like a woman who has turned her back on life and watches it passing in a mirror, so that nothing shall shake the steadiness of her glance, none of those distractions, those sudden blindings, that come from touching what one sees. (Review of *The Waves*, 678)

This comment unmistakably echoes Tennyson's poem "The Lady of Shalott," where the lady's art turns her away from the messiness of life, the reality that threatens to destroy her. Margaret's insight is keen, but she implies rather than asserts, since she admired much in Woolf's writing. She herself would continually experiment with technique in her novels, but she would never renounce the messiness of life that, for her, was an essential ingredient of modernity. It is worth pausing here to note that, while Margaret embraced the messiness of life as a necessary basis for her fiction, she continually fought "mess" in her domestic life, scrubbing, polishing, rearranging, destroying papers. Here, in the personal sphere, she clearly longed for order; and of course in her novels she aimed too for clarity, lucidity, pattern. The "messiness of life" was what she must accept, providing the ingredients she must work on, but that did not mean that she wrote of it messily. What it meant was that she, like writers she admired such as Tolstoy and Dostoyevsky, did not allow aesthetic considerations to exclude elements in the content that she saw as central to life, to humanity.

Permanently short of cash, she had reluctantly agreed to write a short book for a cheap series Sir Ernest Benn was inaugurating. She told E. J. Thompson ruefully that he "promises to print 25,000 copies, at a penny a copy (to me) — and I needed the money so badly." It was no worse, she said, than writing rubbish for the papers, which lately "I have refused to do" (SJ to EJT, 11.7.31). It was small wonder she was struggling, however, as she and Guy had made a momentous decision that would put further strain on her precarious finances, not to mention her health. They were moving to London for three years, for Guy to go back to university; he had been accepted by the London School of Economics for the following October. So now Margaret's writing would be even more essential to their survival, as Guy must be supported for at least four more years, and there was Bill's education to pay for as well. Her Heinemann novel was to come out in the spring, while Hamish Hamilton had "a very nasty spiteful little book of mine that he will publish in January. I think I am very pro-li-fic," she told Thompson, trying to keep a light tone (SJ to EJT, 6.11.31). This little book, however, mentioned so lightheartedly here, would soon become a major headache.

In the public arena, this had been a year of contrasts. There was a campaign in the right-wing press (preeminently, Beaverbrook's *Daily Express* and Rothermere's *Daily Mail*), making a case for Britain to break its ties with Europe, while the League of Nations stood for anti-imperialism, conciliation, and internationalism, a cause that attracted many of the left-wing thinkers of the day. Concerns about the growth of German anti-Semitism were getting some press coverage;[11] but a number of articles were also being published attempting to allay fears about the rise of Fascism in Europe. A German writer who purported to be a former friend and admirer of Hitler brought out a book claiming that, as a revolutionary leader, Hitler had missed his chance and did not pose a threat, while Wyndham Lewis's book *Hitler* expressed positive admiration for his subject.[12] In May, the *Saturday Review* printed "The Expansion of Italy" by the Italian dictator, Mussolini, following this in October with "Germany at the Cross-roads!" by Adolf Hitler himself.[13] Europe was changing by the minute, and while those on the left in Britain were watching the spread of Fascism with growing unease, there were many who saw Communism as the greater threat. Meanwhile, further afield, British interests were being challenged: in September the Japanese Kwantung Army seized control of Manchuria, and the League of Nations could do nothing.

Margaret was increasingly aware of the European situation, and her friendship with people like young Lilo Linke brought her firsthand news of growing violence against Jews and those on the left; for active Social Democrats like Lilo were now being treated as no different from Communists. It was at this time of increasing racism and intolerance that Margaret had been asked to write a story for an anthology, the brainchild of the eccentric John Fothergill, owner of the Spread Eagle Inn in Thame, now established as a rallying point for writers and intellectuals. He had given the outline of a plot to a number of his literary acquaintances, asking each to develop a story from it:

> A man gets into correspondence with a woman whom he doesn't know and he finds romance in it. Then he sees a girl, falls in love with her in the ordinary way, marries her and drops the academic correspondence. Happiness, and then friction. He writes again to the unknown woman and finds consolation till by an accident it is discovered that the married couple are writing to one another.[14]

Margaret's contribution gives a clue to her thinking at the time. Like most of her generation, she could occasionally use language that would now be construed as racist, but this tale, "A Mingled Strain," shows that, in her case, such language was very far from reflecting racist prejudice. The tale centers on a part-Jewish writer, haunted by a fellow soldier killed in the war, and married to a Cockney girl who torments him with racist taunts and jealousy. In the end, his Jewish mother, a poor woman of "incomparable dignity," helps him to accept, even relish, a wry, stoical approach to life as his racial heritage.[15] It is a simple tale, but showed Margaret already, in 1931, starting to confront the insults a Jew might suffer, at home in England.

Toward the end of the year, the novel Margaret had described lightly as nasty and spiteful ran into trouble. Her American publisher, worried about details that seemed to refer to a contemporary novelist, demanded cuts. Rather than make them, since, in her view, they would change the book too drastically, Margaret released her English and American publishers from their contracts, and approached Chatto and Windus instead.[16] They identified the writer in question as Ethel Mannin, the fiery, anarchic working-class writer, who was already established as a force to be reckoned with on the left and something of a bohemian in her lifestyle. Margaret accepted there was a resemblance, but clearly did not think the issue serious, as she sent the proofs to Mannin herself (SJ to Raymond, 12.12.31). Unfortunately, however, Mannin agreed with the Chatto identification. Furious letters from Mannin to Chatto's followed, threatening libel action, and revealing several instances where the book mirrored such events in her life as the suicide of her lover.[17] Margaret was dismayed, as all attempts to placate Mannin failed.[18] One might speculate that the intensity of writing her novel had blurred Margaret's recollection of what was fact and what was invention in the construction of her heroine; it had after all happened at least once before, when she claimed, in that early letter to Vera Brittain, that she was married at nineteen. As it was she apologized to the Chatto editor, saying:

> I come to London so rarely and take so little interest in writing
> people that I probably pick up old and distorted gossip of all sorts
> without taking enough interest in it to remember anything but
> vague memories without names or times. . . . I wrote last week to
> a friend in London asking for the story and heard inter alia that
> within a month of the suicide EM was writing articles about it in
> the Daily Mail and so on. (SJ to Raymond, 12.30.31)

Yet was Margaret being entirely honest? For she was not quite as uninterested in gossip as she maintained here. In a letter to Valentine Dobrée, written in June, a week after she told Thompson about her "very nasty spiteful little book," she mentioned that Rose Macaulay had received a manuscript from a young writer entitled "Have I slept with Ethel Mannin?" Margaret's comment was "Would you say that is Fame?" (SJ to VD, 6.19.31). So at the very least Margaret was not averse to sharing a joke about Mannin with a friend. Whatever the truth of the matter, it cost Margaret dear, for Mannin, always ready for a fight, was threatening to take her to court. Margaret had to refund her advance, and although Knopf did publish *Delicate Monster* in a collection of three novellas in 1933, it was shelved in England until tempers had cooled.[19]

CHAPTER 8

The Growing Crisis in Europe

By the beginning of 1932, Margaret was glad to turn her back on the dispute over *Delicate Monster*, as she and Guy were planning a visit to Germany. A number of writers of their acquaintance had gone or were going to see for themselves what was happening in both Fascist and Communist countries: Amabel Williams-Ellis had visited Russia with her brother John Strachey in 1928, the Woolfs had visited Berlin in 1929, and Naomi and Dick Mitchison would go to Russia in 1932 and visit Austria and Germany in 1934. Over the past few years, Guy and Margaret had visited France and Austria for short holidays, but now they set off for Germany, arriving in Berlin in February, and meeting a range of people, including Lilo Linke.

In 1934, Margaret would recall her first impressions: Lilo and her friends had "our mood of 1913," full of idealism, eagerly debating the shortcomings of their elders and their own hopes and dreams of a better world.[1] Margaret would always maintain that she and Guy did not anticipate the full horror of what was about to happen, but they saw enough to know all was not well. The Social Democrats were not tough enough with the growing extremism, and could not curb the violence on the streets. This failure of a democratic party to tackle extremism would haunt Margaret in the coming years as she saw the growth of right-wing tendencies within her own society. As it was, on her return from Berlin, she wrote an article stressing the continuing signs of poverty.[2] She told how universities were nicknamed "Wartehalle für Unbeschäftigte" (waiting rooms for the workless), and it was from these students, together with the small ruined shopkeepers and the women, "that Hitler draws his support" (*CJ*, 39). At the same time she was wary of a young Communist she had met: she called him "a fanatic of a modern religion," an image she would often use when writing about extremists and their credos (*CJ*, 42). Dogmatism of any kind worried her. In her article, she went on to contrast how she and Guy were guests at a lavish meal in a good restaurant with how, a few Sundays before, "Nazis and Communists staged a bloody fight in this street" (*CJ*, 45). She recognized that Hitler owed his success to Germany's years of weakness in government, in a faltering economy; yet, although she heard Goebbels give an impressive speech, she could not take him entirely seriously. She and Guy remained in Germany throughout March, when Paul von Hindenburg was elected and Lilo and her friends still believed in a bright future. Two years later, Margaret would write very differently about her impressions but, with hindsight, this earlier article is the more chilling. For despite the poverty, the unemployment, the tales of street violence, it was set against signs of a resurgent social life, where Hitler could still seem like a comedian in appearance and Goebbels be mocked for acting like one. Margaret, like many others, while concerned about the dangers posed by the Nazi Party, did not really anticipate its tsunami-like surge to power.

As she and Guy were leaving for Germany in February, two of her books came off the press. One was her contribution to Ernest Benn's new series of "Ninepenny Novels."[3] *The Single Heart* is a tale pared to the bone, laced with dry humor, and unromantic about the relationships of its characters, their love stories interwoven with social comment.[4] It opens with an alluring anecdote: Emily, the daughter of a wealthy shipowner, comes across a salacious novel which her mother snatches away — leaving her to make do with a volume on her mother's shelves, *The Home Doctor*: "Since she had been brought up in a decent ignorance this proved very exciting" (*TSH*, 7). Emily's love for a working-class boy threads through her life, intertwined with her "suitable" marriage; class prejudice, sexual betrayal, and the corruption of ideals are woven together as Emily painfully matures. This little book was not by any means a simple rehash of earlier work; but the reviews were lukewarm when they were not hostile, all focusing on the love story, ignoring the patterning, the mesh of public and private threads.[5] Maybe the husband's condoning of a blatant affair was part of the problem, maybe the lack of glamorizing put the critics off;

or maybe the fact that Margaret was contributing to a cheap series teased them into reading the work as a mere romantic squib. But this novella is a hauntingly modern tale of a woman instrumental in the achievements of two men, while growing into awareness of her own and society's needs.

Margaret's long novel, *That Was Yesterday*, followed hot on the novella's heels, and was very differently received.[6] It picked up the story of Hervey Russell, first met in *A Richer Dust* as the granddaughter of Mary Hansyke, interweaving autobiographical content with development of fictional strands begun in the trilogy. At its core is an unsparing analysis of the protagonist's growing up. But while Margaret was reusing material from earlier works and reworking incidents from her own life, this book was a mature take on material that had, at one point, threatened to bind her inextricably to the past of her student days and unhappy first marriage. As always her descriptions were very fine, linking sight and sound and the thoughts evoked by them; and again she explored elements of a Whitby/Danesacre heredity. But Hervey's early novels, mirroring Margaret's own, are deconstructed, the first described mischievously as "not so much a book as a skittle-alley," because of the way its students delighted in knocking down all shibboleths they disapproved of (*TWY*, 49). Later her writerly claims are scrutinized:

> She . . . was deaf and insensible to the rhythms of prose. She *heard* neither what she read nor what she wrote. Yet she had an acute ear, and tiny sounds, the shiver of grass on grass in light airs, the squeaking of bats, cries of birds in a distant field, creaking of dried roots, the trickle of rain down the walls of a house, were caught by it, and offered to memory. (*TWY*, 278)

Margaret challenges, as she has done before, the idea that the rhythms of prose should be the writer's main concern; for her it is the sounds of nature that call for the writer's attention. Of course she did not mean that style, rhythm in writing did not matter: it was all a question of what the writer should prioritize, and in this passage, so delicately written, she puts her point across perfectly.

The reviews were good; even the curmudgeonly but shrewd H. C. Harwood, who had lambasted her for writing in the evening papers, commented in the *Saturday Review* that "since the death of D. H. Lawrence

I find no contemporary novelist more disappointing, more exasperating or more thrilling than Miss Jameson. . . . This important novelist to become more important has only to break away from a too narrow, too usual circuit of ideas."[7]

In her fiction, Margaret was indeed about to break free from the need to revisit the issue of infidelity that had been a persistent theme in recent novels; she was about to enter an era of rich experimentation. Nevertheless, driven financially, she had also to accept contracts for articles and the odd short story. Back in the summer of 1931, she had written a drily witty essay, in the manner of her best pieces for the evening papers, for Mabel Ulrich's collection *Man Proud Man*.[8] It evoked the life of a certain type of Victorian woman sustaining her man's self-image: "She leaned. He remained upright" ("Man the Helpmate," 109). This pose was then wryly compared with the modern situation, where too often the roles were reversed:

> The change comes about with so much nature that it is tempting to suppose that though men can undoubtedly be induced to act as supporters or helpmates (and were in the past generally so induced) such an attitude is no more natural to them than dancing to a led bear or tea-drinking to a monkey. ("Man the Helpmate," 111)

Margaret also took the opportunity to attack, in a footnote, the eminent scientist and nationalist Sir Arthur Keith, who, in an address at a Scottish university, had recently referred to the necessary "pruning-hook of War." She commented that he was

> under some misapprehension of the uses to which sane gardeners put their pruning-hooks. Did he, perhaps, imagine that they pruned away only the best and lustiest shoots? Now, if in the next War, recruits were strictly chosen from men between the ages of fifty-five and eighty-five, Sir Arthur would be able in person to justify his metaphor. ("Man the Helpmate," 130)

Later she would admit she had been unfair to Sir Arthur, who was not approving war but "passing a judgement on human nature which the future, with its concentration camps and torture cells, did nothing to invalidate."[9] At the time of writing, however, her footnote was responding to a still prevalent attitude in parts of her society that the cost of war in young lives was justifiable, despite the huge losses in World War I.

The book as a whole was well received, Vera Brittain writing enthusiastically that it turned the tables on all the men "who have produced solemn treatises on the Nature of Woman," and she mentioned Margaret's essay with special approval.[10] The friendship between the two women would grow over the next years, even as the friendship with Michael Sadleir dwindled, partly as a result of Margaret's second marriage, for the Sadleirs, barely recovered from their relief at Jesse's departure, were wary of Guy, partly because, fond of Michael as she was, Margaret did not always share his literary tastes. This difference in taste was clear when Queenie Leavis's *Fiction and the Reading Public*, a vivid analysis of the use and abuse of the novel, came out, and Michael attacked it in the *New Statesman and Nation*. Queenie wrote to the journal, protesting that he was attacking her "for not having done what one did not set out to do, and for not having done what one actually *has* done"; and, in the same issue, Margaret was passionate in her support of the book's insistence on the responsibility of the novelist to engage with contemporary society.[11] This defense of Queenie's work would lead to another lifelong friendship with both Queenie and her husband, F. R. Leavis. In 1932, he joined forces with the founders of the quarterly journal *Scrutiny*, becoming its editor by the third issue. This journal, always unafraid to be controversial, would soon attract an intellectual following, and both husband and wife would be seen as two of the most influential and prickly critics of their era, determined to establish an incontrovertible canon of English literature.[12] The journal did much for many writers, championing, for instance, D. H. Lawrence at a time when he was being castigated by the censorship; but its editor's intransigence eventually led to its downfall.

However, that would be in the future. For Margaret in 1932, as these new friendships were forming, an old allegiance was also making fresh claims on her loyalty. While in Berlin, she had read that her mentor, A. R. Orage, had returned to England. He had been out of the country since 1922, falling — as Katherine Mansfield did in her final illness — under the spell of the mystic George Ivanovitch Gurdjieff, first at his institute at Fontainebleau and then, from 1923 to 1931, going to work with him in New York. Now Orage was back in England, taking part in the founding of a new periodical, the *New English Weekly*, which he and his colleagues hoped to make a forum for metaphysical, psychological, and economic debate.[13] On her return from Berlin, Margaret visited him and, no doubt recalling the brilliant *New Age* days and his kindness to an inexperienced young critic, agreed to review for him, unpaid.[14] Moreover, despite her financial difficulties, loyalty would keep her reviewing for him for a full two years (*JN*, 1:329). Yet while the need to read and analyze several works each month was a considerable burden, Margaret took the opportunity to read and assess, with her usual critical acumen, a number of works that impressed her. An early review established Lawrence and Forster as her benchmarks for blending content and style to perfection (*NEW*, May 12, 1932); in June, she analyzed ideas in Queenie's book and backed *Scrutiny* for its insistence on the novelist's responsibility to society (*NEW*, June 2, 1932). In her next article, one of the works she praised was *Nineteen Nineteen* by John Dos Passos, "one of the few living novelists whose consciousness of the contemporary world reaches below the surface. He is the novelist of its disintegration" (*NEW*, June 23, 1932). She admired the way his method reflected a social disintegration that was taking place on different levels, through the narratives of a number of lives, interlocked by means of the juxtaposing of passages written in different registers, reflecting different perspectives not usually seen in company with each other. This would be a method with which Margaret herself would experiment in future novels.

While her critical acumen was always as acute as it was esoteric, it rarely improved her confidence in her own ability. A letter to H. E. Bates in May was typical: asking him if he would review a first novel she liked, she ended:

> You don't know anyone who wants a good cook, do you? I have been reading Mrs. Leavis's book on Fiction, and I believe every word of it. My only comfort is now that I can at least cook. I'm a good darner, too.[15]

Such self-mockery was all too often the way she presented herself in letters; yet in publishing matters, she showed confidence. In July, she signed her last contract with Heinemann for the omnibus edition of her Mary

Hansyke books: *The Triumph of Time: A Trilogy*.[16] Her friendship with the Heinemann editor, Charley Evans, did not inhibit her seeking better terms elsewhere, as had been the case with Michael Sadleir. She had no fears as a reviewer either. That same month she reviewed J. B. Priestley's novel *Faraway*, her good relations with this fellow Yorkshireman not preventing her from a sweeping attack: "Mr. Priestley has not the intellectual, nor the moral and emotional equipment of the great novelist" (*NEW*, July 7, 1932). Margaret was rarely so destructive when reviewing, but no doubt she recalled his highly critical review of *The Pitiful Wife*. Certainly, she had disapproved of the popular success of his novel *The Good Companions*, which she thought dishonest about the war, failing to address the cost so many ex-soldiers had paid mentally and emotionally for their experiences. Indeed, she commented in an earlier review, "most men prefer a good fairy-tale" (*NEW*, April 21, 1932). Whatever her motive, it would take some years before relations between herself and Priestley were mended.

The reviews she wrote for Orage's journal were mostly positive, and gave her the opportunity to develop her views on the role of the modern novelist. She was in fact meditating on her own way forward, for what Margaret asked for was a novelist "great enough to see the whole of his age and controlled enough to present and interpret it as a whole" (*NEW*, Aug. 4, 1932). Here she was showing her own commitment to socially engaged fiction, and her determination to take soundings in the whole of society. Style was to be a servant of this enterprise, and should not dictate a novel's content. This would be her own aim over the next thirty-odd years, as she developed techniques she found in a wide range of works, mostly outside her own culture. A number of German writers impressed her; she was particularly struck by the work of an Austrian Jewish writer, Hermann Broch's *The Sleepwalkers*, recently translated by Edwin Muir and his wife (*NEW*, Dec. 8, 1932). This trilogy covered the period 1888–1918, its narrative complexity weaving together psychological, aesthetic, philosophical, historical, and sociological threads. The first volume centered on an East Prussian landowner, probing the "hollowness and insecurity" of a rigid European tradition; the second turned to the very different world of the lower orders of 1903, where the hollowness and insecurity were more advanced (*NEW*, Dec. 8, 1932). Broch's final volume set reality and unreality in balance, showing how, as traditional values disintegrated, fantasy took over, while a longing for war and slaughter remained constant. In technique, Broch mirrored the growing disconnections experienced within German society, experimenting with shifts in style and story, moving from first-person to third-person narrative, inserting poems, clashing verbal registers, while always maintaining a lucid core; like Margaret, he was committed to clarity of expression even when weaving complex patterns. So, like Dos Passos, Broch would enrich Margaret's reflections on how realist fiction could develop to meet the challenges of the present time. Her inventiveness would use threads of their making.

At the same time, she had become deeply involved in the antiwar movements, and was growing closer to Vera Brittain as a result. Temperamentally, Vera needed female support, but she could be volatile and difficult. Winifred Holtby had been Vera's prop and stay since their student days in Oxford, and her endless patience and understanding would be hard to match; she was always at hand to look after the children, or to comfort Vera through a bout of depression or to explain away perceived slights (Berry and Bostridge, 248). Now, as Winifred's health deteriorated, Vera, having tried and failed to establish a close link with another Yorkshire novelist, Phyllis Bentley, was turning to Margaret and, for a time, it would seem that each had found a reliable friend. Predominantly, they shared anxieties about war: in September, Margaret told Vera, for instance, that the writer and antiwar activist Vernon Bartlett, visiting them at Mooredge at the start of a walking tour, had said that the next twelve months would decide whether there would be another war, because "if the Disarmament Conference fails and if we fail over Japan there isn't a shred of hope left" (SJ to VB, 9.10.32). Four days after Margaret wrote this letter, the German delegation would indeed walk out of the Disarmament Conference, and, soon after, Japan would follow the annexing of Manchuria with the invasion of China.

In October the Chapmans moved into a small flat in London, as Guy was starting his degree course at the London School of Economics without any money of his own. Bill had now returned from Switzerland, still too young to go to Cambridge (he was seventeen in June), and had to be supported. So "this explains my writing day of eleven hours. It gets harder and harder to fill up the crocks with articles on 'Marriage for Love,' and the rest" (SJ to VB, 9.10.32). From now on, the Chapmans would only live in the moorland cottage during Guy's vacations, keeping the small Abercorn flat in Maida Vale throughout Guy's time at the London School. Bill was with them, "cramming" for the matriculation examinations in January that would equip him for a year at University College London before going to Cambridge. Yet despite the financial pressures of two dependent men, Margaret was tempted to buy a second-hand car, planning to sell her small stock of bank shares to make this possible (SJ to EJT, 10.3.32). It was fortunate, under the circumstances, that *The Triumph of Time*, the one-volume edition of her Mary Hansyke trilogy, was due out that month. For there were other demands on Margaret's purse now that they were back in London: Guy's mother visited in mid-October, as did Lilo Linke (SJ to VB, 10.12.32).

But at least Margaret found some solace in sharing concerns with Vera. They were both dismayed by Oswald Mosley's founding of the British Union of Fascists that October, as he argued the necessity for "an authoritative state, above party and sectarian interests," and they were active in their support for the League of Nations.[17] On the writing front, Margaret was supporting Vera's work on her autobiographical *Testament of Youth*; they were now reading each other's work, as well as Winifred's (SJ to VB, 10.12.32, 10.14.32). Encouraged by Vera, Margaret was also refining her attitude to war, developing her own commitment to a peace that would last. However, a certain ambivalence to full-blown pacifism, even at the height of her support for the peace movements, would color her response to the growing crisis in Europe throughout the 1930s, while she would never make the mistake of confusing pacifism with appeasement.[18]

Margaret's writing for periodicals was, indeed had to be, unremitting, given the pressing need to make money.[19] In an article for the *Highway*, she picked up and developed Queenie Leavis's strictures against popular literature, arguing that "a novelist might be said to be more important than a teacher — in the sense that he can do a great deal more harm."[20] For, she insisted, whereas children could resist a formal education,

> the novelist gets past unchallenged. You take up a novel in the definite expectation of being pleased or entertained. . . . What a popular novelist thinks and feels about life affects in the end those forms of life we call the social order. ("Dangers of Fiction," 8)

She went on to equate "certain very popular kinds of fiction" with modern advertising, persuading people to want more, not to think about the real dangers facing contemporary society, and she warned that "between them, the popular novelist, the sensational press, and the cinema, are creating a new civilization." In sum, she concluded, what worried her was that "not one of our most-read novelists has so much as noticed that all is not well with our civilization" ("Dangers of Fiction," 10). Escapism, of course, had its place; but as the decade wore on Margaret would feel more and more acutely that novelists had a responsibility to engage with such problems of their society as poverty, political extremism, and the ever-present debates about war and peace.

This article for the *Highway* anticipated a major theme of her next book, *No Time Like the Present.* She told E. J. Thompson this work would be

> a serious attack on best-sellers for their lightmindedness, on Bishops for their militancy, and on war-mongers and war in general. I don't expect to get any money for it, but I had to write it, and I do hope to get some notice taken of it because I feel very strongly and bitterly about that "next war" and the revolution and so forth. (SJ to EJT, 11.21.32)

She had written this book to broadcast the dangers Western society was facing, given the threat to Europe in America's calling in of debts and loans after the Wall Street crash. Guy had met a "nitrate millionaire," just back from Paris, who told him how nervous the French were about the economic situation; they were very reluctant to pay even the interest on their loan from America (SJ to EJT, 11.28.32). Tensions in Europe were growing. Margaret herself had joined the Writers' Committee of the British Anti-War Council, set up in response to the very successful Amsterdam World Anti-War Congress, held in August of that year, with the aim of organizing resistance to war on a global scale. Fellow members of the British Writers' Committee included Bertrand Russell and Amabel Williams-Ellis, and all were committed to drumming up support.[21] Letters were fired off to the papers; Margaret suggested she and Vera should sign one for the *New Statesman,* and Vera and Amabel could send one to *Time and Tide* (SJ to VB, 12.22.32). However, not all their shared letters to the press were protesting about war. In December, Margaret, Vera, and Amabel sent a joint letter to the *New Statesman*, taking two recent arrests as their cue for an eloquent protest about "the series of prosecutions, imprisonments, and heavy fines, which have this winter been inflicted upon the unemployed and their leaders and advocates."[22] The official crackdown since the general strike showed how fear of the Left overshadowed the rise of Fascism in many British eyes.[23]

Margaret's letters to Vera at this time are full of information and anecdote, as they had so many commitments in common. She shared writer's gossip: a meeting with Frieda Lawrence, who was "rather splendid," and a bad moment at the Anti-War Council where she felt impelled to speak against Bertrand Russell's insistence that Ethel Mannin was a "great intellect" and should be asked to join (SJ to VB, 12.10.32). Margaret confided her own affairs; she now had Nancy Pearn as her agent, a good move, as she was being harassed by publishers who wanted her on their books. She gave news of Bill: he was ill in bed, reading voraciously, but refusing "literature"; she offered to get two writer friends, Helen Waddell and Gerald Bullett, to review Vera's *Testament of Youth*. She felt, she said, like "a broken-down top," her latest short story, "of revolting sentimentality," scattered on the floor (SJ to VB, 12.14.32). In her next letter this unidentified story for a popular magazine is finished, but "a lecture to some Poor Scholars on the Craft of Fiction hangs fire" (SJ to VB, 12.20.32). Her letters were witty, relaxed, and trusting when writing to those she loved and respected, as correspondence with her current confidants — Vera, Valentine, and Thompson — shows.

CHAPTER 9

The Role of the Novel as Hitler Comes to Power

While the need to write bread-and-butter short stories and articles continued to make demands on Margaret's time throughout 1933, the beginning of the year saw a flurry of serious publications.[1] Hot on the heels of *The Triumph of Time*, which had been well received, Knopf and Bernard Tauchnitz in Leipzig brought out *Women against Men*, a collection of three novellas: *The Single Heart, Delicate Monster*, and *A Day Off*, this last about to be published separately in England. Ethel Mannin seems not to have challenged this publication, perhaps because the title of the book hid the presence of *Delicate Monster*. Margaret had enjoyed experimenting with fictional modes in all three novellas; she would say later that they were "tenuously linked," each being

> a portrait of a woman at the turning point, early or late, of her
> life, composed with the utmost scepticism about the feelings
> (love, friendship, loyalty, etc) we all profess, the self-deceptions
> on which we all depend: each was to convey through its form the
> essence of the character. (*JN*, 1:284–85)

A Day Off, an accomplished experiment in Margaret's own "take" on stream of consciousness, explores the mind of a middle-aged prostitute. It is tightly constructed around one day, one outing, tracing the reveries that fend off the moment when a letter confirms the end of the relationship with the woman's last protector, George. The tale may have been suggested by works like Patrick Hamilton's *The Siege of Pleasure* or Jean Rhys's *After Leaving Mr. Mackenzie*, but Margaret's woman is not drawn into Hamilton's "fast" set, and never succumbs to the "sore and cringing feeling" that overwhelms Rhys's Julia.[2] She has too much life to be crushed, even when George's letter arrives, and in that sense is closer to Joyce's one-day work, *Ulysses*. Coming so soon after the publication of *The Triumph of Time* trilogy, the change of approach and subject matter was dramatic, and most reviewers were impressed by the variety of tone in the three works. Harold Strauss in the *New York Times Book Review* summed them up by saying, "So completely is she the master of her art, so instinctively the craftsman, so superlatively the selective artist, that a restrained view of her work is difficult for a student of the novel."[3] Margaret's growing skill at experimenting, pushing at the bounds of realism with tools used by the modernists, was starting to show itself.[4]

For the first time, husband and wife shared a publisher, and almost the same publication date. When Guy's *A Passionate Prodigality* came out in January, its excellence was instantly recognized.[5] Apart from the poignantly chosen epigraphs, the style is crisp and unemotional. The book shows how trench warfare became the only reality for combatants confined in its wasteland during World War I. Guy hated war, was often terrified, but was irrevocably bonded with those in the trenches, and like others of his kind, loathed the times behind the lines for their triviality and *lack* of reality. In the course of the narrative there is both camaraderie and a monklike acceptance of his subsequent, emotionally drained condition. Looking back on the book later, Guy would write:

> I was preoccupied with an attachment, the sentiment of belonging to a living entity and, of course, its death. . . . Montherlant in his Threnody for the Dead of Verdun (*Chant funèbre pour les Morts de Verdun*) talks of the "nostalgia" of the old soldiers for the war and claims that one could really say it had been the most "tender" human experience of contemporary life. Teilhard de Chardin wrote that the invincible attraction of the front lines was that one discovered a lucidity not otherwise vouchsafed[:] "This heightening is not got without pain. All the same it is a heightening. And that is why in spite of everything, one loves the front and regrets it."

And he added, revealingly:

> There is also the other side that I have tried to illuminate in a
> couple of paragraphs — the enormous fascination of war, the re-
> pulsion and attraction, the sharpening of awareness, and as one
> became familiar with one's surroundings an apprehension which
> was not fear — a quickening rather. I was far less scared in 1917
> than I was in the more peaceful days before the Battle of the
> Somme.[6]

Margaret's understanding of what she had and what was gone forever
is confirmed all too clearly in this late preface by Guy himself. But at
the time of the book's publication, she was delighted with the "splendid
reviews," and with a recommendation by the Book Society, while the
spring issue of the *Author* noted that Guy's book was a winter best seller
(SJ to VB, 1.7.33).

For Margaret, work was pouring in, and the debate about the role of
the novel continued. On January 19, she gave her lecture to the "Poor
Scholars" on "The Craft of the Novelist" (SJ to VB, 1.2.33).[7] Much of the
argument reiterated her conviction that the strength in novels was "human worth, and not any fancied aesthetic quality," warning that danger
besets the novelist "who looks too persistently within," as "he is like a man
who tries to tell the time by examining only the works of his watch" (*CJ*,
61, 63, 64). She compared writers concentrating on their characters' lives
in action, writers like Ernest Hemingway and T. F. Powys, with Virginia
Woolf, who explored inner life ("and this, Mrs. Woolf says, is your real
life"), and with D. H. Lawrence, equally concerned with inner life, but
having "emotion issuing in action" (*CJ*, 72). For her it was Lawrence who
came off best. Again, Margaret was right at the heart of current debates
about what should be the primary objective of the novel. Should its main
concern be the working of the human mind, the patterns of consciousness, or should interiority be linked with the social and political patterns
emerging in the world of the 1930s? What writerly priorities expressed
reality, real life, most satisfactorily? For Margaret, interiority could not
be enough; events in Europe strengthened her resolve to engage in her
novels as well as in real life.

In January, Hindenburg appointed Hitler as German chancellor and, at first, the British press was undecided about whether to take him seriously. The left-wing *New Clarion*'s cartoon of the new leader, for instance, appeared with the doggerel:

> A man of Iron, or of Straw?
> What odds? He keeps within the law.
> No one can say just what would happen
> If he should line up with Von Papen![8]

This thinking went along with that of Germany's aristocratic vice-chancellor, Franz von Papen, at this stage: that Hitler was controllable by the German upper class and major business interests. The illusion would not last long. Margaret, along with other left-wing intellectuals, feared that war was a real possibility and was contemptuous about the inconclusive compromises issuing from the Disarmament Conference in Geneva. In an article for the *New Clarion*, she wrote:

> War is only made less probable by changing the social conditions in which the seeds of war are nursed to maturity. If Governments were to pay more and more intelligent and unprejudiced attention to settling in a new spirit the problems of poverty and its results in social and economic instability at home, and less to debating with each other on the quantity of the destructive weapons in their hands, the chances of another war would really recede.[9]

Other humanitarian issues engaged her. In February, she wrote to the *New Statesman and Nation* in support of Hugh Hutchinson, a young reporter on the *Indian Daily Mail*, imprisoned in India in relation to the Meerut Conspiracy Case of 1929, brought by the British government in response to fears about the growing influence of Communism in India. Hutchinson, however, was no Communist: his concern for the conditions of Indian industrial workers was simply humanitarian. Margaret reported that at the eventual trial in August 1932, while the assessors unanimously found Hutchinson not guilty, the sessions judge ignored their decision, sentencing him to "a further four years' rigorous imprisonment."[10] So Margaret was asking for money to finance the appeal for the

Meerut prisoners. Her letter, appositely, was printed under one describing the Dickensian conditions in Indian jails, where the Indian Prisons Act of 1894 was still in force, sanctioning fetters, handcuffs, whipping, and where, the writer asserted,

> prison offences include feigning illness, idleness at work, showing disrespect to a jail officer, refusing to eat the food prescribed (or on the other hand resorting unnecessarily to the night latrine), singing and loud laughing (which must be very prevalent).[11]

Like Winifred Holtby, Margaret was no imperialist, and was brave enough to confront tyrannical behavior in her own backyard (SJ to EJT, 2.23.33).[12]

Yet in family life, Margaret could make decisions that went against her usual perspicacity. When the idea of Bill entering University College London fell through, she had decided to broaden his mind by sending him to live with a German family in Göttingen. By March 1933, as the Nazis grew more strident, she was starting to worry. She had been told that he would be safe in Göttingen, while Berlin would be a different matter, and she vacillated over whether to bring him home (SJ to VD, 3.3.33).[13] Soon she was receiving despairing letters from German friends describing life in Berlin, and was particularly concerned for Lilo Linke, as her work as a left-wing journalist made her a likely Nazi target. Yet life in Göttingen seemed so different, as she told Vera Brittain: "I don't believe the average provincial German has any notion of the atrocities in the cities. Bill's hostess certainly hasn't"; and she could even add humorously, "What ever shall I do if, when I go to meet him in July, a large blond Prussian steps out of the train! I couldn't face it!" (SJ to VB, 3.27.33). A few days later, she was still undecided about bringing him home "unnecessarily. He is staying with Nazis and so ought to be safe" (SJ to EJT, 4.1.33). She was surely being ironic here, but it is hard to be sure of her tone. It is nonetheless extraordinary that she would stick to her original plan to bring him home at the end of July. This whole episode is a fascinating glimpse of how even someone as aware of the growing German crisis as Margaret was could come close to the complacency she had so recently castigated when in Germany herself. Her awareness of the appalling problems her German friends were facing sits oddly with the lighthearted tone of her letters about Bill. But then, not all of those living in Europe who were most threatened by Nazi policies came to a full realization of their peril until it was tragically too late: many Jews would die because they did not leave when they could.

When reviewing for A. R. Orage, however, Margaret was clear-eyed about the growing menace, often using her column as a vehicle to press home a message. For instance, recommending the reissue of Norman Angell's *The Press and the Organisation of Society* for its case against the popular press, she referred to the European situation, saying the easiest way to be popular was

> to appeal to the most primitive emotions and impulses, to shriek "Make Germany Pay" rather than to publish the painful fact that the war had ruined the lot of us and that no one nation could "pay" for it. (*NEW*, March 9, 1933)

An article in the *New Clarion* followed, comparing the expectations for literature before World War I with what came after: in Paris, "the savage railing of the 'Manifeste Dada,'" in England the growth of a popular literature that ignored the current crises. In far too many of these postwar works, responsible engagement with the realities of the contemporary world had been abandoned, she proclaimed.[14]

By now Margaret was again exhausted, had been prescribed rest, and was anxious about the imminent publication of *No Time Like the Present*. She retreated to Mooredge with Guy for the Easter vacation, where she pondered on what was happening in Germany. The Reichstag fire in February had been declared a Communist plot, giving Hitler the excuse to dissolve Parliament, arrest thousands of Communists and socialists, suspend civil liberties, and silence opposition parties and trade unions. She told Vera, "I get such despairing letters from friends there that I carry them about a whole day unopened," and she was particularly distressed by those she received from Lilo, as three out of four of the Social Democrat newspapers Lilo worked for were now prohibited (SJ to VB, 3.27.33). Margaret was eager to get the young woman over to England if she could, but inexplicably, she still did not bring Bill home.

No Time Like the Present came out on April 27. In some sense, this was a two-part book, and yet there are subtle links between its two sections. The first autobiographical section examines the years leading up to 1914. Margaret weaves into passages of self-analysis meditations on language, the importance of a person's roots, and on how to write about memories; she goes on to ask whether people still shared a common understanding of words like "passion" and "decency" (*NTLTP*, 149). Through contemplation of her own life, her love of place and distrust of words, she looks again at the role of the novel, and how inadequate she finds its dealing with reality. Many of Margaret's critical writings could be described as works in progress: a point she made in one would be expanded in the next, so we get clear glimpses of how her thinking was progressing. In this work, her defense of the unemployed and her presentation of the case for peace show her at her most eloquent. The book modulates from memories of her childhood to memories of student aspirations of the prewar period, to the effects of war on its survivors. The writing changes key, from meditation to passionate conviction, and is disturbingly timeless in many of its arguments. She urges that writers should attack "the theory that labour is a commodity, to be bought in the cheapest market"; and she savages an all-too-current idea that "not to work is morally shameful," so the unemployed by definition were contemptible (*NTLTP*, 171, 173). She then turns to the need to resist war, and particularly attacks women who failed to oppose war, saying they had "only added to the quantity of human activity, and little so far to its quality" (*NTLTP*, 230). As a mother, she says, "I feel bitter anger against women who accept war" (*NTLTP*, 237). The ideas in this book were enriched by Margaret's engagement with thinkers of her time like the French philosopher Julien Benda, and hers is an eloquent voice, making the arguments accessible to a wide range of readers. Unsurprisingly, the reviews exemplified the divisions in the thinking of the time.[15]

By the end of April Margaret was still unwell; Vera sent roses, which delighted her, and she acknowledged how their friendship had helped her to pull out of depression (SJ to VB, 4.25.33, 4.26.33, 4.28.33). But events in Europe oppressed her. The Nazi regime in Germany was steadily consolidating its power, even as Count Keyserling published an article in the *Bookman* of June 1933, suggesting that Hitler would probably take a back seat soon. The count still insisted, however, that "[Hitler] it was who awakened German consciousness at a moment when it was at its lowest ebb, and alone made our regeneration possible."[16] Yet a national boycott of businesses owned by Jews had begun two months earlier, and in May there was the notorious burning of the books; increasing numbers of left-wing intellectuals and Jews were either leaving or contemplating flight. Over the summer the list of authors banned in Germany was lengthening: as well as large numbers of German and Jewish writers, including Heinrich and Thomas Mann, Ludwig Renn, and Arnold and Stefan Zweig, Lenin and Karl Marx featured, together with Upton Sinclair.[17] Margaret responded by increasing commitment to the cause of peace: she offered Cape, the publisher, an unsolicited commendation of Beverley Nichols's warning about the slide toward war, *Cry Havoc*, saying "it should penetrate even the thickest skulls," while later in the year she would, despite her phobia about public speaking, take part in a peace film (SJ to VB, 10.28.33).[18]

Guy was approaching first-year examinations at the London School of Economics, his head deep in his books, while Margaret worried that she must sell Mooredge, as she was finding the burden of two establishments too much, and Guy's dislike of life in Whitby showed no signs of abating: "I'm already in tears for my lovely room looking at the moors — the first time I've had a room of my own to write in," Margaret mourned (SJ to VB, 7.4.33). Bill came home from Germany at the end of July and five days later went to Reading to learn to fly. Margaret told Vera: "I'd promised him that, to keep him out of the Air Force. He hasn't been converted to the Nazi faith, thank heaven" (SJ to VB, 8.12.33). But all these distractions had not stopped her embarking on a vast project, as she told Vera in the same letter:

> I am a third of the way through the first volume of a quintet! Can you imagine such madness. I hope that — unless Cassell's rebel — I can keep this vast and foolish work going until Bill is through Cambridge. I daren't send him back to Germany and he doesn't go to Cambridge until 1934. I think of sending him to the Polytechnic for a year, for his soul's sake. Do you suppose Cambridge will sneer at him if I do?

As so often, she made light of any artistic aspiration, implying financial necessity alone was driving her; partly, too, this was to protect Vera's all-too-fragile self-esteem that tended to plummet when confronted by someone else's artistic goals.

But Margaret did indeed have artistic aspirations: she had been deeply impressed by Dos Passos and Broch, and by the first two volumes of Jules Romains's projected series, *Les hommes de bonne volonté* (*Men of Good Will*). Romains's preface was in tune with his American and German contemporaries, and appealed to Margaret as she quested for ways of presenting the current scene. Romains announced that his series would have no central character, and many characters would have no obvious link: "What I see before my eyes is life in the twentieth century, our own life as modern men," and the writer must decide between "a factor of unity or the living truth in our picture."[19] He seems to be advocating the importance of engaging with the messiness of contemporary life rather than a pruning to achieve aesthetic elegance. So his thinking chimed in with arguments Margaret had herself been making in her critical writings.

Margaret honored her political commitments even as she contemplated her proposed novel sequence. In October, she attended the Labour Conference in Hastings as a delegate for Whitby and Scarborough.[20] The conference concerned itself with the rise of Hitler, as this month would see Germany finally withdrawing from the Disarmament Conference, and Japanese imperial expansion. The implications for Europe were debated alongside issues at home: unemployment and the role of the workers. Margaret distinguished herself by voting in favor of the resolution that

> this Conference declares that wage earners of all grades and occupations have a right which should be acknowledged by law to an effective share in the control and direction of socialised industries which their labour sustains.[21]

The motion was carried, Margaret earning a rebuke from the former MP Philip Noel-Baker, who was one of those on the left insisting education must come before managerial responsibility (*JN*, 1:321). But she did not lose his respect; on the contrary, as he was a prominent supporter of the League of Nations, he persuaded her to collaborate on an antiwar project that would give her many headaches over the next few months. The conference also saw Lilo back in England: she had fled Germany, was now jobless and homeless, and Margaret committed herself to help and home her. This commitment would be demanding, for very soon after her arrival, Lilo gave Margaret the manuscript of a book she had written "in what she imagined was English," and Margaret set to work to transform it into a publishable work (*JN*, 1:310). Later she would admit: "I suppose I rewrote every sentence in the book. It remained unalienably her work, her own voice" (*JN*, 1:311). Typically, Margaret was selflessly generous about this labor of love; she sent the rewritten manuscript to her old friend Michael Sadleir at Constable, and he, also generous, agreed to publish.[22]

Voices urging greater awareness of the European crisis were growing in strength. In the *Bookman* (UK), for instance, Hugh Ross Williamson deplored "Literary Detachment," arguing the importance of the link between literature and politics in the widest sense. He pointed to Gollancz's publication of *The Brown Book of Hitler Terror*, a work by the World Committee for the Victims of German Fascism, and proclaimed the young BBC's "power to make political democracy a working reality," if it should choose.[23] Although he was talking primarily about nonfiction, what he said chimed in with Margaret's thinking about the novel. She reflected on this again in an article for the *Bookseller*, this time addressing the role of a publisher faced with the need to make a profit, or to publish a book engaging with serious contemporary issues that would not sell. She accepted that money had to be made, but mourned the fate of the good writer whose work was deemed unprofitable.[24] A few days later, when Orage, who enjoyed a dogfight in his columns, printed two negative reviews of Vera's *Testament of Youth*, both, ironically, from committed pacifists, Margaret defended the book eloquently. She did this partly out of loyalty to her friend, partly as a matter of principle, since two negative reviews of a work in one journal seemed to her unethical, and partly to reinforce Vera's message that lessons must be learnt from the deaths of so many young men in the war.[25] Margaret now finally decided to stop reviewing for Orage, and he was gracious in acknowledging his debt to her: "You've served your time for a dozen volumes, so I still feel in your debt. Best of luck to your new novel."[26]

It was not only reviewing that impeded Margaret's work as a novelist; she had also to contend with heavy domestic demands in the tiny London flat, and with another problem that was growing:

> My life, between German refugee [Lilo], Guy and Bill, is a cross between a boarding house keeper and a receptionist. . . . I cook breakfast for four, make beds for three, run about showing my refugee to people I hope will help her, and in the intervals write my novel. I think I am an ass. (SJ to VB, 11.11.33)

For she was now committed not only to the cause of peace, but to support for victims of Nazi oppression; Lilo was not by any means the only one. Furthermore, as the situation on the Continent worsened, more committees sprang up in response: in November, Margaret attended a Reichstag Trial Defense Committee meeting, one of many committees concerned with the increasingly dark events in Germany. Yet she remained critically alert: she was growing wary of some of the priorities of the Anti-War Council, as its members now tended to focus on the horrors of war rather than on the benefits of peace. Guy, sharing Margaret's concerns, wrote in the *New Clarion* protesting that current antiwar propaganda was unhelpful, as a pacifism based simply on fear was not enough: "The construction of the peace mind is infinitely more vital," he argued.[27]

Increasingly, on the right and on the left, different agendas were being pursued. Many writers who felt a sense of moral responsibility to take sides in the worsening European climate were tempted to move to extremes: the novelist Christina Stead, passionately left-wing herself, noted approvingly in December that "Gide and all the writers of merit and intelligence have gone into the revolutionary camp," vocal in their condemnation of Fascism and their call for active resistance to the growing Fascist threat, wherever it might surface.[28] Reports of German rearmament were coming in by the end of the year, alongside rumors that French firms were involved in the sale of arms to the Nazi regime, even as Margaret's friend Vernon Bartlett was writing "Peace round the Corner," advocating help for a German recovery and urging restraint.[29] Vera was fully committed to the peace drive, while Margaret was willing to write in its support, but not to talk: "Any good I can do writing would be nullified by my ridiculousness as a speaker. I'm far more useful as an unseen pen" (SJ to VB, 12.21.33). On December 30, as the Reichstag trial ended, the *New Statesman and Nation* expressed the hope that the German people would start to ask questions of their leaders about "the purgatories called concentration camps, about the continuous persecution of the Jews, and the steady degeneration of German culture and public life." There was need for writers to respond.

CHAPTER 10

Anti-Fascism, Pacifism, and the PEN

By the beginning of 1934, the threat of war was being taken more seriously in leading journals.[1] The burning of the books and the Reichstag trials had stirred many thinkers on the left. The PEN, founded as an apolitical society, was having its first major crisis: the German Centre's membership had been revoked as it had failed to uphold the PEN's commitment to free speech. Margaret was deeply concerned for the fate of the German writer she most admired, Ludwig Renn, who was imprisoned for "ideological corruption" in January (SJ to HO, 1.18.34). Hermon Ould was sympathetic, but said the PEN was in its usual quandary about issues that could be construed as political; H. G. Wells, as president of the English Centre and with the PEN's constitution in mind, was unwilling to sign protest letters about such prisoners himself, but agreed to letters being sent from Ould and individual members.[2] Margaret, along with all those who had reliable lines of communication with Germany, had good reason to be worried both for the very real sufferings of Ludwig Renn and other prisoners, and for apathy in England, for information from Europe was often contradictory, and therefore easily dismissed. The *Saturday Review*, now under the aegis of the highly eccentric Lady Houston, continued to praise the European dictators, in one issue printing a photograph of Mussolini, "The World's Most Benevolent Ruler," adding underneath, "He dragged Italy out of the mire of Socialism and in a few years has made it the most successful and prosperous country in Europe."[3] The *New Statesman and Nation* offered a very different view, printing an anonymous report from the Sonnenburg concentration camp, in which the writer gave details of torture and suicides among Jews and non-Jews in the camp.[4] Yet soon after this, General Sir Ian Hamilton, who had gone to Germany to receive back the Gordons' drums, lost in the war, told of a fund of goodwill in Germany for Britain.[5] Margaret used her writing skills to plead the cause of prisoners, drafting a letter to Goebbels, while her friend Amabel Williams-Ellis, further to the left than Margaret, was persuaded by the United Front, one of the many groups against Fascism and Nazism, to visit Berlin in an attempt to help the three Bulgarians acquitted over the Reichstag fire but still in jail. She was, of course, unsuccessful (SJ to HO, 2.6.34).[6] Vera Brittain was also active, lecturing and writing, her feminism, like Winifred Holtby's, now inextricably involved in her championing of the cause of peace.[7]

By now, Margaret was also committed to the large peace project she had agreed to collaborate on with Philip Noel-Baker at the Hastings Labour Conference. She was deputed to invite prominent writers they wished to recruit to a dinner, where they would be urged to promote the case against war. This event had to be postponed until Philip, Lord Robert Cecil, and Margaret returned from Brussels after attending the International Conference in Defence of Peace; the dinner finally took place on February 20 at the Wellington Club in Knightsbridge. Cecil presided, with Rebecca West and Rose Macaulay in the seats of honor. From Margaret's point of view, the dinner would be the easy part of what rapidly became yet another all-too-demanding task, as she was assigned the job of editing the book of essays agreed on at the dinner. Later she would claim that this book, *Challenge to Death*, was Philip's idea, although in a letter to Vera in 1934 she would assert that the book was her own suggestion (SJ to VB, 11.5.34). However that might be, she found she had taken on a major chore.

When, overwhelmed by all her commitments, she fell ill again, she lamented "all these totally wasted days — my urgent novel, the Cecil book, an introduction of a noble nature to my refugee's [Lilo Linke's] book, a long article — what an ass I am to get ill" (SJ to VB, 3.2.34). Yet just at this time, the first novel of the promised series, *Company Parade*, came out.[8] Margaret had finished it the previous November, and in her foreword, echoing that of Jules Romains, said it was to be the first of perhaps five or six novels "in which an attempt, necessarily incomplete, is made to depict the contemporary scene" (*CP*, v). The overall title of the series being *The Mirror in Darkness*, she continued, the mirror "may be taken to be the mind of the author, or of the reader, or at times only of the young woman called Hervey Russell." Moreover, the project would need a great many characters "to play their parts in any illusion of the contemporary scene" — hence the title. Interestingly, what she did not say in her foreword was that the first novel picked up where *That Was Yesterday* had ended, with several characters already formed both in that book and in the *Triumph of Time* trilogy; so while she would write no more than three of the promised *Mirror in Darkness* books, covering the period December 1918 to June 1926, by the final volume she had produced seven books that spanned the period from the mid-nineteenth century to the end of the general strike. Nor would she entirely abandon the project: she would pick up some characters again in a number of works over the next twenty years. The mirror of an age would thus reflect so much more than she originally envisaged, being written at intervals over such a dramatically changing time.

There was good reason for Margaret's decision not to link *Company Parade* with *That Was Yesterday*, as she was offering a very differently constructed novel, adapting the nonlinear techniques she had analyzed in works by Dos Passos, Broch, and Romains. She offered a wide perspective on the growing turbulence after World War I and the problems faced by damaged and sensitive minds that had to cope with what war had left in its wake. All is not seen from one point of view but from several, drawing on different backgrounds and experience, cutting from one perception to another, producing a collage effect. There is Hervey herself, hinting at the author's view, there is Penn, petulant and volatile — echoes of her ex-husband, Karl, here. There is Renn, fighting social injustice with integrity and no thought of material gain, unlike Louis, the passionate socialist who gradually succumbs to compromise. And there is Gary, partly recalling the American tycoon whom Dos Passos had named and, by implication, shamed, but in Margaret's novel, shaped by the effects of the war, that for him are catastrophically personal. Margaret was adept at merging dialogue with a stream of consciousness that often runs in a different direction from the words uttered by a character; and increasingly, one of her skills was to blend image and observation with the skill of a poet, as in this description of how Hervey sees Renn:

It was not at all the interest of a young woman, but belonged to a part of her mind which drew the same pure nearly unrealised delight from the flattened places and creases of a man's face; the running of a wave; London when a clear sky gave its buildings that air of delicacy and remoteness; a big careless woman in full sail; a hill; the curve of a lighted road at night. (*CP*, 17)

The reviews were, on the whole, positive. Graham Greene in the *Spectator* particularly admired her style:

For how admirably Miss Jameson writes, with fastidiousness of phrase and tight emotional control. The dialogue is spare, curt, as necessary to the theme as the dialogue in a good play. There is no hazy writing, no padding, and she has the ability to describe her characters quickly and clearly.[9]

Nevertheless, he worried about how she would end the series, since the sense of impending war could not be sustained indefinitely and the series would need, he concluded, "a climax adequate to her beginning." This was a valid point, technically: hindsight alone makes his anxiety ironic. He had one other concern in this review, that she did not produce a "fixed point of view, not even a fixed point of view in each short section, and her novel suffers from the dispersion, is inclined to flicker like an early movie" (Greene, 634) The validity of intellectual uncertainty as a means of portraying the social, moral, and political crises of the time, something that Dos Passos, Romains, and the Broch of *The Sleepwalkers* understood all too well, seemed to have evaded him, at least in this otherwise positive review, and this failure to understand gives a glimpse of how resistant many were at the time to the kind of experiments in fiction developing abroad. Margaret would increasingly find inspiration from fictions being shaped in Europe and the States to cope with the implications of the political and social issues of the time. But many of her British writer contemporaries were either uninterested in or unaware of such experiments. All too often, serious literary debate in England, as against that promoted by European thinkers like Julien Benda and Paul Valéry, was surprisingly disengaged from contemporary events; engagement in

England was too often left to those with specific political affiliations, either to Communism or Fascism.

Margaret was now busy persuading fellow writers to contribute to the book she was editing, *Challenge to Death*. Over the next few months she would write over 174 letters to draw in just 15 authors. Back in Mooredge for the Easter vacation, she was plagued by her family's failure to understand her need for a full-time servant in such a small house, given the work she had undertaken. Exasperated, she could still laugh at herself, at least when writing to Vera:

> We all wear hair shirts, but I put mine on deliberately, under the impression that I was a noble character who would enjoy being pricked. I soon found that far from that, I resented the discomfort intensely and nothing but incessant work and going to bed every night too tired to lift a finger keeps me from behaving like a fiend. (SJ to VB, 3.20.34)

She had reason to feel exasperated: Aldous Huxley responded to her invitation to write the book's epilogue with a long letter of doom-laden prevarication about the threat of war; he ended by refusing. After many other refusals, Margaret reluctantly decided that she would have to write both the introductory essay and the epilogue herself.[10]

She still made time to campaign against war and Fascism. In an article based on a lecture, she inveighed against the realities of Fascism. She implored her readers and fellow writers to "protest against the acceptance of unreason and violence until our tongues are silenced in our mouths," and emphasized her right to "refute those who say that the artist should keep his eyes narrowly on his art."[11] By early April she had completed her careful copyediting of Lilo's book and had written her introduction, highlighting the plight of those persecuted by the Nazi regime.[12] She described her meetings with some of the first refugees in 1933, largely Jewish, but including others who were political dissidents, inviting her readers to see what these refugees could offer "with their love of music, their eager, observing minds, and their genius for conversation" (*TWE*, xxxiv). Then the tone darkened. She told how these refugees were the lucky ones, how a number of hastily formed committees in England were trying to save others, and she gave some cameo portraits of those persecuted. She told of how the Labour Conference at Hastings had been "haunted by the ghost of German Social Democracy," in the shape of a young lawyer or doctor with a pale intelligent face, and no money (*TWE*, xxxiv). She recalled a letter from a young German socialist who had lost his job as his mother was half-Jewish, describing how he and his sister could not get work, and were close to starvation, and how he longed to correspond with an English boy, but must pretend to be discussing something harmless like a wedding (*TWE*, xxxv). This long introductory essay was a crucial addition to the work as a whole, and acted as a foretaste of Lilo's next book, *Restless Flags*, which would deal directly with the growth of Nazism and Lilo's own youthful experience of it.

Margaret had worked herself to a standstill to get this introduction written. As she confessed to Vera:

> It does make a difference that I am the sole bread-winner of my family. If I don't work hard at the Cecil chapter and various "good works" I've let myself in for I shan't get them finished in April. And I *must* start my novel again in May. (SJ to VB, 4.9.34)

She worked on her own essays for the book while Guy was visiting his difficult and demanding mother: he would return, she said,

> in a condition bordering on hysteria, if not actually hysterical. Pray heaven I never have that effect on my child. I don't suppose I shall really, since he doesn't take any notice of anything I say! (SJ to VB, 4.15.34)

Vera was by now a valued confidante and a generous friend, but she had to be treated sensitively. Margaret had to reassure her that she would never put her in a book: "People whom I love and respect elude me if I try to write about them. If I put a real person in a book, they must be dead, or I must hate or despise them. I have a very bad disposition" (SJ to VB, 4.24.34). The last lighthearted sentences would come back to haunt her in a few years' time, when Vera suspected she herself was being satirized in *Europe to Let*.

Driven by the need to make money, Margaret had to write more articles than she liked, but she was writing well. In June she produced a hard-hitting piece, urging that the divorce law should be changed: "As it stands [it] is more an offensive insult to decent people than a deterrent to the light-minded."[13] But there were moments of self-indulgence: in May she told Vera she had spent "more money on myself than I have ever spent for years and years" (SJ to VB, 5.5.34). She had treated herself to a facial, described in sensual detail, bought lots of costly creams, and felt happy despite the current tensions:

> The revolution may be coming and people can't get bread let alone jam, I haven't any new clothes, and I haven't a hope of a holiday. But, for the time, I no longer feel like a piece of chewed leather. (SJ to VB, 5.5.34)

That same month, she brought her mother for a holiday in London. Hannah was now an invalid, her flashing temper long gone, although she could still make emotional demands on her daughter that Margaret found impossible to deny (SJ to VB, 5.19.34). By the time Hannah left, news from abroad, together with the growth of Oswald Mosley's Blackshirt movement at home, was increasingly unsettling: "Don't you wish the world would stop rocking long enough for us to enjoy it for a time?" Margaret asked Vera ruefully (SJ to VB, 6.24.34). By July, as she was typing up chapters of the book, the world was rocking in earnest. She read Dorothy Thompson's firsthand account of the Night of the Long Knives, Hitler's killing of Ernst Röhm and many members of the Sturmabteilung (SA), the Nazi militia Hilter had invited Röhm to command. This was Hitler's cold-blooded way of getting rid of "a friend and followers he had no further use for," as Margaret would put it. She was shattered (JN, 1:320).

Now A. R. Orage approached her again; he was inaugurating a series of pamphlets and wanted her to contribute, offering her a choice of topics (ARO to SJ, 7.22.34). Not very surprisingly, Margaret, overwhelmed by such demands on her time and energy, fell ill again. Guy persuaded her to go to France for a week, but she had to come home early, and was prescribed a month's rest in Whitby (SJ to VB, 7.31.34). Given her pressing commitments, complete rest proved impossible: she was still working on her own and her contributors' essays, in a climate of mounting anxiety over events in Europe. Engelbert Dollfuss, the Austrian chancellor, right-wing himself but not prepared for unification with Germany, was murdered by Nazis supporting the Anschluss; Hitler's expansionist ambitions were becoming increasingly clear. As a result, Margaret was drawn further into a life of action that went beyond writing.

The founder of the PEN, Amy Dawson-Scott (Sappho) had written to Hermon Ould just before she died, telling him to get Margaret and Somerset Maugham on to the PEN Executive Committee. Ould had in fact invited Margaret once before without success; this time, invited at a moment when she felt called to ever greater commitment, she accepted: "I feel as strongly as you do about the international things. But I rather wish the duty hadn't been put before me!"[14] She was, as usual, ignoring medical advice: her doctor told her in August "that if he were examining me for an Insurance Company he would advise them to refuse me!" (SJ to VB, 8.12.34). But between spells in bed, she was writing, had nearly finished her next novel and her two essays for *Challenge to Death*, and was working on an article she had promised Amabel for the *Left Review* (SJ to VB, 9.6.34).[15]

Her letters to Vera were cheerful, but to Edward and Thea Thompson she was more honest about her state of mind. She wrote just after the mining disaster at the Gresford pit in North Wales, where 266 men had died. She said she had been ill all summer, "only from overwork," and was finding writing difficult:

> No-one knows so well as Edward what torture writing can be. I have managed to write every day, but sometimes I wake up in the night and find myself in . . . a fit of despair, only to think that in the morning I must write again. And then something like this ghastly mine disaster happens and I am ashamed I ever grumbled. (SJ to EJT, 9.24.34)

She went on to say how worried she was over what would happen when Guy finished his degree course the following June: "It would be a great help if he had even a small job. I have been meaning to ask you about Extension Lecturing when I saw you next." That autumn, Bill went up to Trinity College, Cambridge, to read for the Mechanical Engineering

Tripos, although, ominously, he was less than enthusiastic, saying it was like going back to school after Göttingen and the aerodrome (*JN*, 1:311; SJ to VB, 10.7.34).

Margaret now had two students to support, but alongside endless articles, her unpaid commitments were growing. Her readiness to commit herself would always outstrip her nervous and physical energy. As soon as she was formally elected to the PEN Executive Committee, Ould lost no time in inviting her to come to a meeting, although she did excuse herself initially, as "my afternoons are now a pattern of doctors and their foul breed, who are patching me up for heaven" (SJ to HO, 11.1.34). It now seemed that "the agonising pain I had for two years before my operation [in the late 1920s], and which the operation was supposed to have cured, was always spinal — and the extra strain of the last three years started it up again" (SJ to VB, 11.5.34). Vera, ever generous where money was concerned, financed an expensive course of osteopathy.

The essay Margaret had promised Amabel for the *Left Review* appeared in November, as a letter "To a Labour Party Official."[16] This was, as she had indicated to Vera, a hard-hitting attack on leaders of the Trades Unions, written before the Labour Party Conference in Southport, which, in the event, only confirmed what she had said (SJ to VB, 10.13.34). In this article, after stating her credentials as continuing president of her small local branch of the Labour Party, Margaret accused union leaders of having become overly respectable, surrendering traditional street-corner speaking to the Fascists and Communists. They had lost sight of their roots; they had betrayed the workers brought out in the general strike, and had recently encouraged members not to attend a demonstration against Fascism. Margaret reminded them, echoing her introduction to Lilo's book, of how the German Social Democrat leaders had failed to oppose the rise of Nazism, adding that "past experience . . . warns us that socialism, like any other faith, loses its power with us in measure as it ceases to be a faith and becomes an establishment" ("To a Labour Party Official," 32–33). Communism, she said, had made no such mistake. "Another Labour Government like the last will write its own epitaph and put up its own tombstone" ("To a Labour Party Official," 34). This was Margaret at her iconoclastic best.

Challenge to Death, due out in November, suffered a few last-minute hitches. Although Margaret, efficient as always, had asked lawyers to read for libel earlier, some "libel trouble" was detected, while Constable threatened to deduct from some contributors' fees for excessive corrections. Margaret, as generous with money as Vera but with far less provision, said she would, if necessary, pay the correction bill herself (SJ to VB, 11.5.34). *Challenge to Death* came out at the same time as another peace initiative instigated by Cecil, a controversial peace ballot, which asked questions about commitment to the League of Nations, to disarmament, and importantly to whether, "if a nation insists on attacking another, the other nations should combine to compel it to stop," either by economic and nonmilitary measures, or by military intervention.[17] This, by way of being the first referendum in the country, polled over ten million votes, with an overwhelming majority voting for peace.[18]

The book Margaret edited, with its foreword by Cecil, shared the ballot's priorities. Margaret did not name herself solely as editor, but ceded the position collectively to the contributors: Philip Noel-Baker, the journalist Gerald Barry, Vernon Bartlett, the poet Edmund Blunden, Vera Brittain and her husband, George Catlin, the critic Ivor Brown, Guy Chapman, the journalist and former MP Mary Agnes Hamilton, the historian and philosopher Gerald Heard, Winifred Holtby, the scientist Julian Huxley, J. B. Priestley, Rebecca West, and Margaret herself.[19] As Cecil wrote in his foreword, they "belong to different schools of thought and approach the subject from different angles," but all recognized that war would be a disaster (*CTD*, vii).

Margaret's introductory article, "The Twilight of Reason" (*CTD*, 1–20), was grave in tone. She attacked what many saw at the time as the essence of Fascism, "an almost religious belief . . . in the supremacy and rightness of purely emotional activity" (*CTD*, 9). She reiterated, as West did in her article, the dangers inherent in nationalism, warning that, "into a world made sufficiently unstable by economic rivalries, Fascism has brought a newly dangerous element of violence" (*CTD*, 16). In her epilogue, "In the End," she concentrated on the practical arguments for opposing war: "It is precisely because I hope for social change that I fear war," for, she said, "poverty and war grow in the same soil and have the same smell" (*CTD*, 322, 323). Better education was vital, concentrating on "each child according to his real abilities," so as to attain "a fully educated and classless society" (*CTD*, 325). She saw this as creating the "first steps towards a European union," rather than the current "irresponsible and half-educated democracy" (*CTD*, 327). In sum, her vision was for "a settled Europe, with England its heart" (*CTD*, 329): for Margaret was always alert to the British tendency to position itself apart from Europe and its problems. The book received wide coverage in the press, at home and abroad.[20] However, despite good reviews, the project had little public impact.

Earlier that year, when Orage had approached Margaret about writing a pamphlet for him (unpaid), she had selected the topic "How would you encourage the right use of leisure?" Orage was delighted, although ironically, he had just visited the Dobrées, where they had agreed that Margaret did too much for nothing (ARO to SJ, 7.22.34, 8.5.34). He would never see the result; he died on November 6. The following week, together with such writers as George W. Russell (AE), G. K. Chesterton, George Bernard Shaw, C. H. Douglas, T. S. Eliot, H. G. Wells, and Augustus John, Margaret contributed to the memorial edition of the *New English Weekly*. She recalled Orage's influence on her generation of 1912, saying it was greater than "any other single person and it was an unmitigatedly good influence, working for an intellectual integrity and honesty" (*NEW*, Nov. 15, 1934).[21] Later, in *Civil Journey* (1939), Margaret would recall her shock when she read of his death, as it was "the end of more than of one man; it ended the story of an age, and the story of my youth as well, though I did not think of that then. . . . I felt silenced and stopped" (*CJ*, 77).

Life at home cannot have been easy for Margaret, and there was in one letter a rare glimpse of the compromises she was making in her marriage to Guy; maybe, too, we have here a hint of something more than the need to earn money in her undertaking such a punishing, relentless workload. For Vera, on a lecture tour in the States, had fallen in love with George Brett, the president of Macmillan in America. She confided in Margaret, and Margaret begged her "to seize with both hands all the love and loving kindness offered to you." Poignantly, she went on to say:

> That vitality and simplicity of purpose which our men lost forever (that's so awful — forever) in 1914–18, is the richest "good" any man can offer to any woman. There are other "goods" which you have from [your husband] and I from Guy — but none of them in the end replace this missing one. None of them are its

intellectual and spiritual, never mind its physical, equivalent. Nothing, finally, makes up for missing it. So, do, dear dear Vera, take all with both hands, and without looking too closely ahead. (SJ to VB, 11.28.34)

Orage, the mentor of her prewar youth, had gone, her marriage, though rich in its way, was irrevocably flawed and, with something akin to monastic self-mortification—a trait she would later come to recognize in herself—she was selling her beloved Whitby house, which Guy had always found uncongenial. But at least the agonizing back pain was better. She had managed to finish her novel, was correcting Lilo's new manuscript, and coping with articles that she hoped to finish by Christmas (SJ to VB, 12.23.34).

The ever-developing European crises loomed large: in December, Margaret was one of the signatories to a letter sent to the press, quoting the widow of the murdered German poet Erich Mühsam, who had begged that

> his death must be made the last in the German concentration camps. The next to be on the list of suicides may be Carl von Ossietzky. The man can write so well! Save Ossietzky! Save all the imprisoned writers![22]

The signatories of the letter were forming a fund to help imprisoned men of letters in Germany, their wives and children, and were supported by such writers as André Gide, Henri Barbusse, and Bertolt Brecht, while funds were also being raised in the U.S., Czechoslovakia, and Holland. To no effect. The German pacifist Carl von Ossietzky, who had been convicted of high treason and sent first to prison and later to a concentration camp, and would be awarded the Nobel Peace Prize in 1935, would die in hospital, still a prisoner, in 1938.

CHAPTER 11

Escalating Violence in Europe, and How to Respond

At the beginning of January 1935, Margaret was preparing to leave her beloved Mooredge for the last time, while Guy, his final examinations approaching, was already looking for jobs. The move from Whitby was very painful for Margaret. She recalled years later the grief of having chosen "to uproot myself from the one place where I am not a stranger," abandoning "the piercing happiness my Whitby view gave me every time I lifted my head from my desk" (*JN*, 1:332–33). But Guy had never felt he belonged there, and the need to be in London was still acute. So she set about supporting Guy in his hunt for a job (SJ to VB, 1.8.35). Back in London, she was plunged into the usual round of social and political activity; her and Guy's friends consisted mainly of foreign correspondents, liberal journalists, and left-wing politicians like the fiery, eloquent Welshman Aneurin (Nye) Bevan and his politician wife, Jennie Lee. R. H. Tawney visited them on occasion, and there were increasing numbers of German and Austrian refugees to look after. Apart from all this, Hannah was ill after suffering a stroke, so Margaret was back in Whitby at the beginning of February to give her sister Winifred a break from nursing her. This postponed treatment for her own continuing bad health (SJ to VB, 2.3.35, 2.4.35).

In March, Margaret went with Guy and Bill to northeast Spain, where they stayed for five weeks. The original plan had been for them to go for two months in the summer and rent a house, "with a cow byre for the ground floor, and no sanitation" (SJ to VB, 2.3.35). The novelist Ralph

Bates was to have joined them; he had lived on and off in Spain since 1923, was very much involved with the labor movement there, and had already interested the Chapmans in the uneasy Spanish situation during Lilo Linke's visit in 1933. However, feeling Guy needed a break before taking his finals, Margaret brought the visit forward to the spring. The family stayed in a simple but well-run hotel, a favorite of writers and artists, the Casa Steyer, in the old village of Tossa. Bates visited them there, bringing them up to date on the unrest in Spain, and trying to tempt Margaret to involve herself in the Spanish workers' cause (JN/TMS, 2:88; SJ to VB, 4.1.35). She was, however, in urgent need of rest, and was worried about already existing writing commitments. The next novel of the *Mirror in Darkness* series was giving her trouble, and she was starting to ponder another, more directly addressing the threat of Fascism (SJ to VB, 4.8.35).

As it was, Margaret was not to be allowed complete rest. The previous October, she had agreed to write an article for a collection of essays on "patriotism," and the proofs reached her in Spain.[1] In this article, Margaret claimed she was

> an unashamed Little Englander. I wish that our Empire were no larger than Norway's, and our population of the same proportion. Then London would still be a habitable city, and the loveliest country in the world would not have been fouled with slums.[2]

She ascribed her pride in England to her place of birth, conceding,

> Had I been born, say, in a colliery town, in one of those streets of small featureless houses, divided from the neighbouring street by a row of closets, I should have felt less respect for my country. ("Patriotism," 123)

Such scenes gave her the core of her message: the appalling disgrace of so many children born in slums and living in poverty, and the fatuousness of those who talked of "national honour," "sacrifice," while doing nothing to make such phrases meaningful to the poor ("Patriotism," 124). This consideration led her to the dishonor inherent in war, the profiteers, the "willful propaganda"; and she voiced astonishment that to be known as a pacifist incurred "the suspicion of being unpatriotic or unEnglish." She savaged the romanticizing of war, since, as it was machines that "deliver the poison gas or a rain of white-hot steel, human courage is as unavailing as human flesh" ("Patriotism," 125). If this was what patriotism meant, then the word had become obscene. She added a touch of irony:

> For ill or good England is a close part of Europe and will remain so until aeroplanes are forbidden to be built. In Europe the majority of the nations have the misfortune to be foreigners, and close enough to us to make living with them uncomfortable and dangerous, if it is not regulated. In such circumstances we ought to sit in conference with them the whole time, for our safety's sake. ("Patriotism," 127)

This was one of Margaret's most eloquent attacks on the blind spots within her society, emphasizing passionately that there could be no safe haven if Britain ignored its closeness to Europe, its inevitable involvement with the crises on the Continent. It still has resonance today.

While the Chapmans were in Spain, *Love in Winter* was published.[3] As in *Company Parade*, Margaret had blended autobiographical material with fictional strains in the self-reflexive manner of her earlier trilogy. She continued to experiment with the collage effect, but in this work the emphasis is rather different: one of the major strands is how memories of the past infect and are transformed by both the present and visions of the future. At one point Hervey opens a box and finds the letters her estranged husband Penn had written to her:

> Half my life is here, she thought. Obeying a strong impulse, she carried the box to the basement, where there was a furnace for heating water (sometimes it did). She filled the boiler with quires of words that had cried, laughed, and suffered passion while they were alive. Now it is really at an end, she thought. Grief choked her and she fought to quiet it. (*LIW*, 248)

Hervey's landlady sees her as she leaves the cellar, and in turn recalls an old photograph of her soldier husband:

> In her mind the photograph had replaced the original, and when she thought of her husband the living image wavered and faded out, leaving its glossy shadow with her. Who's there? she cried, thinking of someone who had come in, but it was eight years ago, and now hurrying into her room she pushed behind the photograph a half-empty jar of cream and curling-tongs. (*LIW*, 249)

The novel also explores how writers measure up in the current world: the war-damaged Renn maintains T. S. Eliot never really knew the wasteland, unlike the fifteenth-century poet François Villon: "He is really and truthfully post-War" (*LIW*, 222). Hervey's strivings to come to terms with her lover, to make sense of herself as a woman and a writer, show how war betrayed youthful promise. In the public sphere, there are other betrayals: Gary, the budding tycoon, mirroring his American namesake in Dos Passos's trilogy, slowly estranges himself from his friends, renouncing the prewar ideals they shared; Earlham as Labour MP moves ever further away from his youthful commitment to socialism. But beyond the current dilemmas are timeless moments. Watching Georgina dance, Hervey

> thought of a wave in the instant before it breaks: shining threads of foam run across the skin of the water; to look at it is like looking at glass which by a miracle is throbbing with life. The green is opaque, faint shivers run through it under and across the foam, the edge thins, rears backward with spumy locks, then rushes down in a welter of green and indigo, with broken flakes of light from the dissolving plumes. (*LIW*, 303)

Among the grim treacheries of society as she perceived it, Margaret never lost sight of such moments of sheer sensual delight in the world around her. As here, she not only captures a picture of the dance, but the movement, a holistic aesthetic experience that matches synesthetic moments in Woolf's writing. This passage shows quite clearly that it was Margaret's choice to prioritize different things in her writing from the high modernists; it was not that she could not, in her mature writing, match them.

Reviews were mostly respectful rather than enthusiastic; critics continued to be wary of Margaret's engagement with political and social issues.[4] But she could not worry about them, being more concerned about her inability to concentrate on the third volume of *Mirror in Darkness* (SJ to VD, 4.27.35). She had by now abandoned the idea of writing the long series of novels she had originally planned, contemplating instead a change of direction as the European situation deteriorated. For in March, Hitler had announced that Germany was rearming. The third volume of what would now be a trilogy may well have felt parochial and backward looking, given the current situation. It was certainly giving her trouble: when she returned to England from Spain, she still felt "in a black hole of despair and dryness" (SJ to VB, 4.30.35).

At the beginning of May she brought her mother down from Whitby for the usual visit; Hannah could always count on her, whatever else was pressing on her mind. For Margaret was increasingly active: in June, she was listed as one of the English writers supporting the principles of the International Congress of Writers, organized by a committee of French writers in Paris, urging that "the perils confronting cultural freedom in a number of countries to-day are such that measures should be taken for their defence."[5] Like Woolf and West, Margaret did not attend the congress, but she soon joined the national section of the International Association of Writers for the Defence of Culture, founded at the Paris Congress.

There was good reason why Margaret could not attend the congress, as in June Guy sat his finals, and she religiously stayed at home each day of the examinations to hear his account of the paper he had taken (SJ to VB, 6.15.35). To their delight, he was awarded a first-class degree, and Tawney, who would remain a staunch friend to both the Chapmans, advised Guy to apply to lecture for the Workers' Education Association (WEA); he got the job. But before taking it up, he set off with Margaret for an island in the Oslo fjord.[6] She now decided to abandon the half-finished third volume of the *Mirror* series for something very different (SJ to VD, 8.10.35). This new novel, *In the Second Year*, would respond to growing anxieties about Fascism, at home and abroad. German Jews were being stripped of their citizenship, Mussolini had invaded Ethiopia (then called Abyssinia). Meanwhile in England, Joachim von Ribbentrop, Hitler's unofficial ambassador, was out to promote an Anglo-German alliance, and, as part of this strategy, had invited members of the British Legion to visit veteran groups in Germany. The British government raised no objection, and the Prince of Wales gave the visit his blessing. Dismayingly, in

July, the delegation, thinking they were on a mission to promote peaceful relations, had found themselves at the center of a propaganda coup, as Hitler decided to meet them. The visit and the resulting propaganda triumph caused consternation in Europe.[7] Given the mixed messages reaching the British people, Margaret had urged Lilo to tell the story of her own experiences in Germany while Nazism gained ground, and had been working on the manuscript the young woman produced, as Lilo acknowledged in her preface.

Restless Flags told the tale of Lilo's growing up and gradual political awakening as German nationalism took hold partly in response to the French chauvinism that threatened it and to galloping inflation.[8] It told how as a politically naive teenager, Lilo nearly joined the forerunner of the Hitler Youth movement, because it offered the allurements of action and adventure. Stopped by a more perceptive boyfriend, she matured politically, and worked with the Leftist opposition until Hitler came to power and she had to flee; although her mother, won over by the Nazi agenda, was convinced that she would return to what she saw as the revitalized Germany that Hitler had brought to birth. Lilo told how she left in tears, and Margaret, gripped by the story, was moved to respond more directly to the European situation in her fiction as well as in articles, as would soon become clear.

Other writers were responding to the growing crisis. This same year, for example, Jean Giraudoux, a favorite author of Margaret's, produced a typically cynical work, *La guerre de Troie n'aura pas lieu* (*The Trojan War Will Not Take Place*), where, in a classical setting, he could mock the all-too-bland international conferences, the exacerbated nationalisms of his world. Naomi Mitchison's *We Have Been Warned*, also out this year, offered a quirky warning about a possible Fascist takeover in England. Now on the island of Ijøme Margaret decided to work flat out on her vision of an England actually under a Fascist regime. By mid-July, she had completed a third of it, by early August two-thirds, writing, for the first time, straight onto her typewriter, working from nine to three each day. In five weeks she had written sixty thousand of the eighty thousand words she was aiming for.[9] In the midst of this intense creativity, Bill arrived for a summer holiday, bringing with him a girlfriend. Margaret was not impressed; she still saw him as dependent, and indulged him "as if he were the child of a rich person" (SJ to VB, 8.5.35). So she reacted to the poor girl all too predictably, describing her as "a dreadful fat girl he seems to love very much," a reaction that no doubt strengthened the bond between the young couple: this young woman, Barbara Cawood, would become Bill's wife (SJ to VB, 8.13.35).

The family was back in England in early September, Margaret with her finished typescript. *In the Second Year* was a major departure from anything she had written before, without an autobiographical element, looking forward, not back.[10] It was set in the near future, in 1940, on one level following the events in the second year of Hitler's rule, culminating in the Night of the Long Knives (June 30, 1934). But it was not a simple transference of German events: Margaret translated them into an English context and idiom. Some of her central characters share traits with Nazi counterparts: Hillier has the physical mannerisms of Hitler when speaking, Hebden recalls the physique and behavior of Hermann Göring. But when among his friends, Hillier is no foreigner, while other characters are based on English counterparts — Towers a barely disguised Tawney, the newspaper magnates very much those of the English press. Crucially, the action offers a plausible projection based on recent trends in Britain, such as the growth of Mosley's following, and developments within the unions. Margaret, as always, had an ear for the debates of her age, in England and in Europe, and was adept at colloquial dialogue, lucid argument, and the painting of English landscapes, lacing them into the action so as to anchor what was happening in an inescapably native setting. In May, for instance, the narrator joins a young couple on a walk:

> Spring was early this year. In the valley, as we crossed it to reach the other moor, the may was full out. I never saw it fuller than that year. The branches fell down under their weight of blossom, white against the blue of the sky and the green of the grass. Never were such colours, except in my memory. The bees were already out as busy as in summer, and in the lilac of the gardens. (*ITSY*, 47)

After this tranquil scene, the shock of finding an internment camp in the middle of the moor is all the greater.

Margaret's first-person narrator is a man and, though English, an outsider living in Norway. Margaret presents this northern country as retaining values being eroded in England; no doubt this was in part due to Norway's one, secret link with herself and her background, since the name Storm still existed there. The narrator is set apart from active participation by a symbolically withered right arm, having a watching brief, yet finding it hard to maintain as he witnesses the cruelties of Hillier's regime. From the first paragraph of this novel, things are going wrong: the Tyne's shipyards are derelict, with grim echoes of the unemployment crisis of the early 1930s. The general strike mirrors that of 1926, making the events that follow all too plausible. The public arena is set against what at first seems a close family circle: Hillier, the Fascist prime minister, is second cousin to the narrator and his sister, who is married to Hillier's best friend and general, Richard Sacker. Margaret was establishing methods of narration she would develop later: a narrator unwilling to be drawn in would reappear in future novels, and Margaret would again mirror major political events in a close family or community, forcing the reader to acknowledge the unbreakable links between public and private worlds. A considerable strength of the novel is the room given to different points of view, from the right and the left: this is no tract, but is sensitive to the different interpretations people place on events, either to shield themselves or to affirm an ideological position. But it also acknowledges the evil that repression brings with it, something Margaret was learning from the refugees she was meeting: "it makes people lie to themselves in the privacy of their hearts" (*ITSY*, 90).

The novel charts Hillier's rise to power, loyally helped by a very English type of soldier in Sacker; the clampdown on freedom of speech, freedom of movement, follows swiftly. The narrator sees how "a disgusting cinematograph psychology becomes actual, as in a nightmare," his brother-in-law like "the hero-gangster of a certain kind of American novel and film [who] steps off the page or screen and plays his horrid part in what is called the regeneration of his country" (*ITSY*, 41). Gradually repression increases as Hillier asserts complete control and, in case the reader should think this could not happen here, Margaret was astute at recalling times of violence in English history, such as the seventeenth-century Civil War. Finally, Sacker meets his end, his wife commits suicide, and the narrator leaves, his thoughts lingering on two young lovers, anglicized equivalents of Lilo and her friends, their vitality and faith offering him hope for some sort of future. But the narrator does not offer any happy ending; he bears Margaret's warning of what could happen, musing as he leaves:

> If all the dead of the past week came to life and met together in one room, still the truth of what each of them had hoped would be hard, no, impossible to tell. . . . The feeling of emptiness in my own spirit returned, and persisted. It seemed that my roots were too firmly and deeply curled round the past, round the old England, the old houses and the old words and thoughts. In between these, the soil was dry and falling away, but my roots only clung the faster to what was left. I was not comfortable any longer in the past. Yet I could neither imagine myself living in a new way, nor wish it. I have lost both worlds. (*ITSY*, 311)

In this powerful passage, Margaret showed herself already empathizing with the lot of those who had exiled themselves or had exile thrust upon them by the growing brutality of the Nazi regime. She was ready for closer involvement.

So it is not surprising that on her return to England, Margaret was soon working more closely with the PEN. At the end of September, Hermon Ould wrote to ask if she would become one of two vice presidents under the president, H. G. Wells. Margaret hesitated at first, as, she said, they would be living wherever Guy was assigned an area of work by the WEA, and she was no good as a chairman. She was, she said, very good at smiling and listening but not at being a "public character" (SJ to HO, 9.25.35). At the same time, Winifred Holtby was almost certainly dying, and Margaret had promised to take Vera away for a week afterward. Winifred did die on September 29, and a memorial service was held at St. Martin in the Fields on October 1. Vera Brittain was shattered, and Margaret did her best to respond. But the week away with Vera was not to be. Back in the London flat, Margaret collapsed yet again; her rigorous writing schedule in Norway, while stimulating, had drained her. She was installed at the Stanborough Hydro in Watford for bed rest and medical care, suffering from severe nervous and mental exhaustion, and she was also having spinal treatment. But she could not agree to the kind of rest they were prescribing: "A writer just can't stop writing and do *nothing*. It's a psychological impossibility quite as much as a financial one" (SJ to

VB, 10.8.35). Such a comment is telling: while Margaret so often insisted she was not by nature a writer, the ideas that she frequently described as crowding her head, along with her constant driving need to perfect her craft, argue against her.

Vera, who had sent fruit and flowers to Margaret, went off to South Cornwall on her own. From there she wrote, begging Margaret to join her, and offering thinly veiled criticism of the pressures she saw Guy and Bill exerting (VB to SJ, 10.17.35). But here was something the friends saw very differently: Vera would always insist on her own independence within her family, pursuing the causes she had espoused with single-minded vigor; Margaret could never feel less than responsible and guilty when she fell short, not only to Guy and Bill, but to family in Whitby, and to the increasing number of refugees who needed help. She did not respond to Vera's comments, and a pattern began to emerge. When Vera became too intrusive, Margaret drew back, always grateful for Vera's extravagant bouts of generosity, always encouraging her in her work, but ultimately unwilling to take on the kind of role Winifred had accepted so readily, responding at Vera's beck and call to her complex emotional needs. Besides, Margaret, fresh from her collapse, was clearing the London flat by the end of the month, having found a flat in Reading (SJ to VB, 10.20.35). While it was being made ready, she and Guy would stay in Oxford, a good temporary base for Guy as he began his lecturing commitment for the WEA, traveling to different venues throughout the area, while Margaret planned to write in the mornings and get the Reading flat ready in the afternoons. All these preparations absorbed what energy she had: her appointment as a vice president of the English PEN went through in her absence.[11]

By November she and Guy had temporary lodgings in 23 Merton Street, Oxford, but almost at once, Margaret was off again, giving a speech at the Scarborough annual meeting of the League of Nations Union. She remained far from happy about speechmaking, telling Ould, "I have already wasted ten days in writing out an hour's speech, and I shall deliver it like a dummy" (SJ to HO, 11.2.35). But this was a time to put commitment above personal inclination. The British Union of Fascists was still flourishing; and when, in this same year, one of the first Gallup polls asked those interviewed whether they preferred Fascism or Communism, 70 percent of those under thirty chose Fascism, and a dis-

turbingly high proportion of the upper classes, while not actively supporting Oswald Mosley, leaned toward Fascism because they feared Communism.[12] Churchill himself trod warily in an article on Hitler where,
though not sanguine, he wrote:

> If, because the story is unfinished, because, indeed, its most fate-
> ful chapters have yet to be written, we are forced to dwell upon
> the dark side of [Hitler's] work and creed, we must never forget
> nor cease to hope for the bright alternative.[13]

Margaret herself was one of those who felt sure, as she told Vera,

> that the next war is about 3 or 5 years off, unless something dras-
> tic is started soon to remove the causes of it. I am sure this re-
> arming means that the Nat. Gov. [*sic*] is also sure and just means
> to be ready. (SJ to VB, 11.4.35)

Back from Scarborough, Margaret had a number of contracts to fulfill.
She had already sent off an Armistice Day article that the *Daily Mail* had
wanted, though "begging me not to be revolutionary"; but she did not
think they would print it as "I'm past telling half-truths any longer" (SJ to
VB, 11.4.35). She had a further article and a five-day serial to write, she
said, along with a piece for the *Woman's Journal*, and then hoped to get
back to the third volume of her *Mirror in Darkness* series in December.
She had completed working on the proofs of *In the Second Year* as she
read Sinclair Lewis's *It Can't Happen Here*, which had been published
in October.[14]

The appearance of Lewis's book was one of those instances when two
writers with similar priorities and anxieties but no knowledge of the other's project produce works that seem almost twinned. Lewis's book was
set in 1936–39 while Margaret's was set in 1940; his was an Americanized
version of a Nazi takeover where, observed by the liberal protagonist, an
earthy farm boy becomes the first tyrant, is ousted by his "gay" right-hand
man, presented as a pervert, who is then shot by a puritanical general.
The book is rich in contemporary comment, with rednecks and finance
playing a large part, and writers like Dos Passos seen as targets for anti-
Red moves. Margaret told Vera she thought it a grand book, "at least,

the second half of it is grand," and she was cross that it got patronizing reviews (SJ to VB, 11.4.35). She felt that Macmillan, now her American publishers, would not like her own novel, as it was a

> restrained English version of the same theme. Sinclair Lewis has just transferred the German horrors bodily to America, and it makes thrilling reading. He hasn't tried at all to think whether American fascism would be different. It wouldn't be much different, perhaps, but I am certain it would be different in England, and I have tried in my book to imagine the English version. (SJ to VB, 11.4.35)

Lewis's work was in fact as American as Margaret's was English, but her knowledge of American society was not, as yet, firsthand. Her defensiveness no doubt sprang from her anxiety about the coincidence of the two novels' publication and the effect on her own book's reception.

The general election of November 14, 1935, saw the third national government voted into power, led by the old Tory Stanley Baldwin. Margaret, like Vera, was disheartened. Moreover, she was working too hard, the flat was not ready, and the removal was proving complicated. All this meant that she still was not able to write her novel, but at least she had one serious publication in November, the pamphlet that A. R. Orage had originally commissioned, *The Soul of Man in the Age of Leisure*.[15] This pamphlet had a rather different focus from the political and social concerns her other works were pursuing, but she had, in fact, tried out her arguments in two short articles earlier in the year, giving her final version time to mature.[16] It was a tribute to Orage's ideas, although the passionate images in her attack on poverty were very much Margaret's own:

> This money god, which has the face of a man, the impulse of a wolf, and no bowels, which kills or stunts the bodies of the very poor, stunts the minds and souls of many others, indeed of the greater part of men and women now living. (*AOL*, 8)

The Age of Leisure is her utopian dream for the future, a dream recalling Orage's own hopes, when there could be a balance between work and rest as against the present, when "Hollywood, the gutter press, and the cozening advertisements, are the natural consequences of a control which *prefers* that the mass of men should remain ignorant and suggestible" (AOL, 15). Education is the key, both for minds and bodies, as "civilisation itself is a tradition, which we are putting in danger by our blind worship of the machine" (AOL, 20); creativity must be nurtured, and a classless society must be the goal. In sum, Margaret's argument stressed the importance of quality of life, not simply the need to alleviate material distress. The pamphlet did not get much critical attention, but it had a good review in *Scrutiny*. Margaret's debt to Orage had been repaid fully and now could be consigned to her past.[17]

After many frustrating delays, the Chapmans moved to the flat in Reading (68a Shinfield Road) in December. Margaret disliked it from the first; she felt it cold and friendless, drafty, the hot water inadequate, although she told Vera she had at least found a household help (SJ to VB, 12.16.35). But she was close to the aerodrome where Bill spent most of his time, his Cambridge tripos a mere sideline now; and importantly, the flat was near the home of her young sister Dorothy (Do). Margaret had grown closer to Do as she grew up, although they could not have been more different in temperament, as Do had her mother's passionate, headstrong nature, and thought Margaret soft. The girl had left university after her second year to take a secretarial course, and had married a fellow student, Robert Pateman. Initially she had kept the London job Margaret had helped her to find, and Margaret helped her again when she needed a gynecological operation "to correct a serious internal deformity" (JN, 1:331–32). Now she and Robert lived in Reading; Margaret had helped them to buy a small house there, and her decision to move closer to them was partly influenced by the fact that Do's first child was expected the following February. For her own part, Margaret felt she must learn to accept her unsatisfactory flat, if only because of the money it had cost them; she was still, in effect, the breadwinner of the family, as Guy's job brought in very little (SJ to VB, 12.20.35).

CHAPTER 12

The Peace Pledge Union and Anti-Fascism

Margaret's firm anti-Fascist stance at this time brought her closer to those on the far left than she had been or would be later, although she never felt comfortable when working with the Communist Party: she never indulged in romanticizing the Soviet world as Naomi Mitchison and Amabel Williams-Ellis did.[1] Margaret's priorities continued to be the case against war together with the threat of Fascism/Nazism. Yet she could still be deflected by a perceived need to defend her own vision of Whitby, writing a passionate letter to the *Whitby Gazette* protesting the influx of red roofs in "the most beautiful town in the world"; she acknowledged that many homes there were unfit for habitation, but urged the use of architects like Clough Ellis to advise on renovation and restoration. This was the forlorn cry of many a conservationist in the modern world.[2] Maybe it was the assault of the red roofs on old Whitby that suggested the subject of Margaret's next long novel, *The Moon Is Making*: Haydn Williams, a Radical stalwart still alive in her youth and much admired by her mother. Margaret would set about reconstructing the Whitby of her mother's and her own childhood, thinly fictionalizing the old man's life in the process.[3]

At the end of January, *In the Second Year* was published, and the reviews ranged from lukewarm to positively hostile, with few exceptions; even the most appreciative could not accept that such things could possibly happen in England.[4] The urge to see England as safe from dictatorship was certainly widespread, but not without some worrying challenges. The *Saturday Review*, for example, was becoming ever more strident in its support for Fascism and Nazism: its journalist "Kim" would soon have an article "England Wants a Dictator," asserting that "it is cheap claptrap to say that England would not tolerate a dictator. Of course she would if that dictator were a great and determined ruler."[5] Other papers, too, suggested that Hitler stood as a bulwark against the threat of Communism, even Beverley Nichols admiring what he claimed was the "moral strength" of Germany (Lovell, 204). But there were others who shared Margaret's concerns. Philip Henderson, for one, a left-wing critic, made a spirited attack on critics who saw the function of the novel "as primarily a form of self-analysis," so inhibiting modern novelists from looking "too closely at social reality lest it lead them to unwelcome conclusions."[6] He pointed instead to great novels, such as *The Brothers Karamazov*, *Madame Bovary*, *The Way of All Flesh*, and André Malraux's *La condition humaine*, that "show an uncomfortable tendency to question everything that most of us take for granted" (Henderson, 14). He set Margaret's work in a chapter on "The Revolutionary Novel" alongside such writers as Henri Barbusse, Heinrich and Thomas Mann, Balder Olden, Ignazio Silone, Malraux, and Mulk Raj Anand, and praised *In the Second Year* as creating a situation that was "terribly real," where "atrocious things are done with perfect manners," without the theatricality of a Mussolini or a Hitler (Henderson, 224). Henderson appreciated how skillfully Margaret had translated European Fascism into a very English setting, not simply concentrating on landscape, but reflecting the behavior patterns of her contemporary society.

Perhaps the hostility of critics to Margaret's foray into the future was another factor encouraging her to set her next long novel in the past, where she could show a thinly fictionalized Haydn Williams having what Henderson called that "uncomfortable tendency to question everything that most of us take for granted." But for the moment she had other preoccupations. Do's son, Nicholas, was born on February 17, yet another member of the family for whom his aunt would feel responsible. Hermon Ould was urging her to attend the Argentine PEN Congress in September, and she was clearly tempted.[7] Indeed, the temptation to get away from England, if only for a PEN Congress, had considerable appeal. The burden of work and the growing threat of war were weighing heavily on her, and she was even tempted by Vera Brittain's plea that she should undertake a lecture tour in the States. She was working frantically to finish *None Turn Back*, the recalcitrant third novel of her trilogy, before she was overdrawn at the bank, and the prospect of a paid-for holiday was alluring. Yet some things gave her pause: she was anxious about Guy and "the lives of an army of people," the family, friends, and refugees who were all too reliant on her, and whom she would have to settle before she could go away (SJ to HO, 2.25.36).

As Margaret finished revising *None Turn Back* in March, Hitler's troops entered the Rhineland and were soon remilitarizing it. Vera wrote to Margaret that the peace structure they had worked for had been smashed, and the fundamental question was "which does one hate most, War or fascism?" (VB to SJ, 3.16.36). Vera knew where she stood: there were three groups as she saw it, one hating murder in Germany but not in Russia, the second doing the reverse, and a minority, like herself, hating it wherever it occurred. Margaret shared her gloom, and for the moment she agreed with Vera that "War to cast out war has been tried and the results are 1936" (SJ to VB, 3.17.36). Inevitably, this was not just a matter of principle for Margaret: Bill's being of fighting age was a major concern. So perhaps it was as an escape from these tensions that Margaret began to write a short experimental work, *Loving Memory*, nothing to do, on the face of it, with the social and political issues that plagued her.[8] It was witty and spare. The core of the tale shows a husband discovering that his dead wife, whom he adored, had apparently, after forgiving him his one lapse, concealed an obsessive belief in his infidelity. He, in turn, becomes obsessed with proving to her in death that she was wrong. In the process he discovers that she has lied about him to her friends, and may well have written her diary as a means of keeping her hold on him in the event of her death "with an almost clairvoyant sense of the effects words can have" (*LM*, 43). Eventually, he is forced to accept that his former view of her and his belief in how she saw him were based on misreading, misrepresentation, and, ultimately, verbal constructs, fiction; the difficulty in reaching ultimate certainty of interpretation is insurmountable. The love story is bound into the journalistic world of two-faced politics, together with manipulation of belief, shown throughout on a personal and public level. The ending, where the protagonist's new love takes him to the very place where his first love began, can be read either as a happy ending or a repeat of what went before. In this little work, Margaret had produced a postmodern prototype, where certainty about meaning is shown to be impossible, interpretation to be profoundly flawed, the fictionality of perception paramount. But this subtle experiment was not the style of book that would make money. Margaret would offer it, under the pseudonym James Hill, to Billy Collins's publishing firm; he would faithfully keep her secret, and enter it for a novelette contest that the American firm Little, Brown had announced.

Loving Memory had been a moment of self-indulgence, but now Margaret again confronted her dire finances. By the beginning of April she was starting work on the book about old Whitby, comforting herself with the hope that her responsibilities might soon lessen: Bill would finish university and get a job; Guy might find something more lucrative, as there was a chance of a better job with the WEA based in Leeds (SJ to VB, 4.9.36, 4.14.36). But Guy was very run-down. His current WEA work involved constant traveling from village to village, and his chest was always vulnerable since the gassing in the war. So Margaret encouraged him to accept an invitation from the eminent zoologist Peter Chalmers Mitchell, who had retired to Málaga. On April 30 Guy set off for what would extend into a five-week visit (SJ to EJT, 4.29.36). Was he simply taking a holiday with an old friend, or was he interested in the Spanish situation? For there was steadily growing unrest there which, in July, would finally erupt into the civil war. He cannot have been unaware of the simmering tensions as he toured with his friend. Moreover, Ralph Bates must have kept both Guy and Margaret informed about the situation; he remained single-minded in his support for the left-wing discontents among the poor in Spain.

Although invited, Margaret did not accompany Guy this time, as she had promised to look after Hannah in Whitby while her sister took a break. Not that she presented herself as a willing martyr: she claimed that she was "violently resentful" about her yearly stint as nurse companion to Hannah (SJ to VB, 5.3.36). But she was also sorry for her sister Winifred, tied all year round, and for Hannah, "old and finished except for her awful will" (SJ to VB, 5.6.36). After the week in Whitby, she brought Hannah back to Reading for the usual May visit; Vera would never succeed in weaning Margaret from such commitments, although she tried. On this occasion, not only did Margaret resist Vera's expostulations, but, despite their shared concerns for the antiwar camp, she failed to confide in Vera that on May 1, 1936, she had accepted, albeit with some hesitation, Dick

Sheppard's invitation to become one of the sponsors of his Peace Pledge Union.[9]

What Margaret termed the "frenzied" start on *The Moon Is Making* was not sustained; it had been laid aside in Whitby, ostensibly because it would need a full year to complete, "by which time I should have been in the workhouse for six months or so" (SJ to VB, 5.6.36). In fact she had another book in mind, one she could finish by the end of the year. But this book, *The World Ends*, was another experimental novel that would hardly be a money spinner. It would seem that just now, despite all the financial pressures, Margaret wanted to prove to herself that she was an artist first and foremost. Making some concessions to the pressing need for money, she agreed to review for the *Schoolmaster* and to continue to write short stories. She was also producing occasional articles on writers she admired and on social issues; she contributed one such to *The Road to Success*, a collection of essays about women's careers, edited by Margaret Cole.[10] Not that Margaret's piece, "The Writer," suggested that writing was an enviable career. Instead, she threw down the gauntlet to any who aspired to write. If any such meant

> to be and to remain free, and to write freely, to throw your inkpot in the face of the public, you must practise an absolute simplicity of living, you must earn it by some other means than writing, and you must learn that the condition of growth is perpetual insecurity. (*RTS*, 114)

For making money would never be Margaret's prime motive: she contributed to a volume raising funds to build a Treatment Block at the Royal Liverpool Children's Hospital, and she was one of those spending time and energy trying to persuade some publisher to accept Mulk Raj Anand's novel *The Coolie*, a book on Untouchables considered too challenging, in the days of the British Raj, for most firms. When E. M. Forster's backing finally prevailed with the left-wing publishers Lawrence and Wishart, Margaret was the only woman writer to be quoted in the *Left Review*'s advertisement for the book, endorsing it as "one of the most moving and impressive novels I have read."[11]

While a lucrative contract had been drawn up by Colston Leigh for an American lecture tour scheduled for January 1938, and while Margaret was still committed to the trip to Buenos Aires, she was, again, ominously exhausted. Her mother's visit had been longer than usual and had proved "ruinous in every way," while Guy's mother had fractured her knee and "since she has quarrelled with all her relations except us there is no one [else] to go to her" (SJ to VB, 6.13.36). Writing had again been interrupted, and there were other claims on her time: she and Guy took part in the June Conference of the International Association of Writers for the Defence of Culture.[12] Margaret was not overimpressed; she told Ould that this conference, held in London,

> confirms my experience that the Latin mind is merely incapable of holding a conference. All they want to do is to make speeches about the "heritage culturel," what Amabel calls "tête-à-tête with the Universe." It is futile and ghastly, and I'm sure you know it. (SJ to HO, 6.24.36)

There were clearly moments when Margaret, Francophile though she was, grew tired of the kind of intellectual debate sometimes indulged in by the French; she wanted specific crises in Europe to be addressed, rather than their philosophical context. In the evening, she and Guy had gone on to Rose Macaulay's flat, "for sherry and strawberries, and being very profound (with some difficulty) with Rebecca West" (SJ to VD, 6.26.36). Margaret would always delight in maintaining she was in awe of the flamboyant, self-confident Rebecca, while slyly implying that Rebecca was not quite what she thought herself to be. She was not above a spot of malicious gossip with a trusted friend.

In the midst of all this, Bill had failed the first part of his Cambridge tripos. Margaret now wished she had sent him to a de Havilland or Avros school, where he would have had to work hard as a mechanic for three years, and maybe got a job on the executive side of civil flying. She was at her wits' end: Guy would not advise, as "he is cross with Bill for not working and with me for spending so much money on him" (SJ to VD, 6.26.36). But despite her anxieties about French impracticality and Bill's insouciance, she was back writing both her short experimental novel and *The Moon Is Making*, "one in the morning and one in the afternoon," or so she maintained (SJ to VD, 6.26.36). Meanwhile, Guy had been called for an interview by the vice-chancellor's office in Leeds for the WEA job based there, and he was successful. He was also editing a book of war reminiscences;[13] both he and Margaret set themselves the deadline of August 15, when they were both to go to Buenos Aires, Margaret working "eight and even ten hours a day to get as much done before I go as I can" (SJ to VB, 6.27.36). Always averse to public speaking, she had decided to forgo the lecturing tour in the States. But this decision, involving a considerable loss of income, did not prevent her from planning to indulge Bill, as if money were no object, with a very expensive summer course at the Massachusetts Institute of Technology (SJ to VB, 6.13.36, 6.15.36).

At the beginning of July, Vera had read in the *Herald* that Margaret supported the Peace Pledge Union (PPU); she wrote to say that she was drawn to it herself. However, she pointed out that support of the PPU, concentrating as it did on absolute pacifism, was "quite incompatible with membership of the Union of Democratic Control and the League of Nations Union or any other organisation which is supporting sanctions or collective security," groups that both Vera and Margaret had supported in the past (VB to SJ, 7.2.36). So Vera still had not decided whether to follow her friend's example; she did not in fact decide until January 1937, joining the PPU just as Margaret was starting to have doubts (Berry and Bostridge, 357–59).

In July 1936, as the Spanish civil war broke out, Margaret had again collapsed and was in St. John's Nursing Home for complete bed rest. The Buenos Aires trip was off and any form of social life was forbidden, although she was allowed to write (SJ to VB, 7.[n.d.].36). Yet again, however, a rest cure was fated not to last. For in August, Margaret had to hurry up to Whitby, as Hannah was seriously ill after a third stroke, confused, living in the past, and Winifred was under severe strain. Margaret did what she could, but, as the weeks passed, she needed to get back to work and to look after Guy (SJ to VB, 8.11.36; *JN*, 1:347–49).

While she was up in Whitby, the final volume of the *Mirror in Darkness* trilogy, *None Turn Back*, was published.[14] This novel still used the collage effect of the previous two, cutting from scene to scene to set disparate groups side by side, but again the emphasis was different. The binding force was subtler, so a first reading, as a number of contemporary reviews showed, could see it as less successful than its predecessors. But Margaret's work was no unsophisticated exploration of the strike, as some reviewers maintained. Images of illness and disability run through the book, offering a diagnostic of what was happening within society at large and within individual relationships. From the first, Hervey anticipates an operation for cancer: she accepts, though fearfully, the need to cut it out, but later has to be reminded that the problem affecting the miners is a social cancer that no one can reform single-handed. As a Jewish doctor says:

> Cancer is on the increase . . . in fact it is our whole life which is out of balance to-day. You could say it is civilisation itself which has begun to lose balance and is breeding tumours instead of more life. (*NTB*, 222)

It is not for nothing that at the start of the book, Hervey is reading Giraudoux's *Bella*, in which the heroine dies trying to reconcile intellectuals and politicians. The power of the recurring cancer image infects the whole structure of the book, but Margaret also used other, more traditional physical images to suggest reasons why some characters develop as they do: Julian Swan has a club foot, a disability that has embittered him throughout his life, making him hungry for a power that would obliterate the weakness he deplores. Gary's war wound, never spelled out in the earlier books, is now revealed as castration, turning him to material power as the only outlet for his formidable energies. These strands of imagery twine around another strand, as many of the characters have a background of camaraderie in the war, which has now gone sour in an atmosphere of postwar betrayal and the corruption of aspirations. Even David Renn's left-wing idealism now has its dangerous side, as Hervey sees that he and his kind may become destroyers, "without knowing what they were doing, through their blind passion for justice" (*NTB*, 180): she would develop this idea nine years later in *Before the Crossing*. On the individual level, Hervey does not absolve herself, pondering on her hospital bed how the strife that prevailed in her first marriage, and the taxing commitment to compromise in her second marriage, mirror aspects within her afflicted society. She has to come to terms with her failures, acknowledging the problems facing the idealist within a society dominated by material interests that threaten to overwhelm the individual. Such thoughts have been prompted by a favorite novel; for just before the operation, she has been reading Stendhal's *La chartreuse de Parme*, a novel that portrays the lover, in search of his ideal, all but crushed by a cavalry charge at Waterloo.

Margaret did not pretend that cutting out the cancer solves everything: in a poignant revelation of postoperative anxiety, Hervey wants to ask if a woman without a womb "can still write books" (*NTB*, 315). For there is always the fear that the cure may remove more than the perceived malignancy. Yet without the risk, there can only be conflict. Compromise is impossible, as in the Germany of the day, where brute force smashes the intellectual radical; the novel observes and reveals, but does not offer answers. Altogether Margaret achieved a great deal in this trilogy that she now laid aside. Read now, it gives a vivid impression of the tangle of strands in the 1920s, the basis for modern Britain, in a world of nascent globalization, with a workforce struggling not to be seen as simply a cog in a money-making machine. Inevitably, however, contemporary themes brought out the contemporary prejudices of reviewers, often obscuring the subtleties of Margaret's structuring.[15]

As August ended, she was still weak, her exhaustion compounded by the need to keep traveling to Whitby to relieve Winifred. She was in touch with Vera, but there were signs of a careful distancing. Margaret told her, for instance, that she had written nothing since finishing *None Turn Back* in May; yet she had, in fact, finished the book in March and written *Loving Memory* in the next few weeks. But she did say she had finished revising *Delicate Monster*, the book Ethel Mannin would not let her publish in 1933. For she had to keep publishing, her finances being so bad; she had borrowed on her life insurance, and even her difficult mother-in-law had been persuaded to send a check for one hundred pounds (SJ to VB, 8.31.36). Worryingly too, Margaret's illness dragged on; despite a holiday, she was not well enough to attend a PEN dinner in honor of H. G. Wells at the end of September.[16] Guy was also under pressure: his new WEA job, while more rewarding than the one nearer home, meant that he was traveling up to Leeds, staying in a hotel for five days each week, and lecturing in Saddleworth, Scarborough, Goole, Selby, and East Ardsley. There were two compensations: his friendship with Bonamy Dobrée, now professor of English at Leeds University, and his own academic work. For Guy was determinedly revising his life of William Beckford, that strange, lifelong passion of his, and reading for his next book, *Culture and Survival* (GC, AKOS, 150).

Margaret was not only struggling with her health but, as would soon appear, with her convictions. Her growing contact with refugees was becoming increasingly important to her, and, while she was as committed to peace as ever, the idea of a peace that was unconditional was making her very uneasy, given the increasing evidence of Nazi brutality. In early October, she tried to resign from both the PEN and the PPU on grounds of ill health, but neither Sheppard nor Ould was willing to part with her.[17] All was not doom and gloom, however: for the moment, she had poured her sense of impending disaster into that other experimental novel which she had been writing, with great enjoyment, throughout the summer. *The World Ends* is very different from *Loving Memory*.[18] Whereas *Loving Memory* had explored the manipulation of perception and rewriting of memory, *The World Ends* looked forward to an apocalyptic future that the protagonist might be experiencing physically or, Kafka-like, within his head. It opens with a dinner party that is the key to what follows: the protagonist, named Blake, inviting a link with the visionary poet, presides at a sophisticated dinner party where a news item about the mountains of the Alps sinking is discussed, then the threat of war. Blake says: "The next war will ruin everything. . . . French civilisation — not to speak of our own — is lost" (WE, 13), and he withdraws to listen to the Third Brandenburg Concerto:

> Fitted against the cellos, the violins flew up with astonishing brilliance; scattering dew from their wings the notes rose to the sun, and Blake felt himself flying up there with them, in a dazzling sky. (WE, 15)

In this work and the next two — *The Moon Is Making* and *No Victory for the Soldier* — music or math is the dominant emblem of Western culture, as it was in Eliot's "Burnt Norton" and would be in his three later quartets, Hesse's *Das Glasperlenspiel* (*The Glass Bead Game*), and Mann's *Dr. Faustus*. In all of these works, the math or music emblem underpins the exploration of a complex visionary experience.

In Margaret's novel, Blake becomes increasingly feverish and unhappy as the dinner guests discuss contemporary news and he finally abandons them in disgust. He drives away, and there is a move from reality to nightmare, real or imagined. Stevie Smith's *Over the Frontier* charts a similar path, where the boundary between reality and a dream experience as vivid as real life is invisible and disorienting, just as it is in so many of Kafka's works. Blake falls asleep outside a country inn;

when he wakes, all has been destroyed, the land under water. When he eventually reaches a farmhouse he finds himself in a primitive rural enclave, with a brutal farmer as patriarch. This is post-Eden primitivism, the old Adam struggling to survive, his sons as different as Cain and Abel. Blake's role in all this is partly snake, for he brings knowledge that has no legitimacy in this stark world. But it is also partly dove, as he tries to instill some sense of beauty into the more receptive of the children, telling them stories of his old, mythical world. In his last moments, Blake hears the Third Brandenburg, a work that will die with him, but which takes the reader back to a moment in Blake's old house. Margaret, like Kafka, like Stevie Smith, gives no clue as to whether his experience is real or visionary, but the sense of cultural loss in a world reduced to brute survival is powerfully conveyed. Blake realizes this:

> His memory mingled with the memories of men dead generations before his birth. It lay in his mind like dust on dry ground, to be scattered by a breath. His mind remembered Chaucer, Karsavina dancing, Bach, Beethoven. . . . This swelling wave of sound, which had seemed to defeat time, was going at last to be defeated by so small a thing as his death. (WE, 108)

The World Ends has a different take on memory than *Loving Memory*: here, what is remembered is not revealed as fiction, but as a shared experience that has gone forever, and Blake's dying memory is poignantly elegiac. Margaret finished the book on October 11, and again decided to publish under a pseudonym, sending her sister Do with the typescript to the publisher Dent. Richard Church, the literary editor, although probably suspecting the young woman was not the author, accepted the book and Margaret signed the contract as William Lamb. A few weeks later, she asked Church if he had any books he could recommend; he said he would send a copy of the Lamb (JN, 1:345).

Spiritually satisfying though this was, money must be made, and Margaret turned back to *The Moon Is Making*; it would indeed be a long book, and she would not finish it until April of the following year. She was still exhausted and could not respond to Vera's frequent barely veiled attempts to persuade her to take Winifred Holtby's place: Vera's urgings of Margaret to put her work before family and friends never included herself. In any case, Guy was in greater need of his wife's support, the continual traveling severely taxing his health, and she fitted in a number of visits to Leeds, on one occasion being interviewed for the still prospering student magazine, the *Gryphon*.[19] Hannah's health was steadily deteriorating too, and Margaret was constantly going up to Whitby to help Winifred. Yet another anxiety was Bill. He was still at Cambridge, but Margaret was coming to accept that she would have to send him to Hamble, the Air Training School near Southampton; for flying was his goal.[20]

The interruptions to her work were endless, but never shirked. She had been helping a friend place a proposed book with a publisher: Hilary Newitt was soon to marry the political journalist Harrison Brown, who had been living in Berlin when the Chapmans visited in 1932. Hilary herself had been working there when she met Harrison, and was deeply involved with women's issues. Her book, *Women Must Choose*, compared the situation of women under different regimes, from democratic to Fascist.[21] Margaret offered to write the preface, and saw the book through all its stages; it was well under way by the end of 1936.

Meanwhile Guy was worrying her. By Christmas, he was looking old and tired, and she felt he could not go on with his work for the WEA in 1937. He recovered a little over the Christmas break, writing an essay for Bonamy's *Introduction to English Literature*; but the resumption of his teaching schedule in the new year, the constant traveling, and the poor food at the Leeds hotel, inevitably set him back. Inevitably, too, the Chapmans' money worries continued to haunt them, which meant that Margaret, with Guy away each week and Bill focused on his flying, was a prey to "all the wildcat schemes and ideas that solitude breeds" (SJ to VB, 1.1.36 [*sic*] for 37).

CHAPTER 13

A Clash of Interests Grows

At least Ethel Mannin had ended her quarrel with Margaret, and the long-postponed publication of *Delicate Monster* by an English publisher finally materialized.[1] In this version, Margaret had been careful to meet Ethel's objections: the novel's protagonist, Victoria, instead of being a writer, had become an actor who saw herself as the equal of Sarah Bernhardt. Her writing became acting, comments on the novels she wrote referred now to novels she read. Her banned novel became her banned memoirs "written to her recipe by the secretary" (*DM*, 99). Despite these changes, however, the work remained mischievously malicious, not only in its portrayal of the central characters, but also in its scorpion attacks on novelists and critics. Fanny, the first-person narrator, is consumed by envy of her actor friend, and the overall impression is of a venting of spleen, controlled but deadly. In sum, Margaret would probably count this work as being a product of what she would term her "jeering northern malice" (*JN*, 1:69).

Ethel had been placated, but Vera Brittain was equally thin-skinned. When Margaret sent her a copy of *Delicate Monster*, Vera's response was ambivalent. She could not put the book down, admiring it but also feeling

> a kind of mesmerised horror at the measure of your bitterness and the uncompromising ferocity of your hatreds. . . . Certainly I think Ethel Mannin had a case! (VB to SJ, 1.17.37)

What dismayed her, she said, was "what the book reveals to me about your psychology." With hindsight, this is a sign of Vera's growing uncertainty about Margaret's view of her. Vera was a profoundly insecure woman, and needed constant reassurance that she was central to her friend's life: Margaret did her best to reassure her, but could never surrender completely to Vera's needs, having too many other needs to address elsewhere. Now, shaken by *Delicate Monster*, Vera insisted on seeing *The Lovely Ship* and particularly *The Clash* as outstanding works (VB to SJ, 1.17.37). As for many of Margaret's critics, this was the Storm Jameson Vera had first admired and saw as Storm Jameson at her best, writing about the provincial North and showing women in love; all too often, Margaret would be dogged by the reputation of early works she had herself long outgrown. Ironically, however, while Vera had feared the jibes at novelists and literary critics might mean that *Delicate Monster* would be reviewed with equal venom, almost all were complimentary.[2] It was a mixed compliment: reviewers were clearly relieved by a woman sticking to what they considered as a subject suitable for the female mind, women attacking women being one of them.

The work schedule Margaret was setting for herself continued to be relentless as she struggled to finish *The Moon Is Making*. Then came a blow: the death of a much-loved friend and fellow Yorkshireman, Ralph Fox, in Spain. Fox was a Communist, but, like Stephen Spender, he was a liberal Marxist, with a strong agnostic Christian underlay, and Margaret quoted him with approval in a number of her nonfictional works of the thirties. In his attitude to the novel, as would become clear in his posthumously published book, *The Novel and the People*, he was very much in tune with Margaret's thinking.[3] The novel, Fox concluded, must restore the historical view, concentrating on the development of man against his social background; but it should not become a scarcely disguised political tract, or substitute an author's opinions for "the living actions of human beings": "it is not the author's business to preach, but to give a real, historical picture of life," where characters must have their own personal history (Fox, 111). Fox's reading was wide-ranging, his appreciation of writers like Malraux, Dos Passos, and Stendhal in tune with Margaret's. This is of course not to say that Fox and Margaret were the only writers who shared this kind of platform in the 1930s. Spender's thinking was similar in *Forward from Liberalism*, as was György Lukács's in *The Historical Novel*, both published that year, while Christina Stead, Gide, and Malraux were all, at that time, "trying to straddle liberalism and orthodox Marxism."[4] This straddling, at the time when many committed Marxists in Britain were still upholding democratic humanist principles, shows why Margaret was able to work closely with a number of Marxist colleagues. Stalinism had not yet fatally tightened its grip on worldwide Communist Party members. Fox was one of the most eloquent of these Marxist colleagues, and was much respected. When he was killed, the signatories to a letter tribute in the *Left Review*, of which he was a cofounder, showed the range of those aligned with him as a man and as a thinker; twenty-nine signed, including Margaret, Ethel Mannin, Sylvia Townsend-Warner, Mulk Raj Anand, Walter Greenwood, Naomi Mitchison, Amabel Williams-Ellis, Bonamy and Valentine Dobrée, Cecil Day Lewis, Henry Nevinson, Olaf Stapledon, Kate O'Brien, and Christina Stead.[5] There is no point in speculating on who influenced whom: the ideas were in the air of the time, discussed at meetings of those politically opposed to Fascism, who were worrying about the responsibilities and aesthetic choices of the socially committed writer. What is worth noting is that each put his or her own signature on and in what he or she wrote.

Margaret was also facing a loss nearer home. By February, Hannah was dying, her heart fading after an attack of influenza. Her last days affected Margaret greatly, and Winifred was in a state of collapse after years of being chief carer. It is all too easy to forget that their father was in the family home as well: he was scarcely mentioned in Margaret's letters to Vera. By now, he had been retired for many years, suffering the humiliation of his pension being cut more than once by the Prince Line that he had served faithfully for so many years. Home in Whitby, he led a strangely solitary life in the family home; Hannah had kept him at arm's length since before the war, never forgiving him for a host of perceived shortcomings such as his tendency to lie when under pressure, and latterly for surviving when her son did not. He never seems to have retaliated, accepting her distant coldness whenever they crossed each other's paths, remembering her birthdays, but living his own life, talking to his seafaring friends, walking the moor, writing his journal. Margaret's attitude to him was very much influenced by her mother, who saw any approach to him as a slight to herself; but his eldest daughter could never feel as vindictive as Hannah or Do, and in later years would admit that she was more like him than she could admit earlier. But for now, she brushed him aside, telling Vera that, being "head of the house now, alas! my father being worse than useless," she must look after Winifred: "I couldn't leave her here" (SJ to VB, n.d.). Hannah had died "like a candle blowing out" (SJ to EJT, 2.17.37); and Margaret admitted, "my mother has always taken in my life a sort of centre-pin place, and anyhow half one's nerves seem to run back there" (SJ to VB, 2.17.37). Difficult as Hannah was, she was a vital ingredient in Margaret's life, and her influence would not die with her. The *Whitby Gazette* gave some idea of Hannah's life in her later years: she had been a member of the Infant Welfare Centre Committee and been associated with the Whitby Subscription Library (now defunct). Her funeral took place in the West Cliff Congregational Church to which she belonged, and she was buried on the cliff top, in the Gallilee grave.[6] The stonemason would make a mistake about her birth, putting 1863 instead of 1862, but perhaps he was misinformed; Margaret was by no means always reliable about dates. After the funeral, the sisters destroyed any papers they felt their mother would not have wanted their father to see: "1914–18 has gone up in smoke again, and all the pitiful, useless and unexplained relics — Memorial Service — all of it" (SJ to VB, 2.21.37). Once they had finished, Margaret took Winifred south with her for a month, and the old man was left alone, with a daily help to do the chores. How far grief affected him is unrecorded; Margaret's found vent in a poem that the *London Mercury* would publish two years later, a poem strangely less lyrical than many an image she would conjure in prose.[7]

Back in London, while coping with Winifred's collapse and her own personal grief, Margaret reluctantly agreed to act as Vera's literary executor (SJ to VB, 3.12.37); and when Amabel Williams-Ellis was concussed in a road accident, Margaret went over the draft of a novel Amabel had written "with really friendly care, reading it three times."[8] She tried to interest the Pelican editor in Edward Thompson, mentioning to Edward that she had approached Pelican about her own *No Time Like the Present*,

> but they said it was unsuitable. I have never had a book in the Penguin series for the reason I have never been asked. . . . My fan circle, as contracted as yours, isn't Left-wing at all, or scarcely at all. It is queer that like you I seem to be distrusted by the

very people I expect to rally to me — they rally all right, but with bricks in their hands. (SJ to EJT, 2.25.37)

The mention of bricks was more to console Edward for his poor sales than to reflect strict truth, for Margaret was in demand and respected by many on the left. By March she was on the editorial board of a new monthly monograph, *Fact*, along with other leading left-wing intellectuals.[9] But Winifred's visit was slowing work down, and Margaret was desperately trying to finish her novel so that she could herself have a proper rest (SJ to VB, 3.12.37).

Vera agreed to become a sponsor of the Peace Pledge Union just as Hitler was overseeing a huge buildup of arms, conscripting labor and capital, and the British were increasing their arms buildup in response. There was something of a security panic in MI5, the domestic arm of the British Secret Service, as Hitler Youth groups were regularly coming to Britain on cycling tours, and were making links with the Boy Scout movement. There were reports of a very amicable meeting between Lord Baden-Powell, head of the scouting movement, and von Ribbentrop. Groups of cyclists were taking breaks at schools, Rotary Clubs, and factories, and were attending church services.[10] At the same time, Stalinism was gaining ground in English Communist circles, snuffing out liberal tendencies. It was an opportune moment for the journal *Fact* to make its appearance, given that developments in England appeared to mirror the polarizations of political positions in France. In the first edition of *Fact*, in April, the editors announced that they aimed to emulate the French encyclopedists headed by Diderot 150 years before, whose "essential work was the spreading of *information*, in a form and in language that any one could understand."[11] The journal was to be an English response to Malraux's French vision for the International Association of Writers for the Defence of Culture that had so irritated Margaret by its vagueness the previous year. The journal would be "an experiment in co-operative publication and authorship," and each of the editorial board would have a specific role (8). Margaret Cole would be responsible for social and economic history, while Arthur Calder-Marshall, Margaret, and Stephen Spender would look after the arts. The entire board made clear where it stood:

We are attached to no group. We are all Socialists, and we are satisfied that only through Socialism can justice and freedom be secured, and the menace of Fascism finally ended. But we are not, for that, tied to any one political group or party to the exclusion of another. We take no notice of bans imposed by the Left or the Right. The Labour Party tabu [sic] laid on members of the Communist Party or the Socialist League, does not apply to our columns; nor the ban laid by Communists upon supporters of Trotskyism; nor any other ban laid by one section of the Socialist movement upon another. (8)

This stance was as iconoclastic as that of Margaret and her student friends so long ago, attacking, like them, widely accepted shibboleths, but now it took her into a grouping that confronted the very different political climate of the second half of the 1930s, and would make her commitment to the PPU increasingly difficult, although not initially. That same month the PPU's journal, *Peace News*, announced that Rabindranath Tagore had just been made president of the newly formed All-India League against War and Fascism; and *Peace News* announced its intention of becoming a major forum for discussion about the end of empire, about Communism, and the link between the personal and the public in the control of aggression.[12] For the time being, Margaret's loyalties were working in tandem.

In April Guy resigned from the WEA, utterly spent. Margaret had managed to finish her novel and begin on the work put aside until the novel was done, after which she intended to take a month's rest and to think about how she saw her future role (SJ to VB, 4.13.37). Hilary Newitt's book, *Women Must Choose*, was just out, in its acknowledgments thanking Margaret "for her unfailing encouragement and interest. If this book can be of service to women today, this is due in no small measure to her help" (Newitt, 7). Margaret's own preface uttered a stark warning about what was happening to women under Nazism:

In my lifetime the position of women in the world has altered radically, twice. There was the change which came during the War. There is now this second change, violently negating the first, which we owe to the spread of Fascism in Europe. Women in the democratic countries have their choice plain before them, as never before. Are we to move forward to a position of much greater freedom, or lose what we have gained? To lose does not mean that we shall be back where we were in 1912 with the problems of 1912: it means that our present problems will be solved, in the way in which death solves problems. It will be in some sort our deaths.[13]

Hilary's book, based on material collected on her travels through Western and Central Europe in the late summer of 1936, and backed up by painstaking research in written records, was in three parts, the first and longest analyzing the position of women under Fascism in its German, Italian, and Austrian manifestations, revealing "the monstrous tale of reaction and repression, of women doctors, teachers, scientists, ruthlessly thrown out of work" (SJ, preface, in Newitt, 14). Women were not simply being repressed but involved in a series of organizations that ensured "the loyalty to the Nazi ideal of the female half of the population and of training this 'second line' of the nation to play its part in emergency situations. The women are part of the machine, too" (SJ, preface, in Newitt, 14). For Margaret, this section was the most valuable part of Hilary's work, as it was in her view crucial that, given von Ribbentrop's skill at presenting his country in an acceptable light, readers should be shown a more accurate picture of how even professional women were being driven back into their traditional domestic role. The second part looked more sympathetically at the status of women in Russia, while the third section looked at women's role in Britain. Hilary condemned the "general apathy and indifference to the wider implications of the women's questions, both among women themselves and in the great Trades Union and Labour Movement" (SJ, preface, in Newitt, 16).

Writing to congratulate Hilary for her book, Margaret mentioned Guy's being unemployed, as he had, she thought, rightly refused to take up the WEA job permanently; his health could not stand the strain. So she was yet again the sole breadwinner, committed to supporting her sister Winifred and Bill at Hamble on the very expensive engineering course he was to start after finishing at Cambridge (SJ to Browns, 4.15.37). Margaret's letter, witty and positive, was full of news; there was no mention of her exhaustion to the newly married Browns, who had recently moved across the Atlantic. She shared instead her hope of coming to the States in 1940, maybe to take up again Colston Leigh's offer for a lecture tour. Her letter was as usual geared to the interests and circumstances of her correspondent. To Vera, the tone was different, admitting her exhaustion (SJ to VB, 4.16.37). By the end of the month this exhaustion was critical and she was back at the Walton Heath Osteopathic Hydro, but she could not rest: Guy, out of work, needed her, while Winifred was clearly proving a burden and irritated him (SJ to VB, 4.30.37). Margaret's letters to Vera always excused her willingness to let Guy's interests dictate their plans; at the same time her way of presenting her situation seems to invite Vera's disapproval of this willingness even as Vera's insistence on Guy's selfishness always met with resistance. No doubt Margaret's coping with her difficult marriage needed safety valves for her inevitable frustrations and exasperation; but she never accepted Vera's pleas to prioritize her own needs. Moreover, events in Europe could not but distract her from her own problems, at least in those moments when she could take action. In April, German and Italian planes had bombed Guernica, and Margaret supported the efforts of Vera and her husband, George Catlin, to coordinate relief work for Spain; she herself was on Priestley's committee, she and he having recently made up their differences. They organized an Ambulance Fund Appeal in memory of Christopher St. John Sprigg, killed in action with the International Brigade (SJ to VB, 5.22.37, 5.25.37).[14]

On June 4, despite their dire financial situation, Margaret and Guy set off for a month in France. They immersed themselves in the French scene; from Royan, Margaret reported to Vera on the political split in France, where the poor were all for Léon Blum and the Popular Front, those who were well-off certainly not. Spain, too, continued to be a preoccupation: the Second Congress of the International Association for the Defence of Culture was first convened in Madrid and Valencia by Nancy Cunard and Pablo Neruda, sponsored by the Soviet Communist Party. It finished its deliberations on June 17 in Paris, focusing on the Spanish situation. With Neruda's help, Nancy Cunard wrote and printed on her own small printing press at her French home a letter titled "Authors Take Sides in the Spanish Civil War," which was sent to writers and intellectuals all over the world.[15] Whether Margaret attended the conference when it reached Paris is unclear, but she would respond to Nancy's letter, showing her commitment to Republican Spain, and this commitment would have its place in her next novel, *No Victory for the Soldier*, which was already taking shape in her head. Later Margaret would tell how, on this trip to France, she was researching music, as her protagonist was to be a musician; she was reading a life of Ferruccio Busoni, the Hector Berlioz memoirs, and an account of the Dutch avant-garde composer Bernard Hélène Joseph van Dieren (*JN*, 1:355). But this next "James Hill" venture would again be kept secret. All she told Vera was that she had almost recaptured her wish to write, the month's holiday was giving her lots of new ideas, and she felt she could improve (SJ to VB, 6.16.37, 6.23.37).

Returning home at the beginning of July, Margaret must have been cheered, although perhaps smiling wryly, to find a letter from H. G. Wells, who had just read her *Delicate Monster* and thought it "superb. Among all the others it's like a live head among hairdresser's busts. Wisdom, good (living) writing clear and clean. . . . Henceforth I am among your readers."[16] But there was not good news from Cambridge: Bill had, all too predictably, only achieved a bare pass degree, although Margaret would tell friends he had done rather better. Nonetheless, she took him to Devon for a ten-day holiday before he went to Hamble, another blatantly reckless expense; he was still intent on marrying his Barbara, but did agree to wait two years until he had finished his course. As for Margaret, Guy's joblessness, her own demanding commitments to family and friends, not to mention her own reckless spending when the mood took her, meant she was back in a frantic writing routine, simply to pay their way.[17]

But this did not mean that she ever became less than serious about what novel writing should be about: she remained much preoccupied by the role of writers in society. In May, she had reviewed three books for *Fact*, including George Orwell's *The Road to Wigan Pier*. She liked the first part — a vivid, bitter, telling document, she said — but found the second less interesting because of its concentration on the problems of Orwell's role as public schoolboy turned socialist and socialist worker. She was not, she said,

> belittling his admirable piece of reporting or questioning the
> reality of his hatred of social injustice. . . . But I must say that I
> think it is time we middle-class socialists shut down on our per-

sonal problem and devoted our energies to direct action of the
sort best suited to us.[18]

In July, her article "Documents" appeared, one of her memorable pleas
for writers to engage with the problems of their day, in tune with writers
like Ralph Fox, but with her own "take" on the subject.[19] The article
began with a clear statement of her credo:

> I believe we should do well to give up talking about proletarian
> literature and talk about socialist literature instead — and mean
> by it writing concerned with the lives of men and women in a
> world which is changing and being changed. ("Documents," 9)

"Change" was, for Margaret, the key to the current world; so no writer
should retreat "into a world made artificially static" ("Documents," 9).
But while she saw change as essential, she also stressed the dangers of
polemic in novels: while Ralph Bates's novels were very fine, she said, his
heroes were least convincing when they were behaving like revolutionar-
ies. Change wasn't restricted to proletarians; and in any case the middle-
class writer shouldn't venture to write about them. Orwell's example was
not one she would encourage. Instead,

> We need documents, not, as the Naturalists needed them, to
> make their tuppeny-ha'penny dramas, but as charts, as timber for
> the fire some writer will light to-morrow morning. The detailed
> and accurate presentment, rather than the representation, of this
> moment, and this society. ("Documents," 13)

Facts alone would not do; there must be speech and action, and perhaps writers could work alongside workers to enrich their own understanding. In all of this, Margaret was very much in accord with the Mass
Observation social research project, founded in the same year; but she
was also concerned as to how a writer should present the material. She
turned to documentary film as the nearest equivalent, while stressing the
importance of language: "Let us write decent straight English, too; not
American telegraphese. Social documents are familiar to our literature"

("Documents," 16). She argued against endless analysis of feeling and thought:

> No more peeling of the onion. . . . No stream of consciousness — that famous stream that we pretend to see flowing, as in the theatre we agree to pretend that the stream on the backcloth flows. No commentary. . . . No aesthetic, moral, or philosophical enquiry — that is, none which is not implicit. ("Documents," 16)

And the writer must be attractive to readers: "People will listen even to what is disagreeable to them if the speaker's tone takes them by the ear" ("Documents," 17). This article was an example of Margaret's thinking in progress. It blurred the boundary, for instance, between literary non-fiction, like Orwell's book, and fiction, between the aims of the editorial team of *Fact* and her own quest for a fiction that could convey more than just one aspect of society. Her vision, while in tune with contemporaries like Fox, and in that sense "orthodox," as she would call it in *Civil Journey*, threw light on her developing response to challenges apprehended but not yet fully experienced. For her increasingly close relations with a number of European refugees would make for the gradual shaping of an aesthetic capable of encasing the implications of the social and cultural turmoil developing in Europe.[20]

Margaret's tone was rather different in "Books to Save Liberalism," an article published in the Bombay journal *The Aryan Path*, that same month.[21] Here she returned to a more humanist argument and to her own concern for self-knowledge, warning that "liberalism as a movement is in danger of becoming extinct," primarily because of "a revolt against reason" ("Books to Save Liberalism," 305). She deplored the "emphasis on national and racial differences," and urged the reinvention of a new liberalism, reasserting the value of men as opposed to money ("Books to Save Liberalism," 306). The external authority of Church or State was useless; it must be replaced "by that inner authority of the man who is striving consciously to know himself" ("Books to Save Liberalism," 306). In other words, each individual must take responsibility for his or her own actions, not relying on any external authority, whether Church or State, whether Nazism or Communism. She pointed to the teachings inherent in the New Testament, setting them alongside teachings of the Buddha, while saying, "I am not a Christian; neither am I a Buddhist" ("Books to Save Liberalism," 307). But such teachings, she said, set the scene for her broad choice of liberating books: *Gulliver's Travels* and the Flemish *Legend of Thyl Ulenspiegel*, Milton's *Areopagitica* and Bunyan's *The Pilgrim's Progress*, passages from Plato's *Republic* and the *Apology*, from Rabelais, from Blake's *The Marriage of Heaven and Hell*, from Erasmus, and from John Stuart Mill's *On Liberty* and *Autobiography*. No commentaries should be read, just the texts themselves; "then [the reader] shall be turned free" ("Books to Save Liberalism," 308). As she showed in this article addressed to a readership in India, Margaret was becoming adept at attuning her articles to very different readerships while maintaining her intellectual integrity.

The Moon Is Making came out in August, showing no sign of the many interruptions it had suffered. Written over the months when Hannah was failing, it brought to life the Whitby of Hannah's day, thinly disguised as the town of Wik. The town still "turned its back to the rest of England and its face to the sea and to the coasts and harbours of strange lands," but things were about to change (*TMIM*, 273). The characters of this savagely independent community are hugely alive, the odd dialect word inserted to underline differences from the Englishness of the south, without letting dialect dictate the novel. The protagonist, Handel Wicker, is based on the defrocked Unitarian minister Haydn Williams, whom Hannah had admired for his resistance to government encroachments on what had been for centuries common land. Hannah's admiration for him, Margaret would recall, gave her daughter her "respect for rebels" (*JN*, 1:346). Handel's family offers a core of characters as extreme in their cunning and savagery as old John in *The Pitiful Wife*. Wicker is portrayed as the exception to the rule, educated, standing for science and spirituality at a time when Darwin's findings, alongside the teachings of Marx, began to challenge traditional religious and social concepts. Handel's life recalls many a Victorian tract, as his one mistake leads to his disgrace and death, but the power of the novel lies in the community around him. Margaret drew in old local customs and superstitions, showing the meanness and generosity, the malice of the old families, their thrashings and toughness with the young — and their courage, too. Memorably, she looked back on the year of the great storm in April 1903 when many boats of the fishing fleet were wrecked, and on one boy, tied to a mast but out of reach of the shore. His mother stands where he can see her, saying, "Hod up, now, hod up: hark tiv thi' mudder, and hod up, there's a brave bairn" (*TMIM*, 166). The boy dies; but somehow, the mother goes on. Handel himself is a visionary, sharing Margaret's lifelong sense of rootedness, her sense of place shaping identity. In all, her portrayal of Wik shows the distance between her home community and the English way of life so often seen as anchored in London and its surrounding area, tellingly known as "the home counties." Whereas Margaret had no need to go further than her own backyard to find her affinity with peasant communities in Europe and beyond; years later she would also find dark echoes in the Russian dramatist Alexander Ostrovsky's depiction of "crushed lives and meaningless cruelties inflicted behind bolted doors of provincial merchants' houses" (*JN*, 1:25). Her novel was, on a profound level, an apologia for the way of life that had formed her, the beauty of its setting, the frequent cruelties of its inhabitants, all helping to fashion her perspective on the world. Old Handel's iconoclastic compassion, his striving for a better world, along with a clear-sighted, critical but appreciative understanding of what gave Whitby its identity, combine to make this novel another key to Margaret's own complex character, both as woman and as writer.

Margaret was very much on the defensive when she sent copies of the novel to friends. She told Frank Swinnerton "it is as uncouth as you must be finding it," and she told Vera to "judge it harshly"; years later she would call it "a Brueghel-like novel."[22] For she had written of characters who were recognizable in the Whitby of her childhood, yet she was aware how grotesque they must seem to sophisticated southern readers; so she preempted criticism with her own derogatory comments. Predictably, some of the London critics did see the novel as exaggerated, feeling that Margaret should have retained the gentler tone of her lovely ships and the people who made them. The need to "place" Margaret continued unabated. However, back in the Whitby Public Library, a copy of the novel had to be removed from the shelves as it had been heavily annotated by readers who recognized various of the characters and had no hesitation in penning their names and what the reader thought of them.[23] The gap between different versions of the English way of life was never more marked than in reactions to this novel.

In September, Guy was offered a part-time post as reader in Jonathan Cape's publishing house. He did not accept immediately; he was well on with his book, and had promised to drive Peter Chalmers Mitchell, with whom he had stayed in 1936, to Pao. As on his previous trip to Spain, Margaret did not go with him, preparing instead to go to Paris with Lilo Linke. Before she left, she wrote to *Time and Tide*, protesting the treatment of two German women by their own government, their only crime being that they had married socialist husbands. They had suffered brutal imprisonment in Brazil, been handed over to the German government, were imprisoned in Germany without charge, and now Mrs. Prestes's child, born in prison, was to be taken from her. Margaret observed:

> No one can feel surprise that the Nazi government should behave inhumanly. But what does surprise is that this same Government claims and expects to be regarded as a civilised government and worthy of respect. I have just received a letter from an English apologist for Nazi Germany scolding me for "not being more ready to extend the hand of friendship to this great country." There is some difficulty in extending a hand both to the Nazi government and its innocent victims.[24]

Virginia Woolf suggested in *Three Guineas*, albeit ironically, that women should renounce their citizenship rather than submit to the rules of a male-dominated society. Such an option was not worthy of mention to the women Margaret was supporting.

Installed in Paris, in a cheap students' hotel with Lilo, Margaret wrote to Vera delightedly about the "grand view of roofs and cats," but, given Vera's tendency to be possessive, she did not mention Lilo (SJ to VB, 9.23.37). She worked until four in the afternoon, then went out with a map, commenting that Paris felt crueler, less safe, than London. But Margaret's love of French culture remained constant; she found an exposition of Independent painters at the Petit Palais "staggering," she told Vera (SJ to VB, 10.6.37). Later, she would describe their meetings with Lilo's friends, such as the Turkish writer Halide Edib, who had served in Atatürk's army. She noted shrewdly the difference between the French and English fears about war, for while the Spanish war "roused violent feeling in England, . . . we did not feel the ground move under our feet," as the French did, being all too close to the hub of the action (*JN*, 1:361). For similar reasons the German Jewish refugees they met in Paris were inevitably more tense and anxious than those in England. Margaret had also met some of those who saw Hitler as the Messiah, hoping an alliance with Nazi Germany would "castrate socialism and the Red swine once for all."[25] She was taking soundings in the European situation from a wide variety of sources, and they were not encouraging.

While she was still in Paris, her first two books written under pseudonyms were published, Dent's advertisement for *The World Ends* by William Lamb in the autumn issue of the *Author* coinciding, by chance, with the appearance of Guy's war anthology, *Vain Glory*, published by Cassell, on the summer best-seller list.[26] Richard Church, Margaret's friend and editor at Dent, had produced a fine edition of *The World Ends*, with wood engravings by the eminent illustrator John Farleigh, who had been, like Valentine Dobrée, a member of the London Group. The reviews were good.[27] Collins brought out *Loving Memory* that same autumn; Margaret would say later that Billy Collins knew she was "James Hill," but had kept her secret; he may well have implied that the writer was American, as *Loving Memory*, in the States, was "one of five novellas chosen for publication from 1340 manuscripts entered in Little, Brown and Comp[any]'s novelettes contest."[28] The reviews of this book were more muted, but respectful.[29] As expected, neither had large sales, but their critical success must have given Margaret pleasure.

Toward the end of October, a week after Lilo had left, Margaret came back from Paris. She had enjoyed her time there, although living on the breadline had not improved her health: "I think I didn't do myself much good physically, but mentally a lot of good" (SJ to VB, 10.18.37). Guy too was back from his travels, and had decided to accept the part-time job with Cape that he would take up in November. Margaret now plunged back into her London commitments, although she had not managed to finish her next "James Hill" novel in Paris. She was now increasingly committed to the PEN, which was still struggling to maintain its apolitical stance against increasing odds. The difficulty of maintaining this stance was made clear by the agenda for the October meeting of the Executive Committee, of which Margaret was a member. For at the end of October, the committee had to discuss plans to hold the 1938 conference in Prague, the increasingly desperate situation of the Jews in Poland,

and the escalating war in China.[30] By now, the spread of war and persecution worldwide was all too clear to those who did not turn a blind eye: W. H. Auden and Christopher Isherwood, commissioned by Faber to write a travel book on the East, had gone to China to see the effects of the Sino-Japanese War for themselves, and Auden, in the sonnet cycle written there, would specifically link what he saw to what was happening in Europe.[31]

At this critical juncture, on October 31, Dick Sheppard, founder of the PPU, died suddenly, and Margaret was, she would say later, disconcerted by the violence of her grief. She contributed one of the articles to the *Peace News* tribute, writing of how

> he believed, and every day proves him right, that war is a crime
> for which there is no excuse. He thought of peace not as a state
> of no-war, but as humanity's chance to grow. This belief, which
> we share, is left in our charge.[32]

Yet Margaret had for some time been concerned as to whether total pacifism could achieve a just peace. In the summer, she had been one of the recipients of Nancy Cunard's "Authors Take Sides" letter, and in November, a *Left Review Pamphlet* gave the responses.[33] The questions asked were: "Are you for, or against, the legal Government and the People of Republican Spain? Are you for, or against, Franco and fascism?" (*LRP*, 3). The response from the British alone was impressive: 127 writers responded positively; 15 declared themselves neutral, for such reasons as pacifism (Vera), the isolation of the writer (Eliot), contempt for the questionnaire (Pound and, in a more ponderous tone, Wells). Five responses were negative, Evelyn Waugh, for instance, maintaining he would fight for Franco, not as a Fascist but as an opponent of Marxism. A few, like Virginia Woolf, had not responded. Margaret responded positively, saying:

> It ought to be impossible to find any writer willing to admit that
> he is for Franco and Fascism. This hideous war, which is murdering Spain and may let war loose again over the whole of Europe, is the deliberate act of the two Fascist dictators, and avowed
> by them as such. It is an act they will not hesitate to repeat.
> (*LRP*, 6)

So already her abhorrence of Fascism sat uneasily alongside her commitment to pacifism; yet, for the moment, she was unwilling to face the growing probability that she would have to choose between them.

In November, Guy had started at Cape's, sharing the reader's job, at a very low salary, with the poet and novelist William Plomer. One of the directors, Rupert Hart-Davis, was Guy's good friend, and Jonathan Cape had an interesting list of writers, if not entirely to Guy's rather conservative taste; Guy would say later that the job offered "variety without depth" (GC, *AKOS*, 171–73). That same month, Margaret was in Leeds, to give a lecture on "The Novel in Contemporary Life."[34] This lecture, not constrained by editorial policy, developed ideas in her article for *Fact*. She began by claiming that "a new Battle of the Books has begun" (*NCL*, 3), concerning how far novelists, *as writers*, should play an active political part; for the novel was "being affected, profoundly, and not in any simple way, by the social and political climate of the present day" (*NCL*, 4). After considering a range of contemporary writers, she spelled out her own developing credo: "The essential concern of the novel is with men and women *in their times*"; so in some way it must depict "the social landscape and climate in which the individual characters move," or so enlarge the individual "that society is mirrored in him and in his actions" (*NCL*, 14). The images Margaret used now were no longer just those of the photographer. The novelist must be a "receiving station" for the voices of his society, rather than clinging to the dead and being deaf and blind to the living; everything depends on the novelist "being sensitive enough to detect the past and the future existing in the present" (*NCL*, 15). She repeated her anxiety that "our great industrial communities have no roots in the past," whereas the healthy life of a community "should grow out of the past experience of the community and towards a steadily developing future" (*NCL*, 15). Here speaks the Margaret who understood the dilemmas of exile for the refugee, being, as she was, a self-imposed exile from the life of her own community, her roots in a past that was rapidly vanishing. But she did not waste time on nostalgia; the novelist must, she said, strive to recognize what was essential in the life of his age, and what was "dead and done for" (*NCL*, 23). And if the whole was too much to encompass, the novelist must "take soundings" (*NCL*, 24); while, however deeply he felt, he must work to detach himself. In the end, words were much more important than character and plot:

We need words that are things. And new and unexpected com-
binations of words to bring out the meaning — as sharply as it is
brought out in a documentary film by choice of significant detail
and the angle from which the picture is made. (*NCL*, 27)

For now Margaret was developing and subtly changing the image of the
photographer in her *Fact* article, allowing for the perspective of the photographer even while stressing the importance of the artist not appearing
to impose himself.

In Leeds, Margaret had stayed with the Dobrées, and while there,
she and Valentine had clearly disagreed about surrealism. Valentine presented a painter's perspective that could evade the head-on clash between
intellect and the irrational that bothered her friend. Returning home,
Margaret had been sufficiently impressed by Valentine's arguments to
write that

> I don't like Surrealism in painting any better than I did, in spite
> of pondering your words. It seems to me on a level with the false
> neo-classicism of some modern musicians. Picasso *is* a great art-
> ist, but . . . I shall never be able to agree that one ought not to
> damn bad writing because "something may come out of it." (SJ
> to VD, 11.26.37)

Three weeks later, she explained her reservations more fully:

> The assumptions of surrealism (I'm talking about literature
> now) have always been true, and always will be. But by mak-
> ing a method of them, writers become self-conscious about their
> unconscious, and what could be worse than that? I don't like my
> arts mixed, either. . . . One only wants the impulses not to get so
> mixed up that the painter tries to do what a poet could do better,
> or the poet to aspire to atonalism. (SJ to VD, 12.17.37)

Margaret was not perhaps entirely honest about her own art here, as her
descriptions of the natural world, of landscape, seascape, and cityscape,
captured the visual through words in ways that often echoed the art and
architecture of her time. But like many of her contemporaries at the

end of the thirties, she saw Nazism, with its mythic connections and its fallacious racial contentions, its espousal of violence, and Hitler's reliance on hysterical rhetoric as the abnegation of rational thinking, and felt writers who favored nonreason above the rational risked condoning such precepts.

In December, there was what turned out to be an amusing distraction. Margaret received a letter "written in a large bristling hand on the notepaper of a distinguished Member of Parliament," from Colette's stepson, Bertrand de Jouvenel, who had, he said, interested the Countess de Beaumont and Horace de Carbuccia in Margaret's *Love in Winter*. The countess wished to translate it and wanted to meet Margaret. This did not appeal to Margaret, as Carbuccia was the editor of the right-wing journal *Gringoire*, and she wrote back, politely declining the honor and pointing out that the novel in question was hardly their kind of work. She also wrote to her French agent, asking her to make sure her photograph did not appear in *Gringoire*, as de Jouvenel had requested, adding for good measure, "*Gringoire*, ça pue" (JN/TMS, 2:132). Unfortunately, the agent "had the odd idea of sending my letter to Carbuccia, who replied 'Tell Madame Storm Jameson that she can go to hell'" (JN/TMS, 2:132). This must have been a welcome absurdity in a darkening world.

Those on the left in England were still working together: Margaret took time to sell books at a *Daily Worker* bazaar in Shoreditch, though she was not a member of the Communist Party (SJ to Brown, 12.31.37). This camaraderie had its limits: by the end of the year, there was growing friction between pacifists and anti-Fascists in the PPU, while fear of Communism continued to blind a worrying number of people to the threat of Nazism. Margaret told Harrison Brown that

> our Germano-philes are more active than ever, the Astors, Dawsons, etc. This Government will fight to save British Capitalism and for no other purpose, and I personally don't believe that Communism will come out of such a war. Not here. A moralising Fascism is far more likely. (SJ to Brown, 12.31.37.)[35]

Abroad, the European situation was steadily worsening, while Japanese activities in the Far East were increasingly alarming: it was reported in the press that the Japanese had sunk four American ships. In this context, Bill's telling Margaret that young pilots were being offered a thousand pounds a month to fly "for China" cannot have been a consoling thought; as it was he had nearly been killed, flying in fog (SJ to VB, 12.12.37). An added irritation was the sudden appearance of Karl, boasting to the improvident Margaret about his unspecified good job; they had "the queerest lunch" in Romano's (SJ to VB, 12.12.37). She was, as usual, suffering a crisis of confidence about the book she was writing, the kind of crisis that more often than not reflected her state of mind rather than the quality of the work: "The only thing I can do is forget it and destroy it or try to publish it under a pseudonym,'" she told Vera dejectedly (SJ to VB, 12.12.37). By the end of the year she was ill with gastroenteritis and was "living on boiled water" (SJ to Brown, 12.31.37). It must have been small consolation that she was one of the authors to appear on Wills's 1937 Famous Authors series of cigarette cards.

CHAPTER 14

Munich, and Margaret's Commitment to the PEN

As 1938 dawned, Margaret was desperate to finish *No Victory for the Soldier*. Inevitably, other commitments intervened; she was in demand as a leading writer on peace issues and agreed to write a short preface for a collection of peace plays. Drama would always be her first love, both as a form and as a vehicle for ideas, as she said in her preface: "The value of drama in bringing alive a theme, and the emotions which belong to it, is greater than that of any other art except painting."[1] Yet *No Victory for the Soldier*, finally completed on January 26, does not have a dramatist or a painter as its protagonist; John Sebastian Knox is a musician, and here Margaret was experimenting with increasing confidence.[2] Her composer Knox is complex, a child prodigy whose name links him with both Bach, who brought math and music together, and either John Knox, the fifteenth-century Protestant reformer, or maybe Ronald Knox, Margaret's priest contemporary who also wrote crime novels and was a regular broadcaster. In fact Margaret, undeterred by the libel problems *Delicate Monster* had caused her, used names wittily throughout, many of them being names from her contemporary literary world. So Priestley is an old soldier like his own hero in the best seller *Good Companions*, Auden is mischievously a woman Knox falls in love with, Greenwood, in life the working-class author of *Love on the Dole*, one of her lovers. Eyles, recalling Leonora Eyles, the *TLS* critic, is an aristocratic patron of Knox, and Neumann, the name of a Jewish refugee writer Margaret knew well, the Jew who loves music and is another patron for Knox.

But this is far from being a roman à clef. The names simply act as a key to literary links, and the wit leavens a serious theme, the role of the contemporary artist, which had preoccupied Margaret increasingly throughout the thirties. For the first two-thirds of the book, Knox meditates on how he should write, his music only reaching the "select few," but in the end, in the Spanish civil war, he is on the brink of appealing to a wider audience. The problem of finding the right aesthetic for one's own time is central. On one level, the novel charts the life and loves of the protagonist, while his career, as he wrestles with how to make "one phrase express everything," is spiced with satirical portrayals of the London salon scene of the 1920s, dinner-party conversations, and vignettes of the women he loves (NVFTS, 104). For all his efforts, he is slated by the critics, and cannot understand their failure to see that his music is

> as simple and sensuous as voices coming out of the darkness, voices of lovers, with street lamps at the other side of the shrubs, and a street of boarding houses, the curtains drawn for the night. Why, there's even a piano playing the notes of a popular tune, squirting its sadness into the sea. The allegretto is happiness itself — if you've ever met it. They didn't say it was trivial: they called it dry, tortuous, without feeling. (NVFTS, 126)

He strives for detachment, for lucidity, even as he sees the effect of Nazism in Europe, the father of a Jewish pupil killed in a Berlin prison. A quixotic idealist himself, Knox works on an opera, *The Night of Sancho Panza*, while visiting refugee friends, glimpsing in Paris, like his author, "a furtive underworld of men and women for whom the possession of a piece of paper was the difference between safety and dread" (NVFTS, 207). Hearing their Yiddish mixing with German, he coins a phrase recalling Auden's poem "Spain" — "It was a fragment nipped off another world" (NVFTS, 208) — for their language marks them as aliens in a land that does not share their experiences or sense of community. Knox lives in poverty, and Neumann asks why he sticks to traditional forms the critics decry. Knox's reply echoes Margaret's point in her *Fact* article: "Because I have something new to say must I invent some hideous new language, atonalism, surrealism, the signs made by idiots, to say it in?" (NVFTS, 222).

In the final stages of the novel, Knox goes to Spain. Margaret sketches the move toward war; conversations with Ralph Bates, and no doubt Guy's experiences in his weeks in Spain, had been thoroughly absorbed. Refusing a friend's urgings to leave Madrid before it falls, Knox insists, as Margaret had insisted a writer should in her recent lecture, that "What I want to know is the *fact*. I need to live it so that I can report on it afterwards" (*NVFTS*, 291). Descriptions of the war itself are graphic: the destruction, the danger of being denounced, the arrests, and inexplicable releases. As Knox says: "You mustn't expect the niceties of justice in a war. . . . We'll be lucky if *any* notion of justice survives another world war. Or any civilization at all — even the most elementary" (*NVFTS*, 326). Ironically, it is in Spain that he has found what he has been seeking. Spain's "icy and sun-scored tablelands were his new thoughts, not yet given bodies in precise sounds" (*NVFTS*, 330). However, discipline has broken down; the anarchists are shooting people at random, and he finally agrees to leave, knowing now what he wants to write. After helping to secure the release of some prisoners, he is walking along the street when he is stopped by an anarchist. Tired, he answers brusquely, and is shot; so this pointless death mirrors other such deaths of artists in Spain, in Germany, their insights dying with them.

The novel is a powerful parable for the life of any artist born before World War I, living through the changing values of the war and its aftermath and attempting to shape a medium to respond to the times. Knox is the modernist artist as Margaret envisions he should be, on a quest to find the right language to interpret his age. He comes to realize the importance of reflecting and reaching out, moving from the personal to observant detachment. Margaret both used and distanced her own experience by making her hero a musician. She had reshaped and made her own the music of Eliot's "Burnt Norton," subtly interspersed with echoes of Auden. Her work, and her use of a musician as protagonist, also anticipate, as I have said, the even darker, World War II vision of Eliot's three later quartets, Mann's *Dr. Faustus*, and Hesse's *The Glass Bead Game*. In these last two works musicians stand for intellectuals who distance themselves from responsibility to their community; for Mann and Hesse echo Julien Benda in their sense that intellectuals had allowed extremism to grow by their own lack of engagement. Poignantly, Margaret's musician dies when he takes time to act rather than compose: from the novel's perspective, he dies just as he has learned the secret of how to communicate.

But Margaret may have had her own subtext here, as she was already finding her increasing involvement with refugees and committees profoundly insightful, even as they eroded her writing energies. And this would be the end of James Hill too; despite good reviews, she abandoned her pseudonymous male counterparts, having broken out briefly to write some of her finest works. The next time she would employ a pseudonymous male, in *Europe to Let*, he would be part of the novel. But it remains an enigma that when Margaret was writing three of her most experimental works, she hid her own writerly identity. Maybe, like Doris Lessing in the 1980s, she wanted to see what critical reaction would be when not influenced by the name that had certain expectations attached to it.[3] Or maybe, like her contemporary Katharine Burdekin, who published *Swastika Night* as Murray Constantine, she thought a male pseudonym might ensure the works would be taken more seriously by male reviewers.[4] But we can only speculate.

Straight after finishing *No Victory*, Margaret wrote, very quickly, *Here Comes a Candle*.[5] This time she put aside considerations of the life of the artist, yet arguably what she wrote fulfilled the vision John Knox had before he died, of writing for a wide audience. Her method in part recalled her argument in *Fact*, where she extolled the photographer of the documentary film; but the type of cinema this novel evokes is more that of the fast-moving film "where half the art seems to consist in the 'Cutting' through which tension is heightened by rapid contrast and emphasis."[6] This method was used to catch the flavor of a poor cosmopolitan London community, living round a wooden yard (reminiscent of Shakespeare's "wooden O"), once part of a great house built at the close of the seventeenth century. The fate of this yard and its community is a parable for modernity's inexorable destruction of an old way of life with its roots in the past, both in England and in Europe. For what the tycoon of the novel wants to do has no roots in the past. He is not even interested in slum clearance to build better flats; and this inhuman face of capitalism tied in with the articles Margaret had written in 1937 about unconcern for the poor. The people in the yard, despite their different cultural backgrounds, form a community, not idealized, but vividly interacting. All have their private worlds; poor as they all are, most dream of escaping in the future, and are shaped by memories of their different pasts. All the little stories make up a collage of ordinary human beings caught up in the plot to fire the failing nightclub so as to make room for a cinema. As the image of fire runs throughout, the inevitability of the end, with all its little tragedies, is what we expect. This was the doomed multicultural world of the late 1930s, all the players caught in a confined space, a technique Margaret was steadily developing. Here was the "continuity with the past" she had talked of in *The Novel in Contemporary Life*, and which the old yard represents as an image about to be lost forever. The wit eases the story along; among the nightclub set, for instance,

> The next best thing to being photographed with your mouth wide open, a cocktail glass in your hand, lips and nails both coming out black in the photograph, is to know by sight the people who are. (*HCAC*, 5)

Alongside such partygoers, the vitality of this wooden enclave "throbbed like an ant-heap with human, animal and insect life" (*HCAC*, 8). The dialogue is threaded through with thoughts that are kept private; most characters are in some sense keeping their present poverty at bay. Margaret's skill with word pictures plays its part: "Towards ten o'clock the light in the yard had a curious bronze tinge, like the water in a moor stream" (*HCAC*, 105); the sheer incongruity of the image is touching, as so much of the thinking within the yard goes beyond its confined limits, the sun itself somehow alien to this slum, functioning, without fuss, as a symbol of what life might be beyond the poverty of the characters' cramped conditions. Margaret, at her best, never indulges in long explanations, leaving the reader to ponder the significance of her lucid, concise prose.

She had finished two novels of quality in the early months of 1938, but, as usual, the world was crowding in, both coloring her writing and impinging on her life outside. She contributed to a collection of essays entitled *What Is Happiness?* by a group of writers in which she was the only woman.[7] Her essay emphasized the irony of a human race still in the grip of escapist fairy tales with just one theme, the pursuit of happiness, despite the cruel lessons being offered daily now by the real world. Indeed, it is as if society is untouched by the cruelties because they have ceased to offer novelty: as Margaret observes, caustically: "Towns have been burned before Guernica" (*WIH*, 33). For, among those with their eyes on Europe, the debates about war and peace were becoming increasingly urgent. This year, H. W. Austin's *Moral Rearmament* (*The Battle for Peace*) established "Moral Rearmament" as the title of a religious movement opposing the military buildup, while Naomi Mitchison's *The Moral Basis of Politics* warned that both the revolutionary cause and the peace movement had lost momentum. For her part, Margaret was growing ever more wary of the extreme pacifism of many in the PPU, her attendance at sponsors' meetings becoming increasingly rare; she was much more involved in the plight of refugees and the work of the PEN. As a result, in early March, she was elected by the English Centre to be one of the official delegates at the Prague Congress in the summer.[8] A few days later, *Peace News* (March 12, 1938) printed a manifesto which was to be adopted by the PPU sponsors the following week, renouncing war and urging appeasement and reconciliation. While it endorsed a global effort to abolish poverty, and backed the end of empire, the timing of such a manifesto backing appeasement was not propitious: the following day, March 13, Hitler annexed Austria.

Writing to Hilary and Harrison Brown, Margaret told of the shock at this news. Not that it was unexpected, but "Hitler always moves faster even than one expects. Next, Czechoslovakia or Denmark"; and England itself did not feel safe. Afraid for her sister and her family, Margaret asked about jobs in Canada for Do's husband (SJ to Brown, 3.12.38). No doubt to counter the tension, she had begun another, much lighter novel, a satirical tale with the working title "Time to Dance," but she would soon lay it aside. For like a number of her fellow intellectuals, she was anxious to come to grips with the intricacies of the Central European situation. Rebecca West and her husband had been exploring the complex world of the Balkans since 1936, which West would write about compellingly in *Black Lamb and Grey Falcon*; and American journalists like Dorothy Thompson and, a little later, Martha Gellhorn were looking to the east of Germany. The Germans were traditional enemies of the Slavs, and the attitude of the Slav Czechs to the Germans living in their Sudeten province was far from easy; memories of the Austro-Hungarian Empire colored their thinking. This province was a place where refugees from Nazi Germany had found sanctuary, a growing concern for the PEN in London, as Nazi sympathizers were by now at work in the province, encouraged by Hitler's successes. Yet despite the growing Nazi threat, the plans for the congress in Prague were still going ahead. Margaret remained an official delegate, while also agreeing to serve on a subcommittee responding to the needs of writers "who had become victims of the new regime in Austria" (SJ to Brown, 4.28.38).

With her understanding of what was happening so rapidly in Europe, Margaret threw herself into action; she was now increasingly involved with Austrian refugees, appalled by the stories they had to tell, and she was fearful about the likelihood of Hitler invading Czechoslovakia in September. But she confused some of her correspondents as to what her own plans really were. She had, over the last two or three months, told her American agent, Carol Hill, that she wanted to go to America, probably to live, if only she could find employment for her husband and child. Accordingly, Carol had offered to put Bill in touch with Charles Lindbergh, saying she could probably find something for Guy as well. Margaret had gone so far as to sign a contract for a lecture tour in the States; "she comes in January," wrote Carol confidently.[9] She must have been less certain of finding work for Margaret's husband, as when she asked the London literary agent, A. D. Peters, what he thought of Guy, she received a less than flattering pen portrait. Guy, said Peters, had

> nothing like the mental calibre or the charm of his wife. . . . He is, in a way, a war victim; not physically but mentally. I am not suggesting that his mind is in any way affected, but he is one of those people who would have had more assurance and less cocksureness if there had been no war. He belongs to the type which is well known to both of us: that is, the husband of a successful female novelist.[10]

It would have shocked and grieved Margaret to know that Peters, whom she respected, and whom Guy himself knew and liked, had noted qualities in Guy that had disturbing echoes of Karl. Yet it is an all-too-common story that a man or woman may choose partners who, to the outside eye at least, are remarkably alike.

Margaret's commitment to the growing refugee crisis was demanding more and more of her energy, and her capacity for leadership was being recognized. In May she was unanimously elected chair of the PEN's Austrian Writers Committee, its main function to accumulate and administer funds to help those who could escape (PEN Exec. minutes, 5.4.38).

She realized that she could not finish "A Time to Dance" before going to Prague; she had also been invited to visit Budapest and Vienna later in the year, but as yet felt she could not afford to go (SJ to VB, 5.15.38). The wranglings in the PPU were an unwelcome distraction. Margaret, increasingly disaffected, missed meetings with growing frequency. Indeed, by the end of May she told Vera Brittain, "I am very seriously thinking of resigning, as a Sponsor, not from P.P.U. membership"; and although, as yet, she took no action, her priorities had shifted, as work with refugees intensified (SJ to VB, 5.28.38). She was all too aware of how little could be done to alleviate their sense of loss of identity, their uprootedness.

As the Prague Congress drew nearer, ideas for the next venue were on the table at the PEN. H. G. Wells was inclined to support an invitation from Japan; given the escalation of the war in China, Margaret strongly opposed him. Her confidence when serving on committees was growing, and she was elected as an English delegate to the International Executive Committee (PEN Exec. minutes, 6.2.38). She attended a dinner in honor of the Czech ambassador, Jan Masaryk, and found him splendid company, remembering him years later as "a miracle of wit and energy," loving wine, talk, and women, "but they did not destroy him"; his "daemonic vigour and cheerful bawdiness" recalled, for her, the English Elizabethans, although she conceded that the more formal diplomats disliked him (JN, 1:368). Back at Wells's house after the dinner, she noted Masaryk's contempt for the British ambassador to Berlin, Sir Nevile Henderson — "a scoundrel and a fascist," he said — his cynicism about the promises of the French and the Russians, his capacity to match Wells in debate (JN, 1:370). Margaret, always at heart the iconoclast, admired wholeheartedly his irreverence, courage, and "passion for justice" (JN, 1:369).

The awareness of the risks writers ran under Fascism and Nazism was ever clearer. A pamphlet issued by the writers' section of the World Council against Fascism listed just some of the writers who had been exiled, imprisoned, or killed. For Germany alone, the list was long, including Erich Mühsam and Carl von Ossietzky (both dead), Thomas and Heinrich Mann, Bertolt Brecht, Ludwig Renn, Ernst Toller, Arnold Zweig, Stefan Zweig, Gustav Regler, Alfred Döblin, Erwin Piscator, Lion Feuchtwanger, and Emil Ludwig. There were also Italian, Basque, and Spanish victims. As an illustration of heartless cruelty, the pamphlet quoted from Mussolini's son Vittorio's "Flying over the Ethiopian Ranges, 1937":

> We arrived unobserved and immediately dropped our explosives. One group of horsemen gave me the impression of a budding rose unfolding as the bomb fell in the midst and blew them up. It was exceptionally good fun.[11]

The awareness of atrocities was growing, as was the realization, at least among such organizations, of the threat to Czechoslovakia; the pamphlet quoted a message signed by a long list of writers, including Karel and Josef Čapek, from the Czechoslovak section of the International Association of Writers for the Defence of Culture, all determined to fight if the necessity arose. Margaret still belonged to the English section of this association as well as to the PEN; clearly the gap between the pacifist priorities of the PPU and these other organizations was reaching critical proportions. It would also put her friendship with Vera at risk. Vera's commitment to pacifism was wholehearted, and Margaret, no doubt fearing her friend's reaction, was for some considerable time unwilling to let Vera know how far she had moved away from the position they had once shared.

Toward the end of June she set out for Prague, traveling by train. The hosts would make this congress very much a Slav occasion. The German threat to the new country of Czechoslovakia awoke old fears of the imperialism that had subjugated the Slavs under the Austro-Hungarian Empire; and, as a result, the Slav attitude to their German citizens was at best lukewarm. But Margaret was not yet fully aware of the tensions: she was deeply impressed by Prague, and quickly made friends with the secretary of the Czech PEN Centre, Jirina Tumova, and her doctor husband, responding to their passionate belief in the new democracy. She was impressed by the Sokol gymnastic displays that the delegates witnessed.[12] She was touched and delighted by the performance, in Czech, of Shakespeare's *Romeo and Juliet*. She met Karel Čapek, originator of the word "robot," and author of the prophetic work *War with the Newts*, a political and moral satire that was one of the influences on Orwell's *Animal Farm*: Čapek was "a world citizen who loved his country dearly, but loved the world more."[13] Margaret met a professor from Komensky University, Otakar Vočadlo, a devoted Anglophile, who knew without doubt that the land of Chaucer, Shakespeare, Keats, and Byron would not let him down. At the grand garden party that Edvard Beneš, president of the Czechoslovak Republic, gave to the PEN delegates, she met another young woman, Liba Ambrosova, who would become a close friend (*JN*, 1:373–81). Despite the massed Nazi troops on the border, the prevailing climate that the congress presented to its delegates in Prague was fresh and optimistic, a great affirmation of democracy. But there were ominous moments: Margaret saw at firsthand the limits of pacifism when put to the test. Čapek himself said he was a pacifist, but "with such neighbours as ours we must be prepared" (Ould, *Shuttle*, 224). She would soon confront something even more challenging, when a young Jewish woman, Kitty Rokoš, asked her help to get her father and mother to England. When Margaret protested that surely they would be safe with the Czechs, she was quickly disabused: "You don't know the Czechs, they are not so kind as you think. Besides, they will not be able to protect us even if they want to" (*JN/TMS*, 2:140–41). So Margaret took their details, noting that the girl had not asked help for herself or her husband, and reflecting on her own ignorance of Europe. Nor did she feel the Czechs understood the West. She and others on the delegation were dismayed by the trust that their Czech colleagues had in the good faith of their Western allies. She tried, with other PEN members, to warn that the West might not be as committed to defending a distant country as their Czech friends believed, but their anxieties were brushed aside.

Margaret now decided to visit Vienna, where she stayed for a few days with the sister of Toni Stolper, wife of Lilo Linke's erstwhile boss in their Berlin days. She found her hostess, Anna, preparing to send her children to safety, and was soon hearing of atrocities: the story of a Jewish surgeon having his hands crushed would be recalled vividly in her raw, passionate novel *Europe to Let*. Remembering a visit to Vienna in 1930, she was bitterly conscious of the change in atmosphere (*JN*, 1:382). After a week, she went to Budapest, short of money and eating as little as she could. She found it dismaying: "this place stank of violence," she would recall, "in a way Vienna, for all its Nazi jails and barracks, did not" (*JN*, 1:387). She was frantically taking notes for a novel — "Two, three, novels" — writing up conversations, a habit she had developed over the years (*JN*, 1:388). She met both Nazi sympathizers and a Jewish journalist; he instructed her about the groundswell of anti-Semitism and the unwillingness of the press in the West to accept Jewish versions of events (*JN*, 1:382–405). After this exposure to the dismaying realities of Eastern and Central Europe, Margaret met Guy in Basel and they traveled on to France, where she could begin to absorb all the implications of what she had learned. Her novel "Time to Dance" was now inevitably laid aside, overtaken by events, and would not be revised for several years.

For now, she wrote letters for Jews to relations outside Austria, letters they dared not write themselves, giving news of their sufferings and asking for help; and she sent her report on the congress to the London PEN, where it was well received. But the article she sent to *Peace News* had a rather different reception. "A Pacifist in Czechoslovakia" described her meeting with an unnamed pacifist couple in Prague. The man had suffered for his strongly held principles in the past, but now he was no longer a pacifist, as he said:

> Don't misunderstand. I believe, as deeply as ever, that war is evil. I believe it is *the* evil of the world. . . . Nevertheless, if my country must fight, I shall fight. (*Peace News*, Aug. 20, 1938, 3)

His wife, who had shared his principles, now agreed with his change of heart: "It is better to fight than to live as slaves." Margaret presented her own response as a weak plea for economic concessions, but the man replied:

> Your government will not give up one square kilometre of your empire, and it is finally your empire which the Nazis, *our* enemies, are determined to have.
>
> You *cannot* make peace with these people. In the end they will not let you. . . . I beg you to face the certainty that you will fail to prevent that war. Do not live in illusions. ("Pacifist," 4)

In the end, Margaret was silenced:

> I am sorry. I could not argue with him. I do not know what answer I could have made to him. I do not think there is an answer.

There is an act — which can be done or not done. But there is no answer in words. ("Pacifist," 6)

The article ended simply with the words, "*What should I have said?*"

The response from her readers was immediate: four letters the following week suggested what she should have said in defense of pacifism (*Peace News*, Aug. 20 and Sept. 3, 1938). All were reasonable arguments, but all came from people who had not confronted the situation that had silenced Margaret, people who did not have Nazi troops massing on their border or suffered oppression in the past. Not that she could ever approve of war; as her James Hill novel showed, she knew all too well the cost people paid when caught up in it. It is worth noting here how Auden and Isherwood responded to their firsthand, traumatic experience of the Sino-Japanese War in China that same year, for their account mirrors the same awareness of simple human cost that so affected Margaret as she witnessed the run-up to World War II in Eastern and Central Europe. As Isherwood would report,

> war, as Auden said later, . . . is bombing an already disused arsenal, missing it, and killing a few old women. War is lying in a stable with a gangrenous leg. War is drinking hot water in a barn and worrying about one's wife. War is a handful of lost and terrified men in the mountains, shooting at something moving in the undergrowth. War is waiting for days with nothing to do; shouting down a dead telephone, going without sleep, or sex, or a wash. War is untidy, inefficient, obscure, and largely a matter of chance. (Auden and Isherwood, *Journey to a War*, 192)

In August, as if on cue, *No Victory for the Soldier* was published to reviews that admired the "terse and unemphatic style, innocent of emotional colouring or fine writing"; Margaret had indeed honed her skills for the world of war and the pity of war in which she would involve her readers.[14] Now her mind was turned toward the East: she was preoccupied with writing up her notes on her recent experiences, and already planning to frame a novel around them. She asked all her contacts for information (*JN*, 1:367, 407). There were just two unanswered questions, she told Vera: "Does Hitler mean war whatever happens? Does 'our Government' mean to keep us out 'under any circumstances?' No one seems to know, not even the Foreign Office" (SJ to VB, 9.5.38). As September wore on, the British prime minister, Neville Chamberlain, had gone to see Hitler, meaning to stay a few days but coming back the same night:

> Which tells us all we want to know of what was said, though so far not a word has been spilled in the press. Now [Parliament is] sitting all day, trying to think of a way to cook the Czechs without the Czechs kicking over the frying-pan. (SJ to Brown, 9.18.38)

Margaret was by now all too well informed; she was bitterly aware that Chamberlain and his government might support Hitler's demands to take the Sudeten province away from Czechoslovakia, treating the Czechs themselves as simply obstacles in the way of peace. She did concede that she had heard "that the Cabinet really is divided quite sharply on giving in to Hitler or standing up to him and risking it," but she was skeptical: politicians stick together, she said (SJ to Brown, 9.18.38).

As Chamberlain continued to negotiate with Hitler concerning the führer's intentions toward his Czech neighbor, Margaret's commitment to the PPU was under review (JN/TMS, 2:178–79). The belligerent attitude of the Berlin press and Chamberlain's increasingly clear preference for a policy of peace at any price was seemingly backed by the French, despite their sworn commitment to the Czechs. And this was ever more worrying to those in England who, like Margaret, knew what "price" many refugees or would-be refugees had already paid or would be paying. On September 24, she was a signatory to a letter printed in the *Manchester Guardian*, expressing the fear that the French and British governments were asking the Czechs to make the supreme sacrifice of ceding the industrialized Sudeten province to Germany without any assurance that this would end the threat of war. They urged that an international settlement should be a condition of this agreement.[15] But they were, of course, too late.

Ever more committed to what was happening in Europe, Margaret was torn, unable to decide whether to go on the proposed American lecture tour (SJ to VB, 9.25.38). But she may well have made up her mind already that she would not be going; as the thirties wore on, she was not always entirely frank with Vera. Moreover, she was about to be persuaded to accept a role that would impel her to remain in England, committed to the fate of the increasing number of refugees turning to the PEN for help. On September 28, at the PEN Executive Committee, since war seemed imminent, Hermon Ould was anxious for a reaffirmation of the principles of the PEN, "calling on our members to counteract any attempt to inflame national hatred" (PEN Exec. minutes, 9.28.38). At this point, the current president, Henry Nevinson, resigned, feeling he was too old to cope with the growing demands on the PEN. Instead, he proposed Margaret to succeed him as president of the English Centre. The following day saw the now-infamous agreement among Germany, Great Britain, France, and Italy concluded in Munich, ceding the Sudeten province of Czechoslovakia to Germany, with some minor conditions. At this decisive meeting, Chamberlain, Édouard Daladier, Hitler, and Mussolini were present, but there were no Czechs. So the Czechs were left with no choice at all; they had no chance, as Margaret had feared, to kick over the frying pan, and they accepted the terms the next day.

At this critical moment, a book by Margaret's contemporary, the foreign correspondent Sheila Grant Duff, was published as a Penguin Special. *Europe and the Czechs* highlighted the "insatiability" of the Nazi regime. It examined the lure for the Nazis of Czechoslovakia as the "arsenal" of Central Europe, its war industries having three times the capacity of Italy, and the often stormy relations between the Czechs and the Germans of the Sudeten province, with its roots in a repressive Hapsburg past: "To this day Czechoslovakia remains as a small Slav promontory in a German sea," wrote Grant Duff.[16] This account could not be definitive, of course, since it was written in the heat of the crisis, but it is still invaluable as an insight of the time, and quite remarkable for its perceptiveness and clarity, given the speed of the response as events unfolded. There was little mention of refugees from Nazi Germany trapped in the Sudeten province, written as the book was before the full ghastliness of their fates came to light. But while Grant Duff, Margaret, and the American journalist Martha Gellhorn could only give partial pictures, they each succeeded in highlighting the sufferings of particular groups as they saw them, providing invaluable humanitarian accounts.[17] Taken together, the three women offered significant insights that have the advantage of immediacy, and such insights were invaluable at the time, since, as Margaret would say on her visit to the States in 1949, knowledge of Czechoslovakia only reached most English people at the time of Munich. Once they were aware of it, many in England had taken the Czech tragedy to heart: Margaret would tell her American audience a touching little story:

> It was an English child of the most ordinary kind who waited on the steps of the Czech embassy in September 1938 with two pennies, her whole fortune, and when Jan [Masaryk] came out asked him, "Are you the poor Czech?" "Yes," he said, "I am the poor Czech." Then these are for you, she told him, and gave him her fortune.[18]

Margaret, all too aware of the plight of refugees, was utterly dismayed by the Munich agreement: she would say later that she lost her last shreds of respect for the president of the International PEN, Jules Romains, when he wrote to the two leading French politicians who had been at that meeting in Munich, Georges-Étienne Bonnet and Daladier, congratulating them for their role (JN, 2:74). His fall from grace was doubly painful for Margaret, as she admired his writing; the early volumes of his great sequence *Les hommes de bonne volonté* (*Men of Good Will*) were some of her favorite French works.

Jirina Tumova had by now sent three appeals from the Czech PEN addressed "To the Conscience of the World," asking fellow writers to keep faith with "the common struggle of mankind" for freedom (JN, 1:411). Soon all communication from her would cease. Soon too, ugly stories were filtering through: a Czech from Prague would tell Margaret that

> Jewish and German refugees, forced into trains by Czech soldiers, were being taken to the occupied areas, where they were jailed or sent off to Dachau. Looking at me coldly, he went on, "We can't hide them. What else can we do except try to satisfy the Germans?" (JN, 1:411)

The brutalities consequent on the Munich agreement were already all too obvious.

Margaret continued to work on ideas for the novel based on her experiences in Central Europe, but these would take time to digest. In the meantime, she put together a collection of essays, *Civil Journey*, written throughout the decade, adding pieces of autobiography at the beginning and end.[19] The "Introduction and Apology for My Life," dated September 1938, spelled out what drew her to the PEN and its ideals:

> A writer should not in any circumstances or for any cause surrender his duty to criticise and to enquire freely into the soundness of any idea, faith, doctrine, delivered to him by the mouth of authority.

They must not surrender their "writer's honesty. . . . I would myself as soon be hanged as let another man think for me" (*CJ*, 12). Writing just before Munich, when "peace and war lie on the balances" (*CJ*, 21), she urged that the writers and intellectuals Benda had castigated for their lack of commitment must hold true to the vision inspiring the young before the last war. They must do this for the sake of the new generation of young people, her son's generation: "They are lively, sceptical, endlessly inquisitive. They are very fine, I think. So were my friends" (*CJ*, 24). The selection of previously published essays covered critical moments of the past decade, and her developing ideas on how a writer should respond. Each was introduced by her current reflections, comparing what she had once thought to where she stood now, and, as so often, she mocked herself for not being quicker to spot where events were heading. But this self-criticism, while honest, could be read as a device that set her, not above her readers, but alongside, a more appealing approach than that of a superior commentator, and one that Orwell also used. The final piece, "Fragment of an Autobiography," ended by deploring the uselessness of writing novels, revealing the pain in a mind battered by those experiences in Prague, Vienna, and Budapest, and ready to turn to a greater commitment to action. For her mood was indeed grim. At the end of the month she wrote to Vera:

> The Czechs are cooked, and Europe is cooked. Nothing has been solved, and we are nearer a fascist England than we ever were. . . . It is peace, but at a price and what a price. (SJ to VB, 9.30.38)

For Margaret saw the Munich agreement as a sign of how easily Britain could introduce policies learned from European Fascist regimes; the autocratic dismissal of Czech opinion had deeply shaken her.

Margaret had begun to write *Europe to Let*, but even as she worked on a draft about Budapest, she turned aside to start a novel with the working title "The Captain's Wife," grounded again in the Whitby of her mother's time (*JN*, 2:13). Quite apart from her need to earn money, alternating between two such very different novels must have given her time to digest her view of Europe, and to ease her mind by the return to old Whitby. She would continue to alternate between them over the next months.

In October, Sheila Grant Duff added a chapter to her book, commenting on the Munich agreement, giving reactions to the Czech sacrifice, and charting the path taken to satisfy Hitler's demands. Her thinking tallied with Margaret's for, in effect, Grant Duff alleged Chamberlain's solution was to hand over Europe to Germany. The Czechs had begged France and Britain to reconsider their arbitrary drawing of new borders to a sovereign state, but their protests were ignored. After they had been forced to agree, the Czech president, Beneš, resigned, exiling himself in England just as Margaret was elected to the presidency of the English Centre of the PEN. She had made her decision to act, and before long her writing would be jostled into the background as the flood of desperate refugees grew. She would work closely with Hermon Ould, a man who treated the great and the obscure with equal compassion, as Margaret would recall: "he could not help giving each the same attention, curiosity, metaphysical love" (*JN/TMS*, 2:188). Over the next years, despite occasional differences of opinion, he would be a steadfast friend and colleague. He and Margaret would prove to be a team of extraordinary commitment to the people they fought selflessly to save and to nurture. Was she influenced by his ideas? Certainly their thinking was very close on love of country, opinions about peace, about spirituality, not to mention the care of refugees, attitudes to the French — and more surprising things, like the importance of horoscopes. In the end, there was a meeting of minds where each influenced the other. They operated at the hub of some thirty or forty centers of the PEN worldwide, which were "all — except the amiable well-meaning English centre — wormholed by literary politics," since European writers, Margaret would aver, had always been political animals (*JN*, 2:18).

Margaret's election to the presidency on October 4 was not without incident: she wrote to Hermon, no doubt tongue in cheek, that she felt "horribly sorry last night that I was a woman, thus bringing dissension into the Club" (SJ to HO, 10.5.38).[20] Nevinson, the retiring president, had no such qualms about her sex, although he was wide of the mark when he wrote, "I think you will not find the work of President at all laborious, dear, so long as Hermon is there to carry on the real work."[21] Hermon himself had intended Margaret for the presidency from the start, and was outraged that "anybody should have objected to you on the grounds that you are a woman. Prejudice dies very hard, but I don't think the PEN ought to do anything to keep it alive" (HO to SJ, 10.6.38).

In the midst of all this, *Here Comes a Candle* was published, getting good reviews.[22] As ever, Margaret herself was dismissive, emphasizing to both Valentine Dobrée and Vera Brittain that she was little more than a hack who could write well (SJ to VD, 10.23.38; SJ to VB, 12.13.38). She was in no mood to see her writing as a worthy contribution to the needs of the moment: the PEN, like the League of Nations Union and others, was hugely concerned for the refugees from the Sudeten province. Margaret agreed with Hermon that they must set up a fund, seeing clearly what lay ahead:

> I see before us a future of opening fund after fund, as one country after another goes down, until the moment when our own fate is so close that we go to the bank to draw out the last two shillings to buy ourselves a ticket to the moon, and the law . . . arrests us for sedition with the two shillings in our hands. (SJ to HO, 10.13.38)

She might joke, but she was all set for action, and the old administrative skills that she had honed when working for the Knopfs back in the 1920s were immediately in evidence. She drafted a letter for the press, and offered suggestions for signatories and distribution. She saw the refugee situation clearly, and did not absolve the Czech reaction:

> The fate of the Germans and Jews driven back into the new German areas is as agonising as the fate of the Czech refugees themselves, worse. I think I'll ask Wells if he can't speak to Masaryk about this. . . . What with the Japanese taking South China, and

the prospect of a sort of Boer War in Palestine, and the colonies screaming against being given back to Germany, . . . and more money wanted for arms, it looks as though this would be the last fund we'd get any money into ever! (SJ to HO, 10.13.38)

The situation was worsening by the minute. The Anglophile professor Margaret had met in Prague, Otakar Vočadlo, described in a letter to her how, across the Danube, he could now see "a huge swastika made of electric light bulbs. The Nazis have occupied the right bank and they don't let us forget it."[23] But, he said, this was nothing compared with the invasion of some purely Czech towns and villages, including Karel Čapek's birthplace. Vočadlo mourned the fact that the Czechs had not been defeated but betrayed by their allies and friends, who forbade them to fight. He was thinking of emigrating, he said; he still had faith in his English friends.

Such letters, and many English writers were receiving them from their contacts in the East, had a profound effect. Priestley, for instance, already supporting the translator Richard Duschinsky, was one of the first to contribute to the fund for the writers of Czechoslovakia, and E. J. Thompson also responded generously. Margaret wrote, thanking him and commenting:

> The lot of the German writers in Prague is particularly bitter, since many of them had been in concentration camps in Germany before they were released and fled to Prague some time since. And now they see the wave overtaking them. We have pulled two of these out, but there are others still there, in imminent danger. And soon there will be purely Czech refugee writers, as reaction gets worse.

She added, "As a German once said to me: 'it is not easy to be living in history'" (SJ to EJT, 10.22.38).[24]

Valentine also contributed readily. Margaret told her, "my own Czech friends send me decent generous letters that cost me blood and tears to answer" (SJ to VD, 10.23.38). She saw her letters from Czechoslovakia as having the "natural eloquence" of the English seventeenth-century letter writers, and in that context she told Valentine, that strong advocate of high modernism and surrealism, that she had seen Picasso's *Guernica* in Paris, but found that it was, for her, a series of fragments

> in themselves stunning, shocking, moving. . . . That was partly
> my own fault, not being able to cope with it. But I think partly
> Picasso, too. I went several times after the first knock-down sight
> of it. All the same it is magnificent.

Speaking of her own work, she concluded, "it matters less all the time. The world is too grim" (SJ to VD, 10.23.38); novel-writing paled into insignificance in the face of all the suffering she was confronting. But she was nonetheless writing, a financial necessity, of course, although "The Captain's Wife" must have been a blessed distraction.

Margaret now wrote a second appeal to the press for money to help writers trapped in Czechoslovakia, cosigning with former PEN presidents, and with Hermon as secretary.[25] There were also personal appeals from friends (R. H. Tawney was one) to help individual writers or intellectuals whom they knew to be in danger (RHT to SJ, 10.24.38). By the end of the month, when Margaret was officially welcomed as president, the appeal for the writers in Czechoslovakia had already raised over three hundred pounds, while she and Hermon wrote to the Czech Writers' Association and personally to Karel Čapek: Margaret was eager to get him to England. She had also written a timely article for the *P.E.N. News*, "Storm Jameson on the P.E.N.," in which she recalled how intellectuals in former centuries had ignored frontiers across Europe, sharing a firm belief in the freedom of intellect. She appealed to PEN members to remember this sense of duty, framed in their founding premise, to all writers under threat and to all exiles:

> In this matter the individual conscience is the judge. A writer
> cannot surrender his conscience to a party to keep for him. He
> cannot evade his responsibility to the future, either, by saying that
> it was not his business to look after the freedom and integrity of
> the intellect. He has no other business. (*P.E.N. News*, Oct. 1938)

Vera had been in America when the presidency was being decided. Coming home on the *Queen Mary*, she wrote that Colston Leigh, the agent organizing British lecture programs in America, was "upset and disappointed" that Margaret had felt it necessary to cancel her lecture tour. Margaret was cautious in her response, masking her doubts about the commitment to pacifism. She simply told Vera "everything has changed since you went away" (SJ to VB, 10.25.38). As for Chamberlain and the government, she saw them as much more authoritarian than Vera did, but here too, she was cautious in her wording. Writing three days later, she was careful to stress her own inadequacy for the job of PEN president, adding that she was sure she would need Vera's help at some stage (SJ to VB, 10.28.38). The conciliatory tone of her letters shows she was aware of the real possibility of a major disagreement. A letter to Harrison Brown shows, too, her growing exasperation with Vera as a commentator on the current crisis. She was critical of Vera's "political ignorance," which would make, she thought, the three "highly-paid" articles Vera was to write for American journals rotten; Margaret was of course writing to transatlantic friends who would read Vera's opinions, opinions from which Margaret wanted to distance herself, but the widening gap between the friends is all too obvious. "She hasn't had a fresh idea since 1920," Margaret wrote; Vera had argued with her that Czechoslovakia was better off, because now it would be more "compact" (SJ to Brown, 5.11.38). Margaret's patience was fraying: deploring war was one thing, basing pacifist arguments on ignorance was another, and Vera, she asserted, never read newspapers. As for herself, she told Harrison:

> I'm sunk trying to get out of Prague in time the group of German and Austrian writers who fled there from the Nazis, some of the Germans after having been in concentration camps. They are of course in urgent danger, the Gestapo is already in Prague, and I'm puzzled they haven't struck openly already. And can we get the Home Office to move? Not with prayers or threats. We have got invitations for these people, we . . . have collected £500 for their immediate expenses when they get here. But the Home Office won't give them their visas, nor refuse them either. I lie awake at night wondering who else I can get at to do something. It is awful. And of course they are only a drop in the ocean of threatened people, Jews, socialists, social democrats, communists. (SJ to Brown, 5.11.38)

At the same time, she was trying to save Bill from call-up, although admitting ruefully he would not be easy to move out of Britain, as his qualifications would be meaningless and he would have to retrain. Moreover, "he isn't the pioneering sort. He's intelligent, a brilliant airman, and all that. But not the sort to go out and live rough" (SJ to Brown, 5.11.38). She swore to Harrison she would come to the States herself if she could move Guy, but he will not hear of it, so "I suppose we'll wait here for the British Gestapo to get to work. Well, I'll get out somehow, if it's only as a refugee" (SJ to Brown, 11.5.38). How honest was she being? Certainly she was worried, not just for Bill but for her sister Do, who now had another child, born in May, just as Hitler was moving his troops to the Czech frontier (JN, 1:367). But given her commitment to the PEN, her comments read more like the spinning of a tale that would please a friend rather than something to be taken as gospel. Nonetheless, the real danger to her family and to herself if war did come was a genuine anxiety that would grow over the next few months.

Margaret's mounting unease about her role as a sponsor for the PPU now made her brave Vera's displeasure by saying, for the second time and more forcefully, that she felt she should resign:

> When Dick Sheppard first approached me and I saw him I explained that I could not take an active, that is speaking and committee-work part, in the Union. . . . I would rather have stayed off his list of Sponsors. . . . I've often regretted it since. The P.P.U. is not a thing one can go into with one foot. . . . And so the only proper, dignified and reasonable thing to do is to stay out altogether. And to take my name off the list of sponsors. (SJ to VB, 11.11.38)

For refugees were now her main concern; the next wave of refugees, she said, would probably come from Spain as the civil war was all but over:

> I wish I could feel certain that non-intervention (as most pacifists believe) has saved Europe from general war and not merely prolonged the agony of Spain itself. I find that there is almost nothing — except the ultimate certainty of the wickedness and futility of war — in which one can *wholly* believe. (SJ to VB, 11.11.38)

Inevitably, Vera wrote back begging her not to resign, as her resignation would be misconstrued as an endorsement of war. Margaret's reply was conciliatory: "If I decide not to take my name off the list it will be because you ask me not to" (SJ to VB, 11.12.38). But she was more concerned about the horror of Kristallnacht on November 9, which heralded a new phase of terrorism against Jews in Germany and Austria, with shops looted, synagogues burned, Jews murdered, and Jewish property appropriated by the Reich. Margaret did prevaricate about resigning for a little longer; her name remained on the list of sponsors for some time after this, but her heart was not in it.

Letters were a major chore, both about writers still trapped abroad, and about the needs of those who had reached England. Margaret took endless trouble to write in a very personal way to individual refugees, sensitive about the need for funding. However many letters she had to write, the friendly tone, the sensitivity never faltered, regardless of how weary or exasperated by demands she might be feeling. Moreover, she did not drop a case if she could help it: she was, for instance, in touch with the Translators' Guild about a range of writers who needed translators. The guild had been apologetic, as they could find few willing "to deal with their work on a speculative basis," as only the best would find a publisher. So they agreed to take on the eminent Austrian Herbert Herlitschka, translator of D. H. Lawrence, Aldous Huxley, Katherine Mansfield, and Thornton Wilder among others, to vet the publishable value of works put up for translation. This was one of Margaret's successes, and he would continue to be someone whose career she would help.[26]

Now Margaret told the Browns that current information suggested England would be Hitler's next target in the spring of 1939, citing Göring's prospecting of Danish harbors for the German fleet. She was rushed off her feet each day trying to help refugees as they arrived, while her novel "has to be written in the intervals and bankruptcy is pretty close!" (SJ to Brown, 21.2.38). She described to them one case, where the PEN had obtained a transit visa for a husband and wife from Prague, had no less than four unimpeachable guarantors in Britain, only to have them sent back to France; if the French were to send him back to Prague the husband would be sent to the torture camps. Such were the anguished frustrations for herself and Hermon Ould: one achievement could be canceled out by red tape, so that pleas and negotiations would have to begin all over again. "I can't afford to lose my temper, or to come out with any open statement about Chamberlain, or my usefulness to these poor devils is finished" (SJ to Brown, 21.2.38). The Home Office seemed capricious, she said: "some people get in with ease, others are kept out for no reason," while the PEN was dealing with three or four writers, journalists, and others every day (SJ to Brown, 21.2.38). She was already exhausted as concerns for Do and the children increased alongside concerns for refugees.

Margaret's mood cannot have been lightened by another letter from Otakar Vočadlo, bringing firsthand news of the encroaching Nazi presence. He wrote that he would leave Bratislava soon for Prague, and then, hopefully, for the United States. He reported that the occupation of South Slovakia by Hungarian troops was very brutal; his wife was taking care of refugees from there (Vočadlo to SJ, 12.4.38). Margaret would not hear from him again until after the war, when he came to England for a spell after surviving Terezín, Auschwitz, and Buchenwald. Other, equally disturbing voices of a different kind were reaching England at this time. In the last weeks of 1938, Guy was sent by his employer, Cape, to Prague, to persuade Douglas Reed, foreign correspondent for the *Times* in Vienna and Prague, to cut out anti-Semitic passages from his book *Disgrace Abounding*. After a grim train journey across Nazi Germany, Guy stayed in Prague for three days while Reed, who had capitulated, deleted passages and rewrote them. This was a small triumph for Guy's publishing house, which was one of those to take a firm line against anti-Jewish comment, following Victor Gollancz's passionate lead (GC, *AKOS*, 126). There was some other encouraging news: *Peace News* was now urging PPU members to help refugees, its editor writing to Margaret asking for details of "her" work. She commented:

> He means the P.E.N., not its poor president. Can you make me
> a short piece about our Catalan, Austrian, and Czech funds,
> and the work we've done and are doing, and add a bit about our
> needs — help to jobs, hospitality, any special cases etc.[27]

Margaret, Hermon, and one assistant, first Margaret's friend Doreen Marston, then Janet Chance with, for a time, a secretary, were working closely now with other organizations, such as the German Jewish Aid Committee, the British Homes for Refugees, the National Council for

Civil Liberties, and the German Freedom League. Besides requests for help coming direct to the PEN's committee, there were desperate appeals sent to individual members of the PEN, all too many of which came too late for help to reach them: one from the Jewish feminist writer and actress Mala Laaser was sent to the novelist Charles Morgan, one from the Jewish poet and playwright Ludwig Fulda to H. G. Wells.[28] Despite all, neither of them could be saved, Fulda committing suicide in the spring of 1939 when he was denied entry to the United States.

Margaret and Hermon worked hard to improve their efficiency in collecting information on people they might be able to help. They could call on a number of refugees who had come over in the early Hitler years, especially the Jewish lawyer and journalist Rudolf Olden, who was tireless in his efforts for his compatriots. Margaret herself was spending long hours writing to the Home Office, all too often with little effect. As she told Vera, it was heartbreaking to read so many appeals for help and to be able to do so little. There was the case of a group of Jewish writers and academics who had fled to Prague from Germany and Austria, and who were now in danger of being trapped there. One of these was Max Hermann Jellinek, who had been a Jewish professor at the University of Vienna, one of "at least thirteen, among them so valuable a writer as Bernhard Menne whose book 'Krupp' not long ago has found a warm appreciation in this country" (SJ to VB, 12.17.38). Olden had discussed Jellinek with the PEN, worrying about extraditions from Czechoslovakia to Germany, where those extradited would face beheading. Margaret was caught up in the case; she wanted Janet Chance to approach a woman on the Czech Committee dealing with visas

> and ask her to instruct us in the method of pressing the Home Office for visas, so that we can take up the cases of the odd dozen writers who are in urgent danger in Czechoslovakia still.[29]

Maybe, she said, they needed influential signatures on letters supporting visa applications; maybe it would be a useless effort, but she insisted they had to make it: "Merely to leave these people in the lurch seems to me, too, as to Olden, impossible." But despite all her and Janet's efforts, Jellinek could not be saved, dying the same year.

They were more fortunate with the writer Bernhard Menne, an eloquent anti-Nazi, whom they managed to get out of Prague. He became the leader of the Thomas Mann Group, a small society of those who had escaped to England from Prague, and also became one of their most reliable helpers in vetting other applications. For at this critical time for writers trapped in Prague, Margaret felt the PEN could not expect the Czech Committee to make special efforts for writers rather than for other professions; although within a very short time, the PEN itself would find its own resources stretched still further, when it was forced to extend its brief beyond writers. Margaret spared no effort in getting things moving. By Christmas Eve, she had asked Olden to make a complete list of the people in danger, and made sure that he and his fellow refugees provided this quickly. For, as she wrote, "You know what these people are! I suppose if I were a refugee I'd lose all sense of time, too, but I hope not" (SJ to Downie, 12.24.38).

Sometimes she had to be gently firm with people keen to help, but expecting the PEN to fund their efforts. Receiving an appeal for money from a poet, Marjorie Battcock, who was keen to set up a shop to help the people of Czechoslovakia, Margaret gently pointed out that all the money she could spare, indeed, more than she could spare, was going into the Refugee Fund.[30] She continued to tread carefully with Vera too; they were not meeting often, but Vera was working for refugees herself, concentrating on German Czechs, a group that the Home Office treated with suspicion, in case they harbored Nazi informers. Margaret now wrote to encourage her, sure that the German Czechs could find work in England if they were allowed to come:

> We're short of agricultural labour and these men are some of them smallholders and all of them could be trained for such work. And they are good decent people. I think we shall regret not being generous. (SJ to VB, 12.31.38)

For some time, Margaret had been trying to attract more high-profile writers to the PEN to give the center more of a voice when lobbying for refugees. She wrote to several distinguished contemporaries inviting them to be vice presidents, including E. M. Forster, Virginia Woolf, Lady Cynthia Asquith, Harold Nicholson, Basil Liddell Hart, and Rebecca West.[31] Rebecca West accepted, as did Liddell Hart; Margaret had told him that the PEN had lost impetus since its early days and she was "eager to make something more of it, while keeping to its purpose — of furthering intellectual cooperation between countries."[32]

Liddell Hart, theoretician of military strategy, with a growing international reputation, was a man whose basic premise was, "If you wish for peace, understand war"; he believed in what he termed "rational pacifism," not a pacifism "of the proverbial ostrich variety."[33] While he was distrusted in the main by the British government, his independent, iconoclastic mind appealed to Margaret, even while she had no illusions about his arrogance and tendency to take offense; and he proved a genuine ally in her search for supporters of PEN campaigns. With Virginia Woolf, however, she failed. Virginia wrote back graciously, saying she was honored to be asked to be a vice president, but that Margaret was right that she did not like societies: "I never join them now, and indeed refused some years ago to join the Club for this reason. . . . But I don't think this means that I am any the less in favour of liberty; and I am sure that the invitation has given me great pleasure."[34]

By now, the time Margaret could give to her writing was extremely limited, yet she was somehow working on her novel and ruminating on her strategy for *Europe to Let*. She still clung to a tenuous hope of a peaceful outcome in Europe: in the Christmas issue of the *Author*, she was a signatory, with Laurence Binyon, Vera Brittain, Gerald Bullett, C. E. M. Joad, Ernest Raymond, Francis Williams, and Philip Gibbs, to a letter supporting the national petition for a new Peace Conference, recently launched by the National Peace Council, along with a large number of national organizations. The letter urged that quick action was essential for this initiative "to influence public policy," and asked readers to sign up.[35] This was, of course, very much a forlorn hope: the swelling flood of refugees could not encourage optimism.

PART III

1939–1949

CHAPTER 15

War Is Declared

Early in 1939, Margaret reported that the October appeals had raised about a thousand pounds, but that was already starting to look inadequate.[1] For now the PEN was being approached by journalists as well as the poets, novelists, and translators they saw as their prime responsibility; they tried to refer such cases to the National Union of Journalists, but soon found they could not draw a clear line.[2]

Apart from the PEN, there continued to be many calls on Margaret's time. Vera Brittain wanted help with her biography of Winifred Holtby, *Testament of Friendship*, also persuading Margaret to act as joint guardian for her children when she and her husband were away (VB to SJ, 1.4.39).[3] Do had taken a large house in the country so that she could grow vegetables for her family if war came; but Margaret, while agreeing to help with the rent, was dismayed to find that, despite its apparently idyllic country setting, the house stood in an area "thick with aerodromes and depots and munition dumps" (SJ to VB, 1.19.39). In letters to Hilary and Harrison Brown, she went on insisting that she would go to the States if it weren't for Bill: "He'll be going into the Air Ministry in March or April, if there isn't a war" (SJ to Browns, 1.7.38 [*sic*] for 39).[4] No doubt she had moments when she wanted to get away from all her commitments, the iconoclast in her always rebelling whenever she found herself tied down. But her priorities were different in a letter to Edward Thompson; she was passionate about keeping the PEN

> out of politics, in a central position, so that if the time comes
> when it is necessary to make a stand for freedom of speech — and

who can say how soon that time will come? — it is there to my hand. (SJ to EJT, 1.14.39)

Yet as Europe unraveled, politics and human suffering were increasingly hard to treat as separate entities. Nancy Cunard described the death throes of the Spanish war, giving sordid details of the thousands of women and children moving through the south of France; and soon she would reveal the horror of the squalid refugee camps the French authorities set up for them.[5] The PEN, as Margaret predicted, would have to add Spain's refugees to its ever-growing list of desperate appeals for help.

Priorities were being challenged in other organizations too. Despite or because of her growing exasperation with the PPU, Margaret took a spirited part in a sponsors' debate on conscription in *Peace News*, echoing the formerly pacifist wife she had met in Prague:

> I do not think that a pacifist has the moral right to attempt, even with pain and danger to himself, to withdraw completely from his society when society is at war. There will be children to save: both their minds and bodies will need to be guarded. I should like to see the PPU preparing to do this. (Jan. 20, 1939)

Yet as Ethel Mannin had pointed out in her Christmas message for 1938, there had been many different agendas in the peace movement from the start: Communist, anarchist, Christian, anti-imperialist — Gandhi's commitment to passive resistance; George Lansbury's commitment to the surrender of the colonies — to name only a few. The present climate could only provoke division.[6]

The PEN was also confronting different agendas. The growing refugee crisis was complicated by the number of small societies trying to help: with the best of intentions, they could get in each other's way. So an Arts and Letters Refugee Committee (A&LRC) was set up, representing a number of societies, including the PEN. However, Janet Chance warned that,

> if we ask for substantial sums, we of the PEN . . . may very well be asked in return to be responsible for all "writers", and this would mean "vetting" them . . . : if accepting them as writers, then look-

ing after them entirely . . . if not, passing them on to be trained "as agricultural labourers or whatever it may be."[7]

Clearly, "vetting" would add considerably to the workload, but Janet felt they should accept the responsibility.

In February of 1939, Margaret was already dismayed at a 50 percent reduction in the funds available for each refugee. She had hoped to postpone further appeals for funding until she knew how many Catalan refugees the PEN would have on its books, but now decided to approach publishers and contacts in the Dominions; none too soon, as the PEN received an urgent request to help thirty-one Catalan refugees stranded in Paris. It was becoming clear that, with ever-increasing demands on the PEN's and other societies' finances, even greater coordination was needed.[8] So the newly formed A&LRC asked to be represented on the overarching Committee for Refugees. The A&LRC pointed out that while all refugees had their sympathy, writers, artists, journalists, and actors, by the very nature of their work, "must reveal their ideas on liberty, democracy, and culture," and so were peculiarly vulnerable to persecutions and reprisals.[9] The appeal was successful; the A&LRC was duly represented on the umbrella committee, and this opened the way for the PEN to apply to other funding bodies. Every penny helped.

February marked the second anniversary of Hannah's death, and in the same month Margaret completed her next novel. Its working title, *The Captain's Wife*, was kept for the American edition; in England it became, much to her displeasure, the heavily punctuated *Farewell, Night, Welcome, Day*, an obvious loss of inspiration on her publisher's part.[10] There was a link with the two trilogies, as this novel incorporated some of the same characters, but the emphasis was very different. Margaret used the same filmic structuring as in *Here Comes a Candle*, "cutting" from moment to moment, but whereas there the "cutting" had been from group to group within the same enclave, dramatic in essence, here the "cutting" was between past and present, as well as between people. Margaret probed mother/daughter relationships, drawing on her own experience. Close to autobiography the novel might be, but it is rich in subtle experiment, responding both to the mother's past and to the shifting world in which it was written. The opening sets the tone; a young pregnant woman sits in a room that hung like a ship in the centre of the cyclone of this world. The walls of the house broke and were held together by the anatomy of the pear-tree nailed against them, and beyond them she saw the bank covered with coarse grass dropping steeply to the road, and behind the wall the glittering steel bones of the railway, and beyond it the harbour, placid sleeping water, mirroring darkness and a gull's feather, and the skeleton of a ship on the stocks, and the ship-master's house, and the road climbing, slowly, grey flint, between stone fences, a long long way, to the moor, the soil black round the gnarled fingers of roots, the circles widening until the farthest coiled itself across the roadstead of the River Plate: and time, turning in her, whipped back, a cold snake, to its centre in her body. (*FNWD*, 7–8)

A few appropriately surreal lines embody the young woman's dreams and the future anchorage of the unborn Hervey, locked in her mother's questing, trapped mind. For the psychological straitjacket stifles this woman. The action alternates between moments her mind re-creates and the shock of the present, exploring what shaped this temperament and what bred the woman's Lawrentian rejection of her husband. But while in *Sons and Lovers* the mother sees her son as lover, Margaret's novel presents this mother differently: "Mrs Russell would have been surprised, she would have refused to believe it, if anyone had said to her, You have been seeking a mother in your own daughter" (*FNWD*, 114). Yet although analysis of the family is central, Margaret had learned to stand back, to shape, and to control, and she plotted the life of Mrs. Russell with a keen ear for a very different stream of consciousness from her own. Opposite her, she set Hervey as a child, intelligent, stubborn, with a near-tragic allegiance to a woman whose maternal feelings are warped, skewed into a bitter need to manipulate and blame.

As Margaret finished the novel, her volume of essays, *Civil Journey*, came out. Most reviews paid the book the compliment of long, largely respectful comment, the *TLS* noting approvingly that "Miss Jameson is no mere doctrinaire or ideologist, but one who writes from convictions, themselves changing but based on experience";[11] but Margaret had already moved on, as March set the tone for the novel based in Central Europe. Hitler's armies occupied the whole of Czechoslovakia now, and arrived in Prague, where their Gestapo agents had preceded them. A week before, in *Peace News*, Margaret had meditated on how people committed to peace should react in war, pointing out that "it is egotism that makes us talk as though war had not yet begun. The living as well as the dead in China and Spain know better" ("If War Comes").[12] She went on to repeat what she had said before: no one could contract out of their society. For the lesson of European societies who had failed to confront the growth of Fascism, of Nazism, of pogroms and persecution, preyed on her mind. She begged pacifists to help refugees who had been "victims of the doctrines of hate" with donations, English lessons, invitations to a meal, and tolerance of their ways "when these are not our ways" ("If War Comes," 4). Margaret might write for *Peace News*, but being named as a sponsor appeared to validate a program that amounted to civil disobedience, an opting out of society that she could not accept, so she now resigned. When messages from the sponsors appeared in the *Peace News* of April 10, 1939, there was nothing from her. Later, Vera would reproach her for not relaying this decision; for although Margaret had been dropping hints over the past year, she had evaded sharing what would have been unpalatable to Vera.[13]

The pressure on the PEN, its president and secretary, was overwhelming. Links with other voluntary groups were changing continually, the government taking more control of various refugee committees. Margaret was immersed in negotiations for political refugees trapped in Prague; there were several writers unable to secure permits to leave. But she was also intent on getting closer to the action in Europe. She planned to go to France for a month, to live in "strict hiding, to struggle with my spoken French, not to speak or read English during that time" and, although she did not say so, to absorb for herself the atmosphere in Paris (SJ to VB, 3.31.39). She did admit ruefully that she would be glad to escape refugees for a while; not all of them were pleasant, sometimes even hostile, little realizing the huge efforts being made on their behalf. As Rebecca West noted, some could be "time bombs in themselves."[14] But while she was away, Margaret assigned Guy the case closest to her heart, that of Kurt and Kitty Rokoš, a young couple trapped in Prague; this was the same Kitty who had asked her at the PEN Congress to help her parents escape. Margaret had spent many hours at the Czech Committee, pleading their cause. She was deeply anxious for them:

God knows if it is going to be possible to get them out at all, now
that the frontiers have been closed to Jews. But we hope this
is only temporary. They could have been out weeks ago if the
Committee had not been so slow. (SJ to VB, 4.3.39)

All news was not bad news: the PEN and other societies were learning
to work together. The PEN now had close links with, for example, the
Royal Institute of International Affairs, the League of British Dramatists,
the Jewish Refugees Committee, the Friends of Europe, the Society of
Authors, the Movement for the Care of Children from Germany, the
Society for the Protection of Science and Learning, and the Alien Artists Recommendation Committee. But despite this growing cooperation,
there were all too often occasions when intervention for an individual
had to wait its turn. Janet, responding to one plea, could only promise
to add the name "to a list of about 70 people in Prague for whom the
P.E.N. has made application for visas."[15] The business of getting people
out was appallingly complex, and in Prague there were problems "in
making contact without further endangering those one means to help."[16]

Until the moment she left for France, Margaret was unsure whether to
go; she had been warned against going by a Foreign Office friend (SJ to
VB, 4.10.39). In the end, her need to see things for herself decided her,
and she set off. By April 14 she was staying with a Mme. Willer, in a Paris
suburb, and was quick to assess the mood there:

I feel now that war is certain for this year (unless we capitulate to
the Germans — in effect — and I don't really believe we shall do
that). I believe the French might, not out of pacifism but out of
a defeated weariness — but this may be only a mistaken impression, drawn from this bourgeois circle. (SJ to VB, 4.14.39)

She was dismayed, she said, but nonetheless paid for a month's French
lessons, although she had prudently "put £10 away to buy a seat in an
aeroplane if war comes now." A week later she wrote that it was hard to
concentrate on irregular verbs:

Paris I find disagreeable in this particular bourgeois monde.
They are so afraid for their money, so incapable of imagining

a world different from their world — safe-for-rentiers. . . . One doesn't blame them for being on edge, but it is a horrid scratchy sensation. (SJ to VB, 4.22.39)[17]

She was planning what to do when she came home, asking Vera whether she could persuade Harold Macmillan to employ her as a reader, for Harold, the future prime minister, headed the Macmillan publishing house with his brother, Daniel. Margaret was

> trying desperately now to get a job — I *can't* go on writing. One of my reasons for coming away was a hope that I'd see things clearer here, but in fact I suffer nightmares of hideous panic about my financial state, which has never been so bad. (SJ to VB, 4.27.39)

After just three weeks, she came home, telling Valentine Dobrée, "Paris is too nervy and on edge — I can't stand it" (SJ to VD, 4.29.39).

Back at home she was immediately in the thick of things, correcting the proofs of her novel and reluctantly taking on the job of writing what she called disgustedly "a lying fake serial of nearly 50,000 words" for the *Woman's Journal*. Such journals paid well, and the serial would be anonymous, which "spares me public disgrace, but not private anguish" (SJ to VB, 5.5.39). On the refugee front, she was delighted that the old Austrian couple who had been hosts on her Vienna visit were now, thanks to her efforts, safe in England (SJ to VB, 5.6.39). She was increasingly concerned about Kurt and Kitty Rokoš, the young Jewish couple trapped in Prague, as she had heard "that further and more stringent laws are going to be put into effect *very soon* in Prague, which will finally ruin anyone's chances of getting out" (SJ to VB, 5.12.39). The process for extricating them was proving incredibly complicated. She had managed to get their names on a quota for the United States, had a photostat of the U.S. affidavit, a duplicate of the U.S. guarantee of support, and a letter from the U.S. consulate in Prague, so she could prove that they were certain to leave England within eighteen months of arrival. She had medical and police certificates from the Prague police and their doctor, and a sum of money deposited for them in a London bank. The British consul in Prague had told them he would give them a visa if they could get a landing permit from the Home Office in England. They would then have every hope of getting an *Ausreise* (exit permit) from the German authorities in Prague, since they had handed over, in its entirety, their small property in Czechoslovakia. But now, in a manner dismayingly worthy of Kafka, she had to battle through the London Czech Committee again, which would take time:

> Meanwhile these two decent people, who have friends here with whom they can live until they go to the States, are not going to be a charge on this country for a moment, are starving in Prague and may be caught there forever by new laws which make their case hopeless. I *must* get this landing permit. (SJ to VB, 5.12.39)

Such a saga lays bare the extent of the problem facing any organization trying to help potential refugees before it was too late.

Margaret's own life was the usual financial and domestic tangle alongside the refugee crisis: "Between writing serials, letters to the Home Office, plans to move, and Guy complaining that he feels ill, I wish some friendly god would turn me into a tree," she told Vera (SJ to VB, 5.15.39). Nor was Margaret's search for a job proving easy: Macmillan's literary editor, the Canadian Rache Lovat Dickson, whom Vera had approached, said they could use her occasionally, but their resident reader had not, as she had thought, retired. So Margaret, although she accepted this offer, was still searching for something more rewarding financially.[18] Meanwhile she and Guy were about to move into Do's "big ugly house" (SJ to VD, 5.23.39). Guy would commute, she said, to Cape's, and they would be saving money, but the arrangement would be

> very awkward in a lot of ways. If I can get a job we shall move to London, and use [Do's] house as a weekend refuge from the noise and smells. . . . My worst trouble now is that Guy really is not well, and ought to have a very long holiday. But it's quite impossible. (SJ to VD, 5.23.39)

Complications in the Rokoš nightmare dragged on; one moment they were all but rescued, the next a further problem kept them in Prague. Margaret was doing all she could, while helping Guy with his book *Cul-*

ture and Survival: he had suffered a *crise de nerfs*, and could not finish a sentence, so she was trying to complete missing sentences and paragraphs for him, while her own work was clamoring for attention (SJ to VB, 5.26.39).

In May, Hitler and Mussolini signed a ten-year military alliance, the "Pact of Steel," as plans were being completed for the next International PEN Congress in Sweden, to be held in September. There was to be a gala performance of *As You Like It*, and in all some three hundred authors were expected to attend. Given recent events, however, the English PEN Executive felt that their center should make a statement about "the present tendency of government to employ professional writers for national propaganda and to call the attention of the members of the P.E.N. to their pledge," their pledge to remain outside politics, which was becoming increasingly difficult to maintain.[19]

In June, it was clear that a grant the English PEN had received would only last five weeks, even though they were referring some of their writers to the German Jewish Aid Committee.[20] It was at this difficult moment that Margaret and Guy moved into Do's house, Heathfield, in the village of Mortimer, while on June 14, Bill married his long-term girlfriend, Barbara Cawood. Quite apart from Margaret's failure to take to Barbara, the timing of the marriage was far from ideal for her. She was desperately busy, packing up, trying to finish some writing jobs, including a further appeal for funds, while also getting ready to take Guy to France for three weeks.[21] Bill's marriage, and a weekend visit from her sister Winifred, inevitably complicated her efforts to furnish two rooms in Do's house; and she was, in any case, "full of dread at the thought of living even for a limited time in someone else's house (though my sister and I get on very well)" (SJ to VB, 6.17.39). To cap it all, Guy was unwell and demanding. A letter to Vera included a piece of classic understatement: "Everything is very confusing just now. . . . I have just been interrupted by Guy, with a page from his book, which he requires elucidating. I call that hard on me. I didn't write it!" (SJ to VB, 6.3.39). In the midst of all this, she was still struggling to get her young couple out of Prague, yet again begging her Home Office contact to send the consul a telegram that might solve their problem.

Do's house was away from the distractions of cities or towns, but Margaret had no time to enjoy a country retreat. The day of their move, she wrote to Hermon Ould suggesting that the PEN might inaugurate debates on the model of Valéry's *entretiens*, and urging that the Executive Committee should discuss, while she and Guy were away, the silliness of having a president for just one year. Whatever she might say in her late memoirs, there was no hint of resigning here; Margaret's commitment to the PEN was paramount, and she tried hard not to take on other responsibilities. Two years before, she had agreed to be a vice president of the Six Point Group, "the Great Feminist haystack built by Lady Rhonnda [*sic*] and Time and Tide and now running on its own will all the warhorses of feminism" (SJ to HO, 6.13.39). She turned down a request to be their chairman; her growing reputation as a desirable leader took no account of her crowded diary. Now too another commitment ended: the last number of *Fact* came out on June 15, its editors all having more pressing obligations in the current climate.[22]

Margaret had every excuse to ignore aesthetic considerations at a time when practical problems loomed so large. But this was far from the case. The June issue of the Leavises' journal, *Scrutiny*, published her essay review, "The Method and Theory of the Bauhaus," of *The New Vision* by the last director of the Bauhaus, the Hungarian painter and photographer László Moholy-Nagy.[23] Margaret's article offered a critique of modernism, showing how her thinking had developed in recent months. She praised the Bauhaus experiment, with its stress on engagement with human biology, although she pointed out that its methods could be misused. Behind her argument must have been her acute awareness of the atrocities committed by the Nazis on those they considered biologically flawed, although she did not refer to this explicitly. She was also wary of too much emphasis on "the painter's obedience to the 'values of the material' in which he works," fearing that this could shift the center of value "from man to things, which marks the death of our society" ("Bauhaus," 81). She was not, she insisted, one of those who claimed there was no "meaning" in cubism, constructivism, and the rest; she was only concerned that the meaning had shifted to a "dematerialized and highly intellectualized formula" ("Bauhaus," 86). She found value in the premise behind Moholy-Nagy's educational work: "art is a function of the whole self or it is, however clever (amusing, brilliant, serious) a trick" ("Bauhaus," 88). The danger for her came when the intellect, that spider, gets out of control and begins to weave a tissue which becomes more and more a "dematerialized and highly intellectualized formula"; equilibrium is overthrown, and what began as a biological function ends (and withers in) — to borrow from Mr. Eliot again — "merely vans to beat the air. The air which is now thoroughly small and dry. Smaller and dryer than the will." A younger growth of painters and sculptors is already profiting as much by the excesses as by the virtues of the experimenters. It is surely safe, and it is certainly time, to talk dispassionately. ("Bauhaus," 88)

This was her most thoughtful and thought-provoking analysis of modern movements yet: she was stressing her continuing wariness of works that drew largely on intellectual abstractions. The context was not only the book on review but Nazism and its ideology, as well as the publication, in May, of Joyce's *Finnegans Wake*, in its entirety. Throughout the years when sections of Joyce's work were printed, reaction from writers had been mixed, and this was so now.[24] Margaret's own reaction to the developing work had been negative, as she had, from the start, seen it as a betrayal of the rational basis of language. But now she was seeing the intellect itself as all too easily led astray by its own cleverness; she was moving toward a fuller exploration of human consciousness, as would soon become clear.

Finally escaping to France, Margaret and Guy settled again in the quiet seaside town of Royan, which seemed ideal for Guy in his run-down and nervy state (SJ to EJT, 6.29.39). But while the town was pleasant, the news in the French press was not; Margaret referred to their "daily dose of depression" (SJ to VB, 7.1.39). She was writing, albeit slowly: "A Russian alliance — on Russian terms, too — fills me with dread. So does the news from Dantzig and Berlin" (SJ to VB, 7.1.39). They were home in the big house by mid-July. Guy had been restless, so they had "hared over half France (or so it seemed). We saw marvellous things, and I'm glad to have seen them, but I got awfully tired" (SJ to VB, 7.18.39). Reflecting on her impressions, she told Vera she found it "as hard to believe that war can come as that Hitler will give up his ambitions because we threaten, or seem to threaten him" (SJ to VB, 7.18.39). A few days later, writing to Harrison Brown, she passed on confidential news from her Foreign

Office contacts, that Chamberlain was pursuing a policy of economic appeasement: "He *knows* he is saving England and his property and he thinks God told him to" (SJ to Brown, 7.23.39). Margaret had a dismaying sense that both in France and in England, Fascism was still seen by many as an acceptable bulwark against Communism. It was this moment of deep concern for a dysfunctional Europe that saw the publication of *Farewell, Night, Welcome, Day*, Margaret's novel based on her own dysfunctional family. It had a number of favorable reviews, some only too happy to have the chance to "place" her again as primarily a provincial novelist.[25]

By August, Hitler was openly threatening Poland, and Britain signed an Anglo-Polish treaty. The next few days were a time of nightmare for Margaret, trying and failing to see Bill, struggling to find homes for refugees; she had her two old Austrian refugees staying with her, turned out of their former lodgings to make room for evacuees. She was dismayed that the need to make money was driving her to "anonymous serials and such basenesses, which pay highly," while she was still endeavoring to work on "proper writing" (SJ to VB, 8.24.39). Moreover, she and Do were expecting four evacuees, despite their village being surrounded by ammunition dumps and aerodromes. She managed at last to speak to Bill, whose firm was under Air Ministry orders; he supposed, she told Vera, that "they were to carry ammunition etc., to France," and after that "would be 'released' to join the Air Force" (SJ to VB, 8.28.39). Margaret commented wryly, "Well, I'm glad I spoiled him and let him have all I could." Now, as war crept closer, she spelled out her current position to Vera:

> Between refugees for whom homes have to be found at a day's notice, others who must be helped with the Home Office, a scheme to prepare for looking after their wives when they are interned (as they all will be, at first) . . . , making room for evacuated children, books and MSS (the last a new development, has anyone yet asked you to take in their library?) I haven't had time to think what I can do when war comes, beyond my wish to do work with the children. . . . I am only clear that if war comes the most important thing to do is to prepare people's minds for a real peace, not another and worse Versailles. There will never

be peace so long as there are a dozen sovereign states in Europe. "Saving" Poland, "restoring" Czechoslovakia, only begins it all over again. I am all in favour of restoring Czechoslovakia as a cultural region, and all against setting it up as a nationalist unit. That is why I liked the idea of Federal Union. (SJ to VB, 8.30.39)

The outbreak of war would see Margaret and Vera adopting profoundly different approaches to peace. Vera would stand for peace at any price, while Margaret remained utterly antiwar, but was not prepared to sacrifice everything to a peace that might not be just.[26] For this moment of crisis, however, the friends drew together: Margaret had already agreed to act as Vera's literary executor, and now Vera asked that, in the event of her death, Margaret would be joint guardian to her children along with Rebecca West's husband, Harry Andrews. Margaret agreed, and she also made time to read the proofs of Vera's *Testament of Friendship*.[27]

On September 3, Britain and France declared war on Germany. Margaret found it hard to believe: "In all this sunshine the wireless announcements are fantastic" (SJ to VB, 9.3.39). There was no word from Bill, she said; his wife had written that she had no idea where he was. At such a moment, Margaret's first thought was to find some kind of war work. She told Basil Liddell Hart:

> I don't know what to do now. It isn't a time for writing words. There are things I ought to write, but it isn't time yet for them. I have too many and heavy responsibilities to volunteer, and I wouldn't put on a uniform anyway. There ought to be some use for me, but I don't know what it is, or what to do.[28]

The only job readily open to her was propaganda, and that, given her aversion to war, "is so repulsive that I think I'd let even my dependents starve rather than touch it" (SJ to VB, 9.8.39).[29] Like a number of other writers, she had already received a letter from the Ministry of Information

> asking me what special knowledge of foreign countries I had that would be useful? I am sending back a formal reply, because I cannot see that they could give me anything to do that would help peace to come quickly, or to be decent when it comes. But

> I haven't refused outright, because I hope to be told more about
> it and to know what is going on. (SJ to VB, 9.9.39)

With the inevitable cancellation of the Swedish Congress, the Executive Committee, under Margaret's chairmanship, decided to send their prepared statement to the other PEN Centres.[30] Margaret and Hermon were elected for a second term at the Annual General Meeting, and were given emergency powers for necessary quick decisions (PEN Exec. minutes, 9.27.39). The advent of war would inevitably mean greater emphasis on the vetting of refugees. A number of the most trusted refugee members of the PEN were already helping with this, among them Rudolf Olden and the writer Robert Neumann, who had headed the PEN in Austria, an intelligent, volatile colleague.[31] The urgent appeals for visas continued, but by October internment would become another urgent issue: a tribunal was set up by the Home Office to deal with all who were now designated enemy aliens. The PEN had already listed those whose integrity was vouched for by Bernhard Menne, leader of the Thomas Mann Group of writers and journalists who had escaped from Germany to Czechoslovakia and from there to England.[32] But a large number of refugees on the PEN books now faced the tribunal. Margaret, Hermon Ould, and Janet Chance were supporting them, by no means always successfully, despite the fact that many of them were proven, active anti-Nazis, and had been persecuted for their views.[33] By November, an increasing number were being brought before the tribunal, including Menne himself and several of the PEN's Austrian refugees.[34]

That same month, despite all the crises and interruptions, Margaret finished *Europe to Let*.[35] Initially she had felt that her experiences in Central Europe would require a number of works to cover different aspects, and this may well have influenced her decision to plan this book as four nouvelles or récits (*JN*, 2:14). For this was a very different book from anything she had written before, both in form and content. Each récit has a different structure, and importantly, although the narrator remains the same for each, each reveals shifts in his point of view. Esk, the name of the narrator taken from a Yorkshire river, inevitably recalls Eric Blair's pen name Orwell, taken from the East Anglian river near his family home. Esk, like the Orwell of *The Road to Wigan Pier*, presides over what purports to be a series of documentaries, but Margaret's way of handling her observer narrator does not conform to the narratorial impersonality advocated in her 1937 article "Documents"; instead it brings out the impact of what is observed on a narrator *attempting* to remain detached. Moreover her narrator is necessarily male, since his emotional responses are affected by his experiences in the trenches of the Great War.

Margaret had started with the Budapest story, "Children Must Fear." Here the narrator is unnamed, "the obscure son of an English fishing village" (*ETL*, 228), an exile from the world he knew before World War I. The action focuses on the simmering hate between races, erstwhile subjects of the Austro-Hungarian Empire, and anti-Semitism is central. Intertwined with this theme is the narrator's view of his own detachment, reflecting his country's unwillingness to engage with Europe's problems. Each time he returns to Budapest, the nightmare grows, caught in a memorable surreal image:

> A round white Easter egg, rolling across Europe, left on the roads traces of blood: Warsaw, Berlin, Vienna, Budapest, Rome, Prague, tomorrow. To be devoured with the mind's salt. . . . I am consenting to the business of jackals. When it is finished, from a safe place I shall condemn what has been done. Do I hear a cock crow? (*ETL*, 258)

Tersely, this macabre image implicates those who betray their Christian principles, the principles on which Western humanism was built, in the Nazi crusade that was crushing so many parts of Europe; for the cock's crow echoes the cock Peter heard when he betrayed Christ at his trial.

Margaret wrote "The Hour of Prague" next, as another "angled" shot, the narrator again unnamed, but no longer able to remain detached. He meets the Czech general Jan Stehlik, married to an English wife, a popular writer and pacifist, Olga Johnson. Through this marriage, two sides of the debate about war and peace confront each other; moreover, Stehlik's love for the Czech woman Hana emphasizes his commitment to his own people's predicament on a personal level, the public and the private reflecting each other. Margaret uses images from history and prehistory, giving a sense of horrific continuity, as the voice of Hitler on the wireless recalls a Roman amphitheater, a Stone Age brawl, or the lynching of a black man, his screams producing "bestial howls from the crowd.

The nerves are still there. They answer when pulled" (*ETL*, 173). In Prague, the narrator sees the beginning of the end, the landowners, the "realists," ready to come to terms. The Jewish and German refugees are forced into trains by Czech soldiers, sending them to the occupied areas, where they will either be killed at once or sent to Dachau.

This récit, involved, passionate, would be the core of the book; but Margaret wrote two more to flesh it out. "The Young Men Dance" was the only one not based on her 1938 visits, drawing partly on Guy's experiences in the occupying force after the Great War, partly on conversations with the American journalist Helen Kirkpatrick, whose book *This Terrible Peace* was published in London in 1939.[36] It is also partly responding to Romer Wilson's extraordinarily prescient novel, *Dragon's Blood*, published in 1926, centering on the right-wing dreams of a group of Germans: it would remain on Margaret's bookshelf for years.[37] Margaret's narrator, Esk, is named this time; he comes to Germany as a guest of the aristocratic Kurt Hesse, four years after the war; only one reviewer, R. D. Charques, would pick up the aristocrat's link with the real Kurt Hesse, "a disciple of Clausewitz, who . . . [announced] the coming of the divinely German Fuhrer."[38] Margaret uses Romer Wilson's device of making the idealist Hesse protector of the seemingly vulnerable Wiedemann, a little man with an "extraordinary air of intelligence and brutality" (*ETL*, 5). This relationship echoes the way in which Hitler was initially supported by well-to-do patrons who thought they could control him. Esk, however, observes the growing violence in debate, Wiedemann's increasing fanaticism, and the beginnings of splits in the group of disaffected young Germans. Margaret developed Esk with just enough rounding of character to convey his sense of guilt for the growing crisis, aware that he can only be tolerated as an observer, not rooted in what is causing the Germans' growing rage and despair. On his last visit in October 1923, Esk witnesses Wiedemann's growing power, Hesse reduced now to the role of victim, a prescient view of how the Hitler situation of the early 1920s might develop. In the event, Esk cannot help his friend: Wiedemann is exposed as betraying his people, while Hesse shoots himself in disgust. In Wilson's *Dragon's Blood*, the fanatic Friedrich Storm is locked up as a madman after shooting his protector; in Margaret's récit, written thirteen years later, Wiedemann is the one left to shape the future, his madness unrestrained. Time had rewritten the ending of Wilson's tale.

Finally, Margaret wrote "Between March and April," based on her visit to Vienna. The narrator reverts to namelessness; his meetings are doom-laden. Throughout his visits, he remains stonily observing. He meets Jews and Gentiles, rich and poor. On his first visit, he meets Emil, a young Jewish surgeon; on his second, after the Anschluss, he meets Emil again, his fingers broken, his life as a surgeon brutally ended. Emil parodies the denial of bitter truths that Western journals had all too often demonstrated:

> It's not true that thousands of people in Austria have been robbed of everything. That thousands are slowly dying of hunger. That the prisons are crowded with people charged with having been born. That others have been existing for weeks on a rotten boat in mid-Danube. It is not true that the postman is authorised to demand a hundred marks for a package containing the ashes of your son, he who was taken away last week by enemies who were amused by your tears. It is not true that when they have forbidden a Jew to work, and knowing that no country will admit him have ordered him to leave at once, officials answer the impudent question, "What am I to do?" by the retort, "There is always the Danube." (*ETL*, 280)

In the book's final form, Berlin came first, then Vienna, the long Czech récit, and finally the récit based in Budapest, each providing a different perspective on Europe's crises. Most of the characters act as "soundings" of actual events or people. The narrator's view of events is rich in implication; through him, Margaret was exploring the role of the observer, of the impersonality claim of the modernists, and merges this with the detachment of governments in the West, not taking action but simply observing developments in Europe. Esk, the former soldier in the first published récit, "The Young Men Dance," is given a name and a personality. He has the peasant temperament Margaret saw as her Whitby inheritance as he reaches out to fellow soldiers on the other side, aware of their shared experience. There are echoes of the British Legion missions here. But as the crises escalate, he becomes symbolically nameless, struggling for detachment, nonintervention, although there are times, especially in "The Hour of Prague," when he reacts, almost despite himself. Margaret's Esk stands both for the common man, unwilling to look beyond his own interests until he cannot avoid greater involvement, and for the unwillingness of the British government to intervene. As throughout her work, Margaret does not allow the reader to evade the links between public and private responsibilities.

She sent the finished typescript to her usual publisher, Cassell, where it ran into trouble. The firm's lawyer found nothing litigious in the book, but the editor, Desmond Flower, first objected to what he termed the attitude to pacifism expressed in the book, and then claimed he was reluctant to publish a work that opposed the government's Munich policy. Margaret was enraged by what amounted to censorship, but neither she nor her agent, Nancy Pearn, could resolve the impasse.[39] In need of money, she fell back on writing articles: in September, she wrote "City without Children," about the first wave of evacuees leaving London as war broke out.[40] She presented the need to save the children as reflecting an age-old fear of Viking raids, centuries of people praying in ancient churches. Margaret's vivid streetscapes reveal a city of middle-aged workers, alongside youngsters barely older than the children earmarked for evacuation. She paused over north and northeast London with its many Jews, "who know the folly of expecting to be safe" ("City," 588). She homed in on the slums, only bearable when there are children to "rush whooping along the cinder tracks, between ash bins and straggling flowers" ("City," 589). There is a pervading sense of unreality in this city, so sparsely peopled, waiting for a catastrophe that does not materialize, barely punctured by moments of awareness; the pause before the storm of 1940 is caught perfectly. Margaret wrote in a different vein for the *Woman's Journal*.[41] For this audience she stressed the importance of sustaining family life throughout the war. She warned against wholesale hatred of the enemy once hostilities took their toll, assigning a key role to women in looking to a future beyond the present conflict:

> Do not accept without reflecting on it anything you hear or read. Try to discover the deep reasons why this war started. Try — above all — try to imagine what sort of a world would make it unlikely that any nation would want to start another. You can see that things have been going wrong for a long time. Try with all your wits to see how they can be put right. Right enough to last.

On what you think, on what you feel today, depends the future of this land, the future of all the children in it. ("In Courage Keep Your Heart," 34–35)

By November, one of Margaret's overriding anxieties was for Robert Neumann, whom an old judge at his tribunal had called anti-English and an enemy alien, despite his being a proven anti-Nazi. Neumann had been in England since 1934 and his credentials were impeccable. The same judge had treated Rolly Becker, the woman Robert was living with and intended to marry, as if she were a prostitute; she had been a journalist on a liberal paper in Germany, and was also anti-Nazi. Yet despite Neumann's problems, about which Margaret and Janet Chance were very active, he continued to help with the vetting of incoming refugees, a task made more difficult by denunciations often emanating from political adversaries, with unsubstantiated claims that some writers were Gestapo agents. As Neumann commented, "if the Czechs join the Stalinists, Trotzkists [sic], Mosleyists, and Nazis in denouncing one another, no one will be left without some secret file about him in some government office pigeonhole."[42]

Meanwhile, as Margaret's problem with Cassell's rumbled on, she contemplated moving to Macmillan, if her current contract would allow. For Flower was now refusing to print the book on the grounds that she had not made the changes he wanted, while he was also stubbornly holding her to her contract. Dismayed, she told Rache Lovat Dickson about her predicament, and he promised to approach Harold Macmillan.[43] Rache was as good as his word, giving Harold the typescript of *Europe to Let*. Harold wrote to Margaret saying how much he liked the novel for its honesty and force, found little risk of libel, and would look at the Cassell contract. At first, Margaret felt optimistic; but Flower proved intransigent, only agreeing to forgo the book if she or Macmillan paid a formidable sum of money, and the fate of the novel continued to hang in the balance.[44]

This exasperating publishing situation added to the strain of the early months of 1940. Hitler was uttering threats against Holland in early January; and the needs of refugees were increasing, whether interned or living in poverty. Even the former president of Czechoslovakia, Edvard Beneš, was living "in a little brick villa in Putney";[45] Margaret made sure that the

PEN did not forget him. Her Jewish friend Humbert Wolfe, both a poet and a high-ranking civil servant, had died suddenly on January 5, robbing her of a valuable contact; yet, in the midst of so many problems, she and Hermon were determined to hold a London Conference in 1941, where intellectuals from several countries might come together.[46]

CHAPTER 16

The Blitz and Increasing Internment

That winter was particularly cold; Guy was now staying up in town during the week to avoid freezing traveling conditions, while Margaret undertook occasional reading jobs for Macmillan and wrote articles.[1] Her awareness of the price being paid in Central and Eastern Europe underpinned her convictions; when she joined Beneš and Jan Masaryk in celebrating Karel Čapek, she presented "this great Czech writer and great European" as dying of a broken heart in December 1938 because his country had "lost everything but its courage and its honour."[2] Her article was unashamedly emotional; what she wanted to convey was the sacrifice of democracy that appeasement could bring, since there were many who still thought there was a case for Britain seeking a settlement with Hitler.

It was hardly surprising that Margaret took the line she did. For each refugee case she, Hermon Ould, and Janet Chance dealt with, whether they achieved a rescue or suffered a heartbreaking failure, there was a mountain of correspondence, while problems at home from a whole range of internments were growing. Many would eventually be released after endless effort from Margaret, Hermon, and Janet, drumming up support, supplying exonerating details they had collected; and by no means all the people they helped were members of the PEN. They had to cope with desperate letters from wives and friends of refugees; they had to respond to those who sent manuscripts of their work, seeking a publisher. By the middle of March, Janet could report that "this Bureau undertakes the translation of articles for refugee writers, if there is some possibility of their being taken"; the PEN had set about using refugee translators.[3]

But the Refugee Fund itself remained tiny, so hard decisions had to be made. Margaret, Hermon, and Janet met with greater understanding from desperate refugees than might have been expected, although some reacted badly when they thought more should be done; at one point they had asked a Mrs. Foden to give a Dr. Weltmann a room — he returned her kindness with torrents of abuse. They continued to work with other organizations, such as the German Emergency Committee of the Society of Friends, the Free German League of Culture, of which Margaret was an honorary patron, the Christian Council for Refugees from Germany and Central Europe, and the German Jewish Aid Committee. They attempted to provide hospitality and activities that gave at least some of their refugees a sense of belonging.[4] They sent out huge numbers of circulars and letters to the papers to try to raise money and to alert readers to the problems refugees had faced in Europe and continued to face in England. But the fund was a hand-to-mouth affair, often supplemented from their own pockets; it was small wonder that Margaret's debts were reaching terrifying proportions. However, many British writers did respond to the PEN's appeal for direct help. J. B. Priestley, for one, now employed Richard Duschinsky to translate his plays into German; Robert Graves, E. M. Delafield, and the Woolfs looked after individual refugees. But the PEN's responsibilities grew all the time; they extended their support to German writers in France, some still free, some interned as were Max Schroeder, Friedrich Wolf, and Gerhard Eisler in the internment camp at Vernet.[5]

By February 1940, a number of refugees in England who had not yet been interned were writing to the PEN anxiously, asking to have rulings on what activities were forbidden them or were punishable offenses. Janet advised that they should simply carry on with their normal lives, and Margaret agreed:

> If they begin asking for definite rulings, they will get far more
> prohibitions than permissions. And surely it will be time enough
> to protest when something innocent is prohibited.[6]

Soon after this, Hermon and Margaret suffered a severe blow, as Janet had to leave; the burden on them both would be infinitely greater without her dedicated assistance. Dismayingly too, the financial backing they sought for their proposed conference from the Ministry of Information (MOI) or the British Council now seemed unlikely, and they tried to think of other backers (SJ to LH, 4.6.40).

The difficulties over *Europe to Let* dragged on. Desmond Flower of Cassell now contended that he was right to reject the book because it was obscene; what was more, the Society of Authors was acting for Cassell and against Margaret. She had let her membership lapse, but was shocked that they were supporting a publisher against a writer, and began to fear she might never be published in England again (LD to SJ, 2.2.40; SJ to VB, 2.2.40). When Vera Brittain wrote from the States, saying she might be able to lend money to cover Cassell's demands if Margaret broke her contract, Margaret said the firm had increased its demands from the original £250 to £1,000. Finally, a compromise was reached: she agreed to fulfill her contract for a further three novels if Cassell released *Europe to Let* to another publisher. For her part, she told Vera, she did not intend to give them any more of her "serious" books, but to write three short, experimental novels, "from which I shall learn a lot about writing" (SJ to VB, 2.27.40). Meanwhile Macmillan, though disappointed not to have her fully on their list as yet, agreed to publish the one book that had given her so much anxiety. Harold Macmillan himself, just back from a special mission abroad, made a point of saying how much he appreciated her presentation of the European situation and the British government's reaction to it.[7]

London was rife with speculation about the war: on the one hand there was talk of a Blitzkrieg, on the other, "peace in June," although this Margaret did not believe (SJ to VB, 3.4.40). Vera, on her way back from the States, was exhausted, unnerved by some poor reviews of *Testament of Friendship* and angry about a news story in the *Evening Standard* attacking the Peace Pledge Union (LD to SJ, 4.5.40). Margaret too was exhausted; trying to save a plate of Guy's porridge, she caught her heel on their stone staircase, tearing ligaments in her back. She wrote to Vera soothingly about the attacks on the PPU, while expressing her own dismay at the German advance into Norway and Denmark:

> I am becoming convinced that there is more good to be done in talking and writing about a just and hopeful peace than by trying directly to end the war. You may think I am wrong. I'm open to be persuaded. (SJ to VB, 4.13.40)

At this point, all seemed well between the two friends. They agreed to take part in a BBC program soon after Vera's arrival. For after some initial confusion at the BBC about what should or should not be broadcast, the speed with which the Nazis had made use of the medium had to be matched, especially after the deeply disturbing effect of the propagandist Lord Haw-haw's broadcasts by Christmas 1939. Women's programs had been recognized as important even before this, and it would be this audience that Vera and Margaret were expected to address.[8]

On the voyage home, Vera read and admired her prepublication copy of *Europe to Let* (VB to SJ, 4.19.40). But on reflection, overwrought and tired, she interpreted Margaret's Olga Stehlik as an attack on herself. Her husband, while agreeing there was some resemblance, as in the woman's double-jointed hands, urged her not to approach Margaret until she had rested. Unfortunately she did not take this advice. She and Margaret met at Paddington Station, Vera hysterically accused Margaret of portraying her unkindly, and Margaret lost her temper (Berry and Bostridge, 395–96). Both women were appalled at their quarrel, and both wrote to apologize, Margaret taking the trouble to explain how she translated people she knew into characters for her books:

> I can either put them in in the flesh, and leave out their actual doings. Or put in their doings and spirit, in some form, and leave out their body. It confuses and clouds my mind to turn actual persons with their actual lives into fiction. I can't do it. (SJ to VB, 4.23.40)

Vera responded with relief, and the friendship overcame this first serious breach. But Margaret's letters were subtly different after this; while her tone remained warm, she would be increasingly guarded. She had long since kept her detailed comments about European politics for Valentine Dobrée, Hilary and Harrison Brown, and, more recently, Basil Liddell Hart. Increasingly, too, she was developing her friendship with Hermon Ould. He had suffered harsh treatment in prison for his pacifism during World War I, despite his work with the Society of Friends. But he now felt, like Margaret, that total pacifism was not the answer. As he would confess in his autobiography, Hitler's war drove him from 100 percent pacifism to 99 percent: "The dropping of this one per cent cost me some searing moments."[9] So he put all his energies into the PEN, and found Margaret a staunch ally: "Above all, we stood firm for tolerance at a time when tolerance was the least popular of virtues" (Ould, *Shuttle*, 329).

At the end of April, Margaret took a much-needed break, going with Irene Rathbone to the Château Bellevue, near Totnes in Devon, from which she could also visit the Liddell Harts (SJ to VB, 5.3.40). The quarrel at Paddington Station had clearly shaken Margaret, and Vera was at her most prickly and vulnerable, not someone Margaret could cope with at the moment. Writing to a friend, Margaret confided:

> I think I must have disturbed a few nerves when I tore the ligaments in my back, because I get so cross and inclined to cry for nothing. As if war-time were a suitable time to develop "nerves."

She added that Basil Liddell Hart had invited her to dinner, but

> He is so abysmally gloomy about the situation in Norway, and about the war itself, that I came away feeling very dejected. I hope he is utterly wrong in everything he prophesied about disaster in Norway in the near future.[10]

Basil Liddell Hart's gloomy view of the situation in Norway was justified all too soon; Margaret would recall later that she was actually visiting the Norwegian journalist Bjarne Braatoy and his German wife, Ria, as the news came through about the British withdrawal (*JN*, 2:42–44). While there she heard that Ria's Nazi acquaintances in Berlin were prophesying that the English would soon be out of Europe, and the royal family in Canada (SJ to LH, 5.3.40). For her part, Margaret thought that Harold Macmillan was too optimistic about the possible consequences of a defeat: "Hitler would not be content with an indemnity and occupation of [English] ports and so on," but would make the British serfs like the Poles, turning England into yet another "Gau" of the German Empire with a German Gauleiter in charge (SJ to VB, 5.6.40). She insisted to Vera that the PPU policy of a negotiated peace "has ceased to be realistic," but Vera must know "with what agony I have come to believe this":

I think more and more that the only useful thing for a pacifist to do is to try to keep alive some spirit of humanity and decency, to keep on and on reminding people that Europe as a whole must be reconstructed after the war (this assumed that we "win"), that one can't punish parts of Europe without poisoning the whole. (SJ to VB, 5.6.40)

Margaret's painful change from full-blown pacifism to the need for a just peace had been inevitable, given her close links with the refugee community: there had been so-called peace in Europe since World War I, but she had seen for herself how brittle and brutal that had been for them. She commuted between Mortimer and London to work on their cases, sometimes staying the night with friends. After a refugee party, mostly for German and Austrian Jews, some Czechs and a few Catalans, each with their own dark experiences, she stayed with Noel Streatfeild (SJ to VB, 5.9.40). She and Noel had rediscovered their friendship and a shared commitment to the PEN strengthened the bond. Back in the 1920s, Noel had been a "young rake of an actress," but now her social conscience reminded Margaret that Noel was a descendant of the great prison and social reformer Elizabeth Fry (*JN*, 2:46). It was while staying with her that Margaret heard of the invasion of Holland and Belgium.[11] The bombing of Antwerp particularly shocked her; she had known it well as a child, on voyages with her mother (SJ to VB, 5.11.40).

Such dire news meant that the fate of Margaret's *Europe to Let* still hung in the balance. She heard that it was getting rave reviews in the States but not selling; in England, Rache Lovat Dickson reported that it had "survived the onslaught of news this week. If only people can be brought to see it, it is the most topical book published since the war" (LD to SJ, 5.13.40). The reviews were in the main complimentary, Rosamond Lehmann admiring "this electrifying and ferocious book."[12] Madame Beneš wrote privately to say she had heard high praise of the book from friends, and found "The Hour of Prague" particularly impressive.[13] Despite disappointing sales, Margaret must have been pleased both with its reception and the reception of Guy's book, *Culture and Survival*, which also came out that month to good reviews. She would moreover be aware that challenging political novels, like her own and Martha Gellhorn's

A Stricken Field, had to compete with works that avoided the current tensions, such as Michael Sadleir's best-selling historical novel, the sensitively feminist *Fanny by Gaslight*, which sustained its popularity throughout the 1940s. For many readers preferred to escape from the realities of the time, and this novel, while by no means purely escapist, dealt with a theme that was away from the shadow of war.

The speed of the German advance was terrifying, yet London life carried on. In May Margaret was at a Chinese embassy reception where Kingsley Martin, editor of the *New Statesman*, introduced her to the Chinese ambassador, Quo, who became a good friend (*JN*, 2:48–50). She stayed that night with Kingsley and his partner, as she was to speak at the Fabian Society's Women's Group annual meeting and dinner the following evening. In a letter to Vera, she maintained she had been "terrorised into it by Margaret Cole" (SJ to VB, 5.3.40).[14] Unfortunately, there is no record of what she said at the meeting, but she voiced her main concerns repeatedly in letters to friends. "At the moment the whole refugee ant-heap is boiling, with the internment troubles," she wrote, as increasing numbers were facing confinement (SJ to VB, 5.20.40). On a personal level, she worried too about the home near Reading, situated in such a vulnerable spot, children being forbidden to go on the heaths, and schools remaining open all summer to keep the children occupied and away from the military areas. She told Vera that the authorities feared an attack on the nearby site of a World War I prisoner of war camp at Bramley, and that Lord Haw-haw "has promised an attack on Woodley," another village with a military base near Reading (SJ to VB, 5.20.40). She was looking for places where Do's children might be safe, in North Wales, in Scotland, then in Canada and the States. The Dobrées had sent their only child, Georgina, to America; Rache was sending his wife and son to Canada (SJ to VB, 5.6.40, 5.20.40).[15]

Margaret's finances were at an all-time low; she had a horrifying bank debt of two thousand pounds, and her banker, Billee Keane Seymour, had been urging her to ask Guy's mother, a fairly wealthy woman, to clear it. Guy approached the lady with some reluctance,

> only to be overwhelmed by reproaches for trying to make her end
> her days in the workhouse, and when he reminded her that I had

spent much more than £2000 on keeping him in the years when he wasn't earning she said "more fool Margaret to spend money on you. *I* wouldn't." (SJ to VB, 5.11.40)

Margaret was furious that she had spoken so offensively to her own son. But there was no denying the financial situation was dire: by May 1940, the magazine market had collapsed, robbing her of a good half of her income, and a paper shortage was beginning to affect all publishers, as overseas suppliers, primarily in Norway, could no longer operate (LD to SJ, 5.23.40). Moreover, Harold Macmillan was leaving his publishing firm as, after Chamberlain's resignation on May 10 and Churchill's coming to power, he had accepted the position of parliamentary secretary to the Ministry of Supply (HM to SJ, 5.23.40). His brother Daniel would now be in charge, but Margaret had lost the director who understood and valued her work.

Throughout May and June, a "seismic shock" ran throughout Europe as the French army fell apart and the Germans, with an unstoppable fleet of tanks, rolled on: "In six traumatic weeks, the cardinal reference points of European inter-state relations changed forever. France ceased to be not just a Great Power but even a power."[16] Kingsley Martin pointed out that, as a known anti-Nazi, Margaret would be a target if the worst happened and Britain were overrun; although she did not appear on all Nazi lists of proscribed people, she knew herself to be on at least one in Berlin, while the PEN as an organization was officially proscribed.[17] Writing no longer seemed a serious occupation, and Margaret wrote to Harold Macmillan, asking if he could suggest some job she could take to help the war effort. He was eager for her to go on writing, as, he said, she was one of a few leading writers whose work would indeed help the war effort, and while he was willing to support her wish to take some more active role, he felt she would be wasted working for the MOI. He must have been aware that the ministry would cramp the independence, the iconoclasm she so valued as a writer (HM to SJ, 5.24.40). She followed his advice for the moment but drove herself ever harder to justify his opinion. In April she had already thought of emulating the Czech letter "To the Conscience of the World," and now, as British troops were evacuated from Dunkirk, she drafted one with a similar title, urging all writers not to indulge in mindless hatred of the enemy but to take a stand for freedom of speech and the free exchange of ideas, and to defend the dignity of the common man. Her appeal was signed by a number of leading writers, and sent to neutral countries (*JN*, 2:56).

By mid-June, Rache reported that *Europe to Let* was selling well in England, which, at such a critical time was, he thought, admirable (LD to SJ, 6.10.40). Jan Masaryk also wrote to Margaret thanking her for the book and the spirit that imbued it;[18] but again, Margaret had moved on. Despite all distractions, she had completed another novel by June 15, as the Germans were entering Paris. In this work, she developed a method she had been exploring for some years, transforming political events into a landscape that would bring them alive for her readers. Now, in *Cousin Honoré*, she drew together many of the strands leading to the French collapse, mirroring them in a small Alsace community. Margaret's central character, Honoré Burckheim, was, as she later revealed, molded from traits of both Hindenburg, the German president at the time of Hitler's rise to power, and Stanley Baldwin, prime minister in England through much of the 1930s, men who, she felt, had pursued a disastrous course (*JN*, 2:58–60). Other characters also drew on real people, but as she explained to Basil a few years later, expanding on what she had told Vera after their quarrel:

> No respectable writer uses a living person, in the sense of copying him down or trying to transplant him bodily into a novel. What happens is that when he meets a highly complex, highly intelligent . . . character, he simply cannot help quarrying in it, or making blood transfusions from it, for characters he invents or imagines. (SJ to LH, 8.17.52)

Characters in a novel had to evolve with the action and could never work if they were too indebted to any one living model. Because of the method she was employing in *Cousin Honoré*, many of the main characters had traits of contemporary actors on the European scene, but if the story was to live, it must have its own integrity, its own dynamic, and her depiction of Burckheim's peasant mentality bore traits of the old Whitby characters she had already explored from *The Pitiful Wife* to *The Moon Is Making*. Moreover, to bring her protagonist to life, Margaret had researched meticulously both the wine-growing area she was using as her base and the whole process of wine production. Nor was Alsace an idle choice of location, since Alsace had been French for centuries, then German in 1870, returning to France at the end of 1918. So Honoré Burckheim, the vine grower, had lived under both German and French rule, his name symbolically drawn from both cultures. He was wary of political involvement, concentrating instead on what appeared to be durable: the local community, his land, and vines.

On one level, this was a tale of Alsace represented by the people of one small community; on another, it brought together all the major components of the present crisis. So there were English and American characters contributing to the action as well as German and French caught up in the current intrigues, all intimately linked to offer "soundings" of the historical moment. To read it straight after *Europe to Let* is to understand why Harold Macmillan valued Margaret so highly as an enlightened commentator on her times, and this despite the difference in their political affiliations; her understanding of Europe in the lead-up to war was far ahead of most contemporary novelists. Nor did she confine herself to one mode of writing: *Europe to Let* is raw and passionate, seen through the eyes of its reluctant narrator; *Cousin Honoré* draws the reader into a close community, the events in the real Europe subtly subtextual.

Hope must have seemed fragile as Margaret finished the novel. The next day she had lunch with her old friend and colleague Rudolf Olden, who was hourly expecting internment as the sweep widened to include even the most dedicated anti-Nazis. He and his wife had already sent their two-year-old daughter, Kutzi, to Canada (*JN*, 2:65). For internment had accelerated. At the outbreak of war it was estimated that there were over sixty thousand German and Austrian refugees in England, not including a large influx from Czechoslovakia. Initially, it was mostly known Nazi sympathizers who were interned, but soon tribunals were examining all refugees, now all classified as "enemy aliens." These were divided into three groups: (A) those to be interned; (B) those whose movements were to be restricted; and (C) the remainder who (like Olden) were allowed to move freely. Now, however, after the French collapse in May, all those classified in the B group were brought in, and when Paul Reynaud's government left Paris for Bordeaux in June, it was clear that all those in the C group who were under seventy would be interned.

On June 22, the French accepted the Armistice terms, and all hostilities in France ceased on June 25. Charles de Gaulle had already left for England, and his broadcast on the BBC, telling his countrymen to fight on, appeared to have gone unheeded. Like so many other families, Margaret's own was increasingly affected by the threat of invasion. Guy was becoming restive at Cape's, had joined the Home Guard, and was trying to join the army, despite being fifty-one; eventually, Margaret's old student friend Archie White, who had won a Victoria Cross in 1916 and was now a colonel in the Army Education Corps, would invite him to join them, but that would be some time later. Margaret did not discourage Guy, although he would be throwing any chance of security to the winds; she understood his hope of recapturing something of what he had experienced in World War I. As his late autobiography would acknowledge, he and Margaret had "no . . . worldly sense" (GC, AKOS, 185). But Margaret had her practical side, and now her first priority was Do and the children.

For the fear of invasion and of collaboration was very real. Writing to Basil about her anger and grief over the loss of France, her dismay that the French premier Reynaud had been outmaneuvered by pro-Nazi sympathizers in government, Margaret wondered, "if we're underestimating the power of our own Lavals and Bonnets" (SJ to LH, 6.26.40). She had good reason to be active on behalf of Do's children, since they were too young to qualify for any government scheme, and must be placed where her American royalties could support them. Meanwhile, she set about destroying any papers that might endanger others. She was, in any case, an inveterate destroyer of written matter, whether to protect her privacy and the privacy of others, or whether to lessen the burden of belongings in her and Guy's peripatetic life, we can only speculate (SJ to VB, 6.28.40; JN, 2:70,71).

There was another matter much on her mind. The increasing and all-too-often inhumane speed of internment was a matter of great concern for the PEN. Rudolf Olden was sent in June to the Warth Mill internment camp in Diggle, outside Manchester, a run-down building with conditions worthy of a nineteenth-century prison of the worst kind. He had been a radical lawyer and journalist in Germany, had fled Germany (on skis) to Czechoslovakia, then come to England, being deprived of his German nationality in 1936 because of his anti-Nazi stance.[19] Now, despite the fact that he and Robert Neumann had been helping the PEN to vet incoming refugees and were proven anti-Nazis, they were both detained in the final tranche. Ironically, Olden had applied for naturalization in January 1939, but the process was held up by the war. At the outbreak, he had offered himself in vain for national service, while his wife, half-Russian, half-British, was forced to leave the Air Raid Precautions (ARP) because she was married to him.[20] Profoundly Anglophile, Olden was heartbroken to be classified as an "enemy alien," and the harsh conditions at Warth Mill destroyed his health. Neumann was interned under better conditions on the Isle of Man. His partner, Rolly (Franziska) Becker, wrote to Margaret, thanking her for her "excellent letter on Robert and Rudolf" which Margaret and Hermon had sent to the *TLS*. It was a powerful protest:

> When the Nazi dictatorship forced all liberal writers into exile, under penalty of the concentration camp, these exiles were received in this country as the representatives of the true German culture. Many of them have been here since 1933. The work of such writers as Rudolf Olden and Robert Neumann, since they came here, has been that of active opponents of the Nazi regime. Now that we ourselves are at war with this regime these representatives of the true German culture are discovered by the authorities to be a danger to the country, and their intelligence and experience are hurriedly interned. . . .
>
> It should be possible, even now, to retrieve from the camps those German and Austrian writers who are known by their works as bitter opponents of Nazi Germany. . . . We need for our own sake to make it clear that the principles those writers hoped to assert in exile are as actively to be defended as our homes.[21]

Margaret and Hermon were following up all such cases, but Robert and Rudolf were peculiarly their concern, as they had made huge contributions to the PEN over the last years. Appeals on their behalf were also being made to the States, as both would have a better chance of release if they had visas for America.[22] Meanwhile the sense of betrayal was all too clear: Robert cabled Margaret from House 14, Morragh Camp, Ramsey on the Isle of Man, saying that in that camp

no less than 40% of the internees have been in German concentration camps. Many of them . . . have fractured skulls, blinded
eyes, wrecked nerves and the like. Many of them have been
condemned to death by the Nazis, and there are Gestapo war-
rants out against scores of them. But their flight from death in
Germany happened too early or too late to please a provincial
tribunal judge.[23]

Margaret was dedicated in her work for such people, often digging
into her own pocket despite her straitened circumstances. Furthermore,
her debts had not prevented her from taking on yet another unpaid job.
A central register had been set up at the Ministry of Labour in February
listing scientists, academics, professionals, and industrialists who might
be drafted into the Civil Service to improve the quality of its support for
the war effort. Now Margaret had been recruited to help "clean up," as
she put it, the register, which had "all kinds of other things injected into
it, and the hours, which were to have been 10–5.30 stretch indefinitely"
(SJ to VB, 7.3.40). These long hours at the ministry, her work for the
PEN, and her efforts on Do's behalf were inevitably haunted by events in
France. In July her friend Denis Saurat, head of the Institut Français, and
at that time close to de Gaulle, told her of a "layer of rottenness that had
spread right across French society, and seeped down" (SJ to VD, 7.20.40).
Indeed many of the French in England supported Philippe Pétain when
he set up his government in Vichy, as they distrusted de Gaulle, believing
he supported the left-wing Popular Front. Saurat said the French premier, Reynaud, was not a strong character and his lover, Helen Bau-
douin, had far too much influence over him. He said Reynaud had been
expecting that Pétain would be forced to reject the German terms and
that he, Reynaud, would "come back stronger, and retreat with a tamed
Cabinet to Africa — but 'he didn't know his Pétain'" (SJ to VD, 7.20.40).
Saurat said "that Pétain is really and truly gaga, and thinks he is Joan of
Arc" (SJ to VD, 7.20.40). What had upset Margaret most, she told Valentine, was Saurat's allegation that there were a number of British Foreign
Office officials who wanted to make a deal with Pétain and Mussolini.
She had no idea whether this was true, and worried about the difficulty
of knowing which rumors to believe. On the home front, one of her prob-

lems had been resolved: Do and her children were off to the States. Margaret was left to cope with a brother-in-law who would be "as melancholy as a gib-cat," a Guy still desperate to get into the army, and a daughter-in-law who was staying with them while Bill was in the Shetlands and who was in a highly emotional state. Margaret felt exasperated and resentful, and ashamed of her reaction in so highly charged an atmosphere (SJ to VD, 7.20.40; JN, 2:72–76). She herself was faced with yet another task: the MOI, in the person of the writer Graham Greene, had asked her to write a thirty-thousand-word booklet on women working in war factories. She was at first reluctant, but would "like the chance to know what they are thinking" (SJ to VB, 7.31.40).[24]

As for Vera, she had run into trouble, having been refused a permit for her next lecture tour in the States by the MOI because of her pacifism, and Margaret was quick to offer support. She was, she said, "mildly surprised" that higher authority had not quashed Graham Greene's scheme for her own factory booklet, but thought it was because she was not primarily seen as a pacifist. She now mentioned to Vera that she was no longer a sponsor of the PPU:

> My loathing of concentration camps and the Nazi creed is as
> deep as my loathing of war, and I've never managed to achieve a
> single mind on the issue since after 1933. Such mental peace as
> I have achieved has only come since I decided that it was dishonest for *me* to be single-minded. (SJ to VB, 8.6.40)

This was the first Vera had heard of Margaret's resignation and, considering the depth of her own commitment to the pacifist cause, she took the revelation fairly well. However, she did say she felt sure Margaret would agree that resigning from the PPU when one might suffer for belonging to it "was rather like playing the part of Peter before the crucifixion" (VB to SJ, 8.7.40). Margaret, quick to spot the danger of another quarrel, replied placatingly (SJ to VB, 8.8.40). At the same time her patience with Vera was sorely taxed by something much more serious. Plans for her own visits to war factories had been going ahead: the Ministry of Supply had sent a list of the places she should visit, places like Woolwich and Cardiff, but suddenly her permits were withdrawn. It appeared that, without telling Margaret, Vera had written to the Home Office asking why Margaret should be given permits when she, Vera, who had wanted to visit factories for her book *England's Hour*, was not. Fortunately, Margaret had the backing of the MOI, and found a copy of her letter of resignation as a PPU sponsor, written in March 1939, so her permits were reinstated. She decided not to discuss the matter with Vera, but this act of treachery, as she perceived it, must have rendered their friendship more fragile (SJ to IR, 8.28.40); the insidious effects of war were all too clear.

Margaret was also finding life difficult at home, as her daughter-in-law was very unhappy, missing her husband. Margaret had an article and a thousand letters to write, and she could neither cope with the housework nor afford a housekeeper if Barbara were to leave. And although Do was determined to come home once the children were settled, Margaret thought she might not be able to get back, as berths on ships were hard to come by (SJ to VB, 8.8.40). Moreover, air attacks were growing in intensity and the village of Mortimer was too close to airfields and munition dumps for comfort. It was therefore all the more extraordinary that the Society of Authors had moved its center of operations nearby; but those responsible for evacuation of various kinds did not always recognize from maps the dangers of a perceived "safe" location. In mid-August, Margaret told Valentine, "I have just been watching an air battle from the lawn, a silly thing to do, I know, but it is the first I have seen" (SJ to VD, 8.16.40). She told how, while waiting for confirmation of the places she must visit for her factory booklet, she was reading books about France alongside works by Gide, Giraudoux, and Valéry, reading that would feed into her next novels. Recently too she had talked to de Gaulle's aide-de-camp responsible for propaganda, and he had told her he had no idea what form the new France might take. "But all these people are very Right Wing too," Margaret said, and she worried that the British government's reluctance to face the need for social change could result in something all too similar to Pétain's policy (SJ to VD, 8.16.40).[25] This fear was compounded by Rudolf Olden's experience as an internee. He had been released in early August,

> but he was too ill to see me. His wife told me that he was in a disused cotton mill, 1500 of them where 400 would have been too crowded, nothing but bare filthy rooms, no latrines, no beds, not

even straw, the food so disgusting that few of them could keep it down. It has nearly killed poor Rudolf. (SJ to VD, 8.16.40)

He had only been released because he had been offered a position at Columbia University in the States, and was now waiting for a ship.

Margaret and Hermon were struggling to free more from internment while they also worked to form links with various European governments in exile: Margaret lunched, for instance, with the Polish foreign minister August Zaleski; and as Beneš had been recognized by the British as head of the provisional Czech government in exile on July 3, the PEN kept very close to him and to Jan Masaryk (*JN*, 2:87).[26] By the end of August, Margaret had to start her journeys to factories "almost at once," and it was now that Margaret's sister Winifred heard she had been successful in her application to work in censorship, and would be based in Bermuda. Margaret was much relieved, as she had worried that her sister had been too badly affected by the years of nursing their mother to be fit for a return to the job she had held in the last war.[27] The appointment was eventually confirmed, only five days before Winifred was ordered to leave, so Winifred and Margaret had to rush round buying clothes, a difficult business, since shops shut for air raids while customers either had to find a shelter or wander the streets until the all clear was sounded (SJ to Brown, 9.7.40).

On one of Margaret's visits to London in September, she found Vera at the end of her tether, what with the refusal of permits and the air raids. So Margaret took her back to Mortimer, where she would stay on and off for several weeks (Berry and Bostridge, 405). By mid-October, Margaret was also housing a pair of refugees; she told Vera, who was on one of her excursions, that these old people were "suffering from the double shock of the bombing of [their lodgings] and a very narrow escape in a daylight raid when they were setting off to come down here" (SJ to VB, 10.14.40). The doctor had said the frailer of the two could not be moved for a fortnight, and Margaret could not write because, as she said, "people would apologise for keeping a man writer washing up and doing chores and running errands, and take it for granted that a woman writer must" (SJ to VB, 10.14.40). She had no domestic help now, she reminded Vera, as Barbara, her daughter-in-law, was on night duty with the ARP and needed her sleep. It was impossible to plan ahead: given the intensity of the Blitz, Margaret was unsure that she would be allowed to visit the arms factories at Woolwich and Enfield the following week, "or whether infuriated managers will tell me to keep out of their works in the middle of a Blitzkrieg" (SJ to VB, 10.14.40). No doubt this long letter was a reminder to Vera of just how much Margaret was having to fit into her overcrowded days.

For inevitably, Vera was adding to her burdens. Living with her at close quarters, Margaret, her own nerves strained to breaking point, found her "a monument of self-pity, vanity, unconscious malice. I have never before understood why people dislike her" (SJ to IR, 10.15.40). Margaret had long-distance responsibilities too: Whitby had been bombed twice and she had to dash up to check on her father and her mother's sister (SJ to IR, 10.15.40). Then her novel was hit by the Blitz, as the binder's warehouse and its stacks of *Cousin Honoré* had been bombed, and some of the stock destroyed. Indeed, during 1940, large quantities of bound and unbound stock were lost in the Blitz — such publishers as Cassell, Gollancz, Lane, Allen and Unwin, Harrap, Duckworth, Baillière, Tindall and Cox, and Werner Laurie all suffered. Fire swept Paternoster Row destroying stock, records, and the actual houses of many of the oldest publishing firms in the country. Hardly any publisher went unscathed.[28]

The Blitz soon made visits to arms factories unfeasible, and Margaret had to give up on the projected booklet. She wrote her report and an article, and hoped to write something more substantial later (SJ to IR, 10.15.40).[29] The notes she had taken were lively, inviting comparison with the Mass Observation project, founded in 1937. For Margaret, like Mass Observation observers, recorded conversations with many women of different backgrounds, bringing them and their concerns vividly alive. She had already realized that "the problem of labour supply differs so widely from locality to locality . . . a general book could only have been a vague and chancy effort."[30] Instead, she offered detailed recommendations on where to attempt recruitment and where to place publicity. Drawing on her own advertising experience, she advised that posters "must make an appeal as direct as a face cream advertisement" (SJ, draft report). She told how a number of the girls had described

> with horror a film called "A Call to Arms". . . . If you want to at-
> tract men into the Army you do not send out pictures of the dying

and exhausted. A film meant to attract vast numbers of women into the factories must not — in stressing the fact of the national emergency — forget to stress the advantages and the pleasures of factory life. Film the keep-fit classes, talent-spotting concerts, the City Hall dances . . . at Curran's (Cardiff); the tennis courts and the Kynoch Follies at Kynoch's (Witton, Birmingham); the kitchen of the canteen at Curran's and the exceptionally varied menu of dinners and high teas there; the white-coated girls in the aeroplane instrument room at Ferranti's (Hollinwood); the big light rooms and ultra-modern equipment at the R.O. Factory Blackburn; the Welsh girls and women singing in the air-raid shelters at Curran's; the smiling young woman operating a capstan and soaking herself in oil at Enfield. ("I always wanted to be an engineer and now I am," she said to me. She used to be a tooth-brush examiner. Good propaganda — that remark). (SJ, draft report)

Margaret's observations were compassionate and pragmatic. Her notes were based on an impressive range of visits to many different areas of the country, given the short time that they were possible. Subsequently, as the danger of air raids eased, others explored and published on the factories; Inez Holden's *Night Shift*, for instance, came out in 1941, as did Edith Summerskill's *Women Fall In*, while Amabel's *Women in War Factories* was published in 1943. But by this time, Margaret was embroiled in very different tasks.

Vera continued to be a trial and an anxiety, talking of suicide, taking lonely walks, and sobbing. Margaret was both exasperated and aware of the pathos inherent in her "blindworm honesty," feeling that she could not consider turning Vera out until George Catlin could return from the States (SJ to IR, 10.21.40). For London was no place to be:

> There is no water or gas from Whitehall to Piccadilly, a bomb has wrecked St James's church in Piccadilly, and a cinema in Leicester Square . . . , Macmillan's office has a 1000lb time bomb outside it, all the lavatories in the War Office or is it the Admiralty are choked, that amuses me, every single night some

other part of London is crumped and you never know when you go up whether your office is still standing. (SJ to IR, 10.21.40)

Yet despite such hazards, Hermon and she somehow kept up their relentless efforts for internees. They would, for instance, with the help of a member of Parliament, newspaper support, and a question tabled in the House of Lords, obtain the release of the eminent German writer Wilhelm (Willy) Schutz by January 1941. But they would be less fortunate with the less well known writer Fritz Seidter, despite very favorable references: he would not be released until January 1945, having spoiled his case, according to the Parliamentary Committee on Refugees, largely because he had threatened a hunger strike.[31]

For Margaret and Hermon one case would always be especially haunting. Rudolf Olden had been released, but the harsh conditions in his camp and the shock of being treated as an enemy alien had left him a broken man. Instead of becoming the naturalized British citizen he had hoped to be, he was only freed because he had been offered a post in the States. Margaret and Hermon tried desperately to stop the deportation, while Rudolf himself continued to advise them on writers still in the camps. He and his wife, Ika, finally sailed for the States aboard the *City of Benares*, a ship full of children. A few days later, Margaret learned that the ship had been torpedoed. Facts about who had survived, who was drowned, were hard to come by: but some time later it was confirmed that Rudolf had been too frail to go to a lifeboat, and Ika had refused to leave him (*JN*, 2:88).[32]

Given all there was to do, Margaret agreed to serve a third year as PEN president. By now the PEN had been designated by the Home Office the official Advisory Committee for reviewing the standing of writers who were interned. Margaret and Hermon agreed to serve on it, with two others. This would inevitably add to the heavy load they were carrying, but they were about to load themselves even more heavily, for Hermon was planning to launch a series of PEN books to give members a voice, and Margaret had agreed to be one of the contributors.[33] She was also managing to write the odd article. In the *Fortnightly Review*, she looked ironically at the way writers and artists were viewed in England, particularly by government. Their capacity to boost the morale of the nation after Dunkirk was being ignored, she said, while Goebbels was given a free hand in his use of propaganda to undermine and mock.[34]

By the winter of 1940, the conditions in the camps had improved when compared with the summer months. A report made for the PEN stated that

> in most cases sleeping in old factories on wet floors, has ceased. Catering is more regular and the care by organisations and friends of the internees makes itself felt.[35]

But most writers were badly in need of clothes, as their garments were old and they had only lightweight coats. Often their footwear was beyond repair, and there was a dire need of warm underwear as rooms were usually cold. Moreover in most camps the food consisted almost entirely of porridge, beans, rice, potatoes, margarine, salted herrings, and kippers, and the helpings were very small. The writers were not fastidious, the report stated, but many had gastric problems and could not eat the food provided; there was a lack of fruit, vitamins, and fats. Furthermore, although there was a trust fund, each internee was only allowed one shilling and sixpence a week, which did not even cover postage; they could not afford paper or books. As a result, "their spirit and their capacity of [sic] mental resistance is getting weaker as the days pass." They appreciated what young British men were suffering, the report said, "but there is still a decisive difference — the barbed wire fence." A note on this report stated that it made grim reading, especially considering the caliber of the men involved: intellectuals, proven anti-Nazis, many of them by no means young.[36] Moreover it was not only those in the camps who needed care. At Leonard Woolf's suggestion, for example, the English wife of Fritz Rudolf Könekamp, a German artist and writer who had been interned and deported to Canada, wrote to Margaret begging her help; if he was to be released his wife could join him in Canada but "I have been refused my application to regain my British Nationality, also my application to join him in voluntary internment."[37] Margaret's reply had cheered her, she said later, "the first human touch from anywhere relating to this," but despite all Hermon and Margaret's efforts, he was not released, because, it would seem, he was accepting his lot too passively.[38] Even when released, refugees could be a source of anxiety.

One was bombed out on his first night back from internment and was left destitute. Although he had proved difficult in the past, when he had rejected a reduced allowance from the steadily shrinking Refugee Fund "as long as the stuff in Windsor [the royal family] is living at such a great rate," this was seen as the protest of a man at the end of his tether, and he was treated sympathetically.[39]

Guy was still working "resentfully" for Jonathan Cape (SJ to VD, 11.12.40). His efforts to get into the army were met with politeness but nothing more. Bill was now based in Liverpool, still flying civilian planes, and Barbara had joined him there. So there was no domestic help for Margaret at a moment when the role of the PEN as official adviser to the Home Office for all writers and men of letters in internment had inadvertently landed them with a wider franchise. While the Royal Academy looked after artists, the Royal Institute after architects, and the Royal Society after scientists, the universities' responsibility for all professors had been eroded since the PEN had been named, Margaret told Valentine, on a government white paper rather than academic institutions. As a result, every kind of scholar was now writing to the PEN from the internment camps, asking for support. Margaret and Hermon were breaking their backs trying to help them (SJ to VD, 11.12.40).

The idea for another novel Margaret had been developing between assaults on the Home Office had started life in September, as "the faceless ghost of a play about both wars . . . , and I made a few notes for it at night" (JN, 2:89). In November she began to write, and since this work started life as a play, the clash of ideas was fought out in dialogue. Normally, when she turned a play into a novel, the meticulous painting of context, the fleshing out of characters would be the next step. But in this case, since Margaret had little time for revision, she decided to let dialogue remain central, capturing different points of view among a group of soldiers caught up in the rapid German advance into France the previous June.

Slowly though her current writing was progressing, *Cousin Honoré* was published toward the end of November (LD to SJ, 11.13.40). The reviews were on the whole approving, although the significance of the setting in Alsace rather than in central France was almost universally missed, as was the transferred political actuality from the public stage to the small village.[40] Margaret was very depressed. However, it must have been a small consolation that, in its Christmas book section, the *TLS* recommended *Europe to Let* alongside Thomas Mann's *Lotte in Weimar* as one of the best novels of 1940.[41]

All this time Vera had remained in Mortimer and Margaret, despite her frustration, still tried to help and encourage her. But things were about to change, for Do had finally come home. She had been unable to get a passage in New York, but had been undeterred, making her way to Canada and sailing from there. The family heard nothing except news of yet more ships being torpedoed; but eventually, in mid-November, Do arrived safely in Liverpool, and was soon back in Mortimer, taking over the running of the house (*JN*, 2:91). Margaret's initial relief must have been considerable, as she could now, in the short times snatched from her work for the PEN, get on with her own writing. Do, however, very much her mother's daughter, did not approve of what she saw as her sister's "soft" attitude, and certainly did not see the need to treat the volatile Vera with "any special sensitivity" (Berry and Bostridge, 405). There were constant arguments, and Do demanded that Vera pay rent. For a number of weeks, this uncomfortable arrangement continued, much to Margaret's embarrassment, with Vera moving between Mortimer and London (VB to SJ, 12.28.40; SJ to VB, 12.30.40).

The Worsening War

In January 1941, Guy was at last invited, thanks to Archie White, to join the Army Education Corps, immediately giving up his position at Cape's and all chance of a future directorship, and leaving for a week's training at the Army School of Education in Brockenhurst (SJ to VB, 1.15.41). Soon after he left, Vera returned to Mortimer for a short visit, when she seems to have further antagonized Do (SJ to IR, 1.20.41). Inevitably, Margaret was caught between her sister and her friend, but managed to keep her head down as she turned *The Fort* from a play into a novel. The book was nearly finished by the end of January, and she was pleased by the way the dramatic form had transformed itself. The confining of the action to a farm cellar in the northeast of France, the classical form, obeying the unities of space, time, and action, and the lack of narratorial comment ensured detachment. Each character represents different elements during the invasion of France; they are types, "soundings" of both World War I veterans, English and French, and of young World War II soldiers, representing tensions between Frenchmen as well as links across national boundaries, even between a young Englishman and a young German prisoner. At the end of the tale, the main German force arrives; there is shooting, then silence. What follows is again in the vein of classical tragedy: the two Englishmen appear to be sleeping, but there is a third, in the stained khaki of the earlier war, by the shaft. The veteran of World War I wakes and exclaims, "Jamie! What luck, when did you get back?" and the novel ends.[1] Some critics complained about this "ghost," failing to appreciate Margaret's aim to show, as she would increasingly show, the repetitive nature of human conflict from ancient times to the present, the timeless tragedies, each one haunted by the last, just as her drama was haunted not only by the past war, but by echoes of Sophocles, Euripides, of Auden's poem "Spain," and of Giraudoux's *La guerre de Troie n'aura pas lieu* (*The Trojan War Will Not Take Place*). The novel is haunted by the previous war throughout, and this haunting is simply given body at the end. Margaret's experiment in transporting into her tale techniques usually associated with classical drama is very much her own, a subtle and unpretentious exercise in a different kind of narratorial detachment than she had explored before.

The article about Margaret's visits to arms factories came out now in the *Atlantic Monthly*.[2] She wrote in the first person, and in story mode, offering a glimpse of an old woman in the street, "preserved in a cocoon of garments by their natural salt," snatches of dialogue, a sketch of girls who had never left home before, the drama of their lives ("Women on the Spot," 169). At one point, she homed in on a first-aid post in a London dock quarter as "the bombers came over the docks and dropped their bombs, one, two, three, four, — an interval — five. The first wounded began coming in about ten o'clock." Then she moved on to a "rest centre" of "two bare rooms, unprotected, where exhausted terrified mothers sat crouched over their children, as if flesh and bone were a protection from the bomber" ("Women on the Spot," 173). Government officials had been shown this: "They didn't think so well of themselves when they went back" ("Women on the Spot," 173). The range of women's experiences was caught with wit and a keen eye for tragic potential.

In the early months of 1941, Vera was also trying her hand at war work, at the Lloyds Shelter in the City (LD to SJ, 1.29.41). She was furious with Do for letting her room and ousting her trunks from the attic, while Margaret apologized, trying to show Do in a more sympathetic light.[3] Writing to Hilary and Harrison Brown, Margaret sounded wistful, saying that their news of a simpler life brought relief from the realities at home. She told them something of the atmosphere in England, where, she wrote, "you'll find in one and the same intelligent person a tremendous admiration for Churchill as war minister with considerable doubts of his interest in post-war reconstruction" (SJ to Browns, 2.25.41).

Unsurprisingly, Margaret's digestion was giving trouble; she was swallowing barium and being x-rayed. There was no respite, as she was courted by a range of committees who wanted her support, either in name or in action. She had rejoined the Society of Authors after they backed Cassell against her; a year later she had been elected to their council, and now they wanted her as chairman.[4] There were requests for talks too: one she recorded for the BBC suggested that a phrase from her Yorkshire childhood, "Watch Out," was more appropriate than the current catchphrase, "Safety First."[5] The subtext of her talk was her recurrent fear that the war against Fascism was being countered by Fascism at home, a fear shared by many on the left, including Orwell and Priestley, as restrictive rules and regulations proliferated, and any criticism of government policy, voiced too loudly, invited quick censure. Margaret was wise to imply rather than state her fears, as there would soon be a further erosion of free speech: in January, Priestley had started a second series of his "Postscript" broadcasts, "aggressively democratic in feeling and tone," only to have the right-wing 1922 Parliamentary Committee raise objections. To his fury, he was replaced by the much less contentious writer and humorist A. P. Herbert.[6] By contrast, Margaret was invited to give another talk on "What I Am Reading Now," which she used to urge listeners not to succumb to disillusionment with France, as "Europe without a strong and healthy France wouldn't be the Europe we hope to rebuild after this war."[7] It was a persuasive talk, with considerable political content woven into its cultural thesis, and was more fortunate than Dorothy Sayers's commissioned talk, "Living to Work." For Sayers's talk would be suppressed "on the heterogeneous grounds that it appeared to have political tendencies," and that "our public do not want to be admonished by a woman."[8] Clearly Margaret, by presenting her argument under the guise of literature rather than as outright polemic, was not seen in the same light; she was becoming astute at evading the vagaries of censorship.

In July 1940, internees being deported to Australia on the *Dunera* had suffered horrific treatment: some twenty-four hundred people, mostly Jews, on a ship equipped to carry half that number, had been systematically robbed and abused by the soldiers supposedly guarding them. Many of the victims had already suffered cruelties in Nazi concentration camps, some could bear no more and jumped overboard. This scandal had gradually seeped into public consciousness, bringing a wave of anger in its wake. Now, as the *News Chronicle* reported, compensation was to be paid to the refugees without waiting for a Court of Inquiry.[9] Several of those affected were on the PEN books, so Margaret and Hermon Ould were involved in their cases. They also had an unwelcome distraction that had rumbled on for some months, as the president of the International PEN, Jules Romains, left for the States, confirming for Margaret her distaste at the poor showing he had made in 1938, when he had congratulated the French representatives for their part in the Munich talks (JN, 2:78). The final breach came when, ignoring Hermon's advice, Romains set up a European PEN in America, without further consultation with the English PEN and its associates in London. Unsurprisingly, since Romains had implied that Europe was finished, the European centers were not impressed, and his cavalier action, savoring of defeatism, was very damaging to morale. This quarrel would escalate over the ensuing months, and Margaret would join Hermon in the fight to support the self-respect of refugee centers and individuals based in England.

By this time, Basil Liddell Hart had become a friend with whom Margaret could debate the European situation; he treated her seriously both as novelist and correspondent. For her part, Margaret was not unwilling to argue with him for while she respected him, she did not by any means share all his opinions. He was still, in 1941, putting forward arguments for some kind of appeasement, but Margaret, despite her loathing of war, was convinced that there could be no kind of compromise with Hitler that he would honor, and she had no hesitation in saying so. And Basil, with all his military expertise and his liking for tough debate, respected her; their correspondence was clearly becoming important to them both. Each made notes on the other's arguments, so they could respond in detail. Moreover, in this year's letters, Margaret was developing the argument for her abandonment of pacifism in favor of the attainment of a just peace, in preparation for the pamphlet she would write for Hermon's PEN series (SJ to LH, 4.19.41). As this correspondence flourished, another was on the wane. For Margaret wrote to Vera Brittain in April, saying she was thinking of writing a kind of autobiography, but was concerned as she had kept so few "documents." She said she thought Vera was

> the only person who has ever kept any of my letters. I shall have
> to have these to read if you still have them. They may remind me
> of a few things I'd otherwise forget. (SJ to VB, 4.10.41)

Vera replied politely, saying she had not written for some time as she was very busy, but would send the letters (SJ to VB, 4.12.41). Margaret would write an autobiographical novel eventually, but her request at this juncture, just after Vera and Do had quarreled, seems very like an excuse to retreat from the former close intimacy. And Vera's cool response would seem to agree.

By this time, the paper shortage had claimed many victims, particularly among magazines and journals. It was all the more pleasing, therefore, when in April 1941, Reginald Moore brought out the first issue of a new quality journal, *Modern Reading*. It would stand alongside John Lehmann's *New Writing* and Cyril Connolly's *Horizon*, attracting over the years an impressive list of contributors including Stephen Spender, Graham Greene, V. S. Pritchett, and R. K. Narayan. Margaret contributed two stories in the first year: one she had published earlier in the *Atlantic Monthly*, "A Day at the Zoo," and a new one, "You Don't Speak French, Do You?"[10] But her writing had much to contend with, as yet again the work of the PEN escalated. The British Council now wanted to cooperate more closely, inviting Margaret to serve on a joint committee, while the PEN's responsibility for internee writers was being widely advertised in the internment camps by the Home Office.[11] The vetting of writers continued to raise problems, as old scores were being paid off, and it was not easy to know whom to believe. The case of Philip Pareth was all too typical. He was a Czech writer whom Beneš himself was prepared to support as an anti-Nazi, according to the editor of the journal *Europa*. However, he had apparently also been imprisoned in various countries for allegedly dubious money matters. In April 1941, a certain W. Necker spelled out instances of his cheating and lying in some detail, saying that in one book he maintained he was a victim of the Nazis, but in fact he had "left Germany rather involuntarily in 1932 and we had no camps then."[12] As a result, the leader of the Thomas Mann Group, Bernhard Menne, concluded that he was "a humbug."[13] So there was evidence that he was a total fraudster, evidence that was backed from various sources, and that had to be weighed against the apparent endorsement Beneš provided for him. The Court of Inquiry about the *Dunera* scandal was also in the offing; by the end of May, many more revelations were being published, the *News Chronicle* telling how a huge dump of articles belonging to detainees had been left on the quay after the ship docked, and that the sergeant major in charge was clearly implicated in the sharing of money made from the possessions stolen from the detainees. The public shock and dismay was profound, and Margaret and Hermon were following events closely, supporting those victims of this scandalous treatment who were on the PEN's books.[14]

Margaret was also trying to concentrate on the pamphlet she was writing for Hermon, *The End of This War*. The Blitz was at its heaviest, and in such circumstances, writing the pamphlet was not proving easy, as she told Vera:

> I forced myself to write 10,000 words on my position as a pacifist who believes that this war became inevitable in 1933 (the alternative being submission to [Hitler's] New Order). Really it was an agony. I've done nothing with them, because even now I'm not sure that I have cleared up my mind. (SJ to VB, 4.14.41)

This letter was a conciliatory gesture, but Vera's response, suggesting Margaret sell the pamphlet to the Ministry of Information, implying it was simply a propaganda document, exasperated Margaret. There was an undertone of simmering resentment now in their correspondence; Margaret regretted that she had not challenged Vera's views about the war in the past, as now she was suspected of too radical a change of mind. She told Vera, "I'm going to put a new page in my pamphlet, and deal with all the frankness I can raise, with a thing you wrote to me about the war" (SJ to VB, 5.5.41). In her reply, Vera appeared to accept the idea of Margaret quoting her: "By all means be as honest and frank with me in your pamphlet as you wish, and make use of any letter that I have written if it serves to help your argument" (VB to SJ, 5.10.41). This exchange, friendly as it seemed, may well have prompted Vera to release Margaret from the role of literary executor and guardian of her children. In her May 15 diary entry, Vera commented: "Don't want someone who disagrees with my views on most vital points to be in charge of either children or books."[15] Unfortunately, she omitted to tell Margaret of her decision.

In May, Guy was promoted to major and had "taken out the crowns he wore on his uniform in the last war, to put them on his new one," while Bill was still based in Liverpool, which was being heavily bombed. Now, unsurprisingly, Margaret had a stomach ulcer and was on a strict diet of milk and potatoes (SJ to Browns, 5.5.41). However, she gave herself no quarter, joining J. B. Priestley's 1941 Committee, which he had recently set up to explore social and political aims both for wartime and for peace; this gave him a platform to develop the ideas that caused his removal from the BBC "Postscript" talks.

Meanwhile, Cassell's truculent literary editor Desmond Flower had agreed to publish *The Fort*, and Margaret, while mulling over her pamphlet, was working on her next short novel, initially called "The Stones Cry Out" (published as *Then We Shall Hear Singing*), while already planning her next "immense" work, *Cloudless May* (LD to SJ, 5.15.41; SJ to LD, 5.20.41). Her fiction would continue to concentrate on Europe now, but she was fully attuned to things nearer home. At the end of May she told Basil:

> I'm balancing in my mind two things said in the last few weeks. The first is a wealthy woman . . . who said of her beautiful house: "If we lose the war, I shall turn the house into a hospital for German officers at once, and run it for them." The other is a brilliant young man in the R.A.F. who was offered the chance to become an instructor, but preferred to stay as a bombing pilot, "because it is such rotten work that I would rather do it myself than teach others." And, alas, he was killed ten days ago. The woman is still alive, so that the sum isn't worked out yet. (SJ to LH, 5.30.41)

It had been a poor spring, so that all the fruit in the Mortimer garden had been lost. The Battle of Britain, fought in the skies over England from July to September the previous year, had offered some respite, but American help was desperately needed — not just support, but total commitment. Moreover, Margaret was finding the French based in England very trying; she complained to the Browns of "an overdose lately of French egoism, which has a kind of exaltation missing from the just as pernicious English egoism" (SJ to Browns, 6.14.41). She worried too that a Central European ambassador had told her:

> "Mr. Churchill is a very great man, but I wish he would sometimes think about Europe. He said to me yesterday, Don't come

talking to me about what is going to happen to Europe after the war, I can't bother about after the war." (SJ to Browns, 6.14.41)

But at least, up in Whitby, Margaret's father was unperturbed. When the town suffered yet another air raid, she had rushed up for a week, as he was now very old and frail, living alone with a housekeeper. His house

> had several windows blown in. . . . He is cheerfully sure that the Germans are going to be defeated, and doesn't mind living in a half-darkened house — he refuses to have new glass put in, to give the Germans the pleasure of blowing it out again.[16]

Then on June 22, Russia entered the war against Germany. At first, many in high places were concerned about having a Communist ally, but attitudes would change as news of Russia's resistance came through. Indeed, the change of mood was echoed by the BBC the following year, when it would be broadcasting Russian plays and music (Briggs, vol. 3). The PEN Executive Committee, while looking to the war in Europe, had to attend to the growing anger at Romains's behavior. He had called his European PEN in America the legitimate successor to "the former P.E.N. in Europe" (PEN Exec. minutes, 6.23.41). So in another talk for the BBC, specifically addressed to the New York PEN, Margaret countered Romains's arguments, describing the arrival in England of soldiers and writers from half a dozen nations alongside several European PEN Centres. She mocked Romains's assertion that "Europe could no longer speak."[17] She went on to appeal to her American listeners, recalling Britain's own reluctance to read the signs of approaching war from the Chinese, the Abyssinians, and the Spaniards. She described how the British did see photographs of dead children but "they weren't our children" ("Britain Speaks"). She told how writers like herself had warned that the bombs would come, but the warnings were useless: "People can't look at what they can't see. And they can't see what they are not living" ("Britain Speaks"). She felt writers had failed to show the pictures clearly, and she urged American writers now to hold them up to view, not to give up on Europe. Her plea was passionate and eloquent, and shows that, much as she hated public speaking, she was developing a gift for it.

Now, formally, it was decided that the London Centre should make itself responsible for the organizing of the proposed International Congress in London that same autumn, from September 10 to 13. Their Anglophile friend Denis Saurat, as head of the Institut Français, welcomed the idea that the congress should be held there, and the writer Wyn Griffith proposed that its theme should be "Literature and the World after the War." This was a theme after Margaret's own heart, for she was increasingly concerned about the need to plan for the end of the war; she was desperately anxious that there should be no repeat of the mistakes made after World War I (PEN Exec. minutes, 6.23.41). Accordingly, she began to recruit writers. One of the people she invited, Arthur Koestler, would become a good friend, despite his complex and difficult character. In some ways, Koestler was a symbol of recent years in Europe. Jewish, born in Hungary, he had been exiled, fought in the Spanish civil war, been captured and sentenced to death; his experiences would form the basis, along with the Moscow Purge trials, for his haunting novel *Darkness at Noon*. From Spain he escaped to France, only to suffer the ghastliness of the French detention camps, was finally released, made his way, via the Foreign Legion, to England and had joined the Pioneer Corps in April of 1941.[18] He was already in contact with the PEN, as Cape's agreement to publish a translation of *Darkness at Noon* in 1940 had brought him into contact with Guy, as well as with Margaret at the English Centre. Margaret wrote to him in early July, telling him she had just read the proofs of his book *The Scum of the Earth*: "It's absolutely first-rate, a magnificent book. I've willingly become its advance agent."[19] It was the first book Koestler had written in English, telling how aliens were treated in the France of 1939–40, based on his own experience of harassment, bureaucratic obstructionism, the brutality of the internment camp at Vernet, and his service in the Foreign Legion before finally reaching England. He compared the camp at Vernet with Dachau, telling how survivors of the International Brigade that had served in Spain were abandoned and savaged in the French camp. He told of the French government's treatment of the two thousand in Vernet along with tens of thousands of other refugees. Their fate was sealed by Pétain's acceptance of paragraph 19 of the Armistice Treaty, providing for the extradition of political refugees to Germany. Koestler claimed that prisoners were used as scapegoats, their condition never investigated, despite the adverse public opinion about their treatment that was growing in America and England.

At the French collapse, he said, prisoners could have been sent to North Africa, allowed to escape, but they were kept behind barbed wire to be handed over, complete with confidential reports on them.

Margaret was working on her next short novel while recruiting for the congress and writing letters to the Home Office about people in internment camps. She was lonely in the big house, her sister and brother-in-law both working, Guy away:

> I start the day with a ration of energy, and spend it all before the evening. . . . It is so easy to do the same thing over and over again when one is alone. I find myself talking aloud. (SJ to Legrand, 7.12.41)

There had been a three-month lull in her correspondence with Vera. But in August, Margaret invited her to come and possibly contribute to the congress, although she rather spoiled the effect by adding that a PPU speech might not be suitable. Vera's reply was curt. She had no wish to make a speech, and had in any case distanced herself from the PPU: "The Christian pacifists are much closer to my position," she said (VB to SJ, 8.13.41). But then came the revelation of the decision made in May:

> I ought to have written to you long ago to tell you that in re-making my Will I finally did as you requested and relieved you of the responsibilities of guardianship and literary executorship which would obviously have been a great burden to you. (VB to SJ, 8.13.41)

Margaret had never asked to be relieved of these responsibilities; she had only ever said she did not want to be left money in Vera's will, and she was quick to protest in no uncertain terms:

> You have, you know, behaved very shabbily to me in the matter of your literary executorship and the guardianship of the children. I did not ask you for either of these privileged tasks, but I accepted them willingly and seriously. . . . You now wait "a long time" before casually telling me that you don't need me. . . . It

would be dishonest of me to pretend that this makes no difference to our friendship. It closes it, in effect. (SJ to VB, 8.19.41)

Margaret was in no fit state to make allowances for what must have felt
like a calculated kick in the teeth.

She was stretched far beyond her strength. Her father was ever frailer,
involving her in frequent dashes up to Whitby; she was deprived of Guy's
company, and the congress was imminent, involving a massive increase
in her correspondence (PEN Exec. minutes, 8.18.41). She wrote to
Koestler's commanding officer, for instance, to ask that the writer be
granted leave to attend; she approached the Ministry of Information,
now keenly supporting the event, asking them to use their influence (SJ
to AK, 8.18.41, 8.28.41). She sent invitations to a wide range of intellectuals, for the number of European centers based in London meant that
the congress would be "truly international and representative," making
the event a rallying point for intellectual debate.[20] The theme was confirmed as "Literature and the World after the War." Movingly, as news
of the congress reached the internment camps, Hermon and Margaret
received good wishes from anti-Nazi internees. One was Jan Petersen, the
German socialist writer, who recalled the first worldwide rally of writers
against cultural barbarism, at the International Authors Congress against
Nazism and for the Defence of Culture, in June 1935.[21] Fresh from Nazi
Germany, he had been one of the speakers, he recalled, alongside E. M.
Forster and Aldous Huxley.

While the planning was in progress, Margaret was facing yet another
upheaval, leaving the "huge inconvenient house" at Mortimer (SJ to Legrand, 9.3.41). Do and her husband would return to their small house,
and Margaret would join Guy in London at the end of September. There
was no area of her life that was secure and peaceful, and Vera kept writing
long, self-justifying letters, with added layers of reproach, accusing Margaret unfairly of quoting her letter in the forthcoming pamphlet "without
consulting me beforehand" (VB to SJ, 8.23.41). Not very surprisingly,
Margaret's replies, while clearly trying for a reasonable, patient tone —
"Your pacifism is one of the things I respect in you " — did not always
achieve it (SJ to VB, 9.4.41).

The congress itself was a great success. The guest list alone was impressive, including Beneš, King Haakon of Norway, and Jan Masaryk. Margaret was particularly delighted to welcome two American writers, John Dos Passos, whose American trilogy, *U.S.A.*, had so impressed her, and Thornton Wilder, author of another of her favorite novels, *The Bridge of San Luis Rey*. The American ambassador, John Winant, also came, and would become a friend. The editor of *Horizon*, Cyril Connolly, was there, and Koestler was given the requested leave. Jules Romains had, despite all Margaret's efforts, refused to come, and was voted out as international president. H. G. Wells declined at the last minute to replace him, and after a few skirmishes, it was decided to set up a presidential committee of Wilder, Hu Shih (the Chinese ambassador to Washington), Denis Saurat, and Wells.[22]

On September 11, Margaret gave the inaugural speech, on "The Responsibilities of the Writer."[23] She threw down the gauntlet at the outset, a daring act when the war hung so precariously in the balance. Recalling the Prague Congress, she said, "The writer must decide whether his work justifies him in ignoring a crisis which may lead to millions of deaths" (*TWS*, 165), but she did not linger on the war itself. She argued that

> writers lucky enough to be free to act as writers can . . . turn their energies to the task, so complex that it alarms all but the stupid and frivolous, of preparing to renew life after the war. . . . Anything like the moral collapse after the last war, the idiot rejoicings, the ignorance, the short-sighted greed, the apathy, would ruin us. (*TWS*, 168–69).

This would be her message for the congress: the future was what mattered, not the current war, not the past. And she went on to sketch her own idea of how their thinking should develop. Future isolationism was no use; there must be "a responsible and strong German government," and writers must remind those who would head reconstruction commissions that "the unit of value in the world is not a mile of frontier territory or a dollar or even a bushel of wheat, but a single human being" (*TWS*, 171). This "unit of value" must also be the priority of the writer, she insisted, brushing aside, by implication, any narcissistic concentration on exclusive interiority; the writer must look out, at fellow human beings, and explore their individual needs.[24] Margaret's address, in fact, voiced a theme which most of the speakers would echo: nothing less than the future of a world that was now ravaged by war. It was an extraordinary act of faith, given how dire the situation seemed in the Europe of 1941.

She closed the congress with a speech of rather different tone and content.[25] She stressed the symbolic value of representatives of all parts of Europe being in London: "Their presence makes London, perhaps for the first time in its history, a European capital" (*TWS*, 180). She then moved on to the importance of French culture. She offered an apologia for capitulation, echoing, without judging, old Honoré's love of his vines:

> Is he to be blamed, by an Englishman who has drunk his wine, has laid a caressing hand on the stones of his walls, for being too civilised to like the idea of total war? (*TWS*, 186)

This speech earned Margaret the reproof of one French delegate for over-romanticizing his country. However, it was not as naive a speech as it might appear; indeed, Margaret would be much more analytical in an essay written later that year, showing herself fully aware of the complexities of the French situation. This closing speech of hers was simply a gesture of friendship, a morale booster, aimed at the French in England at a moment when de Gaulle's Comité National Français had been constituted, but not as yet recognized by the British government. It was responding to a moment when a number of Frenchmen in London, including a few militants of the old Popular Front, were uneasy about both de Gaulle and his committee; and when Denis Saurat was putting his own friendship with de Gaulle in jeopardy by speaking too frankly about the general's increasingly autocratic methods. The French in England were, for various reasons, unhappy, and Margaret was simply reminding them of the symbolic role their country and culture played.

Responses to the congress were pleasing, both at home and in the States.[26] Margaret told Koestler his paper "was one of the Congress's good moments," and thanked her friend, the poet Eleanor Farjeon, fervently for her support (SJ to AK, 9.15.41).[27] There was the odd bonus too: Jan Petersen thanked both Hermon and Margaret for their efforts on his behalf, resulting in his release from internment in time to attend the congress.[28] And now Hermon was putting together a publication, *Writers in Freedom*, containing most of the congress speeches and messages from many who could not be there. Beneš contributed an introductory piece, and several Americans, including Archibald MacLeish, the U.S. Librarian of Congress, saluted their colleagues in England. The sheer range of participants from so many different countries, at such a critical time in the war, recorded in print what a triumph of organization the congress had been.[29]

Its success could also be measured by the large influx of new PEN members it brought in its wake. Relations with *La france libre*, which Hermon and Margaret had fostered for the past year, were also at their warmest.[30] Congratulations flooded in from many sources, the one sour note coming from H. G. Wells, who suddenly accused Margaret, on no evidence whatsoever — he just "felt it instinctively" — of making the PEN a lackey of the British Council, which Wells saw as "part of the machinery of the Foreign Office," and so, by implication, undermining the PEN's nonpolitical ideals (PEN Exec. minutes, 10.10.41). However, this manifestation of elderly truculence did not deter Margaret from being one of the writers contributing to a seventy-fifth birthday "Homage for H. G. Wells" in the *Adam International Review*. In this piece she acknowledged "that he changed the mental outlook of more than one generation, and not in his own country alone."[31] It was a generous tribute, and Wells relented, but the whole incident underlined the blurred distinction between remaining outside politics and being drawn in. For that same month, as Margaret would later recall, a Soviet writer who had translated and published the section "Between March and April" from *Europe to Let* cabled the Ministry of Information to say Margaret now had rubles to her name, whereupon she donated them to the Russian Red Cross. Subsequently, through the MOI, she exchanged "passionate telegrams and letters" with the secretary of an official Soviet body (VOX), who urged her to stand with them against the tyrant Hitler, to which she, "a little more austerely," agreed (*JN*, 2:56).

This same month, rather appositely, the *Fortnightly Review* carried a discussion of the Political and Economic Planning (PEP) broadsheet entitled "The Future of Germany," with Margaret as one of the participants. She commented mischievously that pamphlets were

> one of the horrors of war. Every man with a bee, spider, or death-watch-beetle in his bonnet conceives himself his fellow-country-

man's guide, and gives his passions and prejudices a run at the public's expense. To such the problem of Germany's future is especially attractive, and every solution from extirpation of the enemy to taking him to our bosom is offered with a naïveté only equalled by the author's vanity.[32]

While she was pleased to be part of a measured, thoughtful debate, she reiterated an anxiety she had voiced a number of times in the past months concerning the complacency of both Conservative and Labour MPs who put England's self-interest first: "Will such oratorical, romantic, un-inspired and half-educated representatives of the people make the peace the editors of *Planning* recommend?"[33] Her witty, pugnacious tone was very much that of the iconoclast of old, and here it was employed to warn against a tendency to stand back from Europe and its affairs in the future. For this had been and would continue to be a tendency of British governments, whenever European interests did not seem to mesh with their own.

There was no time for Margaret to rest on her laurels. She was now in post as chair of the Society of Authors, having been formally elected in July; she had agreed to serve for one year. In his retiring speech St. John Irvine welcomed her,

> first, because she is a gallant and courageous soldier in the struggle for intellectual liberty, a fighting woman who will not falter nor submit no matter how fierce the fight may be; and second, because she is the first woman to occupy a presidential position in our Society.[34]

Willing she might be, but she was seriously overstretched, and was never good at conserving her energies, choosing this moment when she had too many committees, alongside many and various writing commit-ments, to restart lessons in French conversation (SJ to Legrand, 9.16.41). Somehow, she was also managing to work on *Cloudless May*, even if its progress was slow, for, when Reginald Moore inaugurated a second jour-nal, *Selected Writing*, in October, Margaret contributed a chapter of the novel to his first issue.[35]

Guy was now established at the War Office, and as Do and her husband moved to their small house in Reading, Margaret finally left the old house in Mortimer, taking a flat in London: Flat 19, 88 Portland Place, close to Broadcasting House. She took the opportunity to return such letters from Vera as she had kept, excusing the address of the flat:

> Not the most salubrious neighbourhood, but I had to go some-
> where central, so that Guy was within walking distance of the
> War Office if communications break down at any time. He'll be
> travelling a lot, and I'll often be alone, so I've taken 2 rooms and
> a cupboard, and shall bring up enough things to make them into
> 2 bed-sittingrooms (SJ to VB, 10.9.41)

She had her own place again, but the move to the flat meant that she

> cooked, dusted, stood in queues in shops, listened to the sorrows
> and problems of exiled writers, listened with a more sardonic
> attention to the buzz of deliciously or wryly believable scandal,
> and went on writing a novel in any time left over. (GC, *AKOS*,
> 191–92)

Margaret's pamphlet, *The End of This War*, was now in print; while it was dated March 1941, she had continued to work on it sporadically since then. Her letter to Vera on May 5 affirmed the addition of a new page that quoted from one of Vera's letters; she would bitterly regret adding, at proof stage, a savage few lines on W. H. Auden, Christopher Isherwood, and Ralph Bates, who by now were in the States. The essay reiterated arguments rehearsed in letters, speeches, and articles over the past two years. It began by quoting a fourteen-year-old boy's letter to the *Times* in 1938, just after Munich, begging that war should be averted; Margaret's argument responded to his plea. She stressed her own hatred of war and its horrors, discussing the case for submission and quoting, anonymously, Vera's letter arguing the value of compromise. Margaret dismissed this argument as "wishful thinking" (*ETW*, 13). She then traced the reason for her own abandonment of pacifism, quoting the Czech experience of concentration camps and the attack on the life of the mind: "God help their alien subjects," she wrote, "on the day a German scientist discovers how to remove the brain and leave the body living and able to work" (*ETW*, 15), an idea central to the short novel she was writing, *Then We Shall Hear Singing*. She described the Polish experience of merciless bombings, the obliteration of villages. So far her case was carefully balanced, weighing the horrors of war against the horrors of submission to the Nazi ethos, but now she inserted the short passage she would later regret. Angered by what she saw as the intolerable tone of a letter from Bates, and another from Isherwood, she lost her temper, and added a few lines about them and Auden abandoning England, ending, "I don't condemn them: I have enough to do judging myself . . . [but] they are not our contemporaries" (*ETW*, 28). In other words, they had not shared the sufferings that Britain had endured since 1940, and so could not understand what they had failed to experience. So Margaret, rather dramatically, excluded them from the British present. After this outburst, the conclusion of her pamphlet was again measured, looking at the problems inherent in a reconstruction of Germany after the war. What her respected friend R. H. Tawney called "the Acquisitive Society" must end, the government must accept "that economic security is not an end in itself, but the means of a good life. . . . No one, no comfortably placed politician, should deceive himself into thinking that we are fighting to restore the England of doles, distressed areas, slums" (*ETW*, 40–41); for Margaret was always alive to the inequalities in prewar British society. We were, she said, "fighting for England, bad mother as she has been to many of us. But let her treat us better when it is over" (*ETW*, 45). Again she was looking to a postwar world where she hoped the poverty of the past, the poverty that had endured during the interwar years, would finally be eradicated.

She had taken risks in this pamphlet, she knew, but the attack she feared from higher authority did not materialize. Instead, she received a long, critical response to the pamphlet from Vera, implying that Margaret, and the PEN itself, failed to appreciate the atrocities of the Russian state. Vera lectured Margaret on how totalitarian states developed, and accused her of encouraging "people's blind and passionate hatreds"; this could not but anger Margaret, fully aware as she was of Stalin's doings in Russia, and wary as she always was of the extremes of nationalism. Vera did not stop there; she accused Margaret of quoting her letter "without permission," although indeed she had given this, and of misusing her words (VB to SJ, 11.10.41). Margaret clearly responded sharply, as Vera wrote again a day or two later, justifying herself at some length (VB to SJ, 11.13.41). But the breach was final. Margaret could no longer cope with Vera's increasingly frequent bouts of taking offense, and was too hard-pressed herself to prolong the correspondence. Other responses to the pamphlet were more heartening. Margaret received "hundreds of letters," including one from a committed champion of the poor, the archbishop of York, William Temple (*JN*, 2:96). In a *TLS* leading article, headed "Dilemma of Pacifism," the writer quoted her pamphlet in a passionate attack on pacifist "extremists" and their impracticality, provoking a lively debate. For there were pacifists who insisted that the evils of war were far worse than any of the atrocities committed by the Nazis, and that by going to war, the British were no better than their enemies.[36]

Margaret had now agreed, if required, to serve as president of the English PEN Centre for another year, and the committee was only too anxious for her to continue in office. But the war situation, the burden of work, the unhappy end to her friendship with Vera, and her own increasingly poor health meant that her mood was steadily darkening. In an article for the *TLS* in November, she observed how this war recalled "the catastrophes of the past, the destruction of cities, the collapse of empires, the return of poverty and barbarism, as a possible future."[37] Disturbingly, she said,

> Words no longer mean the same thing to men of equal intelligence in different nations — or to two men of the same nation. The word for justice, the word for pity, the word for truth has a different meaning according as it is spoken by a Russian or a German or a Frenchman. Or by two Englishmen, one of whom is a party communist and the other an old-fashioned liberal. (*TWS*, 137)

This whole article was an elegy for the shared values that Margaret felt had been eroded by the different ideologies evolving during the interwar years: Communism, Fascism, and Nazism. She feared the self-interest of different groups within society would diverge disastrously, reaching a point where they would be in danger of interpreting key notions, each according to their own point of view, ending the mutual understanding that, for her, was embodied in liberal humanism. For a time, her depression brought her close to idealizing the past. But for Margaret, the answer to depression was to work harder. As chair of both the council and the management committee of the Society of Authors, she wrote on the paper quota for publishers, along with issues of copyright, and a wartime problem by which publishers who could no longer issue an author's work because of the paper shortage sometimes blocked their writers' attempts to publish elsewhere. There were also issues with the BBC: Margaret was involved in establishing the Corporation's Minimum Terms Agreement (*Author*, Winter 1941).

CHAPTER 18

America Joins the War

The escalating paper shortage was seriously affecting writers, and Margaret, as both chair of the Society of Authors and president of the PEN, drafted a letter to the *Times*. It was hard-hitting: "In a war of ideas and machines it is folly to let half your line of defence founder from neglect. Our enemy has not made this mistake."[1] She was again attacking the government's tendency to undervalue its writers and artists as defenders of the West's ideas, while the Nazis used the skills of their writers all too cleverly. Stanley Unwin, the publisher, was delighted with the letter. Its appearance in the press was well timed; the Book Production War Economy Agreement was published the same day, spelling out the paper quotas for publishers.[2] Sadly, in the ensuing weeks, the atmosphere would deteriorate, with comments by reviewers about some books being a waste of paper, along with allegations that some publications were getting more than their fair share of paper, a tendency to snipe that was distressing.

On December 5, Margaret was formally reelected as president of the English PEN Centre (HO to SJ, 12.5.41; SJ to HO, 12.7.41). Two days later, the Japanese attacked Pearl Harbor, and American entry into the war was now inevitable; there was suddenly cause to hope. At this turning point in the war, Margaret's little novel *The Fort* was published in early January 1942, dedicated to Hermon; in the context, it must have seemed to readers like the closing chapter of an earlier phase of the conflict. Most reviewers failed to note its structure was based on the classical unities and disapproved of ghosts in what they determinedly saw as a straightforwardly realist novel, while some even managed to ignore Margaret's carefully sustained detachment, accusing her of "spilling sympathy" for even the German prisoner.[3] She was dismayed that it should be thought "foolish and wicked to show any sympathy for Germans or naughty Frenchmen" (SJ to HO, 1.10.42). But she had little time to waste on reviewers. By the beginning of January, she had finished her next short novel, *Then We Shall Hear Singing*, the tribute she wanted to pay to the Czechs.[4]

The idea of how to present this had come to her the previous spring when, meditating on the Czech experience of concentration camps, torture, and attacks on the life of the mind for her pamphlet, she had written: "God help their alien subjects on the day a German scientist discovers how to remove the brain and leave the body living and able to work" (*ETW*, 15). Clearly this idea was not realistic, and Margaret had to find a way of conveying what she meant by it. The answer came to her from Slavonic tradition, for the Slavs, as Margaret well knew, had a long literary history of presenting political or social ideas in folktale or fabular mode; Karel Čapek himself had written a number of works in this tradition, as had Kafka before him. So as an experiment, Margaret paid homage to a foreign tragedy by not attempting to empathize with events beyond her own experience, using instead a form that would be recognizable to Eastern European readers and pay homage to their literary tradition.[5] She was also determined, despite the harrowing nature of the Czech experience, not to allow her novel to be a vehicle for racial hate. As in *The Fort*, she remained true to her determination not to castigate all Germans; she drew a distinction between German officials following the old tradition of service, and the Nazi scientist, a man both fanatical about rising in society, riven with racial prejudice, and lost without his own peasant roots.

Occupied Europe, unnamed, although suggestive of Czechoslovakia, supplies the scene, while the Nazi scientist's name, Hesse, recalls Rudolf Hess, Hitler's close colleague who had so recently and inexplicably flown to Scotland.[6] Margaret uses an extended surreal image to reflect the man's mentality, an image suggesting a fusion of man and machine, the world opening to his surgical instruments:

> The aeroplane . . . seemed to be taking off from some promontory in his own life. . . . He rose with it, he lifted its metallic bones and webbed silk. His heart pumped blood into the engine

and drove it up and through low-lying clouds and sustained it without effort above the dazzling upper floor of the clouds in a light without bounds. When he wearied of the whiteness below him he moved his hands, and in a moment or two it parted, he saw the anatomy of the earth spread out as if for dissection, the open veins of rivers, the nerves of roads, the bony metacarp of hills stretching from a central plateau. (*TWSHS*, 14–15)

Margaret has Hesse share with the reader a scene that Bill must have described: clouds and the earth below seen from a plane flying high above. The scene delights Hesse; yet this is no pastoral moment. Hesse sees this world as something to be dissected; his pleasure is in his awareness of his power over all that lies below him. It is as if he is a god, controlling the movement of the clouds, supplying the energy to the engine that carries him. Here is the abuse of science, the hubris that Margaret would always warn against, even as she accepted its potential for good. For this man is a brainwasher extraordinary, with the skill to destroy "the higher functions of the brain without affecting the body in any way," leaving his victims "amiable, docile, obedient," literally brainwashed (*TWSHS*, 17, 19). Yet Margaret's story also stresses how folk memory keeps a people together, secured by their roots; the language is very simple, evoking a peasant community. Margaret had learned well from helping refugees to cope with the loss of language skills, and she must also have recalled Čapek's own championship of the Czech language in the short years between the end of the Austro-Hungarian Empire and the invasion by the Third Reich, both eras of imperialism imposing the German language of the conqueror. So in this work the District Commandant is compelled to admit the importance of language: "A man's own tongue is his only way back to his ancestors, to all that store of memories, commands, certainties, they left for him in the caves under his own few memories" (*TWSHS*, 53). Hesse takes young men away from the village he has chosen for "training courses . . . in citizenship" (*TWSHS*, 68). When they return changed, brutalized, Hesse turns to the women. But the Leader back home is dying and without his support Hesse goes to pieces, while in the village that he has ravaged, it is the old woman, Anna, so old that Hesse has ignored her, who gropes toward an understanding of what is needed for recovery.

For the novel insists that in all such invasions, the women are the repositories of true folk memory, and it is Anna who reminds the villagers of their roots and slowly revives their sense of their past. She appeals to the old traditional ways of the women, the embroidery, the cooking, the quiet talking while working on household tasks. She guides them to notice the value of something as simple as an old cracked cup that revives memories of the past as surely as Proust's madeleine biscuit. And she reminds them of the binding force of songs shared; it is the promise of singing together again that gives the novel its title. Gradually, at great cost, the women and their menfolk learn to resist their conquerors. Inevitably, the story is open-ended, but throughout, Margaret allows a subterraneous paean of faith in survival. Into this tale, she had put her sense of the tragedy of occupation, her faith in the resilience of peasant life to ensure the future of Europe, and she was devastated when Guy disliked the result.

As this would be Margaret's last book on her Cassell contract and she would be moving to Macmillan, Rache Lovat Dickson now proposed a way out of her financial difficulties. Margaret had been forced to take out a loan of two thousand pounds from the Midland Bank, and she had wondered whether, on joining Macmillan, they could hold on to her English royalties, lend her a thousand pounds toward her bank loan, and give her just a hundred pounds each time she submitted a book. In the meantime, she said optimistically, she would live off her small American royalties and occasional fees, and Guy could make a contribution. A fortnight later, Daniel Macmillan wrote to Margaret welcoming her to their list and announcing that he had just sent a check to Billee Keane Seymour at the Midland Bank, repaying her loan. A few days later, Macmillan made a contract with Margaret for her next three books, and a new phase was opening up for her as a novelist.[7]

Back at the PEN, Margaret and Hermon Ould, together with Cyril Connolly and Tom Harrisson of Mass Observation, were now members of a subcommittee, Young Writers and the War Effort, drawing up proposals for ways in which young writers in the forces might be given special leave when a particular "job of writing" was needed (PEN Exec. minutes, 1.21.42). The PEN's role had by now undergone many changes:

> What had been the comparatively simple and insoluble problem of finding money became the fearfully complicated business

of visas, permits, and later the back-breaking task of persuading Higher Authority to release the Germans and Austrians it had hurriedly and, when all is said and done, excusably swept into internment at the time when we here were looking with horror at the abyss of treachery and panic which had gaped open suddenly in France. None of this made any easier our first simple job of finding money for men and women exiled not only from their country, which is bad enough, but from their language — which is a kind of death. Especially for a writer.[8]

At least she and Hermon could congratulate themselves on helping to secure a large number of releases from internment toward the end of 1941 (PEN Exec. minutes, 1.21.42). One of those they were able to help was Richard Friedenthal, devoted friend of the eminent Austrian Jewish novelist, playwright, and journalist Stefan Zweig; Zweig's support had been instrumental in obtaining Richard's release as was the fact that Zweig, by now in South America, had procured a visa for Richard; Margaret and Hermon looked after him as he waited for a ship.[9] Yet Margaret's and Hermon's pleasure was just as great when they won the release of the unknown as well as the well connected. There had also been good news for Margaret on the family front: at 3:00 p.m. on January 24, she became a grandmother, as Barbara gave birth in Whitby to a son, Christopher, a grandson with whom Margaret would be closely involved in the future.[10] For the time being, however, she had no private life: she was working all day and deep into each night to honor all the commitments she had undertaken.

In February, the Royal Air Force (RAF) began its controversial blanket bombing campaign, sanctioned by the government with the aim of destroying the morale of the German people, despite evidence that the German Blitzkrieg on Britain had only achieved this in patches.[11] Margaret and Hermon, with their aversion to the horrors of war, were dismayed. Margaret told Rache she wanted to shed all her responsibilities and simply write; a few days later, hearing news of Singapore's surrender to the Japanese, she told Hermon she wanted to emigrate to the States (SJ to LD, 2.9.42; SJ to HO, 2.14.42). She regularly shared such escapist fantasies with her friends when she felt she had reached the end of her tether. In reality, she had taken on another major project. Soon after the

United States had entered the war, the Ministry of Information asked her to edit an anthology of prose and poetry by leading British writers, as a way of strengthening transatlantic bonds; so she was busy recruiting writers for this publication.[12] She worked with her usual intensity, while juggling her PEN commitments: the inevitable needs of refugees, a question as to whether Rebecca West would be willing to chair a Slav lunch. "I think she is pro-Russian, but is she pro-Pole?" Margaret asked Hermon warily; he replied briskly that, even if West were anti-Pole, she would, as chair, have to be polite (SJ to HO, 2.8.42; HO to SJ, 2.9.42). Sometimes she could combine more than one task: when Basil Liddell Hart asked the PEN's help for the artist and poet René Hackett, originally from the Weimar Bauhaus and currently supported by Robert Graves, she agreed to help with money and with letters of support to the British Council, the BBC, and the MOI, while taking the opportunity to ask Basil for an essay, which he agreed to give (LH to SJ, 2.9.42; SJ to LH, 2.11.42).

Somehow, Margaret was working on her long novel *Cloudless May*, even as she coped with a stream of refugee visitors and all this extra work. The pressure was too great; on February 23, the day Macmillan wrote to say he had paid off her bank debt, she told Hermon she had fainted twice and must slow down. Hermon, shocked, replied: "You and I have become such a perfect team that I shall feel like a one-armed man without you saying Yea to my Yea; but fights have been fought before with one arm tethered" (HO to SJ, 2.24.42). Margaret made light of her illness at first; then, at the beginning of March, Guy contracted mumps, and the gassing he had suffered in the last war slowed his recovery. This worried Margaret for more than one reason, as the lease on the empty old house in Mortimer ended that month, and she had to pack up what remained there, including their vast collection of books; it would take three or four days, she thought, and she was right in her estimate. She was also angry with the doctor, who "clearly thinks that women were born to nurse, and takes no interest in my problems."[13]

Unsurprisingly, she finally collapsed. By March 13 she was ordered to bed, with suspected heart problems. Again she made light of it, telling Hermon,

> I hereby authorise you to reject any attempt on the part of Vera
> Brittain to organise a memorial service for me. Engage the ball-

room at the Dorchester yourself, and invite all the refugees to free coffee and buns. (SJ to HO, 3.13.42)

But her doctor insisted on no more than four hours a day out of bed, and she had to shed as many burdens as possible, her own problems making her increasingly aware of how Hermon had sacrificed his own career as a playwright and poet to the needs of the PEN. For his part, Hermon was genuinely concerned for her health, but he would not contemplate her resigning from the presidency of the PEN, and finally she agreed to stay on "for a bit," admitting "the P.E.N. has become so awfully important a part of my thoughts" (SJ to HO, 3.28.42). Moreover, she had been deeply moved when, hearing of her illness, one of the refugees, Ernst Meyer, very poor and shabby, brought her a bottle of milk and four eggs. Noel Streatfeild and her housekeeper would also bring her two oranges, such a scarcity in war-torn London that Margaret would remember them in her old age as a miracle (SJ to HO, 3.28.42).[14]

It is at this time that Margaret's respect for astrology is increasingly obvious. Astrology, the reading of horoscopes, had become very popular since World War I, astrological journals regularly outselling more serious publications, as, after the traumas of war, people longed for some secure reading of the future. Nor was this interest confined to the uneducated: George Orwell and many other intellectuals regularly asked for their horoscopes to be read, often before deciding whether to undertake a project. Margaret had become a devotee as early as 1919, as were Mrs. Thoresby, wife of the *New Commonwealth* editor, and Margaret's first publisher, Michael Sadleir; and now she frequently sought readings from Hermon's great friend David Carver (SJ to MS, 12.12.19; SJ to HO, 4.7.42). Her need for readings would intensify over the years, and Guy too would pay them great attention. The psychological shocks administered by World War I could add this craving to have some certainty about the future to their many legacies.

By April, Margaret had regretfully resigned from the Books and Periodicals Committee of the British Council (SJ to Unwin, 4.3.42). She had also resigned from J. B. Priestley's 1941 Committee and was determined to relinquish her chairmanship of the Society of Authors. She was desperate to avoid the expense of a nursing home, only leaving her bed when she absolutely had to, as she fainted at the slightest hint of exertion. In the end, as Guy was away on a tour of duty, she accepted an invitation from Janet Chance, her former colleague at the PEN, shut up the flat, and stayed with Janet for ten days. Hermon urged her to be patient with her role as invalid; he wrote about things that would interest or amuse her, such as the lunch for the Slavs. He reported that it had gone remarkably well, and was clearly rueful that this, "the FIRST PUBLIC APPEARANCE of the four Slav peoples at a common table was completely overlooked by the press" (HO to SJ, 4.20.42). Margaret returned home at the end of April, but quickly realized that she could not stay in their London flat, as there she was inundated with visitors; many were demanding, some genuinely kind, but she was clearly too easy to access. Moreover, Guy's situation was uncertain; it seemed likely that he would be posted away from the War Office, and if so, she intended to follow him.[15] She was desperate to get the American book off her back, and was fretting as some contributors were, all too inevitably, late in delivering their essays (SJ to LH, 4.28.42). Mercifully, by the end of the month, Hermon was helping with the editing, which eased the burden.[16]

Margaret had written to the BBC a year earlier, asking if they might be interested in her original play of *The Fort*, although she felt "it is too gloomy and cerebral to be any use for broadcasting."[17] An internal memo of January 27, 1941, records that she had sent the script to one of her BBC contacts, but nothing seems to have come of it.[18] However, after the novel came out the following January — Desmond Flower having dragged his feet over publication — Val Gielgud, head of drama at the BBC, had himself written to Margaret's agent, Nancy Pearn. He said he found the novel quite absorbing and beautifully written, wanted to consider it for adaptation, and would like to discuss it with Miss Jameson.[19] Accordingly, on January 30, Margaret invited him to tea or a drink. "Wait while I look at the sherry situation," she wrote to him, "Yes — it's weak, but will hold for a few days"; and they clearly came to an agreement.[20] Political clearance was sought (a standard procedure) and granted on February 7, and the play was scheduled for broadcasting in May.[21] Three months later, Margaret told Hermon that "your book, *The Fort*" — she had dedicated the novel to him — "is being broadcast on May 9, late at night. They are being very cagey about showing me the script." In fact she was referring to the hour-long play that had been adapted from the novel by Barbara Burnham, an adapter for the BBC since 1933, who would become Margaret's mentor for later ventures into radio drama (SJ to HO, 4.7.42).[22] Margaret did not listen to the broadcast, but Hermon wrote that he thought "they made a pretty good job of it" and felt the adaptation had caught "the poetic quality in the language. It might almost have been written in verse. The actors felt this and did justice to it" (HO to SJ, 5.12.42). Margaret was apathetic, having decided to forgo parties, committees, and other functions at least until the fall. She told Hermon: "My will has never been so feeble. I know I must make a change in my life, but I do nothing, plan nothing, and just wait and wait for someone to say This is what you must do" (SJ to HO, 5.23.42). She was still completely exhausted, and agreed to go to North Wales in June, to stay with Amabel Williams-Ellis for a week.

Portmeirion, the village built, and still at that time being built, by Amabel's eccentric architect husband, Clough Ellis, as a response to the horror and destruction of World War I, had delighted Margaret when she and Guy first visited it. Clough had bought the site in 1926 and filled it with things he rescued from buildings being demolished. The overall design was Italianate, adapted to his idiosyncratic vision; he called it a sort of "home for fallen buildings," and housed such fragments as a baroque Italian doorway, an oval grille from the Old Bank of England, a Venus statue from Stowe, and dancing figures from Siam.[23] It was undeniably quirky, but Clough was passionate about preserving the integrity of the landscape; moreover his village was becoming a favorite meeting place for many intellectuals from home and abroad. Margaret enjoyed much of her stay there, but her break from responsibilities came to an end all too soon. When she got back to London, Hermon insisted that she must not get back into "another quagmire of engagements" (HO to SJ, 6.13.42). He had good reason to worry: she was one of the patrons and honorary members of the Free German League of Culture, and in June she was named as a member of the Honorary Exhibition Committee for an event titled "Allies inside Germany." There was no letup in the stream of people and organizations at her door (SJ to HO, 6.15.42).[24]

She decided to send the manuscript of *London Calling* to the States without one or two overdue items. The list of contributors was impressive, including Phyllis Bentley, E. M. Delafield, Walter de la Mare, T. S. Eliot, E. M. Forster, Harold Laski, Rose Macaulay, Phyllis Bottome, John Masefield, J. B. Priestley, Dorothy Sayers, Edith Sitwell, Frank Swinnerton, Rebecca West, Helen Waddell, Osbert Sitwell, and Edmund Blunden; the quality of the essays and poems was very high (SJ to HO, 6.19.42).[25] The book was to be published in November by Harper, and the proceeds would go to the United Services Organization. Margaret supplied the introduction (SJ to LH, 7.17.42).[26] In it, she acknowledged that the English were not always liked, recalling an American who "talks about our greed, brutality, . . . and our conduct in India, Ireland, Africa, and accuses us of pacifism, blood-thirstiness, servility, and arrogance" (*LC*, 2). The truth was, she said, that Americans "know too much about us, and not enough" (*LC*, 3–4), so she now offered details of the Blitz, the refugee crisis, and the work of the PEN. Her essay was a deftly nuanced plea for American understanding, thanking those in the States who were supporting the victims of war and the battle for a better Europe. She used touches of the personal to give abstract argument a human face, and one anecdote stands out. It tells of a woman passing the ruins of a bombed house, and an air raid warden asking if anyone can sing as there is a child trapped under the rubble who has asked for a song. The woman has no voice, but lies down in the dust and sings an old nursery rhyme. The child asks for it again, and she sings it a number of times, until there is no response. It is daylight before the rescuers can reach the dead child, the lower part of her body crushed. Was the woman Margaret herself? The rhyme was one she cherished, and she always said she had no voice. This anecdote, so simple, so redolent of an emotion that is left to the reader, makes the essay hard to forget.

Margaret's own immediate plans remained uncertain, as Guy had been promoted to lieutenant colonel, and a posting seemed likely. While she waited, news filtered through from Czechoslovakia: the assassination of Hitler's favorite, Reinhard Heydrich, had been quickly avenged by the wholesale massacre and destruction of Lidice. News of the full scale of the atrocities against Jews, both in and out of concentration camps, was now reaching Parliament and those with connections to it; for people like Margaret and Hermon, such news could only increase the conviction that all-out pacifism was no longer a tenable option. It was in this context that Margaret asked Vera Brittain again for the return of all her letters, gently suggesting closure to any further debate (SJ to VB, 8.1.42).[27]

Such news from Europe could only induce a feeling of helplessness, but there was no respite for Margaret from a stream of visitors, not just refugees but Americans eager to find out more about England at war (Judt, *Postwar*, 232). She was soon, as Hermon had feared, inundated, but she enjoyed securing contacts for Maxine Davis, whom she considered "one of the most intelligent — and best known — American women journalists" (SJ to LH, 7.12.42). She set up the meeting Maxine wanted with Basil, telling him that Maxine "will do more for us there than any of them" (SJ to HO, 7.13.42). She did not find the others in Maxine's party as impressive, but did her best, trying to coax Dorothy Sayers to meet a Mrs. Zenith. Sayers, ever the eccentric, protested:

> I always contrive to present [Americans] with everything they most dislike in the English character — stiffness, insularity, violent hatred of personal publicity, curt refusal to discuss my own work, and a cynical distrust of any sort of idealism.[28]

She was not good, she said, at parlor tricks, but would cooperate if Margaret really insisted. So there were light moments in coping with these visitors: on one occasion, Margaret told Hermon that a Mrs. Leslie Brown "is declining an invitation from Lady Louis Mountbatten for tomorrow evening in order to come out with me, clearly preferring intellect to blue blood (is it blue?)" (SJ to HO, 7.21.42).

But such moments of fun were few. Margaret was also involved, as chair of the Society of Authors, in "an exhausting struggle with the Publishers' Association" on the society's behalf, for the acute paper shortage had claimed many victims and occasioned many quarrels between writers and publishers.[29] By July, she was too ill to attend the Annual General Meeting of the society, but sent her address as chair.[30] In it she stressed again how the Nazis had made use of writers' talents, while the British government was much less imaginative: "No doubt it is very difficult to decide whether any given writer would be better employed driving a tank or peeling potatoes than in using a mind which has been trained to observe and persuade" (S of A speech, 7.29.42). But her main argument centered on the effect of the shortage of paper and labor, threatening to "whittle down" the rights of authors as against publishers, particularly in the matter of contracts (S of A speech, 7.29.42). The address was well received, and when John Strachey was voted chairman of the Committee of Management, "a sincere vote of thanks was passed to Miss Storm

Jameson for her generous services and valuable help during the period of her chairmanship."[31]

Given all the distractions, Margaret's writing was suffering, but when the radio play of *The Fort* was broadcast for a second time, she felt sufficiently encouraged to write to Val Gielgud, asking his advice on how to write plays for radio herself: "I do not know how much can be done in an hour. My ignorance is one reason why I should like to tackle such a job. I'm more interested in experimenting in forms than in anything else."[32] She was also involved in planning the PEN's twenty-first birthday celebration, due in November, with the now-agreed theme "The P.E.N. of the Future." All foreign groups in London would be invited, and Margaret realized that, with such a theme, the question of politics would inevitably come up. Could the PEN remain apolitical in the future? She thought not:

> My own view is that we can no longer avoid politics, in the sense that we can no longer avoid expressing an opinion on certain fundamental questions. We should however stick to the word ethics or some other word which lifts it out of the region of parties inside a nation.[33]

Meanwhile, the day-to-day pressures were unrelenting. The quest for funds to help indigent refugees was a necessary chore, as was the need to find jobs for them. Margaret and Hermon had to be on the alert for political attitudes that might affect the kind of work they suggested; Hermon spoke of one couple from France, "not at all pro-British, and almost chauvinistically French," which did not prevent them from expecting the PEN to help them find employment (HO to SJ, 8.31.42). But there were all too many poignant cases. A refugee friend of Margaret's, Lutz Weltmann, wrote to her at the end of August, clearly desperate. He had sent an idea for a propaganda book to the MOI, who were interested and had agreed to support his application for three months' leave in London; he was serving with the Pioneer Corps Detachment in Carmarthen. But the War Office had refused to grant him leave, as the Pioneer Corps were now being upgraded for service overseas; he had not even been reexamined for fitness despite having heart trouble and a limp. He said the Pioneers were treated as the black sheep of the British Army since internees had been blackmailed into joining their so-called volunteer companies. What was more, his Welsh wife had lost her job because she was married to a foreigner, and had then lost her unemployment pay because she was married to a British soldier. So she and their child were living a kind of "gipsy's life."[34] All this, he commented wryly, although he had been trapped in a ghetto in Hitler's Germany from 1933 to 1939. This was just one of the many cries of distress that came to Margaret and Hermon, involving constant letter writing and visitations to government departments with just a very small chance of a happy ending.

By September, Guy's posting had been confirmed: he was to be commandant of the new Army Bureau of Current Affairs (ABCA), the second of its kind, which had just been set up at Coleg Harlech in North Wales. Margaret was to join him there on October 16, although lodgings would be hard to find. In the meantime, a visit to her father revealed that he was destroying everything her mother had left, "I think deliberately — unconsciously" (SJ to HO, 9.11.42). There had been, she said, two air raids while she was there, the bombs sometimes falling without warning. This visit to the old man had been dispiriting, and Margaret was worn down by the preparations for her move and by Guy's mood; he was "so choked with work and troubles that he cannot help me in my domestic problems. Indeed, why should he?" (SJ to HO, 9.11.42). For Margaret could be thoroughly old-fashioned about the allotment of roles when she chose; Guy was incompetent when it came to domestic chores, and Margaret seems to have become reluctantly resigned to her role as a housewife. Over the years, her acceptance of this role existed alongside occasional diatribes in print or in letters against the housewife's lot, but rebellious thoughts never seem to have led to active revolt. On this occasion, Hermon was sympathetic as ever, comforting her with David Carver's astrological predictions: he was "emphatic in his belief in an improvement in your affairs," although Hermon himself felt the only redeeming feature of Harlech might be the absence of Margaret's stream of visitors and supplicants (HO to SJ, 9.14.42).

She continued to be very unwell. Her consultant insisted she must rest every afternoon and, if she did not improve in Wales, must go into a nursing home. "I am so anxious to avoid this that I am keeping my promise" (SJ to HO, 9.14.42). Under the circumstances, she had been wryly amused by a letter from Amabel suggesting that the demands of refugees in London just about equaled Amabel's duties for the Women's Royal Voluntary Service (WVS) in Harlech. She went on with packing up the flat, ruefully aware that Harlech could prove a difficult place in which to live and write as it was crammed with commandos and "a tank corps or training school, I'm not sure which" (SJ to LH, 9.18.42). There were no houses or rooms to let and the St. David's Hotel could not warm its bedrooms; Margaret protested she could not work in an "icy-cold bedroom" (SJ to LH, 9.18.42).

She left for Wales at the end of the first week in October, sad and apprehensive. She told Hermon:

> This year of closer work with you has been such fun, and profit and pleasure. And I've a strange and unhappy sense that a whole section of my life is closing. I can hear doors banging shut, and keys being turned. (SJ to HO, 10.7.42)

Hermon too was distressed: "I don't hear doors banging behind me, but in front of me" (HO to SJ, 10.9.42). Arriving in Harlech, Margaret's fears about the St. David's Hotel were confirmed, and "every village near" was crowded; she was miserable, trying to work, and the journey had "knocked me up badly" (SJ to HO, 10.12.42). Moreover, she had not timed her departure from London well. Guy had not yet arrived; she had let their flat too hastily, and was consequently stuck in Harlech before a planned move to

> two tiny rooms in a tiny house . . . exposed to Atlantic winds, rain, mist. This must be a lovely place in a hot summer. It is crammed with troops, and I had trouble to find even these uncomfortable rooms. I think I'm too old to live in my suitcases, but I hope not only to survive but to escape the angina my doctor threatened me with. (SJ to EJT, 10.16.42)

As she moved to those rooms, Margaret wrote to the ever-helpful Barbara Burnham at the BBC, who had adapted *The Fort*, about an idea for a play on William the Conqueror. She saw William as a much subtler character than he was usually presented, and was interested in the ways 1066 had its echoes in the current war: the pro-Norman fifth column had its equivalent in the modern scene, as had the English nobles who joined William once he had won. Barbara approved, and Margaret meant to begin at once, provided she could survive the cold:

> I seem to remember a broadcast play — it must have been in the primitive days — in which the wife of a whaling boat went mad and played the harmonium muttering about "the cold, the misery, the brutality." Have you a harmonium handy? There ought to be one in this Welsh home but there isn't.[35]

Despite a determined lightness of tone in letters to people she did not know well, Margaret was very unhappy: "I think I am too old to fit into a tiny house, already full of people, among strangers. Why did the school have to be in this lost place?" (SJ to HO, 10.21.42). This was a lament that would find its way into most letters of the time to close friends. Yet despite her remoteness, she and Hermon continued to work well together. He wrote about their planned November conference, and about how Robert Neumann had irritated him by saying provocatively that the PEN "must go into politics and give up our art-for-art-sake policy. I asked him where he would be if we had only had an art-for-art-sake policy" (HO to SJ, 10.23.42). Of course, Hermon had not been advocating that the PEN should become a political organization; he consistently defended the PEN's apolitical stance. What had irritated him was Neumann's implication that the PEN had never been engaged with the crises of its time; for Neumann and innumerable other refugees had depended on the PEN's commitment to their causes. Neumann undoubtedly had a gift for raising hackles, but then he was one of those struggling to come to terms with writing in a foreign language. In a preface to his little book *Scene in Passing* (written in English), he told how hard this was; the first version of this slim novel had taken him thirty months to write, being partly written, destroyed, and lost in British internment camps.[36] For one of Neumann's volatile temperament, completing this book and having it published had indeed been an achievement of some magnitude. And despite the odd confrontation, both Margaret and Hermon valued his help in vetting refugees and his commitment to the PEN.

Margaret was struggling with a keen sense of her inadequacy as an absentee president, but Hermon was firm in quashing her doubts about her usefulness, saying, "I have no manner of doubt that you are the best president we could have at this epoch in our history," and that H. G. Wells, all tiffs with Margaret forgotten, had voiced his "admiration for the work you have done and are doing to sustain a civilised attitude towards many of the luckless misunderstood" (HO to SJ, 10.26.42). A few days later, the Executive Committee of the PEN voted unanimously against her attempt to resign (PEN Exec. minutes, 10.28.42). But while this was gratifying, the publication of *Then We Shall Hear Singing* did not improve Margaret's mood. The reviews were on the whole uncomprehending, and Margaret was understandably disheartened. She told Edward Thompson, "I don't think it ever happened to me to get not one good notice" (SJ to EJT, 11.22.42).[37] She was particularly irritated by the young Philip Toynbee, who had sneered at what he saw as a lack of realism in the work; there was no recognition of the genre with which she was experimenting, no pondering on the difficulties faced by the novel writer who was attempting to represent a catastrophe within her contemporary world that went far beyond her own experience.[38] Rightly, under these circumstances, Margaret had felt realism could not contain her theme and had turned to the kind of fable familiar to Eastern Europeans, just as Orwell was doing in *Animal Farm*.

By the beginning of November, Guy still had not joined Margaret in Wales; she was stunned at the possibility that he might remain at the War Office in London (SJ to HO, 11.2.42). Yet there she was, in her tiny rooms, with a row of books by Kierkegaard for company, and starting to have time to meditate, a luxury that had evaded her for the past three years. She could never share Guy's strong conventional Christian outlook and faith, but she was drawn to Kierkegaard. Like him, she could not accept a materialism that denied spirituality, so she responded to the difficult wrestlings of the Dane, who, while deploring the hypocrisies of the Church and the way religion was presented, never abandoned the importance of the values for which it stood. His presence would lurk behind many of the books she would write now.

Nonetheless, Margaret was missing London and looked forward to attending the twenty-first birthday conference she and Hermon had planned for that November. It was not to be. By the middle of November, she was in Whitby, as her father was dying after a stroke, and attendance at the conference was out of the question. Despite all, she did manage to write the speech she had intended to give, and sent it to Hermon just before the old man died (SJ to HO, 11.16.42, 11.17.42). Years later, she meditated on her father's character and their relationship, recalling how "he did not expect from me more than the little he got" (JN, 2:123). She thought of the handsome man her mother had once loved, of what an "obdurate liar" he was, of the lonely life he lived when he retired, in the same house as a wife who would have next to nothing to do with him (JN, 2:124). Margaret knew that in some ways she was like him, "some buried nerve in my mind or body knew him," while Do detested him and mocked Margaret for her moments of understanding (JN, 2:124). Yet it came as a surprise to encounter the respect those in the town felt for him.[39] After his death, Do came to help her clear the house, and they found forty large, folio logbooks, full of his comments, thoughts, incidents. Margaret hesitated over them, but Do insisted they should be burned; and Margaret, exhausted and bowing to the implacable will that echoed their mother's, gave in. Later, she felt remorse when the director of the Literary and Philosophical Society asked for them, because the old man had promised to leave them as a legacy for the town (JN, 2:128). It was a sad end to a life, and a bitter example of the dysfunction in the family that Hannah had nurtured so determinedly. The loss of those logbooks is remembered in Whitby to this day.

By the end of November Guy was confirmed in his post in Wales, much to Margaret's relief, although, she said, "he never seems sure whether the Germans or the War Office is the enemy" (SJ to EJT, 11.22.42). She was still uneasy about remaining president of the PEN when living at such a distance, but Hermon was convinced that she must stay on, and she reluctantly agreed to stand with him for another year (PEN Exec. minutes, 12.4.42). Not good at shedding responsibilities, she still represented the Society of Authors over unilateral decisions taken by some publishers.[40]

CHAPTER 19

Life in Wales

Life in Wales was not easy. Guy was living in Coleg Harlech and faced constant harassment from London, not helped by the fact that Churchill thought the idea of giving young officers courses on current affairs was somewhat subversive (*JN*, 2:129). But the Chapmans had the compensation of breaks in Portmeirion, with its range of stimulating visitors. There Margaret went walking with the brilliant Hungarian Jew Michael Polanyi, a Fellow of the Royal Society and professor at Oxford, a polymath whose expertise ranged across chemistry, economics, and philosophy. There she continued her friendship with Arthur Koestler, admiring his formidable intelligence and kindness, if not his sudden fits of black temper and volatile lifestyle.[1] But by the end of 1942, intellectual morale was at a very low ebb, as news of atrocities committed against Jews was growing in volume. In December, despite the House of Commons being fully aware of the mass executions, and while the Nazi policy was condemned by the Allies, the British Cabinet was reluctant to grant asylum to a larger quota of Jews. Hermon Ould and Margaret discussed how best to express their concerns, Margaret being keen to address the way officialdom was excusing its decisions:

> It has been stated that there are fears in official quarters that any attempt to save Jewish children by bringing them to England would rouse anti-Semitic feeling here. [We should say] that we think this is a slander on our people. But then add that ugly weeds do grow in a war atmosphere, and that we desire to

express our loathing of the vulgar and hideous doctrine of anti-Semitism. And that it is the duty and privilege of every non-Jew in this country to stamp on it wherever they see any trace of it. And not simply for the sake of the Jews, but to prevent ourselves from becoming stupid and callous by indulging in inhuman deeds and thoughts. (SJ to HO, 1.4.43)[2]

With the Executive Committee's approval, she drafted a passionate letter, as the fate of Europe's children had been close to her heart since her *New Commonwealth* days. To her and Hermon's surprise, the response of the committee was mixed. Ironically, the phrase that raised the hackles of Philip Guadella and of Alan Thomas, a prewar ally of Margaret and Ould, "It is not easy to be a Jew," was a straight quotation from the distinguished old Jewish historian Margaret had met in Vienna after her visit to Prague (HO to SJ, 1.16.43; SJ to HO, 1.20.43). Margaret was particularly dismayed by Guadella's comment that "he belonged to one of the Spanish race of Jews who did not believe in whining" (HO to SJ, 1.16.43). She exploded to Hermon, "I hope he is doing more for his racial victims than just sit[t]ing not whining" (SJ to HO, 1.20.43). Guadella did in fact apologize later for a comment made in the heat of the debate.[3] Yet often in their letters, Margaret and Hermon could themselves sound like a surgical team, grimly joking over a difficult operation; one has to be cautious in reading too much into flippant or exasperated references to "the Jew" at this date. Political correctness had not yet been engulfed by issues relating to the use of language rather than the appropriateness of actions, and many of the PEN's refugees and colleagues were undoubtedly difficult to deal with. Racial jokes, not just about Jews, were common both among intellectuals and across social classes, and Margaret and Hermon were of their age. But their actions, their passionate commitment to justice and mercy, remained constant, whatever the pressures and difficulties.

Despite all the discomforts of Margaret's crowded lodgings, Wales was gradually proving a good place for writing. Toward the end of 1942, she had finished her play for the BBC and had written two-thirds of *Cloudless May*. She had also produced, in response to the Lidice tragedy, her short story "The Last Night."[4] The tale is narrated by a young German boy, who tells of his happy childhood on a farm in East Prussia. But then comes the reversal of the English perspective on the war, for he tells how "England attacked Germany for the second time — this time through Poland" ("TLN," 51). He longs to serve the Leader, and eventually, despite his lameness, joins the army. Gradually, through his eyes, the humiliations imposed on the Czechs become clear, and he loses his illusions as murders continue. When his company is attacked by the Czech resistance, the leader of the Czechs spares him, and the boy realizes the man is like his own father. This shared humanity shocks him as does the moment when he is sent away, with a note of safe conduct; the doors of the Czech home that has treated him compassionately are firmly closed behind him. Margaret weaves the chance of reconciliation into episodes of tragic conflict, and prejudices are eroded by experience. The young German, crippled in body, and at first warped in mind, is taught greater understanding by his experiences, like a boy in a folktale. In the end, he is shown compassion simply because he is weak; but he has not yet earned acceptance. The tale, open-ended like *Then We Shall Hear Singing*, does not state whether he ever will.

In the introduction to this story in the *Saturday Evening Post*, Margaret is quoted as saying, "It is very hard to write now, and it is particularly difficult to do a long, sustained piece of writing."[5] This was a constant complaint of many novelists in wartime, but Margaret, while she was writing more slowly than usual, was in fact nearing the end of *Cloudless May*. Then tragedy struck. Her sister Do was killed in an air raid on Reading, and Margaret rushed to support her brother-in-law (SJ to HO, 2.11.43).[6] She told Hermon:

> It's an awful world when one has to be glad that death was "outright" — she must have been killed by blast when the British restaurant where she was doing her weekly turn of W.V.S. work got its direct hit. 38 people were killed in the restaurant itself, but of the six work[ers] in the kitchen only our poor Do. (SJ to HO, 2.20.43)

Touchingly, back at the house, there were signs everywhere of Do's eager planning for the children's return: "I could have been crying all the time, and much good that would have been. There is so much death about, one can't make an indecent fuss over one person — or forget it" (SJ to HO, 2.20.43). Rob would sell their house and stay with friends until he went into the forces. Guy would soon get him a commission in the RAF as an Armaments Officer (JN, 2:132).

Inevitably, given the aspect of her temperament that maintained a more generous version of her mother's matriarchal aspirations, Margaret felt she alone must be responsible for her family. For some considerable time she was adamant that she wanted to raise Do's children and keep Robert under her wing. She corresponded with the Leakes, the family looking after the children in the States, constantly stressing her determination to take on Do's responsibilities. Much later, she would look back on this urge to carry all the family's burdens and judge herself harshly:

> Like Oedipus when he still had his eyes, I was blind without knowing it; like him blinded by what seemed, by what I imagined to be my virtues of energy and goodwill. I made one hideous personal blunder after another, involving me in mental anguish. (JN/TMS, 2:336)

She concluded that she did not see "into other people, even those close to me. Nor did they see that I was spiritually unable *not* to rush forward, recklessly, to try to help" (JN/TMS, 2:336). This was both true and unsparing, for it left out the state of the world at the time, and its effect on decisions taken. Hermon gave some sense of the mood at this stage of the war: "Your depression synchronised with mine. . . . The world is terribly black. If one were a cynic by nature it would be easier to cope with it" (HO to SJ, 2.20.43). In such a state of mind, the yearning to protect family after the shock of Do's death must have been the strongest of urges for someone of Margaret's temperament. To Hermon she confided, "The fact is that I relied on my young sister to provide me with all the colour, including the annoyances, of family life" (SJ to HO, 2.24.43). For she had not just lost Do; she had lost, through Do, the last link with the family life shared and protected by women, the life she had celebrated in *Then We Shall Hear Singing*. This was something she could never share with Guy.

In March, Arthur Koestler asked Margaret to contribute to a book of short stories about what life might be like in 1975, most of the royalties to go to the PEN Refugee Fund. Margaret reacted cautiously:

All my visions of the future are nightmares. I think we are in for a Dark Age. I don't think it is the end of the human race, I think it is just another interregnum, unpleasant while it lasts, and it might last a couple of centuries. . . . I can't help feeling that to offer such a vision would be all wrong — in your book. (SJ to AK, 3.1.43)

She suggested she might try "a Dialogue in the Valéry manner . . . and get out that way the picture of an England which is adapting itself very wisely and cleverly to becoming a third-rate power" (SJ to AK, 3.1.43). Her tone here is ironic, for she could never feel that detached intellectual debate was as strong in England as it was in France, and she was convinced that the future great nations would not include Britain. Since World War I, she had been certain that America would take over Britain's old role.

It seemed increasingly likely that Guy might be posted away from Wales, and that Margaret would have to follow him, possibly to London. Anticipating this, she was tempted to join more than one of the new enterprises involving PEN members. One committee, the Génie Française, set up by the English novelist beloved by the French, Charles Morgan, aimed to promote French cultural interests in England, and would be closely linked with Denis Saurat and the Institut Français. Cyril Connolly, meanwhile, was Churchill's choice for promoting French culture and, while a member of the PEN, he was branching out on his own, both personally and through his journal *Horizon*.[7] The two enterprises mirrored the splits in the French camp, as Saurat, increasingly supportive of the Left, lost de Gaulle's favor. Margaret was always loyal to her friends, and in any case was closer in thinking to Morgan and Saurat, both more liberal than the increasingly autocratic general. She was happy to support them (SJ to HO, 3.2.43). The second enterprise she was drawn to was one promoted by another good friend, Olaf Stapledon, the visionary science fiction writer. He wanted to edit an anthology of essays in which the PEN could reaffirm its fundamental principle of "integrity of the spirit," a project close to Margaret's Kierkegaardian heart (HO to SJ, 1.2.43).

The urge to promote some sense of certainty inspired both projects, for fact and rumor were increasingly hard to separate, as the war dragged on and fears for the future were rife. Responding to these anxieties,

Koestler decided that although most of his prospective contributors, like Margaret, could only conceive of a nightmarish future, he still wanted to publish his book as a warning. However, Margaret was anxious to produce something more positive. This had been her aim in all her writing in wartime, but she was finding it difficult to sustain:

> I'll try to write the dialogue, describing 1975 as it might be if we were not damned. If I find that I simply cannot keep this up, if it is coming out superficial and unreal because I don't believe it, I'll write a nightmare, and you can reject it if you like. (SJ to AK, 3.17.43)

Indeed, the need for some kind of hope was acute. In her quest for spiritual sanctuary, Margaret had been reading Lao-tzu, the reputed founder of Taoism, only to find that Hermon had produced his own translation; he sent it to her, and she was delighted, seeing his work as one of "discovery, uncovering, excavation, re-birth — there is no one word" (SJ to HO, 3.22.43).

Margaret might be living in Wales, but she was far from stuck there. At the end of March, she rushed up to Liverpool to see Barbara, Bill, and Christopher, then spent a night in Whitby on business for her sister Winifred; the following week she was in London where she heard that, while the sales of *London Calling* had been modest in the States, all the contributions had been broadcast or reprinted widely.[8] *Cloudless May* was now with Macmillan, and she joked to Basil Liddell Hart: "I have not quite George Sand's persistence, to begin the first sentence of the next when I finish the last of the one in hand. It may come!" (SJ to LH, 3.29.43). Macmillan gave this novel enthusiastic backing: in their announcement of "outstanding writers of to-day," they placed her alongside Churchill and presented the book as "by far the most important novel this author has written."[9]

Cloudless May, dedicated to Guy, was her first novel for Macmillan after the Cassell contract ended.[10] Margaret used the same technique as in *Cousin Honoré*, mirroring large political and social concerns in a small community, but here a larger cast of characters brought together a wider range of issues. In a French provincial town she had characters reflecting leading French politicians as France fell in May 1940. The usual disclaimer at the beginning was cleverly worded: "The characters in this book are imagined though not imaginary." The novel had been thoroughly researched, written slowly, starting in 1941, partly through choice, partly through necessity, and she had enjoyed writing it.[11] She would comment later that, as in *Cousin Honoré*, "the initial act of transposing an unmanageably vast national theme into a narrow local one releases immense energies," freeing the writer from the "basic artificiality of novels placed supposedly on a national level" (*JN*, 2:132).

Her protagonist is the French officer Rienne, his roots in the peasant community that Margaret always presented as the stable element in European culture. In the old town, the history of a civilization confronts present betrayal and destructiveness, while Rienne's integrity is set against the vulnerability of his old friend the prefect Émile Bergeot (the Reynaud figure), too ready to listen to his mistress, Marguerite. Strands of plot are intertwined with word against deed, misreadings, self-promotion, and self-deception. But there is so much more, lyrical evocations of setting contrasting with the human hurly-burly. Rienne, steeped in French culture, is haunted by the words of Charles Péguy, poet and passionate supporter of Dreyfus, and in this Rienne is of his time, for Péguy, who died in World War I, was still widely regarded as symbolizing the French spirit, a questing mind despite his frequent descent into ferocious rhetoric.

The sheer range of characters in this work reflects the extent of the French tragedy: Jewish Mathieu, the committed Republican; de Thivier, the man of wealth, a devout Catholic; and the old generals, relics from a bygone war, to name but a few. As the novel progresses, Bergeot is unmasked as an actor, assuming different roles for different people, clever, but shallower than he first appears. Such details of characters emerge gradually; the writing is witty and crisp. Marguerite's friendships encircle her with intrigue, so that while she will provoke Bergeot's downfall, she never entirely loses the reader's sympathy. It is as the threat of invasion becomes real that those ruled by self-interest set out to undermine resistance. In this the character of Mayor Labenne, based on the self-serving politician Pierre Laval, is the overwhelming force, all for capitulation if it eases his way, only too ready to trample over anyone: he was "always ready to give up a principle for the sake of a phrase" (*CM*, 88). By contrast, Rienne, both soldier and poet, watches growing corruption govern the actions of those with power. He gains strength from friends in his sister's village, set in the light of the Loire valley, its scents, sounds, old stone, a profound sense of place and of memories. As invasion nears, Labenne shows his true colors, terrifying in his determination to gain and keep power. The weaving together of disparate elements as the Germans advance forms a rich pattern of those who can accept another's rights and those who think only of their own advantage. There is an intricate mingling of dialogue and hidden thoughts, as money, ambition, and plots drive individuals. Bergeot is outflanked by Labenne and weakened by Marguerite's fear as the first refugees reach the town. The capacity for misinterpretation is everywhere; young Marie is shot by her adored husband, Pierre, who deserted when sent a poison pen letter accusing her of an affair; Bergeot and Marguerite flee, her terror overpowering his reason. The frontline soldiers are deserted by their leaders; the Jew Mathieu is tortured, Marguerite killed in a car crash, Bergeot lost. When Rienne reluctantly decides duty means he must leave for England, his village friends remain and he thinks, "If anything good of the past were saved, it would be between the hands of these two of his friends" (*CM*, 495), while a young couple offers another strand of hope for the future. As the eminent American historian Henry Steele Commager would say nearly thirty years later, *Cousin Honoré* and *Cloudless May* were "the best novels on the fall of France yet written."[12] This was high praise at a time when aspects of World War II were being revisited and reassessed by historians and writers alike. Margaret's *Cloudless May* is strikingly similar in its insights to those of Irène Némirovsky's *Suite Française*, the Jewish writer's group of nouvelles written in France during the French Occupation, and only published in 2004, long after her death in a German concentration camp.

For some time now, Margaret had been trying to draft what she called "a sort of post-war admonition" that she had hoped to submit to Koestler for his book (SJ to HO, 4.20.43). By May she had given up on this idea. In exasperation, she complained that

> everyone thinks because of the appalling number of words I turn out that I can run them off like that. But it is only my habit of a daily 12–14 hours grind. If I did 1000 words a day on a book it would be 365,000 words long instead of a mere 240,000! I have

been struggling for a fortnight to write Koestler's piece. At last I've written about 5000 words — a short story, the André Chenier story hacked up (and spoiled) — very pale. I'm vexed I can do no better. (SJ to HO, 5.1.43)

As usual, she did not do herself justice. The tale of Chenier, a principled poet at the time of the French Revolution, embodied the tragedy of a refusal to compromise with those who advocated the violent overthrow of the old regime; he was guillotined in 1794.[13] This may have given Margaret a starting point, but the tale she created was spun from her own fears of a totalitarian state spawned by war. "The Young Prisoner" looks to the future, to 1975, not to the past.[14] The action is set in an English penal colony where prisoners are housed in "dormitories for munition workers during the 1939–46 War." Andrew, his fate echoing that of Chenier, whose verses weave through his thoughts, is in prison for "making foolish little speeches in foolish little gatherings. You wrote foolish little books" ("YP," 114). Recalling his father's death in 1954, Andrew thinks he could hardly "have foreseen the problems of the next twenty years, with their Government of Order and Plenty, their Labour Centre, Youth Camps, and all that benevolent unrelenting authority" ("YP," 115). The prisoners must attend improving concerts and lectures, friendships are discouraged, attempts to escape doomed. But Andrew is an idealist like Chenier and has written poems about "the awful inhumanity of men without love" and about a young woman he met at the Remand Centre, who has become for him "everything that mustn't be trodden into the ground" ("YP," 116, 117). When his one friend is sent to another camp Andrew is isolated, except for an old mathematician who tells how, at the end of the war, what emerged was "an ineffectual fascism, a sham air of order, with violence, hypocrisy, cruelty, given the status of virtues" ("YP," 122). For a time Andrew remains convinced they will live through this Dark Age. But then he hears that the woman who gave him hope has married his friend; he feels "this had happened before, he had been trapped, punished, betrayed before this time; he recognised the feeling, like a man passing his hand over objects in the dark" ("YP," 124). As so often, Margaret shows how readily history repeats itself, in this case, the principled Andrew's fate mirroring that of Chenier, 150 years before; for Andrew's death at the hands of a guard, servant of a brutal regime, follows the same pattern. The warden reports his death as suicide, and "in a few hours, he would believe it" ("YP," 126).

Margaret had achieved a tale powerful in its simplicity. Koestler was delighted with it, and here it is tempting to speculate. For Koestler was a close friend of Orwell, and Orwell, having all but finished *Animal Farm* in 1943, was already making notes for a new book, looking to the future. Did Koestler show him Margaret's story? It is tempting to think so, and that the drab, totalitarian program, banning friendships, disapproving of love, punishing free expression, and showing the iconoclastic influence of past writings, might have offered details beyond what Orwell or indeed Margaret herself could already find in such works as Yevgeny Zamyatin's *We*, Olaf Stapledon's *Last and First Men*, and Katharine Burdekin's *Swastika Night*.[15] Whatever the truth, Koestler thought the tale "outstandingly brilliant" (HO to SJ, 6.7.43). Reluctantly, however, he had abandoned the anthology by the end of June, as he found other contributions disappointing. Margaret eventually published her story in *Modern Reading* (SJ to AK, 5.20.43).[16]

She was starting to find her Welsh lodgings claustrophobic, complaining to Hermon, albeit making a comedy of her complaint,

> that I am shut in this tiny room, with 3 Welsh in the rest of the house, that I cannot go anywhere in the house but my bedroom, that I would sell my soul for a cup of tea but cannot go and make one or otherwise acquire one, that no one will talk to me or come in and I shall be simply forced to spend the evening reading a GOOD BOOK. And if you tell me that this is pure laziness and a neurosis of selfishness I shall go in [*sic*] insisting that it is claustrophobia, and prove to you that I have been suffering from it all my life with appalling results. (SJ to HO, 5.6.43)

She might mock her mood, but she was still grieving for her sister and starting a deeply personal work, tearing up her old diary as she did so, "in the interests of my vow not to leave one single piece of paper, however small" (SJ to HO, 5.6.43). She was trying to persuade Macmillan that she needed to write this book, not as straight autobiography, but like the one she had wanted to write after *Europe to Let*. For she wanted to write about "what one has thought, felt or seen," a quite different sort of book, in which all these experiences and thoughts and feelings are concentrated down to their essences, so that you get not only the event or the feeling but its meaning. (SJ to LD, 5.10.43)

As always, she was at heart more concerned to experiment than to replicate what her publisher knew would sell: "I cannot get rid of the conviction that this is the next stage of learning to write and I must go through it, and if I bye-pass [sic] it I'll never be able to write the novels I want to" (SJ to LD, 5.10.43). It would be an elegy to the past, a way of exorcising grief for all that was lost.

Inevitably, other issues intervened. Margaret had been horrified by private information as to the government's reluctance to accept Hitler's offer to release Jewish children from the camps and, if the statement due to be made in the House of Commons was not satisfactory, she urged that the PEN should write to the press (SJ to HO, 5.20.43). She was also dismayed by the bombing of the German dams: "It feels like a crime to me" (SJ to HO, 5.22.43). In the midst of the horrors, there was a moment of surprised delight when Bill asked for books that would help him to "understand something about the teleological and spiritual forces in the world, the mind of man, the nature of reality" (SJ to HO, 5.24.43). Life, he had told his mother, "has no meaning if there is no free will, and all his mathematical reading had assured him there is none. He has read Freud, Jung, Adler" (SJ to HO, 5.24.43). He was interested in the occult, but Margaret hoped to deflect him into

> Buddhism, mysticism, or at least towards eastern and Chinese philosophy, which has an [sic] clear exoteric meaning as well as an esoteric one and which would let him learn to swim by degrees. He is deeply dissatisfied with the materialist conception of life. . . . He is really attracted to eastern philosophy. (SJ to HO, 5.24.43)

This was a rare meeting of minds between mother and son, and also confirms what her own reading of Lao-tzu suggests about her state of mind in 1943. But an interest in the East was not the whole story; there was also that other need to have some certainty about the future that did not always reveal what she wanted to hear. For someone had read Margaret's horoscope for her and she commented wryly: "Odd how everyone refers to my disastrous aspects for marriage. Possibly they might be disastrous for some people, but they suit me all right" (SJ to HO, 5.26.43).

The essay she was writing for Olaf Stapledon was ready by June, and it showed how far she had moved since the days of "Documents."[17] She laid great store, as before, on the importance of a writer being detached, but at the same time,

> the field of contemplation is widened to take in as many objects as possible, both within and without the writer, who notices how they are related to each other — how this emotion joins itself to many others, this object reassembles an infinity of objects — in a pattern as just as it is complex. ("For Olaf Stapledon")

This continuing insistence on pattern goes beyond "Documents" and suggests what she was contemplating as she began to write *The Journal of Mary Hervey Russell*. For she now argues that if the writer is to engage his readers, "he does so by finding images, of emotions, actions, persons, through which his knowledge, the fruits of his conscious attention to himself and the world, becomes audible and visible" ("For Olaf Stapledon"). Passionate about issues like that of the Jewish children, Margaret had some sympathy for the propagandist as "he burns to destroy tyrants and set prisoners free," although ultimately, this was not the writer's main function ("For Olaf Stapledon"). Turning to ways and means, she pointed to *The Waste Land*, where Eliot, she said, could only separate his despair and dislike of the social and psychological conditions of the contemporary world "by projecting them into the images which startled his readers" ("For Olaf Stapledon"). While the effect of *The Four Quartets* was not as striking, it was probable that

> a faithful reading of these poems, in which the poet has been able to concentrate a vast number of thoughts and feelings, not his although he has felt and thought them, will affect the reader to a depth left untouched by his reading of the revolutionary *Waste Land*. ("For Olaf Stapledon")

She felt she now appreciated a writer's proper aim: "to understand the figures, the types, the emotions, which stalk through my brain" ("For Olaf Stapledon"). For this, she believed,

> the imagination is a readier pupil than the reason, that to present to the imagination a shape of evil, in all its horror and with all its littleness, a shape of good, with all its weakness, is the most potent thing a writer can do. . . . The deeper [the writer] penetrates the nature of human beings, the farther he pushes his enquiry into their motives, the more clearly he sees their differences are superficial, their brotherhood real. ("For Olaf Stapledon")

Margaret had moved far away from her earlier insistence on reason; by this stage in the war she had seen too much horror that was justified by logic. Instead, this paper heralded the thinking behind not only the book she was beginning, but much that she would write in the years to come: it marked, in many ways, an artistic watershed to which the rich experimentation of the last ten years had been moving. Margaret was allowing her poetic mind to coalesce with her intellect more readily than she had done before. Imagination would be given a higher priority than reason, since imagination had the greater chance of penetrating the chaos that war had brought in its wake, and of revealing what lay beneath, what bound human beings together.

Guy's future at the college remained uncertain, although Margaret thought they might be in Wales for another winter. Accordingly she was moving further inland, leaving her cramped lodgings for the Oakeley Arms in Tan-y-Bwlch. This hotel would become a favorite; it was run by "a slender handsome woman, gay, friendly, sharp-tempered," a good businesswoman who enjoyed life, providing hot water, well-cooked food, and a friendly, "faintly louche" atmosphere, patronized at times by occasional commandos from a nearby Rehabilitation Centre (JN, 2:134). But for all the congenial atmosphere, Margaret remained in low spirits as she corrected her proofs of Cloudless May and struggled to shape the Journal. This last was, she said, "a 'luxury' book, written against Macmillan's will, and may never be published" (SJ to HO, 6.11.43). She was depressed, not only by Koestler's abandoning of his book, but by the poor response to Stapledon's call for papers: "I begin to think it is no use pretending that English writers are intellectual. They are not" (SJ to HO, 6.11.43). This was a cry of frustration rather than a wholly serious comment; Margaret had wanted the intellectual debate that Stapledon had hoped to stimulate to succeed. Yet she does signal something else: increasingly, her inquiring mind found its soul mates among European writers and thinkers of the past and present; Stendhal, Tolstoy, Dostoyevsky, and to a lesser extent such different minds as those of Giraudoux and Valéry were those she turned to with growing frequency.

On Monday, July 5, at 9:25 p.m., Margaret's play *William the Defeated* was broadcast on the BBC Home Service.[18] When her own version of the play had been approved in February, certain amendments had been needed, but in the aftermath of Do's death, Margaret had struggled to comply, and so Barbara Burnham came to her aid, and the eventual result pleased both Barbara and Val Gielgud.[19] In the one text available, that of the version Hermon printed, *William the Defeated* explores the follies that conflict brought in its wake through the relationship between a Saxon landowner, Lucius, and the conqueror, William.[20] The play looks at responses to invasion through a moment of English history, when tyrannical feudalism — here, a reflection of Fascism — was taking over from a kind of mutual, muted respect between thane and serf, suggestive of democracy. The dialogue is lucid and in the modern idiom, with no pretentious archaisms; the cast is small. William himself is a challenging character, showing the savagery alongside the consuming need for friendship and approval that Hitler himself had shown in, for instance, his dealings with the British Legion delegations before the war. These were uneasy themes at a time when hatred of the enemy made a simpler option. Margaret did not hear the play broadcast, as she had no access to a radio. Although Hermon said he had liked it, the reviewer in the *Listener* disagreed, one of his less than professional objections being that Margaret's William did not fulfill "our not unreasonable preconceptions."[21] But Margaret herself was upset about the casting; her William was played by Ernest Milton, Naomi Royde-Smith's husband, and Margaret had seen him once act King John, where "he tore everything in sight to fragments, and his eyes flashed green and red lights, like a traffic signal" (SJ to HO, 7.7.43).

The play was a welcome but slight distraction. The Génie Française was in trouble; René Cassin and his wife, Theodora Ohenberg, had not produced any evidence of official French backing from de Gaulle. Furthermore, they were adamantly opposed to allowing Saurat on the committee, no doubt because both Cassin and Saurat aspired to the same postwar post in a future French government. Margaret and Hermon were losing patience with the internal wrangling. Broadly speaking, the supporters of de Gaulle, like Cassin and his wife, were at daggers drawn with those on the left, like Saurat, who had now lost de Gaulle's friendship. Margaret shared Hermon's gloom while clinging to the hope "that the French at home will sweep away both houses and begin to rebuild a nation" (SJ to HO, 6.14.43). Disheartened, she acknowledged also that "they do NOT like us, and I begin to feel that we have exaggerated wildly the existence in this country of Francophilism" (SJ to HO, 6.14.43).

By the autumn, Margaret had settled happily in the Oakeley Arms, despite the discomfort of a mattress with unwieldy ridges (SJ to HO, 9.4.43). When Guy was free, they walked the hills while they could, for the likelihood that he would be posted somewhere else was growing. He was in trouble with his superiors, no longer allowed to invite guest speakers, as his invitation to the iconoclastic Basil Liddell Hart, for one, had earned him disapproval: Liddell Hart was out of favor with the War Office (GC, AKOS, 1975). Margaret kept her head down as Guy fumed. She was part of a symposium with other leading writers on "Reviewing Reviewed" for the *Author*, where she argued that reviewing should not be confused with literary criticism.[22] For criticism, she said, was a form of inquiry into the human condition, not far from the literature alongside which it operated. Reviewing, on the other hand, should be more of an occupation, simply presenting works to the reader, and should not be a vehicle for the reviewer's own views:

> A foreigner has the impression sometimes that all our reviewing is done by maiden aunts, when he reads plaintive scoldings about the unpleasantness of Mr. So-and-so's characters. "What a horrible time Balzac would have had with your reviewers of novels!" a Frenchman said to me. (*Author*, Summer 1943, 69)

Margaret had another article in the Bombay journal the *Aryan Path*, addressing the question "Should the enemy be punished after the war is over?"[23] Revenge was only self-destructive, she argued, and Europe's self-destructiveness had already involved the whole world in its ruin. Consequently, "the spiritual rebirth of Europe involves a change in the European attitude to other civilisations — to take a pressing instance, in the attitude of Great Britain to India."[24] Beneath her article was a short announcement: "Under instructions from our esteemed contributor . . . we have forwarded her honorarium for the above article to the Bijapur Famine Fund." Margaret's support for causes she believed in was never inhibited by her own financial needs.

Cloudless May was published on September 20, and it would do well.[25] The novel was the Book Society choice for October, but Margaret confessed to Hermon this would have meant much more had her mother been alive, as "such things seemed to her really a triumph — and perhaps to me then would have so seemed" (SJ to HO, 6.27.43).[26] Pleasingly, Europeans in London were impressed; Stanley Unwin forwarded a request from a leading Czech publisher, a member of the Czech State Council in London, asking permission to have the novel translated as he was "of the opinion which I share, that yours is one of the first books which should be available in Czech after the cessation of hostilities" (Unwin to SJ, 10.18.43).

By the end of the month, Margaret was quietly working on her next book. Unhappily, it now seemed inevitable that Guy would move at the end of the year "to one of the Commands, to be a full Colonel in charge of the education for a Command" (SJ to HO, 9.14.43). All too soon, a posting to the Northern Command in York was in fact confirmed, and he was told to report there by the end of October: "The full hideousness of the move is breaking over us both" (SJ to HO, 9.19.43). Yet again Margaret was "frantically packing books and papers to go into store," her one comfort being that Guy would be out of the Army Bureau of Current Affairs that had so frustrated him (SJ to HO, 10.13.43; SJ to LD, 10.15.43).

In June, Margaret had received a letter from the vice-chancellor of Leeds University, saying the university wished to confer the degree of D.Litt. on her, "if it would give you pleasure to accept this honour," and she had accepted.[27] Accordingly, on October 27, the degree was conferred, with her friend Bonamy Dobrée giving the eulogy.[28] The *Whitby Gazette* carried an article about the ceremony, while the *TLS* devoted its second leader to "Storm Jameson."[29] It was a generous tribute, placing Margaret firmly at the forefront of contemporary English novelists:

> Few English novelists in the uneasy years of truce between the two wars have so surely captured in imaginative content the common themes of that distinctive and warning phase of European society.

Margaret described the ceremony for Hermon, half mockingly: the crimson robes on the platform, the solemn speeches, the disrobing so that they all "became grubs again" (SJ to HO, 10.30.43). She was sad that there was "no Family to be pleased and impressed. It meant and means just nothing" (SJ to HO, 10.30.43). This is a revealing comment; clearly she felt that Guy and Bill could not be expected to react as Do and especially Hannah would have done.

Certainly Guy was in no mood to be pleased. He loathed York, which he found "a slum round a Roman ghost" (SJ to HO, 11.3.43). By contrast, Margaret admitted, "I must confess that after Leeds I find Harlech an earthly paradise in spite of not being able to move my shoulders with the usual Harlech rheumatism" (SJ to HO, 11.3.43). So she decided to stay put in Wales until December: "By then I shall, D.V. [God willing], have finished the first draft of my book" (SJ to HO, 11.8.43). Her literary output this year had been prodigious, and even as she finished this book, she was taking on other tasks. She helped Amabel Williams-Ellis with an essay competition for the war factories in Wales, the subject designed by Margaret "to get the workers thinking about the real conditions in occupied Europe, so that they will be willing to go on being rationed etc for the benefit of these countries"; and she asked Hermon to get representative writers from a wide range of European countries to write vivid descriptions of experiences in their homelands (SJ to HO, 11.16.43). This, she said, was a chance to do "some real propaganda," as the project would involve a large number of Welsh factories (SJ to HO, 11.16.43). Overall, despite all the commitments, her letters to friends showed that she was more relaxed. She engaged in friendly debate with Koestler, whose essay review, "The French 'Flu,'" had opened with an attack on British attitudes to France:

The people who administer literature in this country . . . have lately been affected by a new outbreak of that recurrent epidemic, the French Flu. Its symptoms are that the patient . . . is lured into unconditional surrender of his critical faculties when a line of French poetry or prose falls under his eyes.[30]

Margaret cheerfully confessed that she was subject to the disease:

But I know what it is — it's being shut up in this damned cold country for five years, with no sun and no cheap wine. I can't stand the curious snobbery which goes about pretending that there is only one English writer, Shakespeare, to an army of French, as if we hadn't had a 17th and 18th century of our own. I give them their 19th century. As for the 20th, I've no call to jeer at anyone, because I've only just got over an attack of Giraudoux which has lasted years, with intervals of sanity. (SJ to AK, 11.27.43)

This was lighthearted in tone, for in essence she agreed with Koestler. As always, her love of France was largely directed to its culture and literature, not to its politics. And she was not one to adulate French literature at the expense of its English equivalent. Each had their greatnesses, and Margaret knew how to keep her sense of proportion.

She was equally lighthearted when discussing with Nancy Cunard how to promote a positive English image to the French; and she joked about Margaret Kennedy joining the PEN Committee, as, Margaret averred, she was said to be "near-Fascist, but this may be spiteful Yorkshire slander" (SJ to NC, 11.22.43; SJ to HO, 11.25.43). More seriously, she debated with Hermon the imprisonment without trial of the former leader of the British Union of Fascists, Oswald Mosley. Hermon thought it "a dreadful gaffe" on the Home Secretary's part (HO to SJ, 11.27.43); and Margaret agreed:

Morrison would have done better to leave him in a prison hospital. He, Mosley, has acted as a catalyst for all the floating discontents with the Government and its Tory manners. That sort of thing is dangerous. (SJ to HO, 11.29.43)[31]

For there were still right-wing elements in Britain who regarded Mosley, who supported Hitler, as a hero, and as so often, Margaret dreaded an escalation in their influence as the war drew on.

Throughout December she was still in Wales. She visited Guy over Christmas, but was back in Harlech by the end of the year, having hated the dirty hotel in York; she had found nowhere to live, and now had vague plans about renting a small flat for the duration: Guy wanted her to try Oxford. In the meantime she was bracing herself to speak to the French Chamber of Commerce; she was the first woman to do so, singled out, as the chairman said, because "English to the bone, she is at the same time more Europe-conscious than any English novelist — certainly any English woman novelist — writing today," while her heading of the English PEN Club demonstrated "her ardent interest in countries other than her own."[32] Whatever the French might think of the English, this accolade showed Margaret as a woman and a writer who was held in respect.

CHAPTER 20

Illness Takes Over

By January 1944, Margaret had finished her next book, *The Journal of Mary Hervey Russell*. The idea had been in her mind since her mother's death in 1937, when she told Tom Moult to check with her before using poems of hers in his next anthology, "because I am writing or going to write a book into which one of them might go, and they are not worth printing over and over again."[1] In 1940 she had made clear to Harold Macmillan the kind of book she had in mind:

> I wrote all the straight autobiography I could in NO TIME LIKE PRESENT [*sic*], and it didn't take many pages. But one cannot write of what one has thought, felt, or seen, *in vacuo*—so that there has to be a personal thread running through such a book. If I am impressed by something Beneš said, it is after all I who am impressed, although Beneš and what he said is the important thing. And if I spend hours or days in Rouen or Bordeaux trying to imagine where my Mother, who is dead, went when she was in those cities, it is I who am walking in that hot sun, though it is my Mother who is the real figure.
>
> So it seems to me that there would be enough of what is hideously called "personal interest" to carry the book. (SJ to Macmillan, 3.9.40)[2]

This statement shows Margaret's continuing fascination with the nature of memory, with the impossibility of absolute objectivity, with the subject's inevitable involvement in what is observed or recalled. Such ideas had been developing over the past decade, of course, and would develop further throughout Margaret's long life, finding their apotheosis in her late autobiography.

However long the proposed work had been in mind—she often said she kept ideas for books in her head for years—what she eventually wrote mirrored her thinking in her essay of 1943 for Olaf Stapledon's failed "Fundamental Values" project. It was an experiment in nonfiction. For the first time Margaret signaled that Mary Hervey Russell was herself. The impulse to disguise, she would say later, "had been encouraged by reading Kierkegaard" (JN, 2:135); the self she revealed was viewed with the detached penetration she had advocated in her essay, and it was a portrait of the artist as a woman. Events are for pondering; stream of consciousness is explored together with the questions it raises: what role do the senses play, how are memories summoned, how do they seduce the mind, and above all, how does a writer's mind function? The book is written literally as a journal, a journal with jottings. It is for the most part a meditation, and much of it works like poetry, although a very different kind of poetry from Woolf's. Here is a meeting with four German Jewish refugees:

> I set myself the task of giving each of them in turn his proper importance. It is so simple that you can scarcely make a mistake. You have only to listen and become nothing or a mirror, in which they see themselves before they were refugees. When they had gone I felt myself as hollow as a reed, and at the same time exhausted, and scattered about a continent. As very slowly I washed cups and glasses, swept up tobacco ash, and straightened chairs, the scattered pieces returned to their places. But it had been, I might even say, a near thing.[3]

In this passage Margaret shows the stripping of the listener's ego to such an extent that she is in danger of losing herself in each refugee's own world; she is fragmented, as she negates herself for each of them. It is the simple household tasks that restore her, the kind of tasks she had celebrated in *Then We Shall Hear Singing*, the normality that is her own and no one else's. It had been a near thing: she had all but lost herself in their sufferings, emptying out her own life source to receive them.

Metaphysical existentialism underpins this work; it contemplates not what consciousness is but how it operates for the Mary Hervey Russell who is Margaret the creative being, exploring in depth how an artist might live in the same skin as a social creature. This is a work that makes its own exploration of interiority, sometimes using the modernist stream of consciousness techniques, but never remaining engrossed by the subject's own reactions: observation, interconnection with the world beyond the individual consciousness is paramount, how such encounters can be absorbed and conveyed, and what risks the ego takes when it sacrifices itself to the experiences of others. This is a work to be read closely, as the much later *Journey from the North* does not allow the reader into precisely the same mind as is found here. It marked a critical moment of self-assessment for a writer at the height of her powers.

The book was dedicated to Do, but the first part begins in one of Hannah's favorite places, Bordeaux. This leads on to contemplation of the remote past represented by prehistoric cave drawings and paintings. Meditating on this art, Mary explores the artist's need to "detach" an object from the mind before it can be "created" in art; and she realizes such skill was already there in the caves. These first sections set the tone of the *Journal*, as they move from a contemplation of abstract art to the subconscious image worked on by the surrealist, revisiting a prewar thought that abstract art could be motivated by the "fear of a repellent civilisation which is dominated by the power of things" (*JMHR*, 9). But the *Journal* is never trapped in one mode. First-person meditation gives way to third-person exploration of "she," the original narrator, practicing the detachment Margaret had advocated in her essays, and seeing her afresh. Nor is this a chronological account. The exploration of the self involves an archaeological dig into memory by way of the links stream of consciousness provides. Facts are viewed through the workings of the artist's mind, her own and others who have helped her to make creative choices. Many of these fellow artists are French — Mallarmé, Baudelaire, Péguy — but whatever she may take from them becomes her own.

The second part of the book is organized differently, with years given in chronological order, while events, madeleine-like, evoke memories more insistently. Does this change in form suggest that Margaret had drafted the first part earlier, before her sister's death and after her mother's? This section is very much an elegy for Do, intertwined with a lament for the post-Munich world, and what had been lost, in Europe and at home. Fact and the fictions people tell themselves confront each other: at one point, Mary dreams a fairy story—a surreal dream with a happy ending—which is shattered by a shock encounter with a "good gently-spoken" German woman who speaks easily about the "servant races" (*JMHR*, 112) and how they must be trained and used: the lack of a "happy ending" is not voiced, the point simply made by the clash with the fairy story. At another moment, it is the mirroring of experiences in different places which she reveals, as when a London air raid, in 1941, is described as first lived elsewhere:

> It is only now, when the smoke of our ruins joins the cloud above theirs, and our dead are confounded with a vague crowd coming from many countries and all now speaking a common language, that we keep the same time as Chinese, Poles and the others. In their cities and villages the Americans are not yet our contemporaries. (*JMHR*, 179–80)

What Margaret evokes here is the way suffering over the centuries and over continents not only mirrors and echoes itself, but links those who suffer. In a strange way, they all speak the same language because they have shared the same experience. And that is what she means when she says as yet Americans are not our contemporaries: they had not yet, in the twentieth century at least, suffered the brutal occupations of foreign powers, the carpet bombings of towns and cities. Contemporaneity she redefines as linking the modern experience with that of Bede, Alcuin, Dante, Montaigne, and Alfred-Victor Vigny. It is Margaret's modernism, soaked in blood, sweat, and tears. Toward the end of the book, there is a short play with a cast of dead soldiers of both wars, but it is not simply concerned with the tragedy of war. At its core the whole work has looked at the function and enduring quality of memory, however it is shaped. In this little play, the dead are lived by their memories, are haunted and claimed by them. The book ends in 1943, contemplating Do's death, and assessing what is left for Mary. Yet always there is the return to the self, "when, in me, someone, a child, always begins again" (*JMHR*, 228). No wonder this intricately crafted, cleanly flowing work remained Margaret's favorite to the end of her life.

January saw her still in Wales; she had not found anywhere in Oxford, and she worried about Guy, living as he was in atrocious conditions (SJ to LH, 1.4.44). But on the writing front, things were encouraging: she was still receiving letters praising *Cloudless May* from English and French readers. Inevitably there was the odd reader who could point out a mistake, but when they were truly knowledgeable, Margaret took it in good part: "I don't at all mind having my moon put right. Really, the things a poor author ought to verify," she told Rache Lovat Dickson, and proposed to buy a book listing several years of weather (SJ to LD, 3.9.44).

She continued to work closely with Hermon, drafting responses to various refugee organizations, discussing diplomatic means of approaching ministries (HO to SJ, 1.10.44; SJ to HO, 1.10.44). There had been a momentary threat to family life that alarmed her: Guy was invited to India as colonel in command of British education, if the War Office would sanction the project. Guy's commanding officer in York reacted quickly, obtaining a promise that Guy would not be sent, but Margaret said, "I still tremble a little — it has only just happened. Guy says he won't go, he'll take to the hills!" (SJ to LD, 1.12.44). At least he was able to leave the unhealthy York billet, as Valentine had offered to put him up in her Leeds home, "a god's-gift in his gloom" (SJ to VD, 1.17.44).

This was cheering, but by February Margaret's blood pressure was dangerously low. She had been taking some drug to sustain her energy levels; now her doctor had "viciously cut off all my dopes, I have as much energy as a winter fly" (SJ to HO, 2.8.44). However, she and Hermon Ould were still undertaking tasks that went far beyond the line of duty: Margaret was busy cutting fifty thousand words out of Lilo Linke's huge book on South America for the publisher, and was also having to "English the Anglo-German. It is a frightful job, I find" (SJ to HO, 3.9.44). She had also agreed to write a preface for the long-overdue translation of Maria Kuncewiczowa's novel *The Stranger* (SJ to HO, 3.11.44). The effort proved too much, and she started to have blackouts again. She was admitted to a nursing home in Harrogate for four weeks to be near Guy in York, hoping this would effect a complete cure, even as she insisted she meant to keep working, planning to correct the translation of Maria's book (SJ to Rathbone, 3.18.44; SJ to HO, 3.23.44).

Once in the Harrogate nursing home, she had to accept that she was really ill. On April 3 she wrote to Hermon, "You'll have to convey to the committee that I'm forced to resign everything, and live in slow motion for a time, a pretty long time" (SJ to HO, 4.3.44). Health had been something she could joke about, but now it looked as if she was on the brink of being a permanent invalid. Hermon was inevitably upset, but too sensible not to realize that this time she must resign; he promised to try Forster for the presidency, at least in a temporary capacity. On April 8, Margaret sent her formal resignation, stressing her "great grief" and congratulating the PEN on its growth during her time in office.[4] The next day she wrote again to Hermon, saying she felt "as if I'd a limb amputated" (SJ to HO, 4.9.44). The doctor had diagnosed a range of problems: anemia, fibrositis, heart, thyroid. For her part, she still hoped to join Hermon at the postwar congress in Stockholm, and "to live on as your Best Female Friend. It means a lot to me" (SJ to HO, 4.9.44). By mid-April she had left the nursing home for one hotel after another (SJ to HO, 4.14.44, 4.24.44). But she was bored in Harrogate, and spent a few days with the Dobrées in Leeds before moving into rooms that Guy had unexpectedly found in York, with a kindly Austrian landlady (SJ to LH, 4.24.44).[5]

Margaret's grief at resigning from her PEN presidency, together with the severity of her illness, may well have supplied the context for "Cloud Form," a sonnet recalling her mother that appeared in *TLS* later in the year. The love is there, but interlaced with the harsh legacy of those beatings:

> Your hands, less kind, shaping the future, invite
> Me to know noon's bitter pulp, a tear
> Born of my body's sterile salt and the fear
> Of some betrayal. . . .[6]

Those few lines with their tight-packed, enigmatic images hint at inner griefs she would be wary of expressing in prose.

Margaret remained very weak. Pernicious anemia looked increasingly likely; she was being given liver injections, but was impatient as they were slow to take effect. She joked with Hermon: what would he like her to leave him in her will? He replied in the same vein: if she left him anything it should be "a little of your courage, please" (HO to SJ, 5.11.44). After a month, the rooms in York were more than she could bear: "the mixture of filth, bad food, discomfort and Austrian schwarmerei is too much for me" (SJ to HO, 5.14.44). Guy, increasingly anxious, suggested that she should go south, to stay with David Murray and his wife, Leonora Eyles, in Hove, and he was right: the move would be a godsend for a bored invalid, as it would take her into a part of England that had restricted access because of the imminent invasion of Europe. Accordingly, she stayed with the Dobrées for the rest of the month, waiting for permission to enter the restricted zone.

Margaret arrived at 24 Hove Street by June 3, "armed with a Journalist's card which admits me to banned areas" (SJ to HO, 6.3.44), for a stay of three months. She knew David well as editor of the *TLS*; he did not share Margaret's love of France, but admired her as a writer and intellectual. For her part, she remembered him later as having little male energy, no vanity; the household, she recalled, was dominated by his eighty-seven-year-old father, Charles, and Leonora, herself a talented journalist, was becoming a household slave, a role that would always be Margaret's worst nightmare (*JN*, 2:138). But she herself was well placed to absorb the atmosphere of D-day, June 6, when the Allies finally invaded France; Basil Liddell Hart wrote, teasing her that "you seem to have been trying to get a front seat for the Second Front" (LH to SJ, 6.12.44). Despite this, she was dismayed at her own enforced inaction; the doctor had told her she must rest completely for six months, and she was finding it hard to bear. Pernicious anemia had now been confirmed, "and if I don't rest I'll die. I am resting" (SJ to HO, 6.17.44). Nonetheless, she was writing the promised preface for Maria Kuncewiczowa, although she was forbidden to type. "I am all but forbidden to breathe, but I do" she told Hermon, adding as an afterthought that they had had three air raids the previous night (SJ to HO, 6.17.44). There were a lot of "noisy nights" on the south coast as the big guns responded to the pilotless planes, the V1s, Hitler's latest weapon (SJ to HO, 6.21.44); Margaret had seen one "neatly shot into the sea by the A.A. [*sic*] gun at the end of the street. I saw another caught in the searchlights and falling falling. At least I hope it was pilotless, I don't like even Germans to be roasted alive" (SJ to LD, 6.21.44). Living in the restricted zone, she had to be careful what she wrote in letters, as they were subject to censorship. Her birthday letter to Bill, "was hacked about, though fortunately not his birthday cheque! I expect I have been too realistic in my account of our most exciting night" (SJ to LD, 6.24.44). Later she wrote that the Hove nights were "sometimes disturbed, and even our days, but not with the appalling regularity of your London plague" (SJ to LD, 6.30.44). By July, she was asking Hermon not to risk going up to London:

> Some nights I hear and watch one of the brutes rushing across the sky, and it seems fantastic to be lying in bed, staring at death going to look for someone else. Also it is a foretaste of the inhumanity of the next war, and that is worst of all to think on. (SJ to HO, 7.1.44)

By now, Margaret was casting round for ways to shore up her dwindling finances, not only because of her enforced rest, but because of a hole in her bank account caused by "rather lavishly" helping a writer's wife who had left him, complicated by the fact that Margaret and the husband "went to school together — and anyhow he is not sane" (SJ to LD, 6.27.44). She was always generous: a few weeks later Jan Masaryk himself would write to her that he had heard she was going to let the Czechs have the rights of three of her books on Europe. He assured her that he would personally make sure they were published in Czechoslovakia once Hitler was in hell (Jan Masaryk to SJ, 8.17.44). Margaret was by now desperate to be allowed to work, while Guy was desperate to be allowed to resign, "to avoid being sent to occupy Europe. If I could have gone with him I'd have encouraged him to go, but I shan't be able to, so I think he has had enough war," she told Rache (SJ to LD, 6.24.44). She had managed to finish the preface for Maria's book by the beginning of July, but it had cost her considerable effort.[7]

Margaret was hoping to leave Hove soon and retreat to a country pub; her doctor was insistent she must not take a flat (SJ to HO, 7.24.44). Guy had been granted four months' leave to look after his wife, and she thought of going to the Welsh seaside town of Tenby. By August, the desire to move on was acute; she had to confess to Basil that she had behaved outrageously, sending a telegram in his name to his friend M. Thierry, proprietor of a hotel in Tenby, asking for rooms for his good friends Storm Jameson and Guy Chapman (SJ to LH, 8.10.44). It worked, and Basil, amused rather than cross since he had already offered help, forgave her. Before she left Hove, there was an awkward moment: when Guy arrived to collect her, Leonora disliked him on sight. Margaret admitted: "Of course he is exhausting, he has a genius for freezing one up or stabbing one to the heart at the most unexpected moments. But he doesn't bore me, and most men do. I am pretty tough" (SJ to IR, 8.19.44). For her part, Margaret had reservations about her host, David Murray, not as a man but as an editor, telling Hermon, "He's terribly prejudiced, leaves far too much to what are obviously bad subordinates, hates anything he can label highbrow" (SJ to HO, 8.13.44).

Given Margaret's health, Tenby had to have priority over the PEN Conference at the end of August. E. M. Forster's opening address began with a tribute to her, claiming he was a poor substitute, as she

> would have given a lead, a direction, most necessary for our de-
> liberations. Not only has she a sense of contemporary tragedy
> (many of us have that), but she has a vision and inspiration as re-
> gards the future. She can see, as it were, round this nasty corner,
> and she would have helped us incalculably.[8]

Murray too was keen to honor her: when the Allied forces entered Paris on August 25, he asked her to write, anonymously, as was usual, the lead-ing article for the *TLS* on the liberation of Paris.[9] It was a long piece, its emotion understandable given the symbolic nature of the moment; it concentrated on a vision of French culture restored, an emblem of free-dom and light for war-weary Europeans. The mood of rejoicing was soon dimmed, however, as news of atrocities under the name of "justice" be-gan to emerge. Margaret found in one French news sheet a vindictive story about a young Frenchwoman who had married a German officer; the story fired her imagination and she began to sketch out the skeleton of a play (*JN*, 2:139–40).

In November, she sent Hermon a cutting from the journal *Vendredi* with a blacklist of French writers accused of collaboration, and an ar-ticle from *Time and Tide* on wartime publishing in France, reporting the deaths of a number of writers (SJ to HO, 11.21.44).[10] Giraudoux had died on January 31. He had defended capitulation and served briefly under Pétain's Vichy government; Margaret asked Hermon about the rumor that he had been murdered. News of their friend the Jewish writer Ben-jamin Crémieux was sadly incontrovertible: he had died in Buchenwald. "It breaks my heart to think that I'll never be able to be angry with Benjamin and his ways again," Margaret wrote, "and never read a new Giraudoux again" (SJ to HO, 11.15.44). The end of the war brought other worries; concessions to the USSR bothered Hermon, the appeasement of the Russians recalling for him Chamberlain's appeasement of Germany and Italy. Margaret shared his anxiety, but, like him, she responded to the perceived threats with attempts to build bridges. She joined the writers' section of the Society for Cultural Relations between the Peoples of the British Commonwealth and the Union of Soviet Socialist Republics (SCR). Founded in 1924, by 1944 the society was promoting itself as vital to the Twenty Years' Treaty of Friendship between Great Britain and the USSR, offering a range of cultural links. The membership was by no means all of the Far Left: in 1944 one of its vice presidents was R. H. Tawney, while Hermon was already on the committee and J. B. Priestley was president of the writers' group. In December Margaret was voted on to the SCR Council, joining a range of eminent writers, including Somerset Maugham, Walter de la Mare, Sean O'Casey, and G. M. Trevelyan; she would remain on the council until 1951.[11]

Back in the Oakeley Arms after the Tenby holiday, Margaret had a number of visitors. Robert Neumann and his wife came, then Arthur Koestler on his way to Palestine, with a "charming young creature he calls, mysteriously, Mermaid"; Margaret had preferred his former partner, Daphne, but, as she said, it was not up to her (SJ to HO, 12.11.44). She was never judgmental about Koestler's tempestuous private life, although she did comment to Irene, "I think he is rather a corrupter of youth" (SJ to IR, 12.19.44). For their own part, she and Guy hoped to be in London in the first week of January: Bill was being transferred to the Air Ministry as he had eye trouble, so Margaret planned to buy a house for Bill and Barbara "to share . . . with me while they look for a house for themselves" (SJ to HO, 12.11.44). This would mean another bank loan, "but I guess it is worth it to be settled in life. We want to get the children back in May, so that they have the summer to accustom their Texas-thinned blood to our winters" (SJ to LD, 12.10.44). Fortunately, she had finished a short, forty-thousand-word book, inspired by the *Vendredi* article, and first drafted as a play: "I told Arthur Koestler the plot, and he was or pretended to be excited" (SJ to LD, 12.10.44).

The Other Side is a sparely written tale; here again, Margaret offered "soundings" of an international crisis in a domestic space, this time engaging a German family of the old Junker class with its French occupiers and the French widow of a German officer. The novel opens with a brief picture of a French officer's sister whose husband was killed in June 1940; she was in the Resistance, but now runs a nursery and hospital for orphans traumatized by their experiences in the war. Her brother, Michael Aubrac, is a former prisoner of war who had been tortured. So the introductory chapter suggests the potential for a return to the vindictiveness that France showed to Germany after World War I. The scene shifts to the German family's château, the older generation recalling their house being requisitioned by the English after the first war, while the child Heinrich, fresh from the Hitler Youth, hates the French. The dilemma that soon confronts the young French widow, Marie, is clear: Aubrac, ordered to requisition the house, is a hostile force, yet they are both French; her family by marriage is German but always reminds her that she is Other. For those regarded as outsiders always run the risk of being treated as Other, when they appear to pose a threat to the normalities that give a society its illusion of a fixed identity. Such was the fate of the Jews under Hitler; and Marie, while the widow of a German officer, is also, for his family, a potential outpost of the enemy force intruding into their domestic space. The dynamics established, clashes ensue with a finely honed inevitability. As in her other war novels, Margaret creates a realism that is, in effect, fabular. The critical moment comes when the child Heinrich, who loves and trusts Marie, tells her of a plot to kill an English officer, and Marie has to decide how to act. When she reveals the plot to the French, they revile her, ignoring her confusion and pain. In the end, Aubrac relents and offers her a kind of redemption: to work with his sister, succoring children traumatized by war. The final touch, when she has left for France and her new task, is the child Heinrich salvaging from the fire the poems of Pierre de Ronsard she had given him, poems of love. This is indeed a fabular ending, a vision of reconciliation; Margaret was far too knowledgeable about the effects of war and unreconcilable hatreds to claim it as everyday reality.

CHAPTER 21

The End of the War and Visits to Eastern Europe

After Christmas, Guy was swept back into the army while Margaret headed for London. She had sent Rache Lovat Dickson *The Other Side* and was delighted when he praised it. On the strength of this, she asked if Macmillan would act as guarantor for a loan from the Midland Bank. She had seen a large, deluxe bungalow in Virginia Water, a village on the edge of Windsor Great Park. The bungalow was designed by an Austrian architect, just big enough to house herself and Guy with Bill and family. The price, astronomical for the time, was £5,500; she had just £2,000 (SJ to LD, 1.14.45). Macmillan agreed to lend her enough to make the purchase possible, and Margaret hoped the two books that her publishers now held would "clear off the financial part of my debt" (SJ to LD, 1.25.45).

In recent months, her plans for Do's family had suffered a sea change: her brother-in-law had suddenly announced that after demobilization he would look for a job in the States so that he and the children could settle there. Margaret, despite putting a brave face on this, was devastated (SJ to HO, 1.28.45). She retired to the Oakeley Arms at the end of January, worrying now about the prospect of sharing a house with Bill and his wife. For not all was well: Bill was established as a civilian examiner in the Air Ministry, but Margaret thought that he seemed to be "consuming his own intelligence in a dangerous isolation" (SJ to HO, 1.31.45). In February, the family descended on the Oakeley Arms in penny numbers: her brother-in-law, soon to be going to Canada for three months with the RAF before exploring possible jobs in the States, then Bill for a week, and Barbara until the end of the month. "I might as well take over the Oakeley for my family," she told Irene Rathbone, sounding rather exasperated, "meantime I can't get on with my new book, which is needed, to pay for all these excursions" (SJ to IR, 2.6.45). Guy at least was cheerful; to his pleasure, he had been posted to Oxford and was living "in rooms provided by his old college, dines at High Table, drinks port afterwards in the SCR [senior common room], and feels himself back in the Middle Ages — it must be rather comforting" (SJ to LD, 3.16.45). There is no doubting the ironic tone of this last comment; Margaret must have had a moment of déjà vu, recalling Karl's carefree residence in a similar Oxford college, all those years ago. By the end of the month, Guy had found himself one room in the town, and Margaret planned to visit him in April to see if she could find anywhere until he was out of the army. Here again there must have been echoes of Karl, contributing to the bittersweet quality of this difficult but happy second marriage.

News from France continued to distress. Guy heard that their friend Denis Saurat had been dismissed from the Institut Français by the French government; Hermon Ould confirmed the news, saying that Saurat had not been discreet about de Gaulle. He had told Hermon once that he knew for a fact de Gaulle planned on being a virtual dictator, and he now saw the present French government as fundamentally anti-British (HO to SJ, 3.8.45). Margaret was anxious for him, and furious with de Gaulle: "It seems a pity . . . to pull down one dictator and set up another in Paris" (SJ to HO, 3.10.45).

At the end of April there was a family crisis: Margaret's sister Winifred, just back from her wartime censorship job in Bermuda, had been taken ill, so Margaret moved to London to be near her. This brought more money problems, as she told Rache:

> My sister from Bermuda is being rushed into hospital for a major operation tomorrow, and will need, when she comes out, a month in a country nursing home followed by a month in a country hotel. . . . It is costing me the earth, as these things do. Do you think I could have £100 . . . — thus reducing my debt to you to a round sum of three thousand (very round)? (SJ to LD, 4.29.45).

As ever, Margaret felt herself responsible for her entire family and felt that they must have the very best care available.

The Journal of Mary Hervey Russell was published in May, its dust jacket designed by Cecil Bacon, an outstanding exponent of scraper board etching;[1] Macmillan had again done Margaret proud. As ever, the reviews were mixed: the *Listener* reviewer reproved her for showing "too naïve a view of how literature works"; he already took T. S. Eliot, E. M. Forster, and Virginia Woolf as the only valid touchstones.[2] But more penetrating readers were quick to praise: Edith Sitwell, touched that one of the epigraphs was hers, sent Margaret a sensitive analysis, while R. H. Tawney told her she had the gift of endowing the recent past with "the permanence and significance of history."[3] The sales showed a readership with faith in her too: by May 24, 16,000 copies of the book had been sold, a good number for a time of austerity (SJ to LD, 5.24.45). By this time, Margaret was back in Wales, as her sister's operation had been a success. For now the Oakeley Arms was a place of refuge, and Margaret could treat its eccentricities lightly: when she requested from Rache twenty extra copies of her book, she asked him to send them in five or six parcels:

> That will create less excitement in this hotel, which is more like a Noel Coward country-house than anything else, every one of the old inhabitants knows all about the others, counts their letters, and asks: What was in that box you got from Harrod's? (SJ to LD, 4.16.45)

Comfortable though she might be, anxieties about the future were increasing. She told Hermon in confidence that Guy, due to be demobbed in June, had been offered the chance of an assistant professorship in Chicago for eight or nine months, and she was "in a flat spin," making herself ill with worry in case Guy at fifty-five was "too old and tired" to make a success of it (SJ to HO, 5.31.45).

Before long, she and Guy had decided not to take up the Chicago offer, partly, it would seem, because of an adverse reading of their horoscopes (SJ to HO, 6.16.45); but this may have been simply an excuse, as Margaret for one did not feel ready to spend eight to nine months abroad just as the war was ending. As it was, she stayed on in her comfortable refuge in Wales to finish her next novel. Once that was accomplished, she intended to move to the bungalow bought for Bill and his family until she could find somewhere for Guy and herself to live. But there was a shock in store: having decided not to go to Chicago, Guy had applied for the history chair at Leeds University and had been short-listed, despite Margaret's objections to his moving to Leeds, and to living there herself: "I have a feeling that I am turning aside at the cross-roads that would have taken me somewhere I ought to go," she told Hermon (SJ to HO, 7.16.45). She was, despite her willingness to serve Guy's needs, very much averse to becoming an academic wife; and she very much feared that this might become her role, away from London. At moments like these Margaret's letters reveal her feminist core, which could only be appeased by the knowledge that serving Guy was her choice, and which nonetheless fought against any risk of a descent into subservience. Against the odds, Guy was appointed to the chair of modern history, and Margaret poured out to Hermon some of the reasons for her dismay:

> All my plans are in ruins about me. I meant to take a small modern flat, and if necessary shut it up and go to the States to start my brother-in-law and his children off there, if he decided on that. Alternatively, I was not at all depressed by the thought of taking a big house and bringing up two nice children. Everyone said I was going to sacrifice myself, but I didn't see it that way, though I preferred the thought of the small flat and freedom to travel. What I have got is a narrow university circle, professors' wives, a house to be run for two people and their university guests from the staff. I am sunk. It seems pretty feeble to be sunk about what millions of people would be thanking God for. But there you are — I wasn't meant for domestic life. (SJ to HO, 7.24.45)[4]

This personal catastrophe meant that the general election of July 26 did not excite much comment in her letters, despite the landslide Labour victory, Churchill's move to the opposition benches, and Harold Macmillan's return to his publishing house. Margaret was more concerned about her own fate and her brother-in law's confirmation that he intended to settle with the children in the States.

Such preoccupations did not result in any slackening of Margaret's discipline as a writer. She finished her novel by the end of July as she had planned, leaving the Oakeley Arms for the bungalow in Virginia Water.[5] She had just settled down there and begun revising the book as the atom bombs were dropped on Hiroshima and Nagasaki. Despite the huge implications for the future of this nuclear attack, the focus of the letter pages in the daily papers was largely on Europe; Margaret was one of the first to respond to what had happened in Japan. Her letter to the *Manchester Guardian* appeared on August 13, making no secret of her disgust:

> Sir, It is difficult to imagine on what grounds Mr. Churchill and the leader-writers base their pious hopes that the atomic bomb will "conduce to peace among the nations" or "become a perennial fountain" of anything but death. Since we have not refrained from using it to blot out a city of 300,000 inhabitants, why should we hope that the consciences of future users will be more sensitive or merciful? The example has been set.[6]

Writing to Basil Liddell Hart, who had said her letter did honor to her, she looked at the atom bomb from a rather different perspective:

> I feel that as a form of human activity it is "better" than torturing people in prison. I have just had my first letter from a friend in Prague [Jirina Tumova], who was in prison with her husband; she was shown him after he had been questioned for some days, he was unrecognizable, and so terrible that she could not look at him for more than a minute: a few days later he was strangled. . . . I think that what I am trying to say is that my despair is not increased at all by the new discovery. I only hope that something will survive — China perhaps — so that there is more than ruins for mankind to start again from. (SJ to LH, 8.22.45)

Her despair at the revelation of the sheer scale and variety of the human potential for cruelty would inform most of her postwar novels.

At the bungalow, life was, for a time, peaceful, but Margaret was not allowed to steep herself in family life for long; she was invited to Cracow by the Polish government. The party Margaret would join consisted of Val Gielgud for the BBC, Bernard Newman, a journalist, David Cleghorn Thomson, a Scottish playwright whose work centered on political issues, and a number of Polish writers, painters, and diplomats, including her friend, the poet Antoni Słonimski. They left on September 9, and the sights of Europe from the air would haunt her, as she noted in a diary of her visit: "Hanover looks like a shell, empty in its ring of suburbs."[7] When they arrived in Warsaw, she jotted down a vivid, impressionistic account of what she saw: "broken colums [sic] defaced carvings clinging to the facades, which are sometimes a whole front, more often part of one . . . piles of rubbish untouched." She described people selling their possessions, "barefooted dirty children. . . . People are killed every day by bits of wall collapsing on them." Yet there was a "terrific sense of life and energy, everyone working." She met Kowalski, the minister of culture, "writer of peasant novels . . . a cheerful old boy, rather like Tawney." All told her the same story: half the writers and artists were dead, and the survivors unable to write or paint, yet the people were hungry for books and they were bringing in translations. She met the essayist and translator Jan Parandowski, chair of the Polish PEN; she felt the Russian influence, heard how "the Russians take all." She gave a staccato description of the horrors of the ghetto, its fired ruins scorched and bleak; she recounted horror stories of the occupation, ending with the stark tale the ambassador told of how "as a curiosity he was shown in a hospital one Jewish child." Margaret never pampered her readers, or herself, with unnecessary commentary on such revelations.

From Warsaw the party traveled to Cracow, where Margaret met Czesław Miłosz, the future Nobel Prize winner, at the time "a solid smiling young man who has been translating *The Waste Land*, he finished it the day the [Warsaw] Rising began." She met Eugenia Kocwa, who had been in the Ravensbrück concentration camp for five years: "Like all these people out of the camps she has curiously withdrawn eyes." Margaret was keen to find some way of conveying to her readers back home the enormity of what had happened, while Miłosz and his friends were more interested in what was happening in England, asking:

Is there no revolt, critical and creative, against the outmoded Marxism of the Spenders etc, and what are the new young English writers providing to set against the blast of Russianism coming from the Continent. Answer by me. No revolt, but a turning away rather.

She found these Poles still very Anglophile; their old society was dying, and they were braced for the advent of "secret police, the arrests, the censorship, the grip over the police, the army, and propaganda . . . a bad thing." She found to her dismay that anti-Semitism survived: one woman repeated the old story of Jews drawing off Christian children's blood. "It is a disease," Margaret wrote. She watched films of two camps, Oświęcim (Auschwitz) and Majdanek; she met the pianist Chlapowski, who had escaped almost naked from his burning house. Back in Warsaw, she spent a day writing a broadcast talk for the Polish radio. One diplomat at the British Embassy urged her to tell the truth when she was back in England, how the young were demoralized by war and years underground: "To kill, lie, rob, loot is heroism one day and evil the next." She was shown German photographs of a street shooting in Warsaw; a young man told her "we are all obsessed, imprisoned in the house of our memories." By the time she returned to England, she was exhausted physically and emotionally. But she told Hermon, "I shall now try to go straight back to Prague" (SJ to HO, 9.21.45). She was not shying away from further grim revelations; while Hermon thought Prague would be less painful than Warsaw, Jirina Tumova's letters about her own imprisonment and her husband's torture and death had told her otherwise (SJ to HO, 9.21.45; HO to SJ, 10.1.45).

While waiting for a flight, Margaret sent her latest novel to Rache. *Before the Crossing* had been written in the first seven months of 1945. While in *Journey from the North* Margaret would say the novel was meant to be a fourth volume of her *Mirror in Darkness* trilogy, and while it did indeed follow the lives of a number of characters from those books, it was quite different in mood and emphasis. For by this time, Margaret was no longer a part of the action; she had moved a long way from the often thinly veiled autobiographical input that was a key factor of her early novels. The Renn of the trilogy now stands as protagonist; and now Margaret's anxiety about Fascist tendencies within the state developing under wartime conditions, and her recognition that such tendencies could be reflected in the individual, come to fruition. For while Renn attacks these tendencies in others, his own fight for justice has become an obsession, dangerously clouding his capacity for compassion. This, for Margaret, was a major stumbling block raised by Sartre's philosophy, an existentialist philosophy that had emerged in the 1930s: "how to reconcile, except in the practice of a Resistance or Revolution, the belief that conflict is the only relation of one human being with another, with the belief that respect for the freedom of others is a basic virtue?"[8] Margaret thought Sartre could not, "within the human situation as he conceives it, erect brotherly respect as a universally valid human value" (TWS, 25). This is the problem confronting Renn, and influencing the behavior of those around him. In this book, there is not the large cross-section of society found in the earlier trilogy. Instead, a searchlight is directed on a group of interrelated people in the Britain of 1939, focusing very much on the dark side of the human spirit. The opening paragraph identifies Renn as observer, recalling Margaret's description of the writer's stance in her essay for Olaf Stapledon's "Fundamental Values" project:

> Renn sat down, to wait for his friend, at a table outside a café. He drew everything towards him — the street, the girl hanging on the arm of her pallid furtive young man, the sharp corner of the rue Soufflot, railings of the Luxembourg, the light. This light ran against him from all sides: he saw himself as a dark knot at its centre, which it did not penetrate. He felt its warmth on his hands pressing the iron table.[9]

The "dark knot" is the key: such detachment will be shown to have its dangers, as the observer ceases to engage readily with other human beings and their predicaments. This is the problem Margaret had already explored through her narrator in *Europe to Let*: the detachment of the observer, the narrator, might give the illusion of objectivity, but by his standing back from the events observed, he risked abandoning compassion and responsibility for the suffering of others.

Many of the characters around Renn started life in the trilogy: Swan, for instance, his Fascist leanings accentuated, while the once exuberant Gary, castrated in World War I, has "lost his nature," becoming nothing more than an "international usurer" (BTC, 145). The state of the world seeps into these characters, each in their own way corrupted. But there are new characters: young Arnold represents a generation that may break free of the older generation's corruptive influence; and there is also young Marie, victimized by both Hunt (the murderer) and Renn (the man who pursues him). For Renn's detachment has indeed grown monstrous, disturbingly echoing Margaret's ideal writer: "his mind was withdrawn and alert, he had become an instrument for registering other people's emotions" (*BTC*, 126). A danger of becoming dehumanized clearly lurks here; through her war experience, Margaret had come to see that reason and detachment can both be corrupted. Many of the characters in this novel are nihilist, perilously adrift from any stable humanist code of values; this situation leaves others vulnerable to the illusion of stability that the Fascist code offers. It is only in his final confrontation with Hunt that Renn realizes his commitment to justice has deteriorated into revenge, that he has slipped over the brink, espousing the lack of humanity that he has condemned in others. For Hunt demands to know what he has done to Marie. There is a terrible irony in the villain accusing the "good guy" and being justified, for Renn realizes "he had pressed roughly on the human being least able to bear it" (*BTC*, 279), bullying little, fragile Marie who was already a victim of Hunt's own callousness. Yet the novel ends: "The light, when he stepped from the dark sunken lane into the road, pressed against his eyes, so warm, massive, living, that it was purely a joy" (*BTC*, 279). This sentence picks up the image of the first paragraph, without the stress on Renn's darkness, offering a hint of hope.

Undoubtedly, in its overall grimness, this was as much a work of its time as anything by the Sartre of the late 1930s or the Malraux of the 1940s. For Margaret, like other leading British intellectuals of her time, was looking to France for the kind of philosophical theorizing that addressed the contemporary era clear-eyed. As she had found increasingly throughout the interwar years, the suffering in Europe was a good breeding ground for intellectual debate. Yet for many of Margaret's English contemporaries, the novel's concentration on a British heart of darkness would prove hard to take after the sapping of energy and morale during the war years. Her letter to her old friend Harrison Brown at the end of September reflected the mood in her novel: "We are all tired to death, we are all sick of short rations, we all used up our last strokes of energy during the flying bombs and rocket months" (SJ to Brown, 9.27.45). She had one piece of good news to impart: Bill had been commended in the New Year's Honours list of 1944 for his services flying civilian planes — in all weathers, seven days a week, throughout the war (SJ to Brown, 9.27.45).

She herself moved north at the beginning of October when Guy took up his chair at the University of Leeds. Not having found a house, they would be living in the Ghyll Court Hotel, in Ilkley, well away from the grime and overcrowding of Leeds itself (SJ to HO, 9.23.45). The hotel was meant to be a temporary perch while they waited for the housing problem to ease; instead, they would stay there for seven years, and Margaret would be able to take daily walks on the moors above the town. She would be going to Prague soon, she thought; but October would fade into November before she could get a flight. In the meantime, she was keen to sit down in a room that was large and airy, sort out her mind, and work on her next book, *Black Laurel*, the sequel to *Before the Crossing*. Later she would claim they were really one novel; but in 1945 she did not suggest this. The working title was "Europe for Sale," since corrupt business deals would be paramount (SJ to HO, 10.1.45).[10]

Margaret finally got a flight in November, and found the city of Prague barely damaged. Her reunion with Jirina was inevitably painful, not only because of the terrible death of Jirina's husband. Jirina was upset that Margaret had been to Poland since there had been friction between Poles and Czechs both before and after the war. She was also unhappy that Margaret wanted to see, among other things, the internment camps where German civilians were being held. Margaret found the Czechs, like the Poles, aware that they must keep on friendly terms with the Russians; unlike the Poles, the Czechs spoke of their "Slav brothers," who would not betray them unlike, Margaret felt, France and Britain. Jirina took her to the prison where she herself had spent many months, now housing German prisoners. There were horrific anecdotes of what German guards had done to their Czech victims; Margaret would recall that she "brought down inside my skull the shutter cutting off emotion" (JN, 2:175).[11] Later in her visit, she had tea with President Beneš alone; he talked to her for two hours, explaining his policies for survival, such as tolerance of Communists at the core of government, and, in a move that still has repercussions today, the expropriation of lands belonging to ethnic Germans and Hungarians who had lived there for centuries; huge numbers of them were deported. Margaret could only listen.

Then there were her visits to the internment camps. Moderaty was bad enough, its inmates living in mud and squalor, but Hagibor was much bigger, its inmates enduring a "suffocating stench" (*JN*, 2:190). Margaret was near the end of her tether, but insisted on seeing the hospital, where certain rooms stayed in her mind over the years: one housed four old men, Germans, one a distinguished brain surgeon, another a heart specialist, all starving, all dying. In another room she was shown young German women and a few Czech girls who had relations with German soldiers, awaiting deportation. She was shown their newly born babies who would die when their mothers' milk dried. Gazing at one dying baby, Margaret had a horrifying insight:

> The tiny face dissolved and for less than a breath I saw through its soft skull the guillotine in Pankrác . . . , the terror of a boy in the instant before he is killed, the decent bodies of women heaped, naked as maggots, in Terezín and Auschwitz — the spume of agony flowing back and forth across Europe. (*JN*, 2:194)

She came away believing that undamaged Prague was more profoundly damaged than Warsaw: "if both were forced to turn religiously towards the east, the Poles might, it was conceivable, ride lighter, with a margin of ironic reserve" (*JN*, 2:197). For what she had seen was that the Poles had, despite all, kept their sense of identity, had not been betrayed by the West; but the Czechs and Slovaks were citizens of a new country whose roots went no further back than World War I, and whose time in the Austro-Hungarian Empire had left them with a bitterness toward ethnic Germans and Hungarians to which they could now give free rein. And this bitterness was not only against the ethnic Other, but against any who could be seen as collaborating or fraternizing. Certainly the sheer scale of retribution in Czechoslovakia for perceived collaboration, fraternization, and vague "crimes against the nation" was dismaying (Judt, *Postwar*, 50).[12] The determination to be Slav alone, wholeheartedly Slav, encouraged the turn toward Russia.

Margaret reached home at the end of November with a very heavy cold, due to "travelling at 15,000 feet in an unheated Dakota, and also without food" (GC to LD, 1.12.45). She communicated none of the horrors she had seen to Rache or to her old friend the publisher Stanley

Unwin, and was uncharacteristically reticent with Hermon (SJ to HO, 12.2.45). She was finding it hard to get over her disgust with what the Nazis had done, had been distressed by the atrocities she had witnessed in its wake, but would, in her writings, strive to keep faith with a European future which could transcend this disastrous past.

CHAPTER 22

War's Aftermath and Visit to the States

From November 1945 to October 1946, the trials of the surviving members of the Nazi leadership were taking place in Nuremberg and given wide press coverage: Rebecca West was one of the journalists writing about them.[1] It was in this context that Margaret wrote articles on her visits to Poland and Czechoslovakia for the *Fortnightly Review*. The article on Poland, drawing on her diary, was vivid and fresh, urging readers to recognize the extent of the devastation that the country had endured, yet showing the extraordinary capacity to regroup and rebuild. Hoping as she did for a better future, she did not dwell on the lingering anti-Semitism she had found there, but concentrated on what was worthy of Western support. This was not because she was naive; she knew all too well from her work with refugees what horrors lay there in the past. But she was also seeing in Eastern Europe, in France, the hatreds that were being appeased in the aftermath of war, and knew that stoking the flames did not bode well for the future.[2] And the article on Czechoslovakia must have posed problems for her that were just as great.[3] She wanted to present Beneš as a statesman, while she could not avoid discussing the forcible expulsion of vast numbers of ethnic Germans. She decided not to excuse, but to explain, thus challenging her English readers' right to judge the brutality spawned by the brutalities of the German occupation. Again, she was not being naive; she had no illusions about what even a friend like Jirina Tumova could countenance after her own ordeals. As in the war, she looked to the future, aiming for reconciliation rather than vindictiveness (Judt, *Postwar*, 51). As it was, she was deeply concerned about the spirit of vindictiveness reaching into the PEN, where there was a move to blacklist writers perceived as collaborating or fraternizing:

> I am totally opposed to old writers like Hamsun being punished, and if anything is to be done or can be done, count me in. Some time ago I signed a petition for Ezra Pound, which had Eliot's support, so I am sure he would support anything we cared to do for Hamsun. (SJ to HO, 1.16.46)[4]

Given their commitment to reconciliation, Margaret and Hermon Ould were consistent in their opposition to vindictiveness wherever they found it, even when there was good cause; they would have had much in common with Nelson Mandela and Archbishop Tutu in the aftermath of South Africa's apartheid. So Margaret risked the anger of those who had suffered as she fought against the punishment of writers who had fallen foul of their colleagues. Quite as readily, she was helping the younger generation of writers from countries that had suffered. Czesław Miłosz, for instance, whom she had met on her visit to Poland, had been appointed to the Polish Consulate in Chicago as Public Relations Officer; and as he and his wife passed through London, Margaret introduced him to Rache Lovat Dickson as one of Poland's leading poets. Rache in turn gave him a letter of introduction to Harold Latham, head of Macmillan in New York, as Czesław needed contacts in publishing.[5]

More personal problems were looming. Margaret, deeply apprehensive about the future in Europe, shaken by what she had seen in Eastern Europe, and not happy about her role as the wife of an academic, must have unburdened herself to Valentine Dobrée. Valentine, highly strung herself, could not, it seems, cope with her friend's distress and Margaret wrote to apologize:

> I have been foolish lately, as so often, in crying for a freedom I know to be illusory. . . . You must please try to forgive me for forcing my unreasonable inexcusable feelings on you. I didn't realise I was doing it so unbearably. (SJ to VD, 2.19.46)

There was a further complication: Guy appeared to think he could stay with the Dobrées during the week in term time, but Valentine was not happy with the idea. She had been willing to have him stay in the war when his billet was so unpleasant, but now he had a hotel and a wife not too far from Leeds, so circumstances were very different. Regardless of these very different circumstances, Margaret set about pleading Guy's cause, while stressing she would not impose herself. Her letters make it all too clear that she was asking more of their friendship than Valentine was willing to give; the warning signs were ominous.

The Other Side was published on March 15, 1946. Margaret's fear that it might no longer have relevance was not justified, for while the reviews were, as ever, mixed, they had small impact on her readers.[6] The novel did so well that Margaret was quite taken aback: "Nearly every day I get another letter or letters from anywhere in England and Europe, praising it in terms more suitable for Shakespeare. I must have stumbled on one of the nerves of Europe at the moment" (SJ to LD, 6.21.46). But as she corrected the proofs of *Before the Crossing*, she had been taken aback less agreeably: "However did I come to write a book in which there is not a single pleasant character, or only half a one? It really is a terrible book. I must have been in a black mood which lasted months" (SJ to LD, 6.21.46). Her own reaction would soon find a distressing echo.

Margaret, with Hermon, attended the Stockholm Congress, postponed from 1939. It was predictable in its priorities. There was a blacklist of collaborators, drawn up by those centers whose countries had been occupied, which Margaret and Hermon opposed vigorously. As Margaret later commented to Irene Rathbone, "the real villains, as usual, are safe in other countries . . . and the only people who will suffer are little people who just weren't very brave" (SJ to IR, 7.1.46). There were lighter moments, however, as when old Prince William, a staunch Anglophile and president of the Swedish Centre, too deaf to hear the arguments, sent her a note saying: "Let me know how the English are going to vote, and I'll vote with you" (JN/TMS, 3:74).

Margaret was away for ten days, and returned to a full-blown family crisis. Bill had been worrying her for some time; by the end of 1945, he had walked away from the Air Ministry, joining a new company, British South American Air Lines, as a navigator. But this move mirrored deeper splits: by June, his marriage was breaking up, and Margaret, who had retired to Ilkley to write, thought she might have to go back to Virginia Water "to save something from a sticky ruin. For the first time I am really shocked, and trembling as I type" (SJ to HO, 6.24.46). Matters got worse over the next fortnight with awful scenes between husband and wife, but then there was an uneasy truce. Clearly, despite her love for Bill, Margaret knew he was behaving badly. She had not interfered, she told Hermon, "but Barbara had a very bad time" (SJ to HO, 7.5.46). Not surprisingly, her greatest concern was for her grandson.

In early July, Margaret and Guy took a flat for the summer vacation in Scarborough, the Yorkshire seaside town where Margaret had studied for her county scholarship.[7] Despite this return to her past, she had no time for nostalgia:

> The amount of drudgery in this small flat is astonishing. I don't write, I just do the cleaning, cooking, queuing — and write my letters. Guy is writing madly fast — there is no point in both of us being sacrificed — and this is his only chance to get on with a book. (SJ to HO, 7.5.46)

This passage gets to the heart of Margaret's problem with domesticity: she was incapable of *not* doing everything in the old-fashioned, physically demanding way, while hating the drudgery. What with this, and the rift in Bill's marriage, her next novel was suffering: "My monster of a book on Germany is perishing of inanition, in my mind. . . . I did begin, and wrote four short chapters, but so difficult a novel as it promises to be needs more peace" (SJ to HO, 7.5.46). More practical matters she could handle, for example, helping a young Polish couple she had met in Warsaw, both of whom had been in concentration camps; Margaret had left most of her clothes with Tamara in Poland, "but it wasn't much for a woman who only possessed one skirt and one jumper and nothing more" (SJ to LD, 7.16.46). Now they were on a six-month leave in England to study "the latest economic books," and she was doing what she could to help them (SJ to LD, 7.16.46). The plight of the Poles Margaret had met still haunted her; old Jan Parandowski, president of the Polish PEN, had been threadbare in Stockholm, and she made over her Swedish royalties to him — five hundred kronor (SJ to LD, 7.16.46).

From the moment it came into print, *The Other Side* had attracted offers from dramatists wanting to adapt it for the stage. Macmillan had discouraged some lesser talents, but the actor, writer, and dramatist Ronald

Millar had won their approval. Margaret had read his first draft and found it passable if rather unsubtle. She was, in fact, more distressed at having to refuse $25,000 for the film rights — because, in the contract to which she had agreed, "they belong with the play rights" (SJ to LD, 6.21.46). As she noted ruefully, her American agent, Carl Brandt, would be furious. In mid-July she heard that Millar's play would be produced at the London Comedy Theatre in four weeks' time; but she had no intention of seeing it: "The young man has made a very neat slick play out of it, but it is not *my* play," she told Hermon (SJ to HO, 7.18.46). Then Millar wrote that the cast would be offended if she were not there: "I'd MUCH MUCH rather sit through an air raid," she protested (SJ to HO, 7.18.46). Eventually agreeing to attend the first night, she traveled to London at the end of July and went to a rehearsal. She was horrified: "Since I saw and approved the first draft of the play, the young man has largely rewritten it. It is awful. What meaning and what restraint the book had has completely vanished" (SJ to VD, 8.1.46). One day, she vowed, she would try to write her own play: "Never again will I let myself in for this humiliation" (SJ to VD, 8.1.46). In the event, the reception of the play was not as bad as Margaret feared; although the first night, she told Hermon, was "pretty grim," she was too tired to care and allowed herself to be pushed on stage (SJ to VD, 8.10.46). It ran for some weeks and was broadcast in part on August 20. The reviewer in the *Times*, however, who had clearly preferred the novel, agreed with Margaret's appraisal of the play: the dialogue was too banal, and if it did not kill the play, "the explanation may be looked for in the strength of the story, and of some of the performances, rather than in the subtlety of the adaptation."[8] So all the play's good qualities were Margaret's own, which must have given her some gratification.

Back in Scarborough, she buried her head in a mountain of letters from all over the world. She took time to visit her mother's sister in Whitby and to see if there was room on "his family gravestone" for her father's name, buried as he was away from her mother (SJ to VD, 8.1.46). But she was growing weary of domesticity, especially of the constant cooking. On August 16 she and Guy left, as planned, for a fortnight in Zurich, while Winifred took a holiday in their flat.[9] However, when they got back, Margaret found her sister in bed with a leg infection, a nurse installed, and the flat, by her standards, filthy. So, she told Hermon crossly, she was "again cook, scrubber, bedmaker, sweeper etc. etc. What a life!" (SJ to HO, 9.4.46). Fortunately Winifred soon recovered, returning to her own flat in London, while Guy and Margaret went to Wales. And despite the domestic crisis, Margaret had managed to correct the "final page" of *Before the Crossing,* and sent it off to Rache (SJ to LD, 9.8.46).

Family problems showed no sign of abating: the split between Bill and Barbara was widening. Margaret was trying to help them both, while desperately anxious for the child. In November she had Barbara and Christopher to stay, both overwrought. The crisis intensified, Bill insisting on divorce, while Barbara, in her anguish, was threatening violence to Bill, the child, and herself. Margaret confided in Kathleen Liddell Hart that it was like living in a thunderstorm (SJ to KLH, 11.21.46). By the end of November, after three weeks of violent scenes, Bill announced he was leaving Barbara, and her mother came to the Ilkley hotel to take her daughter away. Margaret was left exhausted and ill herself, asking for horoscope consultations in her despairing need to see into a murky future (SJ to HO, 11.31[*sic*].46). Hermon, while sympathetic, sought to distract her with a new project. Some time earlier, he had been offered a job with UNESCO (United Nations Educational, Scientific, and Cultural Organization). Feeling too old to take this on, he had compromised, by setting up links between UNESCO and the PEN (HO to SJ, 12.4.46). Now he wrote of the immense possibilities of the UNESCO idea if it could only recruit the right sort of people. He was, moreover, determined to keep Margaret active for the PEN, making sure she had a formal request to be the English Centre's representative on the International Committee. Accordingly, in January, Margaret prepared for her first International Executive Committee meeting while trying hard to build bridges with Barbara, spending time with her whenever she came to London. The PEN meetings, preoccupied as they were with postwar issues and with the increasing invasiveness of Stalinist values, were inevitably fraught; but Margaret was clearly pleased to return to the fold.

By mid-April 1947, despite all the interruptions, Margaret had "written (for the third time) the last page of *The Black Laurel*" (SJ to LD, 4.12.47). The research for this novel had been all the more stringent as she had not visited Berlin, the principal setting for the book, since the early 1930s. On the other hand, she had been to Warsaw, "and it was there that I learned how people live in ruins."[10] The idea of the novel had, she claimed, come to her "when I was flying uncomfortably across Europe in a Transport Command plane in 1945" on a clear day in summer, looking down on the ruins of Europe ("Background"). The writing had taken longer than usual, as she digested information about Berlin. There was a letter from a friend of Guy's in the army of occupation, Robert Wakeford, giving details of postwar military matters in Berlin, while later Margaret would report that ten people had given her information about intelligence in Germany.[11] The subject was inevitably one to make her publishers nervous, given that it dealt with issues right at the heart of the former enemy's homeland and was unsparingly frank about the shortcomings of some British characters: Rache would raise a number of objections, but Margaret was deeply committed to what she had written, and the changes made would be few. A large run was planned, but the subject matter, being what it was, needed careful legal vetting and delayed publication in England until February 1948 despite the date on the book being 1947.[12]

In this novel, characters from *Before the Crossing* move into a very different context: a postwar Europe, its elements all present in Berlin, developing the "soundings" technique that Margaret had made her own. The first chapter takes place during the last days of the war, in a prisoner-of-war camp in Scotland, where two opposing "just" codes come into conflict: the duty of a POW to escape, making betrayal an act worthy of execution, as against the British code of murder, the betrayers having helped the British authorities to thwart a planned escape. This first chapter of clashing codes, of betrayals, establishes key themes in the novel. There is much that is grim, but through it all, Gary's young pilot, Arnold, learns to pursue a more hopeful path to the future, together with his girl, Lise. When the action moves to Berlin, expediency and material advantage inject their own infectious ugliness. The dilemma at the core of the novel is the loss of moral perspective that war brings in its wake, where an individual's private agenda all too often becomes sufficient justification for a decision as to what is "right." Gary and his kind represent the heartlessly opportunistic element in war's poisonous brew, but on the German side the poison is working as well, fragmenting the defeated community. From his plane, Arnold sees the devastation that has been inflicted, a disturbing variation on Hesse's vision in *Then We Shall Hear Singing*:

Bridges sagged like torn wires into the rivers. The rotten teeth of the bombed towns. For the first time he saw what had happened. The hangmen had done their work thoroughly, the body of Europe, flayed while still living, was stretched below him in the sunlight, the nerves exposed and torn, the fractured bones, the nails rotted, decomposing flesh, a death terrible, sordid, poisoned. (*BL*, 35)

There is none of Hesse's godlike triumph in the earlier novel as he sees the earth as a living body to do with as he pleases: young Arnold's vision is of a landscape already dead, of death by torture, the countries below him reflecting the cruelties of the camps and the battlefields in unsparingly human images. Margaret homed in on individuals caught up in the ruins: a young German, physically and mentally warped by war; his uncle, a humanitarian, trying to reassert humanist moral values. Into all this comes Renn, now attempting to reinstate his own humanity, and here also comes little Kalb, a Jew returning to Berlin on a mission, who will become a victim of a corrupt expediency, treated by Gary and his kind as expendable. Kalb is presented as an innocent, not particularly likable but utterly vulnerable, and quite oblivious to his peril until it is too late. He has been a refugee in England, and has a touching faith in British fairness and compassion. Only too soon this faith is betrayed by Gary, together with a few other rapacious individuals, who will destroy poor little Kalb for their own ends. Margaret dares to show here something of the credo that spawned the death camps lingering on in the minds of an ugly and frightening group of British and German entrepreneurs. Indeed, the web Margaret weaves in this novel is awesome in the challenges it threw down to the postwar reader. A digression that Rache initially tried to have omitted, Renn's visit to Prague, where Margaret exposes him to the horrors of the dying babies she herself had seen, is an ingredient in Renn's rehabilitation. He sees how easy it is to justify such callousness when there has been so much suffering to account for. Ruins punctuate the storylines, distorting the landscape and the mentalities that are trapped inside:

In broad daylight, the city of a nightmare. Façades, broken off half way, at a line of defaced sculpture. Sprawling pyramids of dust, of shattered brick; the skeletons of buildings leaning over ossuaries of splintered stone and dust. A single column erect in acres of reddish dust. Carcasses of tanks, burned-out cars. The torn-out megalithic bones, corroded by fire, of a railway-station. Perspectives, beyond those he could see, only of ruins. (*BL*, 36)

Young Arnold's experience, as he walks a Berlin street for the first time, is telling:

He walked through a stench he recognised, though he had not smelled it before. Whole streets, he thought, must have died here in a moment, from intestinal rupture, and there were hundreds, thousands, perhaps, of bodies rotting under the dust. (*BL*, 37)

Renn too is appalled, although the knowledge he brings with him of human frailties and cruelties gives him a broader perspective:

There are some very respectable families living in cellars, over the sewage, and in a few other cellars you can have a quite decent young woman for a bar or two of chocolate. . . . And of course women prepare meals, and put their children to bed, and think the thoughts of anxious women, ignorant . . . and all the other — survivors, all the living, over the entire planet, feeling and acting . . . precisely as human beings have always felt — in the twelfth century, in fourth-century Greece, ten thousand years ago in Tibet — and either they don't know or it doesn't matter to them that they are living through the last years of a civilisation. (*BL*, 39)

The reach of Renn's vision, through time and space, is sobering; this is Margaret's poignant elegy for the end of the civilization she had grown up in, the civilization she and her student friends had hoped to refresh as they matured, and that had, in her view, died in the aftermath of two world wars.

Moreover, Margaret did not let her own bias cloud her determination to convey both sides of an issue; the sacked ruins of Warsaw are depicted after the horrors of a wrecked Berlin, establishing the sufferings of the

German city before revealing the obscenities inflicted on Warsaw, so as to avoid simplistic notions of cause and effect. Margaret uses the collage technique she had used in *The Mirror in Darkness*: she shows Berlin, for instance, through the eyes of Gary, his old compassion warring for a time with his newer pragmatic opportunism, only to succumb in the end; she shows the city through the eyes of its inhabitants, the old man struggling to hand on the culture of Goethe, the young refusing to accept it from him, rendered nihilistic by their loss of Hitler's certainties and the depravations inflicted in their wake. Then there is the Berlin seen by raw young Arnold, and the city seen through Renn's disillusioned eyes. And there is the Berlin of returning little Kalb, who will experience a deeply disturbing rerun of the persecution he had escaped before World War II. The reader is never allowed to settle into one point of view. This is a novel that Margaret, even at her most self-critical, would acknowledge as one she could be proud of; but she was asking questions most of her contemporaries would be reluctant to address for some considerable time. Indeed, the questions she asks in this novel are still being debated now; there are no easy answers.[13]

As she finished the novel, Margaret went back to the Oakeley Arms for the Easter vacation; she was writing a lecture on "The Situation of the Writer" (SJ to HO, 4.17.47).[14] In it, she explored the debate with French existentialism that underpinned her last two novels, developing the ideas in her essay for Stapledon. Citing Louis Aragon, Sartre, and Malraux as three writers who were "trying to hear, then to answer, the question our age asks," each giving different answers to the various questions each saw as key, she went on to analyze Sartre's answer to the paramount question as he saw it: did life have any meaning or purpose? Although she liked his premise that "life has no meaning, no purpose, except the meaning and purpose we give it when we act," he remained, for her, a romantic. He was one who "despairs of a life lived on the knife-edge between sense and absurdity, order and chaos, condemned absurdly to create itself by its own acts," while "the humanly valuable elements in Sartre's philosophy were given him by his Greek masters" (*TWS*, 26–27). For her, the writer must

> listen as carefully as he can to the warnings of the present and
> the future, and give the most truthful account of them. . . . Only
> the artist . . . can tell us how, under what conditions, man can

survive as a fully human being. By this I mean a being who is not only human, not only an existential animal, but a creature who is partly divine, endowed with a divine curiosity and a great, though tragic, destiny. (*TWS*, 35)

This would be Margaret's self-appointed task in her postwar fiction. For while she shared Cyril Connolly's dismay at an England largely reduced to "a vast, seedy, overworked, over-legislated neuter class" and a London "now the largest, saddest and dirtiest of great cities," in her fiction she wanted both to reflect this and to show the potential for a way out of the wreckage (Judt, *Postwar*, 162). For that she needed to stress those aspects of humanity that were "partly divine," in the sense of possessing "divine curiosity and a great, though tragic, destiny," traits that she would emphasize in portrayals of the potential in the younger generation (*TWS*, 35). She was offering a way forward for a generation growing up under the shadow of the Bomb, as the potential for total annihilation would haunt postwar Britain for many years to come.

Before the Crossing was published on May 2. The reviews, even when respectful, were largely uncomprehending; the *TLS* critic was particularly scathing and obtuse about Margaret's presentation of "a group of the most frustrated, purposeless and unhappy people who can have awaited war with apprehension." The ending brought "no great enlightenment, no revelation of human nature."[15] Such incomprehension made Margaret very apprehensive; she had just submitted *The Black Laurel* and feared it would suffer the same treatment (SJ to LD, 5.13.47). However, when Guy eventually found time to read the typescript of *The Black Laurel*, he wrote a note in her diary, which she would copy and keep: "It is the finest work you've ever done. It has quite outstanding intensity, and the real wisdom of the artist. . . . The ideas are stretching the skins of the people."[16] He, for one, could see that the huge questions the novel raised were brought alive by the characters who struggled to contain them. His image of skins being stretched is very apt: Margaret had raised questions that not one of her characters could handle with anything approaching complacency. And Guy's reaction was important to her, even if she did not take it as necessarily meaning her novel would be a success. She wrote to Rache that "it is the first time I have impressed him with a book since *Cousin Honoré*, I don't know whether it is a bad or a good sign"

(SJ to LD, 5.30.47). Providing a kind of coda to Margaret's novel, the *Adelphi* now published the article by Eugenia Kocwa, the woman from Ravensbrück, whom Margaret had met in Cracow.[17] Kocwa's reaction to her suffering was striking, and later commentators might well think it untypical. However, it was one, Margaret said in her introduction, that she herself had heard three more times from camp survivors: "We suffered so terribly that I do not think of punishment for our tormentors. Such things can only be forgiven, and they must be forgiven" ("Mecklenburg," 128). Inevitably, Kocwa's account told a tale of mindless cruelty. Some of the women who had volunteered early to oversee the camps were appalling: "One of them, a certain Lehmann from Silesia, was known for her rages: in a fit of temper, she kicked a young gipsy to death" ("Mecklenburg," 132). Lublin women, especially young girls, were regularly sold to a surgeon from the now notorious Hohenlychen Sanatorium, situated near Ravensbrück, "for experiments on the regeneration of osseous tissue" ("Mecklenburg," 133); many died. It is a searing account, one of many that were emerging from those who had survived. As later in her championing of *The Diary of Anne Frank*, Margaret saw the importance of bringing this testament to British readers.[18]

For the moment, the effort she had expended on her two powerful novels had drained Margaret: she had no impulse to plan another book. She had been told at the PEN Congress in Zurich that the imminent issue of *The Other Side* in France had required great courage; when the publisher had asked the Resistance writer Vercors to write a preface, he had said, "while he admired it enormously, . . . he could not for his life's sake write a preface to a book in which a French girl marries a German" (SJ to LD, 6.25.47). Rache's plea that she should situate her next novel in England was also giving her trouble: "I know you are right . . . [but] all the exciting conflicts are happening abroad—by which I mean that all the conflicts in *personal* lives seem to come much clearer outside this country" (SJ to LD, 6.27.47). Although an English setting would no doubt improve her sales, she felt that translation of such conflicts would not work in a country that had not suffered occupation:

> Take a theme which fascinates me—can you really murder for
> the good of the community, and if you do, what is the effect on
> yourself?—there are any number of ways that could be worked

out in France, say, where people did do murders for the good of the community, but I can't think of a single plausible one set in England, where there has not yet, thank God, been any need for anyone to murder for the good of the country. And then, the true story of the Warsaw Rising is a fascinating personal study of the fate of the middle-of-the-road man between two sorts of fanatics — I keep trying to translate it into English, and failing. (SJ to LD, 6.27.47)

Both of these themes she would mull over, and each would provide the basis for later novels set in Europe: *The Hidden River* and *A Ulysses Too Many*. For while Margaret would often mourn to her friends that she wrote too quickly, she did not acknowledge the time she allowed for ideas to mature, the endless revisions she made as she wrote, and which surviving manuscripts reveal. Nor did she admit that her sales were not as important a goal for her as for her publishers.

In July, she and Guy went to Falmouth, Cornwall, for three weeks. Addresses on hotel notepaper were never a sure way of locating her; Margaret was a great one for taking paper from one hotel and using it later, and now she wrote on paper from the Hotel Rembrandt in Amsterdam. It was a modest holiday; the cost of Bill's divorce, for which she had paid, had been considerable, and she had also bought Bill a boat as a home (SJ to IR, 12.7.47).[19] So she set about planning another novel,

a hybrid form of fiction, drama, philosophical essay, and dream — the last carried by monks of the Benedictine Abbey of Whitby in the twelfth century. The central character was a Mr Antigua, a grotesquely fat man — his physical absurdity a contrast with his sound mind and extreme delicacy of feeling and his friends. (JN/TMS, 3:70)

This sounds like a development from her *Journal* without the autobiographical element, and she was clearly enjoying experimenting with something quite different from her latest novels. Sadly, by the end of September, however, she reluctantly decided it was going nowhere, and (she asserted) tore it up, branding it "a clever fake," although several elements would reemerge twenty years later, in her novel *The White Crow* (SJ to

LD, 9.22.47). But for now, "the germ of a *nouvelle* is growing weakly in the empty place" (SJ to LD, 9.22.47).

About this time, she heard from a young woman in Warsaw who had translated *The Other Side*: it had earned fifty thousand zlotys, which Margaret asked her to donate to the rebuilding fund in Warsaw (*JN*, 2:209). This gift drew a quick response from the city's president; he thanked her warmly, sending her a certificate engraved with a silhouette of the city, workers in the foreground. She also received a letter from the Social Fund for Warsaw Reconstruction, detailing their projects.[20] Generous with money she remained, but she now grew contentious in print. In a letter to the *Times*, she complained about the financial restrictions on foreign travel: "Does this Government so love the under-privileged that it is only happy when increasing their numbers?"[21] She was also embroiled in an argument over the Whitby Spa, another example, in her view, of an encroaching tastelessness that spoiled the idyllic Whitby of her childhood.[22] While she had some local support, a Councillor McNeil reminded her of how many unsanitary buildings there had been in the Whitby of Margaret's youth, how the river was fouled with sewage and stank, how earth closets abounded in the narrow alleys (gunnels) at the backs of houses. Margaret, moreover, lived away; he suggested that she had let her literary ability "outstrip her common sense and judgement."[23] Clearly, the Whitby that was averse to incomers was not going to accept lectures from those who had gone away.

There was, in fact, good reason for Margaret's unusual irritability in print. Bill's divorce had come through on October 14, and it had gone smoothly, but Margaret's own experience had been very different; she had suffered the full force of Barbara's distress. Feeling wretched, she started to flesh out her idea for the short book that had begun to take shape when she abandoned her larger experimental project. Wistfully, she asked Valentine, "Do you suppose that any woman writer, even George Sand, ever really felt that writing was a sufficient reason for living?" (SJ to VD, 10.15.47). Telling Hermon about Bill's divorce, about not being allowed now to see little Christopher, she added simply, "I don't know how to cope with my grief" (SJ to HO, 10.19.47).

Grieved though she was, Margaret never took her eyes off the political developments in her contemporary world. Her new little book was written against the background of the growing aggression of Soviet policy:

in September 1947, the hardening of the Soviet position had taken the Czechs by surprise, ending the idea of peaceful coexistence that had been the bedrock of Beneš's dream of national security (Judt, *Postwar*, 143). As so often, what would be a novel began as a play. Margaret worked on it sporadically, trying several different titles on the way until, as it grew into a three-act drama, *The Moment of Truth* was selected.[24] But work was slow: in November, Margaret strained her back "by pushing heavy wardrobes and cases of books," and she had to rest (SJ to LD, 11.7.47). She was again paying physically for intense nervous strain, as she herself recognized: "I am better, but oddly weak. Too much mental strain about. I am surrounded by lunatics" (SJ to HO, 11.15.47). She was watching swaths of Europe succumb to outside influence, telling Irene that Europe was doomed to be overrun by America or the USSR, she herself preferring America, as "we have a chance of recovering our soul from America in time. From the communists we shall recover neither soul nor body. They are coldbloodedly murdering France at this moment" (SJ to IR, 11.5.47).

As 1947 drew to a close, Margaret was given the first intimations of Guy's plans for 1948: he had been offered an exchange for the following academic year at the University of Pittsburgh, and if he were to go, Margaret was to accompany him. Perhaps these plans to leave an England still suffering the effects of draconian food rationing recalled the passage condemning Auden and Isherwood in *The End of This War* that she had so regretted; for they too had retired from an England that was suffering as war approached. However that might be, the *Gate* published her article on W. H. Auden, "The Poet of Angst," in November.[25] She expressed her admiration for his early work, the imagery of "an extreme sharpness and concreteness" (*TWS*, 84), and she admired his controversial poem *Spain*, published in 1937. By then he had become a symbol for those opposing Fascism, so many were shocked when he left England for America in 1939. Now, in retrospect, Margaret sought a reason she could understand: "Can the poet of *Look Stranger!* have failed to realize . . . that even if a bomb did not destroy him, the fears, the poisons, of Europe might?" (*TWS*, 85). Certainly Auden's sonnets from China suggest the realization that Margaret attributes to him, although these were not poems she expressly admired.[26] Moreover, her view of his later work was mixed. He had not, she thought, developed a large variety or range of metrical forms, but he showed great assurance within his chosen limits.

What bothered Margaret was a verbal skill that she felt did not have emotional depth, and she came back to a prevailing anxiety: since 1930, he showed considerable "intellectual development, the growth of technical assurance, but no or little spiritual development" (*TWS*, 99). She found the influence of Kierkegaard in his later poems overbearing, and here she was on a territory with which she was very familiar; she felt he had been drawn to Kierkegaard by "spiritual kinship," but had failed to note the weight of the Dane's "bolder and more tortured mind" (*TWS*, 100). This article was never meant to be a detailed analysis of Auden's techniques, but a meditation on how his poems responded to the current age. Where she found him wanting was in the failure to quest as she and her fellow students had done so long ago, a failure that she found endemic in her contemporary world, yet which, in her novels, she always suggested was potentially there in such young characters as Arnold in *The Black Laurel*.

In early December, she received a bombshell. She confided in Hermon that

> one of my closest friends, Valentine Dobrée, has just rung me up to say that we must never meet again. After brooding for a year on "Before the Crossing," she has come to the conclusion that the woman who could write so hateful a book isn't fit to know. During this year we have met frequently, she praised the book when she first read it, and it is only a few days since I saw her, apparently sane and friendly as usual. (SJ to HO, 12.4.47)

Years later, Margaret wove her own pattern around the memory of Valentine's renunciation.[27] She renamed Valentine "Leah," the close friend whom

> I admired more than I ever admired a woman before or since. . . . I had a sense of being always several steps behind her, with my slow clumsy mind, always straining to understand her ideas and hoping she was not bored. (*JN/TMS*, 3:78–82)

She had pored over things "Leah" had said "as though I was trying to break a code": she was certain that blame was never one-sided, that she must have shown some disloyalty, and so on and so on (*JN/TMS*, 3:78–

82). However, if we look back to Margaret's arrival in Ilkley, Guy's subsequent long-term lodging with the Dobrées, and Margaret's own mental distress at the time, the roots of the renunciation may well have gone deeper than the one novel. Two brilliant, intense people made for a stressful friendship, always at risk, as that between Vera and Margaret had already shown. But at the time, this renunciation must have mirrored Barbara's.

The year did end with some reassurances. Introducing the *Saturday Evening Post's* selection of stories for 1942–45 the journal's editor wrote:

> The editors of the *Post* challenge anyone to search the short fiction of the past five years and show them a more powerful piece than Storm Jameson's prophetic story "The Last Night," which, incidentally, was written and published before the tide of war in Europe had turned in our favor.[28]

Margaret's story that she had written as a tribute to the victims of Lidice took pride of place.

On the family front, Bill married Ruth (Patchen) on December 18, a woman equipped to cope both with him and with an oversolicitous mother-in-law (SJ to IR, 11.28.47). They were now happily installed on his new boat, and for Margaret, Patchen was "the young woman he ought to have married in the first place, gay, young, brave — she was a ferry pilot herself during the war"; she appeared to have forgotten Barbara's own piloting past.[29] Margaret's sister Winifred had also achieved her ambition to emigrate to the States, where she would live for the rest of her life; and on the work front, Cassell had dropped its blocking tactics, reprinting a number of Margaret's works in their Pocket Library.[30]

So Margaret tried to be positive. The sculptor Anna Mahler, daughter of the composer Gustav, had completed a bust of her by the new year. Margaret liked the "rather gaunt nobility" of the head, and tried to help Anna find new patrons.[31] When Rache said that he did not think the bust caught Margaret's likeness, and even the ever-loyal Hermon commented, reasonably, "it makes you look very masculine," she protested:

> What you don't realise, dear Rache, is that this is really me, the person who writes the books. The smiling person who has lunch

with you . . . is your friend but not the black-hearted author of
'Before The Crossing' etc etc. (SJ to LD, 2.12.48)

She might write cheerfully to Rache, but the Valentine breach haunted
her, as long letters followed the phone call. The condemnation of *Before
the Crossing* particularly dismayed her, as she herself had noted its harsh
presentation of humanity; writing to another friend, she now called it "a
devilish book" (SJ to J. Tawney, 1.20.48). The relationship with Barbara
remained volatile too, although Barbara had agreed to come with Christopher for a fortnight's holiday in North Wales during April (SJ to HO,
1.11.48). Problems with her friend and family left Margaret with little
energy to prepare for the year in America, although plans were slowly taking shape. She and Guy were to set off early so that they could see Do's
children, now in Kansas City with their father and his new Texan wife.
But Margaret viewed with dismay her agreement to teach creative writing
in Pittsburgh. She had agreed to this as she needed the money, because
the allowance she told Hermon she had given to Barbara had sent her
finances into "the whirlpool" (SJ to HO, 1.22.48).

At the end of January, Margaret suffered a bout of gastric flu, distract-
ing herself by planning the North Wales holiday in Portmeirion. Guy,
Christopher, and Barbara were to come, along with Erasmus, the charming nine-year-old, "half-Chinese" son of her old student friend Sydney
Harland; and now she invited Hermon to join them (SJ to HO, 1.27.48).
These preparations helped her over the nervous wait for the publication
of *The Black Laurel.* It had come out already in Canada, but waiting for
the publication in England was "like waiting for an operation," she told
Rache (SJ to LD, 1.28.48).

By February, Margaret had finished the three-act play *The Moment of
Truth*, and at once began converting it into a novel (SJ to LD, 1.28.48;
JN, 2:210). While working on this, she sent Rache an account of the prov-
enance of *The Black Laurel.* The fact that she had not actually visited the
ruins of Berlin clearly worried her, as she warned Hermon not to tell anyone

that all I know of postwar Berlin is seeing it 4 times from the
air in 1945. I'd get no credit for imagination, but discredit for
making-up. But I have questioned so many people who did live

there in 1945, and I did know it before the war, and I do, from Warsaw, know what a ruined city smells of. (SJ to HO, 3.2.48)

She insisted that

> it would be misleading to say that *The Black Laurel* is a continuation of *Before*, but it is true that *Before* is a prelude, a sort of curtain-raiser, to this new book. The two books *are* linked, but more loosely than is implied in the word "continuation." I should be glad if this book sent some people to *Before* — which a Frenchman has just called my "roman noir."[32]

It may well be that, at the time, she did not want *The Black Laurel* to be too closely related to a work that had ostensibly ended her friendship with Valentine.

The Black Laurel was published on February 27.[33] The reviews were on the whole disappointing: Margaret's work never lends itself to a quick appraisal.[34] She was disheartened: "It used to seem to my ignorance very feeble of Thomas Hardy to give up writing novels because the critics scorned them, but I see that he had to" (SJ to LD, 3.6.48). Writing ten days later, she commented ruefully: "I must give up prophecy — no one loved Cassandra" (SJ to LD, 3.16.48). For her awareness of Europe, insightful as it was, was largely disparaged when it was not ignored. Yet Europe remained in the throes of the turmoil that Margaret had explored in *Black Laurel*. The war against Fascism was hardly over before Stalinism spread through Eastern Europe at astonishing speed. Beneš's hope for his country's democracy had already been shattered as Czechoslovakia was taken over by the Communists. Now Margaret feared that Jirina, mortally wounded by Nazism, would defend the Soviet move, and she was concerned about the reaction of Communists in England; she worried too that if the economy worsened in England, many could turn to Communism. Then came the shock of Jan Masaryk's death after a "fall" from a window on March 10; Jirina had written to break the news (HO to SJ, 3.18.48). Margaret and Hermon had come to know him well, and were unimpressed by the official Czech claim that he had committed suicide. As a result, Margaret started to worry about the fate of the Polish writers she knew, also at risk as Stalinism took hold. She thought of Miłosz — was he still in the States or not (SJ to HO, 3.18.48)?

All too appositely, given the spread of Stalinist Communism, *Moment of Truth* was finished on Easter Sunday.[35] This little novel was written with deceptive simplicity, set in a future England undergoing a Soviet takeover, just as *In the Second Year* had envisaged a Hitlerite England a decade before. As in *The Fort*, the action recalls the classical unities of time and space as a group of disparate people aim to leave the country on the last plane. However, space on the plane will be limited, so who must be left behind? There are echoes here of a child's game, but that echo makes the reality all the more sinister. There are frictions: old General Thorburn cannot abide scientists and Breuner, the foreigner, is one; Lackland reveals he is under orders to organize a Home Army, opening rifts among those waiting to leave. At times, Breuner has the role of chorus, identifying what he sees as typical English traits in his companions; his comments feed into Margaret's ongoing thoughts about narratorial detachment, as his perception of Englishness is inevitably shaped by his own European viewpoint. The musings of each character at this critical time are delicately choreographed, each revealed, despite their contributions to debate, as intensely alone in their priorities and memories. But debate they do: will European culture survive, should artists leave if they cannot work under a totalitarian regime, is flight the practical option, resistance purely for romantics, and so on. The debate about war and violence is tied throughout to the dilemmas of exile, while underlying the debates is the larger theme: what definition of an abstraction like "justice" could be shared by such a disparate group of people? For justice is a key issue here, as in Margaret's two preceding novels. Here, although all characters are victims of their zeitgeist, and divided by generation, they are not all slaves of their context. They make different existential choices, while Nature is used throughout as contrast to the affairs of men, untouched by what they do. There is so much in this little work, its intricacy handled so deftly, that most reviewers, all too predictably, would fail to see more than the bare essentials. Elizabeth Bowen, however, would be deeply impressed, writing in the June 1949 *Tatler*:

> This tense story is a masterpiece. So much carried along was I
> by the excitement, the rapid twists and turns of events that I took

for granted the excellence of the writing. But re-reading *The Moment of Truth*, how I relished it!

Bowen would capture concisely the subtlety of Margaret's lucid prose: the storytelling grips the reader first, and it takes a second reading to appreciate the aesthetic quality of the writing that never obtrudes, but underpins the content.

Now was the time for the holiday in Portmeirion; Barbara and the boys came, as did Hermon. In a fit of exuberance Christopher broke Margaret's typewriter, "so that it jumps like a young ram upon the mountains"; he begged her "with sobs" not to tell his mother and she did not, but the strain of the underlying tensions proved the last straw (SJ to HO, 4.18.48). She felt she could not go to the PEN Congress, to be held in Copenhagen this year, as she could not face people anymore, "like one of Tcheckov's [Chekhov's] more tiresome characters, the man whose (moral) back broke and he couldn't do anything any more" (SJ to HO, 4.18.48). She poured out to Hermon her distress at going to the States, at having to write a speech, at losing her seat on the PEN Committee while she was away. The last year had been very bad, she said:

> The Valentine stroke went in very deep, and the Port Meirion fortnight broke my heart. I made myself look through *Before The Crossing* again last week — you know she made this book and its "hatred and evil" the starting-off point for the appalling fantasy she had been evolving for so many months. And I could not see that it was so evil as that. (SJ to HO, 4.18.48)

Along with her all too ready tendency to savage her own personal failings, Margaret's writerly confidence had been severely affected by Valentine's rejection; her belief in her own powers was always fragile. Nonetheless, *Moment of Truth* had been sent to Rache, and by June a contract was in place. Margaret asked for no blurb, largely as "it would, I am sure, be fatal to try to tell the story of this book, because that would involve saying that it was dated in the future, which always puts people off, I think" (SJ to LD, 6.12.48). She need not have worried; next year, the success of Orwell's new book, *Nineteen Eighty-Four*, would show that a future setting was not always a disaster.

Since Valentine's rejection, Margaret had seemed on the brink of complete breakdown and Hermon had begged her to take note of the danger signals (HO to SJ, 5.6.48). Replying, she confessed to some of the demons that troubled her in bad moments:

> I never had any confidence in meeting people properly, in being able to, I mean. I've trained myself to do it as well as I can, but there are always times when such a show as I can put up is knocked down by a sort of black wave of diffidence ("You are the laughing stock of the neighbourhood") . . . I guess . . . why Valentine's dismissing me had such an effect was that it touched off a lot of buried memories of being laughed at. People shouldn't laugh at children.[36]

Hannah was an ever-present ghost at her shoulder, and Hermon was a much needed antidote. Moreover Margaret's distress was compounded by the European crises: Czech refugees from the Soviet takeover had told her that her friend Jirina was complicit in "expelling people from the Syndicate of Writers on very personal grounds — but who knows the motives of so fanatical (and brave) a heart as hers? I am sure she is not happy" (SJ to HO, 5.26.48). Too accustomed to the hearsay evidence of factions and their frictions, Margaret was careful not to judge; but she did fear for another war, and she did not want to be in the States if it should start. The tensions in Europe were certainly building; Berlin had been sealed off from Western Europe by the Soviets, and in June the Berlin airlift began and would continue for nearly twelve months.

The departure for the States was getting close, and Margaret was still wary: "Three months would be splendid, a year too much" (SJ to LD, 6.1.48). However, she was planning her next creative venture, as she told Rache:

> I should now like to spend at least three years writing a long novel. If I can save up all the money from Black Laurel and this short book, perhaps I can manage to live until 1952. But no — even if there isn't a war there'll be a family crisis. (SJ to LD, 6.4.48)

Margaret was always a woman of great complexity: indecisive and apparently broken in some ways, forceful and thoughtfully planning ahead in others. But it was also true that family crises were all too frequent. Even as she and Guy prepared for their departure, there were problems with Guy's mother; her mental state was deteriorating (SJ to HO, 6.14.48). By the end of June she had finally been placed in a mental nursing home, "a quite ghastly business, and now we have to clean up the appalling house" (SJ to LD, 6.25.48). Margaret admitted it would be sensible to postpone sailing, but she longed to see Do's children. Indeed, as the date of sailing neared, she was almost going into overdrive, firing off letters to Hermon about PEN matters and her own concerns. On July 27, she and Guy set sail for the States: Rache, for Macmillan, had loaned her a thousand pounds to buy their passage, which she repaid, rather rashly, with an American draft.[37] They rested in New York for just over a week, visiting Margaret's sister Winifred and seeing old friends.[38] Years later, Margaret would reflect that Winifred

> was in reality more vulnerable than Do had been at any time in her short life, yet I had never felt — as I felt about Do as a girl and a young woman — that I ought to indulge her. The only reason for it that I could give myself is that she is so much closer to me in age, we grew from the same hard root, so that I feel as little impulse to protect her as to protect myself. (JN/TMS/UNCAT, 3:109)

From New York, Margaret traveled to Kansas to see her brother-in-law, his new wife, Louise, and Do's children. It was a moving encounter, as Margaret soon realized that the children were now wholly American: she was secretly horrified to find them addicted to gangster comics (SJ to HO, 9.10.48). Then she and Guy were off to Pittsburgh, where Stanton C. Crawford, dean of the faculty that was receiving Guy, welcomed them.[39] For Margaret, the introduction to Crawford's wife, Ruth, would be particularly important. The women had much in common, not least the fact that Ruth had close connections with Czechoslovakia since first going there with a YWCA unit in 1919. She had known the first president, Tomáš Masaryk, and had worked with his daughter Alice in the founding of the

Czech Red Cross. So she did much to alleviate Margaret's disorientation in a land where there was "a machine for doing everything," something that seemed particularly alien to a woman who believed in scrubbing her floors at home (SJ to IR, 8.10.48). Installed in a Pittsburgh flat, she was struggling to find her feet, loving the people yet distinctly wary of the "gadgets and pin tables and juke boxes" (SJ to HO, 9.10.48). Ruth worked to make Margaret and Guy feel at home, inviting them to dinner and helping Margaret over unfamiliar vocabulary; a doctor had referred to her "basal metabolism," which bewildered her (SJ to RC, 9.14.48). Ruth also helped Margaret over her initial panic at having agreed to teach creative writing at the university, as Margaret would recall later:

> Do you remember gently reproving me on that lovely walk you took me outside Pittsburgh in September 1949[*sic*]? It was before term started, I was in black despair thinking of that Creative Writing course I knew I was incompetent to teach. You encouraged me and told me not to give way to such misery.[40]

By October Margaret was more settled, despite complaining to Blanche Knopf that Pittsburgh's smoky atmosphere was making her cough constantly, and her tiresome job was stopping her writing (SJ to BK, 10.29.48). She enjoyed a weekend in New York with Guy when he was the official Leeds University delegate for the inauguration of Dwight D. Eisenhower as president of Columbia University.[41] Such experiences were stimulating, but she was missing her close connection with the PEN and with Hermon. He had passed through Prague just after the death of Beneš; Margaret responded to this death of an old friend with an article in which she reminded readers of the scars which the Munich agreement had left, and defended him over his failure to establish the kind of *entente cordiale* he had wanted with Russia.[42]

Margaret sent food parcels to friends in England, where food rationing was still very strict. To the Leavises she sent a box of twelve dozen eggs; Queenie reported that they were "quite overwhelmed at the sight of so many eggs and all boiling ones," and thought "the millennium must have come when they can have a boiled egg for breakfast, egg and cress sandwiches for tea, and apple sponge at dinner."[43] Another parcel was for

Hermon, who sent suggestions of what to say to the American PEN, as Margaret had accepted an invitation to visit them. He asked her to thank them for the food parcels they were sending, and to mention the growing link between the PEN and UNESCO, especially over a project on translation (HO to SJ, 11.15.48).

At the end of November Margaret was increasingly worried about not writing, and about the drain on their finances. Life in the States was not cheap, and they had to forgo the services of a maid, so she was forced to take on household tasks again (SJ to HO, 11.29.48). She also worried about Czesław Miłosz. She and Guy had spent Thanksgiving in Washington, D.C., with Margaret's journalist friend Maxine Davis and her husband, Jimmy McHugh. While there, she had met Czesław and noted that he had "certainly moved Left since he came to America"; she feared that he would pay dearly for the comments he was making (SJ to RC, 12.2.48). Christmas brought an enjoyable family-centered visit to Gracechurch, Rye, New York, when Margaret and Guy stayed with their historian friend Henry Steele Commager. Henry was a man after Margaret's own heart, an outspoken defender of civil liberties, who would soon be fighting against McCarthyism. The visit was a great success. It was a "very Tchekov" (Chekhov) house, Margaret told Rache,

> where meals may be at 12 or 4 or not at all, and where three charming and intelligent children make antic hay all day and most of the night, and the huge coloured cook cooks when she feels like it, and what she feels like. . . . It is very amusing, very kind, and very exhausting. (SJ to LD, 12.29.48)

But she was shocked by the enormous work American wives and mothers undertook to make Christmas a success; these women,

> who also work in shops or offices . . . sit up all night wrapping and preparing, then rise at dawn on the 25th to begin cooking, still smiling, and then on the 26th go back to work. Why they don't all die of exhaustion is more than I know. In the street-cars I hear them saying how tired they are but they go on just the same. (SJ to LD, 12.29.48)

She herself was increasingly worried about having no time to write, although "the long English novel . . . hovers in my mind now" (SJ to LD, 12.29.48).

At the end of December, Hermon asked her if she could contribute to the first PEN annual that he was editing. At first she feared she would not have time, as "here I run from university to PENN: College for Women" to teach (SJ to HO, 1.7.49). She had housework to do, and she and Guy had to accept a great many invitations since they were like "ambassadors," as they were the first "official English" in the city (SJ to HO, 1.7.49). She recalled that, before leaving England, she had revised her original play, *William*, and said he could have that when she came home. She also undertook to support Arnot Robertson, the novelist and film critic, who had been banned by MGM from the screening of their films for allegedly "hostile" reviews (SJ to HO, 1.17.49). The appeal was backed by a number of leading writers, such as Agatha Christie, T. S. Eliot, E. M. Forster, John Lehmann, and George Orwell, while Margaret herself guaranteed a donation of twenty pounds for the appeal. Sadly, Arnot lost.

In March, Margaret gave a speech to the university's Czechoslovak Room Committee, for the Masaryk Birthday Commemoration.[44] The Czech community in Pittsburgh was large and very active, as Margaret acknowledged with due humility. Her speech was determinedly upbeat. She touched very lightly on Communism, stressing rather "the strong pulse of the future beating in these old streets, in these young students, these older young-minded men and women" (Czech talk). She spoke of Beneš, recalling his commitment to building "a free strong Czechoslovakia," and she recalled Jan Masaryk's vitality with respect and affection (Czech talk). She told of the Jan Masaryk memorial fund just then being launched in England with his friend Winston Churchill as chairman, and she stressed the importance of the Masaryk tradition for Europe as a whole, urging her expatriate audience not to lose faith in their country in these dark times. Of course Margaret was leaving out a great deal of her experiences in Eastern Europe; but she knew all too well, from her Polish encounters, the rifts that could grow between expats and those who had remained at home; too often, expats were wedded to the past of their country, or dreamed of a future that no longer addressed the needs of their compatriots who had stayed at home. So Margaret's speech avoided controversy, as it was intended as a bridge builder, and it was well received.

Toward the end of March she flew to Dallas to stay with Sam and Betty Leake, who had fostered Do's children during the war. She met a great many people while there, recalling later a lunch at the *Dallas News*, where she sat opposite the formidable Dorothy Parker, "as terrible as an army with banners, in a Tyrolean hat" (*JN*, 2:242). A few days later, she lunched with the novelist Louis Bromfield and the Knopfs in Ohio. That same month, rather appropriately, given her current sampling of the variety to be found in the States, the *New York Times Magazine* printed the article they had commissioned, "Why I Can't Write about America"; in this piece, while she acknowledged the plethora of material things that had at first dismayed her, she stressed the altruistic generosity of spirit she had experienced.[45] The experiences she had now accumulated had been rich and complex:

> Any temptation I might have felt to write an article on the United States withered in face [*sic*] of the paradox of a people which worships success in its grossest form and bestows its good on impoverished countries it may never have seen. In face of the still wilder paradox of a people with such an instinct for piety, for religion, that it makes a faith out of the right to possess, and the right to push higher and yet higher the famous American standard of living. ("Why I Can't," 384)

Ultimately what had impressed her most was the "limitless energy. The sense that anything is possible," and, above all, the "strong sense of purpose" that claimed her respect and admiration ("Why I Can't," 385).

She had yet another speech to compose "for the Writers Conference that takes place through 2 days in the University every May," and attended the PEN dinner in New York in April, where she enjoyed meeting several Jewish writers who greeted her warmly, no doubt because of her wartime work for refugees (SJ to HO, 3.19.49). To her relief, she had managed to get away with a very short speech, and felt "I'm getting better at speaking, though I loathe it" (SJ to HO, 4.16.49). One aspect of the dinner concerned her. While she was increasingly worried about the growing threat from Communism, she was by no means a "Communist-baiter"; and much as she liked Dos Passos, he had become passionately anti-Communist, "too fiercely so, to my sceptical English taste. But maybe scepticism is out of place now" (SJ to HO, 4.30.49). She was trying very hard to keep her balance as the fear of Communism intensified in the States.

Guy's year in Pittsburgh was drawing to a close. There was one last visit to Kansas to see the children, and then she and Guy were off to New York in early June. Margaret enjoyed this break before returning home. She met up with her old friend Noel Streatfeild, "very loquacious and buxom," and wondered mischievously whether Noel had gotten more aggressive as she became "more public-spirited and capable."[46] She had time to read Orwell's *Nineteen Eighty-Four*, telling Hermon it was "awful and terrific. Is it true he is dying? I hope not" (SJ to HO, 6.19.49). She was so impressed that she wrote to Orwell, saying:

> To read Nineteen-Eighty-Four here is a strange experience — the book itself is superb and would disturb, profoundly, read anywhere. Read here it's as disturbing as an earthquake must be. Let me say, briefly and humbly, how much I respect the nervous courage and admire the imaginative energy which joined to bring off this magnificent job — . . . . I don't want to say more about the book, you'd be bored — except that I am quite certain it is not because, since 1926 or so, I have never been free from that same sense of disaster, the sense of the abyss, which obsesses you, that I feel Nineteen-Eighty-Four to be the novel which should stand for our age.[47]

However, she also said how much she wished he could spend time in the States, how she too had felt it very alien when she first came, but how she had come to admire much that she found there. She was gently reproving Orwell for his denunciation of the States without ever having sampled America's complexity and variety, and so she ended, "It doesn't matter tuppence whether most novelists get their sums right or not — it does matter when an Orwell is in question" (SJ to Orwell, 7.1.49).

After visits to Winifred, and her old friend the writer Ida Wylie, Margaret joined Guy at the Commagers before leaving for Montreal; they sailed from there, on a ship bound for Liverpool, on July 15.[48] This break between Pittsburgh and the return to London had insulated her from her habitual fears when a new novel was being published. *The Moment of Truth* came out in June to the predictable mixed reviews, although R. D. Charques was deeply impressed, as was Elizabeth Bowen.[49] But in 1949 Margaret's reputation did not depend on her reviewers. Her work was available in German, Czech, French, Swedish, Danish, Norwegian, Spanish, Polish, and Italian, while the British *Who's Who* for 1949, quoting from "Twentieth Century Writers," described her as "one of the strongest as well as one of the most interesting of contemporary English novelists and one of the few women who can create credible male characters who are both male and human."[50]

Margaret and Guy returned to Ilkley on July 22. She was looking forward to seeing Hermon again, but her priority was of course her family. She went first to visit Barbara and Christopher in Denham before going to see Bill, Patchen, and their new baby in Chichester (SJ to HO, 7.23.49). When she reached Chichester, the news was not good. She had worried for some time that, because of the current economic slump, Bill's job was under threat, and she now learned that he would be out of work by mid-August (SJ to LD, 7.30.49). Moreover the loss of a job brought another anxiety: Bill and family might decide to emigrate to Australia. "My rather battered heart will finally break if they go, since it is too far for me to hope to do more than see them perhaps once again" (SJ to LD, 9.18.49). Financially, this crisis had come at a difficult moment for Margaret, as she was determined to write the book she had been incubating for over a year, taking time to let it mature. Inevitably her publishers were concerned, both about the gap in her production and about the financial implications. But she was adamant:

> This is something I've got to decide for myself. I am convinced that I mustn't indulge myself in any more short novels just now, and I have five or six long ones I want to write and one especially. (SJ to LD, 7.30.49)

Despite these anxieties, Margaret agreed, as Hermon had hoped, to act for the PEN link with UNESCO, which was currently suffering some sort of deadlock on its translations subcommittee.[51] Then in September, she went with Guy to Venice, as guests of honor at the PEN Congress. It was a good week, and she enjoyed the return to Europe, the mellow air of Venice itself. On her way home she went to see Barbara again, but there suffered another devastating scene. Bill, jobless, had stopped paying maintenance, and Margaret took the brunt of Barbara's desperation and fury (SJ to LD, 9.21.49). Much later she still recalled how "I stumbled away from the house, physically broken. I felt old, old. There seemed nothing I could do. I could go on helping a little, from a distance, but I had lost all that mattered" (JN/TMS, 3:250).

It was probably just as well that Margaret had more than one idea for a story or novel in her head at this time, for despite her commitment to family and wider issues, writing was not only her profession but also a kind of sanctuary.[52] Her main project was, as she told Basil Liddell Hart, the long novel,

> not about America, about England. I haven't really the wing-spread for long novels, but I hope, by taking it very slowly, to do it as well as possible, and if it only half comes off I shall send it to you. "Moment of Truth" didn't seem good enough, quite. (SJ to LH, 10.28.49)

Central to the action would be "a scholarly Christian gentleman and radical eccentric, not unlike R. H. Tawney," and it would be set in the thirties and forties, with their "shifting moral currents" (JN, 2:249). Only a single character, the Jewish newspaper proprietor, Cohen, would survive from the *Mirror in Darkness*, while a host of other characters had "pushed themselves forward during the year in America when I was unable to write" (JN, 2:249). She spent time shaping and planning her new work, as she and Guy settled back into their comfortable, familiar Yorkshire hotel. But the need to write was growing:

> My excuses for not beginning the actual writing of a novel are almost used up, and I'll have to begin any day now. I can't go on brooding about it any longer. Well, I could, but I daren't. If I shiver on the brink any longer my nerve will go forever. (SJ to RC, 11.22.49)

She and Guy spent Christmas in Portmeirion, and then borrowed a flat in London. Margaret insisted to Ruth Crawford, perhaps not entirely honestly, that she liked "these breaks when I become a domestic woman, and cook and dust and shop for rationing. I shouldn't like them to go on for too long. But they keep us human" (SJ to RC, 12.16.49). Then at last she was writing, trying to make up for lost time.

PART IV

1950-1986

CHAPTER 23

Reassessing the Road to Now

To ease her financial problems while writing the long novel (*The Green Man*), Margaret persuaded Macmillan to publish a collection of her essays, including a new piece, "The Form of the Novel," that summed up her current thinking.[1] She addressed the growing critical tendency to give preferential treatment to writers like James, Woolf, and Joyce, for their "purity of form" or poetic techniques, countering this tendency with D. H. Lawrence's assertion that form in the novel could be legion. If, she argued, you wrote *War and Peace*, you would have no energy left for perfecting form. The greatest novel was

> a work of which the form is determined by the writer's conception of life, even to the point where this contains lumps of primitive clay, . . . unsolved questions, the contradictions, unacceptable as these are, of human nature, felt, experienced, in a crisis where the writer is reduced to stammering out his report: or offering it with a gesture of amusement or irony. (*TWS*, 49)

As before, she argued, not against the high modernists, but against privileging them at the expense of other writers who were exploring and experimenting. If the impulse to create style came first, she said, the novelist was "beginning to separate himself from his age" (*TWS*, 56). She ended by reaffirming her own credo:

> Either we exhaust ourselves to write against [our age's] pressure, or we add ourselves to its decadence, its hinting at death. . . .

> The pure novelist, intent on easing the bulges out of his form, is forced to exclude too much, and without being able to achieve the evocative precision and concentration of the poem. (*TWS*, 60–61)

By the beginning of 1950, Margaret was again working ten hours a day. She always found time for those refugees who still needed her support and for her family, but she was trying to avoid unnecessary social ties. Yet while she remained committed to taking time over her novel, her money worries inevitably increased. She seems to have been tempted by a lucrative job, but by March had given up on the idea. She told Blanche Knopf that she could not divulge what the job was as she was sworn to secrecy, but that she felt too old to juggle writing and work that was too exacting. Interestingly, she added that she had realized this job would have meant she must stop writing, and that, much as she grumbled, she knew she would resent giving it up (SJ to BK, 3.6.50). This was a rare admission from Margaret that she was indeed a writer, whether she liked it or not. Those ideas that stayed in her mind for years, and the conviction with which she proclaimed her stance over novel writing, insisted on being heard, even as the birth pains were severe.

All too predictably, her punishing work schedule was taking its toll, and by May another bout of anemia meant that she was back on liver injections. Anxiety about Bill's plans must have been a contributory factor: he had been too long without a job, despite having been awarded an Order of the British Empire (OBE) in 1944, and having taken part in the latter stages of the Berlin airlift from May to July 1949.[2] Now he confirmed that he and his family meant to sail their boat to Australia. Accordingly, Margaret stopped work on her novel to spend time near Bill's yacht *Nina* at Birdham Pool, and for the next three months she would shuttle between Chichester and Ilkley. Bill got a temporary job with an airline, flying to South America and to the Middle East, while Margaret helped his sailing preparations financially, asking Rache Lovat Dickson to forward the rest of the money he was holding for her, which was about five hundred pounds. The demands on her purse were daunting. At one point she even thought of putting the long novel aside and writing another short work; Rache urged her not to do this. For her part, Margaret tried to sound optimistic when writing to him: "I begin to see daylight at the end of the tunnel (provided the tunnel isn't running straight into another war), the strain has been awfully heavy, but I'm sure I shall get through — I always do" (SJ to LD, 6.28.50).

In July her book of essays, *The Writer's Situation*, came out, including essays from before, during, and after the war.[3] She was pleased with the presentation, although Guy pointed out that her D.Litt. did not appear on the dust jacket. However, she admitted, "as a matter of fact, I didn't forget, but I felt that with all these Dr Sitwells and Dr Phyllis Bentleys, it is becoming ridiculous, so I said nothing" (SJ to LD, 7.21.50). Reviews were slow in coming, but were for the most part good, the essay on Auden earning special praise.[4] Margaret was as self-deprecating as ever when writing to Basil Liddell Hart about the developments in her thinking that the collection revealed: "My mind is always shifting its ground — or at least its angle of interest" (SJ to LH, 12.25.50). She could indeed change her mind as the chaos of the thirties and forties grew, meeting each crisis thoughtfully and with a keen eye for its implications; but while the "angle of interest" might shift, her fundamental values remained remarkably steady.

In mid-August, she was in Chichester, as she told Rache,

> to stand by until the yacht sails. I needn't tell you that my heart sinks a little lower every day (Bill's has risen, since he imagines now that he'll be able to get into the A.R.A.F. Why he should think he'll be that much younger when he arrives in Sydney I don't know). I'm finding it hard to keep on at the novel, but so far I'm managing it. (SJ to LD, 7.28.50)

Bill, Patchen, and the baby set off in their twenty-one-ton ketch at the beginning of September, together with an ex–petty officer, Jonny. Margaret would hear nothing of them for thirty-nine days, a supposed rest at the Oakeley Arms in the second half of September doing nothing to ease her anxiety. Then, in October, she heard that Jonny had jumped ship at Falmouth, and they had to return. The tales they told were certainly dramatic. Margaret heard that at the height of a storm Patchen could not get to little Frances, down in the cabin, for three hours. When eventually she did, there was her dripping child, sitting up in her cot, drenched and cheerful, telling her mother it was "raining" (SJ to BK, 11.14.50). For the time being they were back in England; Bill got another job as a pilot with an independent airline, and Margaret, freed from listening to news of westerly gales, went back to her novel (*JN*, 2:251–54).

Earlier in the year, the BBC had suggested an adaptation by Anthony Gittings of Margaret's novel *The Moment of Truth*. The adaptation was agreed and duly completed, the performance recorded, and the play scheduled to be broadcast on September 11. It was not to be: the international situation deteriorated badly over the summer; in June, North Korea invaded South Korea, and the Allies became involved. The theme of Margaret's novel must have seemed all too pertinent, and on August 3 the Controller of the Northern Region wrote to her:

> At a time of very grave international tension, the BBC would be open to very serious and justifiable criticism if it broadcast a programme of which the background was the defeat and occupation of this country by (unambiguously) Russia, with particular reference to the inadequacy of our Allies.[5]

Margaret did not raise any objection. But she then learned that, as the play was not to be broadcast, she would receive no fee, although the cast and adapter were paid. Unfortunately, Margaret had dispensed with her agent Nancy Pearn at the end of the 1940s, and acting for herself, had simply failed to see a snag in the agreement she had made; this meant she was out of pocket, as she had spent money in anticipation of payment. Despite this setback, she refused to be distracted from her novel, although assuring Blanche that its growing size had certainly cured her of any ambition to write *War and Peace* (SJ to BK, 11.10.50). Nevertheless, despite her lightness of tone, she was seriously worried about the financial demands she would have to meet over the next two years. Fortunately, Rache was quick to offer help, promising to work out how to save her tax on the thousand-pound loan Macmillan now proposed to give her, and how to arrange a life insurance policy to cover it with the least bother for herself (LD to SJ, 12.1.50).

At the end of the year, Margaret was involved in a new PEN initiative: in a letter to the *TLS*, she and other members announced that the International Executive Committee had decided "to form a special committee concerned solely with writers in exile."[6] She herself, Hermon Ould, and

Stephen Spender would be the British sponsors, while Maria Kuncewi-czowa would act as chairman, and their letter invited interested writers to come forward. It was not without relevance to this initiative that Margaret had recently endowed a "Storm Jameson" Cup in Whitby, to be awarded annually for the best play at the Ryedale Festival written in the dialect of the North and East Ridings of Yorkshire.[7] This defense of the language of her birthplace was another pointer to Margaret's empathy with exiles from Europe.

In January 1951, despite a severe bout of influenza, she was hoping to finish her novel by the middle of the year, but the financial strain was still acute, after her recent failure to extract a fee from the BBC. Now therefore, she felt the need of a good agent; so when, after hearing about her misfortune from her American agent, the formidable A. D. Peters contacted her, Margaret gladly turned to him, recalling his kindness to her over her problem with Ethel Mannin in 1933.[8] Peters and his colleagues acted quickly to put her affairs in order at home and in Europe, and worked closely with her American agents in New York.

Yet no sooner were her own affairs in safe hands than Margaret acquired an eminent emigré who would need considerable support. Since their meeting in the Poland of 1945, Margaret had kept in touch with Czesław Miłosz. Like many of his fellow intellectuals, he had been keen to serve Poland as it regained its freedom from Nazi oppression, but as the Communist Party threw over its democratic pretensions and Stalinism dominated, the vision of a free Poland faded. After his posting as cultural attaché in Washington, Miłosz had been moved to Paris, leaving his wife in the United States as she was pregnant with their second child. As 1950 ended, he was summoned to Warsaw and told that he must now live and write in Poland. He was promised a fine apartment and a good position, but realized that he would become subject to the Communist Party and lose all the intellectual freedom he cherished. Returning to Paris, he decided to defect, intending to rejoin his wife in Washington. Now he ran into trouble: anti-Communism was at its height in the States; he had been a servant of a government dominated by the Communist Party; and so he failed to get a visa (JN, 2:263). In the wake of the Internal Security Act of 1950 and of Alger Hiss being found guilty of spying, Senator Patrick McCarran's Senate Security Subcommittee, working alongside J. Edgar Hoover's FBI, went into action. Very soon Senator

Joseph McCarthy joined the newly formed Senate Permanent Subcommittee on Governmental Operations; and police departments in many major cities worked to identify any Communists or those who had at any time Communist affiliations, however tenuous. Britain too would have its spy scandals, starting that same year with that of Klaus Fuchs, and later followed by the defections of George Blake, Donald Maclean, and Kim Philby. Yet in Britain the public reaction never quite reached the fever pitch sweeping the States.[9]

So there was Miłosz in Paris, cut off from his wife and family, desperately writing to all his contacts for help. Margaret's letters to him are prime examples of her ability to gauge the mind-set of a correspondent. Her letters to Miłosz were long, attuned to his own wavelength, taking account of his Catholic background. From early February, she was offering to approach influential contacts in America. She gave him addresses of friends; she advised him on the best way to support his own case, and asked if she might arrange financial support for his wife.[10] In her first letter she was optimistic, clearly unwilling to believe the intransigence of the anti-Communist elements in the American government. By her second letter she had heard from Maxine Davis that, as he had been an official representative of a Communist government, not to mention his having openly expressed left-wing views on capitalism, things would be very difficult. Margaret was tireless in approaching further contacts, while shielding him from conservative Polish exiles in England. She had learned by bitter experience of the frictions that could develop between nationals whose loyalty was each to their own version of their home country, and which often had little to do with the reality, experience that would feed into her later novel, A Ulysses Too Many.[11]

When the intransigence of the McCarran Internal Security Act was confirmed by both Blanche Knopf and Arthur Koestler, Margaret turned her attention to helping Miłosz with publishing matters, which were of prime importance now that he must establish himself in exile (SJ to BK, 2.23.51; BK to SJ, 3.12.51; SJ to CM, 3.16.51). Importantly, she encouraged him to write about his reasons for not accepting the role he had been offered in Warsaw; his response would be his impressive work The Captive Mind, in which he would chart the effect of totalitarianism on intellectuals caught in its net (SJ to CM, 3.21.51, 4.10.51, 5.5.51).

At the end of May, Margaret was in Paris for a week as the English delegate on a UNESCO committee, but she still hoped to complete her novel by the middle of June. Then yet another family matter intervened: on June 7, the day the news broke of the defection of Guy Burgess and Maclean, her much-loved aunt Jenny (Jane), the last of her mother's sisters, died in Whitby at eighty-eight years of age. Margaret would recall later that this aunt was "drolly kind" to stray animals. She lived alone with her old servant, without a bathroom, and was "completely fearless." Although Margaret would call this the last thread that bound her to Whitby, she meant simply the Whitby of now: "I could not live in Whitby again, but in a sense I live nowhere else" (*JN*, 2:255–56). On a less metaphysical level, her aunt's death meant she "had all that to cope with, solicitors, a decayed house, an ancient maid to provide for — oh, all the complications imaginable" (SJ to LD, 6.13.51). So her book was delayed; the last chapters, she told Rache, needed a second, or maybe a third rewrite, and she also had to write an article for America that she dared not refuse.

She wrote the article as soon as the book was finished; it underlined what her preoccupations had been while writing that long novel.[12] Again she voiced her concern about native contemporaries who "concentrate their interest and curiosity on personal relations," at the expense of "that theme of the greatest novelists of the past, of Stendhal, Tolstoy, Balzac — man in his relation to society" ("British Literature," 24). This article also bore testimony to the priorities she continued to share with R. H. Tawney. Margaret had long proved herself her own woman, distancing herself from some of A. R. Orage's ideas in her youth, and later arguing with the formidable Basil Liddell Hart whenever their ideas parted company; on the other hand, she was always close to Tawney in her thinking, while he admired her work. Their continued affinity was clear when his book *Social History and Literature* was published in 1950. In this work he argued that

> each generation must write its history for itself, and draw its own deductions from that already written, not because the conclusions of its predecessors are untrue, but for a practical reason. Different answers are required, because different questions are asked. (Tawney, 7)

For the past year, Margaret had been working to achieve just this in *The Green Man*.

This long novel develops the method she had used in *Cousin Honoré*, capturing the crises of the age in the dealings of a family, their friends, and associates. On one level it is a family saga, but on a more profound level it takes "soundings" of a great swath of English society over the years, employing wit, irony, and many shifts in tone and pace. The different generations of an English family represent both the variety within each generation, and the differences between generations. The cast is large, cutting across class, race, and culture. At times, leading characters meditate in solitude on their priorities and the shifting ground on which they stand. The countryside and different houses stand for tradition and the challenges it faces, while the imagery often mirrors vogues in the art of the time. No character is simply good or bad — except perhaps the literary poseurs who take their image too seriously, about whom Margaret's irony sharpens into satire — even the best of the cast have flaws, while the worst have their generosities. It is, for instance, very important that old Richard's beliefs are quixotic, while his son Andrew will also be an idealist but in a different mold; and young Benedict, the immigrant child without family, his roots in what Richard, his *chosen* ancestor, and Andrew give him, has yet another vision of where he should make his contribution to his world. And there are dark moments, deliberately provoking contemporary ideas of victory and what was justified in attaining it. Margaret was never afraid of uttering the unpopular point of view, as when her young airman, echoing the pilot she had known herself, says of saturation bombing: "You treat people as vermin, just as they do in the concentration camps," adding, "I don't believe in the civilisation I'm killing for, that's all. Not any longer."[13]

This is not by any means a "didactic" novel, but a novel of ideas, worthy of such European antecedents as Stendhal. Margaret was a Geiger counter for the main crosscurrents of her age and their effect on a complex range of personalities. The elements of family saga and demise of the country house are reshaped over a period when the world shifted and changed. Wit and absurdity play their part, alongside intensity and grimness; the debates are rarely presented as offering simplistic solutions. This is one of Margaret's finest works, which requires more than one reading for its quality to emerge fully, like works by Flaubert or Tolstoy; but for the most part, her reviewers would, as they would increasingly during the next decade, try to cram her into a preexisting box, and then get cross when she did not fit.

The length of the typescript caused alarm at Macmillan's. Even before it was received, Rache was warning that publishing costs were rising (LD to SJ, 6.14.51). In an internal memo, he showed how superficial his reading of her work could be, maintaining that her characters were too often symbols for a point of view, and did not "grow"; that the book was "too intellectual, too thoughtful"; there were things in it that would irritate "the ordinary reader."[14] Margaret's view that the Continental tradition of the novel of ideas was not really at home in England was certainly not without justification; moreover, sales were now the chief concern for many publishing firms that, in prewar days, would have risked publishing a novel of quality that they knew would not sell. Despite his misgivings, Rache remained supportive, writing to Daniel and Harold Macmillan to suggest that they should make Margaret a substantial loan, safeguarded by another life insurance policy.[15] Margaret herself was anxious for Macmillan to act as her banker, holding royalties back for her rather than putting them straight into her hands. As she said, with disarming self-knowledge:

> I do realise that monies have to be presented for tax in the year they are earned. But you know what I am like, with money actually in the bank I imagine I can support Barbara for life or send someone on a holiday to Scotland or buy myself expensive books. Whereas, if I have to write and ask you for it, I do at least hesitate a few minutes. (SJ to LD, 6.30.51)

Eventually it was decided that the novel could not be cut but must be published in its entirety, although the cost of production had to be considered against the sales her previous books had enjoyed, and Rache was still trying to persuade her to changes she did not want to make.[16] Rather than battling these herself, Margaret was clearly relieved to have Peters and his team fight for her: "I hope you won't regret taking on this reformed rake" (SJ to ADP, 6.22.51). By mid-July, Peters had read the novel and liked it. Margaret's relief was palpable.

While these negotiations were taking place, she was writing a foreword for *The Diary of Anne Frank*.[17] She kept it simple, capturing the tone of Anne's own writing. She wrote of the pressures on a lively child in hiding, of the diary's "instinctive gaiety" (*DAF*, 6), Anne's refusal to despair, the first stirrings of love. She showed how the girl had a novelist's capacity for detachment, able to draw clearly the people around her, while "her lucidity, her extraordinary powers of observation, do not betray her when she turns them on herself" (*DAF*, 9). Margaret did not spare her readers:

> Let us press just for a moment on the feeling — of stupefaction — that must start in us when we think that, in our lifetime, side by side with the amazing achievements of scientists and inventors, there exist these vast slaughter-houses for human beings, and that, to a number of her fellow human beings, to send Anne Frank to one of them seemed a natural thing to do. (*DAF*, 9)

She pointed out that in Russia and its satellites, such atrocities continued. This was Margaret at her passionate best, knowing when drama was justified.

Czesław Miłosz may not have suffered the ultimate fate that growing numbers were faced with in Eastern Europe, but he had written to Margaret saying he felt that he had committed suicide as a writer by defecting. Margaret firmly countered this, concentrating on helping him with the work he was currently writing. For he was following her advice, analyzing the effect of totalitarianism on the intellectuals under its dominance, while Margaret suggested ways of presenting his argument that would capture the imagination of a Western audience. When she had read his draft of the first chapter , for instance, she agreed with him that it was not the right introduction. Much of the content, she said, was important: "All the pages . . . which describe the condition, physical and mental, in which a writer must work in the popular democracies, are admirable and *must* appear somewhere in the book" (SJ to CM, 7.15.51). But she went on to urge him that, if he wanted his book to be successful in Britain and in the States, he must, in the first chapter, create himself:

> We need several pages in which you give us briefly yourself, as a living figure, coming out of pre-war Poland, out of the Occupation and the Rising, and out of the Poland of 1945. Unless

English readers have this living figure, they are (except for pure intellectuals) little inclined to listen to what he has to say. This applies to almost all intelligent English readers: they must have a man, not only a mind speaking. . . . Yet if they do not see that, they do not see you. They can be made to see it *through* you. . . . And they will be made to see at the same time why you were right to accept work in Washington . . . ; the right thing is to let it appear from a statement of your choice in 1945, the rightness of which any English reader will recognise, if once you have made him see Poland in 1945. (SJ to CM, 7.15.51)

He took the point, and presented himself in the prologue of *The Captive Mind* just as she had suggested. It is clear from the correspondence how much Margaret contributed to the publication of this book in English over the next two years, and how much she and Czesław had in common. Miłosz stressed how the New Faith of the East did not satisfy the broadly spiritual needs of humankind, something that worried Margaret too. He argued that those who had lived through twentieth-century atrocities admired the vision of Koestler and Orwell; he attacked institutionalized religion, very much as if he were a Kierkegaardian. His iconoclasm spoke to Margaret's, as did his insistence that art had a duty to reflect the human condition in its entirety, both personal and social. No wonder he found in their correspondence a rich source of consolation. For she understood his situation so much better than many of her younger contemporaries, knowing as she did the tales of so many refugees, so many friends trapped under unfriendly regimes. As she wrote later:

All the sharpest problems of our time, the ones that cut to the bone, are visible only outside England, in the countries which have been through the European civil war. No wonder our novelists are so appallingly provincial. (JN/TMS, 2:106–7)

CHAPTER 24

The Death of Hermon Ould and Advent of Harder Times

In August, Margaret and Guy went to Portmeirion for what was becoming a traditional break. Clough and Amabel Williams-Ellis had been much involved recently in opposing a scheme to flood Welsh valleys so as to provide water for the north of England. Aiming to arouse public interest, they had published a clever little novel, imitating the work of Shelley's friend Thomas Love Peacock's satirical debates in *Headlong Hall*. Their Headlong Hall and its cottages were modeled on Portmeirion, and the characters based on themselves and their guests, Margaret appearing as Miss Sebastiana Tempest.[1] She is teasingly described as

> a novelist whose compositions were noted for their deep melan-
> choly, and she commonly slept in a hair shirt, with a volume of
> Kirkegaard as a pillow. Her conversation was usually in marked
> contrast to all this, for neither her philosophical convictions nor
> her habit of doing the washing-up wherever she might be staying,
> nor even the shocking nights consequent on Kirkegaard, were
> able to quench her good nature and curiosity. (Williams-Ellis, 41)

Miss Tempest takes a lively part in the debates, presented as an authority on heresies, on France, and on politics; and she is clearly seen as a formidable intellect.[2]

Time spent in Portmeirion was always a restorative; but by the end of August there was bad news. Hermon Ould had attended the June congress in Lausanne, but was ill on his return, and two months later was dying of an inoperable cancer. A valued friendship was all too suddenly ending; he died in September. Margaret wrote a long letter to the *Times*, stressing all he had done for the International PEN with "what amounts to his genius for personal relationships"; and she came to London in October to attend his memorial service.[3] The volume of tributes published the following year gave some idea of how much he was missed.[4] In her contribution, Margaret recalled how he had sacrificed his burgeoning career as a dramatist, when the PEN became not just a job, but "a spiritual community to be fostered" ("In Memory," 8). This was Margaret writing as former president; but to Eleanor Farjeon she opened her heart as a personal friend. Margaret had visited him in hospital a number of times, yet what haunted her was "that I shall be damned for having too little love."[5] This was something she would accuse herself of all too frequently; yet in her writings, in her response to those in need, in her letters, compassion was always in evidence, as Hermon himself knew.

In August, it had looked for a moment as if the BBC had renewed its interest in the play of *The Moment of Truth*, largely because of a query from Val Gielgud. He had, he said, seen an adaptation of the book for television in New York, had been much impressed by its dramatic quality, and he wanted the North Region to let his team hear their recording. Yet the matter was dropped by October 23, and subsequent attempts to revive interest would also fail.[6] Meanwhile, Margaret spelled out for Rache Lovat Dickson three synopses she saw as possibilities for future novels. The one she most liked was a study of treachery: "I want to try to find out what makes a man a traitor," she explained (SJ to LD, 10.26.51). This was indeed a topical plot, since the defection of Maclean and Burgess and the trial of Fuchs; Rebecca West had written a work of nonfiction on this same theme.[7] But Margaret was not simply interested in defectors and spies; she wanted to explore whether anyone had the moral right to take justice into their own hands, an idea that would see the light in *The Hidden River*. Margaret's second plot, she said,

> concerns the head of a family and an important business, who knows exactly what is best for his family . . . is ruthless in keeping them in order, revels in the use of power (He is not a devil, he is a fallen angel). The plot turns on the escape of one son — at great cost to himself, but his children are saved. (SJ to LD, 10.26.51)

This idea would also be developed later. But the third plot was the one Rache liked, although Margaret protested that it was "scarcely worked out." It was to be the tale of "a brilliant English economist (or something), taken abroad to a South American country to put its railway system right" (SJ to LD, 10.26.51).

By the beginning of November she and Guy had found a flat in Leeds. To Basil Liddell Hart, Margaret confessed she had not wanted to move until Guy retired in 1953; however, the last winter's train journey from Ilkley to Leeds, though short, had been too much for him. Predictably, she was less than happy, complaining that "Leeds is hideously uncivilised," that the flat they had found was too small and had no central heating (SJ to LH, 12.7.51). Nonetheless, she had started planning the South American novel, saying it "has come alive, and I see a whole lot very vividly" (SJ to LD, 11.9.51). She needed the money; she had already borrowed from Macmillan £1,000 of the £1,600 she had negotiated against her general royalties, and had just asked for a further £300. Her insouciant letter to A. D. Peters about money he might be holding for her says a great deal about her continuing lack of financial hardheadedness, as she cheerfully comments, "If you don't send it, and quickly, none of my family and dependents will get a Christmas box this year" (SJ to ADP, 11.9.51).

On Christmas Eve, she and Guy were finally installed in their tiny flat, 12 North Hill Court, in Leeds, while Margaret tried to keep her horror at another bout of domesticity from Guy, a horror exacerbated by her hatred of domestic mess, leading to endless polishing and scrubbing; she loathed cooking too, although she cooked well. But she coped, however unwillingly, for Guy's sake. As she would confess later, "without Guy my life would lack its salt and honey, but our two needs pull diametrically opposite ways." He was, she said, "the scholar-bachelor" at heart (JN, 2:262–63).

This enforced domesticity, hard though she found it, was just a backdrop for continuing commitments. Margaret remained firmly with the PEN, although, with Hermon gone, she did not find the new international secretary, Hermon's old friend David Carver, nearly as congenial. However that might be, the PEN was only part of her responsibilities: she always made time for fellow writers like Czesław Miłosz. Although she does not say so, it seems clear from her letters that she was doing what she had done for Lilo Linke and for others, improving the English version of Czesław's book herself (SJ to CM, 2.12.52).

Margaret did have less weighty distractions: her new American publishers, Harper's, requested a photograph, and she wanted "that man in the Sunday Times, Douglas Glass, who makes photographs of people covered with their own wrinkles, which is so infinitely preferable to the usual frightful studio portraits" (SJ to LD, 2.16.52). After a visit to London in February, knowing the American interest in British royalty, she reported to Ruth Crawford that she had seen the king's funeral:

> To me, the most impressive thing was . . . the naval party "piping the coffin on board" when it was carried from Westminster Hall to the gun carriage, exactly like the scream overhead of a seagull. (SJ to RC, 2.21.52)

In March, she went to France for four days, attending UNESCO and PEN meetings (JN, 2:263). This was a welcome break:

> But the prices! Never have I known anything like it. Paris for the English is now really impossible. . . . But I had some good meals, and one exquisite concert of Italian music. (SJ to LD, 3.13.52)

Money as always was on her mind. She worried about the sales of *The Green Man*, conscious of the huge loan she had taken out against it. Moreover, she needed to borrow more:

> Any money I may have made on "The Writer's Situation" is owed to you, I know too well. But the writer's situation is that, having just paid Christopher's current school bill, I have only ten pounds in the bank. (SJ to LD, 4.22.52)

She had run through all her back royalties, but Rache was able to send her the necessary ninety pounds (LD to SJ, 4.25.52). She had some income from the sale of short stories and translations, and on May 4, a "sad little comedy" she had been commissioned to write for the BBC.[8] But the cost of Christopher's education was heavy.

Then came a shock: without consulting her, Macmillan had decided to print only five thousand copies of *The Green Man*. Margaret was desperate at the prospect of small returns when she needed to pay off her debt to the firm. She wrote to Daniel Macmillan at once, and he, while stressing how much more difficult it now was to sell novels, ordered a reprint of a further five thousand copies.[9] When he realized that she was seriously upset, he tried to reassure her, though without expressing great enthusiasm: "As regards THE GREEN MAN, everyone who has read it, including Lovat Dickson and myself, thought it was, like everything you write, extremely intelligent, interesting, and well written" (D. Macmillan to SJ, 6.18.52). But she had been seriously shaken, all the more so as, by the end of May, she had finished her South American novel only to realize that it was not up to her usual standard; it had, she thought, a good plot but no theme (*JN*, 2:263). Later, she would claim that she destroyed it, but the manuscript of "The Gamble" survives, handwritten, with her usual massive corrections, additions, and changes.[10] She was, however, right about its quality: the plot is full of promise, but the characters do not come alive, the dialogue has no vitality — it is never more than a story. She had wasted precious time on a fictional South American world that was not, ultimately, her own.

She was depressed, what with the rationing that was more drastic now than during the war, her financial worries, the lack of household help, the failure of her South American venture, and fears for the fate of *The Green Man*. By contrast there was good news for Czesław; she had found the publisher Secker and Warburg for him (SJ to CM, 7.1.52). At the same time, she was offering support and encouragement to her friend Nancy Cunard and had been struck by a piece Nancy had written about her mother, comparing it to her own experience:

> The line between your denial of your mother and the dreadful anxious love I had for mine, and the feeling of responsibility for her happiness which crushed me, is very thin. The mother-daughter relationship is the queerest thing in the world. Its dark side . . . is scarcely ever touched. (SJ to NC, 7.9.52)

This letter also shows how dismissively she could, on occasion, write about Guy, however much she prized their difficult marriage. She dreams of sharing "a large lovely tranquil house" with Nancy and Irene

Rathbone, "or a husband, if need be. But I haven't a lot of need for a husband, and where could we store Guy?" This is lighthearted, of course; but it is also a reminder not to take the intensity of her comments on him in old age as the only truth, when she would write: "He is my closest friend, my marriage rests on a rock of confidence and gentleness, given and taken" (*JN*, 2:269).

Earlier in the year, Margaret had taken part in a forum responding to C. P. Snow's observation that current novels tended to dwell disproportionately on horror. Margaret saw such writing, when it was "crude, coarse, witless, as a comic strip," as likely to wither away. For her, the much greater damage came from the effect on language:

> The great writers of the past produced their effect of horror and tragedy by seeking and finding the words which would convey it to the reader in the most direct and concentrated form — as in the single terrible phrase in which Stendhal records the guillotining of Julien Sorel. They did not muffle it in thousands of repetitive strokes or by a flood of obscene and violent words. *They knew when to stop.*[11]

The debasing of language was, as always for her, the greatest crime. She knew the value of leaving intense feeling between the lines, implied rather than stated, trusting to the reader's imagination.

She and Guy headed for France just as the reviews of *The Green Man* were coming out; increasingly, she liked to be away, if she could, at these times. In fact, most were respectful, only the *TLS* being vicariously hostile.[12] The fortnight in France was enjoyable; and in mid-August, she and Guy took Christopher to the New Forest (SJ to LD, 9.1.52). There was a weekend in Chichester, seeing Bill and family, and then a few days in London, before attending the UNESCO Conference in Venice. Margaret would tell Basil that the conference itself was "foolish, unnecessary and confused as UNESCO Conferences usually are," but she loved Venice itself (SJ to LH, 1.4.52 [*sic*] for 53).

John Montgomery, working for A. D. Peters, had achieved a number of successes in placing her stories in journals that paid well. Now he scored another success with a long short story, at first entitled "Miggy," then "The Commonplace Heart," sent to the BBC. Michael Barry, Head of Television Drama, felt it could be adapted, all the more so because Margaret had first written it as a play, and when turning it into a story, had kept it mainly as dialogue. A meeting was set up with her, where she was adamant that she wanted to work on the adaptation herself, since "I want to learn to write for television."[13] But she had little time to acquire the different skills needed and while she worked hard at the suggested changes, the ultimate adaptation had to be made by professionals within the BBC. Nevertheless, maybe mindful of the failure to pay her for *The Moment of Truth*, the BBC gave her full recognition: a memo of December 9 referred to "an original play by Storm Jameson, adapted for Television by Nigel Kneale and George Kerr," recommending she be paid as much as possible, as she had done a great deal of work on the original story and had turned the whole lot into dialogue.[14] So Margaret was shown the respect due to a writer of reputation.

By November, Margaret was already working on another novel, picking up on what had been the first of her suggestions to Rache: a French version of the Orestes story. As was becoming her practice, she drafted it first as a play, adopting a tight classical structure. Her spirits were in fact rising by the end of the year. The sales of *The Green Man* were buoyant, and her debt to Macmillan was well on the way to being cleared. Moreover, Harold Macmillan wrote personally, saying he had now read the novel and was proud that his firm had published it (HM to SJ, 11.18.52).

The year 1953 began well. Macmillan was reprinting *The Green Man* yet again, and Margaret had cleared her debt. She was also able to report that she was halfway through her next "shortish" novel (SJ to LD, 1.11.53). The play *The Commonplace Heart* was televised on January 13, and Margaret could look forward to a fee of 130 guineas.[15] Yet all was not well: there were signs that Guy's health, always under threat from the gassing in World War I, was giving serious cause for concern: he was ill in January and he was overworked. Margaret put his condition down to undernourishment, the result of the continuing food rationing, with eggs, butter, and meat in very short supply. After reflection, Guy made the decision to retire early, in July, hoping to persuade the Treasury he needed months in France to research for his book on the Third Empire, a project that had occupied him for the last decade.[16]

Margaret was working on her new novel at speed since she was to look after her four-year-old granddaughter, Frances, for a few weeks; Patchen was expecting another child. She duly finished the first draft, and was pleased that Rache liked her suggested title, "The Hidden River" (LD to SJ, 2.20.53). In March there was more good news: *The Green Man* was doing well in the States. The review in the *New York Herald Tribune* was detailed and very intelligent, the work of Margaret Parton, who was a leading commentator on contemporary affairs. Her review ended thoughtfully:

> Is it a great book? In breadth, sweep, motivation of living human beings, and message it seems to be so. But to say so unreservedly is like taking the measure of our times in the midst of them. In the future they may fade into insignificance. But this reviewer does not think that they, or *The Green Man* which pictures them so accurately, will be forgotten in a very long time.[17]

Being taken seriously by a fine reviewer must have been particularly gratifying for Margaret after the dismissive tone of some of her British critics.

She was slow to revise the draft of her new novel, aiming to get back to it after the International Executive Committee of the PEN in Paris at the end of the month, which she felt obliged to attend. By the end of April, she submitted the manuscript, and it was scheduled to be published in the autumn (ADP to LD, 4.28.53). But then the American journal the *Saturday Evening Post*, wanting to serialize the novel, insisted on a rewrite of the second half of the book, and Margaret's American agent was pressing her to agree, as the revision would bring in a lot of money. Unfortunately, it would also, because of the terms of the contract, delay Macmillan's publication. Margaret was torn between the financial advantage of serialization and a sense that her integrity as an artist was at stake. She wrote in distress to Rache, saying what the Americans wanted was "not MY story which was (in essence) the Orestes-Electra story" (SJ to LD, 5.27.53). The changes would mean "the plot turned and twisted to give prominence to the English character . . . and to play down what — to me — was the part of the book which really mattered, that is, the effect on Jean Monnier and his conscience of his act of 'justice'" (SJ to LD, 5.29.53). Nonetheless, Rache was in favor of the revision while commenting, rather ominously, that Art was all very well, but royalties were necessary too (LD to SJ, 6.17.53). Financial consideration won the day, and resigned but far from happy, Margaret set to work.

In June, as a vice president of the International PEN, she went to the

Dublin Congress, a brief respite from housework (*JN*, 2:279).[18] Later that month, Guy retired and Margaret was finally free to escape from Leeds and the hated flat. Duly abandoning the city, they spent a fortnight at their old hotel in Ilkley, before heading south. It had not been an easy few weeks. Apart from the complications about the novel, Guy's mother had finally died, "after five years of death-in-life in a mental hospital." Her affairs were very complicated and came under the jurisdiction of officials termed the "Masters of Lunacy," who, Margaret told Rache, "are sitting on her will and refusing to let Guy's solicitors look at it" (SJ to LD, 5.23.53). To make matters more difficult, the old lady had stipulated that her ashes were to be buried in the north of Scotland.

This was not the only matter that had to be cleared up before the much-anticipated departure for France. In May, Arthur Koestler had a major falling out with Graham Greene over an apparent promise Greene had made to give the European royalties stemming from *The End of the Affair* to Koestler's Fund for Intellectual Freedom, which he had housed with the PEN. When the time came, Greene failed to deliver and Margaret was called on to intervene, and to mediate too with the PEN, since David Carver had none of Hermon's tact, and had made matters worse. Margaret, ever the diplomat, spent much time trying to smooth severely ruffled feathers; unfortunately, Greene proved intractable, and Koestler, who could be equally touchy, resigned from the PEN. Yet he continued to value his friendship with Margaret highly, saying, even as he told her of his resignation, that he hoped their personal relations would not be affected, "or, to put it more formally: rest assured of my undying affection" (AK to SJ, 7.6.53).[19]

At the beginning of August, Margaret and Guy spent three weeks with Christopher in Brittany, before setting off for several months in France, using most of Guy's pension entitlement as, despite his disapproval of Margaret's monetary madnesses, he was no more realistic about finance than his wife when his own projects were involved. Over these months, Guy would work on his history of the Third Republic, and Margaret would steel herself to revise her novel — but not at once. She soaked herself in the landscape, looking for the "bare hard line" that she loved, for the moors and cliffs of the North Riding of Yorkshire ensured that she was addicted to the clean lines favored by modernist architects and sculptors (*JN*, 2:287). In their old Citroën, she and Guy drove across France to Haut-Cagnes, where they spent a week with "a kind American writer" (SJ to KLH, 12.26.53). Then there were four days in Arles with Irene Rathbone before they headed south to Aix-en-Provence. By the end of September Guy was bored by this "charming and dead and dusty" town, and its university library disappointed him, so they struck out west for Bordeaux. They stayed first at Madame Beaumont's Aux Bons Soins, where Margaret admitted to Rache, "I'm quite horrified by the length of time I've done nothing," while Guy settled down in the university library to work on his book (SJ to LD, 9.23.53). A ritual was soon set up: a drink in the evening at a café on the Cours Georges Clemenceau, and then a meal at their lodgings, although madame, Margaret said, kept very odd hours for meals. Rache had suggested they should meet a friend of his, Jacques de Rancourt, who had the oldest wine caves in Bordeaux; Margaret worried that her spoken French would let her down as, unlike her reading of the language, it was still "a slow agony" (SJ to LD, 10.2.53).

By mid-October, she was ready to write again and was more than half-way through the revision of her novel, moving quickly because of "the prolonged brooding" she had put in throughout the summer (SJ to LD, 10.2.53). She was now trying hard to salvage something from what must have seemed like a submission to commercialism. She insisted that the version she had made for the American journal should not be the version she would offer to Macmillan and Harper's: for them she would write a different ending (SJ to LD, 10.16.53). Commercialism was not going to undermine art completely.

By the end of the month Margaret was desperate to move on, for as she told Nancy,

> as long as we stay here Guy will go on finding and reading delicious documents in the libraries, and never never begin to write. It is a disease, which he has had for ten years. (SJ to NC, 10.17.53)

The task of finding the right hotel was daunting, as Guy's needs were very specific:

> warmth, a *good* table, cleanliness and reasonable comfort. My own needs press hardest on the warmth and table — I can do with less comfort than Guy. But we do need two rooms, two tables, and if possible one bathroom, and we can't pay more than 3000

or 3500 francs a day for us both, for full pension. (SJ to NC, 10.17.53)

Another letter to Nancy has one of Margaret's rare character sketches of Guy:

> Yes, Guy is a fantasy-man. He moves with the greatest of ease from one world to another, but is never . . . in the world which at any given moment surrounds him. In Bordeaux, for example, when I murmured against Mme Beaumont's ghastly meals . . . Guy insisted that he really liked such meager meals, they were healthy. . . . Here, he talks freely of his sufferings during those jours maigres, and blames the appalling exhaustion from which I am just emerging on to them. Both attitudes are perfectly honest and felt. In short, he is always SOMEWHERE ELSE. (SJ to NC, 11.3.53)

Guy as "a fantasy-man" recalls Karl; did Margaret ever note the echoes? It is impossible to know, but whether or not, she and Guy suited each other.

They now made their way east to the "naked stone country" around Vence (JN, 2:290); but by the end of November they were on the move again:

> Guy refuses to stay in the isolation of this small hill town. We are moving into the Brighton of France [Nice] next week, where there is at least a theatre, a Centre des Hautes Etudes, whatever they are, and the Saurats and other literary people. I am indifferent. (SJ to LD, 11.28.53)

They would stay at the Hôtel Hélios, not very comfortable, with a memorable "stinking bathroom" (JN, 2:294). Despite the poor accommodation, however, Margaret declared to Rache, "I will *not* move again, until it is time for us to go to Paris for Guy to work in the Bibliotheque Nationale" (SJ to LD, 11.29.53).

What she found really disturbing was the atmosphere in France. She told Kathleen Liddell Hart that, having seen the country from several angles, she felt

> the wounds France is suffering from are too complicated and poisoned to be probed by an Englishman, however friendly. What could one say to an Old French lady whose husband and son were both shot by the French milice? (SJ to KLH, 12.26.53)

This was the France that she was probing in *The Hidden River*, and she must have been exasperated at having to simplify and spell out for the serial version what was so complex and subterranean.

Whatever her feelings, by mid-December, she had finished not only the serial version of the novel, but also the revised version she intended for her publishers. Despite her regrets at abandoning her own, austere version of *The Hidden River*, Rache did not share them; while the first version was a restrained, artistic work, he said, this version gave the story much more emphasis, and was a more dramatic narrative (LD to SJ, 1.1.54). Ironically, given Margaret's own reservations about this novel, it would be one of her most successful.[20] In the revised version, English Adam was no longer the shadowy chorus that she had first intended; for her original spare version, on the lines of the Orestes myth with only a hint of a love story, had been fleshed out. However, despite Margaret's continued preference for her first version, the sense of timeless tragedy rooted in Greek myth is not lost, and while Adam becomes more of a catalyst than a chorus, he is never allowed to reach the core of what is a profoundly French tragedy. The opening is sparse, with old Cousin Marie, the Nemesis of the tale, immediately showing her intransigence, as Jean Monnerie announces the arrival of the Englishman he saved in his Resistance days. Adam compares the France he knew in 1944 with the France of his return in 1949, always as an outsider. He ponders on the ways in which war brutalizes, as he observes the gradually unfolding tragedy in Jean's family, while throughout the novel the serenity of the Loire country provides the backdrop to human passion. As each turn of the plot dismays him, Adam is constantly driven to reflect on how the English might have behaved under similar circumstances, so universalizing the central theme. For Jean's much-loved younger brother, François, introduced as the young hero, is revealed as a Judas, while old Daniel, at first castigated as a villain, emerges as much less blameworthy. Marie, in her uncompromising role as Nemesis, goads old Daniel to his death "as singleminded, as innocent, as Electra sentencing her mother to be butchered" (*THR*, 122). Her act of retribution serves as prologue to Jean's anguished decision to execute justice on his brother. Jean, the Orestes of this tale, is now shown confronting his own act: he feels he had no option about doing what he did, but now he must pay. Adam's right to judge is not allowed to stand, even as Jean's right to act as judge is not condoned. In the end, Adam taking the girl Elizabeth away is as much a rescue from an untenable situation as the flight of lovers, while Jean sacrifices what he loves most: Elizabeth, his vines, and his family home. The fundamental dilemmas remain with no easy answers.

But how right Margaret had been to insist that the novel version should not follow the serial she had written for the *Saturday Evening Post*. The serialized story, entitled "The House of Hate," left out much of Margaret's main theme; and the ending had Jean remain, with a long explanation about his moral responsibilities, to look after his land and Cousin Marie. Orestes and Nemesis had been sacrificed, and at the end, "Elizabeth's voice gave away her happiness, shamelessly, recklessly."[21]

This journal version would continue to claim Margaret's attention throughout the year, for the *Saturday Evening Post* prevaricated over the date for the serial's publication, and there was an undertaking that the novel must not appear before the serial was finished. Margaret's agents on both sides of the Atlantic were tetchy with each other, with Margaret trying to keep the peace.[22] Serious work was out of the question, so she distracted herself by revising a work she had written before the war, *A Month Soon Goes*, regarding it simply as a potential money-spinner.[23]

She and Guy left Nice in early March to go to Paris, where she attended the PEN Conference.[24] By April, they had left Paris, heading south again for Vence. The problems with the *Saturday Evening Post* pursued Margaret there as she learned that the serial would not end before December,

> and when I think how they made me sit down and re-re-rewrite, at top speed, and spend a fortune sending new chapters etc by airmail, they were in such a desperate hurry to have everything in their hands before last Christmas, I gnash my own teeth with rage. (SJ to LD, 4.24.54)

Now publication of the novel must wait until January 1955.

CHAPTER 25

Homelessness and Two Narrow Escapes

Margaret and Guy stayed in France until May 23, their dwindling supply of French francs supplemented by entertaining an American visitor — only named as Virginia — visiting Cahors and lunching with Nancy Cunard. From there they moved on to St. Jean de Luz, but then they vanished from publishers' and agents' sight, as Margaret intended, until their return to England a fortnight later (SJ to NC, 4.26.54, 5.10.54). Once back, she was faced with the old problem of where they should live, made all the more urgent because Guy was now retired. They took refuge in one of their favorite haunts, the Burningfold Hall Hotel, "having failed to find a temporary home," which would be the pattern of their existence for some considerable time to come (SJ to JM, 6.16.54). Over the next months Margaret would also face what must have felt like one of life's little ironies: *The Hidden River*, which, because she had caved in to financial pressures, she would always feel somehow disgraced her, was proving a huge success. Rache Lovat Dickson announced to A. D. Peters that it had been chosen as Book of the Month for January 1955, and Margaret's dry response was that "Rache now believes I am a real writer. Can I hope to live up to this" (SJ to ADP, 6.17.54).

Before long John Montgomery, Peters, and Rache, among others, would realize the pressing need to help Margaret find a place to live and all were generous in their suggestions and advice. Long before leaving France, she had told Ruth Crawford:

I am half tempted to settle in London. The other half craves for the north of Wales or the west of Scotland or the south of Devon. I suppose that in the end I'll compromise both halves, and settle in the Home Counties — but they are not the real country. Only, nowadays, the real country usually means endless trouble with domestic help, and I cannot, ever again, face being my own domestic help! (SJ to RC, 2.20.54)

Brushing away offers of help, she and Guy put their immediate problems behind them, as they often would do, traveling to Amsterdam for the PEN Congress. This gathering had its distressing side, as the two Czech delegates "mixed with no one, not even with their colleagues from other Iron Curtain countries," and Margaret felt it would be unsafe to send messages to friends in Prague (SJ to RC, 7.24.54). The draconian effect of Stalinism was still, despite his death the previous year, all too evident: the Poles were friendly, but of the three Hungarians one was spying on the other two. There were problems farther west as well: there were a lot of East Germans, but only one West German, as the others had taken offense at an article in the English *P.E.N. News* on the sufferings of the Dutch during the occupation. Margaret was exasperated. Later she would recall that during the congress someone had asked her novelist friend Charles Morgan where she was. "He smiled his one-sided smile. 'I have no doubt that dear Margaret is breaking her heart in some corner with a refugee'" (JN/TMS, 3:197).

Back in England, she continued to look for a home. Guy wanted a room large enough to house a library; she wanted "modernity, comfort and a view. You see how much grosser a soul I have" (SJ to ADP, 7.15.54). Grossness of soul was on her fastidious mind, for she found it extraordinary that people kept buying *The Hidden River*. "I shan't be surprised now if . . . Levers have bought it to advertise soap," she told Montgomery, trying to laugh off her unease (SJ to JM, 7.15.54).

She and Guy took Christopher to Cornwall in August, going on themselves to stay in Castle Yard, Portmeirion.[1] The frequent visits to Portmeirion suited them both. Amabel and Clough Williams-Ellis were of course old friends, and their stream of intellectual visitors was invigorating. But the Chapmans had grown particularly fond of a couple of younger residents, Rupert and Elizabeth Crawshay-Williams. Rupert was a philosopher and Elizabeth was just as clever but "content to read, bake cakes and converse in her witty and pleasantly malicious Irish way."[2] Margaret's friendship with her would be a lasting one, offering a vision of the simple life that Margaret always aspired to and never managed for herself.

The precise dates of the serial in the *Saturday Evening Post* were still not confirmed, to the exasperation of Peters and publishers alike. As they waited, Margaret added her name to a Society of Authors protest against publishers who wanted to claim a share in any subsidiary rights their authors might have.[3] The *Cornhill* accepted her article, "A Note on France," in which she diplomatically set postwar happenings within the context of what had gone before, ending on an optimistic note.[4] When it was published, a French friend protested that she had implied most Frenchmen were bitter about the Germans. In a letter to Nancy she said that those she had met were indeed bitter, and her aim in the article had simply been "to explain to American and English people why it isn't just bloodyminded of the French to hate the thought of rearming Germans" (SJ to NC, 11.20.54). She herself, she said, was very much against the rearming of Germany, but she admitted that "the whole situation is so grim and difficult that I no longer have confidence in any but instinctive judgements" (SJ to NC, 11.20.54). Increasingly now, she contemplated the eruption of barbarism in Europe from a philosophical angle, meditating on the nature of evil. In an article for the *TLS*, she debated the problem of evil in the context of the gas chamber, concluding that "it needs no intellectual training to feel what reason we have to despair in 1954."[5]

For much of the summer, Margaret and Guy had looked for houses without success. So for the time being they had taken a small furnished flat in London, so that Guy could get on with his monumental work on France (SJ to ADP, 9.9.54). But Margaret was there for just under a week before going to Cyprus to see Bill and family, as he had recently taken a job out there, still flying. Margaret told Peters she was "leaving Guy in charge of a smooth old lady who says she will cook his breakfast and dust him. If you see him at the Savile [his club] with straws in his hair you'll know she is a bad duster" (SJ to ADP, 9.29.54). In Cyprus, she was the farthest east she had ever been. "I never smelled jasmine so strongly before, or saw so much old dust and bones of hills, or minarets against a blazing sky" (SJ to JM, 10.22.54). But she also found herself spending an exhausting domestic month . . . as mother's help, cook, washer and ironer, and kitchenmaid, oh and nursemaid, too, of course. It wasn't all loss, because I learned a lot about that strange close tribe, airline pilots and their wives stationed abroad, and a little of their peculiar, limited vocabulary. I had sun, too, and cloudless skies, more of them than in all the summer in this grey island. (SJ to NC, 11.20.54)

While Margaret was away, the serial of "The House of Hate" began in the *Saturday Evening Post*, calming fears about the publication of the novel. There was huge overseas interest in buying rights for *The Hidden River*, and Macmillan's were bringing out *Cloudless May* in their Modern Fiction Library (SJ to ADP, 11.13.54; LD to SJ, 11.3.54). But she and Guy were no nearer to finding a house, Margaret herself always haunted by that vision of old Whitby that she could never share with Guy, yet which underpinned the empathy she had for exiles. That November, she showed this continuing empathy in a talk given to an audience of such exiles.[6] The BBC recording of her speech brings a rare echo of her living voice: there is no regional accent; her voice is soft and conveys emotion held firmly in check. She said exile was "the most profound experience of our age . . . , not inhuman —*entirely* human." The exiled writer was, she said, *forced* to be reborn, not smothered by the familiar, and she stressed the key importance of literature working against "the religion of the closed mind" (BBC speech).

Margaret reached out her hand again as the year drew to an end. The American romance writer Faith Baldwin was in England, and had asked to meet Vera Brittain. Margaret arranged this, and there was a warm exchange of notes between herself and her former friend (SJ to VB, 11.25.54). As she and Vera had predicted, the end of the war had gone some way to healing their wounds, but the scars would always be there. Margaret did not feel able to accept invitations to family occasions, although she always wrote affectionately about John and Shirley.[7]

With Christmas approaching, Margaret drew out three hundred pounds from the monies held for her by Peters (SJ to JM, 12.2.54). *The Green Man* was doing well in Europe, ten thousand copies being printed in Italy alone, while requests for rights to *The Hidden River* came pouring in from Europe and from Israel.[8] So the Chapmans went to North

Wales for Christmas in good heart. Rache had now read *A Month Soon Goes* and was suggesting alterations, but both he and Margaret seemed to assume it would be ready for publication the following October (LD to SJ, 12.21.54). However, as 1955 opened, Margaret was increasingly unhappy with the novel, thinking it too long for its weight, and one character "completely wrong" (SJ to LD, 1.10.55). She decided to abandon the book for the time being, asking Montgomery to try to sell the old version for serialization (SJ to JM, 1.13.55).

Margaret was not "lying on the parish, as my grandfather said of lazy people," but she was finding it hard to work in London:

> Part of my trouble is that my head is too full of unwritten books, they push each other out of the way, and I find myself attending to one ghost and then to another. This always happens when I'm not actually writing. The rest of the trouble is . . . the dilemma of deciding between two ways of living: either one sets up an establishment with housekeeper and daily woman . . . , or one goes right out of reach of all time-wasting distractions and does nothing at all but write and cook supper. I change my mind daily between these two schemes, and so never find the right place, and never decide anything. (SJ to LD, 1.18.55)

This does not sound like the dilemma of a woman who was not by temperament a writer, as Margaret would claim in her late memoirs. But then, whenever she writes about herself, she plays down her own abilities. Now, however, she had on her mind that *The Hidden River*, proving so popular before publication, was about to come out. The sales were excellent, but the reviews were poor, and Margaret was exasperated:

> I don't see why I should go on writing, only to be cut up in The Listener, patronised by John Betjeman in the Daily Telegraph, made mock of in the TLS and downright insulted in the Times. I propose to start my life again, as a literary agent, and die rich and happy and respected. (SJ to Margaret Stephens, 1.22.55)[9]

By March, the lease on the London flat was coming to an end, and Margaret, dizzy with house hunting, decided on yet another retreat to a country hotel; for she was desperate to get away from London. Financially at least she was in a good position, as the *Housewife* had paid seven hundred guineas to serialize her first version of *A Month Soon Goes*. But she needed to write a new novel, "which may have died of the time it has been lying on a couch in the back-room of my brain" (SJ to JM, 3.18.55).

In early April, she asked Montgomery to send five hundred pounds of the savings she had lodged with A. D. Peters to the Midland Bank, as she was going into the University College Hospital "for ten days (only 'for observation')" (SJ to JM, 4.3.55). However, by mid-April it was clear that she was in hospital for a much longer stay. She told Rache laconically that, after a minor operation, "I haven't behaved awfully well" (SJ to LD, 4.13.54). In fact, she had nearly died, been resuscitated and then spent four hours "clinging to an oxygen mask" (SJ to JM, 4.16.55). Later she suffered a second relapse, her original lung embolism being followed by deep thrombosis (JN, 2:309). As a result, Guy moved down to the Burningfold Hall Hotel, and all thoughts of a house were suspended.

Margaret had hoped to leave the hospital by the end of April, but the doctors kept her there for another fortnight (SJ to LD, 4.21.55). She then joined Guy at the Burningfold Hall Hotel and settled down to plan her next novel (SJ to JM, 5.6.55). By the beginning of June she was writing, but her doctor had warned her that it would be

> months before I'm moderately fit, and two or more years before I'm truly fit. . . . We've decided therefore to live in Oxford (good doctors, hospitals, bookshops, and the chance of domestic help). (SJ to LD, 6.4.54)

As it was, she was "still chained, . . . only able to walk a very short way and not able to stand more than a few minutes" (SJ to JM, 6.13.55). The writing was going very well, however, and by the beginning of July she was halfway through the second draft of a novel (SJ to JM, 7.2.55). Typically, too, she was determined not to spoil the planned holiday in Guy's beloved Scotland, and on August 2 they and Christopher duly arrived in Elgin, staying for three weeks. Not surprisingly, she had yet again pushed herself too far. She confessed to Nancy, while keeping her tone light, that she was shivering in the north of Scotland, and had been mad to come:

I limp round cooking, very inefficiently — I have forgotten the simplest things. Guy walks and climbs. The cooking and sweeping done, I fall asleep over my book. . . . I must go and cook a most curious Scottish joint. The animals seem to be shaped differently up here. This I don't recognize at all, but the gentleman in the shop said it was just fine. I hope. (SJ to NC, 8.6.55)

Back in Dunsfold, her leg was still giving trouble, so she and Guy decided to remain in the hotel for the time being. Sales of her novels at home and abroad were still going well, but Margaret was not resting on her laurels. She refused an invitation to a party, as she was

just going to begin the third and I hope final version of my dry biscuit of a new novel. . . . I have to keep interrupting myself to go and look at another hateful house, and I must cut other interruptions ruthlessly. (SJ to LD, 10.12.55)

Typically, she did allow family interruptions. She was trying to help Barbara, who was at the time manageress at Fullers and wanted to move, as "the work gives her no scope for her immense competence and capacity for hard work, nor is there any future in it" (SJ to Stephens, 10.12.55).

By the winter Margaret had completed her novel, *The Intruder*, and Rache promised it would be a "splendid leader for our next autumn list" (LD to SJ, 11.8.55). Her formidable American agent, Carl Brandt, had other ideas; he was insisting she should rewrite the book for serialization, as he was determined to turn her into a best-selling author. Margaret had given in over *The Hidden River*, but this time she rebelled (SJ to ADP, 12.3.55). She might be a reckless spender, but she was not prepared to go on putting her integrity as a writer in jeopardy simply for more cash (SJ to JM, 12.10.55). She must have recalled how galling it had been to take on lucrative journalism for the evening papers, back in the thirties.

The Intruder, in any case, was not a novel to be trivialized.[10] Margaret had written three drafts between June and November, wrestling with ideas that others of her contemporaries were confronting. Rebecca West, for one, had pondered on betrayal and the betrayed at the Nuremberg trials, and was now meditating on the spy scandals of the time.[11] Neither

Rebecca nor Margaret was driven by nostalgia for the old world as such, both being fully aware of its follies and unfairnesses; but they did hold to a vision of what "civilization" should be about. While Rebecca addressed problems of betrayal, treachery, and treason through literary journalism, Margaret wrote a number of postwar novels exploring similar themes, linking private and public acts of betrayal as old loyalties disappeared and the world was defamiliarized; and in this she was in tune with a younger writer, Doris Lessing, whose work she would follow with approval. Margaret's depictions of treachery have similar traits to Rebecca's and Doris's, for they did not allow their villains to be black all through. All were capable of kindnesses, as was even Hitler; all were recognizable human beings who did not allow readers to distance themselves from their uglier moments.

Margaret's novel opens in Provence at an archaeological dig, a place where past and present meet and anchor the timelessness of the theme. The dig's old director, Carey, is dying and has sent for his estranged son, Nicholas, although Daniel, a born manipulator, has been his trusted assistant throughout the dig. To the end, the reader cannot be sure who is the intruder of the title, for in a sense both Nicholas and Daniel are. Old Carey points to the timelessness of this modern drama as it unfolds: "the single unbroken thread in the history of man is the thread of cruelty and torture"; and he, like his creator, is haunted by the question *why* (*TI*, 53). Daniel is gradually revealed as a corrupter of those around him, yet he himself has been corrupted by his early experiences as a child fleeing the cruelties of Nazism, while Nicholas has been corrupted by his war experiences. Hatred in this novel is shown to be all consuming. Nicholas only just manages to avoid killing Daniel, realizing that "if he killed one he killed both," that in some strange way Daniel is his alter ego, and that "I am my own devil, I created my own hell" (*TI*, 229). This time, Margaret made sure that the theme came through strongly, and refused to dilute it; but she had a hard time with Carl and then with Rache, who wanted her to cut five chapters. As she protested to Peters: "One trouble is that [Rache] thinks it is a love story. It isn't at all, it's a book about a state of possession, and about the man in possession, Daniel" (SJ to ADP, 12.14.55).

By the end of this year, she was more relaxed, as her chatty letters to Czesław Miłosz, still in France but now reunited with his family, showed

(SJ to CM, 12.16.55, 12.31.55). She told Peters whimsically: "I am awfully bored with my position as the invisible aunt of English letters, [although] I'd have been worse bored, I know, by a life spent making friends and influencing people" (SJ to ADP, 12.30.55). Was she thinking of Rebecca West, a great self-publicist? Be that as it may, however Margaret might protest about being invisible, she was less and less inclined to sell herself, withdrawing, step-by-step, from public life.

She wrote a short story on New Year's Day, 1956, with the apposite title "No Home to Go To," for their house hunting was going nowhere (SJ to JM, 1.1.56).[12] But she was more concerned about the pressure from Brandt to rewrite *The Intruder* for serialization, telling Nancy, "Publishers have taken to wanting to rewrite books. It is an infection from America, I think, where the so-called editor . . . bullies the author shockingly" (SJ to NC, 1.5.56). Rache had now caught the infection, she felt; she made some of the cuts he wanted, but by no means all, as they would have "emasculated the book, and turned it into something I never wanted to write" (SJ to LD, 1.15.56). Rache, to her relief, accepted her decisions, and Macmillan agreed to print ten thousand copies. Rache and the firm at large were no doubt encouraged by the sales figures for *The Hidden River*: of the thirty-five thousand printed, over thirty-two thousand had been sold at home and abroad.[13]

There was an unpleasant moment in January when Margaret's first husband, Karl, applied for membership in the PEN. She wrote at once to David Carver, telling him that Karl fantasized about his high connections:

> He will be silent for years and then out of the blue write me four or five immensely long letters, full of fantastic stories, horribly facetious and vulgar, and often downright obscene. . . . I shudder when I think that stories about me may be circulating, of a fantastic, vulgar or obscene kind, which naturally I shall never hear about. (SJ to DC, 1.18.56)

And indeed, when David sent her Karl's letter, it was full of fantasies about his birth and lineage; it would seem that the lying which had always dismayed Margaret in the past had grown out of all proportion.[14]

She and Guy were still comfortably installed at Burningfold Hall, postponing further house hunting until after the winter (SJ to BK, 2.6.56). Margaret was hard at work on her next novel, but there was yet another twist in the fate of *The Hidden River*. Over the past year, there had been requests from various quarters to adapt it for the stage, and toward the end of March, Margaret heard from Carl Brandt that a contract was all but certain with "a man or woman called Goetz" (SJ to JM, 3.20.56). Margaret was amused to hear that these Americans had approached the French star Gérard Philipe to play the lead, as she could hardly think of a less suitable casting: "I can only hope he laughed and refused" (SJ to ADP, 4.4.56). But the success of the book was having its drawbacks. Soon, Margaret faced the prospect of vast income tax demands because of the dollars the novel and its offshoots had earned, so she asked whether Macmillan could hold back payment for two years. She was beginning to worry that there was little prospect of saving for her old age. As she explained to Rache:

> My expert tells me this: it is not officially legal, but, he says, it is done, and so far the Inspector of Taxes has raised no trouble. . . . Another benefit of leaving the money with you is that I am not tempted to buy anyone a yacht! (SJ to LD, 4.4.56)

Peters, at Guy's instigation, sent the names of two accountants who dealt specifically with income tax for authors, but Margaret felt she must stay with her own man for a time as Christopher had started at Westminster School in September, and her own accountant had "just fixed the Trust I have set up for my grandson's education . . . , which pray God I don't break down on" (SJ to ADP, 4.8.56). No matter how bad her financial position was, Margaret could never contemplate not supporting family and friends.

Despairing of finding a house that suited them both, yet by now tired of hotel life, she and Guy had taken another tiny unfurnished flat in London at a low rent in "a large ugly building" owned by the firm that made Schweppes and situated

> on the north side of Hyde Park (the wrong side for fashion and the right side for the sun). . . . There were two flats too many, and the head of Schweppes is a friend of Guy's, so he offered one to

us. Almost with tears, I have agreed to take it, and move in a lot of Guy's books, and a few pieces of furniture — so that we shall have a sort of a home at least. I am sure (nearly sure) I am right, but I do so loathe the noise and dust of London — and the people and the parties. (SJ to CM, 5.29.56)

Inevitably, getting the flat ready was Margaret's job. She told Rache, "there will be straws in my hair — [what with] preparing a totally raw flat for habitation. I shall try not to gibber" (SJ to LD, 6.2.56). Margaret was again protecting Guy from discomfort. The Victorian coat hanging behind the door was often taken down, as she and her fellow students had anticipated before World War I.

Margaret's one consolation as she toiled in the flat was that this year's London Congress was not her responsibility as the last one had been. She told Arthur Koestler that the whole event had gone well. There had been

argument, intelligent discussion, and no, but no, quarrels. The London Poles talked to the Warsaw ones, the East Germans talked to the West, and the French talked kindly to us. I tell you this because I'm told there is a bitchy article in The Spectator, by someone who wasn't present, speaking of ill feeling. It is a complete lie, not a half one. (SJ to AK, 7.14.56)

Soon afterward, she and Guy installed themselves in Flat 2 Clive House, 5 Connaught Place, London W2.[15] This tiny apartment had just one redeeming feature for Margaret: "a fine view — of the trees in Hyde Park, and the penthouses for millionaires being built in Park Lane on the top of the Grosvenor" (SJ to CM, 8.1.56). There she meditated on the impending visit of John Foster Dulles to London, on the *Times* thundering against the Egyptian president, Gamal Abdel Nasser — and on the persistent cough which was troubling Guy (SJ to CM, 8.1.56). They were determined to go to Sweden, taking Christopher for a fortnight's holiday, but on their return, Guy had been told he must go to St. Thomas's hospital for a lung operation: "This all blew up in the last four days, and after some dazed thought we decided to do as much of Sweden as possible rather than hang around here" (SJ to ADP, 8.4.56). They managed the fortnight they had planned, and on their return, Guy went into

St. Thomas's Home, the private wing of St. Thomas's, to have part of his left lung removed. The operation went well but left him very weak, and Margaret had suffered some very anxious days. He came home in September, a month before *The Intruder* was published. Writing to thank Peters for sending ear plugs for Guy, Margaret quipped that she would "wear ear plugs to read the *TLS* notice of my new novel and then I shan't hear it" (SJ to ADP, 9.7.56). As publication day loomed, both Margaret and Rache worried over *The Intruder*'s reception, but when the novel came out on October 11, the reviews were not as bad as they had feared.[16] The book, in fact, exceeded Rache's expectations, soon going into a second printing.

Guy remained "terribly weak and in some pain," while Margaret was "so running from bedroom to kitchen to Selfridge's Food Department to front door and back to kitchen, that I am mindless except as a cook-nurse" (SJ to LD, 9.11.56). She wanted to get him out of the dust of London, but had to find somewhere without hills, so their much loved haunts in Wales or Scotland were out of the question for the time being. The doctor had told her Guy would need great care until Christmas but she was determined to get him away, "and then maybe I'll get started writing again, too" (SJ to LD, 9.16.56). In early November, she finally succeeded in driving Guy down to the New Forest, to another familiar hotel, the Parkhill in Lyndhurst, and there, with help at hand to see to his needs, she was again working hard on a novel. She had completed the first draft in June, writing it in the first person. Now, in the second draft, she reverted to her more usual third-person narration. The need to keep writing made her respond bleakly to the Soviet Union's brutal clampdown in Hungary. As she told Rache, "If you know of a more futile occupation than writing novels while the world cracks, don't tell me. I go on with it, because my hands weren't made to be folded, but my goodness what is the use?"(SJ to LD, 11.4.56). Rache agreed, while grimly observing that this would be a good subject for a novelist like her (LD to SJ, 11.5.56). In fact, Margaret's new novel, while set in England, was indeed relevant, for she had, as always, her finger on the pulse of her age.

She and Guy were comfortable in their hotel, which was shabby, warm, with quite good food and a charming garden, "in fact a good hotel for a writer" (SJ to LD, 11.13.56). And she was relieved of the worst of her anxiety about Guy. She was, however, soon having to arbitrate between Rache and Peters over whether Pan or Penguin should have works of hers to print in paperback. Rache was all for Pan, who wanted *The Intruder* and *The Hidden River*; Peters was all for trying Penguin with *The Hidden River*, judging it too soon to give them *The Intruder*. Rache said Pan would have the bigger sale. Peters tried, without success, to stop him involving Margaret herself in the argument, and Margaret wrote to Peters saying she preferred Pan to Penguin "out of amour-propre, since Penguin have never wanted to do a book of mine in their lives, which I think morally shocking of them" (SJ to ADP, 11.14.56). Peters stormed back that he thought Penguin might have ignored her books because Rache had never offered them one. Margaret replied soothingly, grateful that he was her agent, and later assuring him, no doubt tongue in cheek, "I will be a good pawn. That is, I won't tell one Knight what the other says. I will sit and wait, and give my tongue to the cat" (SJ to ADP, 11.24.56). The spat went on into the following year, Rache now accusing Peters of preventing Margaret getting into paperback; but eventually Peters won Margaret's support, and Penguin was to have *The Hidden River* (SJ to Stephens, 6.1.57).

Another potential quarrel erupted. In November Koestler, unsurprisingly desperate about the savage response of the Soviet regime to the Hungarian uprising, was urging prominent writers in England to go out to Hungary, hoping they might have the effect of stopping the brutality. Margaret was convinced this was not a practical move, writing of her "dislike of play-acting about a serious thing."[17] It says much for Koestler's respect for her and for her views that he wrote back temperately (AK to SJ, 12.1.56). Margaret in turn apologized for the tone of her curt refusal to sign up, adding news about Guy's operation and slow recovery. Koestler responded with instant generosity, saying he had just bought a house "which you may possibly have known in days past when it belonged to Harold Nicolson and Victoria Sackville-West," and which he planned to divide in two, letting one part to people "equally middle-aged and given to the contemplative life as I have become" (AK to SJ, 12.6.56). He offered it now to Guy and Margaret. Margaret, clearly touched, wrote back tactfully, saying that, while they loved the idea of sharing the house with Arthur, frequent visits from noisy grandchildren would make it untenable (SJ to AK, 12.7.56). It must have been impossible in any case, but the kindness was certainly appreciated, and the friendship endured, unsullied by occasional disagreements.

Margaret meant to take Guy to Portmeirion after Christmas, as they had been offered a cottage there for January and February (SJ to Stephens, 12.6.56). She had, as she had planned, finished her new novel. The title, which Alan Maclean, the new young editor at Macmillan, had approved while Rache was away, was to be *A Cup of Tea for Mr. Thorgill*.[18] It was a quirky one, she admitted, as "Mr Thorgill is a minor character who only appears twice, but his cup of tea is almost the centre of the book, and I know he and it will be overlooked if not called attention to" (SJ to LD, 12.22.56). She was right: no one would spot that he was the measuring rod of the tale. Rache, predictably, was not impressed, but Margaret had her way. The year ended with a nice gesture from Vera, who sent reviews of Margaret's work that she had seen in the States; Margaret responded warmly, with a long letter (SJ to VB, 12.23.56).

By the new year, she and Guy were installed in Portmeirion, where they stayed in the Gate House for the two months they had planned. The village remained a perfect place for writing, and their friends the Crawshay-Williamses were close by. There too was the usual grouping of intellectuals, the most formidable still being the philosopher Bertrand Russell, for whom Margaret would later say she had "a cold respect and small liking." He did not, for her, have the integrity of her much-loved R. H. Tawney, as she found him capable of an "intellectual cruelty . . . a shocking anger, . . . cold metaphysical unkindness" (*JN*, 2:327). Given Margaret's view of how easily reason could be seduced, his passionate belief in reason did not encourage her to feel he could address the whole human being. Yet for Margaret, Portmeirion was

> as exquisitely beautiful as always, more so in winter than in summer, I think. But far too many of the . . . intelligentsia for me, beginning with Bertrand Russell and working downwards, and as many cocktail parties as in a smart novel, far far too many. (SJ to LD, 1.9.57)

Guy too gained from the holiday, for he found he could walk more easily. He had begun work again on the Third French Republic, while Margaret put the final touches to her novel.

She would say later that she had wanted, years before, to write a book about the split between "militant communism and a liberalism gone in the tooth." More recently, after the Hungarian uprising and its brutal suppression by the USSR in 1956, "the split was already beginning to lose every quality of a religious war except its bad temper, and the excuses it offers for cruelty, intimate betrayals, devotion" (*JN*, 2:319). In *A Cup of Tea for Mr. Thorgill*, Margaret used echoes of religious language ironically, to suggest the Communist credo that had been debased by recent events. The setting of the novel is Oxford; it opens as young Nevil Rigden travels in a car with his wife, Evelyn, and her brother, Thomas Paget, both committed Communists. Symbolically, as will appear later, Rigden is alone on the back seat. Rigden, of working-class background, is portrayed from the start as out of his element, his judgment clouded by his anxiety to be one of the Pagets' crowd. The action is seen through the eyes of Henry Gurney, a keen-eyed observer of the Oxford of the 1950s, unwilling to commit himself to any group or cause, more ready to criticize than to act, in tune with other of Margaret's narrators. But Gurney's view as narrator does not dominate, for characters meditate on each other and on what is happening in the light of their own commitments or prejudices, so that the "true" picture of any one person or event is fluidly subjective. Gurney himself has his own prejudices: at the outset he dislikes Rigden for being "a lower-class phoenix" (*CTT*, 33). But paradoxically it is Gurney who appreciates old Thorgill, a man who "never accepted anything offered him . . . [remaining] as much the shrewd caustic deep-living northerner, as when he came" (*CTT*, 34). Thorgill is Margaret's touchstone: an independent working man, not taking handouts, his characterization recalling R. H. Tawney's insistence after World War I that human rights must be linked with responsibilities. Not that he is portrayed as a particularly pleasant man, just one who is stubbornly principled, counting himself free, as did Poskett in Margaret's very first novel. From the same background as Rigden, Thorgill sees the younger man as a "Johnny-come-up" and does not trust him (*CTT*, 37). Meanwhile, the lure of Communism in Margaret's depiction of Oxford, the intellectual hothouse of the time, is brought vividly alive. For many, it is a playground for the wits, as it is for the "rich, licensed enfant-terrible" Craddock, who, as a fellow traveler, is "going faithfully through all the rites: adoration of Russia, reverence for that fabled beast, *the proletariat*" (*CTT*, 48).

Margaret was writing in the decade of McCarthyism and the defection of Burgess and Maclean, the emergence of the welfare state and issues of rights, class, and, as she saw in Europe and elsewhere, a too frequent evasion of responsibility for another's pain as different mores clashed. The crisis comes when Rigden is one of two candidates for promotion and at the same time starts to realize, faced with his dying mother, the Sally of *Company Parade*, what he has abandoned in his quest for success — Margaret had shown in the Hesse of *Then We Shall Hear Singing* the debilitating effects of abandoning peasant roots in favor of power and prestige. Rigden is pilloried when he confesses to the master of his college that he had been an active Communist but had left the party. Yet the master accuses him, not of his political links, but of lying about them earlier; when Rigden leaves, the master rages that this was the result of educating nobodies. Margaret, as always, draws a very thin line indeed between those on "our" side and those who are the "enemy." Rigden loses his wife, his hero, and his job, as those around him combine to destroy him with lies and rumors that are never questioned since they are spread by the more acceptable classes in society. But as Rigden falls, Gurney is driven to act, helping him to become a modern-day successor to old Thorgill, a latter-day inheritor of the old man's refusal to accept "charity," conformity, and dependence, a true inheritor of the Whitby spirit that was always Margaret's touchstone for integrity. In this novel she showed, through images of power, cruelty, and the expendability of the individual, some of the uglier aspects of her society; yet she also showed love and integrity, and the realization of potential in various characters, brought out by suffering. This novel was a powerful moral fable for her time and so, inevitably, risked being castigated by the reviewers. Yet it was a work she did not regret writing (*JN*, 2:326). She was, through the slippery identities of most of her characters, reworking modernist preoccupations with the subjectivity of reality, the subversion of gender roles, and the fragmentation of the individual. In these reworkings, she showed herself again as very much in tune with such emerging writers of the next generation as Doris Lessing.

Margaret now heard that Ruth Goetz's adaptation of *The Hidden River* had opened in New Haven and would soon reach New York. Peters was in the States on business, and she urged him to see it, although warning him, "It is as like the novel as I am like the Queen. I won't tell you what I think of it" (SJ to ADP, 3.1.57). She had good reason to be dismayed.

Goetz had so mellowed the action that no sign of Orestes or Nemesis was left; the result was far from the French truth of Margaret's tale.[19] Later, she sent the *New York Times* review to Rache, saying she could not throw it away before sharing a laugh with him and Alan Maclean: "Guy regards it with a grim eye, and thinks I am a disgrace to the family, but I think it is funny. I hope you do" (SJ to LD, 2.4.57). The review was lively, appreciative, but unfortunately accompanied by an absurdly melodramatic photograph of Lili Carver (Marie), with the two male leads — Marie dominating in a pose reminiscent of Noel Coward's comic medium Madame Arcate in his play *Blithe Spirit*.[20]

Margaret wasted no time in Portmeirion; she had already started a novel with the working title "The Exiles" (SJ to LD, 1.9.57). A letter written later in the year explains something of why she was writing with such intensity: "Of course I shan't be able to go on writing novels much longer, shall I? I see that Colette gave up novels at 60, and did journalism after that. She said that after 60 — oh, bother Colette" (SJ to ADP, 8.10.57). This is relatively lighthearted in tone, but Margaret was clearly determined to write as much as she could while she felt able. Her and Guy's old age would depend on her resources, and Guy's serious brush with cancer had cast a shadow over the future, however she strove to ignore it. Yet Portmeirion was restful for them both.

Back in London at the end of February, Margaret wrote to Janka and Czesław at their home in France, with an impressionistic account of the two months in Wales:

> It was a long way from the nearest post-office to the cottage, and one day when there was a cable from New York the postmaster was so excited that he got on his bicycle in a hurricane of rain and wind, and came to deliver it in person.

She told them that she was happy that Guy was so much better, but confessed to her continuing anxiety "in the back of my mind, like an old coat that I may someday have to take down and put on" (SJ to CM, 3.2.57). Poignantly, Margaret now resurrected the image of the coat she had used long ago for the Victorian values she and her fellow students once rebelled against; but now it stood for the intimations of mortality that she could not brush away since Guy's recent illness.

On the publishing front, all was well. Penguin was pursuing *The Hidden River*, and *A Cup of Tea* was the Book of the Month Club choice for May in the States.[21] Margaret was already working on the second draft of "The Exiles," and had the germ of an idea for her next venture (*JN*, 2:335). She wrote concentratedly for months: she had finished "The Exiles" by the beginning of August, and so had completed yet another major novel in a mere seven months (SJ to ADP, 8.8.57). But the speed of writing should not overshadow the fact that the book had been gestating for some years. It explored the complex world of exiles with different experiences and expectations of their homeland. It was of course based on Margaret's long association with refugees from Nazi persecution, but also owed a great deal to her close links with Czesław Miłosz. In 1951 she had comforted him over abuse he was suffering from fellow Poles whose allegiance was to a prewar Poland that had vanished forever:

> They have set up an imaginary Milosz, several imaginary Miloszes (since each of them has a different reason for abusing you), and by drinking his blood they come to life. But you are not any of their imaginary Miloszes. (SJ to CM, 7.26.51)

This insight is at the core of "The Exiles," published as *A Ulysses Too Many*.[22] The novel is set in Nice, where Margaret and Guy had met a group of Poles during their long sojourn in France. In the novel, a number of Polish and Russian exiles from before World War II form a community in Nice; but gradually, as postwar exiles join them, their different experiences divide rather than unite them. It is the return of the writer Nadzin that stirs them up, each character eventually interpreting Nadzin's life and work differently, each making their own imaginary Nadzin, just as Polish emigrants had each constructed their own Miłosz in 1951. This is a deeply insightful work about exile from the past as well as from place. As Margaret assured Peters, it was all too true that Nadzin was suspected by his fellow Poles: "I have been told such stories by sane people as I could never make feasible in writing" (SJ to ADP, 8.8.57).

On August 12, she, Guy, and Christopher left for a three-week holiday in Switzerland, staying on the Bodensee near St. Gallen (*JN/TMS*, 3:236). Immediately after their return Margaret and Guy set sail for the States, where Guy had been offered a semester's visiting fellowship at

Princeton. On arrival, Guy was installed at the Institute for Advanced Study, while Margaret quietly worked on the idea for her next novel. What she would recall with the greatest pleasure was a meeting with George and Zara Steiner. George invited Margaret and Guy to dinner, "an evening marked in my mind as a turning in a lonely road is marked by a single bright light." Zara, pregnant with their first child, reminded her a little of Elizabeth Crawshay-Williams, "in so far as she belongs to a rare order of women not denatured by their strong intellect, incapable of sinning through egoism, or vanity" (JN/TMS, 3:239). George, "a young man overflowing with intelligence, kindness, malicious irony, incomparable energy of mind and body, erudition, gaiety," would, with Zara, become a friend for life, whose appreciation and care for herself and Guy would mean more and more in their old age (JN, 2:342). But during the visit to the States Margaret also received a blow: Carl Brandt, her formidable American agent, died suddenly in October. It was "a shock and a grief," and she was quick to visit Carol, who had been both friend and agent for some years before she married Carl (SJ to LD, 10.14.57). Writing later to Czesław and Janka she would sum up her impressions of this third visit to the States:

> America seemed to me to have changed — . . . the same extremes
> of generosity and violence, the same invincible ignorance of any-
> thing beyond the continent[,] the same kindness and warmth,
> the same instability, but all a stage farther on.

She commented too on the current scale of "anti-Russian talk — not just anti-communism but anti-Russian — all the Methodist passion of a country turned against the horned devil" (SJ to CM, 12.24.57).

A *Cup of Tea for Mr. Thorgill* was published on November 14, and Margaret found herself glad to be in the States, as the reviews at home were, as she was coming to expect, mostly disapproving, this time rushing to the defense of Oxford. Even those critics who enjoyed the novel interpreted it as an exposure of Oxford as a nest of Communism and were shocked at the way her Oxford dons were portrayed. By contrast, the American reviews (apart from the *Commonweal*) were deeply appreciative.[23] Did she feel, ruefully, that the warm reception that A *Cup of Tea* had enjoyed in the States might have been due to the increased antipathy to Communism and Russia? Certainly when sending the novel to Czesław and Janka, she felt the need to explain what it was about:

> It is a story of what happened to and inside a man who stopped being a communist. It is not, as everyone in England supposed (but not, oddly, everyone in America) a story about traitors and "communists in high circles."

Wryly, she added, what made the English reaction so ironic was that "the story itself is a true one, so naturally no one believes it, and I am scolded for imagining unnatural horrors" (SJ to CM, 12.24.57).

Margaret told Ruth Crawford that Guy was having a wonderful time at the institute in Princeton, with

> a pleasant room to himself, the use of a secretary, unlimited stationery, free transport to and from, free tea and cakes in the afternoon, a cheap and good cafeteria. . . . He has got on with his work, having no other obligations.

But a planned visit to Pittsburgh to see her friend was regretfully canceled, as Margaret had to sail home early, "to make a family Christmas for my two small grandchildren," their other much-loved grandmother having recently died (SJ to RC, 12.2.57). Guy would follow her in January, avoiding her anxious planning of how to cram the family into their tiny flat for a week (SJ to LD, 12.18.57). The Christmas spent with Bill and his family brought other anxieties; they now planned to sail across the Atlantic, and were busy making their boat ready (JN, 2:348). Inevitably, Margaret felt the need to help them, both financially and physically, her only comfort being that the abortive voyage of 1950 had given them life-saving lessons. She was exhausted by the Christmas gathering and worried about the projected voyage; the fact that her two small grandchildren were going with their parents made the whole plan seem a nightmare.

Margaret's confidence in her writing was again wavering. She was disappointed at the critical reaction to *A Cup of Tea*, although it was selling as well as *The Intruder* (LD to SJ, 1.9.58). She was a little encouraged when she heard *A Cup of Tea* "described as a major work on the wireless," and she had been cheered by a few of the later, more appreciative reviews (SJ to LD, 1.18.58). Inevitably the literary scene was changing, as younger novelists like Kingsley Amis and John Wain came on the scene, and Margaret was starting to feel that she had lost the energy of her iconoclastic youth. Yet her own values as a writer were strikingly close to those of the young, like Doris Lessing, with experience of a world beyond Britain's shores; and opportunely, even as Margaret was lamenting her loss of energy, the Campaign for Nuclear Disarmament (CND) was founded, and Margaret had a cause she could back wholeheartedly.

CHAPTER 26

The CND and a Secret New Venture

Since Margaret had written one of the first letters deploring the dropping of the atom bombs in 1945, there had been a gradual growth of protest movements in Britain against the inhumanity of nuclear weapons. There was the Stockholm Appeal in 1950, signed by five hundred million people worldwide. In 1952, A. E. Coppard founded the Authors' World Peace Appeal, while in 1955, Bertrand Russell and Albert Einstein issued a manifesto highlighting the massive genetic damage caused by nuclear weapons. In February 1957, in the wake of the Suez Canal crisis and the Soviet invasion of Hungary, the National Committee for the Abolition of Nuclear Weapons Tests (NCANWT) was set up, followed by the Direct Action Committee (DAC) protesting against atomic weapons. Public opinion was gathering force, with marches led by Donald Soper in early 1957 and a march from London to the Aldermaston Atomic Weapons Research Establishment at the end of the year. Then, between January 21 and February 17, 1958, the CND came into being.[1] Margaret does not appear to have been formally linked with the movements before 1958, although records are by no means complete. When the CND was founded, J. B. Priestley's wife, Jacquetta Hawkes, one of the most active women against nuclear weapons, immediately set about forming a women's group, which would, in 1962, become the formally organized body, the CND Women's Advisory Committee.[2] Jacquetta approached a wide range of eminent women, and Margaret was one of them. She replied:

As you knew I would be, I'm wholly with you on the question of Nuclear Disarmament. The thing that makes me hesitate to say at once Yes I will join anything that you are organising, is that I might be very little use. It isn't laziness that has made me drop out entirely from all committees and causes. It's being breadwinner and cook, it's having to find money for old aunts and grandson's school fees, and such — and no longer having the endless energy I had when I was young. . . . I'm ashamed to appear to be supporting causes for which I am doing little, and that is why I've stepped out of things.[3]

Jacquetta persisted, and Margaret agreed to join (SJ to JH, 2.22.58).

After a much-needed break in Cornwall, taken as Guy's health was giving increasing concern, Margaret was back in time for the International Executive Committee of the PEN. This was a committee she had not given up, whatever she might say of her reluctance to act. Then, as Bill's sailing date was rapidly approaching, she and Guy moved to the Parkhill Hotel to be near him and his family on their yacht, the *Tally Ho*. Bill was taking a year's leave of absence from his airline, and he and Patchen had decided to sail without a further crew member. When Margaret commented on this she was reproved by nine-year-old Frances: "Nana, you forget. Troy [her little sister] is a passenger, I am a member of the crew" (*JN*, 2:348). Yet despite the preparations for departure, Margaret was working on her next novel, "writing one gloomy chapter after another, like whizzz." For there was nothing she could do "except make myself useful on the yacht . . . some afternoons, and since the yacht is ten miles away and I don't know a peak halyard when I see it even that is a rest" (SJ to ADP, 5.23.58). By now writing was not only a professional necessity for Margaret; increasingly, whenever a family crisis threatened, her writing was her bolt-hole, where art could for a time blot out anxieties that threatened her personal life.

Bill and family sailed in mid-May, Margaret and Guy returning to London for a fortnight so that Margaret could attend the meeting of Jacquetta's women's group on May 29 (SJ to JH, 5.15.58). That was as much as Margaret could offer by way of support for the time being; soon after the meeting she and Guy set off for Portmeirion, planning to stay for three months, so missing Jacquetta's major event, "Women against the Bomb," on June 27 (SJ to JH, 6.9.58). Portmeirion had long become a favorite refuge for Margaret, amused as she was by its eccentricity. As she told A. D. Peters, the village was

> crammed with domes and colonnades and campaniles (playing records of hunting horns) and God knows what. When the sun shines it manages to look perfectly lovely, in spite of the nonsense. I live in an attic [of the hotel] looking down on the estuary. (SJ to ADP, 6.14.58)

There she worked on her next novel, breaking for meals and the inevitable drinks parties. She enjoyed the odd diversion:

> There is a film company, with Ingrid Bergman, making a film about China. They have built a charming Chinese hill village in a bare Welsh valley six miles away. It seems that this countryside is just like North China, so I need never go there if moved to write a book about China. (Not to worry—I won't be).[4] (SJ to ADP, 6.14.58)

By the end of August, working almost uninterruptedly in her attic room, she had finished the novel that would become *The Road from the Monument*. In a passage cut from her memoirs, Margaret told of a story she had heard about the head of the Bank of England being abroad and pursuing a woman. She thought that Stendhal would have noted it in his journal

> without caring whether it were true or not, and used it to animate his view of human nature as a cauldron of passions, generous, mean, self-destructive, driving the most exalted persons to commit *des folies qui rougirait un sous-lieutenant*. I to my grief cannot use it: I know nothing about the world of high finance, and the ironical point of such a novel would be the contrast between the social and political importance of the man and the levity of his passion. (JN/TMS, 3:107)

This disclaimer was not entirely true. No doubt when she wrote this passage, *The Road from the Monument* had not yet been published, since its appearance was delayed until 1962, so she could enjoy a private joke. For while she had not written a tale of high finance, she had relocated the scandal to the cultural world she knew and explored the consequences. The story begins in Danesacre, the name Margaret habitually used for old Whitby, as Paul Gate retires from his teaching post. In this novel Gate inherits the role of old Thorgill, albeit as a gentler version, providing a yardstick for the career of one of his pupils, the supremely successful Gregory Mott, now head of an arts institute. Gate had loved this boy, but Mott's values are soon under scrutiny as the old man, with his northern perspective, visits him in London. Much of the action of the book takes place in London, most memorably in Mott's magnificent house. The view from its windows, at different times of year, by day and by night, offers silent witness to changing personal and social perspectives as the novel develops. The exploration of the workings of the mind, the tales it tells itself, spiritual worth vying with material gain, are balanced and assessed against the bitchiness of self-aggrandizing literary salons. Many of the novels Margaret was writing in the postwar years read as variations on a theme, by no means repetitious, but subtly viewed under different lights, elements echoing from book to book, always from a different perspective. Her last few novels move from close scrutiny of the deception of others to the effects of self-deception. Mott's self-created world of choreographed excellence is revealed as a fiction, the truth as bumpy and complex where nothing runs smoothly. Yet this, in turn, is part of a larger choreographed structure, with many characters the prey of self-deception, some confronting this, some remaining locked in their own fictions. Townscapes dominate here, for most of these people, Gate excepted, are the product of city cultures, with a hidden suggestion that here it is easier to deceive oneself and others than in the old northern town and generation that Gate represents.

The novel finished, Margaret and Guy left Portmeirion for home on September 1, and almost immediately decided, Guy with some reluctance, to go to Las Palmas, "to catch the yacht there before it sets out on its endless and risky voyage to Barbados. . . . It is a crazy thing to do, but never mind. I will set up again as author as soon as we are back"

(SJ to ADP, 9.9.58; *JN*, 2:350). They embarked on a Spanish ship, the *Montserrat*, their own voyage proving far from luxurious, as they were on a smelly and very shabby vessel, full of emigrants bound for Venezuela. Margaret was delighted to put aside her fears for the family's safety during two short weeks in Las Palmas, bathing, babysitting, eating "large rough meals," and exploring the surrounding countryside. Her only fear was being rowed ashore in the tiny dinghy, as "it floated like a leaf, and unless you stepped down into it quickly and lightly, steadying yourself in the centre, it would turn over and throw you into the dark harbor" (*JN/TMS*, 3:245). Leaving Bill and family was hard; and Margaret timed her return to London badly, as she was in time to confront the dreaded reviews of *A Ulysses Too Many*. As she feared, they were all too often condescending.[5] Very few of her English reviewers understood how true her reading of expatriates was; but the reception in the States (apart from the *Commonweal*) was again superb.

Margaret's fears for her family returned as they continued their voyage. There was some distraction, apart from contemplating the germ of another novel; back in April, Peters had suggested an idea of his own for a series of short television plays, and Margaret, always eager to try her hand at drama, had shown interest.[6] Then in May, Associated Rediffusion had approached her for permission to adapt *A Cup of Tea* for television, and she signed a contract for one performance, valued at £150.[7] The play of *The Hidden River* was also coming to London with a very good cast, headed by Leo Genn, Catherine Lacey, and David King-Wood. When she saw the script, Margaret was not amused, finding it "incredibly crude and silly." Recalling her own early dramatic version, she lamented that "it was a perfectly good play before the Goetzes got their hands on it."[8]

At the end of October, Rose Macaulay died. A sense of the end of an era was growing; at Rose's memorial service, Margaret felt a pang as she recalled the young, slender Rose, with the head of a Greek statue, and the despairing Rose after her lover died (*JN*, 2:352). On the positive side, Margaret was in funds, and for the first time was in a position to postpone the publication of a novel, which was a relief because, as she told Peters, "I hate publishing novels now" (SJ to ADP, 11.13.58). Accordingly, *The Road from the Monument* would not be published until 1962, and Macmillan would keep the typescript in their safe for security. Margaret was certainly wise to request this, knowing her own propensity for destroying papers (SJ to ADP, 11.18.58, 11.20.58).

Writing and looking after Guy were her main occupations now, but she could still take action when she felt strongly. On December 10, she joined a deputation from the Women's Group of the CND which met with twenty-eight women members of Parliament. They demanded that Britain should take unilateral action to cease nuclear tests if the international negotiations in Geneva should fail. The delegation saw this as the first step toward nuclear disarmament, and they insisted that the public should be made fully aware of the dangers of nuclear warfare. The deputation was impressively wide-ranging, including the eminent women scientists Dorothy Hodgkin and Kathleen Lonsdale, the actor Peggy Ashcroft, and the writers Iris Murdoch, Marghanita Laski, and Margaret.[9]

Two days later, Margaret completed a story that she had promised to Alan Maclean for the following year's *Winter's Tales*, and it was one of her most evocative. She had described it to Peters back in July:

> I'm haunted . . . by an elderly lady who went to Cyprus with her small savings, was picked up to be preyed on by the god Hermes in the shape of a charming young Cypriot Greek, and when her money ran out he stole money for her (the god Hermes, you remember, was a thief), and when her repellent relative arrived to take her back to the horrors of life as a poor relation, he gently painlessly killed her. (SJ to ADP, 7.1.58)

Margaret fleshed the idea out simply and sensitively, its subtext her continuing meditation on what constitutes evil: in this case, is the villain the thieving, murdering young man or the portentous relative, disapproving of the joy of living?[10] The idea may have been sparked by Tennessee Williams's *The Roman Spring of Mrs. Stone* or by Sylvia Townsend Warner's *Lolly Willowes*, as all three works have women leaving their old, drab reality for a more magical world. But that is all they have in common: the telling of their tales bears the signature of each writer and no other.

By the end of 1958, Margaret knew that Bill and his family had safely arrived in Barbados, and the relief was beyond words. By now she was far from well, and the house hunting was still unresolved. It had gone on far too long, and she felt "so old and tired and foolish that my twopennyworth of energy needs a gracelessly easy life" (SJ to LH, 12.18.58). By the beginning of 1959 she wrote wistfully to John Montgomery: "Perhaps if I could offer Guy a nice flat with a nice balcony on which he could grow pot herbs he might feel less sad about not having a garden in which to grow them" (SJ to JM, 1.3.59). But in January they lingered on in the New Forest, as Margaret had picked up a virus in Las Palmas that was slow to clear and felt too weak to drive round looking at potential homes.

She was, despite her own loss of confidence, still a major literary figure of her time with a large following abroad, as well as a strong following in England and among her fellow writers. She shrank from the limelight, however, even as the feeling that she was invisible grew. The New Year's Honours list announced that Rebecca West had been made a Dame of the British Empire (DBE), and Margaret duly wrote to congratulate her. Rebecca's reply had honest roots:

> I see you so rarely, but I always think of you as a sort of sister —
> but a much superior one. . . . You have written so many good
> books and done so much public service, and I've written less
> than I should and done far too little for the causes I believe in. I
> never see you without feeling much the better for it.[11]

The next weeks were dominated by the arrival in England of the Goetz adaptation of *The Hidden River*. Margaret had taken considerable trouble to make the Goetz text more suitable for the English stage, but in January her American agents had written somewhat apprehensively, to warn that "the matter of changes is rather a delicate one and should be done only with the consent and approval of Mrs. Goetz."[12] How right they were. After meeting Mrs. Goetz, Margaret commented that she was "a nice woman . . . apart from this odd notion that what she writes is Holy Writ" (SJ to ADP, 2.7.59). For Margaret's careful work on the text was brushed aside, making her determined — for the second time — never again to let anyone dramatize one of her novels. The play opened first at the Theatre Royal in Brighton in early March, where Margaret and Guy went to see it, Margaret by now referring to it as "this farcical play Mrs Goetz has made" (SJ to NC, 3.6.59).[13] The review in the local paper was respectful, although admitting the conclusion was not very profound. As it happened, the adaptation by Associated Rediffusion of *A Cup of Tea* was televised on March 10 with the title *The Face of Treason*, and the reviewer for the *Times* was unimpressed.[14] Margaret was not being well served by adaptations.

On April 13, the play of *The Hidden River* opened at the Cambridge Theatre in London with a new producer, more malleable to Mrs. Goetz's wishes. Margaret dutifully took six seats in the stalls for herself and friends, although she was not looking forward to seeing "Mrs God's play" again (SJ to ADP, 4.3.59). The critics took her view, the *Times* reviewer saying the plot "writhes like a roughly tortured strand of wire, and at every fresh twist one or other of the characters is called on to make a sacrifice of psychological plausibility."[15] Margaret commented rather magnanimously to Alfred Knopf that the blame was not entirely Mrs. Goetz's, but she did feel very sorry for the admirable cast (SJ to AAK, 4.17.59).

Now Margaret resolved to put the play behind her, as the first priority was to get Guy to France. They set off for six weeks in May, as Margaret wanted to be back in time to welcome Bill and his family, due to return in July. She was still plagued by the shadow of Mrs. Goetz, as a German translation of her play was to be produced in Vienna at the Josefstädter Theater in November. Margaret hated the thought of its being performed in a place that remained, for many in her generation, the epitome of taste and sophistication (SJ to JM, 7.20.59). She was again feeling disheartened, as is clear from the tone of her contribution to a forum on "British Books around the World." Margaret commented wryly on

> the half-pained, half-ironical anxiety of an aging writer sitting ignored in a room full of chattering, self-absorbed young writers who, he more than suspects, if they have heard of his books at all, have not read them and never will.[16]

Clearly, Margaret no longer felt part of the English literary scene; her affinities were elsewhere as she addressed "the spiritual malaise which the English intellectual shares with his European colleagues," sensing that the betrayal of humanist values in the cruelty of the gas chambers had lost the West the ear of the rest of the world. She was not optimistic, but wrote that she hoped some day someone in Africa or Indonesia might hit upon a line from Milton or some other English writer, and a new renaissance might ensue.

Once Bill and his family were safely back, Margaret could relax, and she settled down to write another novel. She finished the first draft by mid-September, in time to take a fortnight's holiday in Scotland. She told Peters:

> Guy loves Scotland, and indeed when my teeth are not chattering I do, too. We stand and look at these damned hills, while I turn slowly blue with cold, but daren't interrupt his happy dream. One of these days I shall turn to frost-bitten stone, like Lot's wife — no, that was salt, not ice. (SJ to ADP, 9.18.59)

But for all that, she was happy to indulge Guy: he was about to turn seventy, and she promised Peters to keep quiet about his plans to give Guy a birthday dinner at the Savile Club, where the two men were both members.

Margaret was, as always, dreading publication of her next book, a collection of earlier novellas and short stories entitled A Day Off, but the reviews were not as bad as she had feared.[17] Encouraged by them, she was about to embark on a new project by October, confiding in Blanche Knopf that she had an autobiography in mind (BK to SJ, 10.31.59; SJ to BK, 11.2.59). How to write it was proving a challenge, as a little later she confessed that one of her problems was the form the book should take. She was wondering, she told Blanche, whether to follow Alfred's example, writing fragments and seeing what came of that (SJ to BK, 11.16.59). This is the first we hear of what would become one of her best received works, and may perhaps offer a clue as to her method when writing it.

After another hectic family week over Christmas and New Year's Day, Margaret took Guy off to recover in their familiar, shabby Parkhill Hotel (SJ to ADP, 1.10.60). Nonetheless, while they might be relaxing she kept abreast with the thinkers of her time, deciding she preferred Albert Camus's sense of the absurdity of life to Sartre's postwar adapting of his philosophy to Communism. When she heard of Camus's death, she wrote to Blanche, his publisher and friend, saying that he was the only contemporary writer whose books were for her completely satisfying to mind and spirit (SJ to BK, 1.4.59 [*sic*] for 60). She kept up, too, with the work of younger writers, and while she disliked those who went in for tales of the kitchen sink, she was quick to acknowledge others. She was impressed by Muriel Spark, for instance, reviewing her and recommending her quirkily brilliant novels to the Knopfs (SJ to JM, 1.6.60; SJ to BK, 7.21.60). She was also keeping abreast with the growing influx of postcolonial fiction from writers in countries emerging from former empire, and her own new novel, now completed, while continuing her meditation on cruelty, had a postcolonial theme (SJ to ADP, 1.10.60).

In this book, *Last Score*, the action is set in a landscape clearly reminiscent of the Cyprus Margaret had visited, where independence from British rule was being fought for even as she wrote. But while the landscape might be Mediterranean, the main characters are English, allowing no easy identification of the ensuing drama as simply Other, exotic, not something "we" do. The indigenous people act as chorus to the main thrust of the action, the English being seen only as

> the latest invaders. You won't be the last. Even the violence here is innocent, because it is so old, and never changes. The victims and their murderers change — and change sides. Only the violence remains the same, and the grief and the cries.[18]

It is into this timeless setting that the "civilized" Westerners have intruded. Ormston, the governor, is a product of the old school, confident of his superiority to the native, dismayed when his son falls for the daughter of a man he loathes, courteous but cold to his own wife, yet under his mother's thumb. There are apposite Shakespearean echoes here, the mother/son relationship recalling that of Coriolanus and Volumnia, while the young bring Romeo and Juliet into a contemporary setting. The action focuses on the man who heads a brutal eruption of terrorism/ insurgency and the reaction of the representative of civilized law and order. By making the rebel leader Ormston's old friend, Boyd, by showing an undercurrent of psychological abuse within the governor's home, and by having the younger generation observe, learn, and make their own choices, the novel offers a succinct account of changes in thinking in the postwar years, both for good and for ill. Margaret provides no answer to the ethical problems she poses in this work about violence and torture, but by having the man in power colluding in the torture of his rebel friend, she makes a public dilemma shockingly personal. Ormston has to face what he has become by condoning a professional soldier's cruelty and so losing his son's respect. As so often in Margaret's mature fiction the self-deluding hypocrisy of the older generation, the generation that allowed World War I to evolve into World War II, evokes revulsion in the young.

Margaret continued to respond to international crises as they emerged. New waves of arrests, for instance, were reported from Spain; the writer Luis Goytisolo, winner of several major literary awards, was arrested in Barcelona, and Margaret joined a number of other writers in sending a letter of protest to the *Times*.[19] Moreover, her continuing commitment to the founding principles of the PEN soon persuaded her to take further action when her friend the Hungarian writer Paul Tabori suggested an International Committee for Writers in Prison to investigate the cases of writers imprisoned solely for their writings and opinions and to coordinate the actions of the centers. The committee was formed in 1960 and initially had just three members: Margaret, Victor van Vriesland from Holland, and David Carver.[20] The following year, another organization would follow the PEN's lead: Amnesty International would come into being in 1961.

CHAPTER **27**

The Move to Cambridge

With Guy already seventy, and her own seventieth birthday close, Margaret went on trying to boost their income while she was relatively fit. She accepted a six-month contract to review for the *Sunday Times*, as the year looked like being one of "infernal muddle and chaos." Guy had still not finished his book, and her sister was coming to stay for four months, so reviewing "would at least keep my mind from rotting away quietly" (SJ to ADP, 3.1.60). She grumbled about her ignorance and dislike of contemporary novels and novelists, but in fact her reviews by no means confirm such wholesale dismissal. While she had no qualms about making "a polite protest" against writing she did not like, she was rarely condemnatory.[1] She liked, for instance, Michael Baldwin's *Grandad with Snails*, "a poet's novel," and Edna O'Brien's first novel, *The Country Girls*, "a buoyantly youthful novel, with all the freshness in the world and undertones of something more lasting."[2] She admired *The Crossing Point* by the Anglo-Jewish writer Gerda Charles (Edna Lipson) and the translation of Friedrich Dürrenmatt's *A Dangerous Game*, even if she did not take to Jack Kerouac's *The Subterraneans*. She warmly praised Stan Barstow's *A Kind of Loving*, where she found "every character has the stir of West Riding life and incoercibility, worked from the real."[3] Such careful reviewing was very time-consuming. As she told Norah Smallwood of the publishers Chatto and Windus:

> I haven't learned the trick of reviewing without reading the book, which I am sure that a proper reviewer of novels practises. I never shall learn it, with the result that I spend far too long on the work.[4]

For much of the summer Margaret was also writing a version of *Last Score* for serialization by the *Saturday Evening Post*, as despite having sworn she would never do so again, the money was too good to refuse. And she had finally found a publisher for her essay on the writer Morley Roberts, who had left her all his papers. Her essay reads as what it was, an act of love and gratitude to someone whose ideas had walked beside her own.[5]

In August, a publication came up against the censors, just as it had in the 1920s, but now the cultural climate was very different. Penguin had decided to test the limits of the Obscene Publications Act of 1959 by publishing the full unexpurgated text of D. H. Lawrence's *Lady Chatterley's Lover*, and the publishers were put on trial. The trial attracted huge public interest, not least because it tested the new law, as the 1959 act had made it possible for publishers to escape conviction if it could be shown that a work had literary merit. Margaret was quick to support the publication, writing to her friend Sir William Emrys Williams at Penguin to congratulate him on making "easily available an important novel by a great writer."[6] When asked to be a witness for the defense by Penguin's legal representatives, she agreed at once.[7] In the event she was not called; but she was delighted when the verdict, delivered on November 2, was "not guilty." It was a memorable moment for publishing.

At the end of November, after so many years of house hunting, Margaret and Guy moved to Tiberias Lodge, not too far from the old Parkhill Hotel and the place where Bill's yacht home was moored.[8] From the start it was clearly a mistake, largely dictated by Guy's pressing need to have his books round him. Margaret was predictably unhappy. As she told Czesław and Janka Miłosz, now at last back in the States:

> I always thought that Ovid made too much fuss about missing Rome when he was in Scythia. Now I see how I misjudged him. My laments are silent but deep, and not even poetic. (SJ to CM, 12.30.60)

However, she was managing to work on the memoirs she had discussed with Blanche Knopf; indeed, she may well have turned them into a refuge from the horrors of a return to full-scale domesticity. Was she following Alfred Knopf's pattern, writing fragments and then piecing them together? Had she by now gotten an idea of how she wanted to shape the work? We can only speculate; in December she gave no sign of what she was about in letters to her friends.

The move to the bungalow had severely taxed her strength. At seventy, she was still the breadwinner, as Guy had only a tiny pension, and what was left of his mother's estate seems to have vanished. Yet again Margaret had put Guy's needs above her own, and at least she could take pleasure in the fact that he was now able to finish his big book on the first phase of the Third Republic of France. Ironically however, this gave her another problem, for having finished his book,

> Guy is also the most bored man in the country. All his friends told him he would be, but he wouldn't believe it. See what it cost me in anguish and money to convince him he cannot live in a bungalow in Prinsted! I don't think I have the energy to move this year, but next I must. (SJ to LD, 3.21.61)

Since she felt she could not write a new novel in the lodge, and at this stage, did not think her memoirs publishable, she had resurrected the typescript of *A Month Soon Goes* under its working title, *The Comedians*.

This book was very much a stopgap and does not read well alongside her subtle, postwar works. She had begun the work in 1938–39, but by 1961 its theme had been taken over by others. The young playwright as an Angry Young Man was John Osborne territory, as was the shabby, awkward, well-bred young girl.[9] There are passages of wit, a Noel Coward treatment of social comedy with bitter twists. But now the resurrected text could only hope to be a potboiler, as Margaret herself was fully aware (SJ to ADP, 4.8.61). Spring was proving a low point all round, as the *Saturday Evening Post* version of *Last Score* had been cut to meaninglessness, serialized as "The Lion and the Dagger" in three April episodes.[10] At least Panther had taken up *Last Score* and *Black Laurel* for paperbacks and had options on *Cloudless May* and *The Intruder* (JM to AM, 4.10.61). But while the money was good, Margaret's self-esteem was suffering. She and Guy had timed a holiday in Greece to coincide with the publication of *Last Score*, and Margaret tried to sound lighthearted as she sent Rache Lovat Dickson their Greek address, "just in case I'm charged with high treason or something in *Last Score* (in which case I shan't come home)"

(SJ to LD, 4.11.61). In fact Greece proved a tonic; it was Margaret's first visit and she was enchanted by "the clearest light, a light from the first day of creation, joined to the clearest line"; it symbolized all she wanted to achieve in her use of language (*JN*, 2:367). She was dismayed, however, at the savagery of some of the reviews of *Last Score*.[11] She told A. D. Peters, to whom she had dedicated the novel:

> Some soldiers come home with their shields, some on them. I came home UNDER mine. . . . I'm full of guilt towards you, and full of what the cruel young men would think base fears — that they will so harm me that I shan't be able to keep my dependents in the state to which I've accustomed them. Writing novels has in any case become a terrible burden. What can I do? (SJ to ADP, 5.13.61)

The patronizing — and often less than intelligent — tone of many of these reviews, written by men of the younger generation, wounded her more deeply than she cared to admit. But money was again becoming a problem, although her work was still selling well overseas, in Europe, Israel, and South America, and her earlier works were attracting interest in paperback circles. But her income was not large.

Depressed by reviews of *Last Score*, uncertain whether her reputation could be sustained as the literary climate changed, Margaret was invited to chair a dinner on November 17 to celebrate the fortieth anniversary of the PEN. As chair, she gave the speech of welcome, then a toast was raised to "the distinguished women writers present, Dr Veronica Wedgwood, Dame Rebecca West, Miss Rosamond Lehmann." Margaret saw this as being "publicly confronted by my own invisibility," and left as soon as the dinner ended (*JN*, 2:142). Yet surely this was never the intention: she was chairing as a celebrity who had done so much for the PEN in its finest hour, and the person proposing the toast may simply have been addressing distinguished guests rather than the chair who was in the position of host. Margaret's reaction was a measure of how deeply scarred she was by the slighting reviews of the past few years. As she confessed to the novelist Phyllis Bottome, with regard to reviews, "at a deep level I do not mind, but there is quite a long way to go before I reach that deep level and all the way I feel disgraced."[12] Moreover, the one who flinched was "the beaten child, afraid with an old fear" (*JN*, 2:143). Yet crises of confidence and the introspection consequent on them had not prevented her from remaining active in the PEN for the Writers in Prison Committee, and David Carver also approached her about chairing the Finance Committee as, despite her protests, she was an excellent chair (DC to SJ, 5.30.61).

As 1962 dawned, Margaret was increasingly nervous, given her present state of mind, as the delayed publication of *Road from the Monument* approached (SJ to ADP, 1.15.62). As she feared, the Sunday papers were indeed dismissive, although the daily papers were not so unkind.[13] But it was the adverse criticism that she took to heart. As she told Peters, trying to sound insouciant, "I wish I was Agatha Christie or a polar bear" (SJ to ADP, 1.24.62).

Over Easter, she and Guy spent time in their much-loved Portmeirion, and in May Margaret went to Belgium for a meeting of the International Executive Committee of the PEN in Brussels, from which she brought back information for the Writers in Prison Committee about victims "in countries where imprisonment is an occupational disease of writers" (*JN/TMS*, 3:260). After the meeting, she went to Antwerp for the first time since visiting with her mother in 1908, but, as she commented tersely, "The night spent [there] was an error. It was absurd to expect to find either the city I loved, or the captain's wife and her little girl" (*JN/TMS*, 3:260). Memories were one thing; trying to relive them quite another.

That summer, Alfred Knopf reminded her that in 1965 his firm would celebrate fifty years of publishing, and he wanted something of hers to publish that year (AAK to SJ, 6.11.62). Replying, Margaret gave the news of her autobiography's progress. She had, she said, finished the first volume, ending in 1932, although it was as yet unrevised; and she felt there should be two more volumes but was unsure whether they would ever be written (SJ to AAK, 6.13.62). A few days later she wrote that in the second or third volume of her memoirs she intended to have a chapter on her year in America; would this appeal to him? (SJ to AAK, 7.8.62). Alfred was delighted, and she started work on the piece. Meanwhile, she gave Blanche more news about the memoirs, saying they had turned out rather differently than she had expected. She had intended to produce something short and rather sophisticated, full of anecdotes, but what had emerged was much more long-winded, and very personal (SJ to BK, 6.29.62). Three weeks later she wrote that the first volume must be rewritten or revised, and that the next one, or maybe two, would need a lot of thought (SJ to BK, 7.20.62). It would seem she was wavering about her determination not to publish.

Be that as it may, this was not a time for thinking or writing, for she and Guy were in the process of selling Tiberias Lodge for a handsome profit, as they had decided to buy a house or flat in Cambridge, as yet unbuilt. Yet again, this move would be entirely for Guy's benefit. Margaret was none too happy about living in another academic community. Telling Blanche that she felt she should have been a tramp, she had to explain that she was using the word "tramp" in its English connotation (SJ to BK, 7.8.62). Meanwhile, she occupied herself by working on the pamphlet she had promised Alfred. She wrote to Ruth Crawford in Pittsburgh for some documentary information: "I probably don't want to quote any of them, but I hate writing about anything without a background in my head." This is a reminder of the research she always did before writing the many prefaces, forewords, and introductions she had provided over the years (SJ to RC, 8.8.62).

In the fall, Margaret finally resigned as delegate to the International Executive Committee of the PEN, while remaining on the Writers in Prison Committee, and on the translation project that linked the PEN with UNESCO (SJ to RC, 10.22.62). She continued to work assiduously for her friends too, advising Blanche, who had asked for her help on how to approach Muriel Spark; Margaret advised caution, warning her that Muriel could be difficult, as indeed she could be. Clearly Blanche made a suitably diplomatic approach, as she secured a contract with Muriel for two books, and thanked Margaret profusely for her help.[14]

By now Margaret and Guy were back at the Parkhill Hotel. Guy's *The Third Republic of France* was out, a respectable, solid volume of traditional scholarship, and he was working on what was intended to be the second volume, which would occupy him for the next five years. The new year of 1963 saw the Chapmans snowbound and suffering from the bitterly cold winter, but hoping to move by October into their Cambridge flat, still unbuilt. Margaret was starting to make her mark on the paperback scene: Panther was bringing out *Last Score* in February and paying in advance for a further two books, *Cloudless May* and *The Intruder*, while Macmillan was publishing *A Month Soon Goes* on February 21.[15] Margaret was increasingly anxious about providing for her and Guy's old age; she worried about the amount of income tax her earnings would generate, and how she might spread it out over lean years (SJ to ADP, 1.7.63).

She had now taken the plunge with her memoirs, sending typescript copies of the first volume to a few friends to test their reactions. At this stage the volume was largely an exposure of her dark side, a confessional, an exploration of the thrashed child she had been, and it should be remembered that it was written at a time when, in her seventies, her confidence was at an all-time low. At the end of the month, she asked Peters if she might send him a copy of "the unpublishable," telling him she had heard

> in a roundabout way that it very deeply shocked both Rache Lovat Dickson and Alan Maclean — I knew they were a bit upset, but had not realized the depth of their soul disturbance. I do *hope* it won't disturb yours too much. (SJ to ADP, 3.27.63)

Margaret's view of herself did not tally with the Margaret her male readers knew and admired, and Peters too would be dismayed.

Before leaving for a seven-week break in France, Margaret had sent her little book *Amica America* to Alfred, saying if he did not like it, she would weep and forgive him (SJ to AAK, 3.27.63). But this was simply a courteous comment; after checking facts and tone with American friends, Margaret had no reason to think Alfred would disapprove.[16] To her dismay, Alfred rejected the book, as he said it gave the impression that she and Guy had not liked the States (AAK to SJ, 7.27.63). Margaret was genuinely puzzled: American friends, such as Ruth Crawford and Maxine Davis, whom she had consulted while preparing the book, did not share Alfred's view. Hurt though she was, she did not let this rejection sour her friendship with the Knopfs. Nonetheless, it did involve her in some embarrassment, having to tell friends who were expecting the book that it was not now coming out.[17]

In the meantime, she had completed another novel, *The Aristide Case* (SJ to ADP, 7.22.63). She linked her style in this novel with that of the volume of memoirs, telling Peters:

There were moments when I thought that I had at long last broken through into a freer way of writing—and that writing the volume of autobiography you can't approve of had made this possible. (SJ to ADP, 7.27.63)

For she had let it grow alongside her memoirs, trying a further experiment in style and patterned form. The setting is Provence, where the Greek Aristide Michal has a restaurant. It is a modern tale, taking to extremes the idea of a mobile society, of those who know nothing of their roots: Michal was brought to France as a child, so he is an immigrant. His wife, Lotte, is not his wife: he had picked her up in Marseille when she was ill and half-starved, abandoned by her husband and unsuccessful as a whore. Neither is his son Philippe his son, but a child taken in when he was four, found abandoned by the road after a bombing. This is a work rich in self-deception and deception, about betrayal and masks. The women, at the dawn of new-wave feminism, are viewed dispassionately, their flaws exposed, just as Margaret was exposing her own in that first volume of her memoirs; she was never one to look at her own sex through rose-colored spectacles. There are a number of characters damaged physically or psychologically by war, set against those who try to repair damage. There are those who represent the law, and those who have a wider sense of justice. Light and shade complement each other, but they do not stay still, reflecting the shifting amoral sands of the postwar world. Margaret creates in this novel a postmodern world where meaning continually evades the reader.

It was also a work that had given her breathing space. As she handed the typescript of the novel to Peters, Margaret turned back to volume 2 of the memoirs. Three days later, she tore it up and started again: "With many tearings-up en route, it does now progress slowly. I'll give myself to the end of the year to waste time on it, but I'll go on making notes for the Balzacian novel I thought of in Dax at the same time" (SJ to ADP, 7.27.63).

By August of 1963, the flats in Cambridge were still only half-built and would not be ready before the end of the year. Guy was "in a state of very much not repressed fury," and Margaret was half inclined to abandon the prospect and look elsewhere, but decided against it (SJ to RC, 9.7.63). She and Guy were now living in a two-room cottage in the grounds of the Parkhill Hotel, "with a fraction of our books and none of our other possessions. . . . I do not mind this unsettled life, and I like being able to dine in the hotel when I don't want to cook, but Guy hates it" (SJ to CM, 8.1.63). She was still uneasy about life in a university city; Guy would have historians to talk to, but she was not looking forward to academic gossip. "The temptation, an old one, to go and live in a remote place and never see or be seen again is very strong" (SJ to CM, 8.1.63). Invisibility had its attractions for her, even though she flinched at what she saw as others failing to see her; the cloak should be hers to wear, not others to impose, it would seem. She was never a simple soul. Whatever the truth of her feelings about public exposure, she could not abandon what she saw as her responsibilities: in August, her sister Winifred had a nervous breakdown, and Margaret paid the New York doctor's bills (SJ to DC, 8.17.63).

By early September, she had written several chapters of volume 2 of the memoirs, but anxieties about her financial position in future years meant that she put it aside again "to try to begin another novel, to be put away against a rainy day in 1965. Then perhaps I'll go back to the unpublishable" (SJ to RC, 9.7.63). Her anxieties stemmed from the fact that Peters was engaged in a long wrangle with Macmillan over reduced royalties for *The Aristide Case* that had to end in acceptance as publishing costs had risen dramatically (SJ to ADP, 10.3.63). The prospect of these lower royalties meant that Margaret turned to other ways of raising money. She decided to sell some of the manuscripts still in her possession, and asked Peters's advice about whether to respond to an American buyer, a Dr. Schwarz, recalling ruefully that she had given some of her finest manuscripts, including *The Journal of Mary Hervey Russell*, to be auctioned in the States for a war charity. She also regretted that so much of her work had been destroyed or lost. Peters was quick to offer to approach "a man called Feldman" as a more reliable prospect, as he bought on commission for the University of Texas at Austin (ADP to SJ, 10.23.63).[18]

This year Margaret declined invitations to visit friends as the weather worsened. She told Ruth Crawford, who was in England at the time, "winter driving isn't one of Guy's better skills — he's very bad at it (at any driving, if I am to be unkindly honest)," and since his operation, she rarely left Guy on his own (SJ to RC, 11.28.63). She was in any case hard at work, and by mid-December had finished the first draft of her next novel, its working title "The Bay Tree," which would eventually become *The Early Life of Stephen Hind*. Having got so far with it she now decided to put it away for a year, as she wanted to get on with her memoirs. She had been extraordinarily productive in the last twelve months:

> From my diary I see that since this time last year I have written the two final drafts of The Aristide Case, nine chapters of my infelicitous autobiography Volume Two, and now the first draft of this unpleasing novel called at the moment The Bay Tree. I think that is a very hard year's work, when you consider that for every 50,000 finished words I write *at least* a million. (SJ to ADP, 12.11.63)

There was good reason why she was working so hard. She and Guy were to leave the hotel in the new year, moving to a furnished flat in Cambridge or a hotel nearby while she turned her hand to making their new home fit for Guy to live in. "I can't get a nakedly new flat ready for occupation in a week," she told Peters; "Guy is frenzied with impatience to leave this hotel, and I sympathise with him. The Forest is an odious morass, bog and bare trees" (SJ to ADP, 12.11.63). She was, as ever, putting Guy's needs first.

However, the Cambridge flat was still far from ready and they would not move into 11 Larchfield until April 16, 1964. This, their last move, was

> so infinitely more exhausting than any I ever did, a series of unforeseeable disasters, that I am still physically broken. I'll recover — and start my memoirs, since the thought of writing another novel makes me shudder. I am more than ever sure that for a writer a comfortable remote hotel is the only way of life — a woman writer, anyhow. (SJ to RC, 4.25.64)

To Ruth as a woman friend, Margaret could admit her own preferences as she would never do to one of her male correspondents. She had been for some time suffering from arthritis in her hands, which made writing painful, and the positioning of the flat was not ideal: on the fourth floor, with no lift, and sadly vulnerable to the Cambridge damp. And she dreaded being sucked into the university way of life, firmly keeping their phone number (51540) off her letterhead, "to discourage dons' wives who ask me to coffee at eleven in the morning (I refuse and give offence, alas)" (SJ to LH, 7.8.64).

In May *The Aristide Case* (*The Blind Heart*) was published, and the reviewers this time were quite respectful.[19] The following month, Margaret and Guy were guests of honor at the PEN Congress in Oslo, spending some time visiting places they had enjoyed years before and returning home in early July (SJ to KLH, 7.5.64). Margaret was working steadily on her memoirs now and resented interruption. She made one exception: late in 1964, the Standing Committee of the Convocation of the University of Leeds was planning its 1965 convocation lecture, and Margaret was asked to speak, the latest in a distinguished line of writers and intellectuals. Clearly, her dislike of public speaking must have been allayed by this proof that she was not, as she had thought, invisible as a writer, and she agreed to speak on "The Writer in Contemporary Society."[20]

CHAPTER 28

Settling Down

The new year brought fresh family anxieties, as Bill had developed angina and was axed from the flying he loved: "we don't know yet what his chances are, or what sort of half-life he can live, and how," Margaret told Ruth Crawford.[1] She took on even more responsibility as head of the family, helping him and his young family. At least she was beginning to settle in Cambridge, cheered by the presence of old friends; the Steiners were already installed there, the Leavises were old inhabitants, and the Commagers owned a Cambridge house in which they spent their summer vacations. Margaret wrote to Blanche Knopf asking for Alexander Watt's *Paris Bistro Cookery*, as an American friend (a Commager or a Steiner?) had it and she loved it (SJ to BK, 3.23.65). Blanche sent not only this, but the classic *Mastering the Art of French Cooking*, and Margaret was delighted, explaining mischievously the need to brush up on new recipes as in the Cambridge academic community there was intense cooking rivalry between the wives and that, despite her own preference for simple food, she felt she must master recipes for steak and poultry. She was close, she joked, to retreating to a nunnery (SJ to BK, 4.2.65). Guy now had dining rights at Peterhouse and the new Churchill College, where George Steiner was a founding fellow, so he had some respite from the domestic scene, while Margaret was now

> struggling, under difficulties, to finish my own memoirs. . . . The
> difficulties are chiefly my sister from New York, who is a compul-

sive talker, and insists on telling Guy how to write history. . . . I am rather surprised that Guy has not left me. (SJ to LH, 5.22.65)

In July, Margaret and Guy went up to Leeds for her convocation lecture, "The Writer in Contemporary Society."[2] Margaret began by describing Joyce as a writer who handled words "much as an abstract painter uses line and colour, to embody a reality intelligible only in reference to the workings of the writer's mind, not by relation to the objective world." Her reaction to him was split: "with one half of my mind I admire Joyce as the bold experimenter; the other half sees him as the nihilist, the antihumanist, the atomizer of meaning" ("WCS," 68). Then she looked at why so many critics saw the novel as in decline, but this time she did not offer the growing complexity of the world as the reason. She looked instead at the growth of the electronic media, threatening the novel's existence because "they are creating mental habits that are not simply unlike, but directly opposed to the habits of a man who sits down to take part in a dialogue with the writer of the book in his hand" ("WCS," 69). It was not that she was against "the electromagnetic discoveries which have revolutionised our world, especially the computer"; they had their uses. But everything had its place,

> a place for that extension of our brain and senses which is the computer . . . , and a place for the one-to-one communion in which we come face-to-face with ourselves. Neither our dead nor our unborn can reach us by any but this single living channel, this naïvely human miracle. ("WCS," 77)

The concentration on computers made this a very modern argument for the continuing value of the printed book.[3]

In July Czesław Miłosz suddenly materialized in Cambridge. Although Margaret was delighted to see him, she worried about his profound unhappiness. All she could offer was a Yorkshire dose of tough love, insisting that he must not stop writing. It was, she admitted,

> damnably hard to write out of a well-padded centrally-heated prison. But unless you can contrive to do it, you're not even sell-

ing your soul like Faust, you're shockingly betraying it. I have read your poems in the anthology, and even in translation they reach the core of the mind. (SJ to CM, 7.6.65)

She drew on her experience with refugees. Knowing him well personally, despite the long absence, she was aware that a goad offered with love could be more use than maudlin sympathy. What she did not as yet know was the root cause of his unhappiness, something he would reveal later.

Margaret had asked Basil Liddell Hart to look over three chapters of the memoirs where she had referred to him, to make sure he approved. For she had now completed the whole work:

> The monster is in three volumes, because it seemed to divide that way. The first ends in 1932, and is purely personal. It has been read by four people, two of them were impressed and said it was marvellous etc, the other two (both men) detested it and said it was a vile and misleading slander on the writer [she added a marginal comment here: "no one has read volumes two and three"]. The second runs from 1932 to the end of the war and is a great deal less personal, indeed hardly personal at all. The third runs to 1962 and ends there, beginning with Poland and Czechoslovakia in 1945. Only the concluding chapters are personal.[4]

She repeated her insistence that she would not publish in England, "or not until I am on my deathbed," only in the States: "I don't mind (for more than a minute) the contempt of the young men for the novel, but I should hate them to laugh at or dismiss briefly this book" (SJ to LH, 7.5.65).

Basil wrote back teasing her about the way she misdated her letters, although this was not, in fact, a recent phenomenon, for she had been misdating for years. He also asked her how she managed to recall conversations, held long before, well enough to write them in dialogue form (LH to SJ, 7.8.65). She replied:

> From some time in 1933 until 1946 or thereabouts I used to make notes in the evening of conversations which had impressed

me that day as important or unusually interesting. Now that this autobiography is written I am about to burn the lot, so that they don't fall into the hands of careless people.

She added:

> I have a queer memory, I can read a printed page almost at a glance and reproduce it almost entire — for 24 hours. After that it vanishes. . . . When I am reading to remember, I read very slowly, and do remember for years. I can remember almost wholly a conversation to which I have listened attentively for several days, even weeks. But I don't trust my memory that far, and in writing this book I never strayed from my notes, though of course I didn't use more than a fraction of them. (SJ to LH, 7.10.65)

In this instance, she was talking of the "public" parts of her memoirs. Happenings which only concern her private life were much less accurately recalled, so her memoirs are not to be trusted entirely when referring only to herself. As has become clear, her letters over the years often give a very different picture.

Having seen her sister off on her boat to New York, Margaret finally gave in to Basil's demands to see volume 1. Given the reaction of her other male readers, she must have anticipated what Basil's would be, although he voiced his impression more temperately than the other men appear to have done. He commented shrewdly that

> the memory of the many thrashings you received from your mother seems to have induced a habit of self-flagellation in the psychological way. This can become wearisome and is better conveyed at times by implication than by direct statement. (LH to SJ, 8.6.65)

Kathleen wrote separately with her reaction, which must have agreed with that of Elizabeth Crawshay-Williams:

> You describe the painfulness of guilt feelings better than anyone I have ever come across (I suffer acutely too, and know what di-

vided loyalty can mean — the physically torn feelings that leave scars that never really heal). (KLH to SJ, 8.12.65)

Tellingly, there was a clear distinction between male and female responses. For her part, Margaret acknowledged that

> it is not possible, in a personal memoir, to be truthful — that's one thing I learned as I went on. One tells the truth, but all the time there is a contradictory or different-in-some-way truth being ignored. (SJ to KLH, 8.14.65)

Basil sent his own detailed suggestions for improvements, some of which she would accept. What is particularly striking is his agreement with her comment that Guy continued to live in the world of 1914–18. He said that this was very common among his own friends, although less so among those who had made their mark after the war. He saw all too clearly that Guy had never really settled to anything in those interwar years, a perception that must have made Margaret wince. But he and Kathleen were at one in protesting:

> In your anxiety to be honest you tend to become untruthful in emphasizing your own faults out of all proportion to the good qualities — and it is only at the end of the book that you get the balance better adjusted. (LH to SJ, 8.16.65)

There was a poignant interlude in September when Do's daughter came over from America on her first visit to England since she was two years old. She was now, Margaret found, a "young American woman, 27, very elegant, and very pleasant and with a sort of simplicity which I liked," but she remembered nothing of her mother (SJ to RC, 10.9.65). Margaret did not indulge herself with reminiscences that would mean nothing to the girl, although it must have hurt her to see the vibrant Do descend into invisibility.

A little later she set off with Guy for Portugal, as he wanted to indulge his old enthusiasm for the writer William Beckford, exploring the country round Lisbon that haunted Beckford's writing. As Margaret confessed, she thought Beckford, apart from his diaries, vastly overrated, but Guy had written on him in the years after World War I and remained "one of a small band of enthusiasts which in every century gathers around him. And indeed Guy's life of him, *Beckford*, is still the definitive life" (SJ to RC, 10.9.65). Despite her reservations about Guy's literary hero, Margaret enjoyed Portugal. There was not so much of the "angry poverty" she had met in the Spain of the thirties, she told Kathleen. And while Portugal was indeed a police state, she had watched with delight, in Cascais, "the fishwives terrorising the policeman officiating at the fish auctions. They might have been Whitby fishwives" (SJ to KLH, 12.10.65). The downside had been to find their central heating had broken down when they got home; it would not be mended for three months. Fortunately, they were away again for Christmas and New Year's Day, first in London, then in Twickenham to be with Bill and his wife, now living on an island in the Thames. After that they went to Portmeirion to stay with the Crawshay-Williamses over the New Year holiday (SJ to AAK, 12.31.65; GC to S. C. Crawford, 1.25.66).

While in Wales, Margaret wrote a witty article looking at what she mischievously presented as a current obligation in women's novels to include "a clinically detailed description of copulation or an obsessed account of an abortion or the trials of menstruation, or a slight case of incest or clap."[5] Perhaps, she speculated, it was the latest stage of becoming a "free woman," but she found that in some novels "these anxiously free women are caught in their sexuality like flies in treacle"; were their authors seriously interested in a woman examining the stains on her underclothes, or were they "simply frisking in the sun, ungainly but happy, after years of stifling moral censorship?" ("Love's Labours"). This article was never meant to be a serious attack on feminism, for Margaret never felt other than a feminist; nevertheless, she was impatient with what could be seen as a betrayal of the freedom it advocated. Admiring as she was of Doris Lessing, she criticized some aspects of *The Golden Notebook*, disliking what she saw as "its involuntary and complete misconception, parody, of the very thing it was supposed to be about — freedom, 'free women'" (JN, 2:309). Lessing's women were, she said, struggling in the "sticky web" of their sexual needs (JN, 2:309). But then, Margaret had schooled herself to have very different priorities in her difficult but happy marriage; and Lessing herself was all too aware of the traps Margaret deplored, as later works would show.[6]

Margaret was now seventy-five, and inevitably age was taking its toll not only on her but on her friends. Both Basil and Alfred had serious illnesses during the year, and then in June Blanche died in her sleep (AAK to SJ, 6.9.66). Margaret knew all too well from her own experience that Blanche, dynamic, charismatic, and ambitious, could be difficult, and her condolences to Alfred took sensitive account of this, which he appreciated. Margaret had loved Blanche despite all, and would miss her, just as she missed Lilo Linke, who had died a few years before. In all, 1966 was not proving a good year. In April, Bill had suffered a heart attack and, although he recovered fairly well, all chance of flying had ended, and he had to resign himself to a desk job with his old firm (SJ to AM, 4.14.66). Margaret's anxiety was acute.

Toward the end of 1965 she had decided to revise her novel "The Bay Tree," which would have the published title *The Early Life of Stephen Hind*.[7] In this novel, one generation's perspectives are set against another's, those of old Chatterley against those of his young secretary, Stephen Hind. Chatterley's name is not chosen by chance: perhaps as a response to the trial of Penguin for publishing *Lady Chatterley's Lover* in 1960, Margaret now presented D. H. Lawrence's ill-assorted husband and wife as the older generation, while Stephen has the attitude of a younger generation to the role of lover. The theme of memoirs is also paramount: Chatterley intends his memoirs for the British Museum, not for sale. While he is of a different stamp from the Mott of *The Road from the Monument*, he too is a great man with secrets that threaten to diminish him, while Hind is a manipulative, attractive young man, using calculation to achieve his ends. The role of the memoirs obsesses both men, while the whole idea of what is truth, along with the private individual's view of himself, is presented as affecting and infecting public life, as when Chatterley says of Chamberlain, the real-life prime minister at the time of Munich,

> years of telling himself and the country that he was a man of peace and leader of the only party which knew how to avoid war acted on him like a tranquillising drug, so that with his own eyes shut he led the nation, blindfold, all but disarmed, its belly full of wind, to the very edge of extinction. (*ELSH*, 23)

Reading such passages in these intensely personal memoirs, what Hind sees is arrogance: Chatterley has not forgiven people; he just sees them as not worth hating. The young man learns from the way he perceives Chatterley. He masks his inner impulses behind the impression he gives to others. The chasm between Lawrence's sexually driven characters and Margaret's Stephen, who uses sex to advance his cause, is reflected in each generation's attitude to the memoirs and what constitutes their value. Reviewers saw nothing of Margaret's meditation on the differences between the generations and were, for the most part, unkind.[8] Indeed, such was their venom that they inspired a letter to Margaret from the biographer and novelist Margaret Lane, Countess Huntingdon, protesting at the "extraordinary *animosity*" of some of the reviews, which seemed to stem from a need to knock down anyone who had been writing for a long time. "Brutality is the fashion," she concluded, and might have added that this was indeed an underlying theme of Margaret's novel.[9] Yet other writers of Margaret's generation did not necessarily attract such hostility; it would not escape Margaret's notice that another Macmillan publication, Rebecca West's *The Birds Fall Down*, brought out the same year, received many accolades and was hugely successful.[10] But then, while Margaret steadily withdrew from the public stage, Rebecca had become something of a grande dame of literature in her later years.

The beginning of 1967 found Guy "slaving to finish his book" on the defeat of France in 1940. Margaret had read the typescript in October and had thought it only needed revising, "but I see to my alarm that he is expanding" (SJ to RC, 1.6.67). Meanwhile, she herself had withdrawn her memoirs from Harper's, as they wanted

> to cut too much and to present a smooth portrait of Storm Jameson which offended my sense of truth and justice. So it is back on its shelf in a cupboard. If I can't do anything else with it, I'll have it duplicated and distribute a few copies. (SJ to RC, 1.6.67)

Meanwhile, she told Ruth she was working "in a desultory way at a grotesque novel," which would become *The White Crow*. The idea clearly came in the wake of her and Guy's visit to Portugal on the quest for Beckford. For while her novel had thematic links with its predecessors and indeed its roots went far into the past, Margaret was developing a fascinatingly gothic twist.

By the middle of the year, it was clear that, despite Margaret's first reaction to Harper's insistence that the memoirs must be cut, they would not find a publisher in their present three-volume form. So she reluctantly set about reducing the three volumes to two. She was also struggling to finish a ten-thousand-word essay on Stendhal for "an improbable American, who publishes coffee-table editions of French classics in translation, with essays by English writers. His money comes from Geneva, so I am in the pay of the gnomes" (SJ to KLH, 10.23.67). At the end of the year, Guy's book *Why France Collapsed* was accepted by Cassell. He still thought that the book needed another three years' work, but Margaret told the Liddell Harts that she had felt it was "right to harry him," to draw a line "under (at least) seven years' writing and wrestling with a nearly intractable bit of history." She hoped Basil would like it when it came out, although, "Guy himself doesn't hope, he groans and mutters" (SJ to LH, 12.21.67). Margaret did not say, but it is clear that she was worried that Guy was exhausting his increasingly dwindling strength.

The traditional visit to North Wales had been clouded by the Vietnam War and by Bertrand Russell's last days; Margaret told Ruth Crawford, "He is still dying, so slowly, and still living in a sort of dream which sometimes turns to nightmare, remembering old things and dead people and failing to recognise living friends" (SJ to RC, 2.8.68). She shared another dark moment with Ruth since they both cared deeply about Czechoslovakia. Back in Cambridge, she and Guy had been visited by one of their old Czech friends, Liba Ambrosova's husband, Miloš; the couple had been in England throughout the war but had returned to Czechoslovakia when it ended. At first all had gone well but then:

> He had been in prison — some conspiracy charge — and what he called "an accident" there has left him with a heavy limp. After prison, poverty, no job, his marriage breaking down — his wife, of whom I am fond, is (like him) high-tempered and self-centred — a son's suicide. (SJ to RC, 2.8.68)

Such tragedies spawned by repressive regimes of the Right and now of the Left were all too frequent, something Ruth and Margaret understood only too well.

Margaret had now finished the novel she had mentioned to Ruth, *The White Crow*.[11] Like her last, it was written while she was deeply engaged with issues of memory. Indeed, the book had its origins back in 1948, after the writing of *The Black Laurel*. It is worth recalling the passage cut from her memoirs in which she recalled details of the novel she had abandoned then:

> It was to be a hybrid form of fiction, drama, philosophical essay, and dream — the last carried by monks of the Benedictine Abbey of Whitby in the twelfth century. The central characters were a Mr Antigua, a grotesquely fat man — his physical absurdity a contrast with his sound mind and extreme delicacy of feeling and his friends. (JN/TMS, 3:70).

Margaret may have abandoned the novel back in 1948, but now, twenty years on, she had developed its ideas in ways that show her engaging with recent developments in fiction. The time frame, 1890s to 1940s, provides a background of the major events in the first half of the twentieth century, but the tone is very different from anything Margaret had done previously. The grotesque in tragic and comic guise figures largely, in the main character's body, his view of the world, and his interaction with it. The epigraph, from a northern folktale, signals a work responding to Angela Carter's magic realism and anticipating, or perhaps inspiring, William Golding's *Darkness Visible*. The first pages set the tone:

> In deep sleep the traveller heard — did he hear? — a broken sound, a phrase, the same phrase, repeated, without intelligible words, less speech than an animal whimper with human undertones. (WC, 1)

The same phrase will end the book, a variation on the device used in *The Black Laurel*. In the late-nineteenth-century world, in Portugal, the traveler takes on an orphaned baby with "two long puckers of skin stretching from the shoulder-blade so far as the third rib" (WC, 9–10). Gradually the novel develops this excursion into the grotesque, suggesting that the true grotesque lies at the core of society. All are judged by how they respond to the appearance of this child who will become Antigua. As he matures, Antigua sees the changing Europe on the brink of World War I, but his observations are increasingly out of tune with "realist" interpretations of his world and culture, as his mind creates a medieval monastery where he can take refuge. This gripping work shows Margaret at home with preoccupations that absorbed younger writers: what exactly constitutes, for instance, madness and sanity, something Doris Lessing was exploring in *The Four-Gated City* and *Briefing for a Descent into Hell*. Aesthetically, too, Margaret was showing the grotesque as a way of presenting a Europe capable of Holocaust. The slaughter of World War I, the gas chambers, the refugees, and in a sense her own resurrection of the dead as her judges, which the dedication of her memoirs makes clear, all these things are woven through this novel alongside her own sense of herself as a clownish Quixote.

Guy was as anxious as Margaret when a book was finished and out of his hands. In February, he was, she told Basil, "growlingly going out on an errand, his life a total failure, his mind a ruin, his books worthless" (SJ to LH, 2.10.68). Fortunately, a snippet on *A Passionate Prodigality* from the *New York Times* sent by Basil "not only restored him to sanity but sent him out smiling." "Thank you," wrote Margaret, no doubt with heartfelt sincerity; a grumpy Guy must have been a trying companion (SJ to LH, 2.10.68). But this was not a good spring. The news from Vietnam was dismaying, as were the implications of the new immigration law, aimed at restricting the entry of Asians holding British passports. Margaret told Ruth she felt "bitterly ashamed" (SJ to RC, 3.1.68). In April she and Guy spent ten days in Portmeirion before he went into the hospital for another operation, coming out very weak and, she told Alfred, having to put up with the amateurish nursing of his wife instead of the pretty young nurses who had tended him in the hospital (SJ to AAK, 5.23.68). From now on, Margaret's first preoccupation would be Guy; he recovered, but far too slowly, which made him very cross (SJ to KLH, 5.24.68). She was now acting as nurse, cook, and general dogsbody, and she could not leave him (SJ to AAK, 5.29.68).

Toward the end of the year, Guy's *Why France Collapsed* and Margaret's *White Crow* were published, but their private troubles overshadowed this joint event. On the broadcasting front, there was some good news, as Douglas Allen of the BBC was enthusiastic about *The Early Life of Stephen Hind*, suggesting its adaptation for television, and unlike previous disappointments, this project would indeed take shape.[12] This interest was small comfort at a time of international unrest and personal worries. Margaret shared with Ruth her anxiety about Czechoslovakia: "There is an awful sense of déjà vu about the Czech troubles, I half expect to wake up and find myself writing 1939 on my letters." She was, she said, now busy writing begging letters for Czech students over in England: "And that, too, is like the years after 1933, when one spent so much time trying to keep afloat the first wave and then the second and the third of refugees. What a world, what an age" (SJ to RC, 12.18.68). Yet her own preoccupations did not deter Bill and family from coming for Christmas again, and Margaret, always one for a challenge, decided to buy a goose, although she told Kathleen she had no idea how to cook it. No doubt the family invasion meant extra shopping trips, and sadly,

> running along King's Parade, I fell and cut my eyebrow, and by next morning a vast swelling, like a blood-red sunset, covered half that side of my face and still does. I look like something out of one of the grimmer of Brecht's plays, and have to wear a large patch when I go out, lest people should swoon at the horrific sight. (SJ to KLH, 12.20.68)

She still delighted in self-mockery when writing to her friends.

All this time, Margaret had been cutting and reshaping her memoirs so as to achieve a two-volume version that would be publishable. By the end of 1968 she had virtually completed the transformation. She had, when she started, two closely related versions of the three-volume work to hand. One would be given to the University of Texas in 1975, and carries Margaret's own note stating:

> This is the original version of my memoirs, written directly on to the typewriter. These memoirs have not been published, and will possibly not be published in my lifetime. Therefore they can only be sold on the understanding that they are not made any use of in my lifetime.[13]

The three-volume version, like its two-volume successor, was not structured in strict chronological order, suggesting instead ways in which the mind retrieves information. Memories are recalled from different moments, and while there are many comments dated at the time of writing, these too do not appear in chronological sequence. So much for the structure; it is also important to stress again that these memoirs were written in Margaret's seventies, at a time when she was less than confident about her own worth as a writer and as a person. As a result, the story she told now was not, could not be, the same story that her correspondence told over the years. Furthermore, while on the whole she represented events of public import accurately, drawing on her records which she subsequently destroyed, she was far from accurate when recording more personal events. Her dating, for instance, was often wildly astray, as it so often was in her correspondence. Crucially, she set down the truth about herself as she saw it, which did not by any means always tally with the view of her that others had.

This was certainly true in the three-volume version, where, in the first volume, she laid great stress on her sense of guilt and of failure. She would, in the printed version, cut long passages that poured scorn on herself as a person and also as a writer, as here:

> I suspect that when I indulge in eloquence it is always an impure act, that I am taking pleasure in the words *for their own sake*, even if, at the same time, I am using them in a cause I believe to be good, and which does not profit me in any way.
>
> The friend to whom I read this last paragraph said, "My God, you are either out of your mind or a hopeless Calvinist." (*JN/TMS*, 1:188)

Constantly the image of her mother's thrashing obtrudes, far more frequently than in the published text, shaping her life. The first volume does indeed give a bleak view of how she saw herself in her later years, and this was the view her friends could not accept. In volume 3, she commented (dating the passage November 23, 1964):

> I should have known better than to show the first volume of this work to four persons only alike in so far as each of them is well-educated and my friend: . . . The first, a woman some twenty years younger than I am [Elizabeth Crawshay-Williams] thought well of it. The others [men] were disturbed or shocked: my friend A. D. Peters called it "an unfair, incomplete and inadequate portrait of the author. . . . If anyone else had written this book one

would say: You don't know Storm Jameson at all — neither what she is nor what she has done nor what she stands for."

Discouraged, I was almost inclined to destroy most of what I had written and go no further with the book. I am surrounded by English gentlemen, I thought. Frightful . . . But I knew I should regret it: something between stubbornness and patience — the patience of the old sea-captain, my father, filling folio after folio with details. (*JN*/TMS , 3:1)

Nonetheless, she added another passage that would be cut, the full text of what her Polish friend Maria Kuncewiczowa, "one of the subtlest and least facile of writers," wrote to her before she started the memoirs, suggesting something of the "glow" that Sydney Harland had first noted in Scarborough, so many years before:

I simply want you to remember that you are much more than your books, your words, your magnificent talent, or even your presence, and that many people are aware of it. Please do be proud of yourself. . . . You sometimes say and write about yourself things which cannot be emphatically denied for the ridicule [*sic*] of the idea itself. And, I know, you think even worse things. But this is so discourteous on nature (not to speak of God), and so unfair on your friends who love you because you are what you are. (*JN*/TMS, 3:2)

However, Margaret was unwilling to abandon her harsh view of herself, even as she acknowledged that it might not be the whole truth. A passage she clung to in both unpublished versions reveals what this view meant to her:

Certain incidents in this memoir appeared in the *Journal* [*of Mary Hervey Russell*], with the important difference that I was not then, as I am now, trying to be nakedly truthful, to mistrust appearances, to be ruthlessly skeptical about myself, to penetrate illusions. . . . It is perfectly possible that the *Journal* is as truthful, even, perhaps closer to truth, than this second desperate attempt. I don't know. Reality, the reality of oneself, is *that which cannot be grasped*. (*JN*/TMS, 2:234–35)

The two volumes of the published version kept much of the spirit of the two three-volume texts and the overall structuring: the more personal years up to 1932, greater concentration on the public and political sphere after that. But the compression had been far from simple. The ordering of passages was thoroughly revised, and phrasing was reviewed. Large chunks of self-criticism, not to say flagellation, were cut but by no means was this element omitted, while a great deal about Bill and Christopher disappeared, along with some of the more critical passages about people she had met. The lack of precise chronological sequence was maintained throughout both volumes, with occasional comments from one of the years in which she was writing, although again not in chronological order. But it must be stressed that in this work, the memory is that of the 1960s, and while the ruminations on her life, her times, are a superb achievement, this work is not the ultimate source for an understanding of her earlier life. As she says, in the course of writing she constantly tore up and rewrote passages in the interests of accuracy; and even then could not be sure about what constitutes "truth."

It is tempting, too, to see this work as made up of layers of "writing back," and not just to Bloomsbury modernism. When she says of Doris Lessing's *Golden Notebook* that she was struck "by its involuntary and complete misconception, parody, of . . . 'free women,'" she is seeing them as so unlike Lilo Linke's youthful free spirit of the 1930s (*JN*, 1:309). Yet the web that restrained Margaret was that of her mother, who shaped so much of her own story right up to the time of writing. What Margaret achieved in this work was to catch echoes of the many voices of her time, as they impinged on her, the flawed observer. We move from the cliffs and seascapes of Whitby through London, to Europe, deft sketches giving us a background of street or room, turns of phrase hinting at cultural difference. Family, refugees, politicians, writers, and journalists flock through its pages; no one strand dominates, but the cohesion of public and private inspires the work as a whole. For like her novels, this autobiography will not allow the public ever to be separated from the personal: Margaret cannot dissociate herself from her world, and her errors, her enduring sense of guilt, of lack of love, mirror those of the Europe she loved at this stage in its history. It is interesting to compare what another Yorkshirewoman says in her own autobiography, produced at about the same time. Barbara Hepworth comments:

All landscape needs a figure — and when a sculptor is the spectator he is aware that every landscape evokes a special image. In
creating this image the artist tries to find a synthesis of his human experience and the quality of the landscape. . . . [There is] a
rhythm of form which has its roots in earth but reaches outwards
towards the unknown experiences of the future.[14]

Barbara goes on to speak of the great United Nations secretary-general
Dag Hammarskjöld, who had watched the progress of her sculpture
Single Form, embodying ideas of compassion, courage, and creativity,
commissioned for the United Nations building in New York, and she
says of him:

He had a pure and exact perception of aesthetic principles, as
exact as it was over ethical and moral principles. I believe they
were, to him, one and the same thing. . . . In the lives of most
men there is some form of tension between the attraction of the
world outside and their yearning for home. (Hepworth, 99)

This, in her own distinctive way, was true of Margaret too. Her aesthetics
could never be divorced from her values; and her roots in the Whitby she
had left behind and lost were what gave her such lifelong compassion
for the exiles of the world. She was, like Hepworth, like Hammarskjöld,
inextricably committed to addressing the spirit of her age.

CHAPTER 29

The Shadows Gather

On January 6, 1969, Margaret and Guy got away from Cambridge and the demands of the family Christmas, staying in a "fantastic Count's fantastic country house," La Capella, in Mallorca (SJ to KLH, 12.20.68). Margaret was amused by the very wealthy, jet-setting people there: all, she told Kathleen Liddell Hart, "could be erased from the world with no loss to it (except of elegance), but they are not intolerant, not ill-meaning, not stupid, not lazy" (SJ to KLH, 1.13.69). She and Guy stayed there for three weeks. On the whole, it was an enjoyable interlude of "extreme luxury and idleness," she told Alan Maclean, who had sent her copies of the *White Crow* reviews: "I was silly enough to begin looking at them before shuddering and tearing them up" (SJ to AM, 1.29.68 [*sic*] for 69). They were poor, as her reviewers could not comprehend Margaret's gothic experiment. Despite her not-unfounded dread of English reviewers, she had now steeled herself to sign a contract with Collins for her memoirs, as Alan, now in Rache Lovat Dickson's place as Rache had retired, had been reluctant to publish them; he had been devastated by her unsparing presentation of her dark side. This refusal did not spoil their growing friendship; she told him cheerfully that "now all I have to do is think where, what remote continental shore, to go to the week before publication" (SJ to AM, 2.7.69).

For publication of the memoirs was not her prime concern. Quite apart from Guy's health, there were other serious family concerns. British Eagle, the firm employing Bill, had collapsed, and he was without work. Margaret was desperately anxious: "It seems hard that a responsible-minded intelligent fifty-year-old young man is unwanted anywhere. His own fault for electing to be only an air-pilot, I know, but it cuts to the heart." Moreover, Guy was "more than usually prickly," as there had been no reviews of his book (SJ to LH, 2.1.69). In April, she and Guy managed a welcome holiday in Jersey, which was, she told Ruth Crawford, "full of daffodil fields and miles of gorse on the tops of cliffs looking down on empty beaches and bays." They returned all too soon to yet another family crisis. Barbara was dying,

> too slowly, of cancer, and I keep going up to York, where she and my grandson are. . . . I am desperately sorry for my poor ex-daughter-in-law, but much more anxious about my grandson, whose days are portioned out between a heavy load as a University lecturer and two long daily sessions at the nursing home, and who shows signs of the prolonged strain, too heavy for his 26-year-old shoulders. (SJ to RC, 5.3.69)

Finally, at the beginning of June, Margaret heard from Christopher that his mother was close to death, and she rushed up "to help him through"; the funeral was on June 11 (SJ to KLH, 6.2.69). Then in August, Guy had a slight stroke.[1]

The first volume of the memoirs, *Journey from the North*, was published on September 5. Up to the last, Margaret had been calling it "my unnecessary autobiography," for she was very nervous about its reception (SJ to LH, 8.7.69). She need not have worried. The reviews were excellent, and she received many letters admiring the book.[2] The reception clearly delighted her, although she still regretted much that had been cut out.[3]

Despite Margaret's relief that the first volume was doing well, a shadow hung over her. Guy did not make a good recovery from his stroke, and she told Alfred Knopf that it felt as if they had each been tapped gently on the shoulder. She found herself watching Guy nervously, and he was rather nervous himself (SJ to AAK, 11.11.69). She hoped to take him away to Malta in the winter; she thought too of moving to a more comfortable flat. As an interim measure, she got him to Torquay for ten days in November, but it was clear he was not really recovering. He seemed, she told Basil Liddell Hart,

> to have jolted down a step or steps. . . . In Torquay he couldn't
> walk up even the gentlest slope without stopping for breath two
> or three times, and he complains that his missing lung pains him
> when he walks any distance. (SJ to LH, 11.21.69)

His chest pains proved to be angina. Margaret had to decide between risking him falling ill abroad or being bored and cold at home (SJ to LH, 11.30.69). Serious work was out of the question for her. At the end of the year she did manage a letter to the *Adam International Review*; she was fond of its redoubtable editor, Miron Grindea, who, despite huge financial problems and rapidly changing literary tastes, had kept his journal going throughout the times of austerity. It was now in its thirty-fourth year, and Margaret contributed one of several letters from contemporary writers on Georges Simenon. She did not praise his detective fiction, as the genre, she said, bored her; but his other novels appealed to her.[4] They constituted, she said, a *comédie humaine* that was "stripped of superfluous flesh and gestures." A writer, in fact, after her own heart.

In the new year, Margaret and Guy did travel to Malta in search of the sun, and so heard sad news from a distance. Basil would never see the second volume of her memoirs: he died on January 29. The Chapmans grieved for him, as they stayed out the winter in Malta, only returning on March 9. This meant they missed the broadcasts of Margaret's two BBC interviews, coinciding with the publication of the second volume of *Journey from the North*, which was as well received as the first.[5] For the first broadcast, she had been interviewed by a fellow Yorkshireman, Jack Singleton.[6] The mood was relaxed, and when he asked about her name, "Storm," she told him her father was William Storm Jameson and so she as the eldest child inherited the name. This was of course a delightful fiction: Ethel as her middle name had long been airbrushed out of her history. There was laughter in this interview, even while she recalled that nothing in her writing career had been very easy. The interview with Jeanine McMullen broadcast the next day was much darker in tone: Margaret said she had not been punished for her mistakes and sins as she should have been, insisting that she had never devoted herself to anyone completely, had not always answered pleas for help. Praise of her own generosity was never willingly received, and she was increasingly dissatisfied not only with her own achievements but with the attitude of British novelists as a whole, commenting in an article that there was a

> curious lack of tension in so much intelligent well-written present-day English fiction, as compared with the novels reaching us from countries where freedom has to be exercised with cunning or bought at a steep price.[7]

Looking to Russia, Hungary, and Greece, she said that persecution and danger meant "that a lean wolf develops muscles that a domestic dog rarely needs" ("Now and Then").[8]

She had now abandoned Macmillan as her publisher. Pleased with what Collins/Harvill had made of the memoirs, she had given them her forthcoming volume of essays, while remaining with Harper's in the States. Her friendship with Alan Maclean stayed firm despite her defection, but she never felt he was up to the intellectual level of old friends like Basil and Alfred Knopf. With Basil gone, Alfred's correspondence became all the more important to her. In September 1970 she told him that after the memoirs and a short book on the modern novel, she would not be writing anything else. She confided that Collins had asked her to write a companion guide on Normandy, and that she had spent some time preparing an exciting itinerary. But then at the last moment Guy had said he did not feel he could go. As she would not leave him, she sadly withdrew from the project (SJ to AAK, 9.12.70).

The short book on the modern novel, *Parthian Words*, was published that same month.[9] Standing where she now felt herself to be, outside the fray, Margaret pulled no punches as she meditated on the modern novel. In her foreword she presented this work as a kind of bedfellow to the memoirs. Indeed, she had introduced some of the passages she had expunged from that into this, making this book, in a sense, "a moral autobiography of a writer as well as an essay in criticism" (*PW*, 7–8). She now challenged her image of the photographer in "Documents," or rather she developed it, saying we are misled

> by the notion of the novelist as a camera-eye into supposing that a truly honest picture of the collapsing world we live in will

emerge from collapsed sentences. The camera itself, even the television camera, cheats, showing us the distorted face but not the thoughts passing behind it, perhaps only thoughts of a street corner or a piece of new bread. (*PW*, 44)

Her range was broad: she had, for instance, changed her mind about André Breton's surrealist manifesto of 1924. It was not, she said, that he had "an intellectual interest in the paradox of totally irrational thinking," but he had been engaged in a lighthearted but violent rebellion against established society in the wake of the utter wasteland of young death in World War I (*PW*, 59). Nonetheless, she said, even fantasy needs the control, acute intelligence, and profound gaiety of the Argentinian writer Jorge Luis Borges to succeed (*PW*, 61). She analyzed the *nouveau roman*; she attacked, as she had elsewhere, pornographic tendencies in the modern novel, but remained against censorship: "perhaps there are no unusable subjects, there are only good, bad, and mediocre writers" (*PW*, 103). She gave one chapter over to a dissection of the critic's role and warned against the current growth of literary theory, with

> the dangers of retreating into a Platonic realm of forms and essences where the practice of criticism is neglected for the pleasures of constructing scholastically intricate general theories addressed to the circle of initiates. (*PW*, 109)

She looked at the relation between the novel and film, and she challenged the idea that there could be any novel, even the most bravely experimental, actually free of tradition: "Like Sterne, Joyce was a seminal jet from the centre of the tradition" (*PW*, 125). She then asked: "Will it be impossible to write a novel in the old mode with a new intention? . . . Should we now give up looking for the 'great' novels, those which are . . . human history?" (*PW*, 127). This was nothing if not a plea to look again at what she had been doing so subtly for so long. In the end, the novel must go on evolving, she said, for there was no one kind of novel: "I am too profoundly convinced that there is no right or solely respectable form of fiction, no one technique. No sacrosanct rules" (*PW*, 150). And she ended with her own unpretentious credo:

I write from the still warm ashes of a society given me by my birth and growth in it, I cannot write in the language of any other. If this begins to lose its idiomatic cogency, when I am too old to learn to think and feel in the new idiom I become a survivor, talking my obsolete personally shaped language to deaf ears. The past remains to me, as strong and hard as Yorkshire stone, as green as a sapling. Luckily, to my intense happiness, I may still use my ears and eyes. (*PW*, 156)

The reviews were inevitably mixed.[10] Margaret, having set out to be combative, was not unduly worried by the reception.

She had in any case far greater worries at home (SJ to KLH, 10.11.70). Guy was getting frailer, and at the end of the year a bad attack of bronchitis was a major threat, given his limited lung capacity. He had, she told Czesław and Janka Miłosz, been convinced "that his doctor was concealing from him the inevitable fatal end, and that I, his devoted amateur and clumsy nurse did not really know what he was suffering" (SJ to CM, 12.24.70). At least he had completed his book, *The Dreyfus Trials*, reworking, in the light of recently released documents, a subject he had researched years before. He had also managed a review of Basil's *History of the Second World War*, a fitting tribute to an old friend.[11] But the attack of bronchitis pulled him down, and was exhausting for Margaret too. They were due to go to Cornwall in January 1971, when she suddenly developed a thrombosis in her leg.[12] As she recovered, they set off as planned, but after a week Guy suffered an apparent heart attack that proved to be a return of his lung problem. Rather than go into a hospital in the Cornish town of Truro as the local doctor advised, he insisted on going home and Margaret somehow got him back by car, a nightmare journey. By April she admitted to Kathleen that he kept going on drugs, while she still dreamed of getting a ground-floor flat "nearer shops with pleasing gardens he can sit in" (SJ to KLH, 4.26.71).

With all this anxiety, reviews of the American publication of her autobiography must have passed almost without notice; certainly she did not comment on them in letters to friends. Stephen Spender, in the *New York Times Book Review*, might have irritated her in former years, as he described the book as the "self-portrait of a woman who sees herself divided between the egoist who is also an artist, and the altruistic lover of humanity," with little mention of her work for the PEN.[13] His comments provoked a quick response from Henry Steele Commager, praising Margaret as "one of the most distinguished novelists in the English language." As a historian Commager singled out for praise her *Cousin Honoré* and *Cloudless May*, calling them "the best novels on the fall of France yet written."[14] This in turn elicited a pained response from Spender, saying he had been misunderstood, and insisting he admired Margaret as a writer, that he had drawn "attention to her generosity, her gaiety and her selflessness, which I am glad to salute again," and that he had read and admired several of her novels.[15] Had she not been so absorbed in her concern for Guy, Margaret might well have enjoyed this traffic of arms between her American friend and her old sparring partner from the days of *Fact*.

At the end of April, Margaret told Alan Maclean that she had, "before this riot began, in January finished a 50,000 word draft of a novel, with exquisite reluctance. Goodness knows if I shall ever be able to get back to it, though" (SJ to AM, 4.28.71). Guy was very ill. In the autumn, the Crawshay-Williamses offered to collect them both for a break in Portmeirion, but Margaret had to say no; Guy was quickly exhausted, and she was afraid to take him away from the doctors he trusted (SJ to RC, 10.10.71). By December his remaining lung was deteriorating, although he was "kept alive on two of these wonder drugs which have such unhappy side effects. His mind — except that he forgets — is as good as it ever was, thank goodness" (SJ to CM, 12.29.71).

Against all the odds, or indeed as an antidote for her fears, by the beginning of 1972 she managed to revise the novel she had finished in draft at the start of 1971.[16] *There Will Be a Short Interval* would be her last novel, but it was by no means an unworthy end to her novel-writing career. It tells the tale of a man, SJ, faced with a dangerous operation, taking stock of his life. Margaret sets him firmly in the present, meditating on the future of England and the wider world, the future of family and Western civilization, while his Jewish surgeon and friend calls up memories of Europe's harrowing past. Before deciding to have the operation, SJ takes steps to make contact with his estranged son, whose former partner, twice his age, has recently killed herself. Thus, the generation gap is analyzed, a gap that goes "to the roots of civilization. In short, to syntax" (*TWSI*,

16). But that is not the only generation gap: SJ's mother, recently made a Dame of the British Empire, is still alive, having deserted both him and his father many years before. The narrative weaves the links between the three disparate generations, disparate in their values and experiences, undergoing the problems in communication that such differences make. The relationships between the young man, Simon, the iconoclast of now, his father, SJ, and the predatory writer, the grandmother, are at the core of the novel. The second half of the book centers on the old woman being found dead, the mystery of the circumstances of her death running in parallel with demands for the right to write her biography. As he contemplates this biography, SJ, engaging with the postmodern world, realizes that it will lie, for "words fob us off with a construction or a concept as films cheat us with an image" (*TWSI*, 142). Yet he also acknowledges the case for

> contradiction, contraries, antithesis — double necessary root of the ambiguous human tongue. Transformational grammar of the natural world (including man), to be read off as plainly and lucidly in myth as in molecular biology. . . . The artist, poet, biographer, novelist, who can't trust himself to his words as confidently as the mathematical logician trusts to his symbols, is a moral eunuch or a deliberate waster of his seed. (*TWSI*, 143)

Margaret showed herself in touch with the present generation of thinkers like Noam Chomsky, who theorized transformational grammar, without herself trying to be part of it, giving an honest view of one of her own age confronting the new world of the young, as Lessing would do a year or two later in *Memoirs of a Survivor*. This was both meditation and confrontation, personal and cultural. The style was relaxed, the easy modernity of Margaret's own memoirs.

CHAPTER 30

Guy's Death and the Aftermath

Margaret's letters were now devoted to her growing exhaustion and her fear for Guy, broken by occasional flickers of optimism that, she told Alfred Knopf, might only be the product of her Yorkshire obstinacy (SJ to AAK, 1.14.72). In March Guy managed a note to Kathleen Liddell Hart, thanking her for an article and adding: "We go on alas! much the same, and Margaret has far too much to do with both looking after the house and looking after me" (GC to KLH, 3.1.72). In the midst of all this, A. D. Peters let Margaret's *There Will Be a Short Interval* go to Collins/Harvill without her noticing, a move which unhappily coincided with the Macmillan editor, Alan Maclean, being seriously ill, and causing Margaret some distress when she realized he had not been informed.[1] By June, Guy was terminally ill, but she refused to let him go into the hospital. She acted as "nurse most of the day and at night, and ward maid during the very few hours when a real nurse takes over" (SJ to AM, 6.3.72). When he died, on June 30, she collapsed into an all-too-common maelstrom of grief and self-blame: she had not loved enough, she had put her writing before his comfort, he was a better person than she was, a better mind, a better writer, and she must continue to serve him. She immediately set about sorting his papers, writing to Bonamy Dobrée about a large file of his letters she had found: did he want them? Bonamy, himself old and frail, replied, and Margaret made a poignant attempt to heal the breach which had so distressed her in the late forties. Bonamy responded: if she would visit them, it would be good to talk.[2] But both Valentine and Bonamy died two years later, and the reconciliation remained incomplete.[3]

To Basil's widow, Kathleen, Margaret poured out her grief:

> You walked this cold road before me, and there is nothing I need say to you about it. I think of my failures and I cry and cry, for Guy who loved living but for myself too. Egotist that I am. (SJ to KLH, 7.11.72)

She had set herself a formidable task, struggling to decipher a mass of manuscript he had left, for, she told Alfred, Guy's handwriting was more like an Assyrian script than anything else. Two years before, when he realized he could not write any more history, the Steiners had persuaded him to start an autobiography; and it was this that she was determined to put in order. She told Alfred this would be a daunting task, but it was all she wanted to do. She said she would stay in their flat, full as it was of Guy's absence, until she had worked through the huge pile of his disordered notes (SJ to AAK, 8.30.72). On September 11, she went with Christopher to Scotland to scatter Guy's ashes. The spot in the Cairngorms that he had chosen years before, a place he had visited every summer from his fifth year to 1914, had been built over, but Margaret was determined to find somewhere similar: "It means a lot of walking — roads are few in those hills — but I must find the right unspoiled place" (SJ to KLH, 9.7.72). She herself was now over eighty, but "by walking and scrambling and half-wading upstream," she found what she was looking for: "nothing but heather, trees, rocks, mountains, and the fast-running peat-brown stream" (SJ to BD, 9.24.72).

In December *There Will Be a Short Interval* was published, and attracted a number of good reviews, including a long, acerbic but appreciative one from Auberon Waugh.[4] Then there was a moment that could have developed into a crisis: in the new year a number of people, including the lady herself, had identified the autocratic grandmother in Margaret's novel, Dame Retta Sargeant, with Rebecca West. Alan drafted a letter to Margaret suggesting she write to Rebecca, but then, sensitive to her current anguish, decided not to send it.[5] He turned instead to placating Rebecca, who did not, in the end, bear a grudge. Or not for long, as she had some reason for seeing the link. There were passages in the novel that were mischievously apt, as when Retta's occasional stylistic excesses, closely mirroring Rebecca's, are dissected. Retta's novels are clever, subtle, sensible, you can say intelligent; you start to read one of them with pleasure or at the worst interest; and before you've turned the fifth page you're up to your hocks in a paragraph of high-powered eloquence, all but senseless. There's a streak in her mind of — as well as a streak of near-lunacy — oh, call it fatuity. Her admirers call it speculative depth. (*TWSI*, 61)

Fortunately, Margaret seems never to have been taken to task, and there was no repeat of the Ethel Mannin spat.

As time wore on, Margaret made some attempt to take up her life again. The following Easter, she went to Portmeirion, and there read Richard Hughes's *The Wooden Shepherdess* for Ian Parsons at Chatto's. She remained firmly professional and generous in her approach to works she reported on or reviewed, while in her own mind she built up a story of a Guy that helped her to deal with his death, even as it exaggerated his intellectual achievements and his literary ability. By July, she had all but completed her work on his papers; she dreaded being at a loose end, deprived of the task that had kept her from confronting her loss too closely during that first year (SJ to AAK, 7.28.73). So she worked over her draft repeatedly, cutting and reordering, meticulously checking names, dates, and quotations, filling gaps from information in his letters, for these, despite her tendency to destroy paperwork, she had kept, since the 1920s. She would be adamant that she had resisted the temptation to add any material of her own. After consulting Guy's old friend Rupert Hart-Davis, she offered this memoir to a number of publishers, but they all said it would not sell. She was depressed: "I feel that I am failing him as — it now seems to me — I failed him again and again" (SJ to KLH, 12.19.73).

While both Margaret and Guy had had their horoscopes read regularly in the past, Margaret was now seeking some other form of reassurance. Spiritualism was something a number of her contemporaries, including Elizabeth Bowen and Aldous Huxley, had tried. Initially Margaret, by nature a skeptic, unable to find sustenance in Guy's simple but firm Christian faith, was hesitant to take this new path; but she had heard that the novelist Rosamond Lehmann, after the death of her daughter Sally, had a number of psychic experiences.[6] Such was Margaret's desolation by the new year of 1974 that she wrote to Rosamond out of "the empty completely meaningless place in which I live, have lived for the past eighteen months."[7] Her need, she said, was to have the chance to say to Guy: "Forgive me my unforgiveable failures" (SJ to RL, 1.11.74). Much as she wished for comfort, however, her Yorkshire spirit could not wholly submit; and she reverted more readily to practical ways of sustaining Guy's memory. She took some comfort from a snapshot of Guy sent by a relative, taken with Bernard Law Montgomery in the Germany of 1919, before Margaret had known him and before he knew of his first wife's betrayal: "It gives me pleasure to look at it. Perhaps because, taken before he was so unkindly hurt, it is of a gay untouched person, smiling and confident" (SJ to RL, 3.8.74).

In April, she had a lucky escape: a large car knocked her down, fracturing six ribs. Impatient as she always was with physical problems, and no doubt suffering from shock, she told Alfred she had fought her way out of the hospital, determined to get home, since the only remedy was to wait for the bones to heal and the pain to stop (SJ to AAK, 4.22.74). It mattered more to her that Guy's memoirs were now with Gollancz, while she tried to find some meaningful way to live (SJ to AAK, 4.29.74). Grandchildren were ministering to her, especially Christopher; while she was grateful, she knew she must learn to cope on her own.

As she would confess to Alan, she now lived on a spartan diet: coffee and toast at breakfast, no lunch, and a boiled egg in the evening. No more of the two cooked meals a day she religiously provided for Guy throughout the years (SJ to AM, 10.19.74). Unsurprisingly, her friends were anxious about her: Alfred, for one, offering support in the only way he could, by continually sending books. Receiving one batch, she told him she was particularly happy to see the Doris Lessing essays, as Lessing was the one contemporary novelist she always wanted to read.[8] She added that Guy's memoirs would be published in the spring by Livia Gollancz, now head of her father's firm. She hoped, she said, to live until the memoirs came out, but had no wish to survive much longer (SJ to AAK, 10.30.74).

The irony was, as Margaret was losing interest, she was coming to public notice again. In May of 1974, the BBC paid half of a £750 fee for the right to adapt *The Early Life of Stephen Hind* in three episodes: the adaptation was duly televised at the end of the year.[9] Margaret took little pleasure in such things. She confessed to Rosamond:

If I'd been told, before June 30 1972, that I wrote my books for Guy I would not have understood. It turns out to be true. (Paradoxically so, since he didn't care for novels, though he faithfully read and criticised mine.) Perhaps because he was the first person to tell me what a bad writer I was. When I had known him about a fortnight in 1924 he said: I'm so sorry — I couldn't read your novel, you write so emotionally, writing should be clear and direct.

I have spent the rest of my writing life since then trying to be just that. (SJ to RL, 12.7.74)

Margaret had by now convinced herself that this was true, and she was determined to keep no credit, no critical acumen for herself. All her writerly skills were to have been Guy's gift to her.

For now, she continued to concentrate on the publication of his memoirs, with no inclination to write herself.[10] When Alan Maclean asked her for a story for his next issue of *Winter's Tales*, she said she had a "rather fine plot, but I don't think I'll ever get round to writing it. . . . So wait and see if I ever as they say take up my pen. Which I doubt" (SJ to AM, 1.28.75). She didn't. Nevertheless, while she felt unable to write, she responded quickly enough to a PEN emergency. The writer Kathleen (Kate) Nott, a woman of great intellect but not given to suffer fools gladly, was an old friend; she had dedicated a book to Margaret back in 1963.[11] She was now president of the English PEN, but there was a problem. Although she had in fact been asked to act for just one year before Stephen Spender could take up the post, she had not understood this and was devastated when she found that she was not to be reelected. Knowing Kate's admiration for Margaret, Rosamond asked Margaret to mediate, which she did with all her old compassion and good sense. She spent time and trouble to persuade Kate not to make an issue of what was clearly a wretched misunderstanding, but had to confess to Rosamond that

Kate, unlike me, and I think unlike you, loves a fight. I don't know whether it has occurred to her that a fight of this sort will certainly injure P.E.N., and I don't know how much that would weigh with her if it did occur to her. (SJ to RL, 4.16.75)

Despite her efforts, Kate refused to be mollified; Margaret's reading of her character appeared to be justified.

This storm had blown up just as Guy's memoir, *A Kind of Survivor*, was published by Gollancz. In Margaret's preface to the book, Guy emerged at his best. She quoted Bonamy's comment that Guy

> grumbles his way through life with indomitable gaiety. Though he has no rose-coloured view of the future of humanity, he refuses to live in a slough of despond as if life were not to be lived here and now. . . . He . . . has a great talent for friendship.

She herself described Guy as the "most instinctively honest and straightforward of mortals," with a wide range of interests, his knowledge of French memoirs encyclopedic, while he had Sir Thomas Browne's seventeenth-century writings, she thought, by heart. He was, she said, "a volcano of enthusiasm and sensibility," with "a natural capacity for self discipline." She wrote of how World War I had branded him, and yet he had "a genius for happiness" that she depended on. She drew, she said, on "his familiarity with worlds in which I am blind or deaf or ignorant, on the sweep of his reading, on his knowledge of music and architecture." In the end, "he made all other company a little dull" (Preface, *AKOS*).

This was a moving tribute, growing out of Margaret's deep sense of loss. It certainly revealed what enriched their marriage; but there was no hint of how difficult that marriage often was, something she had admitted from time to time in her letters. The Guy who emerges from those letters was cheerfully self-centered, and could rely not only on Margaret's readiness to put his interests before her own but on her willingness to be the breadwinner at a time when this was by no means the norm. He expected two cooked meals a day; he could scold her for her profligate generosity to others without, it would seem, too troubled a conscience about his own expectations. All that being said, he suited her, and the qualities she spoke of in this preface far outweighed, for her, the difficulties; she had never been able to put him aside, as Vera wanted her to, when his wishes clashed with her own. Her own deep-rooted sense of herself as a lesser human being fed into her insistence that he was wiser, more gifted than herself. Yet in the text of his "autobiography," Margaret's relaxed style, developed in her own memoirs, makes for a fine piece of writing; and the form too recalls her own work, as it is not chronological, but plays on the connections that memory makes as it weaves together a life. In the end, it is impossible to know how much was her work, how much his: she always insisted that she intended to be true to his text, but how possible that was in fact, given the huge difficulties she had faced in deciphering and piecing together chaotic notes, can never be ascertained with confidence. However that might be, the few reviews were excellent.[12]

No doubt heartened by the good reception of this book that mattered so much to her, Margaret contemplated going to Marjorie Watts's garden party in June of 1975; the link with Sappho's daughter Marjorie and her family, the link with the PEN, was tempting. But by the end of the month, as the anniversary of Guy's death approached, she lost heart and failed to go. She was deeply depressed: "Being too much, far too much, of a coward, to kill myself, I try to die in another way. . . . I used to think I was intelligent and sensible and rather horribly 'managing' — who'd have thought I'd be so — so *nothing*."[13] That summer Christopher drove her to Scotland, where she enjoyed a visit to the National Trust gardens in Ross, "where Guy's birch tree is growing," carrying the label she wanted. But she had insisted on visiting the place where Guy's ashes were scattered, to make sure it was still unspoiled, and clearly the scramble "along the pathless side of the mountain stream" had exhausted her (SJ to MW, 7.20.75). She would never go again.

What she now undertook in her need to find ways of serving Guy was the retrieval of the manuscript of *A Passionate Prodigality*, sold to the Harry Ransom Center at the University of Texas, Austin, some years before, and beyond all expectation she was successful. The Research Center was extraordinarily generous, as they had paid Guy a very good price; they simply asked Margaret to give them a manuscript of her autobiography, the three-volume version. Margaret handed it over cheerfully, saying, "I think they made a bad bargain."[14] What overjoyed her was the chance to give Guy's manuscript to Churchill College, Cambridge, where his books were now lodged.

She confessed to Alan that the exchange of her manuscript for Guy's did not involve a payment. She ruminated:

> It is the solitary typescript I have. I have nothing else, typed or handwritten — six universities, in England and America have

manuscripts, for which they asked as gifts, Leeds, St Andrews, Boston, I forget the others, and am too lazy to get up and look in the files. Others have all been destroyed — apart from the few Mr Feldman bought [for the Research Center]. And there will never be any more. (SJ to AM, 9.22.75)[15]

She had never been businesslike about making money out of old work. Many years before she had given the diary of her Polish visit to a Dr. Hey, who now gave it to the Churchill archive; so that at least had found a safe home, as had her notes on her visit to Czechoslovakia which Basil had borrowed and never returned. They remain in his archive.[16] But Margaret was not being strictly truthful to Alan about having no more manuscripts. In April 1976, Arthur Koestler (who was writing his own memoirs), asked for a letter from Graham Greene which he knew she had received. Margaret apologized, saying she had slipped the letter into one of "two copies of the complete uncut script of A Journey to [sic] the North (autobiography) in 3 [sic] volumes. . . . And, alas, that was the copy I posted to Texas: I had hoped it was the one I still have" (SJ to AK, 4.14.75). So when she told Alan she had no further manuscripts, the second copy of her three-volume memoirs was still in her keeping. It would reach Texas at a later date. It is in fact a further revision, differing in certain passages from the copy given to the Research Center in 1975.[17]

Margaret had drawn back from Rosamond's somewhat intrusive spiritualist evangelism; she knew it was not for her (SJ to RL, 10.18.75). Instead, she turned increasingly to Alfred, the old friend who had known both herself and Guy, and found some comfort in their correspondence (SJ to AAK, 11.27.75). Otherwise, although there were many good, intelligent people in Cambridge who wanted to see her, she told Marjorie Watts, with whom she could take some pleasure in exchanging PEN news, that she preferred to be "left to growl quietly in the back of my cave. . . . The older I get, the more I care for old friends, and the less I want to meet new ones. I should have fled as soon as Guy died" (SJ to MW, 12.24.75).

Just as it seemed she was completely giving up, back she came in response to the world of now. As 1976 dawned, she wrote a letter of protest to the *Times* on the Sex Discrimination Act:

I am and always have been a passionate advocate of political and economic equality for women, but I cannot be the only woman in England who is surprised and grieved by the efforts of perhaps only a few women to force themselves, unwanted, into masculine social haunts. . . . It is sensible and pleasant for women to have places and occasions from which men are barred and sensible and pleasant for men to be able to drink and talk among themselves, whether in wine bars or in their clubs. For pity's sake, do not let us lose now not only our manners but our worldly good sense.[18]

This was Margaret in iconoclastic mood, not looking back but rebelling against a current trend, her pen as cutting as ever.

The need for links with Guy remained acute. Just as she had loved the photo of Guy with Montgomery, she was now delighted that Marjorie Watts had found a Ronald Boswell who had worked with Guy in 1920; Margaret was even prepared to go to London to meet him, something she had not done for a long time (SJ to MW, 1.21.76). In the meantime she had another task: Christopher had thought of something to occupy her formidable mind, sending his book on the coal mining industry for her to copyedit (SJ to MW, 1.27.76). She worked steadily through Christopher's folders of notes and drafts, only mourning the fact that her water heater had broken down, so she could only "bath in a basin" (SJ to MW, 2.11.76). Maybe this disaster encouraged her to make the promised visit to London in early March to see Marjorie and the man who had known Guy. She clearly enjoyed the meeting: "I liked those Boswells, and I liked listening to him talking about Guy. I do such a lot of talking *to* Guy in this empty flat that it was a happiness to listen to someone talking about him" (SJ to MW, 3.5.76). In the aftermath of this pleasant evening, she accepted a dinner invitation in Cambridge, "the first dinner party I've been to since Guy fell ill." It was not to be repeated; she came home "crying with rage that I'd let myself in for further invitations from other guests — invitations I just have to refuse." She could not, she wrote, "attempt social life. Truly I can't. I'm not fit for company" (SJ to MW, 9.2.76).

Margaret's determination to withdraw from social events remained firm. She told Marjorie she would not come to the PEN Congress in

London: "I don't want to get *involved* again with all the good and pleasant people I should get involved with." But she willingly helped Marjorie with the book about her mother, Sappho, offering herself as "a ruthless publisher's reader" (SJ to MW, 7.5.76).[19] And while she did not attend the congress in September, she certainly followed its fortunes; she was exasperated by articles in the *New Statesman* and the *Sunday Times* which implied that the PEN "has become a sort of venerable institution that idiots like to chuck stones at" (SJ to MW, 9.2.76).

After the congress, one old friend broke into her determined seclusion, giving her unexpected pleasure: Czesław Miłosz came to Cambridge, bringing her books and sharing ideas (SJ to CM, 9.23.76). She continued to be stimulated by Alfred's book offerings too, meditating in October on a volume containing Ottoline Morrell photographs. She felt that Ottoline was a much better human being than the men and women who enjoyed her generous hospitality and then mocked her behind her back (SJ to AAK, 10.10.76). Margaret could never bear unkindly laughter.

Over the last several years, Margaret's literary agents had served her well: she had come to have great faith in the Brandts in New York, where Carol carried on after Carl died, and in A. D. Peters in London. But Peters had died in 1973, a loss of both a wise counselor and a friend; and Carol retired after negotiating, in 1975–76, for a number of Margaret's books to be reissued in paperback by Berkley Medallion Books, based in New York, so that Margaret would continue to have some income trickling in from the States. On the English front, she sorely missed Peters's advice, turning increasingly to Alan Maclean rather than to younger agents, for his quietly staunch support despite her defection from Macmillan could always be relied on. She worried that her "total indifference to my books, once they are published," would give Christopher, her literary executor, trouble, so Alan helped her in her efforts to have the rights to all out-of-print books revert to her (SJ to AM, 2.22.77). However, another old publishing friend exasperated her: Rache Lovat Dickson, now long retired in his native Canada, had asked Christopher, "if I am able to answer letters. Thoughtful of him to ask. He also hopes I am not in want. That's thoughtful, too" (SJ to AM, 8.10.77). Margaret was not amused.

She was far from intellectually incapacitated. In August of 1977, she offered to show Alan the typescript of a short book she had written on Stendhal. After she had finished her work on Guy's memoirs, she had looked up the "mass of notes I had been making at intervals over fifteen or so years for a life of Stendhal — and found that I no longer cared to write" (SJ to AM, 8.10.77). Yet Guy had always wanted her to write this book, and no doubt that weighed with her as another service she could offer him. *Speaking of Stendhal* is a concise, lucid appraisal of the author who, above all others, Margaret described as a friend.[20] It is also possible to read, as subtext to this work, her measuring of herself and her priorities against his. She claimed that great writers were of two kinds: self-destroyers like Balzac and Byron, and self-preservers like Goethe; Stendhal, she said, was of the first kind as, one might say, was she. She described him as an iconoclast, with an undiminished passion for social justice. She analyzed his work with her usual concise clarity, exploring the density of his narrative, woven from experiences, memories, reflections, reveries. She spent time on *Le rouge et le noir*, showing how, in his male protagonist, "he chose to put a narrow but perceptible distance between himself and his creation" (SS, 111). Looking at his memoir, *Vie de Henry Brulard*, she commented:

> All autobiography is distorted, the writer is looking inward at a figurant who is himself, is recalling joys and agonies which are in a significant sense done with. The fresco, as Stendhal himself says, is partly obliterated; there are vivid fragments. (SS,134)

This is a perceptive assessment of Stendhal, as man and as artist, but it also underlines how Margaret and he were in many ways soul mates. They had so much in common, each perceptive about their age, way ahead of so many of their contemporary critics. Ironically, the link was still being played out in 1977, as Alan's readers in their reports rejected Margaret's work, and she was without a publisher.[21]

She was resigned, if disappointed; but she was much less resigned to being misrepresented at the PEN over the issue of whether to invite the Russians to join:

> Perhaps if I write a terse letter to the Broadsheet just saying that I think it would be extremely naïve to accept a Russian Centre so long as the USSR remains an autocracy — or sharper words to that effect?

"Shall I do that?" she asked Marjorie (SJ to MW, 9.1.77). Clearly she had not lost her commitment to the PEN and its dealings, but she still drew back from being visited, begging Marjorie

> never to tell anyone, especially any PEN character (no names, no pack drill), that I am fit to be visited. . . . It is just that I am less and less able to cope with people I respect for their great minds and so on, if they make demands I can't meet. And after all I *am* an ancient, practically one of Shaw's Methusalahs (that can't be the way to spell it), I ought to be allowed to behave badly. (I can't even type!). (SJ to MW, 9.1.77)

Margaret might not wish to see new people, but she greatly valued old friends, none more so than Rupert and Elizabeth Crawshay-Williams, who had so often invited herself and Guy to their home in Portmeirion. Her dismay must have been great when she heard that they had made a suicide pact and died together; she made the effort to attend the memorial service, although it must have been hard to cope with the distress of the Portmeirion community, who reacted badly to what, for them, seemed a rejection of close friends.[22]

By March 1978, Margaret heard that both Macmillan, despite all Alan's efforts, and Harper's had rejected her Stendhal book, and she asked for the typescripts to be returned to her. Then a happy accident brought a fresh opportunity: she upset a bottle of ink over her sole copy of *A Kind of Survivor*, and wrote to Livia Gollancz asking for a replacement. Gollancz had only printed a short run of Guy's book, and it had gone out of print in 1976, but Livia managed to track down a copy, sending it with the firm's compliments (SJ to MW, 3.30.78).[23] This may well have given Margaret the idea of approaching Livia about her Stendhal; she did so, and Livia, who was very fond of her, asked to see it (SJ to LG, 4.12.78; LG to SJ, 4.14.78). The book was duly sent, and the Gollancz readers' reports were excellent.[24]

It must have done Margaret good to have such a positive response; moreover she was feeling better in herself, even visiting Arthur Koestler and his wife, Cynthia, in their Suffolk home (SJ to C. Koestler, 4.26.78). In May, she heard that the American Academy and Institute of Arts and Letters had elected her to an honorary membership; and she also heard that a portrait of her from the 1920s was to be included in the exhibition of E. O. Hoppé's work at the National Portrait Gallery.[25] Then at the end of the month, Gollancz confirmed that her Stendhal would be published (LG to SJ, 5.25.78). What was more, the publication of this book had clearly brought to Livia's mind the number of writers who had been honored in recent years: Rebecca West was a Dame Commander of the Order of the British Empire (DBE), and Lettice Cooper had been awarded a CBE (Commander of the Order of the British Empire), while all that Margaret had achieved as a writer and as president of the English PEN had gone unrecognized. To promote someone for such recognition, there had to be support from distinguished people, and accordingly, in July, Livia set about seeking support for Margaret, writing, for instance, to Victor Bonham-Carter of the Society of Authors, and to Baroness Lee (Jennie), widow of the Labour politician Aneurin Bevan, a move that prompted Jennie to write to her old friend Margaret about her own memoir of Aneurin, asking Margaret to visit.[26] There was, Livia found, plenty of support, with a consensus feeling Margaret should have a DBE like Rebecca. However, when Kenneth Stowe, principal private secretary to the prime minister, wrote to Margaret asking for her consent to her name being put forward for a CBE, Margaret politely declined.[27] She could not but be hurt that she was valued less highly than Rebecca West and maybe too she had no wish to earn a greater reward than her menfolk: both Guy and Bill had accepted awards of an OBE. A few days later, when she heard from George Steiner that Livia was behind the move to have her on the New Year's Honours list, she wrote to thank her, saying she was touched by Livia's kindness, might have accepted if Guy had been alive, but felt too old and tired now to cope with the formal presentation by the queen. In reply, Livia said that since in her view Margaret should have been offered a DBE, she would be philosophical about the refusal of the lesser award (SJ to LG, 12.2.78; LG to SJ, 12.5.78).

Recently, Margaret had been approached by the international secretary of the PEN, Peter Elstob, to write a piece on the PEN of the war years. She produced a succinct, telling account: she and Hermon were, she said, "in the situation of a man with a piece of frayed rope trying to drag hundreds from a quicksand. . . . For one person we got out, five hundred sank."[28] The writing of this account must have stirred many memories: of Ulrich Boschwitz, perhaps, a young writer interned in Australia, whose release they negotiated only to hear his ship was attacked "and this most promising and attractive young writer lost his life"; of Elias Canetti, the writer of the apocalyptic German novel *Die Blendung*, translated by Virginia Wedgwood as *Auto-da-Fé* and hailed by the young Iris Murdoch as one of the few great novels of the century, who needed help as there were problems with his nationality: he had Turkish-Jewish parents, was born in Bulgaria, and had a Turkish passport until 1924, when it was withdrawn. So many heartbreaking cases, so much dogged work on their behalf, so many they could not help, despite all their efforts.[29]

Nonetheless, there had been notable successes, and some of them remembered what Margaret had done for them. In December, Alan received a letter from a Mr. Rokoš. The letter, marked "strictly confidential," asked for advice on a very delicate matter. Mr. Rokoš said he and his wife owed their very existence to someone he called X, which Alan had no difficulty in interpreting as Margaret, who had helped them forty years before. They were now deeply concerned, Rokoš said, because Margaret was living in a nearly unheated flat, confining herself for the most part to one room, her hands often too cold to write, and often depressed. Offers of help were, he said, kindly but firmly rejected, and she must never find out they had contacted Alan as she would be hurt, angry, and humiliated. What Rokoš asked was whether there was anything they could do to help her without her knowing: increase royalties perhaps, or sponsor an unpublished manuscript?[30] This, from one of the many Jewish refugees Margaret had helped, must have moved Alan deeply. Moreover, this was the very couple she had been so desperate to get out of Prague in the spring of 1939. These were also people who were running admirably true to type: when Margaret had first met Kitty, on her visit to Prague in 1938, Kitty had pleaded for help in getting her parents out, not herself, and Margaret had promised to do what she could. Six months later Kitty and her husband would themselves have been lost without Margaret's commitment. They had not forgotten, but were themselves appalled at how many had failed to remember what they owed to Margaret's unsparing efforts on their behalf.

And still Margaret did not fail to respond to a friend in trouble. She now heard from Czesław, who finally told her about his wife's long illness. Margaret replied at once, saying simply, "you are a native of a region of my mind." She now understood, she said, why he was spending so much time learning biblical Hebrew, so as to translate psalms, Ecclesiastes, and a gospel:

> Few documents can be better worth your translating, whether
> from a Hebrew text or from the Greek. A time to be born and a
> time to die, and the rest of it. (SJ to CM, 1.4.79)

After writing sensitively about his enduring grief, she added, as a kind of footnote, that she was herself reading "poetry and neurophysics, and [I] get a satisfaction out of the effort to account for the existence in us of self-consciousness — vainly, a vain effort" (SJ to CM, 1.4.79). She may have called it vain, but her interest in consciousness was part of the quest that had started with the examination of Kierkegaard's ideas; she was moving with the times in her research, while sharing with Czesław their mutual fascination with the mysteries inherent in being human.

Margaret had responded just as readily when Queenie Leavis's husband died. She shared with Queenie her own way of coping with grief: taking on a demanding task. Queenie took her advice, editing Frank's uncollected works and writing his biography. She told Margaret how she admired her work and her example; she said Margaret was someone "like Wittgenstein and a very few others I have met, the people whom one needs to know exist, because they fortify one in one's intention to live, in Edward Thomas's fine phrase."[31] The respect was mutual: in a draft of her memoirs Margaret had said of her,

> As I did, she had struggled away from a poor narrow unintel-
> lectual background, with no help except her intelligence and
> energy, and she had worked to exhaustion. Unlike me she had
> never compromised. (JN/TMS, 2:183).

When Queenie wrote again with news of Leeds University, where she had been given an honorary degree like Margaret all those years before, Margaret replied with reminiscences about Guy's time there, and her own, a letter that Queenie sent on to the Leeds librarian as an interesting piece by "an early-day student and one who must be one of the most distinguished women it ever produced."[32]

CHAPTER 31

Journey to the North

Margaret's Stendhal was on the Gollancz spring list for 1979; she was a little startled that her short work was being priced so high (£6.95) (SJ to LG, 1.3.79). But when *Speaking of Stendhal* came out in February, it appeared to Margaret to have attracted few reviews.[1] She was concerned that she had let her publisher down, something she habitually felt when a book failed to impress the critics, although she had received a number of delighted letters from readers. Livia Gollancz, however, pointed to reviews in the *Birmingham Post*, *Yorkshire Post*, and *History Today*, reminding Margaret that a printers' strike had closed the *Times*, *Sunday Times*, and *TLS*; and she insisted, rightly, that Margaret's was a distinguished book.

Margaret was still taking time to respond to budding writers and students of a new generation: Adam Munthe, for one, who sent her his "beginner's novel," and Lu Bruch, who was doing research on women writers and their use of pseudonyms. Replying to Lu, Margaret said her own brief use of pseudonyms was "a fugue": "Faire une fugue, to break out briefly, to run away for a few days." However, she took the opportunity to urge the young woman not to address her as "Ms.": "it is too silly. Perhaps I should add that, as the daughter of a Yorkshire matriarch, I was never in any doubt that women are the equals of men, and never less than enraged by economic injustices. That is why I dislike us to make silly gestures."[2] Her feminism was always distinctively based on the experiences of the strong Whitby women in whose tradition she had grown up, and she found many of the minor gestures of new-wave feminism exasperating. She had protested a short time before about such gestures in a letter to the *Times*:

> I am mortified when supposedly sane grown women sink to demanding unisex pronouns and the use of terms such as chairperson. It is worse than stupidly trivial. As we said where I came from, it is daft enough to make a cat laugh, or cry. (Letter to *Times*, 11.2.78).

On the home front, Margaret continued to struggle to put her affairs in order for Christopher as her literary executor. She made a note of what papers she had kept, "two small thin diaries and a few letters," and seemed to have felt some regret for her wholesale destruction of the records of a lifetime. She sent Bonamy Dobrée's speech at her honorary degree ceremony to Mrs. Stephens in the Leeds University Archive, with comments on what he had got wrong; and she fulfilled a promise to send a piece about life as an undergraduate in 1909–12. She also offered the university the bronze head Anna Mahler had sculpted (Anna had sculpted the head in clay, and Guy had it cast in bronze); the offer was accepted, and Christopher was asked to make the delivery.[3]

Margaret's letters, while always lucid, were becoming rather repetitive; she was under great strain, increasingly worried about Bill's health. In August, she invited Marjorie Watts to lunch, only to cancel as Bill was able to visit that weekend, between appointments at clinics. "He hasn't been for a year because the drive tires him out," she told Marjorie (SJ to MW, 8.14.79). He would in fact be driven "by his devoted worn-out wife," and would stay for two nights (SJ to MW, 8.18.79). She hoped to see Marjorie after they left, when

> all I'll have to do is clear up the debris of two days' cooking (I have nearly forgotten how to cook, but Bill won't go out to meals, he hates to be seen moving across the floor like an old old man) — I try to give Patchen a brief rest. (SJ to MW, 8.23.79)

Clearly, her role as head of the family had not yet been abandoned, and she still kept up with old friends. She wrote regularly to Marjorie, her much-valued link with the PEN, and she spent a day in Suffolk with the

Koestlers again, delighted that Arthur liked her "small Stendhal . . . written to please Guy's shade" (SJ to AK, 12.10.79).

Old friends were inevitably getting fewer: Irene Rathbone died in January 1980, Doreen Marston in May, and Winifred was very ill in the course of the year. Margaret's creative writing was at an end, and it must have seemed strange to see a review of *The Voyage Home*, dated January 30, 1930, reprinted in the *TLS* series "Fifty Years On."[4] Her arrangements for what archive material she still had were nearly complete, and Christopher delivered the Mahler head to the University of Leeds in February. In October, Margaret wrote to Czesław Miłosz, warmly congratulating him on being awarded the Nobel Prize (SJ to CM, 10.10.80). She was also delighted when Ruth Crawford Mitchell's *Alice Garrigue Masaryk: 1879–1966* came out, celebrating Tomáš's daughter and Jan's sister, a gifted and public-spirited woman in her own right. In the preface, Ruth recalled how Margaret herself had "focused the energies of the British Pen Club on the rescue of European writers, first from the Nazis and later from Communist persecution," a tribute that underlined the respect Margaret's friends held for her.[5] Then, as the year ended, Jennifer Pullein Thompson wrote on behalf of the PEN, offering Margaret honorary membership, support, and, in a personal postscript, her own warm admiration for what had been achieved in the war years; and Margaret's dining rights at New Hall, granted when she first moved to Cambridge, were renewed, again with offers of support.[6]

By the following spring, the Virago editorial team finally decided to republish some of Margaret's works, and she was approached about the *Mirror of Darkness* trilogy. She had heard they were considering her works as early as December 1978, and so had hung fire when approached, in July 1979, by Colin Walsh of the Book Production Consultants (The Book Concern Ltd.), who wanted to reproduce a number of her works in batches of four.[7] She needed the money, for even *Speaking of Stendhal* was remaindered in July.[8] But the thread that bound the year 1981 together was the correspondence that linked Margaret to Alfred Knopf. Now in their nineties, they wrote lively letters covering a range of subjects, comparing notes on their own and each other's culture and country. They discussed the state of publishing as the small firms were disappearing, and they reminisced about the Knopf London house. They discussed politics in general, and both Reagan and Thatcher in particular.

Alfred shared his concerns about the economy and abortion; Margaret gave him her views on the English scene, describing the splits in the Labour movement, the strikes that were becoming all too common, and Mrs. Thatcher, who was in her view rather too confident that she had the government completely under her control (SJ to AAK, 5.30.81). She told Alfred prophetically that, while Thatcher had plenty of courage and obstinacy, there were powerful men in her own party who would be all too ready to abandon her if they felt she was becoming a liability (SJ to AAK, 8.4.81). In August, Alfred commented that their correspondence sometimes reminded him, as they debated the failings of their respective governments, of how his step-grandfather and his father would argue over which was the worst town in the Russian Poland from which the family had emigrated (AAK to SJ, 8.26.81). And so these old friends supported each other in their old age, arguing gently, sharing concerns about the present, recalling a happier world out of which they airbrushed the worst things. At the end of the year Margaret told him she spent a lot of time now reading books she only half understood, books on physics which she had to read a number of times before a little light dawned (SJ to AAK, 12.21.81). She might be increasingly reclusive, rather forgetful, but she was not intellectually idle.

This same year, George Steiner's novella *The Portage to San Cristóbal of A.H.*, in which Hitler is found in the Amazon jungle thirty years after the war, generated a great deal of controversy, largely because Steiner, a Jew himself, had allowed Hitler to make a case for his own defense. The fact that the Jewish protagonist warns against allowing Hitler to speak, as speech was his most dangerous weapon, was largely ignored by the protesters. Certainly the case Hitler makes is disturbing: he maintains that Israel could not have come into being without the Holocaust, and that therefore the Jews should regard him as a benefactor. Such controversy can always inspire a dramatist, and Christopher Hampton adapted the tale. The play was staged in April 1982 at the Mermaid Theatre in London, and Margaret went to the first night, joining in "the discussion and disquiet" it provoked, aware as she would be of the reaction many of her refugee friends would have had.[9]

She now braced herself as the first Virago publication date drew near: they were issuing *Company Parade* and *Women against Men* first, and the first interviews began. Margaret did not enjoy being questioned about her life for nearly four hours by Janet Watts, although she did manage to slip in that Michael Foot, Labour MP and leading left-wing intellectual, had told her he had stayed up all night to finish her Stendhal.[10] She was more relaxed when interviewed by the poet Elaine Feinstein.[11] The editions came out in the heyday of new-wave feminism, and Virago's choice of novels reflects this. For they chose works from her prewar writing with female protagonists, so ignoring her commitment to the wider society of suffering Europeans, and the rich maturing of her art from the late 1930s onward. Naomi Mitchison's review of the two Virago editions made some attempt to redress this imbalance, setting them in the context of *Journey from the North*, "one of the best ever autobiographies," and so astutely putting the Hervey of *Company Parade* who had lived through one war against the narrator of the memoirs who had lived through two.[12]

Inevitably, the usual losses and anxieties of old age continued. One of the last of Margaret's lifelong friends, Oswald Harland, died; and Winifred sent news that Alfred had broken his hip in September. Margaret tried to distract him with comments on the coming election in Britain (SJ to AAK, 9.29.82). She drew little satisfaction from the political situation she still followed, despite her growing weariness. In December she told Alfred that Thatcher was running the country with just a few of her closest allies, that the Labour Party was in turmoil, and the Liberals gave her the impression of being nervously self-satisfied. Nothing was being done to solve the unemployment problem, she said (SJ to AAK, 12.18.82).

The following year, 1983, was a dark one for Margaret. Bill, an invalid for so long, died in March. Margaret traveled down to the island in the Thames where, as she put it, he had been trying to live, for his death meant that she had a great deal to settle (SJ to AAK, 5.7.83). The tight-lipped news she sent Alfred echoed the tone of her letters when Do died; what she felt was beyond words. In the circumstances, the joint suicide of Arthur Koestler and his wife must have all but passed her by, echoing though it did the deaths of the Crawshay-Williamses. Virago's letter telling her they hoped to republish *Journey from the North* and asking if she would write a preface also failed to break the surface of her own troubles; the preface would not materialize.[13] By July, Alfred was growing anxious as he had not heard from her, and at the beginning of August she begged his forgiveness for not replying to his earlier letter, saying she had read it a number of times since Bill died. She added evasively that nothing had gone right for a long time after that (SJ to AAK, 8.2.83). This death had hit her very hard.

Virago brought out *Journey from the North* in January 1984, together with the last two novels of the *Mirror in Darkness* trilogy. Naomi Mitchison reviewed the memoirs admiringly, as did Victoria Glendinning. Both saw the two novels as another form of autobiography, but they ignored the experiments with form and the panoramic view of society that they encompassed.[14] However, Margaret was long past being anxious about reviews. In the interview she granted Caroline Moorhead what was most evident was her determined withdrawal from contemporary life; she was quite clear that she had outlived her time.[15] Rebecca West had died in 1983, and 1984 saw the deaths of yet more old friends: Amabel Williams-Ellis, Ruth Crawford Mitchell, and J. B. Priestley died this year, as did her favorite correspondent of the last few years, Alfred Knopf. There was the comfort of her grandchildren, and the fact that Buchan and Enright were issuing a paperback edition of Guy's *A Passionate Prodigality*. Margaret remained a life member of the PEN, an honorary member of the American Academy and Institute of Arts and Letters, and a member of the Council of the Society of Authors. She had done all she could to leave accurate records for her literary executor, together with such letters as she had decided to preserve, but now she was, as Caroline's title had picked up, "just killing time before death." As 1985 dawned, she relied more and more on her grandson, Christopher, as she sank into the obscurity she so much desired.[16] In the course of the year, a bout of food poisoning put her in hospital, and from there into a nursing home outside St. Neots.

In January 1986, the BBC broadcast "A Day Off," a play adapted by Elaine Feinstein from Margaret's novella, starring Brenda Bruce.[17] But a slip of the pen Margaret had made when referring to her memoirs in a letter to Arthur ten years before — calling it "Journey to the North" — has its poignancy, for her own journey was well on its way.[18] Margaret died on September 30, a few months after her sister Winifred, and the obituaries were many, if not all very penetrating.[19]

Margaret was a writer who, despite her constant financial straits, rarely compromised. In many ways, she was ahead of her time in her assessment of what was happening in twentieth-century Britain and Europe; she was adept at diagnosing society's flaws, the flaws inherent in human nature, and her critics often resented the sharpness of her perceptions. But she did not simply document; she had the head of a philosopher and the heart of a poet; she was always exploring the extraordinary vagaries of consciousness, of mind as well as brain. It is sad that in her last years, the tendency to dwell on her sins of omission as she thought them far outweighed any personal satisfaction in her considerable gifts and achievements. Yet even in extreme old age she could impress. Elaine Feinstein recalled how Zara Steiner introduced her to Margaret in 1981:

> In that first conversation I was amazed not only by the precision of her memories, but even more by the range of her continuing interest in the contemporary world. She seemed the least self-absorbed writer of any I have known.[20]

No doubt, being the complex woman she was, full of contradictions, she could be difficult; but not many have given more of themselves to those in need.

In her early writings on drama she had been seen as a Nietzschean; and in the end Nietzsche's own musings, quoted by W. G. Sebald in his essay on the artist and poet Peter Weiss, sum up something about Margaret that was important:

> Perhaps there is nothing more terrible and mysterious in the whole prehistory of mankind than our mnemonic technique. We burn something into the mind so that it will remain in the memory; only what still hurts will be retained.[21]

This was Margaret's burden; yet it also meant that she never forgot what suffering humankind could inflict on itself, whether in the past or in its potential for the future. Despite all discouragement, she always kept faith with her role as a modern Cassandra, telling the truth honestly, lucidly, even when many chose not to listen. And she never failed to hope that a future generation might take steps to bring humanity out of its self-imposed catastrophes. As Stendhal did for her, she speaks to us now.

NOTES

Chapter 1

1. Margaret Storm Jameson (hereafter cited as SJ), *The Pot Boils* (PB; 1919), 303. Unless otherwise specified, works cited parenthetically in the text are by SJ, using short titles of the works in the list of abbreviations. See also the list of abbreviations for the names of correspondents in citations of letters.

2. SJ, "Where Lovely Ships Were Launched," *Everyman*, Aug. 13, 1931.

3. SJ, *There Will Be a Short Interval* (1973), 222.

4. Kendall, "The Streets of Whitby and Their Associations."

5. SJ, letter to the *Times*, Nov. 2, 1978.

6. SJ, *That Was Yesterday* (1932), 44.

7. Details on grave in Larpool Cemetery, Whitby, 4686/4687.

8. See records held by the Whitby Archive and Heritage Centre.

9. See marriage register of Whitby parish church.

10. Details on grave in Larpool Cemetery, Whitby, 6107/6108.

11. SJ, *No Time Like the Present* (NTLTP; 1933), 20; *Journey from the North* (1969–70), 1:21. Is this, maybe, a recollection in the spirit of Wordsworth's poem "We Are Seven"?

12. Keighley, *Whitby Writers*.

13. The late autobiography was published in two volumes as *Journey from the North* (hereafter JN; 1969–70); this quotation is from 1:21.

14. SJ, *No Time Like the Present* (1933); the quotation is from p. 22.

15. Details on grave in Larpool Cemetery, 4686/4687.

16. Details on graves in Larpool Cemetery, 4686/4687 and 6107/6108.

17. See extract from letter from SJ to Bill, her son, 6.17.65 (Christopher Storm-Clark archive, hereafter cited as CSC).

18. Interview with Jack Singleton, March 3, 1970 (British Library: BBC Sound Archive). See King, *Memory, Narrative, Identity: Remembering the Self*.

19. SJ to Secker, 1.27.61 (Secker mss, Manuscript Dept., Lilly Library, Indiana University).

20. SJ to Michael Sadleir (hereafter cited as MS), 10.30.19 (Michael Sadleir archive, General Manuscripts, Wilson Library, University of North Carolina).

21. SJ, "Teaching by Not Teaching. New Methods 'Half Waste of Time and Half Definitely Harmful,'" *Evening Standard*, March 17, 1927, 7.

22. Harland, *Nine Lives*.

23. SJ, typed manuscript of *Journey from the North*, 3 vols. (Harry Ransom Research Center [hereafter HRC], University of Texas, Austin), vol. 1; it was sent in exchange for manuscript of *A Passionate Prodigality*, chap. 8 (chap. 9, 50, in the published version). This manuscript is hereafter cited as JN/TMS.

24. SJ, "The University of Leeds in 1909–12" (University of Leeds Archive, n.p.); hereafter cited as "ULeeds 1909–12."

Chapter 2

1. SJ, "The University of Leeds in 1909–12" (University of Leeds Archive, n.p.).
2. Leeds University Session Records, Sessional Entries of Students for 1905/6–1909/10, 9–11, University of Leeds Archive.
3. See Robinson, *Bluestockings*.
4. Women's Representative Council, 1902–14, Item 16 (University of Leeds Archive, STU/001 [committees doc.]).
5. *Gryphon* 13, no. 2 (Dec. 1909): 25; 13, no. 4 (March 1910): 56; 14, no. 2 (Dec. 1910): 29.
6. *Leeds University Calendar 1910–11*, 592, University of Leeds Archive.
7. *Gryphon* 14, no. 2 (Dec. 1910): 29, 30.
8. The WSPU was a powerful force at the time.
9. Leeds University Session Records.
10. Women's Representative Council, 1902–14, Item 16.
11. *Gryphon* 15, no. 1 (Nov. 1911): 45; 15, no. 3 (Feb. 1912): 47; 15, no. 4 (March 1912): 57.
12. *Gryphon* 15, no. 6 (June 1912): 84.
13. Orage, *Political and Economic Writings*, 57.
14. Orage, *Selected Essays and Critical Writings*, 7, 9.
15. SJ, "Student Days," in *Modern Essays and Sketches* (1935), 164.
16. See Martin, "Contesting Knowledge," 124–47.

Chapter 3

1. SJ, "The End Thereof," *New Age* 3 (March 20, 1913).
2. Lidderdale and Nicholson, *Dear Miss Weaver*, 183.
3. SJ, "The Drama of Ideas Since Ibsen," *Egoist* 1 (Jan. 15, 1914): 29–30.
4. SJ, "The Theatre," *Egoist* 1 (April 15, 1914): 155–56.
5. In *Journey from the North* (1:79), Margaret says Rebecca West replaced her; in fact it would seem that Harriet Weaver saw Margaret as a replacement for West, who had resigned from the *New Freewoman* the previous year after clashing with Dora Marsden.
6. SJ, "England's Nest of Singing Birds," *Egoist*, Nov. 1, 1915, 14–15.
7. See Phillips, *The Ascent of Woman: A History of the Suffragette Movement and the Ideas behind It*.
8. Duckworth report on "The Pot Boils" (CSC archive).
9. Robins, *Modern Art in Britain, 1910–1914*, 12, 36, 108.
10. SJ, "The Scene-Models of Norman MacDermott," *Egoist*, Jan. 1917, 3–4.
11. SJ, *Happy Highways* (*HH*; 1920); SJ to MS, dated 11.9.12 ([*sic*] for 1918). Margaret frequently, throughout her life, misdated letters.

Chapter 4

1. Reviews of *PB*: *Times* and *TLS*, Feb. 6, 1919; see also *Athenaeum*, March 1919; *Saturday Review* 127 (March 1, 1919); *Nation* (UK), April 26, 1919; *Whitby Gazette*, March 14, 1919.
2. See, on this issue, MacMillan, *Peacemakers*.
3. On hardening attitudes to pacifism and sexuality, see Bourke, *Dismembering the Male*.

4. SJ, "The Woman Doctor's Tale: Mother-Love," *New Decameron* 1 (1919): 78–104.

5. SJ to Alfred Knopf (hereafter cited as AAK), 7.9.81 (Knopf archive, HRC).

6. SJ to Moult, 11.26.19 (Brotherton Library, University of Leeds: Moult File).

7. SJ, "The Woman Doctor's Tale: A Player Perforce," *New Decameron* 2 (1920): 158–75.

8. SJ, "Nietzsche in Modern Drama — I ," *Theatre-Craft*, no. 3, edited by Hermon Ould and Horace Shipp (undated but late 1919 by internal evidence from advertisements): 8–14.

9. Anon., "Gentle Death. The Passing of Vienna," *New Commonwealth* (hereafter NC), Nov. 28, 1919.

10. See, for instance, George Gallilee, "The Joy of Work," NC, Nov. 28, 1919; see interview with SJ as author of *Happy Highways*, NC, Nov. 7, 1919. The serialization of *Happy Highways* ran from Nov. 14, 1919, to Feb. 20, 1920.

11. See, for women addressing this issue, Phillips, *The Ascent of Woman*, 258–90.

12. JN 1:158, and John, *William Heinemann*, 220–22.

13. Random House Archive: Heinemann: file on SJ, for *The Happy Highways*.

14. See Random House Archive: Heinemann: file on SJ, for *The Clash*.

15. See Nicolson, *The Great Silence, 1918–1920*, 188.

16. Random House Archive: Heinemann: file on SJ, for *The Clash*.

17. Reviews of *HH*: TLS, Sept. 16, 1920; *Saturday Westminster Gazette*, Oct. 2, 1920; see also *Nation and Athenaeum* (UK) 28 (Oct. 16, 1920); *Bookman* (UK), Oct. 1920; *Nation* (New York) 112 (May 25, 1921).

18. SJ, *Modern Drama in Europe* (MDIE; 1920).

19. For reviews of *MDIE*, see, e.g., TLS, Dec. 2. 1920; *Sewanee Review* 29 (1921).

20. *The Labour Party: Report of Annual Conference* of the Labour Party held in the Albert Hall, Nottingham, Jan. 23–25, 1918, 15, under the heading "Party Reorganisation."

21. Stephen A. Bird in e-mail to Dianne Hayter, 10.22.2007, in response to query of mine.

22. SJ, "England and America: The Post-war Situation," *English Review* (Feb. 1921): 137–41; "England and America: The Blood Bond," *English Review* (March 1921): 213–15; "England and America: Unrestricted Competition," *English Review* (April 1921): 320–28. See also *Saturday Westminster Gazette*, Aug. 20, 1921, for a review by "M.S.J." of A. Travers-Borgstroem, *Mutualism: A Synthesis*, including a précis of her argument in the May *English Review* article.

23. SJ, "England and America: European Reconstruction," *English Review* (May 1921): 437–42.

24. *Bookman*, June 1921 (picture in the National Portrait gallery under Storm Jameson).

25. JN/TMS, 1:247 (cut from published version, 1:203).

26. Galsworthy to SJ, 7.2.21 (CSC archive).

27. Pankhurst, *The Great Scourge and How to End It*.

28. SJ to Blanche Knopf (hereafter cited as BK), 10.5.21.

29. SJ, *The Clash* (TC; 1922). See "The Clash," author's manuscript, heavily revised in two notebooks, HRC: Jameson, S. (Works).

30. See MacMillan, *Peacemakers*, 488–500.

31. Agreement on *The Clash*, Nov. 29, 1921 (Random House Archive: Heinemann: file on SJ).

32. SJ, *The Clash* (Little, Brown ed.), vii–x.

33. SJ, "The Tale of the Solitary English Girl: The Pitiful Wife," *New Decameron* (1922): 56–71.

34. SJ to Mr. Shorter, 3.27.22 (Special Collections Library, University of Michigan).

35. Watts, *P.E.N.: The Early Years, 1921–1926.*

36. See Watts, *P.E.N.: The Early Years, 1921–1926*; and Watts, *Mrs. Sappho: The Life of C. A. Dawson-Scott, "Mother of International P.E.N.,"* with a foreword by Francis King.

37. Ould, *Shuttle*, 48.

38. Reviews of *TC*: *Sphere*, May 27, 1922; Rebecca West, *New Statesman* 19 (May 27, 1922). For hostile reviews, see *Times*, May 2, 1922; *TLS*, May 11, 1922; and especially *Nation and Athenaeum* (UK) 31 (July 15, 1922).

39. Holtby, *Letters to a Friend*, 125–26.

40. Vera Brittain (hereafter cited as VB) to SJ, 1.17.37 (Vera Brittain archive, William Ready Division of Archives and Research, McMaster University Library).

41. Knopf, memo, 7.30.23.

42. SJ, *The Pitiful Wife* (TPW; 1923).

43. For reviews of *TPW*, see *TLS*, Aug. 30, 1923; *Whitby Gazette*, Sept. 28, 1923. See also Dawson-Scott in the *Bookman* (UK), Oct. 18, 1923; *Bookman* (U.S.) 58 (Nov. 1923); *London Mercury* 8 (Oct. 1923); *Saturday Review* 136 (Sept. 8, 1923); *Weekly Westminster Gazette*, Sept. 8, 1923; *New Statesman* 21 (Sept. 8, 1923); *Nation and Athenaeum* 33 (Sept. 29, 1923); *Spectator*, Nov. 15, 1923.

44. SJ, *Lady Susan and Life: An Indiscretion* (LSAL; 1923).

45. For reviews of *LSAL*, see *TLS*, Jan. 21, 1924; *Bookman* (UK), March 1924; *Whitby Gazette*, March 7, 1924; *Spectator*, March 12, 1924.

46. See Harding, *Keeping Faith.*

47. Briggs, *Virginia Woolf*, 19.

48. Williams-Ellis, *Anatomy of Poetry*, 11–12.

49. See Hammacher, *Barbara Hepworth*, 9.

Chapter 5

1. Guy Chapman (hereafter cited as GC), *A Kind of Survivor* (AKOS), 76.

2. See, for instance, A. Knopf to Spalding of Chatto and Windus, 4.21.24.

3. SJ to Bull, 8.21.81 (CSC archive) and Bull, *Noel Streatfeild.*

4. See note of new address, SJ to Raymond, 12.27.24 (University of Reading Archives: Chatto and Windus — CW 11/9).

5. See, for instance, SJ to Raymond: 1.15.25, 1.26.25, 4.17.25, 10.28.25.

6. SJ, "The Bureaucrat's Tale: Monotony," *New Decameron* (1925): 178–94.

7. SJ to Rosamond Lehmann (hereafter cited as RL), 12.7.74 (Rosamond Lehmann archive, Miscellaneous, King's College Library, Cambridge).

8. SJ to de la Mare, 7.5.25 (Bodley. Ms. Eng. Walter de la Mare Collection, Bodley Library, Oxford).

9. Marriage certificate (CSC archive).

10. SJ, *Three Kingdoms* (TK; 1926).

11. Reviews of *TK*: Edwin Muir in *Nation and Athenaeum* (UK) 38 (March 27, 1926); *Whitby Gazette*, March 12, 1926; *TLS*, March 4, 1926; L. P. Hartley in *Saturday Review* 141 (March 20, 1926).

12. James Joyce, *Finnegans Wake* Notebook for 1926 on back flyleaf and on back cover (University of Buffalo Libraries: Special Collections).

13. See SJ to Prentice, 4.7.26 (Chatto and Windus archive) and see Bodley Head/ John Lane archive: Jameson, Storm file, University of Reading Library.

14. SJ to E. J. Thompson (hereafter cited as EJT), 9.14.26 (Bodley. Ms. Eng. C.5292, E.J.Thompson, General Vorr — Jack-Joyce, Bodley Library, Oxford).

15. SJ to Herman Ould (hereafter cited as HO), 11.25.26; PEN to SJ, 11.29.26 and 12.2.26; SJ to HO, 12.1.26 (PEN archive, HRC).

16. SJ, "The Price of a Career: How Women Pay for Success," *Evening Standard*, Nov. 2, 1926, 7.

17. John, *William Heinemann*, 220–22 (Random House Archive: Heinemann: file on SJ, for *The Lovely Ship*).

18. SJ, *The Lovely Ship* (*LS*; 1927); Storm Family Archive, Whitby Archive and Literary Centre.

19. Kenyon, ed., *The Letters of Elizabeth Barrett Browning*, 1:232.

20. For reviews of *LS*, see *TLS*, April 7, 1927; *Spectator*, April 16, 1927; *Saturday Review* 142 (April 16, 1927); *New Statesman* 29 (April 30, 1927); *Nation and Athenaeum* 41 (May 1927); *Whitby Gazette*, May 14, 1927. See also Ella Patterson, in Keighley, *Whitby Writers*.

21. *Evening Standard*, Jan. 3, 1927, 7; Feb. 1, 1927, 7; see also *New York Times* 7, no. 17 (Feb. 27, 1927): 1, under "Part Time Care of the Baby Not Feasible, Says Mother."

22. Berry and Bostridge, *Vera Brittain*, 60.

23. See VB's note on this letter in VB archive, 7.22.42.

24. *Whitby Gazette*, Dec. 23, 1927, 6.

25. SJ to Valentine Dobrée (hereafter cited as VD), 2.14.28 (Dobrée archive, Brotherton Library, University of Leeds).

26. SJ to BK, 5.15.28 (two letters on same day).

27. SJ, *Farewell to Youth* (*FTY*; 1928).

28. Reviews of *FTY*: *Spectator*, June 2, 1928; *Saturday Review* 145 (June 16, 1928); *Times*, May 25, 1928; *New Statesman* 31 (June 2, 1928); *Bookman* (UK), July 1928; *Evening News*, June 4, 1928.

29. SJ to Lidderdale, 8.23.69; see also Lidderdale's reply, 8.25.69 (London Metropolitan University: Women's Library).

30. SJ, *Full Circle* (1928); and see *Vogue*, July 25, 1928, for dating.

31. *Sunday Dispatch*, Aug. 19, 1928.

32. Stories in *Sunday Dispatch*, Aug. 19, 1928; Nov. 4, 1928.

33. Lee, *Virginia Woolf*, 526.

34. SJ to Michael Baker, 3.27.81 (CSC archive).

35. Random House Archive: Heinemann: file on SJ, for *The Georgian Novel and Mr. Robinson* (hereafter GNMR; 1929), contract: 12.7.28.

36. Forster, *Aspects of the Novel*, 151.

37. Woolf, "Is Fiction an Art?" in MacNeillie, *Essays of Virginia Woolf*, 4:461.

38. Desmond Shaw, "What Is 'the Novel'?" *Bookman* (UK), Jan. 1928.

39. West, *The Strange Necessity*, 118.

40. Reviews of GNMR: St. John Adcock, "What's Wrong with Modern Fiction," in "Books and Their Writers" series, *Bookman* (UK), April 1929; *London Mercury*, 20

(June 1929); *Bookman* (U.S.), 70, no. 2 (Oct. 1929); *TLS*, May 30, 1929, issue 1426; *New Statesman* 32 (March 2, 1929).

41. Harwood, "Recent Tendencies on English Fiction," *Quarterly Review* 252 (April 1929): 321–38.

Chapter 6

1. SJ to Frank Swinnerton, 2.16.29 (Special Collection [MS Sw62], University of Arkansas Libraries).

2. SJ to Croom-Johnson, 6.6.29 (PEN archive, HRC).

3. SJ, "Peace and Quest," *Sunday Graphic*, July 14, 1929, 4, 8; "I Want a Good Wife," *Britannia and Eve*, Aug. 1929, 62–63; SJ on "charm" with ad underneath, *Sunday Graphic*, Aug. 18, 1929, 18. See also "Marriage and the New Morality," *Britannia and Eve*, Oct. 1929.

4. SJ, "The Decline of Fiction," originally in *Nation and Athenaeum* 45 (April–Sept. 1929): 594; citations are from the reprint in *Civil Journey* (*CJ*; 1939), 26–33, 26.

5. Random House Archive: Heinemann: file on SJ, for *Farewell to Youth* and *The Voyage Home* (*TVH*; 1930).

6. Reviews of *TVH*: *New York Times Book Review*, Jan. 19, 1930; *Saturday Review* 149 (Feb. 1, 1930); *TLS*, Jan. 30, 1930; see also *Bookman* (UK), March 1930.

7. SJ to Cape, 9.25.30 (Reading: Cape correspondence, 1930).

8. Reviews of *Decline of Merry England* (1930): *New Statesman* 36 (Nov. 22, 1930); *Adelphi*, Dec. 1930; *Spectator*, Nov. 15, 1930. See also Orwell to Max Plowman, 10.24.30 (Davison, 10:189). See also *Quarterly Review* 256 (March 1931).

9. Random House Archive: Heinemann: file on SJ, for *A Richer Dust* (published 1931).

10. SJ, "The Future of the Novel," *Library Assistant* 23 (Nov. 1930): 212–22; *Bookman* (U.S.) 72, no. 6 (Feb. 1931): 557–65.

Chapter 7

1. *Author*, July 1921, July 1930.

2. PEN to SJ, 12.11.30; SJ to HO, 12.12.30 (PEN archive, HRC).

3. SJ, *A Richer Dust* (1931). Citations are to the reprint in *The Triumph of Time* (*TOT*; 1932).

4. Reviews of *A Richer Dust*: *Times*, Feb. 17, 1931; *TLS*, Feb. 19, 1931; *Week-end Review* 3 (April 11, 1931); *Saturday Review* 151 (Feb. 28, 1931); *New Statesman and Nation*, n.s., 1 (March 7, 1931); *New York Times Book Review*, March 29, 1931. See also *Commonweal* (U.S.), June 10, 1931, and also *Adelphi*, n.s., 2 (April 1931), for a hostile review from a critic who had not read the previous two volumes of the trilogy.

5. SJ, "Where Lovely Ships Were Launched," *Everyman*, Aug. 13, 1931.

6. Anon., "The Charms of Whitby," *Whitby Gazette*, Aug. 14, 1931.

7. See Random House Archive: Heinemann: file on SJ, for *A Richer Dust* and "A Picture in the Margin" (published as *That Was Yesterday*).

8. *The Labour Party: Report of 31st Annual Conference, Oct 5–8 1931 in Scarborough*, 158.

9. See SJ, introduction to Linke, *Tale without End* (1934), xii–xiii.

10. SJ, review of Woolf, *The Waves*, in *Fortnightly Review*, Nov. 1931, 677. See also *Time and Tide* reviews: Jameson, Storm Works I, Notebook I, AMS (253 pages), HRC.

11. See, for example, "The Growth of German Anti-Semitism," from a "German Jew," in *Saturday Review* 151 (Feb. 14, 1931).

12. Letter from "German Correspondent," *Bookman* (UK), May 1931.

13. *Saturday Review* 151 (May 16, 1931); 152 (Oct. 24, 1931).

14. Preface in Berdan, ed., *Fourteen Stories from One Plot*.

15. SJ, "A Mingled Strain," first published in *The Fothergill Omnibus* (1931), then as *Fourteen Stories from One Plot*.

16. See SJ to Raymond, 12.6.31 (University of Reading Archives: Chatto and Windus — CW 35/121). The novel at issue was *Delicate Monster*.

17. Mannin to Chatto and Windus, 12.20.31, 12.28.31.

18. SJ to A. D. Peters (hereafter cited as ADP), n.d. (Jameson, Storm, letters, HRC); SJ to Raymond, 12.29.31 (twice), 12.30.31; Mannin to Chatto and Windus, 12.30.31 (University of Reading Archives: Chatto and Windus).

19. SJ, *Women against Men* (*A Day Off, Delicate Monster, The Single Heart*) (1933); see Jameson, Storm — works, Peters A.D., Miscellaneous Correspondence, Box 1 of 3, HRC; SJ to ADP, 1.5.32 (Jameson, Storm, letters, HRC).

Chapter 8

1. SJ, introduction to Linke, *Tale without End* (1934), xiv.

2. SJ, "City to Let: Berlin Now," *Nash and Pall Mall Magazine* (June 1932). Citations from the reprint in *Civil Journey* (*CJ*; 1939) as "City to Let — Berlin 1932."

3. See "Ninepenny Novels: The Case for Paper Covers," *Whitby Gazette*, Feb. 12, 1932.

4. SJ, *The Single Heart* (*TSH*; 1932).

5. For reviews of *TSH*, see *Times*, Feb. 26, 1932; *TLS*, March 3, 1932; *Saturday Review* 153 (March 5, 1932); *Week-end Review* 5 (March 5, 1932).

6. SJ, *That Was Yesterday* (*TWY*; 1932).

7. For reviews of *TWY*, see *New Statesman and Nation*, n.s., 3 (March 12, 1932); *Saturday Review* 153 (April 9, 1932); *Times*, March 11, 1932; *New York Times Book Review*, Feb. 7 1932; *Spectator*, March 19, 1932; *Week-end Review* 5 (April 2, 1932). See also admiring letter to SJ from Charles Morgan, 4.5.32 (in *Selected Letters of Charles Morgan*).

8. SJ, "Man the Helpmate," in *Man Proud Man* (1932), edited by Mabel Ulrich, 103–36.

9. SJ, *Morley Roberts* (1961), 1.

10. VB, *Week-end Review* 5 (April 23, 1932).

11. Letters, *New Statesman and Nation*, n.s., 3, no. 63 (May 7, 1932).

12. See MacKillop, *F. R. Leavis*.

13. See Orage, *Political and Economic Writings*.

14. SJ, fortnightly column in *New English Weekly* 1, no. 1 (April 21, 1932) through 2, no. 15 (Jan. 26, 1933); cited hereafter as *NEW* and date.

15. SJ to H. E. Bates, 5.7.32 (H. E. Bates archive, HRC).

16. Random House Archive: Heinemann: file on SJ, for *The Lovely Ship* etc. (omnibus edition), contract on July [no day], 1932.

17. From Mosley's *The Greater Britain* (1932), quoted in Deane, *History in Our Hands*, 28.

18. The confusion of pacifism with appeasement springs from a common misunderstanding of the French *appaisement*, meaning pacification. It is worth noting that

Margaret's friend Vernon Bartlett would, in 1938, become a member of Parliament, specifically to fight appeasement.

19. See, for instance, SJ, "People Are Queer," *Nash and Pall Mall Magazine* (March 1932): 46; "Strange Landfall," *Strand Magazine* (June 1932): 546–59; "The Release of Mr. Dewey," *Strand Magazine* (Oct. 1932): 357–66; "Abolish Reviewers," *New Clarion* 1, no. 5 (July 9, 1932): 109; "The New Ancestors — An Examination of the Young Hopes of Europe," *Nash's Pall Mall Magazine* (Oct. 1932): 46.

20. SJ, "The Dangers of Fiction," *Highway* 25 (Nov. 1932): 8–10.

21. SJ to Mr. Fletcher, 12.17.32; SJ to Mrs. Fletcher, 12.17.32 (Rare Books and Manuscripts, University Libraries, Pennsylvania State University).

22. SJ, letter headed "The Gagging Act" to *New Statesman and Nation* (Dec. 31, 1932): 854.

23. See, e.g., Wilkinson, *The Town That Was Murdered* (1939); Overy, *The Morbid Age* (2009).

Chapter 9

1. See, for instance, SJ, "The Young Are So Hard," *Strand Magazine* 85 (Feb. 1933): 168–75; "M. Green Loses His Watch," *Strand Magazine* 85 (June 1933): 612–22; "Away to Sea," *Collier's* (U.S.), Sept. 16, 1933, 10–11, 41, 44, 45. See also "Extracts from a Book of Views," *Heaton Review* (Bradford) 6 (1933): 17–20, for a vivid evocation of the Whitby of Margaret's youth.

2. Rhys, *After Leaving Mr. Mackenzie*, 9.

3. Strauss, *New York Times Book Review*, Jan. 1, 1933, 7.

4. For reviews of *A Day Off*, see, e.g., *Saturday Review* 155 (Jan. 7, 1933); *TLS*, Jan. 19, 1933; *Spectator*, Feb. 2, 1933; *Bookman* (UK), March 1933; *Week-end Review* 7 (March 4, 1933) (L. P. Hartley); *New Clarion*, Feb. 4, 1933 (H. E. Bates); one hostile review, *New Statesman and Nation*, n.s., 5 (Jan. 21, 1933).

5. GC, *A Passionate Prodigality* (1933); see, e.g., the review in *Bookman* (UK), March 1933, in the same issue as the review of SJ, *A Day Off*.

6. GC, preface (1966) to *A Passionate Prodigality*, 6. Teilhard de Chardin was a French Jesuit priest and a philosopher.

7. SJ, "The Craft of the Novelist" (1934), in *Civil Journey* (*CJ*; 1939), 53–76. See also Phillips, "The Irresponsibility of Novelists: An Interview with Storm Jameson," *Bookman* (U.S.) 76, no. 2 (Feb. 1933): 114–17, for a repeat of her views.

8. *New Clarion*, Jan. 14, 1933.

9. SJ, "About the Next War: What Are *You* Going to Do?" *New Clarion*, Jan. 28, 1933.

10. SJ, letter to *New Statesman and Nation*, n.s., 5 (Feb. 18, 1933): 104.

11. Dudley Collard, letter to *New Statesman and Nation*, n.s., 5 (Feb, 18, 1933): 187.

12. See further letter headed "The Meerut Appeal," *New Statesman and Nation*, n.s., 5 (March 11, 1933): 107. See also Winifred Holtby, "Cavalcade," in Deane, *History in Our Hands*, 337–41.

13. SJ to Vernon Bartlett, ADMSS (Society of Authors) 59500 Vernon Bartlett (1087, no. 157).

14. SJ, "The Vested Interest of Writers," *New Clarion*, March 18, 1933.

15. Reviews of *NTLTP*: VB, "Aftermath of Calamity," *Week-end Review* 7 (April 24, 1933); Bonamy Dobrée, "View and Reviews, Autobiography Plus," *New English*

Weekly, 3, no. 4 (May 11, 1933); Margaret Wallace, *New York Times Book Review*, June 23, 1933; see also E. M. Delafield, "The Past or the Present? An Autobiography from Miss Storm Jameson," *Morning Post*, April 25, 1933; Eleanor Carroll Chilton, *English Review* 56 (June 1933); Margaret Grant Cook, *TLS*, June 22, 1933.

16. Count Keyserling, "Whither Goes Germany?" *Bookman* (UK), June 1933, 147.

17. See the organ of Society of Authors, etc., *The Author, Playwright and Composer* 43, no. 6 (Summer 1933).

18. SJ to Miss Atkinson, 7.17.33, plus copy of her report (Reading: Cape correspondence, 1933).

19. Romains, *Men of Good Will*, 1:19–20.

20. See *The Labour Party: Report of the 33rd Annual Conference*, held in the White Rock Pavilion, Hastings Oct 2nd to 6th, 1933 (Transport House [South Block], Smith Square, London S.W.1), where Margaret is listed as delegate for Scarborough and Whitby.

21. See report on morning session of 10.5.33, on "The Position of the Workers," *The Labour Party: Report of the 33rd Annual Conference, October 2nd to 6th*, 1933.

22. Linke, *Tale without End* (1934).

23. Williamson, "Literary Detachment," *Bookman* (UK), Oct. 1933; World Committee for the Victims of German Fascism, with introduction by Lord Marley, *The Brown Book of the Hitler Terror and the Burning of the Reichstag* (London: Victor Gollancz, 1933).

24. SJ, "Writers, Publishers and Booksellers," *Bookseller*, Oct. 6, 1933.

25. Letter from SJ, "Symposium or Law-Court?" *New English Weekly*, Oct. 19, 1933; see also letter from Margaret R. B. Shaw, *New English Weekly*, Oct. 26, 1933, and subsequent correspondence from Ethel Mannin, Ezra Pound, and Margaret Shaw, Nov. 9 and 16, 1933.

26. A. R. Orage (hereafter cited as ARO) to SJ, 12.8.33 (CSC archive).

27. *New Clarion*, Dec. 2, 1933.

28. Christina Stead to Florence James, 12.8.33, quoted in Rowley, *Christina Stead*.

29. Bartlett, "Peace round the Corner," *Bookman* (UK), Dec. 1933.

Chapter 10

1. See, for instance, articles on "Rearmament" and on "Whither Germany?" in *Bookman* (UK), Jan. 1934.

2. SJ to HO, 1.18.34, 1.20.34, 1.23.34; HO to SJ, 1.30.34 (PEN archive, HRC).

3. *Saturday Review* 157 (Feb. 3, 1934).

4. Part 1 of report, *New Statesman and Nation*, Jan. 20, 1934.

5. Harding, *Keeping Faith*, 148.

6. Williams-Ellis, *All Stracheys Are Cousins*, 141. Amabel would go again to try to help Thaelmann and von Ossietsky and other prisoners of conscience.

7. Brittain, "Can Women of the World Stop War?" *Modern Woman*, Feb. 1934; Holtby, "Black Words for Women Only," *New Clarion*, March 24, 1934.

8. SJ, *Company Parade* (CP; 1934).

9. Reviews of *CP*: Greene, *Spectator*, April 30, 1934, 634. See also, for instance, *TLS* review (Leonora Eyles), March 22, 1934, 212; *Times*, anon. review, "The Post-war World," March 23, 1934.

10. Huxley to SJ, 3.23.34 (CSC archive); SJ to VB, 3.26.34; SJ to W. Holtby, 3.29.34

(Hull Libraries: Holtby archive); SJ to Bartlett, 3.29.34 (ADDMSS [Society of Authors] 59500 Vernon Bartlett 1087).

11. SJ, "A Faith Worth Dying For," *Fortnightly Review* 141 (April 1934): 413–24; reprinted in *Civil Journey*, 179.

12. Linke, *Tale without End* (TWE). SJ's introduction was reprinted in *Civil Journey* as "The Youngest Brother."

13. SJ, "Providing the Evidence," *Fortnightly Review* 141 (June 1934): 687–95.

14. See Watts, *Mrs. Sappho*, 198–99; SJ to Leslie, 8.3.34 (PEN archive, HRC).

15. See also HRC: MS Jameson, S (Works). MS of *Company Parade* in two note-books, followed by "The Defence of Freedom" (introduction to Lilo Linke's book); *Twilight of Reason*; and *In the End*. Finished Sept. 1934.

16. SJ, "To a Labour Party Official," *Left Review*, Nov. 2, 1934.

17. League of Nations Peace Ballot 1934–35. See also National Declaration Committee (England), *War or Peace? The Workers' Guide to the National Declaration on the League of Nations and Armaments* (London, 1934).

18. Livingstone and Johnston, *The Peace Ballot*.

19. Anon., ed., *Challenge to Death* (CD; 1934).

20. See Overy, *The Morbid Age*, 221.

21. See, for the importance of his influence, chapter 2.

22. *Left Review*, Dec. 1934, 70.

Chapter 11

1. See SJ to Macdonald, 10.21.34, 10.25.34, 1.8.35, 1.12.35, 1.30.35 (PEN archive, HRC).

2. SJ, "What Is Patriotism?" in N. P. Macdonald, ed., *What Is Patriotism?* (1935), 123.

3. SJ, *Love in Winter* (LIW; 1935).

4. For reviews of *LIW*, see, e.g., J. D. Beresford (John Davys), *TLS*, April 11, 1935; William Plomer, *Spectator*, April 12, 1935; anon., *Times*, April 16, 1935; Margaret Wallace, "Miss Jameson's Widening Canvas," *New York Times Book Review*, May 5, 1935; Osbert Burdett, *English Review* 60 (June 1935).

5. Report in *Left Review* 9 (June 1935): 346; see also Christina Stead's report, *Left Review* 9 (Aug. 1935): 453.

6. GC, AKOS, 145.

7. Harding, *Keeping Faith*, 148–57; pictorial record in *Zur Erinnerung an den Besuch der British Legion in Deutschland*, lodged in Royal British Legion HQ.

8. Linke, *Restless Flags: A German Girl's Story*. See also Grass, *Peeling the Onion*, trans. Michael Henry Heim, 19–20, for the lure of the Hitler Youth.

9. SJ to VB, 7.18.35; SJ to EJT, 7.29.35; SJ to VB, 8.5.35; SJ to VD, 8.10.35.

10. SJ, *In the Second Year* (ITSY; 1936).

11. SJ to VB, 10.26.35; HO to SJ, 10.10.35, 10.30.35.

12. See Lovell, *The Mitford Girls*, 195.

13. Churchill, "The Truth about Hitler," *Strand Magazine*, Nov. 1935.

14. Lewis, *It Can't Happen Here* (Oct. 1935).

15. SJ, *The Soul of Man in the Age of Leisure* (AOL; 1935).

16. SJ, "Leisure," *Aryan Path* (Bombay) 6, no. 4 (April 1935): 211. See also "Technique for Living," *Civil Journey* (1939), 238–46, which develops these ideas.

17. Review of *AOL* by D. T., *Scrutiny* 4 (Dec. 1935).

Chapter 12

1. See, for instance, SJ, review, *The Socialist* (journal of the Socialist League, chair Stafford Cripps), n.s., no. 4, 1936.

2. SJ, letter to *Whitby Gazette*, Jan. 31, 1936.

3. SJ, *The Moon Is Making* (TMIM; 1937); and see SJ, *NTLTP*, 28.

4. Reviews of *ITSY*: *TLS*, Feb. 1, 1936; *Times*, Feb. 4, 1936; *London Mercury* 33 (March 1936); *Whitby Gazette*, Feb. 21, 1936; *New English Weekly*, March 19, 1936; *Spectator*, Feb. 7, 1936. For more positive reviews, see *Left Review* 3 (March 1936); *New York Times Book Review*, Feb. 23, 1936; and *New York Herald Tribune*, Feb. 23, 1936.

5. *Saturday Review* 161 (May 2, 1936); and see other issues, e.g., March 28, 1936; April 25, 1936.

6. Henderson, *The Novel Today*, 14.

7. HO to SJ, 2.21.36, 2.26.36 (PEN archive, HRC); SJ to VB, 2.22.36; SJ to HO, 2.22.36.

8. SJ, as James Hill, *Loving Memory* (LM; 1937).

9. For a list of the first group of sponsors, see *Peace News*, Aug. 22, 1936, and Morrison, *I Renounce War*, 11.

10. SJ, "The Writer," in Cole, ed., *The Road to Success* (RTS; 1936), 98–114.

11. SJ, "London in 1913," in Brophy, ed., *Hotch-Potch* (1936), 129–36; Anand, *The Coolie*, 1936.

12. Memo re: International Association of Writers for the Defence of Culture, June 19–23, 1936 (PEN archive, HRC).

13. GC, ed., *Vain Glory*.

14. SJ, *None Turn Back* (NTB; 1936); in HRC: MS Jameson, S (Works), *None Turn Back*, author's manuscript and TMS. Original title "The Bright Day."

15. Reviews of *NTB*: *Times*, Aug. 28, 1936; *Whitby Gazette*, Aug. 28, 1936; *TLS*, Aug. 29, 1936; *New Statesman and Nation*, Sept. 5, 1936; *Left Review*, Oct. 1936.

16. SJ to PEN, 9.29.36 (PEN archive, HRC).

17. SJ to Sheppard, 10.6.36; SJ to HO, 10.11.36; HO to SJ, 11.25.36 (PEN archive, HRC).

18. SJ, as William Lamb, *The World Ends* (WE; 1937).

19. *Gryphon*, Nov. 1936, 76.

20. SJ to Mrs. Fletcher, 11.9.36 (Rare Books and Manuscripts, University Libraries, Pennsylvania State University. Personal Author, Jameson, Storm, 12 Items).

21. Newitt, *Women Must Choose* (1937), with preface by SJ.

Chapter 13

1. Mannin to SJ, 2.6.36, 5.18.36 (Jameson, Storm — works +, from Peters A.D., Miscellaneous Correspondence. Box 1 of 3, HRC); SJ, *Delicate Monster* (DM; London, 1937). MS of novel in HRC in SJ Works I, Notebook I, AMS 253.

2. Reviews of *DM*: *Spectator*, Jan. 29, 1937; *Time and Tide* 18 (Feb. 6, 1937); *London Mercury* 35 (Feb. 1937); *Times*, Jan. 22, 1937; *TLS*, Jan. 23, 1937; *New Statesman and Nation*, Jan. 30, 1937.

3. Fox, *The Novel and the People*.

4. Rowley, *Christina Stead*, 235. See also Sutherland, *Stephen Spender: The Authorized Biography*; Lukács, *The Historical Novel* [1937], 1989.

5. *Left Review* 6 (Feb. 1937).

6. Obituary notice, *Whitby Gazette*, Feb. 19, 1937.

7. SJ, "February 1937," *London Mercury* 39, no. 232 (Feb. 1939): 383–84.

8. Williams-Ellis, *All Stracheys Are Cousins*, 152.

9. See advertisements for *Fact*, in *Left Review* 6 (March 1937): 122.

10. See report on recently released MI5 files in the *Guardian*, March 8, 2010, 11.

11. *Fact* (1937–39) 1 (April 1937): 6–8, 6.

12. *Peace News*, April 3, 1937.

13. SJ, preface, in Newitt, *Women Must Choose* (1937), 13.

14. *Left Review* 6 (June 1937): 259.

15. Report on Second Congress in *Left Review*, Sept. 1937; also see Usandizaga, "The Forgotten Brigade," in Usandizaga and Monnickendam, *Back to Peace*, 240.

16. Wells to SJ, 6.26.37 (CSC archive).

17. SJ to VB, 7.4.37; SJ to VD, 7.5.37; *JN*, 1:358.

18. SJ, review, *Fact*, no. 2 (May 15, 1937), 87–90.

19. SJ, "Documents," under general heading "Writing in Revolt: 1. Theory," *Fact*, no. 4 (July 15, 1937): 9–18.

20. See Bigsby, *Remembering and Imagining the Holocaust*, 78–79.

21. SJ, "Books to Save Liberalism," *Aryan Path* (Bombay) 8, no. 7 (July 1937): 305–8.

22. SJ to Swinnerton, 8.14.37; SJ to VB, 8.21.37; *JN*, 1:25.

23. Told to me by member of Whitby Public Library, recalling grandmother's anecdote.

24. SJ, letter to *Time and Tide* 18 (Sept. 11, 1937).

25. SJ to VB, 9.23.37, 10.6.1937; *JN*, 1:313, 358–66.

26. *Author*, Autumn 1937; SJ, as William Lamb, *The World Ends* (WE; 1937).

27. Reviews of WE: *Times*, Oct. 15, 1937; *Time and Tide*, Oct. 23, 1937; *TLS*, Jan. 1, 1938.

28. On dust jacket of *LM*.

29. Reviews of LM: *TLS*, Oct. 23, 1937; *Time and Tide*, Oct. 30, 1937; *Times*, Nov. 5, 1937.

30. PEN minutes of Exec. Committee, 10.26.37 (PEN archive, HRC).

31. See Auden and Isherwood, *Journey to a War*, sonnets XII, XVII.

32. *Peace News*, Nov. 6, 1937.

33. SJ, contribution to "Authors Take Sides," *Left Review Pamphlet*, Nov. 1937 (hereafter cited as *LRP*).

34. The lecture was printed in SJ, *The Novel in Contemporary Life* (NCL; 1938) and in *Civil Journey* (1939), with added quotation from William Lamb novel and passage on pointillism, and some cuts. Citations are from the first, American, printing as pamphlet.

35. The Astors were a well-known aristocratic family. Geoffrey Dawson (1874–1941) was editor of the *Times* and a member of the Cliveden set that Nancy Astor (1879–1964) hosted.

Chapter 14

1. SJ to Ward, 1.9.38, 1.14.38 (Rare Books and Manuscripts, University Libraries, Pennsylvania State University, Personal Author, Jameson, Storm, 12 Items); Ward, ed., *Ten Peace Plays* (1938), with preface by SJ.

2. SJ, as James Hill, *No Victory for the Soldier* (NVFTS; 1938).

3. See Lessing's three novels written under the pseudonym Jane Somers, *The Diary of a Good Neighbour* (1983); *If the Old Could . . .* (1984); and *The Diaries of Jane Somers* (1985).

4. Burdekin, as Murray Constantine, *Swastika Night* (1937).

5. SJ, *Here Comes a Candle* (*HCAC*; 1938).

6. Comment made in *TLS* review, Oct. 8, 1938.

7. SJ, essay in *What Is Happiness?* (1938), 31–41; hereafter cited as *WIH*.

8. PEN minutes of Exec. Committee, 3.9.38 (PEN archive, HRC).

9. Hill to ADP, 5.3.38 (archive of A. D. Peters, Literary Agent, HRC).

10. ADP to Hill, 5.17.38 (ADP archive, HRC).

11. "Writers Declare against Fascism," Queen's Hall, June 8, 1938; subsequent pamphlet, King's College Cambridge archive, Misc. 42B/11.

12. See Roubal, "Politics of Gymnastics: Mass Gymnastic Displays under Communism in Central and Eastern Europe," 6.

13. Ould, *Shuttle*, 224. See also Elizabeth Maslen, "Proper Words in Proper Places: The Challenge of Čapek's *War with the Newts*," *Science Fiction Studies* 14 (1987): 82–92.

14. Reviews of *NVFTS*: *TLS*, Aug. 27, 1938; and see *Times*, Sept. 16, 1938; *Time and Tide*, Sept. 3, 1938.

15. Letter headed "Conditions of the Sacrifice," subheaded "General Settlement," *Manchester Guardian*, Sept. 24, 1938.

16. Grant Duff, *Europe and the Czechs*, 25, 61.

17. See Gellhorn, *A Stricken Field*.

18. SJ, talk to Czechoslovak Room Committee, University of Pittsburgh, Masaryk Birthday Commemoration, 3.7.49 (Manuscripts Dept., Lilly Library, Indiana University).

19. SJ, *Civil Journey* (*CJ*; 1939).

20. *P.E.N. News*, Oct. 1938, editorial and report on 17th AGM of London Centre, Oct. 5, 38 (PEN archive, HRC).

21. Nevinson to SJ, 10.5.38 (CSC archive).

22. Reviews of *HCAC*: *TLS*, Oct. 8, 1938; *Time and Tide*, Oct. 22, 1938.

23. Vočadlo to SJ, 10.14.38 (CSC archive).

24. Priestley to [Janet] Chance, 10.23.38; Chance to Priestley, 10.14.38 (PEN archive, HRC).

25. Letter re: Czechoslovakia authors, *TLS*, Oct. 22, 1938; *New Statesman and Nation*, Oct. 22, 1938; repeated in *New English Weekly*, Oct. 27, 1938.

26. Translators' Guild to PEN, 12.31.38 (PEN Refugee Writers' Bureau letters, HRC); and, for ongoing correspondence, see Herbert Herlitschka archive, University of Reading.

27. SJ to Downie, 12.8.38 (PEN Refugee Writers' Bureau, HRC).

28. PEN Refugee Writers Fund archive, HRC, 12.12.38, 12.30.38.

29. SJ to Marston, 12.19.38 (PEN Refugee Writers Fund archive, HRC).

30. See correspondence between SJ and Battcock (Bodley, Ms. Eng. Autogr.d.39. Marjorie Battock).

31. PEN Exec. Committee minutes, 10.26.38; Rebecca West to SJ, 2.21.39 (PEN archive, HRC).

32. SJ to Liddell Hart (hereafter cited as LH), 12.26.38, 12.30.38; Liddell Hart to SJ, 12.29.38 (Liddell Hart archive, King's College London, LH1/408).

33. Danchev, *Alchemist of War*, 166–67.

34. Virginia Woolf to SJ, 12.31.38 (CSC archive).

35. Letters to the editor, letter headed "The National Peace Petition," *Author*, Christmas issue, 1938.

Chapter 15

1. Unsigned, undated report, but probably the annual report of the president, c. Oct. 1939 (PEN archive, HRC).

2. See PEN Refugee Writers' Bureau — W-Z file, HRC.

3. GC, *Culture and Survival* (1940).

4. This should be 1939; again Margaret misdates.

5. See Usandizaga, "The Forgotten Brigade," in Usandizaga and Monnickendam, *Back to Peace*, 240.

6. "Ethel Mannin's Christmas Message, Peace on Earth," *Peace News*, Dec. 23, 1938.

7. Janet Chance report, 2.10.39 (PEN: Refugee Writers Fund, A file, HRC).

8. PEN Exec. Committee minutes, 2.22.39; undated letter to publishers (PEN: Refugee Writers' Bureau: Letters, HRC); see SJ to Unwin, 2.22.39 (University of Reading, Archives: Allen and Unwin — AUC 68/15); SJ to Chatto and Windus, 2.24.39 (University of Reading Archives: Chatto and Windus — CW 84/14); HO to SJ, 2.28.39 (PEN archive, HRC); Macmillan to SJ, 3.1.39 (Macmillan archive, Third Tranche, British Library); Priestley to SJ, 2.24.39 (PEN archive, HRC).

9. Application from A&LRC to Committee for Refugees, 2.28.39 (PEN: Refugee Writers Fund, A File, HRC).

10. SJ, *Farewell, Night, Welcome, Day* (*FNWD*; 1939).

11. Review of *CJ* in *TLS*, March 4, 1939, 131. See also *Times*, March 7, 1939; *Time and Tide*, March 18, 1939; *London Mercury* 39, no. 234 (April 1939); *New Statesman and Nation*, n.s., 17 (April 8, 1939). See also *Peace News*, April 21, 1939.

12. *Peace News*, March 10, 1939, 6.

13. See SJ to Irene Rathbone (hereafter cited as IR), 8.28.40 (CSC archive), stating in another context that she had found a copy of her letter of resignation dated March 1939.

14. Quoted in Glendinning, *Rebecca West*, 159.

15. Chance to Mr. Weatherall, 4.13.19 (PEN Refugee Writers' Bureau archive, HRC).

16. Weatherall to PEN, 4.13.39; Chance to Weatherall, 4.19.39 (PEN Refugee Writers' Bureau: Letters — Box N-Schl, R file; file Sm-Sz; file Mi-Mz; J file; W-Z file).

17. See how Margaret's perceptions match with those mirrored in Irène Némirovsky, *Suite Française*.

18. Rache Lovat Dickson (hereafter cited as LD) to SJ, 5.31.39 (King's College London, Liddell Hart Centre for Military Archives: LiddellH: 1/408, 1937–73, 1986).

19. Report in the *Times*, April 18, 1939; PEN Exec. Committee minutes, 6.1.39.

20. Janet Chance report, June 1939 (PEN: Refugee Writers' Fund, File A, HRC); A&LRC report, 6.14.39 (PEN: Refugee Writers' Fund, A File, HRC).

21. SJ to Downie, 6.17.39 (PEN Refugee Writers' Bureau: Letters, HRC).

22. *Fact*, June 15, 1939, "Our Last Number."

23. SJ, "The Method and Theory of the Bauhaus," essay review of L. Moholy-Nagy's *The New Vision* (London: Faber, 1939), in *Scrutiny* 8 (June 1939), 88.

24. See L. A. G. Strong, *John O'London's Weekly*, May 5, 1939; Edwin Muir, *Listener*, May 11, 1939; B. Ifor Evans, *Manchester Guardian*, May 12, 1939; Malcolm Muggeridge, *Time and Tide*, May 20, 1939; Richard Aldington, *Atlantic Monthly*, June 1939; Louis Gillet, in *Babel* 1 (1940), 101–13, translated by D. D. Paige for *Quarterly Review of Literature* 1, no. 2 (Winter 1944).

25. For reviews of *FMWD*, see, for example, *Times*, July 21, 1939; *TLS*, July 22, 1939.

26. See, for instance, SJ to VB, 10.3.39, and VB's reference (in letter to SJ, 10.15.39) to SJ's articles at the beginning of October in *TLS*, *P.E.N. News*, and *Peace News*.

27. See VB to SJ, 9.6.39, 9.11.39, and SJ to VB, 9.8.39, 9.9.39, 9.13.39, 9.14.39, and 9.21.39.

28. SJ to LH, 9.4.39. And see letter of 9.14.39.

29. See White, *The New Propaganda* (1939).

30. PEN Exec. Committee minutes, 8.24.39.

31. See, for example, Neumann to Olden, 9.3.39 (PEN Refugee Writers' Bureau: Letters — Box N-Schl, N-O file, HRC).

32. See PEN Refugee Writers' Bureau: Letters — Box T-V file, HRC.

33. See, for example, PEN Refugee Writers' Bureau: Letters, HRC file H — dealing with Herbert Herlitschka.

34. See, for example, PEN Refugee Writers' Bureau: Letters — Box T-V file, HRC.

35. SJ, *Europe to Let: The Memoirs of an Obscure Man* (*ETL*; 1940).

36. Kirkpatrick was Geneva correspondent for the *New York Herald Tribune*.

37. It is tempting to speculate there may also be a link with the idealistic knight Friedrich von Hess in Burdekin's *Swastika Night*, first published in 1937.

38. Review of *ETL*, anon. (R. D. Charques), *TLS*, May 18, 1940.

39. SJ to VB, no date, but clearly at this juncture according to content.

40. *Atlantic Monthly* 164, no. 5 (Nov. 1939): 585–89.

41. SJ, "In Courage Keep Your Heart," *Woman's Journal*, Dec. 1939, 34–35.

42. See SJ to VB, no date (but from internal evidence, late Nov. 1939), enclosing draft of letter to Humbert Wolfe; Chance to Neumann, 11.29.39, Neumann to Chance, 1.12.39 (PEN Refugee Writers' Bureau: Letters — Box N-Schl, N-O file, HRC). See also Chance to Wistuba, 11.29.39 (PEN Writers' Bureau: Letters — Box W-Z, Wi-Y file, HRC), and Wistuba to Chance, 12.1.39.

43. SJ to VB, 12.22.39, 12.27.39, 12.28.39; LD to SJ, 12.27.39; VB to SJ, 12.28.39.

44. See Berry and Bostridge, *Vera Brittain*, 391; Harold Macmillan (hereafter cited as HM) to SJ, 1.3.40, 1.10.40 (Macmillan LB, British Library); LD to SJ, 1.5.40, 1.10.40; SJ to VB, 1.9.40, 1.13.40; HM to SJ, 1.15.40 (Macmillan LB, British Library); LD to SJ, 1.15.40; SJ to VB, 1.19.40.

45. Lovat Dickson, *The House of Words* (1963), 222.

46. See letters from Madame Beneš to SJ, 1.17.40, 5.25.40 (CSC archive); PEN Exec. Committee minutes, 1.25.40 (PEN archive, HRC).

Chapter 16

1. See LD to SJ, 1.24.40 (Macmillan LB, British Library). See, for instance, SJ, "The New Europe," *Fortnightly Review* 153 (Jan. 1940): 68–79, reprinted in *Living Age* (Boston) as "The Collapse of Sovereignty," 358 (March 1940).

2. SJ, "Karel Čapek and Czechoslovakia" (1940).

3. Janet Chance report, 1940 (PEN: Refugee Writers Fund, HRC).

4. See, for instance, PEN to Warner Bros., 2.9. 40 (PEN Refugee Writers' Bureau: Letters — W-Z file. HRC).

5. PEN Refugee Writers Fund archive, HRC.

6. SJ to J. Chance, 2.9.40 (PEN Refugee Writers' Bureau — J file, HRC).

7. LD to SJ, 2.29.40; HM to SJ, 3.4.40 (Macmillan LB, British Library); LD to SJ, 3.7.40; HM to SJ, 3.8.40; LD to SJ, 3.28.40.

8. LD to SJ, 4.18.40; SJ to VB, 4.18.40, 4.19.40. However, no record of the program has been found; many records were destroyed as a result of war damage. See Briggs, *The History of Broadcasting in the United Kingdom*, 3:22, 128, 145.

9. Ould, *Shuttle*, 324–25.

10. SJ to Evelyn Sharp, 4.30.40 (Bodley, Ms. Eng. Lett. D.279. Nevinson correspondence [wife Evelyn Sharp]).

11. SJ, *JN*, 2:45–46; Bull, *Noel Streatfeild*, 159–60; SJ, *JN/TMS*, 2:240–42 (in printed version, *JN*, 2:46–47, cut and revised).

12. Review of *ETL*, Rosamond Lehmann, *Spectator*, May 30, 1940. See anon. (R. D. Charques), *TLS*, May 18, 1940; John Mair, *New Statesman and Nation*, June 1, 1940; Desmond Hawkins, *Time and Tide*, June 8, 1940; *Times*, May 25, 1940. See also Wallace Stegner, "New Novels," *Virginia Quarterly* 16, no. 3 (Summer 1940): 459–65.

13. Mme. Beneš to SJ, 5.25.40 (CSC archive).

14. Noted in the annual report of the Fabian Society (18/A/26 Executive Committee Minute Book Jan.16 1939 to June 29 1946: 58th annual report for year ending 31 March 1941). There is no record of what Margaret said; the beginning of volume containing the annual report acknowledges many papers destroyed over the years; *JN*, 2:53.

15. See also Lovat Dickson, *The House of Words*, 230.

16. See Judt, *Postwar: A History of Europe since 1945*.

17. SJ, *JN*, 2:47, 52, 61; see *Sonderfahndungsliste G.B.* [the Black Book] (Imperial War Museum), where the PEN is mentioned more than once. Margaret was not named there, but she did appear on other lists in Berlin.

18. Jan Masaryk to SJ, 5.31.40 (CSC archive).

19. See, for instance, Rudolf Olden, *Hitler der Eroberer: Entlarvung einer Legende* (Amsterdam: Querido, 1935). The book was promptly banned by the Nazis and Olden's German citizenship revoked.

20. See Ould to Undersecretary of State, Home Office, 6.13.40 (PEN Refugee Writers' Bureau: Letters — Box N-Schl, N-O file, HRC).

21. Becker-Neumann to SJ, 7.11.40 (PEN Refugee Writers' Bureau: Letters — Box N-Schl, N-O file, HRC); and letter from SJ and HO, *TLS*, July 13, 1940.

22. See, for instance, Robert Nathan, president of the PEN Center in New York, to SJ, 7.17.40 (PEN Refugee Writers' Bureau: Letters — Box N-Schl, N-O file, HRC), sending letter from SJ on Olden, via Stephen Benet, to Archibald MacLeish at the Library of Congress.

23. Neumann to SJ, cable (PEN Refugee Writers' Bureau: Letters — Box N-Schl, N-O file, HRC).

24. See also Sherry, *The Life of Graham Greene*, vol. 2 (1939–55).

25. See details on further reading in SJ to VB, 8.16.40.

26. See also details of Czech broadcast, BBC — Czechoslovak program, Saturday, 8.17.40, 6:15–6:30 p.m. (CSC archive).

27. See SJ to VB, 10.21.39; and SJ to Vernon Bartlett, 12.10.45.

28. See details in volumes of the Society of Authors organ, *Author, Playwright and Composer* 50–51 (1939–41).

29. See SJ, "Women on the Spot," *Atlantic Monthly*, Feb. 1941, 169–76. The longer article does not seem to have been written, and other accounts were coming out by 1941.

30. See draft of SJ's report on this project, undated (CSC archive).

31. SJ to Mrs. Herlitschka, 10.15.40 (University of Reading: Herbert Herlitschka archive, 1409/62/217); see PEN Refugee Writers' Bureau: Letters — H file, HRC.

32. See Herbert Herlitschka to HO, 10.24.40; HO to Herlitschka 10.28.40 (PEN Refugee Writers' Bureau: Letters — H file, HRC).

33. Report in PEN Refugee Writers Fund archive, HRC; PEN Exec. Committee minutes, 10.31.40 (PEN archive, HRC).

34. SJ, "Why Not a Ministry of Fine Arts?" *Fortnightly Review* 154 (Nov. 1940): 449–57.

35. PEN Refugee Writers' Bureau: Letters — Ma-Me file, HRC.

36. PEN Refugee Writers' Bureau: Letters — Ma-Me file, HRC.

37. PEN Refugee Writers' Bureau: Letters — J file, HRC.

38. PEN Refugee Writers' Bureau: Letters — J file, HRC.

39. PEN Refugee Writers' Bureau: Letters — Sm-Sz file, HRC: Heinz Stroh, 11.3.40.

40. For reviews of *Cousin Honoré*, see *TLS*, Nov. 23, 1940; *New Statesman and Nation*, Nov. 30, 1940; *Spectator*, Dec. 13, 1940; *Time and Tide*, Dec. 14, 1940.

41. *TLS*, Dec. 7, 1940.

Chapter 17

1. SJ, *The Fort* (1941), 159.

2. SJ, "Women on the Spot," *Atlantic Monthly*, Feb. 1941.

3. VB to SJ, 1.31.41; SJ to VB, 2.5.41; VB to SJ, 2.6.41. See also VB's long-hand addition, long after the breakup: "Dorothy was subsequently killed in an air-raid on Reading — not much loss, alas, even to her children." Letters between SJ and VB on this crisis continue until March 1, 1941.

4. See *Author*, March 1941.

5. SJ, "Safety First!" (BBC Written Archives, Caversham. Recorded Talks. Script Library: Radio Talks: Storm Jameson). Recorded Wed., Feb. 26, 1941, at 6 p.m. (Home Service).

6. See Briggs, *History of Broadcasting*, 3:295.

7. SJ, "What I Am Reading Now," Thursday, March 20, 1941, Home Service from London, 4:15–4:30 p.m. (BBC Written Archives, Caversham: Recorded Talks. Script Library: Radio Talks: Storm Jameson).

8. Dorothy Sayers, "Living to Work"; the quotation is from the foreword, p. 7.

9. *News Chronicle*, Feb. 25, 1941. See also Eunice Buckley's novel *Destination Unknown*.

10. SJ, "A Day at the Zoo," *Atlantic Monthly* 161, no. 5 (May 1938): 683–91, reprinted in *Modern Reading*, edited by Reginald Moore, no. 2 (July 1941): 11–26; and "You Don't Speak French, Do You?" *Modern Reading*, no. 4 (April 1942): 47–64.

11. PEN Exec. Committee minutes, 3.20.41 (PEN archive, HRC).

12. See letters about Philip Pareth, PEN Refugee Writers' Bureau: Letters — Box N-Schl, P-Q file, HRC.

13. PEN Refugee Writers' Bureau: Letters — Box N-Schl, P-Q file, HRC.

14. PEN Refugee Writers' Bureau: letters in many files; see *News Chronicle* reports for May 22 and 23, 1941, in L file, HRC.

15. VB, 5.15.41, in *Wartime Chronicle: Vera Brittain's Diary, 1939–45*.

16. SJ to Legrand, 6. 21.41 (MSJ Correspondence, Dept. of Special Collections, McFarlin Library, University of Tulsa).

17. SJ, "Britain Speaks," BBC Overseas North-American Transmission, Thursday/Friday, July 3 and 4, 1941. Talk given live (censored by J. W. Macalpine) (BBC Written Archives, Caversham: Recorded Talks. Script Library: Radio Talks: Storm Jameson).

18. See Cesarini, *Arthur Koestler: The Homeless Mind*; Scammell, *Koestler: The Literary and Political Odyssey of a Twentieth-Century Skeptic*; and Applebaum, review, "Yesterday's Man?" 10–11.

19. SJ to Arthur Koestler (hereafter cited as AK), 8.7.41 (Koestler archive, University of Edinburgh Library); Koestler, *The Scum of the Earth* (London: Jonathan Cape, 1941).

20. SJ to St. John Irvine, 8.18.41 (Irvine mss, Manuscripts Dept., Lilly Library, Indiana University).

21. Jan Petersen to the PEN, 9.3.41 (PEN Refugee Writers' Bureau: Letters — Box N-Schl, P-Q file, HRC).

22. SJ, *JN*, 2:102–8. Later, Wilder would aim to mend the breach with Romains: see his letter to SJ, 11.21.41 (CSC archive).

23. SJ, "The Responsibilities of the Writer," delivered at the opening meeting of the London Congress of the PEN, held on Sept. 11, 1941. Printed first as "The Writer's Duty" in the *Fortnightly Review*, Nov. 1941, then with original title in *The Writer's Situation* (TWS; 1950), 164–79. Citations are to the TWS printing.

24. See "Writers Discuss New World Role as London P.E.N. Congress Opens," *New York Times Book Review*, Sept. 12, 1941, 12.

25. SJ, "Creditors of France," spoken at the closing meeting of the PEN Congress, Sept. 1941; printed in "Le congrès internationel des PEN," *La france libre* 2, no. 11 (Sept. 15, 1941): 395–99, and in *The Writer's Situation* (TWS; 1950), 180–88 (citations are to the TWS printing). See also SJ's challenge to writers, *Adam International Review*, edited by M. Grindea, no. 152 (Sept. 1941).

26. See, e.g., *New York Times Book Review* 4, no. 2 (Sept. 14, 1941): 6; Unwin to SJ, 9.17.41 (University of Reading Archives: Allen and Unwin — AUC 121/10).

27. SJ to Farjeon, 9.16.41, 10.25.41 (British Library, Farjeon archive ADD 83146, unbound).

28. Jan Petersen to HO and SJ, 9.17.41 (PEN Refugee Writers' Bureau: Letters — Box N-Schl, P-Q file, HRC). See also *La france libre* 2, no. 1 (Sept. 15, 1941): 395–99.

29. Ould, ed., *Writers in Freedom: A Symposium Based on the XVII International Congress of the P.E.N. Club Held in London in September 1941.*

30. See Denise Amye, "Échanges de livres," *La france libre* 2, no. 12 (Oct. 15, 1941): 541–43.

31. SJ, "The H. G. Wells Age," *Adam International Review*, no. 153 (Nov. 1941).

32. *Fortnightly Review* broadsheet, "The Future of Germany," 156 (Sept. 1941). SJ's contribution, 220–22; the quotation is from p. 220.

33. *Fortnightly Review* broadsheet, "The Future of Germany" (Sept. 1941), 222.

34. Quoted in *Author*, Sept. 1941.

35. SJ, "A Moment of Happiness," in *Selected Writing*, edited by Reginald Moore (1941), 1:96–108.

36. Anonymous leading article, "Dilemma of Pacifism," *TLS*, Sept. 15, 1941, 567. See also letters to *TLS* in response from Dalgliesh, Nov. 22, 1941; Macaulay, Nov. 29, 1941; and Lunn, Soutar, and Tippett, Dec. 6, 1941. See also anonymous review, "Books for Gifts: The World Turmoil," *TLS*, Dec. 6, 1941.

37. SJ, "A Crisis of the Spirit," in *The Writer's Situation* (*TWS*; 1950), 136–63.

Chapter 18

1. SJ, letter to *Times*, Jan. 1, 1942, headed "Books in War Time: 'Disintegration' of the Trade: The Case for Concessions."

2. See SJ to Unwin, 1.1.42 (University of Reading: AUC 141–3); see also *Bookseller*, Jan. 1, 1942.

3. For reviews of *The Fort*, see anon. (R. D. Charques), *TLS*, Jan. 10, 1942; John Hampson, *Spectator*, Jan. 16, 1942; Oliver Warner, *Time and Tide*, Jan. 17, 1942; and Desmond Hawkins, *New Statesman and Nation*, n.s., 23 (Jan. 24, 1942), who was patronizing. See also the good review of *The Fort* and *The End of This War* in *La france libre* 3, no. 17 (March 16, 1942): 430–31.

4. SJ, *Then We Shall Hear Singing* (*TWSHS*; 1942).

5. See, for instance, Čapek, *War with the Newts* (1936).

6. It seems odd that SJ should use the name she had already used in *Europe to Let*; but this Hesse is peasant born, not noble, and the link with Rudolf Hess, since he was in the news recently, seems more likely.

7. LD to SJ, 2.2.42; SJ to Macmillan, 2.9.42; Daniel Macmillan to SJ, 2.23.42; Daniel Macmillan to George Brett, 2.27.42 (British Library: Macmillan files—American 38: Feb 19 1942–Nov 9 1943).

8. As described by SJ, ed., in *London Calling* (*LC*; 1942), 7.

9. PEN Refugee Writers' Fund archive, HRC. See also Matuschek, *Three Lives: A Biography of Stefan Zweig*.

10. Birth certificate (CSC archive).

11. See, e.g., Sebald, *On the Natural History of Destruction*, 14–19; Harris and Cox, *Despatch on War Operations: 23 February 1942 to 8 May 1945*; Boog et al., *Germany and the Second World War*, vol. 6: *The Global War*; British Bombing Survey Unit, *The Strategic Air War against Germany, 1939–1945*.

12. *JN*, 2:116. And see, for instance, SJ to Frank Swinnerton, 2.7.42, 2.12.42 (MS Sw62, Special Collections, University of Arkansas Libraries).

13. SJ to Unwin, 3.2.42; SJ to HO, 3.3.42.

14. See also *JN*, 2:122, and SJ, "Memory of Noel," 8.21.81 (CSC archive).

15. SJ to Marlys Herlitschka, 4.28.42 (University of Reading: Herbert Herlitschka archive, 1409/62/218).

16. PEN to SJ, 4.29.42 (PEN archive, HRC).

17. See excerpt from letter, SJ to Hilton Brown, in BBC internal memo, 1.27.41 (BBC Written Archives, Caversham).

18. See internal memo, Hilton Brown to Mr. Salmon, 1.27.41 (File R Cont I Scriptwriters: Jameson, S, 1941–61, BBC Written Archives, Caversham).

19. Val Gielgud to Nancy Pearn, 1.28.42 (BBC Written Archives, Caversham).

20. SJ to Gielgud, 1.30.42.

21. Memo re: political clearance, 2.7.42 (BBC Written Archives, Caversham: File R Cont I Scriptwriters: Jameson. S. 1941–61).

22. Play, *The Fort*, adapted by Barbara Burnham, BBC Home Service, 10:30 p.m., Saturday, May 9, 1942 (BBC Written Archives).

23. Quoted in *Portmeirion: The Portmeirion Guidebook* (Portmeirion, 1983), 3.

24. See Free German League of Culture archive (LSE archive); SJ to HO, 6.15.42.

25. PEN to SJ, 6.25.42 (PEN: Letters, HRC).

26. SJ, "Introduction, or Ninety Times as High as the Moon," in SJ, ed., *London Calling* (*LC*; 1942), 1–17.

27. Brittain, *Wartime Chronicle*, entry for July 7, 1942, 160. Fortunately, Vera kept copies of Margaret's letters, so that the correspondence has survived.

28. Dorothy Sayers to SJ, 7.18.42 (PEN archive, HRC).

29. See *Author* 3, no. 3 (Spring 1942); SJ to Unwin, 7.19.19, AUC 141–3.

30. SJ, chairman's speech, 7.29.42 (LSE archive).

31. Report on Annual General Meeting, *Author*, Aug. 12, 1942.

32. SJ to HO, 8.26.42, re: payment for second broadcast; Jameson to Gielgud, 8.6.42 (BBC Written Archives, Caversham: File R Cont I Scriptwriters: Jameson S. 1941–6); Gielgud recommended *How to Write Broadcast Plays* (London: Hurst and Blackett).

33. PEN Exec. Committee minutes, 8.5.42 (PEN archive, HRC); SJ to HO, 8.10.42.

34. Lutz Weltmann to SJ, 8.24.42 (PEN Refugee Writers' Bureau: Letters — Box W-Z, Wa-Wh file, HRC).

35. SJ to Barbara Burnham, 10.23.42 (BBC Written Archives).

36. Neumann, *Scene in Passing* (1942). Report in *Bookseller*, June 4, 1942.

37. For review of *TWSHS*, see anon. (R. D. Charques), *TLS*, Oct. 31, 1942, one of the least dismissive.

38. Philip Toynbee, review of *TWSHS*, *New Statesman and Nation*, n.s., 24 (Nov. 28, 1942). By contrast see "Speaking of Books," *New York Times Book Review* 6, no. 2 (Oct. 25, 1942).

39. See obituary for William Jameson, under Local and District News, in *Whitby Gazette*, Nov. 20, 1942.

40. See SJ, letter headed "Planning for Publishing," *TLS*, Dec. 5, 1942; Unwin to SJ, 12.7.42, 12.16.42; SJ to Unwin, 12.10.42, 12.13.42 (Reading); see also *Author*, Winter 1942.

Chapter 19

1. *JN*, 2:129–31; SJ to LH, 12.11.42.

2. See HO to SJ, 1.8.43, enclosing Gollancz pamphlet *Let My People Go: Some Practical Proposals for Dealing with Hitler's Massacre of the Jews and an Appeal to the British Public*. This enclosure lost.

3. For Guadella's apology, see HO to SJ, 1.23.43.

4. SJ, "The Last Night," *Saturday Evening Post*, Jan. 30, 1943; *Argosy* (UK), Feb. 1944; reprinted in *Lidice: A Tribute by Members of the International PEN* (1944), with introduction by Harold Nicolson, 50–84; and in *Saturday Evening Post Stories 1942–1945* (n.d.), 3–30.

5. Introduction, "Writer and War Worker," to SJ's tale "The Last Night," *Saturday Evening Post*, Jan. 30, 1943.

6. GC to LD, 2.13.43 (British Library: Macmillan Jameson files).

7. See Fisher, *Cyril Connolly: A Nostalgic Life*, 232–34.

8. See SJ to Swinnerton, 3.29.43 (MS S3w62, Special Collections, University of Arkansas Libraries); SJ to de la Mare, 3.29.43 (Bodley).

9. *Bookseller*, Feb. 11, 1943.

10. SJ, *Cloudless May* (*CM*; 1943).

11. The disclaimer appears on the verso of the dedication page. See for some source material, Koestler, *Scum of the Earth*, and Bois, *Truth on the Tragedy of France*.

12. Commager, letter, *New York Times Book Review*, April 4, 1971.

13. See Smernoff, *André Chenier*.

14. SJ, "The Young Prisoner" ("YP"), in *Modern Reading*, no. 9 (1944): 111–26.

15. See Crick, ed., *George Orwell: Nineteen Eighty-Four*.

16. See Koestler, "The Fraternity of Pessimists," in *The Yogi and the Commissar and Other Essays*, 106–12.

17. SJ, "For Olaf Stapledon," MSS with author's corrections [1943] (PEN Misc Storm Jameson [Fundamental Values], HRC).

18. *William the Defeated*, broadcast July 5, 1943 (BBC Written Archives, Caversham: File R Cont I Scriptwriters: Jameson, S. 1941–61). No transcript of the actual script survives in the BBC archives.

19. See SJ to Miss Burnham, 3.11.43, 3.18.43.

20. For SJ's play text, "William the Defeated," see Ould, ed., *The Book of the P.E.N.*, 187–230. How far this is her own early version or the actual broadcast text is uncertain.

21. HO to SJ, 7.6.43; Herbert Farjeon, review, *Listener*, July 15, 1943.

22. SJ, contribution to "Reviewing Reviewed" symposium, *Author* (Summer 1943): 68–69.

23. SJ, "Should the Enemy Be Punished after the War Is Over?" *Aryan Path* (Bombay) 14, no. 9 (Sept. 1943): 388–90.

24. In this Margaret was ahead of many at the time. See MacMillan, *Peacemakers*.

25. See Macmillan Jameson files, uncatalogued: Sales and profits on SJ's books, British Library.

26. See announcement of *CM*, *Author* 53, no. 4 (Summer 1943): 17, ad for Macmillan. For reviews, see anon. (R. D. Charques), *TLS*, Sept. 9, 1943; Kate O'Brien, *Spectator*, Oct. 15, 1943; Marie Scott James, *Time and Tide*, Oct. 23, 1943.

27. University of Leeds Archive, Personalia (PER/070 [Jameson doc], Letters, 6.30.43; 7.21.43).

28. Bonamy Dobrée, eulogy for SJ (Brotherton: Dobrée file, MS 408/394).

29. *Whitby Gazette*, Oct. 29, 1943; anon. (R. D. Charques), second leader: "Storm Jameson," *TLS*, Oct. 30, 1943.

30. Koestler, "The French 'Flu,'" in *Tribune*, Nov. 1943, reprinted in *Yogi and Commissar*, 21–27.

31. Morrison was Home Secretary.

32. *Bulletin de la Chambre de Commerce Française de Grand-Bretagne*, Jan. 1944 (CSC archive), 617–21. Headed "Déjeuner Mensuel" (transcript of speech given Dec. 14, 1943).

Chapter 20

1. SJ to Tom Moult, 11.1.39 (Brotherton Library, University of Leeds, Moult file).

2. Harold was the director who was overseeing her at this time.

3. SJ, *The Journal of Mary Hervey Russell* (*JMHR*; 1945), 14.

4. SJ to HO, 4.8.44, from nursing home, although the letter gives her friend Wyn Griffith's address.

5. In Macmillan Archive Box 87, SJ gave her postal address for May 1944 as the Dobrées in Collingham Leeds.

6. SJ, "Cloud Form," in *TLS*, July 29, 1944, 370.

7. SJ, preface to Maria Kuncewiczowa, *The Stranger*, translated by B. W. A. Massey (1944); reprinted in *The Writer's Situation* (1950), 118–25 — dated June 1944, with quite a few alterations.

8. See Ould, ed., *Freedom of Expression: A Symposium* (c. 1945, date suggested in British Library as most likely).

9. Anon., leading article, "Paris," *TLS*, Aug. 26, 1944; reprinted in *The Writer's Situation* (1950): 114–17.

10. The article sent was G. Turquet-Milnes, "Midnight Books," *Time and Tide*, Oct. 21, 1944.

11. See archive of the former Society for Cultural Relations between the Peoples of the British Commonwealth and the Union of Soviet Socialist Republics (SCR), now Society for Co-operation in Russian and Soviet Studies (SCRSS), 320 Brixton Road, London SW9 6AB.

Chapter 21

1. In scraper board or scratch board, sharp knives and other tools etch on China clay with black ink.

2. For reviews of *JMHR*, see *Listener*, May 17, 1945; *TLS*, May 5, 1945; *Time and Tide*, June 2, 1945.

3. Edith Sitwell to SJ, 5.25.45; R. H. Tawney to SJ, 5.16.45; see also Osbert Sitwell to SJ, 5.17.45 (CSC archive).

4. See the *Whitby Gazette* announcement of Guy's appointment, July 27, 1945.

5. Macmillan archive, Box 87, Reading: SJ from 7.31.45 at Masunga, Wellington Avenue, Virginia Water.

6. SJ, letter to *Manchester Guardian*, Aug. 13, 1945.

7. Diary of Polish visit. In later life, SJ sent this diary to Dr. Hey (Churchill Archive JMON2) with a covering letter dated only August 3 from her Cambridge address. In her letter SJ says she does not want the notes back. Hey gave the diary to the archive on 11.12.75. Unless otherwise specified, all quotations in this paragraph and the next are from this document.

8. SJ, "The Situation of the Writer," lecture delivered in May 1947 at Lyceum Club, printed as "The Writer's Situation" in *The Writer's Situation* (TWS; 1950), 1–36; the quotation is from pp. 23–24.

9. SJ, *Before the Crossing* (BTC; 1947), 1.

10. JN/TMS 3:62 (198 in published version), HRC.

11. Note there are very blotchy notes in biro of the Czech visit in the Liddell Hart archive — borrowed by LH but never returned.

12. See also *Guardian*, May 17, 2005, re: statue of Beneš erected on May 16, 2005, and German protests.

Chapter 22

1. See Glendinning, *Rebecca West: A Life*. See also Lyndsey Stonebridge's admirable work *The Judicial Imagination: Writing after Nuremberg*.

2. SJ, "Poland," *Fortnightly Review* 165 (Jan. 1946): 28–34. See also "Poland 1945," in *The Windmill*, edited by Reginald Moore and Edward Lane (1946), 1: 127–32.

3. SJ, "The New Czechoslovakia," *Fortnightly Review* 165 (Feb. 1946): 73–80.

4. Knut Hamsun (1859–1952), the Norwegian writer who received the Nobel Prize for Literature in 1920, was accused of collaboration, tried, and fined in 1947. Ezra Pound suffered more severely, first caged and then held in a psychiatric hospital for twelve years.

5. LD to Latham, 1.26.46 (British Library: Macmillan files: American 40: May 16 1945–May 3 1946).

6. For reviews of *The Other Side*, see *TLS*, March 23, 1946; *Time and Tide*, March 23, 1946; *Commonweal*, April 5, 1946.

7. See Macmillan archive, Box 87, Reading.

8. Review of Ronald Millar's play adaptation of SJ's *The Other Side*, *Times*, Aug. 9, 1946.

9. See the uncataloged second typed manuscript of *JN* in HRC (hereafter cited as *JN*/TMS/UNCAT), 3:208.

10. SJ, "Background to Black Laurel" (A4 typescript, written Feb. 1948; British Library: Macmillan archive, 73144 unbound).

11. See Wakeford to Chapman, 4.7.46 (ADP archive).

12. SJ, *The Black Laurel* (*BL*; 1947).

13. See, for instance, Judt, *Postwar* and *Reappraisals*; Tooze, *The Wages of Destruction*; Usandizaga and Monnickendam, *Back to Peace: Reconciliation and Retribution in the Postwar Period*; Mazower, *Dark Continent: Europe's Twentieth Century*.

14. SJ, "The Situation of the Writer To-day," delivered May 1947 at the Lyceum Club, printed in *Humanitas* 2, no. 2 (Winter 1948): citations are to the reprint (as "The Writer's Situation") in *The Writer's Situation* (*TWS*; 1950): 1–36. This is probably the same lecture she would give in Zurich on 6.2.1947.

15. Review of *BTC*, anon. (Mrs. Michael Roberts [Janet Buchanan Adam Smith]), *TLS*, May 10, 1947.

16. Note in copy of *JN*, vol. 2 (CSC archive).

17. SJ, introduction to Eugenia Kocwa, "On the Sands of Mecklenburg," *Adelphi*, n.s., 23, no. 3 (April–June 1947): 127–35 (introduction on pp. 127–28).

18. One of the striking features of this account is the insistence on forgiveness as the only way of dealing with such appalling brutalities. This is by no means a usual reaction from Holocaust survivors, yet Margaret met with it two or three times.

19. Macmillan archive, Box 87, Reading: SJ letters from July 10 to August 6 at Budock Vean hotel, Falmouth, Cornwall.

20. St. Tolwinski, president of the city of Warsaw, to SJ, 10.6.47 (CSC archive); Naczelna Rada Odbudowy m.st. Warszawy, Komitet Wykonawczy, to SJ, 10.8.47 (CSC archive).

21. SJ, letter to *Times*, Sept. 24, 1947.

22. SJ, letter to *Whitby Gazette*, Oct. 10, 1947.

23. Report on Councillor K. McNeil's speech, "Local Jottings by 'Tattler,'" *Whitby Gazette*, Oct. 31, 1947.

24. SJ, *Moment of Truth*, as three-act play, with all titles. First draft, 94 pp., then full script, 203 pp. (Jameson, Storm Works, HRC). Published in novel form, 1949.

25. SJ, "W. H. Auden: The Poet of Angst," *Gate*, Nov. 1947; citations are from the reprint in *The Writer's Situation* (*TWS*; 1950), 83–101.

26. Auden and Isherwood, *Journey to a War* (1939).

27. See JN/TMS/UNCAT, 3:78–80 (210 in published version). Much of this is cut in the published version.

28. SJ, "The Last Night," in *Saturday Evening Post Stories 1942–45*, introduction by Benn Hibbs (undated): 3–30. This collection was made up of twenty-five stories chosen from eight hundred stories in the journal.

29. SJ to Jeanette Tawney, 1.20.48 (LSE: Tawney Archive, 24/2). Ferry pilots took aircraft from manufacturers to airfields, or from airfield to airfield during the war.

30. See, for instance, *Here Comes a Candle* and *The Lovely Ship* (Cassell's Pocket Library, 2nd ed., 1947).

31. The bust is now in Brotherton Library, University of Leeds; the National Portrait Gallery has the photograph; JN, 2:210.

32. SJ to LD, 2.24.47 [*sic*] for 48, according to stamped date of reception (British Library: Macmillan archive AD73144, unbound).

33. See British Library: Macmillan Jameson files, uncataloged: Sales and Profits on Storm Jameson's novels.

34. For reviews of *BL*, see anon., *TLS*, March 6, 1948, 133; Tullis Clare, *Time and Tide*, March 20, 1948; L. A. G. Strong, *Spectator*, March 26, 1948; V. S. Pritchett, in Feb. 1948 issue of *Bookman* (Book Society News).

35. SJ, *The Moment of Truth* (1949). Note that the dates at the end of the text of the novel, Oct. 1947–Feb. 1948, are those of the play, not the novel.

36. SJ to HO, undated, but content shows it was written in reply to his letter of 5.6.48.

37. SJ to LD, 7.14.47 [*sic*], but she may mean 48.

38. Not as in *JN*, 2:212, Toni and Gustav, as Gustav was already dead.

39. Stanton C. Crawford to SJ, 7.30.48 (Crawford archive, Lilly Library, Indiana University).

40. SJ to Ruth Crawford (hereafter cited as RC), 8.8.62 (Crawford archive, Lilly Library, Indiana University).

41. SJ to Betty Leake, 10.8.48 (CSC archive).

42. SJ, "Edvard Beneš," *Fortnightly Review* 70 (Oct. 1948): 247–51.

43. Quoted in MacKillop, *F. R. Leavis*, 222.

44. SJ, "Talk to Czechoslovak Room Committee, University of Pittsburgh, Masaryk Birthday Commemoration, 7 March 1949" (Manuscripts Dept., Lilly Library, Indiana University).

45. SJ, "Why I Can't Write about America," *New York Times Magazine* 6 (March 27, 1949): 15; reprinted in *Fortnightly Review* 172 (Dec. 1949): 381–85, and in *Reader's Digest* 58 (May 1951): 119–22. Citations are to the *Fortnightly Review* printing.

46. SJ to HO, 6.19.49 (wrongly dated July).

47. SJ to Orwell, 7.1.49 (Orwell archive, UCL).

48. SJ to HO, 6.19.49 (wrongly dated July). Ida Wylie was I. A. R. Wylie, Australian-born, 1885–1959.

49. Reviews of *Moment of Truth*: Elizabeth Bowen, *Tatler*, July 1949; R. D. Charques, *Spectator*, June 24, 1949; anon., *TLS*, July 8, 1949; Tullis Clare, *Time and Tide*, July 16, 1949; J. D. Scott, *New Statesman and Nation*, July 8, 1949; see also Vernon Fane, *Sphere*, July 1949.

50. British *Who's Who* for 1949, quoting from "Twentieth Century Writers."

51. See Słonimski to HO, 8.16.49 (PEN Refugee Writers' Bureau: Letters — Sm-Sz file, HRC).

52. In the TMS of *JN*, 3:123, SJ claimed to have written a twelve-thousand-word story in the wake of this blow, based on a story she saw in a Pittsburgh newspaper. This could be either "This Is It" or the longer "The Commonplace Heart."

Chapter 23

1. SJ, "The Form of the Novel," in *The Writer's Situation* (TWS; 1950), 37–61. Written Oct.–Nov. 1949.

2. See LD to Michael Hillary, 3.23.10 (British Library: Macmillan files: Storm Jameson); see these files also for Bill's curriculum vitae.

3. The choice of title may well have been suggested by the collections of essays by Jean-Paul Sartre: *Situations I* (*Critiques Littéraires*), *Situations II*, and *Situations III*, published in 1947, 1948, and 1949.

4. For reviews of *TWS*, see, e.g., *TLS*, Aug. 18, 1950; *Listener*, Sept. 28, 1950; *Adelphi*, n.s., Nov. 1950; *New Statesman and Nation*, Nov. 25, 1950.

5. Donald Stephenson to SJ, 8.3.50 (BBC Written Archives, Caversham).

6. Letter from SJ and others, *TLS*, Dec. 29, 1950.

7. See announcement of the year's winners, the Pickering Women's Institute Players, in *Whitby Gazette*, Feb. 9, 1951.

8. ADP to SJ, 2.13.51; SJ to ADP, 2.14.51.

9. See Judt, *Reappraisals*, 376.

10. SJ to Czesław Miłosz (hereafter cited as CM), 2.7.51 (Czesław Miłosz Papers, General Collection, Beinecke Rare Books and Manuscript Library, Yale University).

11. SJ to CM, 1.19.51 [*sic*] but must be February from content.

12. SJ, "British Literature: Survey and Critique," first item in "Books and Their Makers" section, *Saturday Review of Literature* (New York) 34 (Oct. 13, 1951): 24–26, 47.

13. SJ, *The Green Man* (1952), 320.

14. LD to Bayliss, memo on *Green Man*.

15. LD to Daniel and Harold Macmillan, memo; see also Bayliss's Reader's Report on *Green Man* (British Library: Macmillan files uncat.: Storm Jameson).

16. See, for comparison, Storm Jameson: Books and Earnings (i.e., the publisher's profits): 1939–40, *Europe to Let*, £279.17.9; 1943–44, *Cloudless May*, £4440.12.3; 1944–45, *Journal*, £1821.11.1; 1945–46, *Other Side*, £2514.2.10; 1946–47, *Before the Crossing*, £1596.1.1; 1947–48, *Black Laurel*, £1583.10.2; 1948–49, *Moment of Truth*, £749.12.3 (British Library: Macmillan files uncat., Storm Jameson).

17. SJ, foreword, *The Diary of Anne Frank* (DAF; 1954), 5–11.

Chapter 24

1. Amabel and Clough Williams-Ellis, *Headlong down the Years* (1951).

2. See Williams-Ellis, *All Stracheys Are Cousins*, 178.

3. SJ, letter to *Times*, Sept. 26, 1951.

4. *Hermon Ould: A Tribute by Various Authors* (n.d.), with contribution by SJ, "In Memory of Hermon Ould."

5. SJ to Farjeon, 10.7.51 (British Library, Farjeon archive ADD 83146, unbound).

6. BBC Writers' File: Storm Jameson, T48/341/1, 8.20.51; Val Gielgud letter, 8.8.51 (BBC Written Archives, Caversham: File R Cont I Scriptwriters: Jameson. S, 1941–61).

7. See West, *The Meaning of Treason*.

8. See note, 2.21.52 (BBC Written Archives, Caversham: File Record: Copyright,

Jameson S, 1950–54); BBC Archive information for 5.4.52, on "I'm Proud of My Father"; *JN*, 2:262. No information on this play other than Margaret's comment and the BBC note has been found.

9. See SJ to Daniel Macmillan, 6.5.52, 6.7.52, 6.19.52 (British Library: Macmillan files).

10. SJ, "The Gamble," MS in notebook with ex libris inscription: "This book belongs to William Storm Clark" (Jameson, Storm: Works, HRC).

11. Forum reply to C. P. Snow, "The Ugliest Trend," *Author* 52, no. 4 (Summer 1952): 83–89.

12. For reviews of *Green Man*, see R. D. Charques, *Spectator,* July 11, 1952; John Mortimer, *New Statesman and Nation,* July 19, 1952; Marghanita Laski, *Observer,* July 13, 1952; Tullis Clare, *Time and Tide,* Aug. 2, 1952; anon., *TLS,* Aug. 1, 1952.

13. See Sir Basil Bartlett to SJ, 10.9.52; SJ to Sir Basil, 10.16.52 (BBC Written Archives, File 28/114, TV Scriptwriters: Jameson, S. File I, 1952–53).

14. See Sir Basil Bartlett, memo, 12.9.52 (BBC Written Archives).

15. Note re: "The Commonplace Heart" and (for "This Is It") report, 2.19.53 (BBC Written Archives: File 28/114 TV Scriptwriters: Jameson. S, File 1, 1952–53).

16. See SJ to LH, 1.14.52 [*sic*] for 53 (from internal evidence).

17. Review of *Green Man*, Margaret Parton, *New York Herald Tribune*, March 5, 1953.

18. See also *JN/TMS*, 3:157 for fuller account.

19. Koestler archive (2399/2): full correspondence involving SJ, Mamaine Koestler, David Carver, and Arthur Koestler. See also *JN/TMS* cut passage, 2:135.

20. SJ, *The Hidden River* (THR; 1955).

21. SJ, "The House of Hate," serialized in *Saturday Evening Post*, Oct. 16, 23, 30, and Nov. 6, 13, 20, 1954.

22. See Carl Brandt to ADP, 1.7.54; SJ to ADP, 1.11.54; ADP to LD, 1.12.54 (ADP archive, HRC).

23. SJ to John Montgomery (hereafter cited as JM) for ADP, 2.6.54.

24. See SJ to LD, 3.3.54; see also Macmillan archive, Box 87, Reading, for March 10, 1954.

Chapter 25

1. For dates, see Macmillan archive, Box 87, Reading; also ADP correspondence files for August 1954, HRC.

2. Excerpt from Lionel Brett's autobiography, "Our Selves Unknown" (1985) (CSC archive).

3. *Author* 54, no. 4 (Summer 1954): 76–79.

4. SJ, "A Note on France," *Cornhill Magazine* 167, no. 1001 (1954–55): 439–52.

5. SJ, "The Dualist Tradition," *TLS*, Aug. 6, 1954.

6. SJ, introductory talk before readings from *The PEN in Exile*, Nov. 24, 1954 (BBC Sound Archive, T2587WR, British Library).

7. See, for instance, SJ to VB, 12.20.54.

8. See ADP archive, Aug. 1954–Dec. 1954, HRC.

9. For reviews of *Hidden River*, see, for instance, anon. (Eric de Mauny), *TLS*, Jan. 21, 1955; anon., *Times*, Jan. 22, 1955.

10. SJ, *The Intruder* (TI; 1956).

11. See West, *The Meaning of Treason* (1949) and *A Train of Powder* (1955); and see, for instance, Murdoch, *Existentialists and Mystics: Writings on Philosophy and Literature*.

12. See also SJ to JM, 2.9.56, where the proposed title is "Somewhere to Live."

13. See note on *The Hidden River*, 1.20.56 (British Library: Macmillan files: Storm Jameson).

14. Clarke to David Carver (hereafter cited as DC), sent 1.20.56.

15. See Macmillan archive, Box 87, Reading: Storm Jameson.

16. For reviews of *TI*, see anon., *Times*, Oct. 11, 1956; anon., *TLS*, Oct. 19, 1956; Isabel Quigly, *Spectator*, Oct. 19, 1956; Reginald Moore, *Time and Tide*, Nov. 3, 1956.

17. SJ to Mrs. Walmsley, 11.23.56 (Koestler archive).

18. SJ, *A Cup of Tea for Mr. Thorgill* (*CTT*; 1957). It was ironic that this was the first book of Margaret's that Alan Maclean handled, as he was the brother of Donald Maclean, the spy who had defected with Burgess to the USSR. His defection had ended his brother's career in the Foreign Office. Future references to Alan Maclean will be cited as AM.

19. See SJ to Coogan-Nielson, 1.16.57 (ADP archive, HRC).

20. *New York Times* review of Goetz adaptation of *Hidden River*, Jan. 5, 1957; Noel Coward, *Blithe Spirit*, first acted in 1941.

21. See Penguin to Stephens, 5.28.57; AM to JM, 5.31.57.

22. SJ, *A Ulysses Too Many* (1958).

23. For reviews of *CTT*, see, for instance, Tom Hopkinson, *Observer*, Nov. 17, 1957; anon., *Times*, Nov. 14, 1957; David Tyler-Wright, *TLS*, Nov. 15, 1957; L. P. Hartley, *Spectator*, Nov. 22, 1957; G. S. Fraser, *New Statesman and Nation*, Nov. 30, 1957; Elizabeth Bowen, *Tatler*, Dec. 11, 1957); Fred Urquhart, *Time and Tide*, Dec. 14, 1957; and see Gerald Weales, *Commonweal* (U.S.), Dec. 20, 1957, for an unusually hostile review for journals in the States.

Chapter 26

1. See Clark, *Second Wind: The Story of the Campaign and the Committee of 100*; see also Taylor, *Against the Bomb: The British Peace Movement, 1958–1965*.

2. Information supplied by Alison Cullingford, archivist, University of Bradford.

3. SJ to Mrs. Priestley (Jacquetta Hawkes, hereafter cited as JH), 2.4.58; see also list of letters sent and responses (Jacquetta Hawkes archive, University of Bradford, Special Collections).

4. This film was *The Inn of the Sixth Happiness*.

5. For reviews of *A Ulysses Too Many*, see anon., *Times*, Oct. 2, 1958; anon. (David Tyler-Wright), *TLS*, Oct. 17, 1958. See also *Observer*, Nov. 17, 1958; L. P. Hartley, *Spectator*, Nov. 24, 1958; *Time and Tide*, Dec. 14, 1958.

6. See letters between ADP and SJ from April to July 1958.

7. Associated Rediffusion to SJ, 5.29.58, 10.31.58; SJ in reply, 11.1.58 (ADP archive).

8. See Harold Freedman (from Brandt) to SJ, 11.10.58; SJ to ADP, 11.25.58 (ADP archive).

9. See paper "From the Campaign for Nuclear Disarmament," not for publication before 5:30 p.m. Dec. 10, 1958 (Jacquetta Hawkes archive, University of Bradford, Special Collections).

10. SJ, "The Friendly One," *Winter's Tales* 5 (1959): 181–215.

11. Rebecca West to SJ, 1.2.59 (CSC archive).

12. Harold Freedman (for Brandt), 1.28.59 (ADP archive, HRC).

13. See program for *The Hidden River*, also copy of review, *Evening Argos* (Brighton), March 10, 1959, in ADP archive.

14. See undated note in ADP correspondence files, Jan. 1958–April 1959; anon., "Battle of Wits Too Pat," review of *The Face of Treason*, *Times*, March 11, 1959.

15. Review of Goetz adaptation of *Hidden River*, anon., "Plausibility Sacrificed," *Times*, April 14, 1959; and see, for example, anon., "This Brand of Hate Is Musty," *Evening Standard*, April 14, 1959; anon. (Philip Hope Wallace), *Guardian*, April 15, 1959.

16. SJ, "Can It Be Done? The Case for Providence," in "British Books around the World" section, *TLS*, Aug. 7, 1959, Axxviii.

17. For reviews of *A Day Off: Two Novels and Some Stories* (1959), see anon. (Marigold Hunt [Mrs. Marigold Johnson]), *TLS*, Oct. 16, 1959; and see, the following year, C. Chaumel's excellent review in *Études anglaises* 13 (1960).

18. SJ, *Last Score; or, The Private Life of Sir Richard Ormston* (1961), 4.

19. Letter re: Luis Goytisolo, *Times*, March 1, 1960.

20. See Josephine Pullein-Thompson, "Standing Aside from Politics," *The PEN Broadsheet of the English Centre of International PEN*, no. 19 (Autumn 1985).

Chapter 27

1. SJ, column in *Sunday Times*, April 3, 1960 (see GC on Stanley Unwin's autobiography in the same issue).

2. SJ, columns in *Sunday Times*, May 1 and 29, 1960.

3. SJ, columns in *Sunday Times*, June 26, July 10, July 24, and Aug. 7, 1960.

4. SJ to Mrs. Smallwood, 6.21.60 (Chatto and Windus archive, University of Reading Archives).

5. See, e.g., *Times* review of SJ, *Morley Roberts: The Last Eminent Victorian*, Oct. 5, 1961.

6. SJ to Emrys Williams, 8.13.60 (Penguin archive, University of Bristol, University Library: Special Collections).

7. See Rubinstein/SJ correspondence, Aug.–Oct. 1960 (Penguin archive).

8. See Macmillan archive, Box 87, Reading; SJ had made a passing reference to "the bungalow project" in her letter to DC, 6.10.60.

9. See John Osborne's play *Look Back in Anger*, first performed in 1956.

10. SJ, *The Lion and the Dagger*, serialization of *Last Score* in *Saturday Evening Post*, April 8, 15, and 22, 1961.

11. For reviews of *Last Score*, see anon., *Times*, May 4, 1961; Marigold Hunt, *TLS*, May 19, 1961; Gillian Tindall, *Time and Tide*, May 18, 1961; see also, for instance, *Evening Standard*, May 9, 1961, and George Steiner's long comment in a cut passage of *JN/TMS*, 2:262 (365).

12. SJ to Phyllis Bottome, 1.2.61 (British Library, Phyllis Bottome Correspondence, Add.Ms. 78861, f.58.).

13. For reviews of *The Road from the Monument*, see *Sunday Telegraph*, Jan. 21, 1962, and *Sunday Times* (Jeremy Brooks), Jan. 21, 1962; *Times*, Jan. 25, 1962; *Daily Telegraph*, Jan. 26, 1962; Marigold Hunt, *TLS*, Jan. 26, 1962; Julian Mitchell, *Spectator*, Jan. 26, 1962; Robert Taubmann, *New Statesman and Nation*, Jan. 26, 1962.

14. See BK to SJ, 11.12.62; SJ to BK, 11.17.62; BK to SJ, 11.20.62; SJ to BK, 11.28.62; BK to SJ, 12.4.62, 1.29.63; SJ to BK, 2.1.63 (Knopf archive).

15. Memos re: Panther and *A Month Soon Goes* (ADP archive, 1963).

16. See Carol Brandt to ADP, 6.20.63.

17. See SJ to AK, 8.7.63; SJ to RC, 9.7.63 re: query from Pittsburgh about printing "Amica America"; SJ to ADP, 9.11.63; SJ to RC, 10.26.63; RC to SJ, 11.1.63; SJ to RC, 11.13.63.

18. See SJ to ADP, 10.22.63, 10.23.63; SJ to Schwartz, 11.24.63; Schwartz to ADP, 11.1.63; Schwartz to SJ, 11.14.63 (ADP archive).

19. For reviews of *The Aristide Case* (*The Blind Heart*), see anon., *Times*, May 14, 1964; anon. (Ann Wordsworth), *TLS*, May 28, 1964.

20. Convocation of University of Leeds: Standing Committee minutes (Leeds Brotherton Library).

Chapter 28

1. SJ to RC, undated; see also this information in SJ to DC, 2.5.65 (PEN archive).

2. Convocation of University of Leeds: Standing Committee minutes; SJ, "The Writer in Contemporary Society," *American Scholar* 35 (Winter 1965–66): 67–77, with some revision from speech to article form.

3. See Convocation of the University of Leeds: Standing Committee minutes, 10.25.65.

4. See SJ to LH, 4.28.65 [*sic*] for June.

5. SJ, "Love's Labours Exposed," *Spectator*, Feb. 4, 1966.

6. See, for instance, Lessing, *The Four-Gated City*.

7. SJ, *The Early Life of Stephen Hind* (*ELSH*; 1966).

8. For reviews of *ELSH*, see, for instance, anon. (Marigold Johnson), "Somebody Up There Likes Me," *TLS*, June 9, 1966.

9. Margaret Lane to SJ, 6.15.66 (CSC archive).

10. See Glendinning, *Rebecca West: A Life*, 230–31.

11. SJ, *The White Crow* (*WC*; 1968).

12. Douglas Allen, TV Script Unit reader's report, 12.11.68 (BBC Written Archives).

13. TMS of *JN*, sent to HRC in exchange for MS of *A Passionate Prodigality*, 1975 (Jameson, Storm: Works).

14. Hepworth, *A Pictorial Autobiography*, 93.

Chapter 29

1. See SJ to Jane Lidderdale, 8.29.69 (London Metropolitan University: Women's Library); GC to KLH, 9.2.69.

2. For reviews of the first volume of *JN*, see, e.g., Ray Gosling, *Times Saturday Review*, Sept. 6, 1969; Alice Hope, interview with SJ, "The Household Gods Couldn't Keep Up with Storm Jameson," *Daily Telegraph*, Sept. 9, 1969; Arthur Calder-Marshall, "The Need to Be Uprooted," *TLS*, Oct. 2, 1969. Reviews also appeared in *New Statesman and Nation*, Oct. 3, 1969; *Irish Independent*, Oct. 18, 1969; *Spectator*, Oct. 25, 1969.

3. See, e.g., SJ to Mr. Wadsworth, 9.16.69 (SJ correspondence, Dept. of Special Collections, McFarlin Library, University of Tulsa).

4. SJ, letter of 12.29.69 to *Adam International Review*, ed. Miron Grindea, nos. 328–30 (1969): 51.

5. For reviews of the second volume of *JN*, see, e.g., anon. (Arthur Calder Marshall), *TLS*, March 12, 1970; Ray Gosling, *Times Saturday Review*, March 14, 1970.

6. Jack Singleton recorded interview with SJ, broadcast March 3, 1970, in "Home This Afternoon" series (British Library: Sound Archive, ILP 195571); Jeanine McMullen recorded interview with SJ, broadcast March 4, 1970, in "Books and Writers" series (British Library: Sound Archive, ILP 196495).

7. SJ, "Now and Then," in "Writing in the Seventies" series, no. 5, *Author* 81, no. 2 (Summer 1970): 59–63. Also published in Richard Findlater, ed., *Author! Author!* (1970); and as "What to Do till the Novel Comes," *Writer* (Boston) 84 (April 1971): 14–15.

8. See Loseff, *On the Beneficence of Censorship*.

9. SJ, *Parthian Words* (*PW*; 1970).

10. For reviews of *PW*, see, e.g., Paul Bailey, *Observer*, Sept. 13, 1970; anon. (Bernard Bergonzi), *TLS*, Sept. 25, 1970.

11. GC, *Contemporary Review*, Jan. 1971.

12. See Doreen Marston to A. Knopf, 1.10.71 (Knopf archive, HRC).

13. Spender, review of *JN*, *New York Times Book Review*, March 7, 1971.

14. Commager, letter in *New York Times Book Review*, April 4, 1971.

15. Spender, letter in *New York Times Book Review*, April 25, 1971.

16. SJ, *There Will Be a Short Interval* (*TWSI*; 1973).

Chapter 30

1. See Doreen [Marston] to JM, 3.26.12 (British Library: Macmillan LB).

2. See SJ to Bonamy Dobrée (hereafter cited as BD), 7.10.72, 7.13.72, 9.24.72; BD to SJ, 8.19.72, 9.13.72.

3. See SJ to the Dobrées' daughter, Georgina, who was her goddaughter, 1.2.75 (Brotherton).

4. For reviews of *TWSI*, see Auberon Waugh, "A Congenial Despair," *Spectator*, Dec. 16, 1972; and see, e.g., Phillippa Toomey, *Times*, Jan. 4, 1973; and a superficial review: anon., "Heroically Fatuous," *TLS*, Jan. 5, 1973.

5. See AM's draft to SJ, 2.2.73; with note saying "not sent."

6. See Hastings, *Rosamond Lehmann*.

7. SJ to RL, 1.7.74 (King's College archives).

8. Lessing, *A Small Personal Voice*.

9. See memo re: terms for television adaptation of *ELSH* (BBC Written Archives).

10. See SJ to Mary Brash (for Gollancz), 1.10.75, 1.14.75, 1.21.75; Brash to SJ, 1.20.75; Livia Gollancz (hereafter cited as LG) to SJ, 2.3.75 (Orion Publishing Group: Gollancz archive: file on SJ, Speaking of Stendhal).

11. See dedication in Nott, *An Elderly Retired Man*: "To Margaret Storm Jameson, in love and admiration."

12. See Francis King to SJ, 5.13.[no year given], CSC archive; see also SJ, letter re: Sir William Haley's review, *TLS*, Aug. 1, 1975, and his letter to her, 8.7.75 (CSC archive).

13. SJ to Marjorie Watts (hereafter cited as MW), 6.3.75 (SJ correspondence, Dept. of Special Collections, McFarlin Library, University of Tulsa).

14. SJ to Stephen Roskill, 10.2.75; and see 10.8.75.

15. See also SJ to Sir William Hawthorne, 10.23.75 (Churchill, Chapman archive).

16. Dr. Hey's gift of SJ's diary of the Polish visit, given Nov. 12, 1975 (Churchill archive, JMON2).

17. At the time of writing, this second version was uncataloged.

18. SJ, letter, *Times*, Jan. 3, 1976.

19. Watts, *Mrs. Sappho.*

20. SJ, *Speaking of Stendhal* (SS; 1979).

21. See memo on SJ's *Speaking of Stendhal* (British Library: Macmillan archive).

22. See Donald Hall to SJ, 9.3.77 (CSC archive); see also Lionel Brett's autobiography, *Our Selves Unknown.*

23. See also memo: LG to SJ (Orion Publishing Group: Gollancz Archive: file Storm Jameson).

24. See readers' reports on *Speaking of Stendhal* (Orion Publishing Group: Gollancz Archive).

25. See Harrison Salisbury to SJ, 5.4.78 (CSC archive): Hoppé Exhibition at the National Portrait Gallery, June 30 to December 3, 1978.

26. See LG to Jenny Lee, 7.7.78 (Orion); see also AM to Victor Bonham-Carter, 7.18.78 (CSC archive).

27. See Kenneth Stowe to SJ, 11.24.78; SJ to Kenneth Stowe, 11.29.78 (CSC archive).

28. SJ to Peter Elstob, 7.12.78 (PEN archive, HRC).

29. See PEN Refugee Writers' Bureau: File of Refugee Writers' Fund notes, HRC.

30. See Mr. and Mrs. K. W. Rokoš to AM, 12.14.78.

31. Queenie Leavis to SJ, 5.1.79 (CSC archive).

32. Queenie Leavis to Leeds librarian Dennis Cox, 6.6.79 (Brotherton). See Queenie Leavis to SJ, 5.21.79 (CSC archive); SJ to Queenie Leavis, 5.23.79.

Chapter 31

1. But see Anthony Burgess, review of *SS*, *Observer*, Feb. 4, 1979.

2. SJ to Lu Bruch, 1.30.79 (CSC archive). See Adam Munthe to SJ, 1.15.79, 2.3.79, 2. 21.79; Lu Bruch to SJ, 1.17.79 (CSC archive).

3. See SJ to AM, 5.12.79 (British Library); part of journal, 6.3.79; SJ, "The University of Leeds 1909–12"; SJ to Mrs. Stephens (two letters), 6.26.79, 7.7.79 (CSC archive).

4. Reprint of review of SJ, *The Voyage Home*, in "Fifty Years On . . ." series, *TLS*, Jan. 1, 1980.

5. Crawford Mitchell, ed. *Alice Garrigue Masaryk: 1879–1966.*

6. Jennifer Pullein Thompson to SJ, 12.17.80; Rosemary Murray to SJ, 5.15.80 (CSC archive).

7. See SJ to MW, 12.20.78; SJ to AM, 7.11.79.

8. A note in Orion Publishing Group: Gollancz Archive; file on Storm Jameson, Speaking of Stendhal, says remaindered July 21 (July 31 according to publicity file).

9. See Elaine Feinstein's introduction to SJ, *Love in Winter* (London: Virago, 1984), ix.

10. Janet Watts, *Observer Magazine*, May 9, 1982 (with photo by Jane Bowen); see SJ to AAK, 8.2.82.

11. Elaine Feinstein, *Guardian*, 9.1.82 (with photos from 1939 and current photos).

12. Mitchison, review, *TLS*, Oct. 22, 1982.

13. See Ursula Owen to SJ, 3.15.83 (CSC archive).

14. Mitchison, "Eye-Opener," *New Statesman*, Jan. 27, 1984; Victoria Glendinning, "The Autobiographies of Storm Jameson," *Sunday Times*, Jan. 29, 1984. See also Patricia Craig, *TLS*, March 9, 1984.

15. Caroline Moorhead, "Just Killing Time before Death," *Times*, March 2, 1984.

16. See Josephine Pullein-Thompson, "Standing Aside from Politics," *The PEN Broadsheet of the English Centre of International PEN*, no. 19 (Autumn 1985).

17. SJ, *A Day Off*, dramatized by Elaine Feinstein, broadcast on Radio 4, Jan. 13, 1986 (recorded Oct. 1985) (BBC Written Archives).

18. See SJ to AK, 4.14.76, for her miswriting of the title "Journey to [*sic*] the North."

19. See anon., "Powerful Writer with a Bleak and Brave Eye," *Times*, Oct. 7, 1986; anon., "Writer Who Fought for Freedom Dies," *Yorkshire Post*, Oct. 8, 1986; *Whitby Gazette*, Oct. 10, 1986; John Cunningham, "Restless Spirit," *Guardian*, Oct. 9, 1986.

20. Elaine Feinstein, "Margaret Storm Jameson," *The PEN Broadsheet of the English Centre of International PEN*, no. 23 (Autumn 1987): 6–7.

21. Nietzsche, *Genealogie der Moral*, vol. 6, pt. 2, of *Works* (Berlin, 1968), 311; quoted in Sebald's essay, "The Remorse of the Heart: On Memory and Cruelty in the Works of Peter Weiss," *On the Natural History of Destruction* (trans. Anthea Bell).

SELECT BIBLIOGRAPHY

Published Works by Storm Jameson
Works are in chronological order. Asterisks indicate editions cited, if other than the first
UK edition.

Novels
The Pot Boils. London: Constable, 1919.
The Happy Highways. London: William Heinemann, 1920; New York: Century, 1920.
The Clash. London: William Heinemann, 1922; Boston: Little, Brown, 1922.
The Pitiful Wife. London: Constable, 1923, popular ed., 1926; New York: Alfred A.
  Knopf, 1924.
Lady Susan and Life: An Indiscretion. London: Chapman and Dodd, 1923; New York:
  Dodd Mead, 1923.
Three Kingdoms. London: Constable, 1926; New York: Alfred A. Knopf, 1926.
The Lovely Ship. London: William Heinemann, 1927, popular ed., 1928, uniform ed.,
  1935; Cassell pocket ed.,1946; reissued William Heinemann, 1971; New York:
  Alfred A. Knopf, 1927; New York: Berkley Medallion Press, 1976; Bloomsbury
  e-book, 2011.
Farewell to Youth. London: William Heinemann, 1928; New York: Alfred A. Knopf,
  1928.
The Voyage Home. London: William Heinemann, 1930, reissued 1971; New York: Al-
  fred A. Knopf, 1930; New York: Berkley Medallion Press, 1976.
A Richer Dust. London: William Heinemann, 1931; Leipzig: Bernhard Tauchnitz,
  1932; New York: Alfred A. Knopf, 1931; New York: Berkley Medallion Press,
  1976.
*The Triumph of Time (*The Lovely Ship, The Voyage Home, A Richer Dust*). London:
  William Heinemann, 1932; Leipzig: Bernhard Tauchnitz, n.d.; New York:
  Berkley Medallion Press, 1976.
That Was Yesterday. London: William Heinemann, 1932; Leipzig: Bernhard Tauch-
  nitz, 1933; New York: Alfred A. Knopf, 1933; New York: Berkley Medallion
  Press, 1976.
The Single Heart. Benn's Ninepenny Novels/Leaders of Modern Fiction, no. 5. Lon-
  don: Ernest Benn, 1932.
A Day Off. London: Nicholson and Watson, 1933; London: Wells Gardner one-shilling
  ed., n.d.; London: Remploy, 1980.
Women against Men (*A Day Off, Delicate Monster, The Single Heart*). Leipzig: Bern-
  hard Tauchnitz, 1933; *London: Virago Press, 1982; New York: Alfred A.
  Knopf, 1933.
Company Parade. Book 1 of *The Mirror in Darkness* trilogy. London: Cassell, 1934;

*London: Virago Press, 1982; New York: Alfred A. Knopf, 1934; New York: Berkley Medallion Press, 1976; Bloomsbury e-book and paperback, 2012.

Love in Winter. Book 2 of *The Mirror in Darkness* trilogy. London: Cassell, 1935; *London: Virago Press, 1984; London: Capuchin Classics, 2009; New York: Alfred A. Knopf, 1935; New York: Berkley Medallion Press, 1976.

None Turn Back. Book 3 of *The Mirror in Darkness* trilogy. London: Cassell, 1936; *London: Virago Press, 1984; New York: Alfred A. Knopf, 1936; Bloomsbury e-book, 2011.

In the Second Year. London: Cassell, 1936; Nottingham: Trent Editions, 2004; New York: Macmillan, 1936.

Delicate Monster. London: Ivor Nicholson and Watson, 1937.

The Moon Is Making. London: Cassell, 1937; New York: Macmillan, 1938.

[William Lamb, pseud.] *The World Ends*. London: J. M. Dent, 1937.

[James Hill, pseud.] *Loving Memory*. London: Collins, 1937; Boston: Little, Brown, 1937.

[James Hill, pseud.] *No Victory for the Soldier*. London: Collins, 1938; *New York: Doubleday, Doran, 1939.

Here Comes a Candle. London: Cassell, 1938, *pocket ed., 1945, repr., 1947; New York: Macmillan, 1939.

Farewell, Night, Welcome, Day. London: Cassell, 1939. As *The Captain's Wife*. New York: Macmillan, 1939; New York: Berkley Medallion Press, 1976.

Europe to Let: The Memoirs of an Obscure Man. New York and London: Macmillan, 1940.

Cousin Honoré. London: Cassell, 1940; *pocket ed., 1947; New York: Macmillan, 1941.

The Fort. London: Cassell, 1941; New York: Macmillan, 1941.

Then We Shall Hear Singing: A Fantasy in C Major. London: Cassell, 1942; New York: Macmillan, 1942.

Cloudless May. London: Macmillan, 1943; London: Book Society, 1943; London: Reprint Society, 1945; London: Panther Books, 1965; New York: Macmillan, 1944; Bloomsbury e-book and paperback, 2012.

The Journal of Mary Hervey Russell. London: Macmillan, 1945, repr., 1961; New York: Macmillan, 1945; Bloomsbury e-book, 2011.

The Other Side. London: Macmillan, 1946; Stockholm and London: Continental, Zephyr Books, 1947; New York: Macmillan, 1946; Bloomsbury e-book, 2011.

Before the Crossing. London: Macmillan, 1947; New York: Macmillan, 1947.

The Black Laurel. London: Macmillan, 1947; New York: Macmillan, 1948; Bloomsbury e-book and paperback, 2012.

The Moment of Truth. London: Macmillan, 1949; New York: Macmillan, 1949; Bloomsbury e-book, 2011.

The Green Man. London: Macmillan, 1952; New York: Harper, 1953.

The Hidden River. London: Macmillan, 1955; Reprint Society, 1956; Harmondsworth: Penguin, 1959; Remploy, 1979; New York: Harper, 1955; Bloomsbury e-book, 2011.

The Intruder. London: Macmillan, 1956; Panther Books, 1963; White Lion Editions, 1977; New York: Macmillan, 1956.

A *Cup of Tea for Mr. Thorgill*. London: Macmillan, 1957; New York: Harper, 1957; Bloomsbury e-book and paperback, 2012.

A *Ulysses Too Many*. London: Macmillan, 1958. As *One Ulysses Too Many*. New York: Harper, 1958.

A *Day Off: Two Novels and Some Stories*, including *The Single Heart* (1932), "The Mask" (1954), "This Is It" (1952), "The Last Night" (1943), "A Friendly Talk" (1958), and *A Day Off* (1932). London: Macmillan, 1959; Bloomsbury e-book, 2011.

Last Score; or, The Private Life of Sir Richard Ormston. London: Macmillan, 1961; The Reprint Society, 1962; White Lion, 1977; New York: Harper, 1961.

The Road from the Monument. London: Macmillan, 1962; White Lion, 1974; New York: St. Martin's, 1962; Bloomsbury e-book, 2011.

A *Month Soon Goes*. London: Macmillan, 1962; New York: St. Martin's, 1962; Bloomsbury e-book, 2011.

The Aristide Case. London: Macmillan, 1964; Pan Books, 1967. As *The Blind Heart*. New York: Harper and Row, 1964; Bloomsbury e-book and paperback, 2012.

The Early Life of Stephen Hind. London: Macmillan, 1966; New York: St. Martin's, 1966.

The White Crow. London: Macmillan, 1968; New York: Harper and Row, 1968; Bloomsbury e-book, 2011.

There Will Be a Short Interval. London: Collins/Harvill, 1973; New York: Harper and Row, 1973; Bloomsbury e-book and paperback, 2012.

Serializations

The Happy Highways. *New Commonwealth*, Nov. 14, 1919–Feb. 20, 1920.

Hate Dies Hard [*The Other Side*]. *Saturday Evening Post* (Pennsylvania), June 30, July 7, July 14, July 21, 1945.

The Hidden River. *Housewife Magazine*, Jan.–April 1954.

House of Hate [*The Hidden River*]. *Saturday Evening Post* (Pennsylvania), Oct. 16, 23, 30 and Nov. 6, 13, 20, 1954.

A *Month Soon Goes*. *Housewife Magazine*, Oct.–Dec. 1955.

The Lion and the Dagger [*Last Score*]. *Saturday Evening Post* (Pennsylvania), April 8, 15, and 22, 1961.

Stories

"The Woman Doctor's Tale: Mother-Love." *New Decameron* 1 (1919): 78–104.

"The Woman Doctor's Tale: A Player Perforce." *New Decameron* 2 (1920): 158–75.

"A Cloke for Two." *New Commonwealth*, n.s., 1 (Jan. 9, 1920): 11.

"The Tale of the Solitary English Girl: The Pitiful Wife." *New Decameron* 3 (1922): 56–71.

Series (later collected in *Lady Susan and Life*) in *The Sketch*: "On Manners," May 30, 1923; "Lady Susan and the Policeman," June 6, 1923; "On Americans," June 13, 1923; "Contentment," June 20, 1923; "Film," June 27, 1923; "Feminine Influence," July 4, 1923.

"The Bureaucrat's Tale: Monotony." *New Decameron* 4 (1925): 178–94.

"Romance Begins at Home." *Nash and Pall Mall Magazine* 78, no. 402 (Nov. 1926): 38.

"The Fortune Hunter." *Sunday Dispatch*, Aug. 26, 1928, 2.

"The Fool of Love." *Sunday Dispatch*, Nov. 4, 1928, 2.

"Peace and Quest." *Sunday Graphic*, July 14, 1929, 4, 8.

"Professor Fabian's Crime." *Sunday Dispatch*, Nov. 3, 1929, 2.

"The Door." In *The Legion Book*, edited by Capt. H. Cotton Minchin, 94–108. London: Cassell, 1929.

"The Seven Little Foxes." *North American Review* 229, no. 1 (Jan. 1930): 73–81.

"Splendid Days." *Argosy* (UK), June 1930, 109–20.

"A Mingled Strain." In *The Fothergill Omnibus*, with introduction by John Fothergill, R. G. Collingswood, and Gerald Gould. London: Eyre and Spottiswoode, 1931. Reprinted in *Fourteen Stories from One Plot*, edited by John Milton Berdan. New York: Oxford Univ. Press, 1932.

"People Are Queer." *Nash and Pall Mall Magazine* 88, no. 466 (March 1932): 46.

"Strange Landfall." *Strand Magazine* 83 (June 1932): 546–59.

"The Release of Mr. Dewey." *Strand Magazine* 84 (Oct. 1932): 357–66.

"The Young Are So Hard." *Strand Magazine* 85 (Feb. 1933): 168–75.

"Mr. Green Loses His Watch." *Strand Magazine* 85 (June 1933): 612–22.

"Away to Sea." *Collier's* (U.S.), Sept. 16, 1933, 10–11, 41, 44, 45.

"According to Plan." *Strand Magazine* 87 (March 1934): 276–87.

"The Storm." *Nash's Pall Mall Magazine* 94, no. 502 (March 1935): 28.

"Fog." *Strand Magazine* 89 (July 1935): 707–17.

"Circa 1942: Scenes from a New Novel" [from *In the Second Year*]. *Left Review* 3 (Oct. 1935–March 1936): 148–54.

"Camilla's Education." *Nash's Pall Mall Magazine* 97, no. 519 (Aug. 1936): 18–25.

"A Day at the Zoo." *Atlantic Monthly* 161, no. 5 (May 1938): 683–91. Reprinted in *Modern Reading*, edited by Reginald Moore, no. 2 (July 1941): 11–26.

"A Moment of Happiness" [from a novel in preparation, *Cloudless May*]. In *Selected Writing*, edited by Reginald Moore, poetry selected by Tambimuttu, 1: 96–108. London: Nicholson and Watson, 1941.

"You Don't Speak French, Do You?" *Modern Reading*, no. 4 (April 1942): 47–64.

"The Last Night." *Saturday Evening Post*, Jan. 30, 1943. Reprinted in *Argosy* (UK), Feb. 1944; *Lidice: A Tribute by Members of the International PEN*, with introduction by Harold Nicolson, 50–84 (London: Allen and Unwin, 1944); *Saturday Evening Post Stories 1942–45*, with introduction by Benn Hibbs, 3–30 (New York: Random House, n.d.).

"The Young Prisoner." *Modern Reading*, no. 9 (1944): 111–26.

"Very Clever People." *Good Housekeeping*, May 1952, 40–51.

"This Is It." *Cornhill Magazine* 166, no. 994 (Feb. 1953): 233–70.

"The Mask." *Harper's Magazine* 209 (Nov. 1954): 59–66. Reprinted in *Winter's Tales* (London: Macmillan, 1955), 1:128–66; *Argosy* (UK), August 1955.

"The Cost of Freedom." In *The PEN in Exile*, edited by Paul Tabori, 35–53. London: The International PEN Club Centre for Writers in Exile, 1954.

"A Friendly Talk." *Harper's Magazine* 216 (June 1958): 44–49. Reprinted in *Cornhill Magazine* 170 (1958–59): 189–200.

"The Friendly One." *Winter's Tales* 5 (1959): 181–215.

Plays and Adaptations
Full Circle. Oxford: Basil Blackwell, 1928; produced in Liverpool, 1928.
The Fort. Adapted by Barbara Burnham (BBC Written Archives: radio broadcast, BBC Home Service, 10:30 p.m., Saturday, May 9, 1942).
William the Defeated. Adapted by SJ and Barbara Burnham (BBC Written Archives: radio broadcast, BBC Home Service, 9:30 p.m., Monday, July 5, 1943). See "William the Defeated" in *The Book of the P.E.N.*, edited by Hermon Ould, 187–230 (London: Arthur Barker, 1950).
The Commonplace Heart. Adapted by Nigel Kneale and George Kerr (BBC Written Archives: BBC television, Jan. 13, 1953).
The Hidden River. Adapted by Ruth and Augustus Goetz (New York: Dramatists Play Service, 1957). Produced New Haven, Jan. 1957; New York, April 1957; Theatre Royal, Brighton, March 1959; Cambridge Theatre, London, April 1959.
The Face of Treason [*A Cup of Tea for Mr. Thorgill*]. Adapted by and presented on television by Associated Rediffusion, 8:30 p.m., March 10, 1959.
The Early Life of Stephen Hind. Adapted for BBC television (BBC Written Archives: presented in three episodes: Nov. 30, Dec. 7, and Dec. 14, 1974).
A Day Off. Adapted by Elaine Feinstein (BBC Written Archives: radio broadcast, BBC Radio 4, Jan. 13, 1986).
The Single Heart. Billed in *Radio Times* as by Storm Jameson (BBC Sound Archive: radio broadcast, BBC Radio 4 Playhouse, at 2:30 p.m., Jan. 25, 1997).

Poems
"February 1937." *London Mercury* 39, no. 232 (Feb. 1939): 383–84.
"Silchester." *TLS*, Oct. 30, 1943, 525.
"Cloud Form." *TLS*, July 29, 1944, 370.

Translations
Guy de Maupassant: Collected Short Stories. Translated by Ernest Boyd and SJ. New York: Alfred A. Knopf, 1928. A reissue of vols. 1–16 published earlier in the 1920s.
88 Short Stories by Guy de Maupassant. Translated by Ernest Boyd and SJ. 4 vols. London: Alfred A. Knopf, 1930. A reissue of vols. 3, 8, 14, and 16 of collected edition (New York: Alfred A. Knopf, 1928). See also BBC Written Archives, Feb. 5, 1943, and Oct. 6, 1944, for broadcasts of individual translations.
88 More Stories by Guy de Maupassant. Translated by Ernest Boyd and SJ. 4 vols. London: Cassell, 1930. A reissue of vols. 1, 2, 9, and 12 of collected edition (New York: Alfred A. Knopf, 1928). See also BBC Written Archives, Feb. 21, 1952; June 3, 1954; Nov. 5, 1957; and July 18, 1991, for broadcasts of individual translations.

Nonfiction
Modern Drama in Europe. London: Collins, 1920; New York: Harcourt Brace, 1921.
The Georgian Novel and Mr. Robinson. London: William Heinemann, 1929; New York: Morrow, 1929.

The Decline of Merry England. London: Cassell, 1930; Indianapolis: Bobbs-Merrill, 1930.

No Time Like the Present. London: Cassell, 1933; New York: Alfred A. Knopf, 1933.

[Anon., ed.] *Challenge to Death*. By Philip Noel-Baker, Gerald Barry, Vernon Bartlett, Edmund Blunden, Vera Brittain, Ivor Brown, George Catlin, Guy Chapman, Mary Agnes Hamilton, Gerald Heard, Winifred Holtby, Julian Huxley, Storm Jameson, J. B. Priestley, Rebecca West. Foreword by Viscount Cecil. London: Constable, 1934; New York: Dutton, 1935.

The Soul of Man in the Age of Leisure. Pamphlets on the New Economics, no. 13. London: Stanley Nott, 1935. Reprinted in *The Social Credit Pamphleteer* (London: Stanley Nott, 1935).

The Novel in Contemporary Life. Boston: The Writer, 1938. Reprinted with added quotation from William Lamb novel and pointillism passage in *Civil Journey* (1939), 277–309.

Civil Journey. London: Cassell, 1939.

The End of This War. PEN Books. London: George Allen and Unwin, 1941.

[Ed.] *London Calling*. New York and London: Harper, 1942.

The Writer's Situation and Other Essays. New York and London: Macmillan, 1950.

Morley Roberts: The Last Eminent Victorian. London: Unicorn Press, 1961.

Journey from the North. 2 vols. London: Collins and Harvill Press, 1969–70. Reprint, 2 vols., *London: Virago Press, 1984; 1 vol., New York: Harper and Row, 1971; Bloomsbury e-book, 2011.

Parthian Words. London: Collins and Harvill Press, 1970; New York: Harper and Row, 1971; Bloomsbury e-book and paperback, 2012.

[Ed.] *A Kind of Survivor: The Autobiography of Guy Chapman*. By GC. London: Victor Gollancz, 1975.

Speaking of Stendhal. London: Victor Gollancz, 1979; Bloomsbury e-book and paperback, 2012.

Introductions to Works by Other Writers

Cazotte, Jacques. *A Thousand and One Follies* (*Les mille et une falaises*) and *His Most Unlooked-for Lordship* (*Le lord impromptu*). Translated by Eric Sutton. London: Chapman and Hall, 1927; New York: Robert M. McBride, 1928.

Hayes, F. W. *A Kent Squire*. 1900. Reprint, London: Hutchinson, 1932.

Linke, Lilo. *Tale without End* . . . . London: Constable, 1934; New York: Alfred A. Knopf, 1934. Reprinted as "The Youngest Brother" in *Civil Journey* (1939), 126–50.

Newitt, Hilary. *Women Must Choose: The Position of Women in Europe To-day*. London: Victor Gollancz, 1937.

Ward, R. H., ed. *Ten Peace Plays*. London: J. M. Dent, 1938.

Kuncewiczowa, Maria. *The Stranger* (*Cudzoziemka*). Translated by B. W. A. Massey. London, New York, Melbourne: Hutchinson's International Authors, [1944]. Introduction reprinted in *The Writer's Situation* (1950), 118–25.

Linke, Lilo. *Andean Adventure: A Social and Political Study of Colombia, Ecuador and Bolivia*. London and New York: Hutchinson, [1945/46].

Roberts, Kate. *A Summer Day and Other Stories*. Translated by Dafydd Jenkins. Cardiff: Penmark, 1946. Preface reprinted in *The Writer's Situation* (1950), 102–13.

Kocwa, Eugenia. "On the Sands of Mecklenburg." *Adelphi*, n.s., 23, no. 3 (April–June 1947): 127–28.

Legrand, Ignace. *The Land Within* (*La patrie intérieure*). Translated by E. H. F. Mills. London: Phoenix House, 1948.

Frank, Anne. *The Diary of Anne Frank*. Translated by B. M. Mooyaart-Doubleday. London: Pan Books, 1954.

Miles, Susan. *Portrait of a Parson*. London: George Allen and Unwin, 1955.

Bullett, Gerald. *Ten-Minute Tales*. London: Readers Union, Dent, 1960.

Linke, Lilo. *People of the Amazon*. London: Robert Hale, 1963.

Stendhal. *The Red and the Black*. New York: Heron Books by arrangement with Collier Books, 1969.

Articles, Chapters, Reviews, Lectures

"The End Thereof." *New Age* 12 (March 20, 1913): 482–43.

"The Drama of Ideas since Ibsen." *Egoist* 1 (Jan. 15, 1914): 29–30.

"Modern Dramatists." *Egoist* 1 (Feb. 16, 1914): 74–75.

"Modern Dramatists." *Egoist* 1 (March 16, 1914): 116–17.

"New Statesman. A Bill Providing for an Economic Basis of Marriage." *New Age* 14 (April 2, 1914): 682.

"The Theatre." *Egoist* 1 (April 15, 1914): 155–56.

"England's Nest of Singing Birds." *Egoist* 2 (Nov. 1, 1915): 175.

"Reviews." *Egoist* 3 (Sept. 3, 1916): 135–36.

"A Plea for the Arbitrary Limit." *New Age* 19 (Sept. 5, 1916): 447–48.

"The Scene-Models of Norman MacDermott." *Egoist* 4 (Jan. 2, 1917): 3–4.

"Divorce." *New Commonwealth* 1 (Oct. 1, 1919): 2.

"Profiteering." *New Commonwealth* 1 (Oct. 8, 1919): 15.

"America." *New Commonwealth* 1 (Oct. 15, 1919): 20.

"America and Britain." *New Europe: A Weekly Review of Foreign Politics, Literature, Art, Drama, Music* 13 (Oct. 23, 1919): 36–39. Reprinted as "England and America: The Post-war Situation," in *English Review* 32 (Feb. 1921): 137–41.

"Shaking Hands with Murder." *New Commonwealth* 1 (Nov. 14, 1919): 2.

"America and Britain." *New Europe* 13 (Nov. 20, 1919): 167–71. First half reprinted as "England and America: The Blood Bond," in *English Review* 32 (March 1921): 213–15; second half reprinted as "England and America: Unrestricted Competition," in *English Review* 32 (April 1921): 320–28.

[George Gallilee, pseud.] "The Joy of Work." *New Commonwealth* 1 (Nov. 28, 1919): 9.

"Nietzsche in Modern Drama," parts 1 and 2. *Theatre-Craft*, edited by Hermon Ould and Horace Shipp, no. 3 (n.d., but internal evidence for 1919): 8–14; no. 4:9–15. Both parts take from first chapter of SJ, *Modern Drama in Europe* (1920).

[George Gallilee, pseud.] "A Philosophy of Youth" series in *New Commonwealth* 1: "On Fear" (Jan. 2, 1920) and "Childhood" (Jan. 9, 16, 23, and 30, 1920).

At the Theatres. Monthly column in *New Commonwealth*, n.s.: "Romance as You Like It," 1 (April 1920): 10; "The Three Best Plays in London," 2 (May 1920): 13; "Two Plays and a Novel," in five parts: 2 (June 20, 1920): 15; 2 (July 2, 1920): 9; 2 (Aug. 20, 1920): 7; 2 (Sept. 20, 1920): 7; 2 (Oct. 20, 1920): 7.

"The Modern Novel." In "Special Literary Supplement Containing Reviews of Current Literature by Thomas Moult and Storm Jameson." *New Commonwealth*, n.s., 1 (April 1920): 29–30.

"England and America: European Reconstruction." *English Review* 32 (May 1921): 437–42.

[M.S.J.] Review of A. Travers-Borgstroem, *Mutualism: A Synthesis*. *Saturday Westminster Gazette*, Aug. 20, 1921.

"Review." *Yale Review*, n.s., 2 (Jan. 1922): 425–26.

"Mr. de la Mare and the Grotesque" (review). *English Review* 34 (May 1922): 424–30.

"The Joy of Work." *Forum* (New York) 68 (Nov. 1922): 965–69.

"Review." *Bookman* (UK), Jan. 1924, 221–22.

"The Price of a Career: How Women Pay for Success." *Evening Standard*, Nov. 2, 1926, 7.

"The Office and the Hearth: Combining a Career with a Home." *Evening Standard*, Dec. 2, 1926, 7.

"The Genius in the Home: Why His Domestic Life Breaks Down." *Evening Standard*, Dec. 15, 1926, 7.

"Man the Hero — in Books: As Our Women Novelists See Him." *Evening Standard*, Jan. 3, 1927, 7.

"What Every Woman Knows: Man as the Incurable Romantic." *Evening Standard*, Feb. 1, 1927, 7.

"The Discovery of Woman: Dream Types of Mr. Bennett and Mr. Wells — Arrival of the Ineffectual Husband." *Evening Standard*, March 6, 1927, 5.

"Teaching by Not Teaching: New Methods 'Half Waste of Time and Half Definitely Harmful.'" *Evening Standard*, March 17, 1927, 7.

"Problem of Sex in Public Life." *Daily Mirror*, March 28, 1927, 4.

"The Wife Who Bilks: Thin Times for the Parasite Woman," *Evening Standard*, April 26, 1927, 7.

"When Brains Wed Brains: A Perilous Experiment — But of Surpassing Success If It Comes Off." *Evening Standard*, May 12, 1927, 7.

"Nothing Wrong with Modern Woman." *Daily Mirror*, May 23, 1927, 6.

"Woman — Poor Wretch! Destroyer of Romance and Ruiner of Men and Manners." *Evening Standard*, June 16, 1927, 7.

"Literary Reputations in the Balance" (comment on Edgar Allan Poe in debate). *Bookman* (UK), Sept. 1927.

"The Double Standard: An Article on Modern Morals — and the Only Thing in Life That Matters." *Pall Mall Magazine* 212 (Dec. 1927): 11–13.

"Can Womanhood Stand This 'Freedom'?" *Evening News*, Jan. 20, 1928, 8.

"Can a Wife Say 'You Must be Mine'?" *Evening News*, Feb. 20, 1928, 8.

"A Woman — a Husband: Children: A Career. 'You Cannot Do Three Things at Once.'" *Evening News*, Feb. 27, 1928, 8.

"Inefficient Wives. She-Who-Must-Be-Worshipped and the Too-Independent Bride. Why Not a Legalised Sharing-Up of Family Income? The Worst-Performed Profession." *Evening News*, March 7, 1928, 8.

"My Fear for the New Child." *Evening News*, March 12, 1928, 6.

"How I Look at Divorce." *Evening News*, March 19, 1928, 8.

"You Can't Keep Women Out!" *Evening News*, March 26, 1928, 8.

"What I Should Tell a Daughter Today." *Evening News*, April 5, 1928, 8.

"No Woman Shall Train My Son." *Evening News*, April 16, 1928, 8.
"Who Gives Up Most in Marriage?" *Evening News*, April 23, 1928, 8.
"Dreams — and Disillusion." In "What Life Has Taught Me" series. *Evening News*, May 21, 1928, 8.
"Women and That 'Next War.' No Mother Can Take That 100th Chance." *Evening News*, May 29, 1928, 6.
"'Rabbit' Husbands." *Evening News*, June 4, 1928, 8.
"What Shall I Make of My Son?" *Evening News*, June 14, 1928, 8.
"'Platonic Friendships' and Peril." *Evening News*, June 20, 1928, 8.
"Idle Wives." *Evening News*, June 27, 1928, 8.
"Daughters or Sons: Which Are Best Now?" *Evening News*, July 3, 1928, 8.
"One Child Families." *Evening News*, July 10, 1928, 8.
"Sex Jealousy." *Evening News*, July 17, 1928, 8.
"Dissatisfied Women." *Evening News*, July 24, 1928, 8.
"London (Eng.) Is Good Enough!" *Evening News*, July 31, 1928, 8.
"Separate Holidays." *Evening News*, Aug. 8, 1928, 8.
"That Fatal Tenth Year!" *Evening News*, Aug. 20, 1928, 8.
"The Woman with a Past." *Evening News*, Aug. 29, 1928, 8.
"The New 'Lady': Freedom — and No Code of Honour!" *Evening News*, Sept. 6, 1928, 8.
"Will Not Take Place." *Evening News*, Sept. 12, 1928, 8.
"Marriage Made Possible." *Evening News*, Sept. 20, 1928, 8.
"Bored Wives: Why, After All, Should Their Husbands Have to Amuse Them?" *Evening News*, Oct. 1, 1928, 8.
"The Only Perfect Match I Know." In "Love — as I See It" series, no. 5. *Evening News*, Oct. 13, 1928, 8.
"Men." *Evening News*, Oct. 23, 1928, 8.
"What Are You Going to Do with Your Boy . . . ? A Modern Mother on the Choice Between the Day-School and the Public School." *Evening News*, Nov. 7, 1928, 11.
"Modern Morality Just Means Playing the Game." *Evening News*, Nov. 13, 1928, 11.
"The Best Wife I Know." *Evening News*, Nov. 20, 1928, 11.
"Which Would You Choose — ?" *Evening News*, Nov. 27, 1928, 11.
"Who'd Be a Woman?" *Evening News*, Dec. 10, 1928, 11.
"The Love-Letter of a Modern Girl." *Evening News*, Dec. 17, 1928, 11.
"The Golden Age of Spinsters." *Evening News*, Dec. 31, 1928, 11.
"The Soul of Modern Woman." *Evening News*, Jan. 7, 1929, 11.
"This Feminine Freedom." *Britannia*, Feb. 8, 1929, 76–77.
"The Decline of Fiction." *Nation and Athenaeum* 45 (April–Sept. 1929): 594. Reprinted in *Civil Journey* (1939), 26–33.
"I Want a Good Wife." *Britannia and Eve*, Aug. 1929, 62–63.
"Charm" (a Pears ad). *Sunday Graphic*, Aug. 18, 1929, 18.
"Marriage and the New Morality." *Britannia*, Oct. 1929, 82–83, 196.
"Ha Ha Ha I'm Laughing." *Bookman* (U.S.) 72, no. 1 (Sept. 1930): 15–20.
"The Future of the Novel." *Library Assistant* 23 (Nov. 1930): 212–22.
"Autobiography and the Novel." *Bookman* (U.S.) 72 (Feb. 1931): 557–65.
"Where Lovely Ships Were Launched." *Everyman*, Aug. 13, 1931.

Review of *The Waves*, by Virginia Woolf. *Fortnightly Review* 130 (Nov. 1931): 677–78.

"Man the Helpmate." In *Man Proud Man*, edited by Mabel Ulrich, 103–36. London: Hamish Hamilton, 1932.

Recent Novels. Fortnightly column, *New English Weekly* 1, no. 1 (April 21, 1932) through 2, no. 15 (Jan. 26, 1933).

"City to Let: Berlin Now." *Nash and Pall Mall Magazine* 89, no. 469 (June 1932): 10–26. Reprinted as "City to Let — Berlin 1932," in *Civil Journey* (1939), 36–52.

"Storm Jameson Asks: Why Do *You* Read Novels?" *New Clarion* 1, no. 1 (June 11, 1932): 12.

"Abolish Reviewers!" *New Clarion* 1, no. 5 (July 9, 1932), 109. Reprinted in *Bookman* (U.S.) 75, no. 6 (Oct. 1932): 600–601.

"Films, the Opium of the People." *New Clarion* 1, no. 9 (Aug. 6, 1932): 205.

"The Lost Generation." *New Clarion* 1, no. 14 (Sept. 10, 1932): 321.

"No Escape: Two Books Which Keep to the Facts." *New Clarion* 1, no. 17 (Oct. 1, 1932): 39.

"A Novel of Quality." *New Clarion* 1, no. 29 (Oct. 29, 1932): 490.

"The New Ancestors — an Examination of the Young Hopes of Europe." *Nash's Pall Mall Magazine* 90, no. 473 (Oct. 1932): 46.

"The Dangers of Fiction." *Highway: The Journal of the Workers' Educational Association* 25 (Nov. 1932): 8–10.

"The Christmas Snob." *New Clarion* 1, no. 26 (Dec. 3, 1932): 605.

"Salients." *New Clarion* 2, no. 30 (Dec. 31, 1932): 63.

"Extracts from a Book of Views." *Heaton Review* 6 (1933): 17–20.

"About the Next War/What Are *You* Going to Do?" *New Clarion* 2, no. 34 (Jan. 28, 1933):144.

Review of "How to Read," by Ezra Pound. *New English Weekly*, March 9, 1933, 9.

"The Vested Interest of Writers." *New Clarion* 2, no. 41 (March 18, 1933): 285.

"The Cultivation of Values." *Highway* 25 (March 1933): 28–29.

"'A Bad-Tempered Footnote' to Life in 1933." *New Clarion* 3, no. 53 (June 10, 1933): 11.

"Writers, Publishers and Booksellers." *Bookseller*, Oct. 6, 1933, 13.

"Fifteen Years Ago — We Said 'Never Again.'" *New Clarion* 3, no. 71 (Oct. 21, 1933): 325, 327.

"Love in England and in France" (joint article by André Maurois and SJ). *Nash and Pall Mall Magazine* 92, no. 487 (Dec. 1933): 16.

"The Twilight of Reason." In *Challenge to Death* (1934), 1–20. Reprinted in *Civil Journey* (1939), 184–210.

"In the End." In *Challenge to Death* (1934), 322–32. Reprinted in *Civil Journey* (1939), 212–25.

"The Craft of the Novelist." *English Review* 58 (Jan. 1934): 28–43. Reprinted in *Civil Journey* (1939), 54–76.

"A Faith Worth Dying For: The Defence of Freedom." *Fortnightly Review* 141 (April 1934): 413–24. Reprinted as "The Defence of Freedom" in *Civil Journey* (1939), 152–80.

"Providing the Evidence." *Fortnightly Review* 141 (June 1934): 687–95.

"To a Labour Party Official." *Left Review*, Nov. 2, 1934, 29.

Contribution to tribute to A. R. Orage. *New English Weekly*, Nov. 15, 1934.

"Leisure." *Aryan Path* (Bombay) 6, no. 4 (April 1935): 211.

"Marriage Is Worth Fighting For." *Woman's Journal*, Nov. 1935, 32, 111.

"Student Days." In *Modern Essays and Sketches*, edited by J. W. Marriott, 164–69. London: Nelson, 1935.

Chapter in *What Is Patriotism?* edited by N. P. Macdonald, 123–33. London: Thornton Butterworth, 1935. Reprinted in *Civil Journey* (1939), 248–60.

Review. *Left Review*, Jan. 4, 1936, 156–59.

Contribution to "Some Remarkable Dreams," in response to Alfred Adler, "What Is a Dream?" *New Current Digest: Outstanding Articles of the Month*, Sept. 1936, 4–8.

Review. *Socialist* (Journal of the Socialist League), n.s., no. 4, 1936, 16.

"London in 1913." In *Hotch-Potch*, edited by John Brophy, 129–36. Council of Royal Liverpool Children's Hospital, 1936.

"The Writer." In *The Road to Success: Twenty Essays on the Choice of a Career for Women*, edited by Margaret Cole, 98–114. London: Methuen, 1936.

"Genius or What Have You?" *Writer* (Boston) 49 (June 1936): 173–74, 199. Reprinted in *Civil Journey* (1939), 228–35.

"Socialists Born and Made" (review). *Fact*, no. 2 (May 15, 1937): 87–90.

"Documents." *Fact*, no. 4 (July 15, 1937): 9–18.

"Books to Save Liberalism." *Aryan Path* (Bombay) 8, no. 7 (July 1937): 305–8.

Review. *Fact*, no. 7 (Oct. 15, 1937).

"We Must Not Fail Him." *Peace News*, Nov. 6, 1937, 7.

Contribution to "Authors Take Sides." *Left Review Pamphlet*, Nov. 1937.

Chapter in *What Is Happiness?* by Martin Armstrong et al., 31–41. London: John Lane, Bodley Head, 1938.

Review. *Fact*, no. 15 (April 1938).

Obituary on Claude Napier. *TLS*, June 11, 1938, 398.

"A Pacifist in Czechoslovakia." *Peace News*, Aug. 20, 1938.

"Storm Jameson on the P.E.N." *P.E.N. News*, Oct. 1938.

Review. *Fact*, no. 23 (Dec. 15, 1938).

Contribution to debate on conscription. *Peace News*, Jan. 20, 1939.

Response to Ben Greene on Sudetenland. *Peace News*, Feb. 3, 1939.

"If War Comes." *Peace News*, March 10, 1939.

"The Method and Theory of the Bauhaus." *Scrutiny* 8 (June 1939): 81–88.

"Fighting the Foes of Civilization: The Writer's Place in the Defence Line." *TLS*, Oct. 7, 1939, 571. Reprinted as "Writing in the Margin" in *The Writer's Situation* (1950), 189–200.

"Writers between Two Wars." *Writer* (Boston) 52, no. 11 (Nov. 1939): 327–30.

"City without Children." *Atlantic Monthly* 164, no. 5 (Nov. 1939): 585–89.

"In Courage Keep Your Heart." *Woman's Journal*, Dec. 1939, 34–35.

"Karel Čapek and Czechoslovakia." *Central European Observer*, n.s., no. 1 [o.s., 17] (Feb. 1, 1940).

"The New Europe." *Fortnightly Review* 153 (Jan. 1940): 68–79.

"The Cultivation of Values." *Living Age* (Boston) 358 (March 1940): 7–12.

"Why Not a Ministry of Fine Arts?" *Fortnightly Review* 154 (Nov. 1940): 449–57.

"Women on the Spot." *Atlantic Monthly* 167 (Feb. 1941): 169–76.

"Le congrès internationel des PEN." *La france libre* 2, no. 11 (Sept. 15, 1941): 395–

99. Reprinted with original lecture title, "Creditors of France," in *The Writer's Situation* (1950), 180–88.

Front page message. *Adam International Review*, edited by M. Grindea, no. 152 (Sept. 1941).

Contribution to discussion of PEP (Political and Economic Planning) broadsheet entitled "The Future of Germany." *Fortnightly Review* 156 (Sept. 1941): 220–22.

"The Writer's Duty." *Fortnightly Review* 156 (Oct. 1941). Reprinted in *Writers in Freedom: A Symposium Based on the XVII International Congress of the P.E.N. Club Held in London in September 1941*, edited by Hermon Ould. Hutchinson, 1942. Reprinted with additions and original lecture title, "The Responsibilities of the Writer," in *The Writer's Situation* (1950), 164–79.

"The H. G. Wells Age." *Adam International Review*, no. 153 (Nov. 1941).

Review. *La france libre*, no. 18 (April 17, 1942).

"Introduction, or Ninety Times as High as the Moon." In *London Calling* (1942), 1–17.

Contribution to "Reviewing Reviewed" symposium. *Author*, Summer 1943.

"Should the Enemy Be Punished after the War Is Over?" *Aryan Path* (Bombay) 14, no. 9 (Sept. 1943): 388–90.

"Literature between the Wars: The Tyranny of Things." *TLS*, Sept. 18, 1943, 450. Reprinted as "Between the Wars," in *The Writer's Situation* (1950), 126–35.

[Anon.] "Paris." *TLS*, Aug. 26, 1944, 415. Reprinted in *The Writer's Situation* (1950), 114–17.

"A Seeker after Value: Views in a War-Torn Mirror." *TLS*, Dec. 9, 1944, 594.

"Poland." *Fortnightly Review* 165 (Jan. 1946): 28–34. Reprinted as "Poland 1945" in *The Windmill*, edited by Reginald Moore and Edward Lane, 1:127–32. London and Toronto: William Heinemann, 1946.

"The New Czechoslovakia." *Fortnightly Review* 165 (Feb. 1946): 73–80.

Contribution to "Tribute to Hermon Ould." *Adam International Review*, March 1946.

Contribution to symposium on BBC rates of pay, "Personal Comments from Leading Authors." *Author*, Summer 1947.

"W. H. Auden: The Poet of Angst." *Gate*, Nov. 1947. Reprinted in *The Writer's Situation* (1950), 83–101.

"Edvard Beneš." *Fortnightly Review* 70 (Oct. 1948): 247–51.

"The Situation of the Writer To-day." *Humanitas* 2, no. 2 (Winter 1948). Reprinted, with full text of Lyceum Club and Zurich lecture (1947) as "The Writer's Situation," in *The Writer's Situation* (1950), 1–36.

"Why I Can't Write about America." *New York Times Magazine* 6 (March 27, 1949): 15. Reprinted in *Fortnightly Review* 172 (Dec. 1949): 381–85, and in *Reader's Digest* 58 (May 1951): 119–22.

"The Novelist Today." *Virginia Quarterly*, May 1949. Reprinted as "The Novelist To-day: 1949" in *The Writer's Situation* (1950), 62–82.

"British Literature: Survey and Critique." First item in "Books and Their Makers" section. *Saturday Review of Literature* 34 (Oct. 13, 1951): 24–26, 47.

"In Memory of Hermon Ould." In *Hermon Ould: A Tribute by Various Authors*. PEN English Centre, Slough: Kenion Press, n.d.

"A Young Girl's Diary." *Everybody's*, April 19, 1952, 10, 26.

Contribution to "The Ugliest Trend" forum, replying to C. P. Snow. *Author*, 52, no. 4 (Summer 1952): 83–89.

"Inner and Outer Worlds" (review). *TLS*, Sept. 26, 1952, 628.

"The Dualist Tradition." *TLS* Supplement, "Special Autumn Number: Personal Preferences," Aug. 6, 1954, Axxxvi.

"The Sad State of English Writers." *P.E.N. News*, Autumn 1954, 5–8.

"A Note on France." *Cornhill Magazine* 167, no. 1001 (1954–55): 439–52.

"Somewhere to Live: A Long Search." *Manchester Guardian*, Feb. 25, 1956.

"Can It Be Done? The Case for Providence." *TLS* Supplement, in "British Books around the World" section, Aug. 7, 1959, Axxviii.

"A Sense of Proportion." *Adam International Review*, nos. 284–86 (1960): 169–79.

"One Man in His Time." *Sunday Times*, magazine section, Jan. 31, 1960, 15.

Fiction of the Week. Column in *Sunday Times*, magazine section: April 3, 1960, 18; April 17, 1960, 17; May 1, 1960, 18; May 15, 1960, 17; May 29, 1960, 18; June 12, 1960, 28; June 26, 1960, 28; July 10, 1960, 28; July 24, 1960, 24; Aug. 7, 1960, 23; Aug. 21, 1960, 23; Sept. 4, 1960, 27.

"Portrait of a County: Yorkshire." *Vogue* (UK) 116, no. 14 (mid-Oct. 1960): 70–73, 138, 143. Reprinted in 1962 edition of *Vogue's Gallery*.

"Morley Roberts: The Last of the True Victorians." *Library Chronicle* (University of Pennsylvania, Philadelphia) 27, no. 2 (Spring/Summer 1961): 93–127.

"A Writer's Sermon." *Writer* (Boston) 75 (Oct. 1962): 13–15.

"A Bolster to Young Mr. X." *Books and Bookmen*, 1962.

"The Writer in Contemporary Society." *American Scholar* 35 (Winter 1965–66): 126–32.

"Love's Labours Exposed." *Spectator*, Feb. 4, 1966.

"Now and Then." "Writing in the Seventies" series, no. 5. *Author* 81, no. 2 (Summer 1970): 59–63. Reprinted in *Author! Author!: A Selection from "The Author: The Journal of the Society of Authors since 1890,"* edited by Richard Findlater (London: Faber and Faber, 1984); and as "What to Do till the Novel Comes: A Lean Wolf Develops Muscles" in *Writer* (Boston) 84 (April 1971): 14–15.

Selected Printed Letters

Egoist, Nov. 1, 1916, 14–15.

New Statesman and Nation, n.s., 3, no. 63 (May 7, 1932): 582–83.

"The Gagging Act" (joint signatory). *New Statesman and Nation*, n.s., 4, no. 97 (Dec. 31, 1932): 854.

New Statesman and Nation, n.s., 5, no. 104 (Feb. 18, 1933): 187.

"The Meerut Appeal." *New Statesman and Nation*, n.s., 5, no. 107 (March 11, 1933): 288.

"Symposium or Law-Court?" *New English Weekly*, Oct. 19, 1933.

Joint signatory. *Left Review*, Dec. 1934.

Whitby Gazette, Jan. 31, 1936.

"A Popular Front." *Time and Tide* 17, no. 23 (June 6, 1936): 811.

Author, Summer 1936. Reprint of two letters from *Times*, March 13, 1936, and March 17, 1936.

Left Review 6 (Feb. 1937).

Time and Tide 18 (Sept. 11, 1937): 1196.
"Mrs. Crozier" (joint signatory). *Peace News*, Feb. 5, 1938.
"Conditions of the Sacrifice," subheaded "General Settlement" (joint signatory). *Manchester Guardian*, Sept. 24, 1938.
"Czechoslovakia: Authors." *TLS*, Oct. 22, 1938, 677; *New Statesman and Nation*, n.s., 16, no. 4000 (Oct. 22, 1938): 606.
"The National Peace Petition" (joint signatory). *Author*, Christmas issue, 1938.
"Refugee Writers." *TLS*, July 13, 1940, 339.
"Books in War Time: 'Disintegration' of the Trade: The Case for Concessions" (joint signatory). *Times*, Jan. 1, 1942; *Bookseller*, Jan. 1, 1942.
"Planning for Publishing." *TLS*, Dec. 5, 1942, 595.
Manchester Guardian, Aug. 13, 1945.
"Books for Poland" (joint signatory). *Times*, Oct. 24, 1945, 5d.
TLS, Aug. 3, 1946, 367.
"Writers in Conflict: Nationalism at PEN Conference." *Manchester Guardian*, June 12, 1947.
Times, Sept. 24, 1947, 5e.
Whitby Gazette, Oct. 10, 1947, and subsequent responses.
Joint signatory on exiled authors. *TLS*, Dec. 29, 1950, 827.
Times, Sept. 26, 1951, 6d.
"Lament for the Muffin." *Times*, Nov. 10, 1952, 7g.
TLS, Dec. 19, 1952, 837.
Joint signatory. *Author* 54, no. 4 (Summer 1954): 76–79.
TLS, Feb. 4, 1955.
Joint signatory. *Times*, Nov. 14, 1955, 9d.
"The Author and the Public." *TLS*, May 10, 1957, 289.
Times, Nov. 7, 1959, 7d.
Joint signatory. *Times*, March 1, 1960, 11d.
TLS, April 13, 1962, 249.
Times, Oct. 19, 1965, 13e.
Times, Feb. 8, 1967, 11c.
New York Times Book Review 4, no. 11 (Aug. 11, 1968): 4.
Adam International Review, nos. 328–30 (1969): 51.
TLS, Aug. 1, 1975, 874c.
"Sex Discrimination Act." *Times*, Jan. 3, 1976, 13d.
TLS, Aug. 20, 1976, 1032b.
"R. H. Tawney." *TLS*, Jan. 28, 1977, 106d.
"Unsexed Pronoun." *Times*, Nov. 2, 1978, 17g.
"Margaret Storm Jameson in Her Own Voice: Correspondence of Storm Jameson with Hilary Newitt Brown and Harrison Brown," edited by Chiara Briganti and Kathy Mezei. In *Margaret Storm Jameson: Writing in Dialogue*, edited by Jennifer Birkett and Chiara Briganti, 164–206. Newcastle: Cambridge Scholars Publishing, 2007.

Interviews and Recorded Talks

"The Author of Our Serial, 'The Happy Highways': A Chat with Storm Jameson." *New Commonwealth* 1 (Nov. 7, 1919): 6.

"The Irresponsibility of Novelists: An Interview with Storm Jameson," by R. le Clerc Phillips. *Bookman* (U.S.) 76, no. 2 (Feb. 1933): 114–17.

"Safety First!" BBC Home Service, 6 p.m., Feb. 26, 1941 (BBC Written Archives, Caversham: Recorded Talks. Script Library: Radio Talks: Storm Jameson).

"What I Am Reading Now." BBC Home Service, 4:15–4:30 p.m., March 20, 1941 (BBC Written Archives: Recorded Talks).

"Britain Speaks." BBC Overseas North-American Transmission, July 3 and 4, 1941 (BBC Written Archives: Recorded Talks).

Introductory talk before readings from *The PEN in Exile*, Nov. 24, 1954 (British Library: BBC Sound Archive, T2587WR).

"The Household Gods Couldn't Keep Up with Storm Jameson." Interview with Alice Hope. *Daily Telegraph*, Sept. 9, 1969.

Interview with Jack Singleton, in "Home This Afternoon" series. March 3, 1970 (British Library: BBC Sound Archive, ILP 195571).

Interview with Jeanine McMullen, in "Books and Writers" series. March 4, 1970 (British Library: BBC Sound Archive, ILP 196495).

Interview with Elaine Feinstein. *Guardian*, Sept. 1, 1982.

Interview with Janet Watts. *Observer*, Sept. 5, 1982.

"Just Killing Time until Death." Interview with Caroline Moorhead. *Times*, March 2, 1984, 17a.

Obituaries and Reminiscences

"Powerful Writer with a Bleak and Brave Eye." *Times*, Oct. 7, 1986, 22f.

"Writer Who Fought for Freedom Dies." *Yorkshire Post*, Oct. 8, 1986.

Cunningham, John. "Restless Spirit." *Guardian*, Oct. 9, 1986.

Whitby Gazette, Oct. 10, 1986.

New York Times Book Review 1, no. 7 (Oct. 11, 1986): 3.

Feinstein, Elaine. "Margaret Storm Jameson." *The PEN Broadsheet of the English Centre of International PEN*, no. 23 (Autumn 1987): 6–7.

Parsons, Diana. Centenary tribute in *This England*, Autumn 1991.

Selected Works by Other Writers

Adcock, St. John. *The Glory That Was Grub Street: Impressions of Contemporary Authors*. London: Sampson Low, Marston, 1928.

Allsop, Kenneth. *The Angry Decade: A Survey of the Cultural Revolt of the Nineteen-Fifties*. London: Peter Owen, 1958.

Anand, Mulk Raj. *The Coolie*. London: Lawrence and Wishart, 1936.

———. "A Writer in Exile." In *Voices of the Crossing*, edited by Ferdinand Dennis and Naseem Khan, 16–21. London: Serpents Tail, 2000.

Anon. *The Author and the Public: Problems of Communication*. London: Hutchinson, 1957.

Applebaum, Anne. Review, "Yesterday's Man?" *New York Review of Books*, Feb. 11, 2010, 10–11.

Auden, W. H., and Christopher Isherwood. *Journey to a War*. 1939. London: Faber and Faber, 1973.

Bates, Ralph. *The Dolphin in the Wood*. London: Rupert Hart-Davis, 1950.

Bedford, Sybille. *A Legacy*. London: Weidenfeld and Nicolson, 1956.

Benda, Julien. *The Great Betrayal* (*La trahison des clercs*). Translated by Richard Aldington. London: Routledge, 1928.

Benjamin, Jessica. *Like Subjects, Love Objects: Essays on Recognition and Sexual Difference*. New Haven, Conn.: Yale Univ. Press, 1995.

Berdan, John Milton, ed. *Fourteen Stories from One Plot*. New York: Oxford Univ. Press, 1932.

Berry, Paul, and Mark Bostridge. *Vera Brittain: A Life*. London: Virago Press, 2001.

Besant, Annie. *A Study of Consciousness: A Contribution to the Science of Psychology*. London: Theosophical Publishing, 1904.

Bigsby, Christopher. *Remembering and Imagining the Holocaust: The Chain of Memory*. Cambridge: Cambridge Univ. Press, 2006.

Birkett, Jennifer. "(En)countering Globalisation: Resistances in the System." In *Globalisation and Its Discontents*, edited by Stan Smith, 47–69. Cambridge: Boydell and Brewer, 2006.

———. "A Fictional Function: Storm Jameson and W. H. Auden." *English* 56, no. 215 (Summer 2007): 171–85.

———. *Margaret Storm Jameson: A Life*. Oxford: Oxford Univ. Press, 2009.

Birkett, Jennifer, and Chiara Briganti, eds. *Margaret Storm Jameson: Writing in Dialogue*. Newcastle: Cambridge Scholars Publishing, 2007.

Blackham, Robert J. *Woman: In Honour and Dishonour*. London: Sampson Low, n.d. [1936].

Bluemel, Kristin. *George Orwell and the Radical Eccentrics: Intermodernism in Literary London*. London: Palgrave Macmillan, 2004.

———, ed. *Intermodernism: Literary Culture in Mid-Twentieth-Century Britain*. Edinburgh: Edinburgh Univ. Press, 2009.

Bois, Elie J. *Truth on the Tragedy of France*. Translated by N. Scarlyn Wilson. London: Hodder and Stoughton, 1940.

Boog, Horst, et al. *Germany and the Second World War*. Vol. 6, *The Global War*. Translated by Ewald Osers et al. Oxford: Oxford Univ. Press, 2001.

Bottome, Phyllis. *The Mortal Storm*. London: Faber and Faber, 1937.

———, ed. *Our New Order or Hitler's?* Harmondsworth: Penguin, 1943.

Bourke, Joanna. *Dismembering the Male: Men's Bodies, Britain and the Great War*. London: Reaktion Books, 1996.

Bowen, Elizabeth. *The Bazaar and Other Stories*. Edited by Allan Hepburn. Edinburgh: Edinburgh Univ. Press, 2008.

———. *People, Places, Things: Essays by Elizabeth Bowen*. Edited by Allan Hepburn. Edinburgh: Edinburgh Univ. Press, 2008.

Bradley, Fiona. *Surrealism*. Movements in Modern Art. 1997. London: Tate Gallery Publishing, 2009.

Brett, Lionel. *Our Selves Unknown: An Autobiography*. London: Victor Gollancz, 1985.

Briggs, Asa. *The History of Broadcasting in the United Kingdom: The War of Words, 1939–45*. Vol. 3. Oxford: Oxford Univ. Press, 1995.

Briggs, Julia. *Virginia Woolf: An Inner Life*. London: Penguin, 2006.

British Bombing Survey Unit [Michael Beetham and Sebastian Cox]. *The Strategic Air War against Germany, 1939–1945*. London: Frank Cass, 1998.

Brittain, Vera. *England's Hour*. London: Macmillan, 1941.

———. *On Becoming a Writer*. London: Hutchinson, 1947.

———. *The Rebel Passion*. London: George Allen and Unwin, 1964.

———. *Testament of Experience: An Autobiographical Story of the Years 1925–1950.* London: Victor Gollancz, 1957. Reprint, London: Virago Press, 1979.

———. *Testament of Friendship.* London: Macmillan, 1940. Reprint, London: Virago Press, 1980.

———. *Testament of a Peace Lover: Letters from Vera Brittain.* Edited by Winifred and Alan Eden-Green. London: Virago Press, 1988.

———. *Wartime Chronicle: Vera Brittain's Diary 1939–45.* Edited by Alan Bishop and Y. Aleksandra Bennett. London: Victor Gollancz, 1989.

Broch, Hermann. *The Sleepwalkers: A Trilogy (Die Schlafwandler).* Translated by Edwin and Willa Muir. London: Martin Secker, 1932.

Brook, Donald. *Writer's Gallery: Biographical Sketches of Prominent British Writers and Their Views on Reconstruction.* London: Rockcliff Publishing, 1944.

Bull, Angela. *Noel Streatfeild: A Biography.* London: Collins, 1984.

Bulletin de la Chambre de Commerce Française de Grande-Bretagne. Jan. 1944. Christopher Storm-Clark archive.

Burdekin, Katharine [Murray Constantine, pseud.]. *Swastika Night.* 1937. London: Victor Gollancz, 1940; London: Lawrence and Wishart, 1985.

Burton, Elaine. *And Your Verdict?* London: Frederick Muller, 1942.

Calder, Jenni. *The Nine Lives of Naomi Mitchison.* London: Virago Press, 1997.

Čapek, Karel. *War with the Newts (Válka s mloky).* 1936. Translated by Allen and Unwin. London: Allen and Unwin, 1937. Reprint, Evanston: Northwestern Univ. Press, 1985. Translated by Ewald Osers. London: Unwin Paperbacks, 1985.

Cesarini, David. *Arthur Koestler: The Homeless Mind.* London: Random House (UK), 2000.

Chapman, Guy, ed. *Beckford: A Biography.* London: Jonathan Cape, 1937. Reprint, London: Rupert Hart-Davis, 1952.

———. *Culture and Survival.* London: Jonathan Cape, 1940.

———. *The Dreyfus Case: A Reassessment.* London: Rupert Hart-Davis, 1955.

———. *The Dreyfus Trials.* London: Batsford, 1972; New York: Stein and Day, 1972; London: Granada, Paladin, 1974.

———. *A Kind of Survivor: The Autobiography of Guy Chapman.* Edited by Storm Jameson. London: Victor Gollancz, 1975.

———. *A Painted Cloth.* London: Cassell, 1930.

———. *A Passionate Prodigality: Fragments of an Autobiography.* London: Nicholson and Watson, 1933; New York: Holt, Rinehart and Winston, 1966; Fawcett, 1967, with preface by Chapman.

———. "The Publisher's Reader." *Author,* Autumn 1943.

———. "Put Peace in Its Place." *New Clarion* 3, no. 78 (Dec. 2, 1933): 1–2.

———. Review. *Sunday Times,* April 3, 1960.

———. Review of *History of the Second World War,* by Basil Liddell Hart. *Contemporary Review,* Jan. 1971.

———. *The Third Republic of France.* Vol. 1, *The First Phase, 1871–1894.* London: Macmillan, 1962.

———. *The Travel-Diaries of William Beckford of Fonthill.* Vol. 1. London: Constable, 1928.

———, ed. *Vain Glory: A Miscellany of the Great War, 1914–1918.* London: Cassell, 1937.

———. *Why France Collapsed.* London: Cassell, 1968.

————, with John Hodgkin. *A Bibliography of William Beckford of Fonthill*. London: Constable, 1930.

Clark, George. *Second Wind: The Story of the Campaign and the Committee of 100*. London: Workshop Publications, [March 1963].

Clark, Ronald W. *The Life of Bertrand Russell*. London: Jonathan Cape and Weidenfeld and Nicolson, 1975.

Clarke, I. F. *Voices Prophesying War, 1763–1984*. Oxford: Oxford Univ. Press, 1966.

Cockburn, Claud, ed. *Week*. Journal published March 29, 1933, through Dec. 18, 1946 (suppressed by Government Order, Jan. 15, 1941–Oct. 23, 1942).

Cole, Margaret, ed. *The Road to Success: Twenty Essays on the Choice of a Career for Women*. London: Methuen, 1936.

Colls, Robert, and Philip Dodd, eds. *Englishness: Politics and Culture, 1880–1920*. London: Croom and Helms, 1986.

Conradi, Peter J. *Iris Murdoch: A Life*. London: HarperCollins, 2001.

Crawford Mitchell, Ruth, ed. *Alice Garrigue Masaryk: 1879–1966*. University of Pittsburgh: University Center for International Studies, 1980.

Crick, Bernard, ed. *George Orwell: Nineteen Eighty-Four*. Oxford: Clarendon, 1984.

Cunard, Nancy, ed. *Poems for France, Written by British Poets on France since the War*. London: La France Libre, 1944.

Danchev, Alex. *Alchemist of War: The Life of Basil Liddell Hart*. London: Weidenfeld and Nicolson, 1998.

Dane, Clemence. *The Women's Side*. London: Herbert Jenkins, 1926.

Davison, Peter, ed., assisted by Ian Angus and Sheila Davison. *The Complete Works of George Orwell*. 20 vols. London: Secker and Warburg, 1998.

Deane, Patrick, ed. *History in Our Hands: A Critical Anthology of Writings on Literature, Culture and Politics from the 1930s*. London: Leicester Univ. Press, 1998.

de Gourmont, Remy. *Les saintes du paradis*. Paris: Éditions R. Kieffer, 1922.

Dell, Edmund. *A Strange Eventful History: Democratic Socialism in Britain*. London: HarperCollins, 1999.

Dobrée, Valentine. *The Emperor's Tigers*. London: Faber and Faber, 1929.

————. *Your Cuckoo Sings by Kind*. London: Alfred A. Knopf, 1927.

Dos Passos, John. *Big Money*. Vol. 3 of *U.S.A.* London: Constable, 1936.

————. *The Forty-Second Parallel*. Vol. 1 of *U.S.A.* London: Constable, 1930.

————. *Nineteen Nineteen*. Vol. 2 of *U.S.A.* London: Constable, 1932.

Dowson, Jane, ed. *Women's Writing, 1945–1960: After the Deluge*. London: Palgrave Macmillan, 2003.

Etlin, Richard, ed. *Art, Culture, and Media under the Third Reich*. Chicago: Univ. of Chicago Press, 2002.

Fabian Society. Annual Report (18/A/26 Executive Committee Minute Book, January 16, 1939, to June 29, 1946: 58th Annual Report for Year Ending 31 March 1941).

Fisher, Clive. *Cyril Connolly: A Nostalgic Life*. London: Macmillan, 1996.

Fitzroy, A. T. [Rose Allatini]. *Despised and Rejected*. London: C. W. Daniel, 1918; London: Gay Modern Classics, 1988.

Ford, Hugh, ed. *Nancy Cunard: Brave Poet, Indomitable Rebel, 1896–1965*. Philadelphia: Chilton, 1968.

Forster, E. M. *Aspects of the Novel*. London: Edward Arnold, 1927; London: Hodder and Stoughton, 2012.

Fowler, Bridget. *The Alienated Reader: Women and Romantic Literature in the Twentieth Century*. Hemel Hempstead: Harvester Wheatsheaf, 1991.

Fox, Ralph. *The Novel and the People*. London: Lawrence and Wishart, 1937.

France, Anatole. *La révolte des anges*. Paris: Calmann-Lévy, c. 1914.

"From the Campaign for Nuclear Disarmament." Jacquetta Hawkes archive, University of Bradford, Special Collections.

Furedi, Frank. *First World War: Still No End in Sight*. London: Bloomsbury, 2014.

Gardiner, Juliet. *Wartime Britain, 1939–1945*. London: Headline Book Publishing, 2005.

Geissmar, Berta. *The Baton and the Jackboot*. London: Hamish Hamilton, 1944.

Gellhorn, Martha. *A Stricken Field*. New York: Duell, Sloan, and Pearce, 1940; London: Jonathan Cape, 1941; London: Virago Press, 1986: Chicago: Univ. of Chicago Press, 2011.

George, W. L. *The Intelligence of Woman*. London: Herbert Jenkins, 1927.

Gielgud, Val, ed. *Radio Theatre: Plays Specially Written for Broadcasting*. London: MacDonald, 1946.

Gindin, James. "Storm Jameson and the Chronicle." *Centennial Review* (U.S.) 22, no. 4 (Fall 1978): 400–409.

Giraudoux, Jean. *Bella*. Paris: Bernard Grasset, 1926.

——. *Intermezzo*. Paris: Bernard Grasset, 1933.

——. *La guerre de Troie n'aura pas lieu*. [1935.] Paris: Larousse, Petits classiques, 2009.

Glendinning, Victoria. *Rebecca West: A Life*. London: Phoenix, 1998.

Gollancz, Victor. *Let My People Go: Some Practical Proposals for Dealing with Hitler's Massacre of the Jews and an Appeal to the British Public*. London: Victor Gollancz, 1943.

Grant Duff, S[heila]. *Europe and the Czechs*. Penguin Special. Harmondsworth: Penguin, 1938.

Grass, Günter. *Peeling the Onion (Beim Häuten der Zwiebel)*. Translated by Michael Henry Heim. London: Harvill Secker, 2007; London: Vintage, 2008.

Hall, Radclyffe. *The Well of Loneliness*. London; Jonathan Cape, 1928; London: Falcon Press, 1949.

Hamilton, Cecily. *Marriage as a Trade*. London: Chapman and Hall, 1909.

Hamilton, Mary Agnes. *Dead Yesterday*. London: Duckworth, 1916.

Hamilton, Patrick. *The Midnight Bell*. London: Constable, 1929; Boston: Little, Brown, 1930.

——. *Twenty Thousand Streets under the Sky*. London: Constable, 1935; London: Vintage, 2004.

Hammacher, A. M. *Barbara Hepworth*. Translated by James Brockway. London: Thames and Hudson, 1968; reprinted with additions, 1987.

Hanley, James. *Boy*. 1931. Richmond, Surrey: Oneworld Classics, 2007.

Harding, Brian. *Keeping Faith: The History of the Royal British Legion*. Barnsley: Leo Cooper, 2001.

Harland, Sydney Cross. *Nine Lives: The Autobiography of a Yorkshire Scientist*. Edited by Max Millard. Raleigh, N.C.: Boson Books, 2001.

Harris, Arthur Travers, and Sebastian Cox. *Despatch on War Operations: 23 February 1942 to 8 May 1945*. London: Taylor and Francis, 1995.

Hartley, Jenny. *Millions Like Us: British Women's Fiction of the Second World War*. London: Virago Press, 1997.

Hastings, Selina. *Rosamond Lehmann*. London: Vintage, 2003.

Henderson, Philip. *The Novel Today: Studies in Contemporary Attitudes*. London: John Lane, Bodley Head, 1936.

Hennessy, Peter. *Having It So Good: Britain in the Fifties*. London: Allen Lane, Penguin, 2007.

——. *Never Again: Britain 1945–51*. London: Jonathan Cape, 1992.

Hepburn, Allan. *Intrigue*. New Haven, Conn.: Yale Univ. Press, 2005.

Hepworth, Barbara. *A Pictorial Autobiography*. Edited and designed by Anthony Adams. London: Tate Publishing, [1970].

Herf, Jeffrey. *Reactionary Modernism: Technology, Culture, and Politics in Weimar and the Third Reich*. Cambridge: Cambridge Univ. Press, 1984.

Hillary, Richard. *The Last Enemy*. London: Vintage, 1997.

Hirsch, Pam. *The Constant Liberal: The Life and Work of Phyllis Bottome*. London: Quartet, 2010.

Hobsbawm, Eric. *Interesting Times: A Twentieth-Century Life*. London: Allen Lane, Penguin, 2002.

Holtby, Winifred. *Letters to a Friend*. Edited by Alice Holtby and Jean McWilliam. London: Collins, 1937.

Humble, Nicola. *The Feminine Middlebrow Novel, 1920s to 1950s: Class, Domesticity, and Bohemianism*. Oxford: Oxford Univ. Press, 2001.

Hutchins, Bessie Leigh. *The Working Life of Women*. London: Fabian Society, 1911.

Hutt, Allen. *The Post-war History of the British Working Class*. Left Book Club. London: Victor Gollancz, 1937.

Jackson, Julian. *France: The Dark Years, 1940–1944*. Oxford: Oxford Univ. Press, 2001.

James, Norah C. *Sleeveless Errand*. Paris: Henry Babou and Jack Kahane, 1929.

John, St. John. *William Heinemann: A Century of Publishing, 1890–1990*. London: William Heinemann, 1990.

Judt, Tony. *Postwar: A History of Europe since 1945*. 2005. London: Pimlico, 2007.

——. *Reappraisals: Reflections on the Forgotten Twentieth Century*. 2008. London: Vintage, 2009.

Keighley, Marion. *Whitby Writers: Writers of Whitby and District 1867–1949*. Whitby: Horne and Son, 1957.

Kendall, Hugh P., ed. *Ten Reprints of Local History from the "Whitby Gazette."* Sold for the benefit of the H. P. Kendall memorial fund, Whitby: Whitby Gazette, n.d.

Kenyon, Frederic G., ed. *The Letters of Elizabeth Barrett Browning*. 2 vols. London: Smith, Elder, 1897.

Kershaw, Angela, and Angela Kimyongür, eds. *Women in Europe between the Wars: Politics, Culture and Society*. Aldershot: Ashgate, 2007.

Kershaw, Ian. *Fateful Choices: Ten Decisions That Changed the World 1940–1941*. London: Penguin, 2008.

King, Nicola. *Memory, Narrative, Identity: Remembering the Self*. Edinburgh: Edinburgh Univ. Press, 2000.

Kirkpatrick, Helen Paull. *This Terrible Peace*. London: Rich and Cowan, 1939.

Klein, Yvonne M., ed. *Beyond the Home Front: Women's Autobiographical Writing of the Two World Wars*. Houndmills, Basingstoke: Macmillan, 1997.

Koestler, Arthur. *The Scum of the Earth*. London: Jonathan Cape, 1941.

———. *The Yogi and the Commissar and Other Essays*. London: Jonathan Cape, 1945.

Lassner, Phyllis. *Anglo-Jewish Women Writing the Holocaust: Displaced Witnesses*. London: Palgrave Macmillan, 2008.

———. *British Women Writers of World War II: Battlegrounds of Their Own*. Houndmills, Basingstoke: Macmillan, 1998; New York: St. Martin's, 1998.

———. *Colonial Strangers: Women Writing the End of the British Empire*. New Brunswick, N.J.: Rutgers Univ. Press, 2004.

Lawrence, Margaret. *We Write as Women*. London: Michael Joseph, 1937.

Leavis, Queenie. *Fiction and the Reading Public*. 1932. London: Bellew Publishing, 1990.

Lee, Hermione. *Virginia Woolf*. London: Vintage, 1997.

Lefanu, Sarah. *Rose Macaulay*. London: Virago Press, 2003.

Lessing, Doris. *The Four-Gated City* (Children of Violence, volume 5) [1969] (London: HarperCollins, 1993; New York: HarperPerennial, 1995).

———. *A Small Personal Voice: Essays Reviews Interviews*, ed. Paul Schlueter [1974] (London: Flamingo, 1994).

Lewis, Sinclair. *It Can't Happen Here*. 1935. New York: Signet Classics, 2005.

Lidderdale, Jane, and Mary Nicholson. *Dear Miss Weaver: Harriet Shaw Weaver, 1876–1961*. London: Faber, 1970.

Lidice: A Tribute by Members of the International P.E.N. Introduction by the Hon. Harold Nicolson C.M.G., M.P. London: George Allen and Unwin, 1944.

Linke, Lilo. *Restless Flags: A German Girl's Story*. London: Constable, 1935.

———. *Tale without End*. London: Constable; New York: Alfred A. Knopf, 1934.

Livingstone, Dame Adelaide, with Marjorie Scott Johnston. *The Peace Ballot: The Official History*. London: Victor Gollancz, 1935.

Loseff, Lev. *On the Beneficence of Censorship: Aesopian Language in Modern Russian Literature*. Translated by Jane Bobko. Munich: Verlag Otto Sagner in Kommission, 1984.

Lovat Dickson, Rache. *The House of Words*. London: Macmillan, 1963.

Lovell, Mary S. *The Mitford Girls: The Biography of an Extraordinary Family*. London: Little, Brown, 2001.

Lubbock, Percy. *The Craft of Fiction*. London: Jonathan Cape, 1921.

Lukács, György. *The Historical Novel*. 1937. Translated by Hannah and Stanley Mitchell. London: Merlin Press, 1962.

Macaulay, Rose. *A Casual Commentary*. London: Methuen, 1925.

———. *Non-combatants and Others*. London: Hodder and Stoughton, 1916. Reprint, London: Capuchin Classics, 2010.

MacKillop, Ian. *F. R. Leavis: A Life in Criticism*. London; Allen Lane, Penguin, 1995.

MacMillan, Margaret. *Peacemakers: The Paris Conference of 1919 and Its Attempt to End War*. London: John Murray, 2001.

Malraux, André. *Man's Fate* (*La condition humaine*). Translated by Haakon M. Chevalier. New York: Random House, c. 1934.

Mannin, Ethel. *Women and the Revolution*. London: Secker and Warburg, 1938.

Martin, Jane. "Contesting Knowledge: Mary Bridget Adams and the Workers' Education Movement, 1900–1918." In *Gender, Colonialism and Education: The Politics of Experience*, edited by J. Goodman and J. Martin, 124–47. London: Woburn Press, 2002.

Maslen, Elizabeth. *Political and Social Issues in British Women's Fiction, 1928–1968*. London: Palgrave, 2001.

Mass Observation. *The Journey Home: A Report Prepared by Mass Observation for the Advertising Service Guild*. London: John Murray, 1944.

Matuschek, Oliver. *Three Lives: A Biography of Stefan Zweig*. Translated by Allan Blunden. London: Pushkin Press, 2011.

Mazower, Mark. *Dark Continent: Europe's Twentieth Century*. London: Penguin, 1998.

McCrum, Robert. *Wodehouse: A Life*. London: Penguin, Viking, 2004.

Miłosz, Czesław. *The Captive Mind*. London: Secker and Warburg, 1953; Harmondsworth: Penguin, 1980.

Mitchison, Naomi. *Among You Taking Notes: The Wartime Diary of Naomi Mitchison, 1939–1945*. Edited by Dorothy Sheridan. London: Victor Gollancz, 1985.

——. *The Moral Basis of Politics*. London: Constable, 1938.

Montefiore, Janet. *Men and Women Writers of the 1930s*. London: Routledge, 1996.

Morgan, Charles. *The Fountain*. London: Macmillan, 1932.

——. *My Name Is Legion*. London: William Heinemann, 1925.

——. *Selected Letters of Charles Morgan*. Edited by Eiluned Lewis. London: Macmillan, 1967.

Morrison, Sybil. *I Renounce War: The Story of the Peace Pledge Union*. London: Sheppard Press, 1962.

Munson, Gorham. *The Awakening Twenties: A Memoir—History of a Literary Period*. Baton Rouge: Louisiana State Univ. Press, 1985.

Murdoch, Iris. *Existentialists and Mystics: Writings on Philosophy and Literature*. Edited by Peter Conradi. London: Chatto and Windus, 1997; New York: Penguin, 1999.

——. *Sartre*. London: Bowes and Bowes, 1953. Reprinted as *Sartre: Romantic Realist*. London: Vintage, 1999.

Némirovsky, Irène. *Suite Française*. 2004. Translated by Sandra Smith. London: Virago Press, 2007.

Neumann, Robert. *Scene in Passing*. 1942. London: Hutchinson International Authors, 1945.

Newitt, Hilary. *Women Must Choose: The Position of Women in Europe To-day*. London: Victor Gollancz, 1937.

Nicholson, Virginia. *Among the Bohemians: Experiments in Living, 1900–1939*. London: Penguin, Viking, 2002.

Nicolson, Juliet. *The Great Silence, 1918–1920: Living in the Shadow of the Great War*. London: John Murray, 1909.

Nott, Kathleen. *An Elderly Retired Man*. London: Faber, 1963.

Obelkevish, James, and Peter Catterall, eds. *Understanding Post-war British Society*. London: Routledge, 1994.

Ogden, Charles Kay. *Basic English: A General Introduction with Rules and Grammar*. London: Kegan Paul, Trench, and Trübner, 1930.

Olden, Rudolf. *Hitler der Eroberer: Entlarvung einer Legende*. Amsterdam: Querido, 1935.

Orage, A. R. *Political and Economic Writings*. Edited by Montgomery Butchart. London: Stanley Nott, 1936.

———. *Selected Essays and Critical Writings*. Edited by Herbert Read and Denis Saurat. London: Stanley Nott, 1935.

Ottinger, Didier, ed. *Futurism*. London: Tate Publishing, 2008.

Ould, Hermon, ed. *The Book of the P.E.N.* London: Arthur Barker, 1950.

———, ed. *Freedom of Expression: A Symposium, Based on the Conference Called by the London Centre of the International P.E.N. to Commemorate the Tercentenary of the Publication of Milton's "Areopagitica": 22–26 August 1944*. London: Hutchinson, c. 1945.

———. *Shuttle: An Autobiographical Sequence*. London: Andrew Dakers, 1947.

———, ed. *Writers in Freedom: A Symposium Based on the XVII International Congress of the P.E.N. Club Held in London in September 1941*. London: Hutchinson, 1942.

Overy, Richard. *The Morbid Age: Britain between the Wars*. London: Allen Lane, Penguin, 2009.

Pankhurst, Christabel. *The Great Scourge and How to End It*. London: Lincoln's Inn House, 1913.

Phillips, Melanie. *The Ascent of Woman: A History of the Suffragette Movement and the Ideas behind It*. London: Little, Brown, 2003.

Piette, Adam. *The Literary Cold War: 1945 to Vietnam*. Edinburgh: Edinburgh Univ. Press, 2009.

Plain, Gill. *Women's Fiction of the Second World War: Gender, Power and Resistance*. Edinburgh: Edinburgh Univ. Press, 1996.

Pratt, Mary Louise. "Interpretive Strategies/Strategic Interpretations." In *Postmodernism and Politics*, edited by Jonathan Arac, 26–54. Manchester: Manchester Univ. Press, 1986.

Priestley, J. B. *The Good Companions*. London: William Heinemann, 1929.

Pullein-Thompson, Josephine. "Standing Aside from Politics." *The PEN Broadsheet of the English Centre of International PEN*, no. 19, Autumn 1985.

Raitt, Suzanne. *May Sinclair: A Modern Victorian*. Oxford: Clarendon, 2000.

Rathbone, Irene. *We That Were Young*. London: Chatto and Windus, 1932; New York: Feminist Press, 1989.

Reeves, Mrs. Pember. *Family Life on a Pound a Week*. London: Fabian, 1912.

Renn, Ludwig. *War*. Translated by Willa and Edwin Muir. London: Martin Secker, 1929.

Rhys, Jean. *After Leaving Mr. Mackenzie*. London: Jonathan Cape, 1930; London: Penguin, 1971.

Robins, Anna Gruetzner. *Modern Art in Britain, 1910–1914*. London: Merrell Holberton in association with Barbican Art Gallery, 1997.

Robinson, Jane. *Bluestockings: The Remarkable Story of the First Women to Fight for an Education*. London: Penguin, Viking, 2009.

Rolph, C. H., ed. *The Trial of Lady Chatterley: Regina v. Penguin Books Ltd; The Transcript of the Trial*. Harmondsworth: Penguin, 1961.

Romains, Jules. *Men of Good Will (Les hommes de bonne volonté)*. Vols. 1 and 2. London: Lovat Dickson, 1933.

Roubal, Petr. "Politics of Gymnastics: Mass Gymnastic Displays under Communism in Central and Eastern Europe." *Body and Society* 9, no. 2 (2003): 1–25.

Rowley, Hazel. *Christina Stead: A Biography*. London: Secker and Warburg, 1995.

Sadleir, Michael. *Fanny by Gaslight*. London: Constable, 1940 [reprinted fifteen times by 1947].

Sanger, Margaret. *The New Motherhood*. London: Jonathan Cape, 1922.

Sartre, Jean-Paul. *Critique littéraires (Situations I)*. Paris: Gallimard, c. 1947.

——. *Situations II*. Paris: Gallimard, 1948.

——. *Situations III*. Paris: Gallimard, 1949.

Sayers, Dorothy. "Living to Work." In *Unpopular Opinions*, 122–27. London: Victor Gollancz, 1946.

Scammell, Michael. *Koestler: The Literary and Political Odyssey of a Twentieth-Century Skeptic*. New York: Random House, 2010.

Sebald, W. G. *On the Natural History of Destruction*. 1999. Translated by Anthea Bell. London: Hamish Hamilton, 2003.

Shaw, Bernard. *The Intelligent Woman's Guide to Socialism and Capitalism*. London: Constable, 1929.

Sherry, Norman. *The Life of Graham Greene*. London: Pimlico, 2004–5.

Smernoff, Richard A. *André Chenier*. Boston: Twayne Publishers, c. 1977.

Smith, Stevie. *Over the Frontier*. 1938. London: Virago Press, 1980.

Snowman, Daniel. *The Hitler Emigrés: The Cultural Impact on Britain of Refugees from Nazism*. London: Pimlico, 2003.

Sologub, Feodor. *The Little Demon*. Translated by John Cournos and Richard Aldington. London: Martin Secker, 1916.

Souhami, Diana. *The Trials of Radclyffe Hall*. London: Weidenfeld and Nicolson, 1998.

Spender, Stephen. *Forward from Liberalism*. London: Victor Gollancz, 1937.

Stapledon, Olaf. *Last and First Men*. London: Millennium, Victor Gollancz, 1930.

——. *Old Man in New World*. PEN Books. London: George Allen and Unwin, 1944.

Stonebridge, Lyndsey. *The Judicial Imagination: Writing after Nuremberg*. Edinburgh: Edinburgh Univ. Press, 2011.

Summerskill, Edith. *Women Fall In: A Guide to Women's Work in War-Time*. London: Hutchinson, 1941.

Sutherland, John. *Stephen Spender: The Authorized Biography*. London: Penguin, Viking, 2004.

Swinnerton, Frank. *Figures in the Foreground: Literary Reminiscences, 1917–1940*. London: Hutchinson, 1963.

Tawney, R. H. *The Acquisitive Society*. London: G. Bell and Sons, 1921.

——. *Religion and the Rise of Capitalism: A Historical Study*. London: John Murray, 1926.

——. *Social History and Literature*. Cambridge: Cambridge Univ. Press, 1950.

Taylor, Richard. *Against the Bomb: The British Peace Movement, 1958–1965*. Oxford: Clarendon, 1988.

Thompson, Edward. *An Indian Day*. London: Alfred A. Knopf, 1927.

Tooze, Adam. *The Wages of Destruction*. London: Penguin, Allen Lane, 2006.

Upward, Allen. *The Divine Mystery: A Reading of the History of Christianity Down to the Time of Christ*. Letchworth: Garden City, 1913.

Usandizaga, Aránzazu. "The Forgotten Brigade: Foreign Women Writers and the End of the Spanish Civil War." In *Back to Peace: Reconciliation and Retribution in the Postwar Period*, edited by Aránzazu Usandizaga and Andrew Monnicken-dam, 230–49. Notre Dame, Ind.: Univ. of Notre Dame Press, 2007.

War Factory: Mass Observation. 1943. London: Cresset, Hutchinson,1987.

Warner, Sylvia Townsend. "Apprentice." In *A Garland of Straw*, 14–24. London: Chatto and Windus, 1943.

——. *The Diaries of Sylvia Townsend Warner*. Edited by Clare Harman. London: Virago Press, 1995.

Watts, Marjorie. *Mrs. Sappho: The Life of C. A. Dawson-Scott, "Mother of International P.E.N."* London: Duckworth, 1987.

——. *P.E.N.: The Early Years, 1921–1926*. London: Archive Press, 1971.

Wells, H. G. *The New Machiavelli*. London: John Lane, Bodley Head, 1911.

——. *New Worlds for Old*. London: Constable, 1908.

West, Rebecca. *The Birds Fall Down*. 1966. London: Pan Books, 1978.

——. *The Meaning of Treason*. 1949. London: Virago Press, 1982.

——. *Return of the Soldier*. London: Nisbet, 1917.

——. *The Strange Necessity: Essays and Reviews*. 1928. London: Virago Press, 1987.

——. *A Train of Powder*. London: Macmillan, 1955.

Wheeler, Kathleen. *"Modernist" Women Writers and Narrative Art*. London: Macmillan, 1994.

White, Amber Blanco. *The New Propaganda*. Left Book Club. London: Victor Gollancz, 1939.

Wilder, Thornton. *The Bridge of San Luis Rey*. 1927. Harmondsworth: Penguin, 1941.

Wilkinson, Ellen. *The Town That Was Murdered: The Life-Story of Jarrow*. Left Book Club. London: Victor Gollancz, 1939.

Williams, Gertrude. *Women and Work*. New Democracy. London: Nicholson and Watson, 1945.

Williams, Keith, and Steven Matthews, eds. *Rewriting the Thirties: Modernism and After*. London: Longmans, 1997.

Williams, Shirley. *Climbing the Bookshelves*. London: Virago Press, 2009.

Williams, Tennessee. *The Roman Spring of Mrs. Stone*. London: John Lehmann, 1950.

Williams-Ellis, Amabel. *All Stracheys Are Cousins: A Memoir*. London: Weidenfeld and Nicolson, 1983.

——. *An Anatomy of Poetry*. Oxford: Basil Blackwell, 1922.

——. *Women in War Factories*. London: Victor Gollancz, 1943.

Williams-Ellis, Amabel, and Clough Williams-Ellis. *Headlong down the Years: A Tale of To-day*. Liverpool at the Univ. Press, 1951.

Wilson, Romer. *The Death of Society*. London: W. Collins, 1921; New York: Alfred A. Knopf, 1928.

——. *Dragon's Blood*. London: W. Collins, 1926; New York: Alfred A. Knopf, 1926.

The Women's Who's Who 1934–5: An Annual Record of the Careers and Activities of the Leading Women of the Day. London: Shaw Publishing, 1934.

Wood, Michael. *Stendhal*. London: Elek Books, 1971.

Woolf, Virginia. "Is Fiction an Art?" In *Essays of Virginia Woolf*, edited by Andrew MacNeillie, 4 (1925–28): 457–65. London: Hogarth Press, 1994.

World Committee for the Victims of German Fascism. *The Brown Book of the Hitler Terror and the Burning of the Reichstag*. London: Victor Gollancz, 1933.

Zur Erinnerung an den Besuch der Vertreter der British Legion in Deutschland. "Mögen unsere beiden Völker in Zukunst sich so verstehen, wie das Tommy und Fritz Zwanzig Jahre nach dem Kriegsende tun!" Berlin, July 15, 1935. Royal British Legion Archive.

Archives Consulted

BBC Written Archives, Caversham.

Bodley Library. Gilbert Murray microfilm.

——. Ms. Eng. Autogr. d. 39. Marjorie Battcock.

——. Ms. Eng. C.5292, E. J. Thompson, General Corr. — Jack-Joyce.

——. Ms. Eng. Lett. c. 3163. Fols. 1–23, Sir Arthur and Sybil Colefax.

——. Ms. Eng. Walter de la Mare Collection; Nevinson correspondence (wife Evelyn Sharp).

British Library. Farjeon archive ADD 83146, unbound.

——. Macmillan Publishers Ltd. Archive.

——. National Collection of Newspapers and Periodicals at Colindale.

——. Sound Archive: BBC Sound Archive. Christopher Storm-Clark archive.

Churchill College, Special Collections: Guy Chapman archive. JMON2.

Harry Ransom Center, University of Texas at Austin: Jameson, Storm: Works.

——. Alfred A. Knopf archive; PEN archive; A. D. Peters (literary agent) archive; P. Scott archive; H. E. Bates archive; Lowndes, M.A.B. archive; Louis Golding archive; Nancy Cunard archive.

Hull Central Library, Winifred Holtby Archive.

Indiana University, Manuscripts Dept., Lilly Library: Hughes, R. mss; Irvine mss; Lockhart mss; Secker mss; Crawford Mitchell mss.

King's College Cambridge Library, Rosamond Lehmann archive (Misc 42A/35).

King's College London, Liddell Hart Centre for Military Archives: LiddellH: 1/408, 1937–73, 1986.

Liverpool Record Office, Central Library: James Hanley papers.

London Metropolitan University: Women's Library.

London School of Economics Library: Special Collections; R. H. Tawney archive.

McMaster University, Hamilton, Ontario: The Vera Brittain Archive; Bertrand Russell Archive.

National Portrait Gallery.

Orion Publishing Group: Gollancz Archive.

Pennsylvania State University, Rare Books and Manuscripts, University Libraries, University Park, Pa. Personal Author, Jameson, Storm, 12 Items.

Random House Archive: Heinemann: Storm Jameson: Author file.

Royal British Legion HQ, Special Papers.

SCR Archive (Society for Cultural Relations between the Peoples of the British Commonwealth and the Union of Soviet Socialist Republics), 320 Brixton Road, London SW9 6AB.

Simon Fraser University, Bennett Library, Special Collections: Margaret Storm Jameson letters to Hilary Newitt Brown and Harrison Brown.

Society of Authors Archive, ADDMSS (Society of Authors).

University College London Library, Special Collections: George Orwell Archive.

University of Arkansas, Frank Swinnerton archive, Special Collections, University of
Arkansas Libraries.

University of Bradford, Special Collections, Jacquetta Hawkes archive.

University of Bristol, Penguin Archive, University Library: Special Collections.

University of Central Lancashire, People's History Museum: Labour Party Archive.

University of Edinburgh Library, Special Collections, Arthur Koestler Archive.

University of Leeds Archive, Personalia.

———. STU/001 [committees doc.]. Women's Representative Council, 1902–14.

University of Leeds, Brotherton Library, Special Collections: Chapman file; Dobrée
file; Moult file; Shorter file.

University of Michigan, Clement King Shorter Special Collections Library.

University of North Carolina, Michael Sadleir Archive, General Manuscripts, Manuscripts Department, Wilson Library.

University of Pittsburgh, Archive Services Center.

University of Reading: Special Collections: Bodley Head/John Lane files; Chatto and
Windus files; Allen & Unwin files; Hogarth Press files; Jonathan Cape files;
Routledge files; Herbert Herlitschka archive.

University of Sussex, Special Collections: Elton/Ehrenberg papers; Monks House
papers.

University of Tulsa, Margaret Storm Jameson Correspondence, Dept. of Special Collections, McFarlin Library.

Yale University, Czesław Miłosz Papers, General Collection, Beinecke Rare Book and
Manuscript Library.

personal papers, 245, 302, 419, 439, 462, 467, 476; on poverty, 21, 25, 33, 73, 105, 119, 137, 151, 188, 272; on propaganda, 223, 227; on refugees, 132–33, 181, 192, 202, 241; on religion, 175–76, 291; on retaliation, 307–8, 336; on starvation, 51; on surrealism, 182, 456; on the United States, 361, 362, 411; on war, 38–39, 75, 79, 81–82, 108–9, 113, 114, 119, 122, 137, 141–42, 155, 178, 206, 226–27, 272; on wartime pamphlets, 270–71; on William the Conqueror, 289–90

WRITINGS:

Fiction: anonymous serials, 45, 150, 221; *The Aristide Case*, 431–35; *Before the Crossing*, 160, 326, 327, 329–31, 332, 337, 340, 341, 345, 350, 352, 353, 355; *The Black Laurel*, 332, 338, 340–44, 345–46, 350, 352–53, 356, 427, 445; *The Captain's Wife*, 201, 204, 217–18, 226; *The Clash*, 43, 48, 49, 54–56, 57–58, 166; "A Cloke for Two," 46; *Cloudless May*, 263, 271, 281, 294, 295, 298–300, 305, 307, 316, 396, 427, 430, 458; *Company Parade*, 129–31, 142, 408, 478–79; *Cousin Honoré*, 243–44, 251, 255, 269, 298–99, 300, 345, 376, 458; *A Cup of Tea for Mr. Thorgill*, 33, 404, 406–8, 410, 411–12, 417, 418, 421; "A Day at the Zoo," 261; *A Day Off*, 116–17, 422, 480; *Delicate Monster*, 101, 103–5, 116, 161, 165–66, 185; *The Early Life of Stephen Hind*, 434, 442–43, 446, 463; *Europe to Let*, 133, 188, 194, 201, 211, 218, 228–33, 237, 240, 243, 244, 256, 270, 302, 330; *Farewell, Night, Welcome, Day*: see *The Captain's Wife*; *Farewell to Youth*, 78, 80; *The Fort*, 255, 257–58, 263, 276–77, 283, 354; "The Friendly One," 419; "The Gamble," 382, 384; *The Green Man*, 356, 360, 363–64, 369, 370–72, 375–77, 383–87, 396; *The Happy Highways*, 36, 37–39, 44, 46, 47–48; *Here Comes a Candle*, 188–89, 202, 217; *The Hidden River*, 347, 381, 386–87, 388–89, 391–94, 396–97, 399, 401–2, 405, 408–9, 410, 418, 420–21; *In the Second Year*, 144–48, 150–51, 153–54, 354; *The Intruder*, 398–401, 404–5, 412, 427, 430; *The*

Journal of Mary Hervey Russell, 302–3, 304, 309, 312–15, 325, 347, 433, 449; *Lady Susan and Life*, 59, 63, 66; "The Last Night," 294–95, 351; *Last Score*, 422, 423–24, 426, 427, 430; *Love in Winter*, 142–43, 183; *The Lovely Ship*, 45, 74–75, 78, 82, 166, 177; *Loving Memory*, 155–56, 161, 163, 164, 179; "A Mingled Strain," 102–3; *The Mirror in Darkness* trilogy, 51, 98, 129–30, 141, 144, 150, 155, 159, 217, 329–30, 344, 364, 477, 480; *The Moment of Truth*, 348–49, 352, 354–55, 356, 363, 364, 372; *A Month Soon Goes*, 392, 397–98, 427, 430–31; *The Moon Is Making*, 13, 153, 154, 157, 158, 162, 163, 166, 170, 176–77, 243; "No Home to Go To," 401; *None Turn Back*, 141, 144, 155, 159–61; *No Victory for the Soldier*, 162, 173, 179, 184–88, 196; *The Other Side*, 321–23, 337, 338–39, 348; *The Pitiful Wife*, 45, 56, 59–62, 69–70, 74, 111, 176, 243; *The Pot Boils*, 9, 32–36, 37–38, 41, 42, 407; *A Richer Dust*, 93, 97–98, 99, 107; *The Road from Monument*, 415–17, 418, 429, 442; *The Single Heart*, 106–7, 116; "The Tale of the Solitary English Girl," 56, 71; *That Was Yesterday*, 11, 98–99, 101, 107, 130; *Then We Shall Hear Singing*, 263, 266, 273, 277–79, 291, 295, 296, 313, 341–42, 408, 501n6; *There Will Be a Short Interval*, 10, 458–59, 461–62; *Three Kingdoms*, 71–72, 77; "Time to Dance," 190, 192, 195; *The Triumph of Time* trilogy, 51, 75, 90, 93, 97–98, 107, 110–11, 113, 116–17, 130, 141, 217; *A Ulysses Too Many*, 347, 374, 409, 410, 418; *The Voyage Home*, 90–91; *The White Crow*, 347, 443, 444–46, 452; "The Woman Doctor's Tale," 44–45; *Women against Men*, 116, 478; *The World Ends*, 157, 158, 162–63, 179; "You Don't Speak French, Do You?," 261; "The Young Prisoner," 300–302

Journalism and essays: 28, 29–32, 36, 43, 45–46, 48–49, 51, 53–54, 73–74, 75, 77, 78–81, 83–84, 88–89, 108, 113–14, 118, 121, 133–36, 141–42, 150, 157, 174–75, 189, 232, 242–43, 253,

Lehmann, John, 261, 360
Lehmann, Rosamond, 240, 428, 462–63,
   463–64, 467
Leigh, Colston, 157, 172, 204–5
Lenin, Vladimir, 123
Lessing, Doris, 4, 5, 188, 400, 408, 413, 441,
   446, 450, 459
Lewis, Sinclair, 150–51
Lewis, Wyndham, 30, 34, 46–47, 60, 63, 73,
   102
Liddell Hart, Basil, 210–11, 227, 238–39,
   260, 281, 286, 307, 375, 442, 444, 446,
   454, 457, 467; reaction to SJ's memoirs,
   438–40; SJ's letters to, 243, 245, 260, 263,
   298, 318, 319, 327, 364, 371, 453–54
Liddell Hart, Kathleen, 340, 390, 439–40,
   460–61
Lindbergh, Charles, 191
Linke, Lilo, 100, 102, 105, 113, 120, 121,
   125–26, 133, 136, 141, 178, 442, 450; SJ
   as her editor, 125, 129, 132, 136, 139, 145,
   316, 383; in SJ's *In the Second Year*, 147
Listener, 325
Lloyd, Marie, 26
London Group, 76, 179
London Mercury, 168
Lonsdale, Kathleen, 419
Lowell, Amy, 31
Ludwig, Emil, 192
Lukács, György, 166–67

Macaulay, Rose, 44, 50, 73, 104, 129, 158,
   284, 418
MacCarthy, Desmond, 84
MacDermott, Norman, 36
MacDonald, Ramsay, 64, 99–100
Maclean, Alan, 406, 409, 419, 452, 455,
   458, 460–61, 464, 467, 469, 473, 509n18;
   reaction to SJ's memoirs, 431
Maclean, Donald, 374–75, 381, 408, 509n18
Maclean, John, 42
MacLeish, Archibald, 270
Macmillan, Daniel, 221, 242, 279, 281, 377,
   383–84
Macmillan, Harold, 221, 233, 237, 239, 242,
   244, 302, 312, 326, 377, 386
Mahler, Anna, 351, 476–77
Mallarmé, Stéphane, 314
Malory, Thomas, 61
Malraux, André, 154, 166–67, 169, 331, 344
Manchester Guardian, 197, 327

Mandela, Nelson, 336
Mann, Heinrich, 123, 154, 192
Mann, Thomas, 123, 154, 162, 187, 192, 256
Mannin, Ethel, 4, 64, 89, 115, 167, 216; and
   SJ's *Delicate Monster*, 103–4, 116, 161,
   165, 373, 462
Mansfield, Katherine, 62–63, 109
Marsden, Dora, 29–30, 36, 83
Marston, Doreen, 208, 477
Martin, Kingsley, 241, 242
Marx, Karl, 123, 176
Marxism, 167, 180, 328
Masaryk, Alice Garrigue, 477
Masaryk, Jan, 192, 199, 202, 235, 243, 250,
   268, 319, 353
Masaryk, Tomáš, 46, 357, 360
Masefield, John, 284
Mass Observation project, 174, 251, 279
Maugham, Somerset, 135, 321
Maupassant, Guy de, 68, 69
McAlmon, Robert, 52
McCarthyism, 359, 373, 408
McHugh, Jimmy, 359
McMullen, Jeanine, 454
Meerut Conspiracy Case, 119–20
Menne, Bernhard, 209–10, 228, 261
Meyer, Ernst, 282
Mill, John Stuart, 176
Millar, Ronald, 338–39
Miłosz, Czesław, 328, 336, 354, 359, 373–74,
   378–79, 382–83, 384, 400, 437–38, 469,
   477; and Janka, 409–10, 411–12, 426, 457,
   473–74
Milton, Ernest, 306
Milton, John, 16, 176, 422
Mitchell, Peter Chalmers, 156, 178
Mitchison, Naomi, 105, 145, 153, 167, 190,
   479, 480
Modern Reading, 261, 302
Moholy-Nagy, László, 224
Monro, Harold, 46
Montaigne, Michel de, 315
Montgomery, Bernard Law, 463, 468
Montgomery, John, 385, 393, 394, 397, 398,
   420
Montherlant, Henry de, 117
Moore, Henry, 65
Moore, Olive, 90
Moore, Reginald, 261, 271
Moorhead, Caroline, 480
Moorman, Frederic, 20

144, 180, 210–11, 313, 325; SJ on, 46–47, 85–86, 93, 100–101, 118, 369

BOOKS: *Jacob's Room*, 63; *Mrs. Dalloway*, 86, 93; *Night and Day*, 46–47; *Orlando*, 85, 86; *Three Guineas*, 178; *The Waves*, 100

Woolf family, 4, 105, 236

Wordsworth, William, 483n11

World Council against Fascism, 192

World War I, 31, 34, 37, 55, 64, 73, 82, 90, 109, 138; postwar books on, 90, 91, 117, 125; in SJ's *Fort*, 258–59; in SJ's *White Crow*, 445–46

World War II, SJ predicts, 150, 180, 219, 220, 225, 262, 264

Wylie, Ida, 362

Yeats, W. B., 61

York, William Temple, Archbishop of, 274

Zaleski, August, 250

Zamyatin, Yevgeny, 302

Zweig, Arnold, 123, 192

Zweig, Stefan, 123, 192, 280

ABOUT THE AUTHOR

Elizabeth Maslen is a senior research fellow in the Institute of English Studies, School of Advanced Study, at the University of London.